SHELLY Cashman SERIES®

Adobe®
PHOTOSHOP®
CREATIVE CLOUD™

COMPREHENSIVE

JOY L. STARKS
Indiana University Purdue University Indianapolis

CENGAGE
Learning·

Australia • Brazil • Mexico • Singapore • United Kingdom • United States

Adobe® Photoshop® Creative Cloud™: Comprehensive
Joy L. Starks

Product Director: Kathleen McMahon

Senior Product Manager: Jim Gish

Managing Content Developer:
Emma F. Newsom

Associate Content Developer: Crystal Parenteau

Director of Marketing: Michel McTighe

Senior Marketing Manager: Eric La Scola

Print Buyer: Julio Esperas

Director of Production: Patty Stephan

Senior Content Project Manager: Jennifer
Feltri-George

Developmental Editor: Amanda Brodkin

QA Manuscript Reviewer: Danielle Shaw

Proofreader, Indexer and Compositor: Lumina
Datamatics Inc.

Art Director: Jackie Bates, GEX Publishing
Services

Cover and Text Design: Lisa Kuhn, Curio Press, LLC

Cover Photo: ©istockphoto.com/Yuri_Arcurs

Library of Congress Control Number: 2014949275

Student Edition:
ISBN: 978-1-305-26723-7

Cengage Learning
20 Channel Center Street
Boston, MA 02210
USA

Adobe, the Adobe logos, and Photoshop are either registered trademarks or trademarks of Adobe Systems Incorporated in the United States and/or other countries. THIS PRODUCT IS NOT ENDORSED OR SPONSORED BY ADOBE SYSTEMS INCORPORATED, PUBLISHER OF PHOTOSHOP.

Cengage Learning is a leading provider of customized learning solutions with office locations around the globe, including Singapore, the United Kingdom, Australia, Mexico, Brazil, and Japan. Locate your local office at:
www.cengage.com/global.

Cengage Learning products are represented in Canada by Nelson Education, Ltd.

For your course and learning solutions, visit **www.cengage.com**

To learn more about Course Technology,
visit **www.cengage.com/coursetechnology**

Purchase any of our products at your local college bookstore or at our preferred online store **www.cengagebrain.com**

Printed at CLDPC, 02-20

Adobe® PHOTOSHOP® CREATIVE CLOUD™
COMPREHENSIVE

Contents

Appendices

Preface

The Shelly Cashman Series® offers the finest textbooks in computer education. We are proud of the fact that our previous Adobe® Photoshop® books have been so well received. With each new edition of our Photoshop books, we have made significant improvements based on the comments made by instructors and students. The Adobe Photoshop Creative Cloud books continue with the innovation, quality, and reliability you have come to expect from the Shelly Cashman Series.

For this Photoshop Creative Cloud text, the Shelly Cashman Series development team carefully reviewed our pedagogy and analyzed its effectiveness in teaching today's student. Students today read less, but need to retain more. They not only need to be able to perform skills, but to retain those skills and know how to apply them to different settings. Today's students need to be continually engaged and challenged to retain what they're learning.

With this Photoshop Creative Cloud text, we continue our commitment to focusing on the user and how they learn best.

Objectives of This Textbook

Adobe Photoshop Creative Cloud is intended for a course that offers an introduction to Photoshop and image editing. No previous experience with Adobe Photoshop Creative Cloud is assumed, and no mathematics beyond the high school freshman level is required.

The objectives of this book are:

- To teach the fundamentals and more advanced features of Adobe Photoshop Creative Cloud using student-focused exercises

- To expose students to image editing and graphic design fundamentals

- To develop an exercise-oriented approach that promotes learning by doing

- To encourage independent study and to help those who are working alone

New To This Edition

All New Creative Cloud Interface and Tools
Complete coverage of the new cloud-based installation of Adobe apps, including Photoshop and Bridge – all of the skills necessary to obtain certification.

New Smart Guides
Photoshop's improved guides display precise distances between onscreen objects and distances between moved layers.

Linked Smart Objects
In Photoshop Creative Cloud, you can create linked smart objects which update automatically and can be reused across designs.

Image Asset Generation
Save tagged layers and layer groups as individual image files in formats you choose, all collected in a single folder.

Reduce Camera Shake Blurring
Expanded coverage of image improvement tools shows you how to salvage blurry photos caused by camera shake using the Shake Reduction loupe.

Warp Perspective
Adjusting the perspective or viewpoint of a specific part of an image without affecting the surrounding area is a subtle but effective technique that is now covered in Chapter 9.

3D Tools and Modeling
Coverage of Photoshop's new 3D tools include instruction on converting 2D images to 3D; students also use meshes, lighting, and materials to create a 3D model, 3D printing is also covered.

New Touch Screen Support
Chapter projects and end of chapter exercises now include instructions for using Photoshop Creative Cloud on desktop, tablets, or mobile devices.

The Shelly Cashman Approach

A Proven Pedagogy with an Emphasis on Project Planning
Each chapter presents a practical problem to be solved, within a project planning framework. The project orientation is strengthened by the use of Plan Ahead boxes that encourage critical thinking about how to proceed at various points in the project. Step-by-step instructions with supporting screens guide students through the steps. Instructional steps are supported by the Q&A, Other Ways and BTW features.

A Visually Engaging Book that Maintains Student Interest
The step-by-step tasks, with supporting figures, provide a rich visual experience for the student. Callouts on the screens that present both explanatory and navigational information provide students with information they need, when they need to know it. Each chapter presents a real-world, photo scenario with current topics and new Creative Cloud features.

Supporting Reference Materials (Quick Reference, Appendices)
The appendices provide additional information about the application at hand, such as the Help Feature and customizing the application, as well as an appendix for Mac users. With the Quick Reference, students can quickly look up information about a single task, such as keyboard shortcuts, and find page references of where in the book the task is illustrated.

End-of-Chapter Student Activities
Extensive end of chapter activities provide a variety of reinforcement opportunities for students where they can apply and expand their skills through individual and group work.

To complete some of these assignments, you will be required to use the Data Files for Students. Visit http://solutions.cengage.com/ctdownloads for detailed access instructions or contact your instructor for information about accessing the required files.

Instructor Resources

The Instructor Resources include both teaching and testing aids that can be accessed via www.cengage.com/login.

Instructor's Manual Includes lecture notes summarizing the chapter sections, figures and boxed elements found in every chapter, teacher tips, classroom activities, lab activities, and quick quizzes in Microsoft® Word® files.

Sample Syllabus Easily customizable sample syllabus that covers policies, assignments, exams, and other course information.

Figure Files Illustrations for every figure in the textbook in electronic form. Visit http://solutions.cengage.com/ctdownloads for detailed instructions.

PowerPoint Presentations A multimedia lecture presentation system that provides slides for each chapter. Presentations are based on chapter objectives.

Solutions to Exercises Includes solutions for end-of-chapter exercises.

Test Bank & Test Engine Cengage Learning Testing Powered by Cognero is a flexible, online system that allows you to author, edit, and manage test bank content from multiple Cengage Learning solutions and to create multiple test versions. It works on any operating system or browser with no special installs or downloads needed, allowing you to create tests from anywhere with Internet access. Multi-language support, an equation editor and unlimited metadata help ensure your tests are complete and compliant, and it enables you to import and export content into other systems. The Dreamweaver Creative Cloud Test Bank includes 112 questions for every chapter, featuring objective-based and critical thinking question types, and including page number references and figure references as appropriate.

Learn Online

CengageBrain.com is the premier destination for purchasing or renting Cengage Learning textbooks, ebooks, eChapters and study tools, at a significant discount (eBooks up to 50% off Print). In addition, CengageBrain.com provides direct access to all digital products including eBooks, eChapters and digital solutions (i.e. CourseMate, SAM) regardless of where purchased. The following are some examples of what is available for this product on www.cengagebrain.com.

CourseNotes

CourseNotes are six-panel quick reference cards that reinforce the most important and widely used features of a software application in a visual and user-friendly format. CourseNotes serve as a great reference tool during and after the student completes the course. CourseNotes are available for software applications such as Microsoft Office 2013, Windows 8 and HTML. Topic-based CourseNotes, including Best Practices in Social Networking, Hot Topics in Technology, and Leverage the Internet for Your Career Search, are also available. Visit www.cengagebrain.com to learn more!

course|notes ™
quick reference guide

Textbook Walk-Through
The Shelly Cashman Series Pedagogy: Project-Based — Step-by-Step — Variety of Assessments

Plan Ahead boxes prepare students to create successful projects by encouraging them to think strategically about what they are trying to accomplish before they begin working.

Overview

As you read this chapter, you will learn how to edit the photo shown in Figure 1–1a on the previous page by performing these general tasks:

- Customize the workspace.
- Display a photo at various magnifications.
- Crop and straighten a photo effectively.
- Create and modify a border.
- Stroke a selection.
- Resize and print a photo.
- Save, close, and then reopen a photo.
- Add stroked text to the photo.
- Save a photo for the web.
- Use Photoshop Help.

BTW

Gestures
Windows users who have computers or devices with touch screen capability can interact with the screen using gestures. A **gesture** is a motion you make on a touch screen with the tip of one or more fingers, or your hand. Touch screens are convenient because they do not require a separate device for input.

BTW

The Swipe Gesture
When you want to gain access to another portion of the screen such as scrolling, or when you need to gain access to the Charms bar in Windows 8, you can press and hold one finger and then move the finger horizontally or vertically on the screen in a **swipe gesture**. This gesture emulates moving the mouse, or clicking a scroll bar.

BTW

Windows 8 Start Screen
After you sign into a computer running Windows 8, Windows displays the Start screen, which shows tiles corresponding to the installed apps that you use regularly. From the Start screen, you can choose which app to run by using a touch screen, mouse, or other input device.

Plan Ahead

General Project Guidelines
When editing a photo, the actions you perform and decisions you make will affect the appearance and characteristics of the finished product. As you edit a photo, such as the one shown in Figure 1–1a, you should follow these general guidelines:

1. **Find an appropriate image or photo.** Keep in mind the purpose and the graphic needs of the project when choosing an image or photo. Decide ahead of time on the file type and decide whether the image will be used on the web. An eye-catching graphic image should convey a theme that is understood universally. The photo should grab the attention of viewers and draw them into the picture, whether in print or on the web.

2. **Determine how to edit the photo to highlight the theme.** As you edit, keep in mind your subject, your audience, the required size and shape of the graphic, color decisions, the rule of thirds, the golden rectangle, and other design principles. Decide which parts of the photo portray your message and which parts are visual clutter. Crop the photo as needed.

3. **Identify finishing touches that will further enhance the photo.** The overall appearance of a photo significantly affects its ability to communicate clearly. You might want to add text or a border.

4. **Prepare for publication.** Resize the photo as needed to fit the allotted space. Save the photo on a storage medium, such as a hard drive, USB flash drive, or CD, or store it on the cloud. Print the photo or publish it to the web.

When necessary, more specific details concerning the above guidelines are presented at appropriate points in the chapter. The chapter also will identify the actions performed and decisions made regarding these guidelines during the creation of the edited photo shown in Figure 1–1b on the previous page.

Starting Photoshop CC

If you are using a computer to step through the project in this chapter, and you want your screen to match the figures in this book, you should change your screen's resolution to 1366 × 768. For information about how to change a screen's resolution, read the Editing Preferences Appendix.

To Start Photoshop CC

The following steps, which assume Windows 8 is running, start Photoshop CC based on a typical installation. After starting your computer, you may be required to sign in to an account to access the computer's resources. If necessary, ask your instructor how to sign in to your account and how to start Photoshop CC for your computer.

Textbook Walk-Through

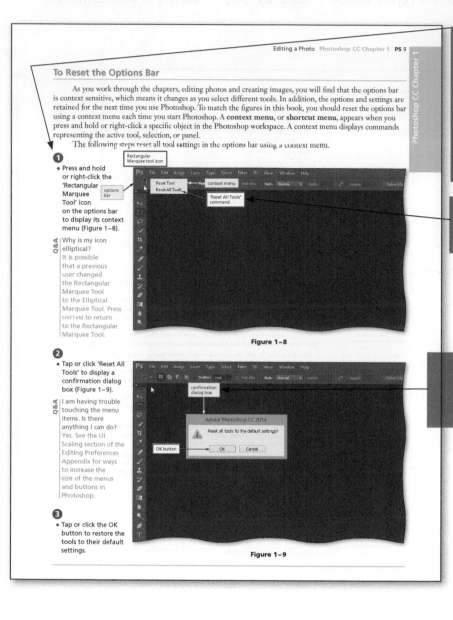

To Reset the Options Bar

As you work through the chapters, editing photos and creating images, you will find that the options bar is context sensitive, which means it changes as you select different tools. In addition, the options and settings are retained for the next time you use Photoshop. To match the figures in this book, you should reset the options bar using a context menu each time you start Photoshop. A **context menu**, or **shortcut menu**, appears when you press and hold or right-click a specific object in the Photoshop workspace. A context menu displays commands representing the active tool, selection, or panel.

The following steps reset all tool settings in the options bar using a context menu.

1
• Press and hold or right-click the 'Rectangular Marquee Tool' icon on the options bar to display its context menu (Figure 1–8).

◁ Why is my icon Q&A elliptical?
It is possible that a previous user changed the Rectangular Marquee Tool to the Elliptical Marquee Tool. Press SHIFT+M to return to the Rectangular Marquee Tool.

Figure 1–8

2
• Tap or click 'Reset All Tools' to display a confirmation dialog box (Figure 1–9).

◁ I am having trouble Q&A touching the menu items. Is there anything I can do?
Yes. See the UI Scaling section of the Editing Preferences Appendix for ways to increase the size of the menus and buttons in Photoshop.

3
• Tap or click the OK button to restore the tools to their default settings.

Figure 1–9

Step-by-step instructions now provide a context beyond the point-and-click. Each step provides information on why students are performing each task, or what will occur as a result.

Explanatory callouts in red show students where to click.

Navigational callouts summarize what is happening on screen.

Q&A boxes offer questions students may have when working through the steps and provide additional information about what they are doing right where they need it.

scroll bar

Figure 1–2

Application bar

Photoshop window

Maximize/Restore Down button

❷
- Tap or click the Adobe Photoshop CC tile to run the Photoshop CC app.

options bar

- After a few moments, when the Photoshop window is displayed, if the window is not maximized, tap or click the Maximize button next to the Close button on the Application bar to maximize the window (Figure 1–3).

workspace

other panels

Tools panel

Figure 1–3

Q&A   Can I use a stylus to tap the correct tile?
Yes. You can tap the tile with your finger, click the tile with your mouse, or tap the screen with a stylus to select and run the app. A **stylus** is a pen-shaped device used to interact with a touch screen by applying the stylus tip to the screen with a light pressure.

0_ch01_REV2.indd   5   8/19/14

PS 44   Photoshop CC Chapter 1   Editing a Photo

❸
- Tap or click the OK button in the Border Selection dialog box to define the selection (Figure 1–58).

Q&A   Is the border 50 pixels wide?
Yes, Photoshop adds half of those pixels to either side of the selection marquee.

 Experiment
- To practice smoothing the border, tap or click the Select menu, tap or click Modify, and then tap or click Smooth. Enter a value in the Sample Radius box and then tap or click the OK button. Notice the change in the marquee. Press CTRL+Z to undo the Smooth command.

double marquee defines border selection

Figure 1–58

Experiment Steps within our step-by-step instructions, encourage students to explore, experiment, and take advantage of the features of the Dreamweaver Creative Cloud. These steps are not necessary to complete the projects, but are designed to increase the confidence with the software and build problem-solving skills.

To Switch Foreground and Background Colors

On the Tools panel, the default foreground color is black and the default background color is white. Photoshop uses the default foreground color in strokes, fills, and brushes – in the previous steps when you stroked, the pixels became black. In order to create a rounded gray border, you will use a white, overlapping stroke. The following step switches the foreground and background colors so white is over black.

❶
- Tap or click the 'Switch Foreground and Background Colors' button to reverse the colors (Figure 1–59).

'Switch Foreground and Background Colors' button

white over black

Figure 1–59

Other Ways boxes that follow many of the step sequences explain the other ways to complete the task presented.

Other Ways

1. Press x

Textbook Walk-Through

To Quit Photoshop

The following step quits Photoshop and returns control to Windows.

❶
- Tap or click the Close button on the right side of the Application bar to quit Photoshop.
- If Photoshop displays a dialog box asking you to save changes, tap or click the No button.

For a detailed example of this procedure using the Mac operating system, refer to the For Mac Users Appendix.

Other Ways
1. On File menu, tap or click Exit
2. Press CTRL | Q

For Mac Users feature provides instructions for users with Mac operating systems.

Chapter Summary

In this chapter, you gained a broad knowledge of Photoshop. First, you learned how to start Photoshop. You were introduced to the Photoshop workspace. You learned how to open a photo, change the magnification, zoom in, and display rulers. You learned about design issues related to the placement of visual points of interest. You then learned how to crop a photo to eliminate extraneous background. After you added a blended border, you resized the image and added text.

Once you saved the photo, you learned how to print it. You used the 'Save for Web' command to optimize and save a web version. You learned how to use Adobe Help to research specific help topics. Finally, you learned how to quit Photoshop.

The items listed below include all the new Photoshop skills you have learned in this chapter:

1. Start Photoshop CC (PS 4)
2. Select the Essentials Workspace and Reset It (PS 6)
3. Reset the Tools Panel (PS 8)
4. Reset the Options Bar (PS 9)
5. Reset the Interface Color (PS 10)
6. Open a File (PS 12)
7. Save a File in the PSD Format in a New Folder (PS 21)
8. Use the Zoom Tool (PS 26)
9. Use the Navigator Panel (PS 28)
10. Minimize the Navigator Panel (PS 29)
11. Use the Hand Tool (PS 31)
12. Change the Magnification (PS 32)
13. Display Rulers (PS 33)
14. Straighten a Photo and Crop (PS 36)
15. Create a Selection (PS 39)
16. Stroke a Selection (PS 41)
17. Modify a Selection (PS 43)
18. Switch Foreground and Background Colors (PS 44)
19. Deselect (PS 45)
20. Save a File with the Same File Name (PS 46)
21. Close a File (PS 46)
22. Open a Recent File (PS 47)
23. Resize the Image (PS 49)
24. Select the Horizontal Type Tool (PS 51)
25. Set Font Options (PS 52)
26. Insert Text (PS 53)
27. Stroke Text (PS 54)
28. Save a File with a Different Name (PS 55)
29. Print a Photo (PS 56)
30. Preview using the Save for Web Dialog Box (PS 57)
31. Choose a Download Speed (PS 58)
32. Preview the Photo on the Web (PS 60)
33. Save the Photo for the Web (PS 60)
34. Access Photoshop Help (PS 62)
35. Use the Help Search Box (PS 62)
36. Quit Photoshop (PS 64)

Chapter Summary includes a concluding paragraph, followed by a listing of the tasks completed within a chapter together with the pages on which the step-by-step, screen-by-screen explanations appear.

Apply Your Knowledge

Reinforce the skills and apply the concepts you learned in this chapter.

Editing a Photo in the Photoshop Workspace

Note: To complete this assignment, you will be required to use the Data Files for Students. Visit solutions.cengage.com/ctdownloads for detailed instructions or contact your instructor for information about accessing the required files.

Instructions: Start Photoshop and perform the customization steps found on pages PS 6 through PS 11. Open the Apply 1-1 Deer file in the Chapter 01 folder from the Data Files for Students.

First, you will save the photo in the PSD format. Then you will crop the photo, add a white border, and save the edited photo, as shown in Figure 1–89. Next, you will resize the photo for printing and print one copy. Finally, you will reopen your edited photo, and then you will optimize it for the web, save it, and close it.

Apply Your Knowledge usually requires students to open and manipulate a file from the Data Files that parallels the activities learned in the chapter.

Figure 1–89

STUDENT ASSIGNMENTS   Photoshop CC Chapter 1

Courtesy of Joy Starks

longer are displayed.

7. To create the border:

    a. If necessary, press the D key to select the default colors. Press the x key to reverse the foreground and background colors, so that white displays over black on the Tools panel.

    b. Press CTRL+A to select all of the photo.

    c. Use the Stroke command on the Edit menu to stroke the selection with white.

    d. Press CTRL+D to clear your selection when finished creating the border.

8. Press CTRL+S to save the Apply 1-1 Deer Edited photo with the same file name in the same location. Press the D key to return the colors to black over white.

9. Use the Image menu to resize the photo width to 5 inches wide to create a custom-sized photo for printing.

10. Save the resized file as Apply 1-1 Deer for Print.

11. Print the photo and then close the file. If Photoshop displays a dialog box about saving again, tap or click the No button.

12. Open the Apply 1-1 Deer for Print file using the Open Recent list.

13. Save the photo for the web, displaying it in the 4-Up tab and zoomed to fit on the screen. Select the preview that looks the best for your download speed.

14. Preview the optimized photo in your browser, and print the browser page. Close the browser.

15. Save the optimized file with the name, Apply-1-1-Deer-for-web.

16. Close the Apply 1-1 Deer Edited file without saving it and quit Photoshop.

Extend Your Knowledge

Extend the skills you learned in this chapter and experiment with new skills. You may need to use Help to complete the assignment.

Exploring Aspect Ratios and Borders

Note: To complete this assignment, you will be required to use the Data Files for Students. Visit solutions.cengage.com/ctdownloads for detailed instructions or contact your instructor for information about accessing the required files.

Instructions: Start Photoshop and perform the customization steps found on pages PS 6 through PS 11. Open the Extend 1-1 Arc de Triomphe file in the Chapter 01 folder from the Data Files for Students and save it on your storage device as Extend 1-1 Arc de Triomphe Edited in the PSD file format.

The photo (Figure 1–90) is to be added to a book a...
be centered, straightened both horizontally and vertically...

Extend Your Knowledge projects at the end of each chapter allow students to extend and expand on the skills learned within the chapter. Students use critical thinking to experiment with new skills to complete each project.

Courtesy of Lourdes Nunez

Figure 1–90

Perform the following tasks:

1. Use Photoshop Help to read about cropping using the 'Select a preset aspect ratio or crop size' button.

2. Select the Crop Tool. Tap or click the Straighten button, and then draw across a line horizontally that should be straight in the arc itself. Repeat the process vertically.

3. Use the 'Select a preset aspect ratio or crop size' button to choose a 5: 7 forced ratio. Drag a corner cropping handle inward, keeping the arc within the grid. Drag the picture to center it within the cropping area.

4. Delete cropped pixels and then crop the photo.

5. Review Table 1–4 on page PS 42. Use the commands on the Modify submenu to set the border options of your choice. Stroke the selection with a color of your choice.

6. After viewing the resulting border, press the CTRL+ALT+Z keys enough times to step back to the photo's original unedited state.

7. Repeat Steps 1–4 several times to experiment with different border widths and colors, then apply the border that best complements the photo and save the changes to the photo.

8. Close the photo and quit Photoshop.

Make It Right

Analyze a project and correct all errors and/or improve the design.

Changing a Photo's Focus and Optimizing It for the Web

Note: To complete this assignment, you will be required to use the Data Files for Students. Visit solutions.cengage.com/ctdownloads for detailed instructions or contact your instructor for information about accessing the required files.

Instructions: Start Photoshop and perform the customization steps found on pages PS 6 through PS 11. Open the Make It Right 1-1 Young Stars file in the Chapter 01 folder from the Data Files for Students and save it on your storage device as Make It Right 1-1 Young Stars Edited in the PSD file format.

Members of your Astronomy Club have selected the Young Stars photo (Figure 1–91 on the next page) for the club's website. You are tasked with editing the photo to focus more clearly on the cluster of stars and its trailing dust blanket, and then optimizing the photo for the web.

Continued >

Make It Right projects call on students to analyse a file, discover errors in it, and fix them using the skills they learned in the chapter.

Textbook Walk-Through

Figure 1–91

View the photo in different screen modes and at different magnifications.

Use the Crop Tool's Golden Spiral overlay to crop the photo to change its focal point and resave it. Then save the photo for the web as Make-It-Right-1-1-Young-Stars-for-web.

In the Labs ◄

Design and/or create a project using the guidelines, concepts, and skills presented in this chapter. Labs are listed in order of increasing difficulty.

Lab 1: Cropping a Photo and Adding a Smooth Border

Problem: A gardening club has accepted your flower photo to publish in its upcoming brochure, but the club would like you to crop the photo more, add a smooth border, and resize it. The edited photo is displayed in Figure 1–92.

Figure 1–92

In the Lab assignments require students to utilize the chapter concepts and techniques to solve problems on a computer.

Found within the **Cases and Places** exercises, the **Personal** activities call on students to create an open-ended project that relates to their personal lives.

Cases and Places

Apply your creative thinking and problem-solving skills to design and implement a solution.

Note: To complete this assignment, you will be required to use the Data Files for Students. Visit solutions.cengage.com/ctdownloads for detailed instructions or contact your instructor for information about accessing the required files.

1: Cropping and Straightening a Photo

Academic

You are writing a paper for your Sociology class about the calming effects of owning pets. As examples, you are using photos of several pets, including a parrot. Open the file Case 1-1 Parrot from the Chapter 01 folder of the Data Files for Students. Save the photo on your storage device as Case 1-1 Parrot Edited, using the PSD format. Select the Crop Tool. Using the rule of thirds, and the information in the chapter, crop the photo to focus on the bird. Use the Image Size dialog box and an appropriate resampling algorithm to create a photo approximately three inches wide. Save the photo again and print a copy for your instructor.

2: Creating a Photo for a Social Networking Site

Personal

You would like to place a photo of your recent tubing adventure on your social networking page. The photo you have is of two people. You need to crop out the other person who is tubing. After starting Photoshop and resetting the workspace, select the photo, Case 1-2 Tubing, from the Chapter 01 folder of the Data Files for Students. Save the photo on your storage device as Case 1-2 Tubing Edited, using the PSD format. Crop the photo to remove one of the inner tubes, keeping in mind the rule of thirds, the golden rectangle, and the direction of the action. Save the photo for the web and upload it to Facebook or another social networking site as directed by your instructor.

3: Creating a Photo for a Brochure

Professional

You are an intern with an event planning business. The company is planning to send out a tri-fold brochure about local churches and chapels used for weddings. The photo named Case 1-3 Chapel is located in the Chapter 01 folder of the Data Files for Students. Save the photo on your storage device as Case 1-3 Chapel Edited, using the PSD format. Resize the photo to be 3.5 inches wide. Create a black border of 10 pixels. Save the file again and print a copy for your instructor.

Ps File Edit Image Layer Type Select Filter 3D View Window Help

Adobe **Photoshop CC**   Feather: 0 px   ☐ Anti-alias   Style: Normal ⬦   Width   Height   Refine Edge...

1 | Editing a Photo

Adobe product screenshot(s) reprinted with permission from Adobe Systems Incorporated;
Microsoft product screenshot(s) used with permission from Microsoft Corporation.

Objectives

You will have mastered the material in this chapter when you can:

- Start Photoshop CC and customize the Photoshop CC workspace
- Open a photo
- Identify parts of the Photoshop CC workspace
- Explain file types
- View a photo using the Zoom Tool, Navigator panel, and Hand Tool
- Display rulers
- Straighten and crop a photo

- Save a photo for both print and the web
- Create a border
- Open a recent file
- Resize a photo
- Insert text and stroke
- Print a photo
- Access Photoshop CC Help
- Close a file and quit Photoshop CC

Ps   File   Edit   Image   Layer   Type   Select   Filter   3D   View   Window   Help

Adobe **Photoshop CC**   Feather: 0 px   Anti-alias   Style: Normal   Width: Height: Refine Edge...

1 | Editing a Photo

What Is Photoshop Creative Cloud?

Photoshop Creative Cloud or **Photoshop CC** is a popular image editing software program produced by Adobe Systems Incorporated. Photoshop CC includes many updates from Photoshop Creative Suite 6 (CS6) and all of the features from the Photoshop CS6 Extended version. Photoshop CC is part of the **Adobe Creative Cloud** app that uses the web to deliver subscription-based access to a wide variety of Adobe programs, including those previously included in the Creative Suite. An **app** (short for application) refers to a program designed to make users more productive. Compared with previous versions of Photoshop, the Photoshop app requires a smaller initial investment for customers, and its frequent updates keep your software current. Unlike other software as a service (SaaS) models, Adobe Creative Cloud and its components are installed and run locally on your own computer rather than running hosted on the web.

Image-editing software refers to computer apps and programs that allow you to create and modify **digital images**, or pictures in electronic form. One type of digital image is a digital **photograph**, or **photo**, which is a picture taken with a camera and stored as a digitized file. Other types of digital images include scanned images, or electronic forms of original artwork created from scratch. Digital images are used in graphic applications, advertising, print publishing, and on the web. Personal uses include private photos, online photo sharing, scrapbooking, blogging, and social networking, among others. Image-editing software, such as Photoshop CC, can be used for basic adjustments such as rotating, cropping, or resizing, as well as for more advanced manipulations, such as airbrushing, retouching, photo repair, changing the contrast of images and balancing or combining elements of different images. Because Photoshop CC allows you to save multilayered, composite images and then return later to extract parts of those images, it works well for repurposing a wide variety of graphic-related files.

Photoshop CC comes bundled with other apps in the Creative Cloud suite from Adobe. It also is sold independently as a stand-alone app. Photoshop CC is available for both the PC and Macintosh computer platforms. The chapters in this book use Photoshop CC on the PC platform, running the Windows 8 operating system; however, Photoshop looks very similar whether you are using Windows 8.1, Windows 7, or the Mac Operating System. All versions present the same tools and similar menus. One of the main differences between the PC and the Mac is in the approach to shortcut keys. Windows uses the CTRL key to access many of the shortcuts in the Adobe Creative Cloud suite; the Mac operating system uses the CMD key represented by the symbol ⌘ and sometimes the OPT key represented by the symbol ⌥. Windows 8 system dialog boxes are presented in the chapters; the corresponding steps for Mac users are presented in the For Mac Users Appendix. In addition, if the Windows 7 instructions differ from those for Windows 8, you will find the Windows 7 steps in a yellow box following the Windows 8 steps.

To illustrate the features of Photoshop CC, this book presents a series of chapters that use Photoshop CC, more commonly referred to as just **Photoshop**, to edit photos similar to those you will encounter in academic and business environments, as well as photos for personal use.

BTW

Creative Cloud Accounts
Businesses and students with Creative Cloud accounts can store files for use on any computer and from any location. Adobe Creative Cloud subscribers receive 20 megabytes (MB) of online storage. A new sync feature allows users to synchronize files, fonts, and settings from one device to another.

Project — Postcard Graphic

A **postcard** is a rectangular piece of mail intended for writing and sending without an envelope. People use postcards for greetings, announcements, reminders, and business contacts. Many times, a postcard is an effective marketing tool used to generate prospective leads at a relatively low cost. One of the most popular uses for postcards involves pictures. Businesses and organizations produce a postcard with a photo or graphic on one side, and a short description with room to write brief correspondence on the other. People purchase picture postcards to mail to friends or to serve as reminders of their vacation. Sometimes a picture postcard is mailed to attract attention and direct people to websites or business locations. A postcard graphic must portray clearly its message or theme in an eye-catching manner, keeping in mind the relevant audience.

Most postcards are rectangular, at least 3½ inches high and 5 inches long – some are larger. A common size is 4 inches by 6 inches. A picture postcard might contain text printed over the picture or a border to add interest. A graphic designed for a postcard should be of high quality, use strong color, and must deliver a message in the clearest, most attractive, and most effective way possible. Photos edited to look good on postcards also make good additions to social media sites and electronic communication.

The project in this chapter uses Photoshop to enhance a photograph of a surfer and add text to create a postcard. The original photo appears in Figure 1–1a. The edited photo appears in Figure 1–1b. The enhancements will emphasize the surfer, straighten and crop the photo slightly, and add text. A shaded border will frame the scene. Finally, the photo will be resized to fit on a postcard, and then optimized for use on a website.

(a)

(b)

Figure 1–1

© iStock.com/VincentsEar

Overview

As you read this chapter, you will learn how to edit the photo shown in Figure 1–1a on the previous page by performing these general tasks:

- Customize the workspace.
- Display a photo at various magnifications.
- Crop and straighten a photo effectively.
- Create and modify a border.
- Stroke a selection.
- Resize and print a photo.
- Save, close, and then reopen a photo.
- Add stroked text to the photo.
- Save a photo for the web.
- Use Photoshop Help.

BTW

Gestures
Windows users who have computers or devices with touch screen capability can interact with the screen using gestures. A **gesture** is a motion you make on a touch screen with the tip of one or more fingers, or your hand. Touch screens are convenient because they do not require a separate device for input.

BTW

The Swipe Gesture
When you want to gain access to another portion of the screen such as scrolling, or when you need to gain access to the Charms bar in Windows 8, you can press and hold one finger and then move the finger horizontally or vertically on the screen in a **swipe gesture**. This gesture emulates moving the mouse, or clicking a scroll bar.

BTW

Windows 8 Start Screen
After you sign into a computer running Windows 8, Windows displays the Start screen, which shows tiles corresponding to the installed apps that you use regularly. From the Start screen, you can choose which app to run by using a touch screen, mouse, or other input device.

Plan Ahead

General Project Guidelines

When editing a photo, the actions you perform and decisions you make will affect the appearance and characteristics of the finished product. As you edit a photo, such as the one shown in Figure 1–1a, you should follow these general guidelines:

1. **Find an appropriate image or photo.** Keep in mind the purpose and the graphic needs of the project when choosing an image or photo. Decide ahead of time on the file type and decide whether the image will be used on the web. An eye-catching graphic image should convey a theme that is understood universally. The photo should grab the attention of viewers and draw them into the picture, whether in print or on the web.

2. **Determine how to edit the photo to highlight the theme.** As you edit, keep in mind your subject, your audience, the required size and shape of the graphic, color decisions, the rule of thirds, the golden rectangle, and other design principles. Decide which parts of the photo portray your message and which parts are visual clutter. Crop the photo as needed.

3. **Identify finishing touches that will further enhance the photo.** The overall appearance of a photo significantly affects its ability to communicate clearly. You might want to add text or a border.

4. **Prepare for publication.** Resize the photo as needed to fit the allotted space. Save the photo on a storage medium, such as a hard drive, USB flash drive, or CD, or store it on the cloud. Print the photo or publish it to the web.

When necessary, more specific details concerning the above guidelines are presented at appropriate points in the chapter. The chapter also will identify the actions performed and decisions made regarding these guidelines during the creation of the edited photo shown in Figure 1–1b on the previous page.

Starting Photoshop CC

If you are using a computer to step through the project in this chapter, and you want your screen to match the figures in this book, you should change your screen's resolution to 1366 × 768. For information about how to change a screen's resolution, read the Editing Preferences Appendix.

To Start Photoshop CC

The following steps, which assume Windows 8 is running, start Photoshop CC based on a typical installation. After starting your computer, you may be required to sign in to an account to access the computer's resources. If necessary, ask your instructor how to sign in to your account and how to start Photoshop CC for your computer.

1

- With Windows 8 running, scroll to display the Photoshop CC tile on the Start screen (Figure 1–2).

Q&A What is the best way to scroll?

You can scroll by swiping the screen, by tapping or clicking the scroll bar at the bottom of the Start screen, or by using the ARROW keys on your keyboard.

Is it OK to use Photoshop CC (64 bit)?

Yes, your computer may run an operating system the uses the 64 Bit version of Photoshop CC. Your steps and screens will work exactly the same way.

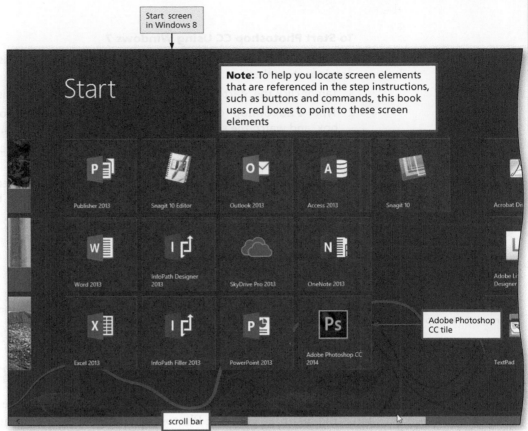

Start screen in Windows 8

Start

Note: To help you locate screen elements that are referenced in the step instructions, such as buttons and commands, this book uses red boxes to point to these screen elements

Adobe Photoshop CC tile

scroll bar

Figure 1–2

2

- Tap or click the Adobe Photoshop CC tile to run the Photoshop CC app.

- After a few moments, when the Photoshop window is displayed, if the window is not maximized, tap or click the Maximize button next to the Close button on the Application bar to maximize the window (Figure 1–3).

Q&A Can I use a stylus to tap the correct tile?

Yes. You can tap the tile with your finger, click the tile with your mouse, or tap the screen with a stylus to select and run the app. A **stylus** is a pen-shaped device used to interact with a touch screen by applying the stylus tip to the screen with a light pressure.

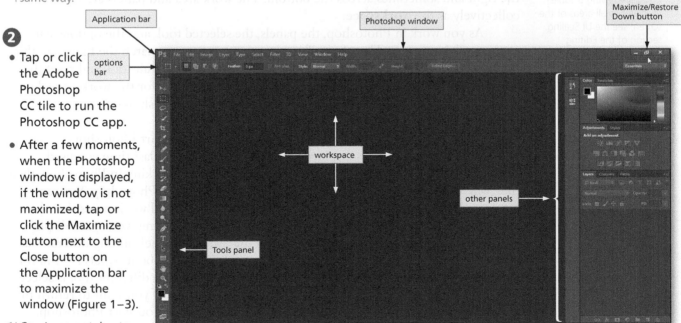

Application bar

options bar

Photoshop window

Maximize/Restore Down button

workspace

other panels

Tools panel

Figure 1–3

To Start Photoshop CC Using Windows 7

If you are using Windows 7, perform these steps to start Photoshop CC instead of the previous steps that use Windows 8.

1. Tap or click the Start button on the Windows 7 taskbar to display the Start menu.

2. Type `Photoshop CC` as the search text in the 'Search programs and files' text box, and watch the search results appear on the Start menu.

3. Tap or click Adobe Photoshop CC in the search results on the Start menu to start Photoshop CC.

After a few moments, when the Photoshop window is displayed, if the window is not maximized, tap or click the Maximize button next to the Close button on the Application bar to maximize the window.

MAC For a detailed example of this procedure using the Mac operating system, refer to the For Mac Users Appendix.

Other Ways

1. Tap or click Search charm on Charms bar, type Photoshop CC in search box, tap or click app name in results list

2. Double-tap or double-click file created in Photoshop CC

Customizing the Photoshop Workspace

BTW

Windows 8 Tiles
Some versions of Windows 8 might display a 'Show All Apps' button with a blue arrow to help you find the correct tile.

BTW

Using a Touch Screen
If you are having trouble touching small areas of the screen, see the UI Scaling section of the Editing Preferences Appendix for ways to increase the size of the menus and buttons in Photoshop.

BTW

Charms
If you swipe in or point to the right side of the screen in Windows 8, Windows displays the Charms bar. The five charms — Search, Share, Start, Devices, and Settings — are quick ways to access the actions you perform often, such as searching the web and your system, printing documents, and emailing photos and links. Charms always are available on the right side of your screen, no matter where you are in Windows.

The screen in Figure 1–3 on the previous page shows how the Photoshop workspace looks the first time you start Photoshop after installation on most computers. Photoshop does not open a blank or default photo automatically; rather, the Application bar and the options bar appear across the top of the screen with a work area below the options bar. The Tools panel is displayed on the left; other panels are displayed on the right and sometimes across the bottom. The work area and panels are referred to collectively as the **workspace**.

As you work in Photoshop, the panels, the selected tool, and the options bar settings might change. Therefore, if you want your screen to match the figures in this book, you should restore the default workspace, select the default tool, and reset the options bar. In addition, users might change the default color for the workspace. For more information about how to change other advanced Photoshop settings, see the Editing Preferences Appendix.

Because of a default preference setting, each time you start Photoshop, the Photoshop workspace is displayed the same way it was the last time you used Photoshop. If you (or another user) move the panels while working in Photoshop, then they will appear in their new locations the next time you start Photoshop. You can create and save your own workspaces, or use Photoshop's saved workspaces that show groups of panels used for certain tasks. For example, the Painting workspace displays the Brush panel, the Brush presets panel, and the Swatches panel, among others — all of which you would need when painting. You will learn more about panels later in this chapter. Similarly, if values on the options bar are changed or a different tool is selected, they will remain changed the next time you start Photoshop. If you want to return the workspace to its default settings, follow these steps each time you start Photoshop.

To Select the Essentials Workspace and Reset It

The default workspace, called Essentials, displays commonly used panels. The following steps use the **workspace switcher** to select the Essentials workspace and reset its default values.

1

- Tap or click the workspace switcher on the options bar to display the list of workspaces (Figure 1–4).

Experiment

- Tap or click each of the workspaces that are displayed in the list to view the different panel configurations. Notice that Photoshop displays the name of the selected workspace in blue. When you are finished, tap or click the workspace switcher again to display the list.

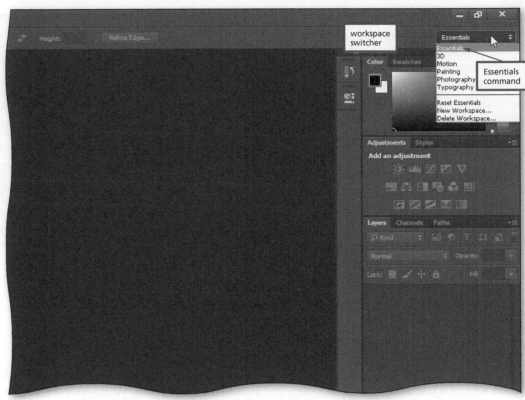

Figure 1–4

2

- Tap or click Essentials in the workspace switcher list to select the default workspace.

- Tap or click the workspace switcher on the options bar to display the list again (Figure 1–5).

Q&A What does the New Workspace command do?
The New Workspace command displays a dialog box where you can create a new workspace based on the currently displayed panels. You also can delete a workspace from the workspace menu.

Figure 1–5

3

• Tap or click Reset Essentials to restore the workspace to its default settings and reposition any panels that previous users may have moved (Figure 1–6).

Q&A

My screen did not change. Did I do something wrong?

If Photoshop is a new installation on your system, you might not notice any changes on your screen.

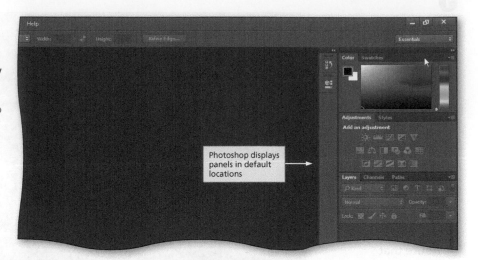

Photoshop displays panels in default locations

Figure 1–6

Other Ways

1. On Application bar, tap or click Window, tap or click Workspace, tap or click Essentials (Default), tap or click Window, tap or click Workspace, tap or click Reset Essentials

To Reset the Tools Panel

The following step resets the default colors on the Tools panel, and then selects the Rectangular Marquee Tool, which is the default tool for a new installation of Photoshop. When you select a tool on the Tools panel, the options bar reflects the settings of that tool.

1

• If the tools in the Tools panel appear in two columns, tap or click the double arrow at the top of the Tools panel to display the Tools panel as a single column.

• Tap or click the 'Default Foreground and Background Colors' button near the bottom of the Tools panel to ensure that the default colors are black and white.

• If the color white appears over black at the bottom of the Tools panel, tap or click the 'Switch Foreground and Background Colors' button to choose the default colors.

• If necessary, tap or click the second button from the top on the Tools panel to select it.

• If the button does not display a square icon, press and hold or right-click the button, and then tap or click 'Rectangular Marquee Tool' on the context menu (Figure 1–7).

Q&A

What appears when I point to the button?

When you point to many objects in the Photoshop workspace, such as a tool or button, Photoshop displays a tool tip. A **tool tip** is a short, on-screen note associated with the object to which you are pointing, which helps you identify the object. The name of the button you selected is the Rectangular Marquee Tool.

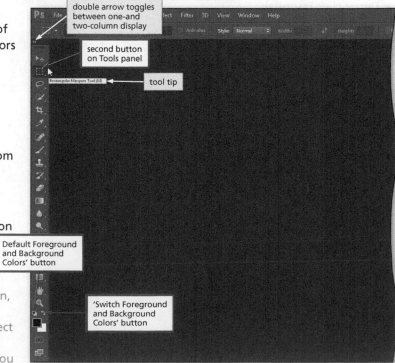

double arrow toggles between one-and two-column display

second button on Tools panel

tool tip

Default Foreground and Background Colors' button

'Switch Foreground and Background Colors' button

Figure 1–7

Other Ways

1. Press D, press M

To Reset the Options Bar

As you work through the chapters, editing photos and creating images, you will find that the options bar is context sensitive, which means it changes as you select different tools. In addition, the options and settings are retained for the next time you use Photoshop. To match the figures in this book, you should reset the options bar using a context menu each time you start Photoshop. A **context menu**, or **shortcut menu**, appears when you press and hold or right-click a specific object in the Photoshop workspace. A context menu displays commands representing the active tool, selection, or panel.

The following steps reset all tool settings in the options bar using a context menu.

1

- Press and hold or right-click the 'Rectangular Marquee Tool' icon on the options bar to display its context menu (Figure 1–8).

Q&A Why is my icon elliptical?
It is possible that a previous user changed the Rectangular Marquee Tool to the Elliptical Marquee Tool. Press SHIFT+M to return to the Rectangular Marquee Tool.

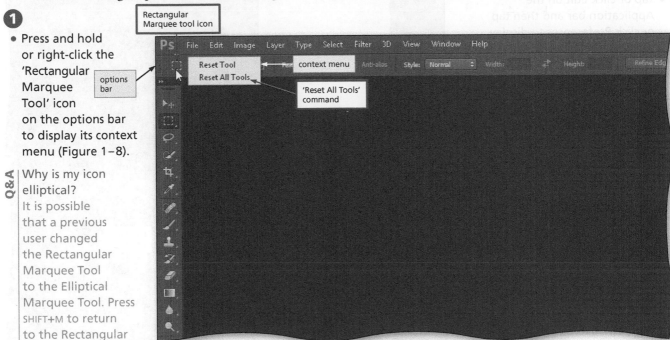

Figure 1–8

2

- Tap or click 'Reset All Tools' to display a confirmation dialog box (Figure 1–9).

Q&A I am having trouble touching the menu items. Is there anything I can do?
Yes. See the UI Scaling section of the Editing Preferences Appendix for ways to increase the size of the menus and buttons in Photoshop.

3

- Tap or click the OK button to restore the tools to their default settings.

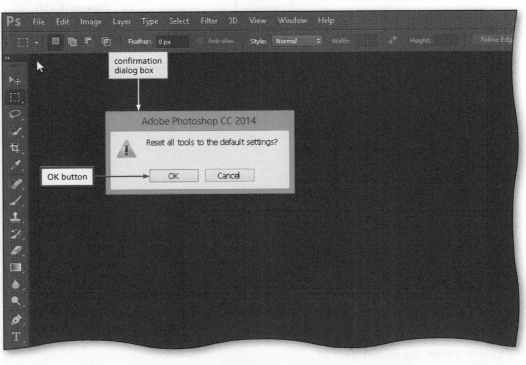

Figure 1–9

To Reset the Interface Color

Photoshop allows the user to choose from among four different color themes for the interface: Black, Dark Gray, Medium Gray, and Light Gray. The color theme you choose depends upon your personal preferences for contrast, focus, and readability.

The following steps reset the interface color to Medium Gray, which displays the workspace in dark gray and the panels in medium gray.

- Tap or click Edit on the Application bar and then tap or click Preferences to display the Preferences submenu (Figure 1–10).

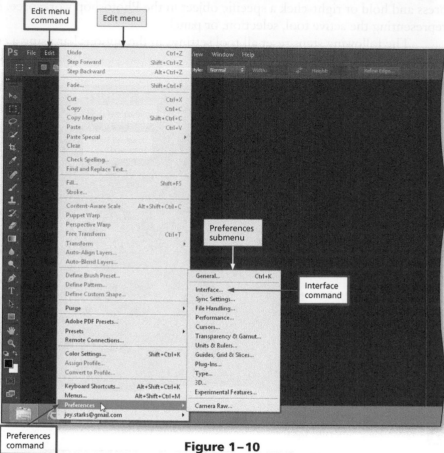

Figure 1–10

2

- Tap or click Interface on the Preferences submenu to display the Preferences dialog box.

- In the Appearance area, tap or click the third button, Medium Gray, to change the interface color (Figure 1–11).

Q&A What other preferences can I change?

You can change the color of certain display features, the number of states in the History panel, and the unit of measure, among others.

Figure 1–11

Experiment

- One at a time, tap or click each of the four color themes and notice how the interface changes. You can drag the title bar of the Preferences dialog box to move it out of the way, if necessary.

3

- Tap or click the OK button in the Preferences dialog box to close the dialog box and return to the Photoshop workspace (Figure 1–12).

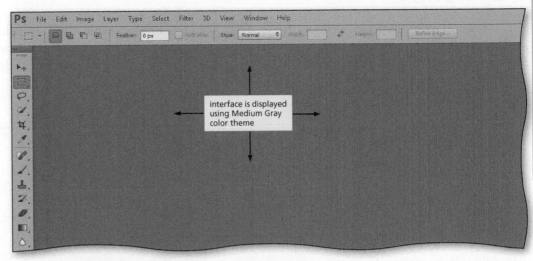

interface is displayed using Medium Gray color theme

Figure 1–12

MAC For a detailed example of this procedure using the Mac operating system, refer to the For Mac Users Appendix.

Other Ways

1. Press CTRL+K, tap or click Interface in Preferences bar, tap or click desired color theme, tap or click OK button

2. Press and hold or right-click any button on vertical dock of panels, tap or click Interface, tap or click desired color theme, tap or click OK button

Opening a Photo

To open a photo in Photoshop, it must be stored as a digital file on your computer system or on an external storage device. To **open** a photo, you bring a copy of the file from the storage location to the screen where you can **edit**, or make changes to, the photo. The changes do not become permanent, however, until you **save** or store the changed file on a storage device. The photos used in this book are included in the Data Files for Students. Visit solutions.cengage.com/ctdownloads for detailed instructions or contact your instructor for information about accessing the required files.

Find an appropriate image or photo.
Sometimes a person or business gives you a specific photo for use in a project. Other times, you are assigned a theme and asked to find or take the photo. An eye-catching graphic image should visually convey a message that is not expressed easily with words. Keep the audience in mind as you choose a photo. Photos generally fall into one of four categories:

- In advertising, a photo might show a product, service, result, model, or benefit.

- In a public service setting, a photo might represent a topic of interest, nature, signage, buildings, or a photo of historical importance.

- In industry, a photo might display a process, product, work organization, employee, facility, layout, equipment, safety, result, or culture.

- For personal or journalistic use, a photo might be a portrait, scenery, action shot, or event.

The images used in postcards must fit into a small space. A picture on a postcard might contain text printed over the picture or a border to attract attention. A graphic designed for a postcard should be of high quality, use strong color, and must deliver a message in the clearest, most attractive, and most effective way possible.

BTW **The Tap Gesture**
When you want to select an object, activate a link, press a button, or run an app, you should use the **tap gesture**, by quickly touching and releasing one finger, one time. This gesture emulates a mouse click.

Plan Ahead

BTW **The Press and Hold Gesture**
When you want to display a shortcut menu or gain immediate access to allowable actions, press and hold one finger to cause a context menu to display in a gesture called the **press and hold gesture**. This gesture emulates right-clicking the mouse.

To Open a File

The following steps open the Surfer file from the Data Files for Students. Visit solutions.cengage.com /ctdownloads for detailed instructions or contact your instructor for information about accessing the required files. A typical installation of the Data Files for Students, on a single system, unzips the downloaded files to the Documents folder in Windows 8.

- Tap or click File on the Application bar to display the File menu (Figure 1–13).

Q&A

Do I need the Data Files for Students?
You will need the Data Files for Students to complete the activities and exercises in this book. See your instructor for information on how to acquire the necessary files.

Can I use a shortcut key to open a file?
Yes, the shortcut keys are displayed on the menu. In this book, the shortcut keys also are displayed at the end of each series of steps in the Other Ways box.

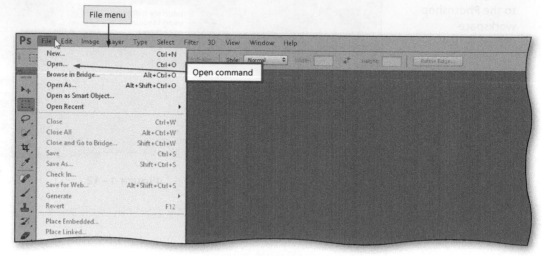

Figure 1–13

- Tap or click Open on the File menu to display the Open dialog box.

- If necessary, tap or click the arrow next to Libraries, or This PC, in the Navigation pane to display the inclusive folders.

- Tap or click the Documents location to display a list of the available folders and files (Figure 1–14).

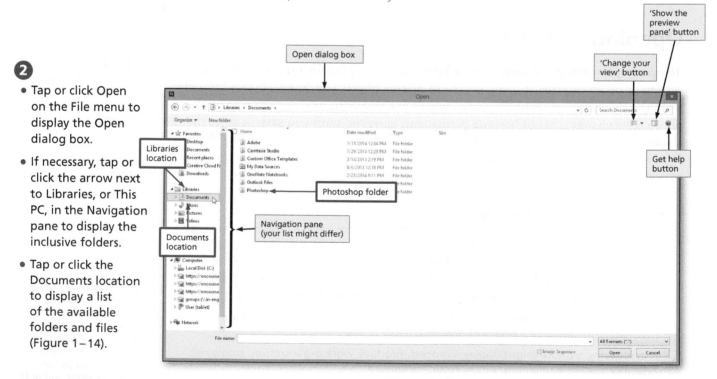

Figure 1–14

Q&A

What do the other buttons in the Open dialog box do?
On the right side of the toolbar are buttons to help you change the view, navigate folders, and get help. Links to common storage locations appear in the Navigation pane on the left.

3

- Double-tap or double-click the desired folder to display its contents (in this case, the Photoshop folder) (Figure 1–15).

Q&A I do not have a Photoshop folder. Did I do something wrong?
You might have downloaded the Data Files for Students to a different location. Navigate to that location using the Navigation pane, or see your instructor for the correct location of the downloaded files.

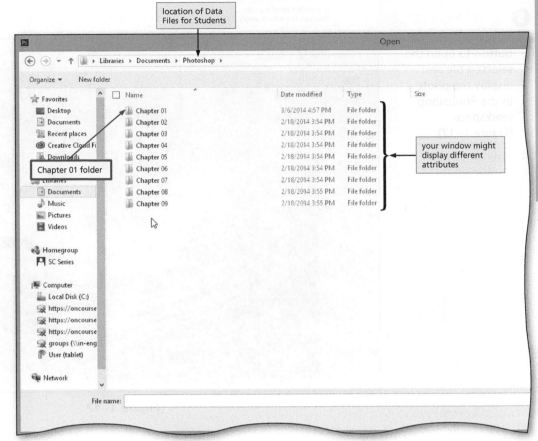

Figure 1–15

4

- Double-tap or double-click the Chapter 01 folder to display its contents

- Tap or click the file, Surfer, to select the file to be opened (Figure 1–16).

Q&A Why is my file list different?
Your list might vary. In addition, the files in Figure 1–16 are displayed in Details view. Tap or click the More Options arrow on the dialog box toolbar to verify your view.

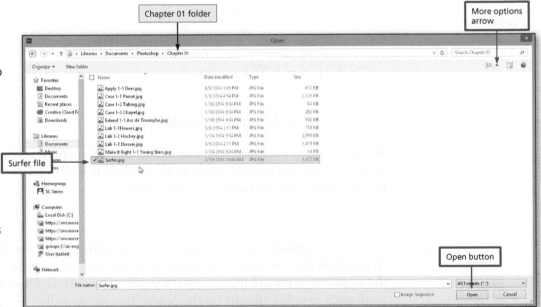

Figure 1–16

5

- Tap or click the Open button to open the selected file and display the photo in the Photoshop workspace (Figure 1–17).

Q&A

How do I edit a printed photo?
Most of the images you will use in this book already are stored in digital format; however, when you have a print copy of a picture, rather than a digital file stored on your system, it sometimes is necessary to scan the picture using a scanner. A **scanner** is a device used to convert a hard copy into a digital format for storage, retrieval, or other electronic purposes. Photoshop allows you to bring a copy from the scanner directly into the workspace.

Figure 1–17

For a detailed example of this procedure using the Mac operating system, refer to the For Mac Users Appendix.

Other Ways

1. Press CTRL+O, select file, tap or click Open

2. In Windows, press and hold or right-click file, tap or click Open with, tap or click Adobe Photoshop CC 2014

3. Double-tap or double-click a Photoshop file icon

The Photoshop Workspace

The Photoshop workspace consists of a variety of components to make your work more efficient and to make your photo documents look more professional. The following sections discuss these components.

The Application Bar

The **Application bar** appears at the top of the workspace (Figure 1–18). The Application bar contains the application button and the menu. On the far right side of the Application bar are the common window clip controls. On a Mac computer, the workspace switcher appears on the Application bar as well.

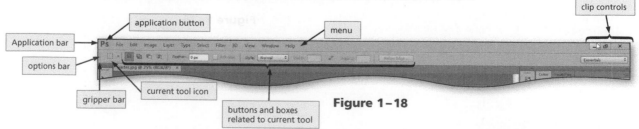

Figure 1–18

The menu displays the Photoshop menu names. Each **menu** contains a list of commands you can use to perform tasks such as opening, saving, printing, and editing photos. To display a menu, such as the View menu, tap or click the View menu name on the Application bar. If you point to, tap, or click a command on a menu that has an arrow on its right edge, a **submenu**, or secondary menu, displays another list of commands. (See Figure 1–10 on page PS 10).

The Options Bar

The **options bar** (Figure 1–18) appears below the Application bar. Sometimes called the control panel, the options bar contains buttons and boxes that allow you to perform tasks more quickly than when using the Application bar and related menus. Most buttons on the options bar display words or images to indicate their functions. When you point to a button or box on the options bar, a tool tip is displayed below the pointer. The options bar changes to reflect the tool currently selected on the Tools panel. For example, a tool related to text might display a font box on the options bar, whereas a tool related to painting will display a brush button. The selected tool always appears as an icon on the left side of the options bar. On the far right, the options bar displays the workspace switcher, regardless of which tool you select.

You can **float**, or move, the options bar in the workspace by dragging the gray gripper bar on the left side of the options bar. You can **dock**, or reattach, the options bar below the Application bar by resetting the workspace. To hide or show the options bar, tap or click Options on the Window menu.

The Tools Panel

On the left side of the workspace is the Tools panel. The **Tools panel**, also called the **Tools gallery**, is a group of **tools**, or buttons, organized into a toolbar. As with the options bar, you can float, dock, hide, or show the Tools panel. Each tool on the Tools panel displays a **tool icon**. When you point to the tool icon, a tool tip displays the name of the tool, including its shortcut key. You can expand some tools to show hidden tools beneath them. Expandable tools display a small triangle in the lower-right corner of the tool icon. Press and hold, click and hold, or right-click the tool button to see or select one of its hidden tools from the context menu. On a Mac computer, you can CONTROL+tap or CONTROL+click to display the hidden tools. The default tool names and their corresponding shortcut keys are listed in Figure 1–19.

When you tap or click a tool on the Tools panel, Photoshop selects the button and changes the options bar as necessary. When using a tool from the Tools panel, the pointer changes to reflect the selected tool.

The Tools panel is organized by purpose. At the top of the panel is a button to display the panel in two columns, followed underneath by the gripper bar. Below that, the selection tools appear, then the crop and slice tools, followed by retouching, painting, drawing and type, annotation, measuring, and navigation tools. At the bottom of the Tools panel are buttons to set colors, create a quick mask, and change screen modes.

As each tool is introduced throughout this book, its function and options bar characteristics will be explained further.

BTW

The Drag or Slide Gesture
When you want to move an item around on the screen, or scroll, you can press and hold one finger on an object and then move the finger to the new location in a **drag gesture**. This gesture emulates clicking the mouse, holding down the button and moving.

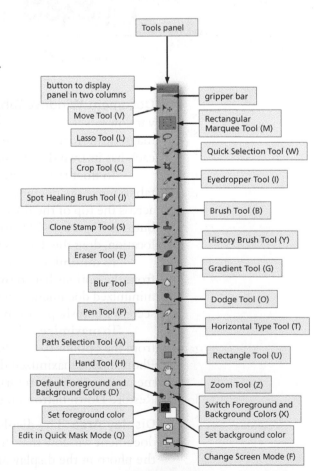

Figure 1–19

The Document Window

The **document window** is the windowed area within the workspace that displays the active file or image. The document window contains the document window tab, the display area, scroll bars, and a status bar (Figure 1–20).

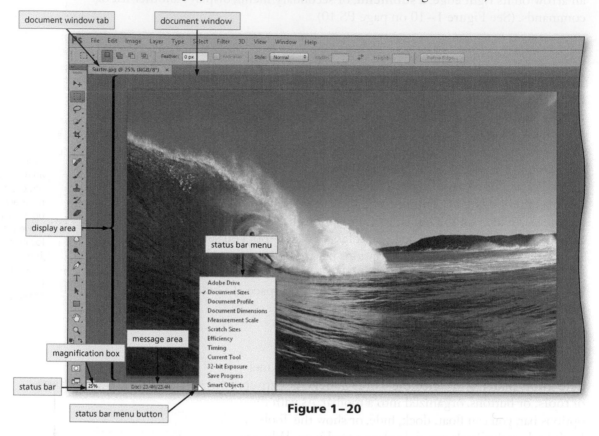

Figure 1–20

Document Window Tab When a file is open, Photoshop displays a document window tab at the top of the document window that shows the name of the file, the magnification, the color mode, and a Close button. If you have multiple files open, each has its own document window tab.

To **float** the document window in the display area, drag the document window tab to move the document window. When floating, the document Window tab expands across the top of the document window and displays Minimize, Maximize, and Close buttons (Figure 1–21). To **dock** the document window again, or lock it in its previous location, drag the document window tab close to the options bar.

To **minimize** a document window, drag the document window tab away from the options bar so that it floats, and then tap or click the Minimize button. A minimized document window does not appear in the workspace; rather, it appears as a second Photoshop button on the Windows taskbar.

To **maximize** a document window, drag the document window tab away from the options bar so that it floats, and then tap or click the Maximize button. In Photoshop, a maximized document window fills the entire screen; you cannot see the menus or panels. To return the document window to a floating state, tap or click the Restore Down button on the document window title bar.

Display Area The **display area,** sometimes called the **canvas,** is the portion of the document window that displays the photo or image. You perform most tasks and edit the photo in the display area.

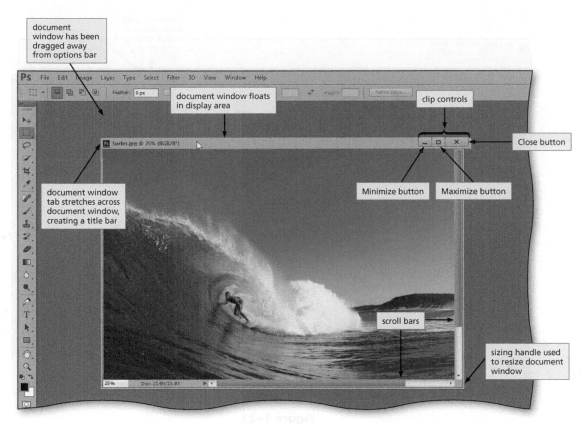

Figure 1–21

Scroll Bars When the photo is bigger than the document window, the **scroll bars** become active and display scroll arrows and scroll boxes to move the image up, down, left, and right.

Status Bar Across the bottom of the document window, Photoshop displays the **status bar** (Figure 1–20). The status bar contains a magnification box. **Magnification** refers to the percentage of enlargement or reduction on the screen. For example, a 50% indication in the magnification box means the entire photo is displayed at 50 percent of its actual size. Changing the magnification does not change the size of the photo physically; it merely displays it on the screen at a different size. You can type a new percentage in the magnification box to display a different view of the photo.

The status bar **message area** displays information about the file size, the current tool, or the document dimensions. When you first start Photoshop, the message area displays information about the document size in storage.

On the right of the message area is the status bar menu button that, when tapped or clicked, displays a status bar menu (Figure 1–20). You use the status bar menu to change the message area or to change to other versions of the document.

Your installation of Photoshop might display rulers at the top and left of the document window. You will learn about rulers later in this chapter.

Panels

A **panel** is a collection of graphically displayed choices and commands related to a specific tool or feature, such as those involving colors, brushes, actions, or layers (Figure 1–22 on the next page). Panels help you monitor and modify your work. Each panel displays a panel tab with the name of the panel and a panel menu button.

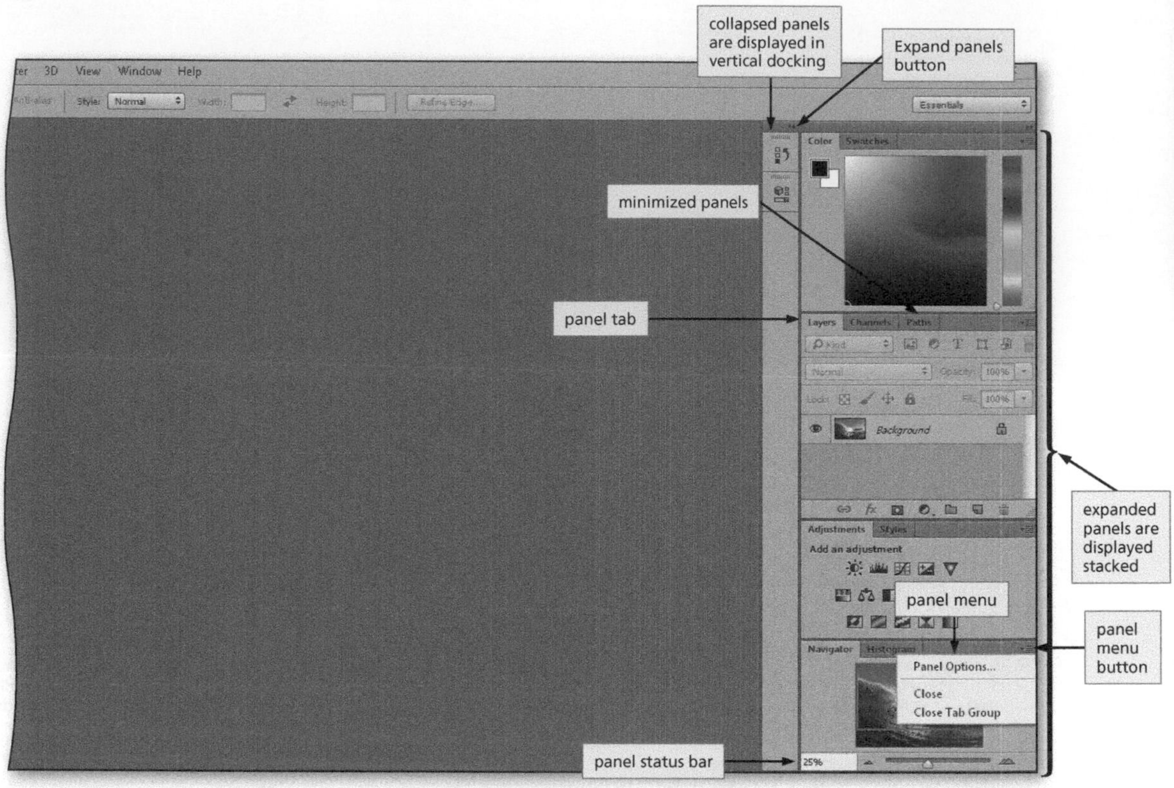

Figure 1–22

When you tap or click the panel menu button, also called the panel menu icon, Photoshop displays a context-sensitive panel menu that allows you to make changes to the panel. Some panels have a status bar across the bottom. A panel can display buttons, boxes, sliders, scroll bars, or drop-down lists.

Several panels appear in the Essentials workspace. Some panels are expanded to display their contents, and are grouped by general purpose. A **panel group** or **tab group** displays several panels horizontally. The panel groups are docked vertically on the right side of the workspace. Other open panels are displayed along the bottom, or as icons or buttons in a vertical dock between the document window and the expanded panels. Panels are **collapsed** when they appear as a button, or **expanded** when they display their contents. Panels are **minimized** or **collapsed** when they display only their tab. To collapse or expand a panel, tap or click the double arrow at the top of the panel, or double-tap or double-click its tab. To close a panel, tap or click Close on the panel menu. To redisplay the panel, tap or click the panel name on the Window menu or use a panel shortcut key.

You can arrange and reposition panels either individually or in groups. To move a single panel, drag the panel tab; to move a group, drag the area to the right of the tabs. To float a panel in the workspace, drag its tab outside of the vertical dock. You can create a **stack** of floating panels by dragging a panel tab to a location below another floating panel and dock it.

Sometimes you might want to hide all the panels to display more of the document window. To hide all panels, press the TAB key. Press the TAB key again to display the panels.

BTW

The Double-Tap Gesture
When you want to run a program or an app, or select a file in a dialog box, you can quickly touch and release one finger two times in a **double-tap gesture**. This gesture emulates a mouse double-click.

In addition to the Tools panel described earlier, Photoshop comes with 26 other panels, described in Table 1–1. These panels can be accessed using the Window menu. As each panel is introduced throughout this book, its function and characteristics will be explained further.

Table 1–1 Photoshop Panels

Panel Name	Purpose
3D	To show the 3D layer components, settings, and options of the associated 3D file
Actions	To record, play, edit, and delete individual actions
Adjustments	To create nondestructive adjustment layers with color and tonal adjustments
Brush	To select preset brushes and design custom brushes
Brush Presets	To create, load, save, and manage preset brush tips
Channels	To create and manage channels
Character	To provide options for formatting characters
Character Styles	To create, load, save, and manage character styles
Clone Source	To set up and manipulate sample sources for the Clone Stamp tools or Healing Brush tools
Color	To display the color values for the current foreground and background colors
Histogram	To view tonal and color information about an image
History	To jump to any recent state of the image created during the current working session
Info	To display color values and document status information
Layer Comps	To display multiple compositions of a page layout
Layers	To show and hide layers, create new layers, and work with groups of layers
Measurement Log	To record measurement data about a measured object
Navigator	To change the view or magnification of the photo using a thumbnail display
Notes	To insert, edit, and delete notes attached to files
Paragraph	To change the formatting of columns and paragraphs
Paragraph Styles	To create, load, save, and manage paragraph styles
Paths	To manipulate each saved path, the current work path, and the current vector mask
Properties	To display characteristics about the file and to assist in creating precise, editable pixel- and vector-based masks
Styles	To view and select preset styles
Swatches	To select and store colors that you need to use often
Timeline	To create a sequence of images or frames, displayed as motion over time
Tool Presets	To save and reuse tool settings

© Cengage Learning

File Types

A **file type** refers to the internal characteristics of digital files; it designates the operational or structural characteristics of a file. Each digital file, graphic or otherwise, is stored with specific kinds of formatting related to how the file appears on the screen, how it prints, and the software it uses to do so. Computer systems use the file type to help users open the file with the appropriate software. A **file extension**, in most computer systems, is a three- or four-letter suffix after the file name that distinguishes the file type. For example, Surfer.jpg refers to a file named Surfer with the extension and file type JPG. A period separates the file name and its extension. When you are exploring files on your system, you might see the file extensions as part of the file name, or you might see a column of information about file types.

Graphic files are created and stored using many different file types and extensions. The type of file sometimes is determined by the hardware or software used to create the file. Other times, the user has a choice in applying a file type and makes the decision based on the file size, the intended purpose of the graphic file — such as whether the file is to be used on the web — or the desired color mode.

A few common graphic file types are listed in Table 1–2.

Table 1–2 Graphic File Types

File Extension	File Type	Description
BMP	Bitmap	BMP is a standard Windows image format used on DOS and Windows-compatible computers. BMP format supports many different color modes.
EPS	Encapsulated PostScript	EPS files can contain both bitmap and vector graphics. Almost all graphics, illustration, and page-layout programs support the EPS format, which can be used to transfer PostScript artwork between applications.
GIF	Graphics Interchange Format	GIF commonly is used to display graphics and images on webpages. It is a compressed format designed to minimize file size and electronic transfer time.
JPG or JPEG	Joint Photographic Experts Group	JPG files commonly are used to display photographs on webpages. JPG format supports many different color modes. JPG retains all color information in an RGB image, unlike GIF format. Most digital cameras produce JPG files.
PDF	Portable Document Format	PDF is a flexible file format based on the PostScript imaging model that is cross-platform and cross-application. PDF files accurately display and preserve fonts, page layouts, and graphics. PDF files can contain electronic document search and navigation features such as hyperlinks.
PNG	Portable Network Graphics	PNG is a format that does not loose data when compressed or zipped. This format can display millions of colors and supports transparency.
PSD	Photoshop Document	PSD format is the default file format in Photoshop and the only format that supports all Photoshop features. Other Adobe applications can import PSD files directly and preserve many Photoshop features due to the tight integration among Adobe products.
RAW	Photoshop Raw	RAW format is a flexible file format used for transferring images between applications and computer platforms. There are no pixel or file size restrictions in this format. Documents saved in the Photoshop Raw format cannot contain layers.
TIF or TIFF	Tagged Image File Format	TIF is a flexible bitmap image format supported by almost all paint, image-editing, and page-layout applications. This format often is used for files that are to be exchanged between applications or computer platforms. Most desktop scanners can produce TIF images.

Saving a Photo

As you make changes to a file in Photoshop, the computer stores it in memory. If you turn off the computer or if you lose electrical power, the file in memory is lost. If you plan to use the photo later, you must save it on a storage device such as a USB flash drive, a hard disk, or in cloud storage.

While you are editing, to preserve the most features such as layers, effects, masks, and styles, Photoshop recommends that you save photos in the **PSD format**. PSD, which stands for Photoshop Document Format, is the default file format for files created from scratch in Photoshop, and supports files up to 2 gigabytes (GB) in size. The PSD format also maximizes portability among other Adobe versions and applications.

To Save a File in the PSD Format in a New Folder

The following steps save the photo using the file name, Surfer Edited. In addition to saving in the PSD format, you will save the photo with a new file name and in a new location, so that the original photo is available in case you need to start again. Even though you have yet to edit the photo, it is a good practice to save a copy of the file on your personal storage device early in the process.

The following steps also create a new folder in a save location called Creative Cloud Files. **Creative Cloud Files** is a storage location on your computer, which is created by Adobe's Creative Cloud app using your Adobe ID. An advantage of using the Creative Cloud Files location is that Adobe **syncs,** or synchronizes, your files with those stored on your Creative Cloud storage service. You must be online for the files to sync. If you do not have an Adobe account or a Creative Cloud Files location, you can save to your hard disk, a secondary storage device, or a location that is most appropriate to your situation.

1

- Make sure your storage device is connected to your computer, if necessary.

- Tap or click File on the Application bar to display the File menu (Figure 1–23).

Q&A Can I save to a USB flash drive?
Yes. You can save to any device or folder. If you have signed up for Adobe Creative Cloud storage, you can navigate to the Creative Cloud Files directory on your computer.

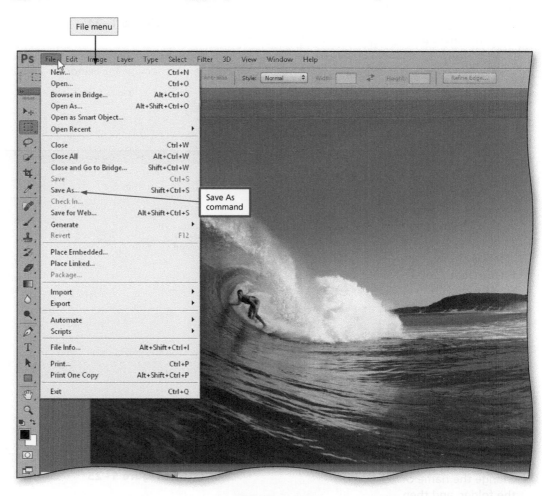

Figure 1–23

2

- Tap or click Save As to display the Save As dialog box.

- Type **Surfer Edited** in the File name text box to change the file name. Do not press the ENTER key after typing the file name (Figure 1–24).

Q&A Why is my list of drives arranged and named differently?
The size of the Save As dialog box and your computer's configuration determine how the list is displayed and how the drives are named. You can resize the dialog box by dragging the lower-right corner. The Save As dialog box in Windows 7 is slightly different. See the steps at the end of this section for Windows 7 instructions.

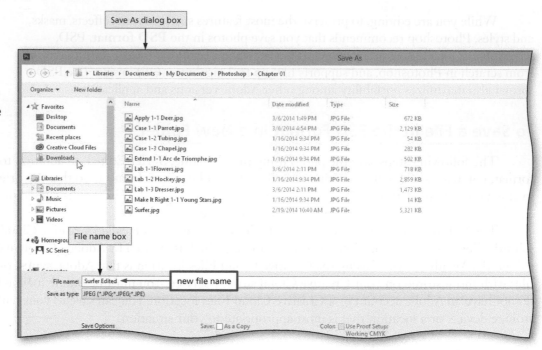

Figure 1–24

3

- Navigate to your storage location by using the Navigation pane or the Previous Locations box arrow to select that drive as the new save location (in this case, the Creative Cloud Files location).

- Tap or click the New folder button on the Save As dialog box toolbar to create a new folder on the selected storage device.

- When the new folder appears, type **Chapter 01** to change the name of the folder, and then press the ENTER key (Figure 1–25).

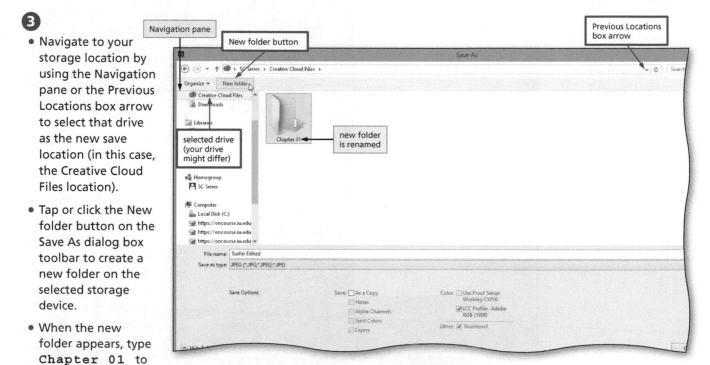

Figure 1–25

Q&A What if my storage device has a different name or letter?
It is very likely that your storage location or USB flash drive will have a different name and drive letter, and be connected to a different port. Verify that the device in your list is correct.

4

- Double-tap or double-click the new folder to open it.

- Tap or click the 'Save as type' button to display the list of available file formats (Figure 1–26).

Q&A Do I have to use the same file name?
It is good practice to identify the relationship of this photo to the original by using at least part of the original file name with some notation about its status.

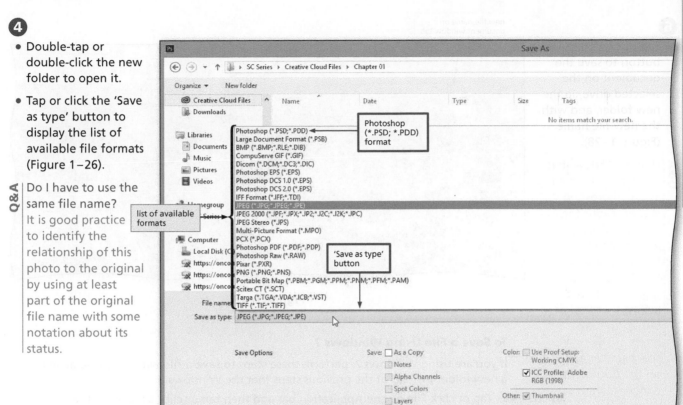

Figure 1–26

5

- Tap or click Photoshop (*.PSD; *.PDD) in the list to select the file type (Figure 1–27).

Q&A What is PDD?
The **PDD format** is used with images created by Photo Deluxe and other software packages. Some older digital cameras produce files with a PDD extension as well.

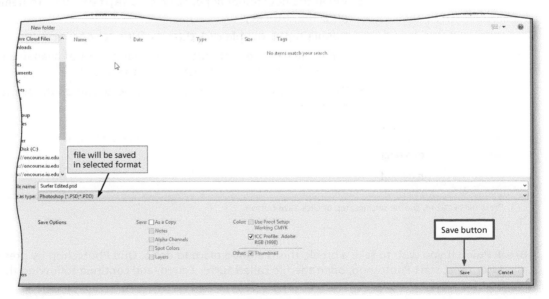

Figure 1–27

6

- Tap or click the Save button to save the document on the selected drive, in the new folder, and with the new file name (Figure 1–28).

Q&A

How do I know that the project is saved? While Photoshop is saving your file, it briefly displays a Working in Background shape. In addition, your drive might have a light that flashes during the save process. The new file name appears on the document window tab.

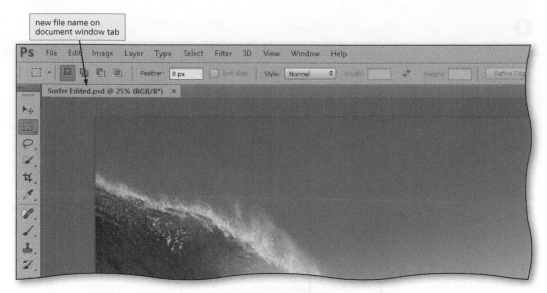

new file name on document window tab

Figure 1–28

To Save a File Using Windows 7

If you are using Windows 7, perform these steps to save a file with a new name and in a new folder instead of the previous steps that use Windows 8.

1. Tap or click File on the Application bar and then tap or click Save As on the File menu to display the Save As dialog box.

2. In the File name text box, type **Surfer Edited** to rename the file. Do not press the ENTER key.

3. Tap or click the Save in box arrow and navigate to your desired storage location.

4. Tap or click the Create New Folder button on the Save As dialog box toolbar.

5. When the new folder appears, type **Chapter 01** to name the folder and then press the ENTER key.

6. Double-tap or double-click the new folder to open it.

7. Tap or click the Format button to display the list of available file formats, and then tap or click Photoshop (*.PSD; *.PDD) to select it.

8. Tap or click the Save button to save the document on the selected drive with the new file name.

MAC

For a detailed example of this procedure using the Mac operating system, refer to the For Mac Users Appendix.

Other Ways

1. Press SHIFT+CTRL+S, choose settings, tap or click Save button

---

Break Point: If you wish to take a break, this is a good place to do so. Quit Photoshop by pressing CTRL+Q. To resume at a later time, start Photoshop, open the file called Surfer Edited, and continue following the steps from this location forward.

BTW

Adobe Creative Cloud

Using the Adobe Creative Cloud app, you can create an Adobe account and move your saved files to cloud storage on an Adobe online storage site. Adobe Creative Cloud also will **sync** or synchronize your cloud files with the data on your computer, updating both with the most recent information. Cloud storage makes your files available on any web-enabled device. For example, cloud storage is any easy way to keep files up-to-date between your desktop and your tablet.

Viewing Photos

Photoshop allows you to view photos in many different ways, by adjusting the document window and by using different tools and panels. Using good navigation techniques to view images can help you edit the details of a photo or check for problems. For example, you might want to zoom in on a specific portion of the photo or move to a different location in a large photo. You might want to use a ruler to measure certain portions of the photo. Or you might want to view the image without the distraction of the panels and menu. Zooming, navigating, scrolling, and changing the screen mode are some ways to view the document window and its photo.

Zooming

To make careful edits in a photo, you sometimes need to change the magnification, or **zoom**. Zooming allows you to focus on certain parts of the photo, such as a specific person in a crowd scene or details in a complicated picture. Zooming in enlarges the percentage of magnification of the photo; zooming out reduces the magnification. Note that zooming does not change the size of the photo; it merely changes the appearance of the photo in the document window.

The Zoom Tool button displays a magnifying glass icon on the Tools panel. You also can press the z key to select the Zoom Tool. Choosing one method over the other is a matter of personal choice. Most people use the shortcut key. Others sometimes choose the button because of its proximity to the pointer at the time.

When you use the Zoom Tool, each tap or click magnifies the image to the next preset percentage. When positioned in the photo, the Zoom Tool **pointer**, or mouse pointer, displays a magnifying glass, with either a plus sign, indicating an increase in magnification, or a minus sign, indicating a decrease in magnification. When you press and hold or right-click in the photo with the Zoom Tool, Photoshop displays a context menu with options to zoom in or zoom out, among others. To make the image fill as much of the available space in the document window, press CTRL+0 (zero) to fit on screen.

Figure 1–29 displays the Zoom Tool options bar, with buttons to zoom in and out. Other options include check boxes used when working with multiple photos, displaying the actual pixels, fitting the entire photo on the screen, filling the screen, and displaying the photo at its print size. A **pixel**, short for picture element, is a single dot or point in a graphic on the screen.

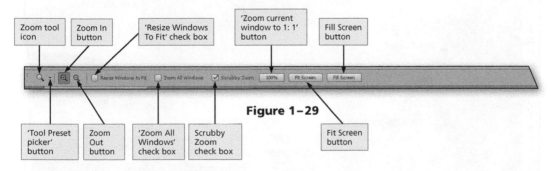

Figure 1–29

To Use the Zoom Tool

The following steps zoom in on the surfer for careful editing later in the chapter.

1

- Tap or click the Zoom Tool button on the Tools panel to select the Zoom Tool.

- Move the pointer into the document window to display the magnifying glass pointer (Figure 1–30).

Q&A Why does my pointer display a minus sign? It is possible that a previous user zoomed out and the setting has carried over. Tap or click the Zoom In button on the options bar.

Figure 1–30

2

- Tap or click the image twice to zoom in (Figure 1–31).

Q&A My magnification is not at 50%. How do I get to exactly 50%? Type 50 in the magnification box on the status bar, and then press the ENTER key.

Figure 1–31

Experiment

- On the options bar, tap or click the Zoom In button and then tap or click the photo. Tap or click the Zoom Out button and then tap or click the photo. ALT+tap or ALT+click the photo to zoom in the opposite direction from the options bar setting. Zoom to 50% magnification.

Other Ways

1. To zoom to 100%, double-tap or double-click Zoom Tool button	2. On View menu, tap or click Zoom In or Zoom Out	3. Press z, tap or click document window	4. Press CTRL+PLUS SIGN (+) or CTRL+MINUS SIGN (-)

The Navigator Panel

Another convenient way to zoom and move around the photo is to use the Navigator panel. The Navigator panel (Figure 1–32) is used to change the view of your document window using a thumbnail display. To display the Navigator panel, select Navigator from the Window menu.

The rectangle with the red border in the Navigator panel is called the **proxy view area** or **view box**, which outlines the currently viewable area in the window. Dragging the proxy view area changes the portion of the photo that is displayed in the document window. In the lower portion of the Navigator panel, you can type in the desired magnification, or you can use the slider or buttons to increase or decrease the magnification.

In Figure 1–32, the Navigator panel menu appears when you tap or click the panel menu button. The Panel Options command displays the Panel Options dialog box.

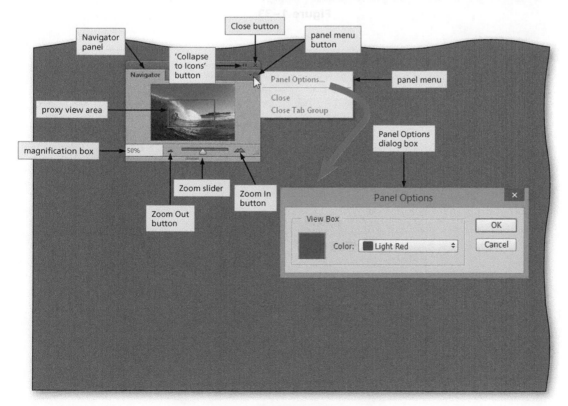

Figure 1–32

To Use the Navigator Panel

The following steps display and use the Navigator panel to reposition the view of the photo using the proxy view area.

1

- Tap or click Window on the Application bar to display the Window menu (Figure 1–33).

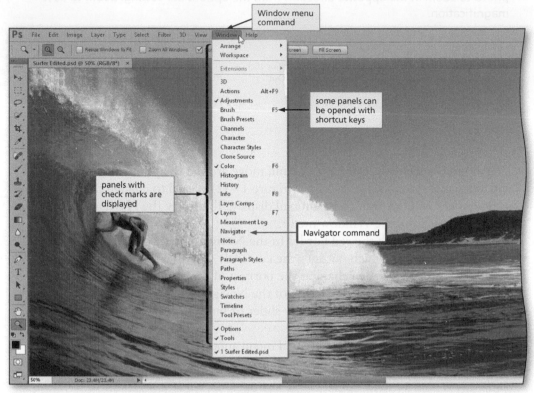

Figure 1–33

2

- Tap or click Navigator on the Window menu to display the Navigator panel (Figure 1–34).

Q&A Why would I choose the Navigator panel over other methods of moving around the screen?
When you are using a different tool on the Tools panel, such as a text tool or brush tool, it is easier to use the Navigator panel to zoom in or out and move around in the photo. That way, you do not have to change to the Zoom Tool, perform the zoom, and then change back to your editing tool.

Figure 1–34

3

- Drag the proxy view area on the Navigator Panel to display the right portion of the photo (Figure 1–35).

 Experiment

- Drag the proxy view area to display different portions of the photo. Drag the Zoom slider and try tapping or clicking the Zoom In and Zoom Out buttons on the Navigator panel. When you are finished, return to 50% magnification, and drag the proxy view area to display the upper-right portion of the photo.

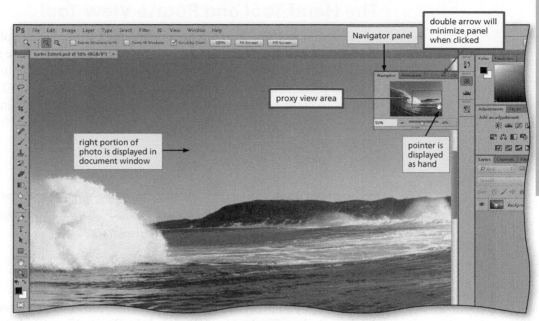

Figure 1–35

To Minimize the Navigator Panel

The following step minimizes the Navigator panel so it is displayed as a button in the vertical dock of buttons. In the right portion of the panel's title bar, the double arrow, sometimes called the 'Collapse to Icons' button, minimizes a panel.

1

- Tap or click the double arrow (shown in Figure 1-35) at the top of the Navigator panel (Figure 1–36).

Q&A How would I move or close the panel? To move the panel, drag the panel tab. To close the panel, tap or click Close on the panel menu, or if the panel is floating, click the panel's Close button.

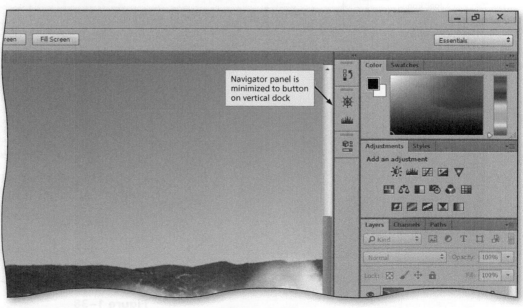

Figure 1–36

Other Ways

1. On vertical dock, tap or click Navigator button

The Hand Tool and Rotate View Tool

The Hand Tool also can be used to move around in the photo if the photo has been magnified to be larger than the document window. To use the Hand Tool, tap or click the Hand Tool button on the Tools panel, and then drag in the display area of the document window. The Hand Tool options bar (Figure 1–37) displays boxes and buttons to assist you in scrolling and manipulating the document window.

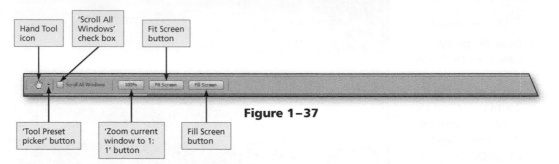

Figure 1–37

When you press and hold or right-click the Hand Tool button, Photoshop displays choices for the Hand Tool and the Rotate View Tool. The Rotate View Tool allows you to rotate the image without making any permanent change, which may help you touch up the photo or paint at certain angles. The pointer for the Rotate View Tool displays a hand with a rotation arrow. When you tap or click the image, Photoshop displays a compass to help you rotate the image (Figure 1–38). The Rotate View options bar helps you choose specific rotation angles and reset the display to its original view.

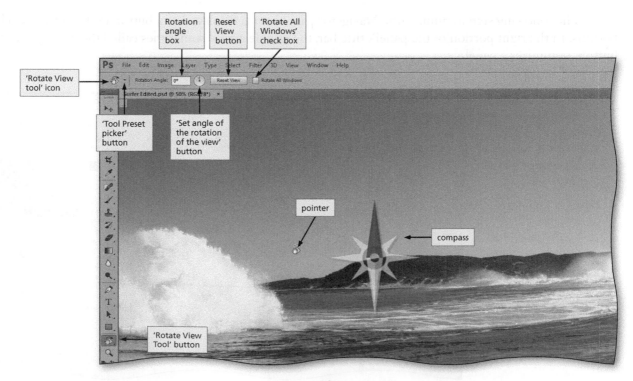

Figure 1–38

To Use the Hand Tool

The following step uses the Hand Tool to view a different part of the photo.

- Press and hold or right-click the Hand Tool button to display the list of tools (Figure 1–39)

Hand Tool button

Hand Tool command

Figure 1–39

- Tap or click Hand Tool to select the Hand Tool.

- Drag in the document window to display the surfer (Figure 1–40).

pointer

Figure 1–40

Other Ways

1. Press H, drag photo

To Change the Magnification

The following steps use the Magnification box on the status bar to change the magnification.

1

• Double-tap or double-click the Magnification box on the status bar to select the current magnification (Figure 1–41).

magnification is selected

Figure 1–41

2

• Type 20 and then press the ENTER key to change the magnification (Figure 1–42).

photo is displayed at new magnification

'Change Screen Mode' button

Figure 1–42

Other Ways

1. On Navigator panel, type percentage in Magnification box
2. On View menu, tap or click desired magnification
3. To magnify to 100%, press CTRL+1
4. To fit on screen, press CTRL+0 (zero)

To Display Rulers

To make careful edits in a photo, sometimes you need to use precise measurements in addition to zooming and navigating. In these cases, you should change the Photoshop document window to view the rulers. **Rulers** appear on the top and left sides of the document window. Rulers help you position images or elements precisely. As you move your pointer over a photo, markers on the ruler display the pointer's position.

The following steps display the rulers in the document window.

1

- Tap or click View on the Application bar to display the View menu (Figure 1–43).

Q&A What unit of measurement do the rulers use?

Rulers display inches by default, but you can press and hold or right-click a ruler to change the increment to pixels, centimeters, or other units of measurements.

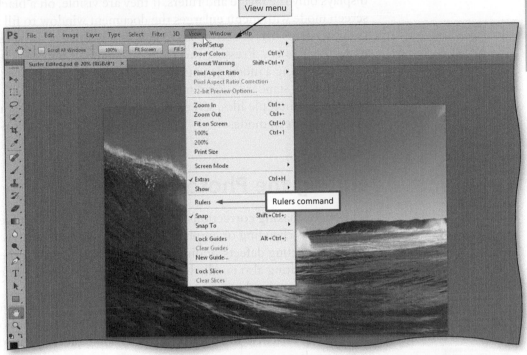

Figure 1–43

2

- Tap or click Rulers on the View menu to display the rulers in the document window (Figure 1–44).

Figure 1–44

Other Ways

1. Press CTRL+R

Screen Modes

To change the way the panels, bars, and document window appear, Photoshop includes three **screen modes**, or ways to view the document window. The Change Screen Mode button is located at the bottom of the Tools panel (Figure 1–42 on page PS 32) and toggles among the screen modes. Standard screen mode displays the Application bar, document window, scroll bars, and visible panels. Full screen mode displays only the image and rulers, if they are visible, on a black background. Full screen mode with menu enlarges the document window to fill the workspace with no title bar, status bar, or scroll bars. A fourth way to view the screen is to hide the panels using the TAB key. Pressing the TAB key again redisplays the panels.

Choosing a mode depends on what you are trying to accomplish. While editing a single photo, standard screen mode may be the best, especially for beginners. If you are working on multiple files, screen space is at a premium and you might want to use one of the full screen modes.

Editing the Photo

Editing, or making corrections and changes to a photo, involves a wide variety of tasks such as changing or emphasizing the focus of interest, recoloring portions of the photo, correcting defects, adding new artwork, or changing the file type for specific purposes. Editing also is called **post-processing**, because it includes actions you take after the picture has been processed by the camera or scanner.

Table 1–3 suggests typical categories and types of edits you might perform on photos; there are many others. When performed in combination, they can even create new editing varieties. You will learn more about edits as you work through the chapters in this book.

Editing the Surfer Edited photo will involve three steps. First, you will crop the photo to remove excessive background. Next, you will add a border and stroke it with color. Finally, you will resize the photo to fit the intended use and size requirements, inserting text for the postcard.

Table 1–3 Photo Edits

Category	Types of Edits
Transformations	Cropping, slicing, changing the aspect, rotating, leveling, mirroring, warping, skewing, distorting, flipping, and changing the perspective
Enhancements and Layering	Filters, layers, clones, borders, artwork, text, animation, painting, morphing, ordering, styles, masks, cutaways, selections, depth perception, anti-aliasing, moves, shapes, rasterizing
Color	Correction, contrast, blending, modes and systems, separations, screening, levels, ruling, trapping, matching, black and white
Correction	Sharpening, red-eye, tears, correcting distortion, retouching, reducing noise, blur, dodge, burn
File Type	Camera Raw, print, web, animated images
Resolution	Resampling, resizing, collinear editing, interpolation, editing pixel dimensions and document sizes

Determine how to edit the photo to highlight the theme.
You always should perform editing with design principles in mind. Look at your photo carefully. Are there parts that detract from the central figure? Would the theme be illustrated better by only displaying a portion of the photo? If you want to emphasize a single object on a fairly solid background, you might need to crop, or trim, extraneous space around the object. Decide which parts of the photo portray your message and which parts are visual clutter.

- Use the rule of thirds to position visual lines.
- Crop the photo to remove excess border.
- Rotate the photo if necessary.

Cropping

The first step in editing the surfer photo is to **crop**, or cut away, some of the extra background so the photo focuses on the surfer. Photographers try to compose and capture images full-frame, which means the object of interest fills the dimensions of the photo. When that is not possible, photographers and graphic artists crop the photo either to create an illusion of full-frame, to fit unusual shapes in layouts, or to make the image more dramatic. From a design point of view, sometimes it is necessary to crop a photo to straighten an image, remove distracting elements, or simplify the subject. The goal of most cropping is to make the most important feature in the original photo stand out. Cropping sometimes is used to convert a digital photo's proportions to those typical for traditional photos.

Most photographers and graphic artists use the **rule of thirds**, also called the principle of thirds, when placing the focus of interest. Imagine that the scene is divided into thirds both vertically and horizontally. The intersections of these imaginary lines suggest four positions for placing the focus of interest. The position you select depends on the subject and its presentation in the photo. For instance, there might be a shadow, path, or visual line you wish to include. In the case of moving objects, you generally should leave space in front of them, into which they theoretically can move. When eyes are involved, it is better to leave space on the side toward which the person or animal is looking, so they do not appear to look directly out of the setting.

Because the surfer photo will be used on a postcard, the photo's orientation should be **landscape**, or horizontal. In most cases, you should try to crop to a rectangular shape with an approximate short-side to long-side ratio of 5:8. Sometimes called the **golden rectangle**, a 5:8 ratio emulates natural geometric forms such as flowers, leaves, shells, and butterflies. Most digital cameras take pictures with a similar ratio.

The Crop Tool allows you to select the portion of the photo you wish to retain. Photoshop automatically displays handles and a rule of thirds overlay for further adjustments, if necessary. Then, when you press the ENTER key, the rest of the photo is cropped, or removed. The Delete Cropped Pixels box on the options bar lets you decide whether the cropped pixels should be removed permanently. The cropping handles continue to appear until you choose another tool.

The Crop Tool is grouped with the Perspective Crop Tool. In a **perspective crop**, when you drag one of the cropping handles, the other handles stay in place creating a distortion.

The Crop Tool options bar displays boxes and buttons to assist cropping activities (Figure 1–45 on the next page). You can specify the aspect ratio, or the exact height and width of the crop. The options bar also contains buttons to rotate or straighten the photo, as well as a View button menu to change the overlay grid.

Embedded with the Crop Tool are the Perspective Crop Tool and the Slice Tools. The Perspective Crop Tool lets you adjust and correct how objects appear from a distance as you crop the image. You will learn about changing the perspective and using the Slice Tools in a later chapter.

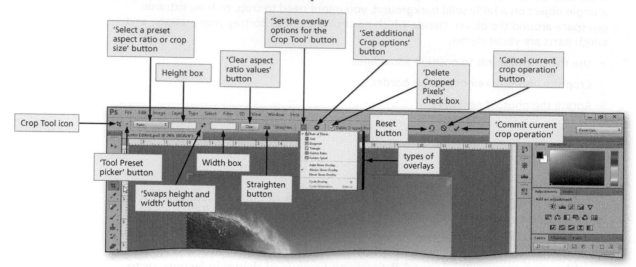

Figure 1–45

To Straighten a Photo and Crop

To make the surfer the focus of the photo, the photo will be straightened and extra background cropped, to provide a line of sight to the right, keeping as much of the wave as possible. The following steps straighten and crop the photo.

1

- Tap or click the Crop Tool button on the Tools panel to select the Crop Tool.

- Tap or click the Straighten button on the options bar to select it.

- If necessary, tap or click the 'Delete Cropped Pixels' check box on the options bar, so that it displays a check mark (Figure 1–46).

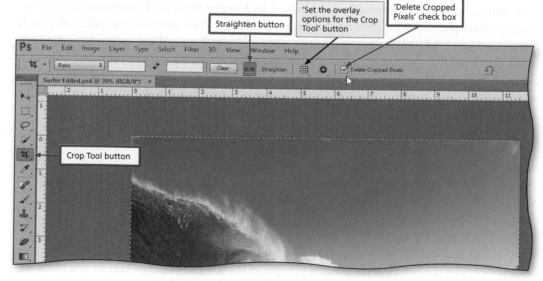

Figure 1–46

 Experiment

- On the options bar, tap or click the 'Set the overlay options for the Crop Tool' button, and then, one at a time, choose different overlays. Tap or click the photo to display the overlay each time. When you are finished, tap or click the button again and then tap or click 'Rule of Thirds'.

2

- Drag along the shoreline to indicate a straight line in the photo (Figure 1–47).

Q&A What happened as I dragged?
Photoshop displayed a straight line and a tool tip with an angle specification.

What happened when I finished my drag?
Photoshop adjusted the image to match the straight line that you drew, and now displays the rule of thirds grid. If you do not like your straighten attempt, press CTRL+Z to undo, tap or click the Straighten button on the options bar, and then drag again.

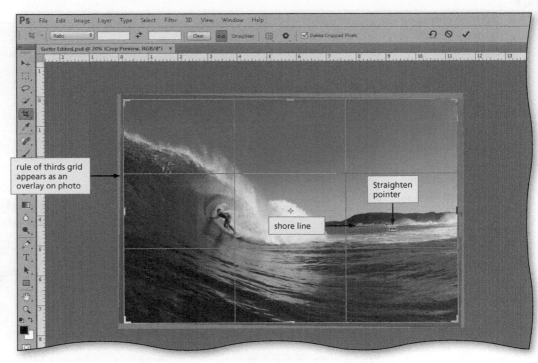

rule of thirds grid appears as an overlay on photo

Straighten pointer

shore line

Figure 1–47

3

- SHIFT+CTRL+drag the upper-right cropping handle until the left vertical gridline aligns with the surfer (Figure 1–48).

Q&A Why should I hold down the SHIFT and CTRL keys while dragging?
SHIFT+CTRL-dragging maintains the aspect ratio of both the grid overlay and the image.

vertical gridline aligns with surfer

cropping handle

Figure 1–48

4

- Within the cropping area, drag the photo straight down, until the lower-left intersection of the grid is centered over the surfer. Keep the cropping grid within the image and do not include any white space within the cropping area (Figure 1–49).

Q&A

What if I change my mind or make a mistake when cropping?

If you make a mistake while dragging the cropping area and want to start over, you can tap or click the Cancel current crop operation button or press the ESC key, which cancels the selection. If you already have performed the crop and then change your mind, you have several choices. You can tap or click the Undo command on the Edit menu, or you can press CTRL+Z to undo the last edit.

photo is moved down so that surfer is at lower-left intersection

Figure 1–49

5

- Press the ENTER key to complete the crop (Figure 1–50).

Experiment

- If you want to practice cropping, drag a cropping handle again. After each crop, press CTRL+Z to undo the crop.

cropped image

Figure 1–50

Other Ways

1. Select portion of image, on Image menu tap or click Crop, press ENTER key

2. Press C, drag in photo, tap or click 'Commit current crop operation' button

To Select the Default Tool Again

If you do not want to use the Crop Tool any longer, or you do not want to see the cropping handles or cropping pointer, select any other tool on the Tools panel. The following step selects the default tool again, as you did at the beginning of the chapter.

1 On the Tools panel, tap or click the 'Rectangular Marquee Tool' button to select the tool.

Creating a Border

A **border** is a decorative edge on a photo or a portion of a photo. Photoshop provides many ways to create a border, ranging from simple color transformations around the edge of the photo, to predefined decorated layers, to stylized photo frames.

A border helps define the edge of the photo, especially when the photo might be included in a collage, used within a newsletter, or displayed on a webpage with a background texture. A border visually separates the photo from the rest of the page, while focusing the viewer's attention. Rounded borders soften the images in a photo. Square borders are more formal. Decorative borders on a static photo can add interest and amusement, but easily can detract from the focus on a busier photo. **Blended borders** are not a solid fill; rather, they blend a fill color from the outer edge toward the middle, sometimes providing a three-dimensional effect. A border that complements the photo in style, color, and juxtaposition is best. In the surfer photo, you will create a border using selections of 75 black pixels with 25 pixels of overlapping white. Recall that a pixel is an individual dot of light that is the basic unit used to create digital images.

Identify finishing touches that will further enhance the photo.
Adding a border or decorative frame around a photo sometimes can be an effective way to highlight or make the photo stand out on the page. A border should frame the subject, rather than become the subject. If a border is required by the customer or needed for layout placement, choose a color and width that neither overwhelms nor overlaps any detail in the photo. Using a border color that complements one of the colors already in the photo creates a strong, visually connected image. For more information about graphic design concepts, read the Graphic Design Overview Appendix.

Plan Ahead

To Create a Selection

Specifying or isolating an area of your photo for editing is called making a **selection**. By selecting specific areas, you can edit and apply special effects to portions of your image while leaving the unselected areas untouched.

Selections can be simple shapes such as rectangles or ovals, or unusually shaped areas of a photo, outlining specific objects. Selections can be the entire photo or as small a portion as one pixel. A selection displays a marquee in Photoshop. A **marquee** is a flashing or pulsating border, sometimes called marching ants.

In the case of the Surfer Edited photo, you will make a selection around the edge of the photo in order to create a border. The steps on the next page select the photo.

1

- On the Application bar, tap or click Select to display the Select menu (Figure 1–51).

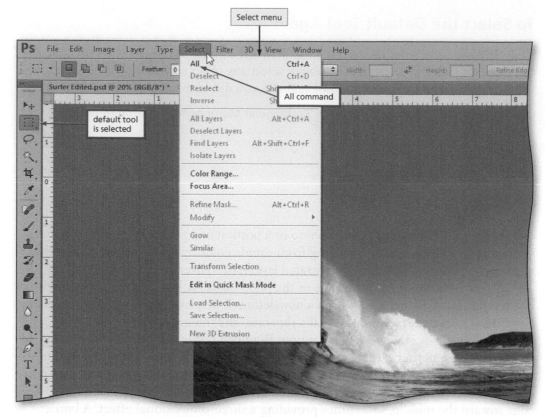

Figure 1–51

2

- On the Select menu, tap or click All to display the selection marquee around the entire photo (Figure 1–52).

Q&A

Am I selecting all of the photo itself?
Yes. Some commands apply to all of the pixels within the selection border, such as copying, deleting, or filling; other commands, such as stroking, apply only to the pixels along the edge of the selection. In this case, the selection will be used to identify the pixels along the edge of the image.

Figure 1–52

Other Ways

1. To select all, press CTRL+A

To Stroke a Selection

A **stroke** is a colored outline or edge. When stroking a selection, you must specify the number of pixels to include in the stroke and the desired color. You also must decide whether to apply the stroke outside the selection border, inside the selection border, or centered on the selection border. Other stroke settings include blending modes and opacity, which you will learn about in a later chapter.

The following steps stroke a selection.

1

- With the photograph still selected, tap or click Edit on the Application bar to display the Edit menu (Figure 1–53).

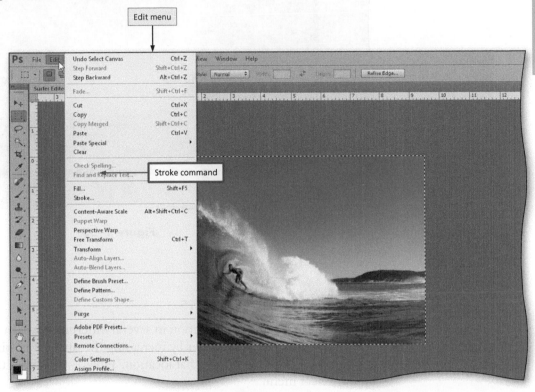

Figure 1–53

2

- Tap or click Stroke to display the Stroke dialog box.

- Type 100 in the Width box.

- If necessary, tap or click the Center option button to select it (Figure 1–54).

Q&A Do I need to select a color?

No, the default value is the foreground color, black. If your foreground color is not black, tap or click the Cancel button, press the D key to choose the default colors and start again with Step 1.

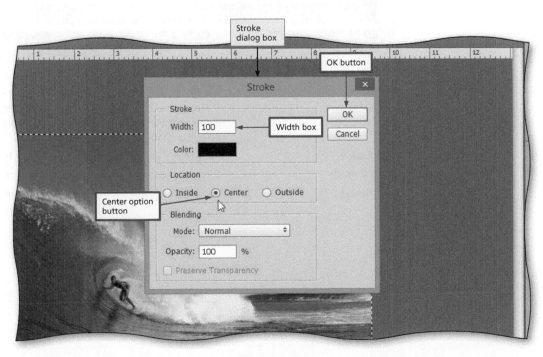

Figure 1–54

3

- Tap or click the OK button in the Stroke dialog box to apply the stroke (Figure 1–55).

stroke is applied to image

Figure 1–55

Modifying Selections

You can modify the selection in several different ways. In the surfer photo, you will modify the selection border by increasing the number of pixels along the border so you can add a second color at that location. Table 1–4 displays the Modify commands on the Select menu.

Table 1–4 Modify Commands	
Type of Modification	**Result**
Border	This command allows you to select a width of pixels, from 1 to 200, to be split evenly on either side of the existing selection marquee.
Smooth	This command allows you to select a number of pixels in a radius around the selection. Photoshop adds or removes pixels in that radius to smooth sharp corners and jagged lines, reducing patchiness.
Expand	The border is increased by a number of pixels from 1 to 100.
Contract	The border is decreased by a number of pixels from 1 to 100.
Feather	This command creates a feather edge with a width from 0 to 250 pixels.

To Modify a Selection

The following steps modify the selection.

1

- On the Application bar, tap or click Select, and then tap or click Modify to display the Modify submenu (Figure 1–56).

Q&A What does the asterisk mean in the document window tab?

The asterisk means you have made changes to the photo since your last save. Once you save the file, the asterisk no longer is displayed.

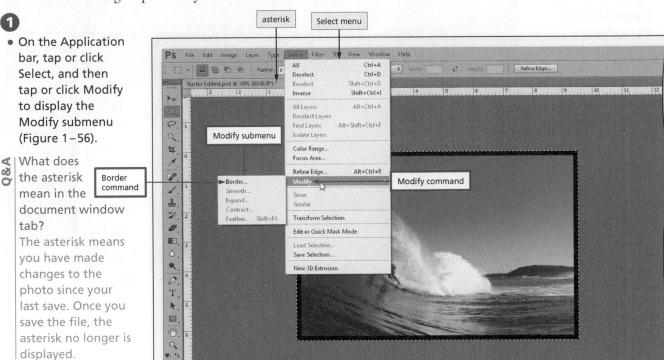

Figure 1–56

2

- Tap or click Border on the Modify submenu to display the Border Selection dialog box.

- Type 50 in the Width box to create a border selection on each side of the marquee (Figure 1–57).

Q&A Could I use the Contract command to contract the selection?

No, you must specify the border first. The Contract command is **grayed out** so you cannot select it before choosing the Border command.

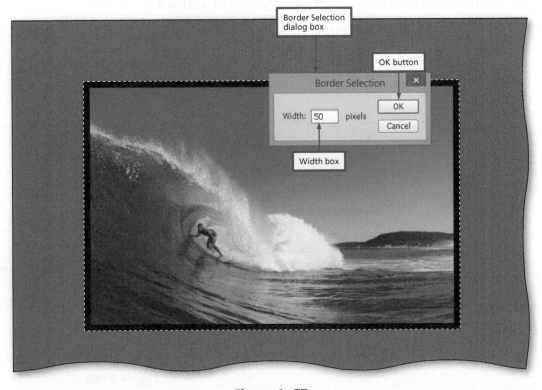

Figure 1–57

❸

- Tap or click the OK button in the Border Selection dialog box to define the selection (Figure 1–58).

Q&A

Is the border 50 pixels wide?
Yes, Photoshop adds half of those pixels to either side of the selection marquee.

🔍 Experiment

- To practice smoothing the border, tap or click the Select menu, tap or click Modify, and then tap or click Smooth. Enter a value in the Sample Radius box and then tap or click the OK button. Notice the change in the marquee. Press CTRL+Z to undo the Smooth command.

double marquee defines border selection

Figure 1–58

To Switch Foreground and Background Colors

On the Tools panel, the default foreground color is black and the default background color is white. Photoshop uses the default foreground color in strokes, fills, and brushes – in the previous steps when you stroked, the pixels became black. In order to create a rounded gray border, you will use a white, overlapping stroke. The following step switches the foreground and background colors so white is over black.

❶

- Tap or click the 'Switch Foreground and Background Colors' button to reverse the colors (Figure 1–59).

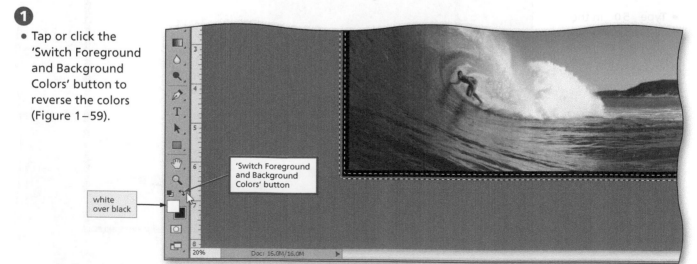

'Switch Foreground and Background Colors' button

white over black

Figure 1–59

Other Ways

1. Press x

To Stroke Again

To create the gray border, you will stroke the selection again, this time with white, and using a narrower width.

1 Tap or click Edit on the Application bar to display the Edit menu.

2 Tap or click Stroke to display the Stroke dialog box.

3 Type **4 0** in the Width box to set the width of the stroke.

4 Tap or click the OK button to apply the stroke (Figure 1–60).

white is stroked over black to create gray border

Figure 1–60

To Deselect

Because the border is complete, you should remove the selection indicator, or **deselect** it, so the marquee no longer appears. The following step removes the selection.

• Tap or click Select on the Application bar and then tap or click Deselect to remove the selection (Figure 1–61).

selection marquee no longer is displayed

Figure 1–61

Other Ways

1. Press CTRL+D

To Switch Foreground and Background Colors Again

The following step switches the foreground and background colors back to black over white.

1 On the Tools panel, tap or click the 'Switch Foreground and Background Colors' button again to reverse the colors.

Saving a Photo with the Same File Name

Because you have made many edits to the photo, it is a good idea to save the photo again. When you saved the document the first time, you assigned the file name, Surfer Edited. When you use the following procedure, Photoshop automatically assigns the same file name to the photo, and it is stored in the same location.

To Save a File with the Same File Name

The following step saves the Surfer Edited file with the changes you made.

1

- On the Application bar, tap or click File to display the File menu, and then tap or click Save to save the photo with the same file name.

Other Ways
1. Press CTRL+S

To Close a File

The following step closes the Surfer Edited document window without quitting Photoshop.

1

- Tap or click the Close button on the document window tab to close the document window and the image file (Figure 1–62).

2

- Tap or click the No button because you have saved the file already.

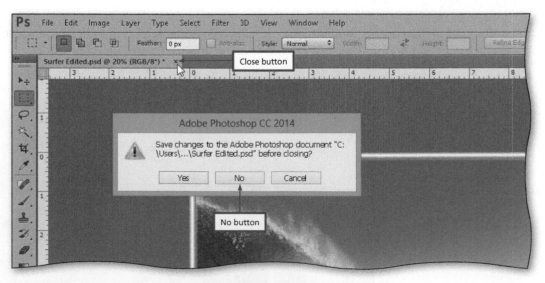

Figure 1–62

 For a detailed example of this procedure using the Mac operating system, refer to the For Mac Users Appendix.

Other Ways	
1. On File menu, tap or click Close	2. Press CTRL+W

Break Point: If you wish to take a break, this is a good place to do so. Press CTRL+Q to quit Photoshop. To resume at a later time, start Photoshop, and continue following the steps from this location forward.

Opening a Recent File in Photoshop

Once you have created and saved a document, you might need to retrieve it from your storage medium. For example, you might want to edit the photo further or print it. Photoshop maintains a list of recently used files to give you quick access to them for further editing. The list is maintained from session to session.

To Open a Recent File

Earlier in this chapter, you saved your edited photo using the file name, Surfer Edited. The following steps open the Surfer Edited file using the Open Recent list.

1

- Tap or click File on the Application bar and then tap or click Open Recent to display the Open Recent submenu (Figure 1–63).

Q&A What does the 'Clear Recent File List' command do?
If you tap or click the 'Clear Recent File List' command, your Recent list will be emptied. To open a file, you then would have to tap or click Open on the File menu and then navigate to the location of the file.

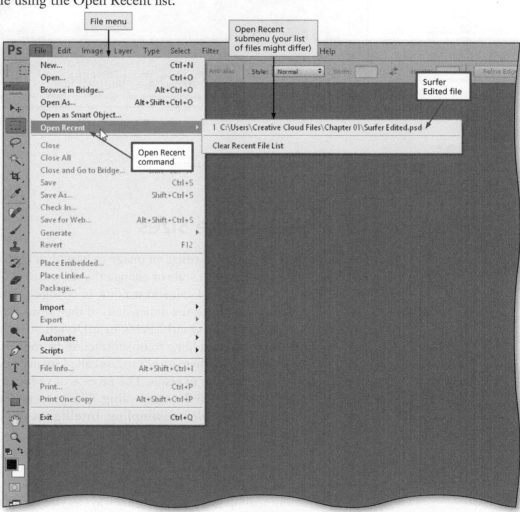

Figure 1–63

2

- Tap or click the Surfer Edited file to open it.
- Press CTRL+0 (zero) to fit the image on the screen (Figure 1–64).

Surfer Edited photo again is displayed

Figure 1–64

Other Ways

1. Tap or click Open on File menu, navigate to file, tap or click Open button
2. Press CTRL+O, navigate to file, tap or click Open button

Changing Image Sizes

Downsampling
Downsampling reduces image data by representing a group of pixels with a single pixel. If during the destruction, black-and-white pixels come next to each other, both pixels are changed using a complex calculation to produce a smoother tonal gradation of gray. The disadvantage of downsampling is the loss of data, or **lossiness**.

Sometimes it is necessary to resize an image to fit within certain print and web space limitations. **Resize** means to scale or change the dimensions of the photo. Zooming in or dragging a corner of the document window to change the size on the screen is not the same as actually changing the dimensions of the photo. Resizing in a page layout program, such as Publisher, QuarkXPress, or InDesign, merely stretches the pixels. In Photoshop, resizing means adding to or subtracting from the number of pixels.

Photoshop uses a mathematical process called **interpolation**, or **resampling**, when it changes the number of pixels. The process of reducing the size of the image by subtracting pixels is called **downsampling**. The process of enlarging the size of the image by adding pixels is called **upsampling**. **Intelligent upsampling** is one of the new features of Photoshop CC. Using a special algorithm, the program interpolates or calculates how to add pixels to the photo to match those already there, preserving the detail and sharpness. Intelligent upsampling retains edge detail and reduces artifacts or blotches normally associated with enlarging images.

While Photoshop helps you in many ways as you resize a photo, you must consider things such as the type of file, the width, the height, and the resolution. **Resolution** refers to the number of pixels per inch, printed on a page or displayed on a monitor. Not all photos lend themselves to resizing. Some file types lose quality and sharpness when resized. Fine details cannot be interpolated from low-resolution photos. Resizing works best for small changes where exact dimensions are critical. If possible, it usually is better to take a photo at the highest feasible resolution or rescan the image at a higher resolution rather than resize it later.

In those cases where it is impossible to create the photo at the proper size, Photoshop helps you resize or **scale** your photos for print or online media.

**Plan
Ahead**

Prepare for publication.
Keep in mind the golden rectangle of well-designed photos and the limitations of your space. Resize the photo. Insert any final text. Print a copy and evaluate its visual appeal. If you are going to publish the photo to the web, determine the following:

- Typical download speed of your audience
- Browser considerations
- Number of colors
- File type

Finally, save the photo with a descriptive name indicating its completion.

To Resize the Image

Because the surfer photo will be printed on a postcard at a specific size, you will change the height to 4 inches. The following steps resize the image to create a custom-sized photo for printing.

1

- Tap or click Image on the Application bar to display the Image menu (Figure 1–65).

Figure 1–65

2

- Tap or click Image Size to display the Image Size dialog box.

- Double-tap or double-click the value in the Height box and then type **4** to replace the previous value.

- Tap or click the Resample button to display a list of resampling choices (Figure 1–66).

Q&A Why did the width change?
When you change the width or height, Photoshop automatically adjusts the other dimension to maintain the proportions of the photo. Your exact width might differ slightly depending on how closely you cropped the original photo.

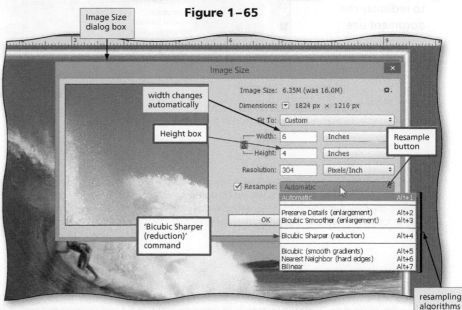

Figure 1–66

3

• Tap or click 'Bicubic Sharper (reduction)' to select the resampling algorithm (Figure 1–67).

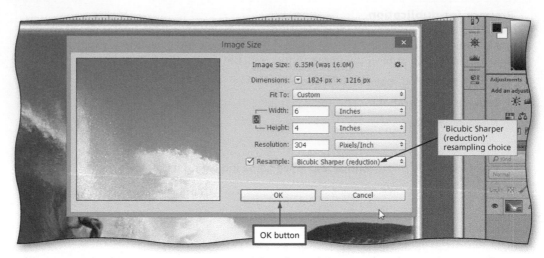

Figure 1–67

4

• Tap or click the OK button to finish resizing the image (Figure 1–68).

 **Experiment**

• Tap or click the status bar menu button, and then tap or click Document Dimensions to verify that the image size has been changed. Then, tap or click the status bar menu button again, and tap or click Document Sizes to redisplay the document size.

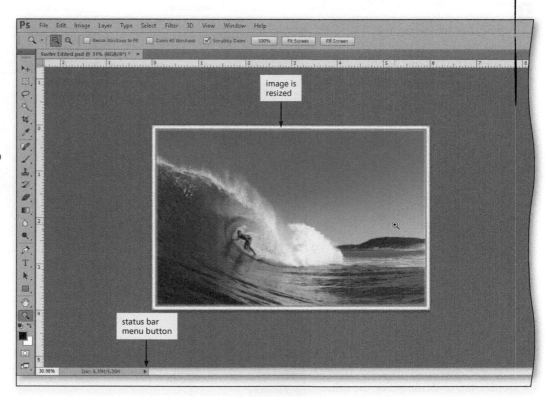

Figure 1–68

Other Ways

1. Press ALT+CTRL+I, change settings, tap or click OK button

BTW | **Upsampling**
When you upsample, Photoshop assigns a new color to the added pixels based on an average interpolation. For example, if an image needs to be enlarged, the interpolation notes where a new pixel should be added. If that new pixel falls at the edge of a yellow insignia on a red sweater, the new Remember that Photoshop cannot insert detailed information that was not captured from the original image. Photos will start to look softer, with less detail, as they are enlarged.

BTW | **Resampling Errors**
No matter what resampling method you choose, it may introduce **artifacts**, or changed pixels, that do not look good and were not in the original image. Blurs or halos may be introduced. Jagged edges, or aliasing, may appear when upsampling, and moiré patterns may appear when downsampling. A **moiré pattern** is an alternating of blurred and clear areas, forming thin stripes or dots on the screen.

Inserting Text

The next steps use a type tool to create text for the postcard. On the Tools panel, the default type tool is the Horizontal Type Tool. The options bar for the Horizontal Type Tool (Figure 1–69) includes boxes and buttons typical of those found in a word processing toolbar, including font family, font style, font size, and justification. A 'Create warped text' button allows you to create text in specialized formations, similar to the WordArt tool in Microsoft Word. On the right side of the options bar are buttons to cancel and commit editing changes. In a future chapter, you will learn about the Character and Paragraph panels that provide additional tools for manipulating text.

Embedded with the Horizontal Type Tool are the Vertical Type Tool and the type mask tools that you will learn about in a later chapter.

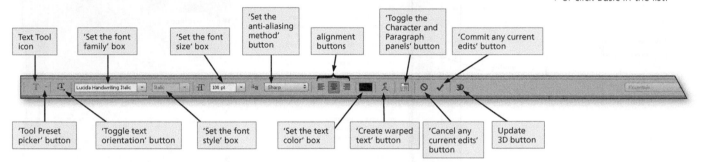

Figure 1–69

To Select the Horizontal Type Tool

The following step selects the Horizontal Type Tool on the Tools panel.

1

- Tap or click the 'Horizontal Type Tool' button on the Tools panel to select it (Figure 1–70).

- If the solid T icon does not appear on the button, press and hold or right-click the button to display its context menu, then tap or click 'Horizontal Type Tool' in the list.

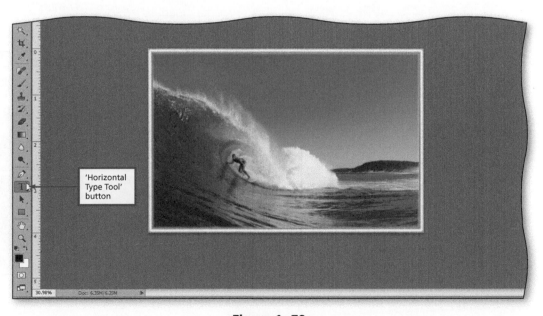

Figure 1–70

Other Ways

1. Press T or SHIFT+T until Horizontal Type Tool is active

To Set Font Options

The following steps select font settings on the options bar. In addition to the font and alignment options, when you tap or click the 'Set the text color' box, Photoshop uses color picker tools, such as a color field and color model boxes, to help you select the text color.

1

- On the options bar, tap or click the 'Search for and select fonts' box arrow to display the list of font families.

- Scroll as necessary (Figure 1–71).

Q&A Does Photoshop let you preview text in the font style?
Yes, if text is selected, you can point to any of the fonts in the list and the document window will display an **instant font preview** or **live preview**.

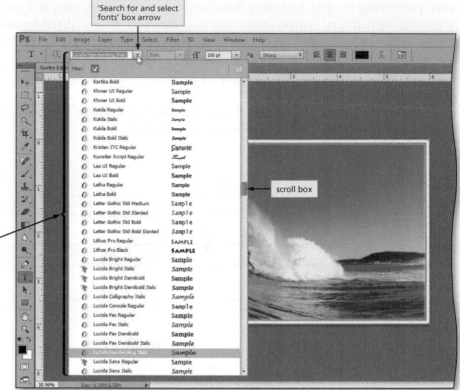

Figure 1–71

2

- Tap or click Ravie Regular or a similar font in the list.

- Select the value in the 'Set the font size' box, and then type 30 to replace the size.

- If necessary, tap or click the 'Left align text' button to left-justify the text (Figure 1–72).

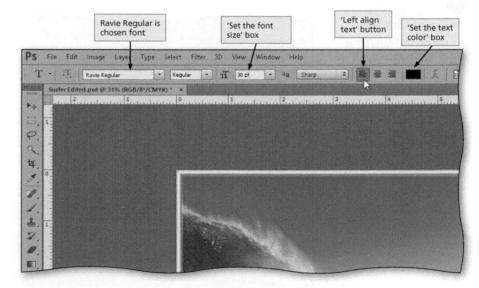

Figure 1–72

3

- Tap or click the 'Set the text color' box to open the Color Picker (Text Color) dialog box.

- Tap or click a white color in the upper-left corner of the color field (Figure 1–73).

Q&A What do the numerical boxes indicate?

Each color mode uses a numerical method called a color model, or color space, to describe the color. Some companies use specific numbers to create exact colors for branding purposes.

4

- Tap or click the OK button in the Color Picker (Text Color) dialog box to apply white as the text color on the options bar.

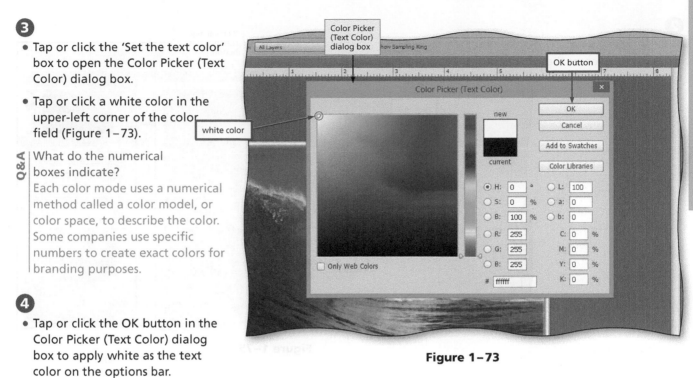

Figure 1–73

To Insert Text

With the type tool selected, you drag a bounding box in the document window to insert text. A **bounding box** is similar to a text box in other applications, with a dotted outline and sizing handles. The pointer changes to a small, open book outline. After typing the text in the bounding box, you use the 'Commit any current edits' button to complete the entry. Then, if the size of the bounding box needs to be adjusted, you can drag the sizing handles. The pointer becomes a cursor when positioned over the text. You will learn about other type tools and features in a later chapter.

The following steps enter text on the postcard.

1

- With the Horizontal Type Tool still selected, drag a bounding box beginning at the top of the image, approximately 1.5 inches from the left side. Drag down and to the right, as shown in Figure 1–74.

Q&A My image went black. What did I do wrong?

In its early releases, Photoshop CC was not compatible with older video cards. Try pressing CTRL+Y to change to proof colors.

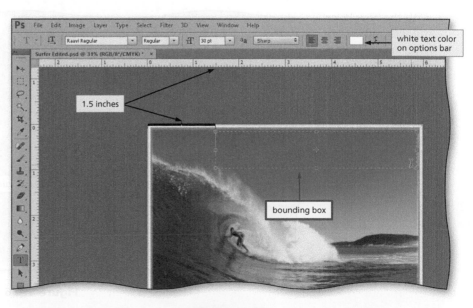

Figure 1–74

2

- Type **Catch a wave...** to enter the text (Figure 1–75).

Q&A Can I make changes and corrections to the text?

Yes, you can tap or click anywhere in the text box, use the ARROW keys, the BACKSPACE key, and the DELETE key just as you do in word processing. If your bounding box is too small, you can drag the sizing handles.

What is the new notation on the Layers panel?

When you create a bounding box, Photoshop separates the text from the rest of the picture in its own layer. You will learn more about layers in a future chapter.

Figure 1–75

3

- On the options bar, tap or click the 'Commit any current edits' button to finish the new layer.

To Stroke Text

Earlier in this chapter, you added a stroke of color to a selection as you created a border for the post card. The following steps stroke the text with black to make the letters stand out. You will use the Layer Style dialog box to create the stroke.

1

- With the new layer still selected on the Layers panel, tap or click the 'Add a layer style' button on the Layers panel status bar to display the list of layer styles (Figure 1–76).

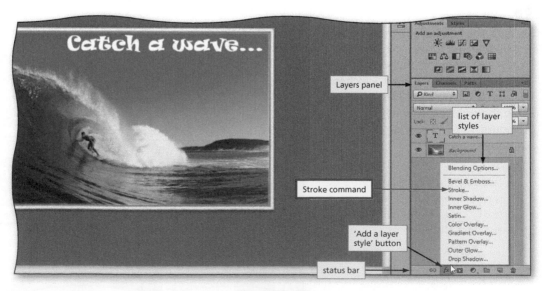

Figure 1–76

2

- Tap or click Stroke in the list of layer styles to display the Layer Style dialog box.

- Type **5** in the Size box to create 5 pixels of black stroke (Figure 1–77).

Q&A

What should I do if my color does not appear as black? Black is the default color; however, a previous user on your computer may have changed the color. Tap or click the Color box to display a color picker dialog box. Tap or click black, and then tap or click the OK button.

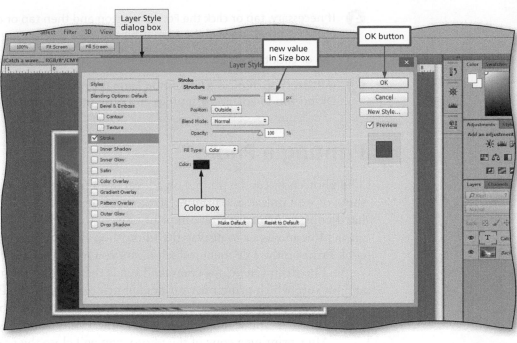

Figure 1–77

3

- Tap or click the OK button in the Layer Style dialog box to accept the settings and add the stroke.

- Press the D key to reset the default colors on the Tools panel. (Figure 1–78).

Figure 1–78

Other Ways

1. On Application bar, tap or click Layer, tap or click Layer Style, tap or click Stroke, adjust settings, tap or click OK button

To Save a File with a Different Name

Many graphic designers will save multiple copies of the same photo with various edits. Because this photo has been resized to print properly, you need to save it with a different name as performed in the following step.

1 Tap or click File on the Application bar and then tap or click Save As to display the Save As dialog box.

2 In the Save As dialog box, type **Surfer Resized with Text** in the File name text box.

3 If necessary, navigate to your storage device and the appropriate folder in the list.

④ If necessary, tap or click the Format button and then tap or click Photoshop (*.PSD; *.PDD) to select the format type.

⑤ Tap or click the Save button to save the image with the new name.

⑥ If Photoshop displays a Photoshop Format Options dialog box, tap or click the OK button to accept the settings and close the dialog box.

Printing a Photo

The photo now can be printed on a local printer, saved, taken to a professional print shop, or sent online to a printing service. A printed version of the photo is called a **hard copy** or **printout**. You can print one copy using the Print One Copy command on the File menu, or to display the Photoshop Print Settings dialog box, you can tap or click Print on the File menu, which offers you more printing options.

The Print One Copy command sends the printout to the default printer. If you are not sure which printer is your default printer, choose the Print command. In the Photoshop Print Settings dialog box, tap or click the Printer button and choose your current printer. You will learn more about the Print dialog box in Chapter 2.

After printing a copy of the photo, you will close the photo. Then, you will return to the version of the photo before resizing to prepare a web version.

To Print a Photo

The following steps print the photo created in this chapter.

①

- Ready the printer according to the printer instructions.

- Tap or click File on the Application bar and then tap or click Print to display the Photoshop Print Settings dialog box.

- If necessary, tap or click the Printer button and then select your printer from the list. Do not change any other settings (Figure 1–79).

Q&A Does Photoshop have a Print button on the options bar?
No. Photoshop's Print commands are available on the File menu or by using shortcut keys.

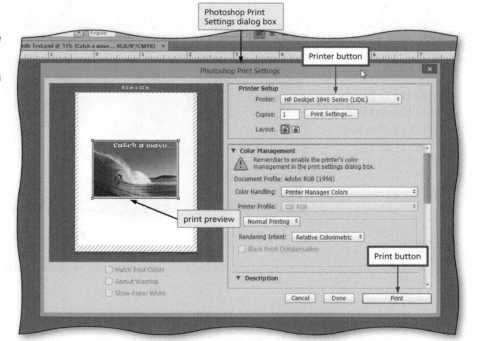

Figure 1–79

②

- In the Photoshop Print Settings dialog box, tap or click the Print button to start the printing process. If your system displays a second Print dialog box or a Print Settings dialog box, unique to your printer, tap or click its Print button.

- When the printer stops, retrieve the hard copy of the photo.

Other Ways

1. To print one copy, press ALT+SHIFT+CTRL+P

2. To display Photoshop Print Settings dialog box, press CTRL+P

Saving a Photo for Use on the Web

When preparing photos for the web, you often need to make a compromise between the quality of the display and size of the file. Web users do not want to wait while large photos load from web servers to their individual computer systems. To solve this problem, Photoshop provides several commands to compress the file size of an image while optimizing its online display quality. Additionally, Photoshop allows you to save the photo in a variety of formats such as **GIF**, which is a compressed graphic format designed to minimize file size and electronic transfer time, or as an **HTML** (Hypertext Markup Language) file, which contains all the necessary information to display your photo in a web browser.

You have two choices in Photoshop for creating web images: the Zoomify command and the 'Save for Web' command. When you **zoomify,** you create a high-resolution image for the web, complete with a background and tools for navigation, panning, and zooming. To zoomify, tap or click Export on the File menu and then tap or click Zoomify. In the Zoomify Export dialog box, you set various web and export options. Photoshop creates the HTML code and accompanying files for you to upload to a web server.

If you do not want the extra tools for navigation and zooming, you can create a single graphic file or HTML files using the 'Save for Web' command. The graphic can be used on the web or on a variety of mobile devices.

Optimization is the process of changing the photo to make it most effective for its purpose. The 'Save for Web' command allows you to preview optimized images in different file formats, and with different file attributes, for precise optimization. You can view multiple versions of a photo simultaneously and modify settings as you preview the image.

To Preview using the Save for Web Dialog Box

To optimize the surfer photo for use on the web, you need to make decisions about the file size and how long it might take to load on a webpage, as you preview the image. These kinds of decisions must take into consideration the audience and the nature of the webpage. For example, webpages geared for college campuses probably could assume a faster download time than those that target a wide range of home users. An e-commerce site that needs high-quality photography to sell its product will make certain choices in color and resolution.

The hardware and software of web users also is taken into consideration when optimizing a photo. For instance, if a web photo contains more colors than the user's monitor can display, most browsers will **dither,** or approximate, the colors that it cannot display, by blending colors that it can. Dithering might not be appropriate for some webpages, because it increases the file size and therefore causes the page to load more slowly.

Many other appearance settings play a role in the quality of web graphics, some of which are subjective in nature. As you become more experienced in Photoshop, you will learn how to make choices about dithering, colors, texture, image size, and other settings.

The steps on the next page use the 'Save for Web' command to display previews for four possible web formats.

• With the Surfer Resized with Text photo open, tap or click File on the Application bar to display the File menu and then tap or click 'Save for Web' to display the Save for Web dialog box.

• Tap or click the 4-Up tab to display four versions of the photo.

• Tap or click the Zoom Level box arrow to display the list (Figure 1–80).

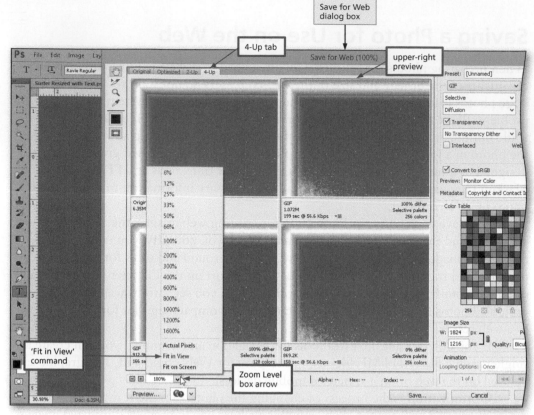

Figure 1–80

Why are there four frames?

Photoshop displays four previews — the original photo and three others that are converted to different resolutions to optimize download times.

• Tap or click 'Fit in View' to see the entire post card in each preview.

Other Ways

1. Press ALT+SHIFT+CTRL+S

To Choose a Download Speed

For faster downloads when the photo is displayed as a web graphic, you can choose a download speed that will be similar to that of your target audience. The **annotation area** below each preview in the Save for Web dialog box provides optimization information such as the size of the optimized file and the estimated download time using the selected modem speed. You will learn more about other settings in the Save for Web dialog box in a later chapter.

The following steps change the download speed to 1 megabyte per second (Mbps).

Photoshop CC Chapter 1

1

- Tap or click the upper-right preview, if necessary, to choose a high quality version of the photo.

- In the annotation area below the upper-right preview, tap or click the 'Select download speed' button to display the list of connection speeds (Figure 1–81).

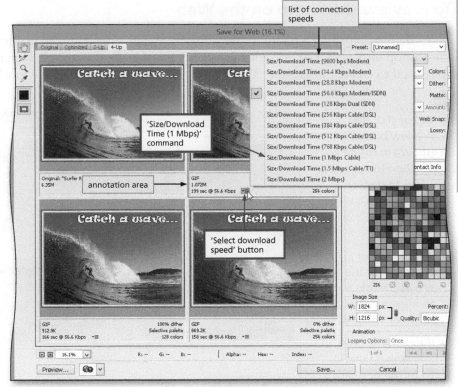

Figure 1–81

2

- In the list, tap or click Size/Download Time (1 Mbps Cable) or another appropriate speed (Figure 1–82).

Q&A How fast will the picture download?

In Figure 1–81, the speed was 199 seconds at 56.6 Kbps. At 1 Mbps, the photo will download in 12 seconds, as shown in Figure 1–82. Your download times might differ slightly.

Experiment

- Tap or click the Select download speed button to display the list of connection speeds and then tap or click various connection speeds to see how the download times are affected. When finished, tap or click 'Size/Download Time (1 Mbps Cable)' in the list.

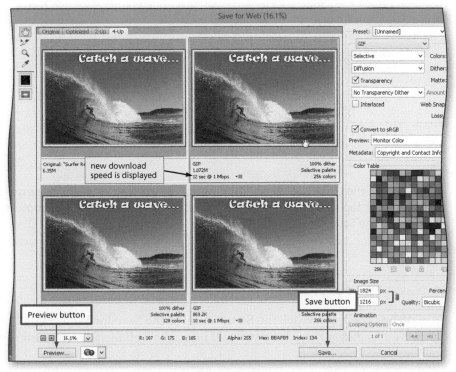

Figure 1–82

Other Ways

1. Press and hold or right-click annotation area, select download speed

To Preview the Photo on the Web

Before uploading a photo to the web, it is always a good idea to preview it to check for errors. When Photoshop displays a web preview of any photo, it also displays the characteristics of the file and the HTML code used to create the preview. The following steps preview the image in a browser.

1

- Tap or click the Preview button (shown in Figure 1–82 on the previous page) to display the photo in a web browser.

- If necessary, double-tap or double-click the browser's title bar to maximize the browser window.

- If necessary, press CTRL+MINUS SIGN (–) to fit the postcard in the browser window (Figure 1–83).

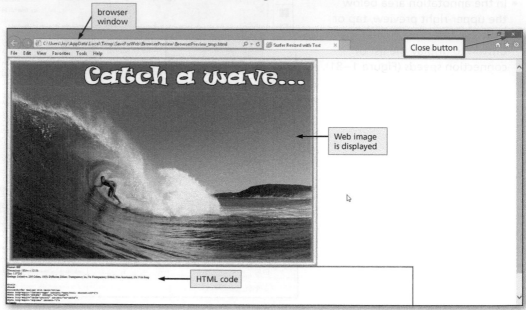

Figure 1–83

Q&A

When I clicked the Preview button, the HTML code was displayed in Notepad. Why did it not open in a browser?
If Photoshop cannot detect a default browser on your system, you might have to tap or click the box arrow next to the Preview button (Figure 1–82 on the previous page), and then tap or click Edit List to add your browser.

How would I use the HTML code?
As a web designer, you might copy and paste the code into a text editor or web creation software, replacing BrowserPreview with the name of the file. After saving, the code, the HTML file, and the photo would need to be uploaded to a server.

2

- Tap or click the Close button on the browser's title bar to close the browser window. If necessary, tap or click the 'Adobe Photoshop CC' button on the Windows taskbar to return to the Save for Web dialog box.

To Save the Photo for the Web

When you tap or click the Save button in the Save for Web dialog box, Photoshop displays the Save Optimized As dialog box where you will name the web file as performed in the following steps.

1

• In the Save for Web dialog box, tap or click the Save button (shown in Figure 1–82 on page PS 59) to display the Save Optimized As dialog box.

• Type **Surfer-for-web** in the File name text box.

• If necessary, navigate to your storage location, and then double-tap or double-click the appropriate folder in the list (Figure 1–84).

Q&A

Why are the words in the file name hyphenated?
For ease of use, it is standard for web graphics to have no spaces in their file names.

My default file format was GIF. Is that correct?
Yes. The GIF format is the default file format when Photoshop saves for the web. It does not lose data when the file is compressed to reduce the file size for quick downloads.

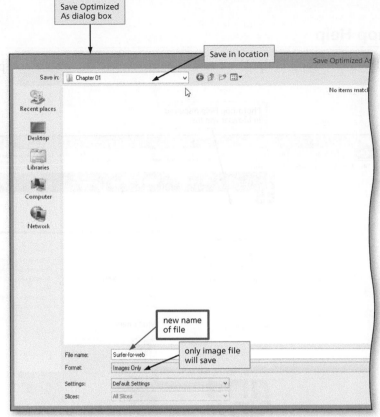

Figure 1–84

2

• Tap or click the Save button in the Save Optimized As dialog box to save the file.

Photoshop Help

At anytime while you are using Photoshop, you can get answers to questions using **Photoshop Help**. You activate Photoshop Help either by tapping or clicking Help on the Application bar or by pressing the F1 key. The Help menu includes commands to display more information about your copy of Photoshop as well as a list of how-to guides for common tasks. The Photoshop Help command connects you, through the Adobe Photoshop Support Center on the web, to a wealth of assistance, including tutorials with detailed instructions accompanied by illustrations and videos. Used properly, this form of online assistance can increase your productivity and reduce your frustration by minimizing the time you spend learning how to use Photoshop. Additional information about using Photoshop Help is available in Using Photoshop Help Appendix.

BTW

Web Formats
If you tap or click the Format button shown in Figure 1–84, you can choose to save the image only or save the complete HTML code and its accompanying files. Photoshop will create the folder structure for you.

To Access Photoshop Help

The next step displays Photoshop Help. You must be connected to the web if you plan to perform these steps on a computer.

- With Photoshop open on your system, press the F1 key to access Photoshop Help online.
- If necessary, double-tap or double-click the browser title bar to maximize the window (Figure 1–85).

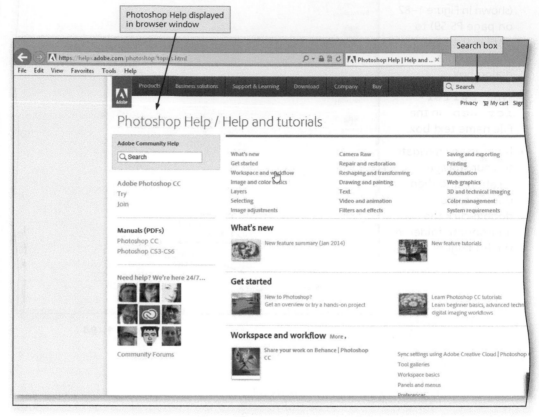

Figure 1–85

Other Ways

1. On Help menu, tap or click Photoshop Online Help

To Use the Help Search Box

The Search box allows you to type words or phrases about which you want additional information and help, such as cropping or printing images. When you press the ENTER key, Photoshop Help responds by displaying a list of topics related to the word or phrase you typed.

The following steps use the Search box to obtain information about the Tools panel.

- Tap or click the Search box and then type **Photoshop CC Tools Panel** to enter the search topic (Figure 1–86).

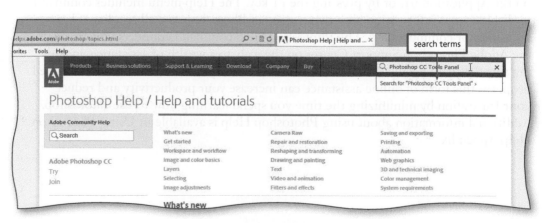

Figure 1–86

2

• Press the ENTER key to display the relevant links (Figure 1–87).

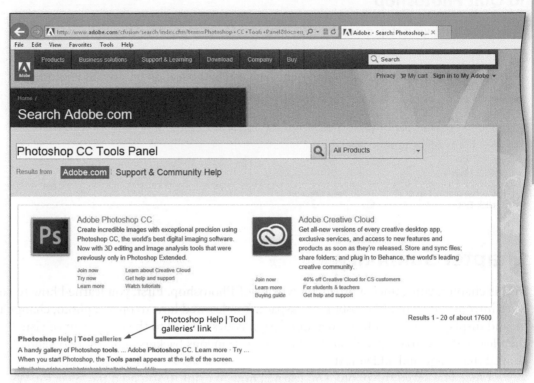

Figure 1–87

3

• Tap or click the link, 'Photoshop Help | Tool galleries' or a similar link to display the contents (Figure 1–88).

• Scroll as necessary to read the information about tools.

Experiment

• Tap or click other links to view more information, or search for other topics using the Search box.

4

• On the browser title bar, tap or click the Close button to close the window, and then, if necessary, tap or click the Adobe Photoshop CC button on the taskbar to return to Photoshop.

Figure 1–88

Other Ways

1. On Help menu, tap or click Photoshop Online Help, tap or click Photoshop Help (web) link, enter search topic

To Quit Photoshop

The following step quits Photoshop and returns control to Windows.

- Tap or click the Close button on the right side of the Application bar to quit Photoshop.

- If Photoshop displays a dialog box asking you to save changes, tap or click the No button.

 For a detailed example of this procedure using the Mac operating system, refer to the For Mac Users Appendix.

Other Ways

1. On File menu, tap or click Exit
2. Press CTRL+Q

Chapter Summary

In this chapter, you gained a broad knowledge of Photoshop. First, you learned how to start Photoshop. You were introduced to the Photoshop workspace. You learned how to open a photo, change the magnification, zoom in, and display rulers. You learned about design issues related to the placement of visual points of interest. You then learned how to crop a photo to eliminate extraneous background. After you added a blended border, you resized the image and added text.

Once you saved the photo, you learned how to print it. You used the 'Save for Web' command to optimize and save a web version. You learned how to use Adobe Help to research specific help topics. Finally, you learned how to quit Photoshop.

The items listed below include all the new Photoshop skills you have learned in this chapter:

1. Start Photoshop CC (PS 4)
2. Select the Essentials Workspace and Reset It (PS 6)
3. Reset the Tools Panel (PS 8)
4. Reset the Options Bar (PS 9)
5. Reset the Interface Color (PS 10)
6. Open a File (PS 12)
7. Save a File in the PSD Format in a New Folder (PS 21)
8. Use the Zoom Tool (PS 26)
9. Use the Navigator Panel (PS 28)
10. Minimize the Navigator Panel (PS 29)
11. Use the Hand Tool (PS 31)
12. Change the Magnification (PS 32)
13. Display Rulers (PS 33)
14. Straighten a Photo and Crop (PS 36)
15. Create a Selection (PS 39)
16. Stroke a Selection (PS 41)
17. Modify a Selection (PS 43)
18. Switch Foreground and Background Colors (PS 44)
19. Deselect (PS 45)
20. Save a File with the Same File Name (PS 46)
21. Close a File (PS 46)
22. Open a Recent File (PS 47)
23. Resize the Image (PS 49)
24. Select the Horizontal Type Tool (PS 51)
25. Set Font Options (PS 52)
26. Insert Text (PS 53)
27. Stroke Text (PS 54)
28. Save a File with a Different Name (PS 55)
29. Print a Photo (PS 56)
30. Preview using the Save for Web Dialog Box (PS 57)
31. Choose a Download Speed (PS 58)
32. Preview the Photo on the Web (PS 60)
33. Save the Photo for the Web (PS 60)
34. Access Photoshop Help (PS 62)
35. Use the Help Search Box (PS 62)
36. Quit Photoshop (PS 64)

Apply Your Knowledge

Reinforce the skills and apply the concepts you learned in this chapter.

Editing a Photo in the Photoshop Workspace

Note: To complete this assignment, you will be required to use the Data Files for Students. Visit solutions.cengage.com/ctdownloads for detailed instructions or contact your instructor for information about accessing the required files.

Instructions: Start Photoshop and perform the customization steps found on pages PS 6 through PS 11. Open the Apply 1-1 Deer file in the Chapter 01 folder from the Data Files for Students.

First, you will save the photo in the PSD format. Then you will crop the photo, add a white border, and save the edited photo, as shown in Figure 1–89. Next, you will resize the photo for printing and print one copy. Finally, you will reopen your edited photo, and then you will optimize it for the web, save it, and close it.

Courtesy of Joy Starks

Figure 1–89

Perform the following tasks:

1. On the File menu, tap or click Save As. When Photoshop displays the Save As dialog box, navigate to your storage device and then double-tap or double-click the appropriate folder, if necessary. In the File name box, type **Apply 1-1 Deer Edited**. Tap or click the Format button and choose the PSD file format. Tap or click the Save button to save the file.

2. Use the Zoom Tool to zoom the photo to 66.67% magnification, if necessary.

3. Use the Hand Tool to reposition the photo in the workspace to view different areas of the zoomed photo.

4. Use the Navigator panel to zoom out to 16.67%.

Continued >

Apply Your Knowledge *continued*

5. Use the Crop tool to crop the photo, maintaining the aspect ratio to place the deer at the lower-left intersection of the rule of thirds grid as shown in Figure 1–89 on the previous page (*Hint*: If your cropping selection does not look correct, you can press the ESC key to clear the selection before you press the ENTER key. Immediately after cropping the photo, you can tap or click Undo on the Edit menu to undo the crop action.)

6. Press the ENTER key to commit the crop. Select a different tool so the cropping handles no longer are displayed.

7. To create the border:

   a. If necessary, press the D key to select the default colors. Press the X key to reverse the foreground and background colors, so that white displays over black on the Tools panel.

   b. Press CTRL+A to select all of the photo.

   c. Use the Stroke command on the Edit menu to stroke the selection with white.

   d. Press CTRL+D to clear your selection when finished creating the border.

8. Press CTRL+S to save the Apply 1-1 Deer Edited photo with the same file name in the same location. Press the D key to return the colors to black over white.

9. Use the Image menu to resize the photo width to 5 inches wide to create a custom-sized photo for printing.

10. Save the resized file as Apply 1-1 Deer for Print.

11. Print the photo and then close the file. If Photoshop displays a dialog box about saving again, tap or click the No button.

12. Open the Apply 1-1 Deer for Print file using the Open Recent list.

13. Save the photo for the web, displaying it in the 4-Up tab and zoomed to fit on the screen. Select the preview that looks the best for your download speed.

14. Preview the optimized photo in your browser, and print the browser page. Close the browser.

15. Save the optimized file with the name, Apply-1-1-Deer-for-web.

16. Close the Apply 1-1 Deer Edited file without saving it and quit Photoshop.

Extend Your Knowledge

Extend the skills you learned in this chapter and experiment with new skills. You may need to use Help to complete the assignment.

Exploring Aspect Ratios and Borders

Note: To complete this assignment, you will be required to use the Data Files for Students. Visit solutions.cengage.com/ctdownloads for detailed instructions or contact your instructor for information about accessing the required files.

Instructions: Start Photoshop and perform the customization steps found on pages PS 6 through PS 11. Open the Extend 1-1 Arc de Triomphe file in the Chapter 01 folder from the Data Files for Students and save it on your storage device as Extend 1-1 Arc de Triomphe Edited in the PSD file format.

The photo (Figure 1–90) is to be added to a book about Paris; therefore, the structure should be centered, straightened both horizontally and vertically, and displayed in a 5 × 7 format.

Courtesy of Lourdes Nunez

Figure 1–90

Perform the following tasks:

1. Use Photoshop Help to read about cropping using the 'Select a preset aspect ratio or crop size' button.

2. Select the Crop Tool. Tap or click the Straighten button, and then draw across a line horizontally that should be straight in the arc itself. Repeat the process vertically.

3. Use the 'Select a preset aspect ratio or crop size' button to choose a 5: 7 forced ratio. Drag a corner cropping handle inward, keeping the arc within the grid. Drag the picture to center it within the cropping area.

4. Delete cropped pixels and then crop the photo.

5. Review Table 1–4 on page PS 42. Use the commands on the Modify submenu to set the border options of your choice. Stroke the selection with a color of your choice.

6. After viewing the resulting border, press the CTRL+ALT+Z keys enough times to step back to the photo's original unedited state.

7. Repeat Steps 1–4 several times to experiment with different border widths and colors, then apply the border that best complements the photo and save the changes to the photo.

8. Close the photo and quit Photoshop.

Make It Right

Analyze a project and correct all errors and/or improve the design.

Changing a Photo's Focus and Optimizing It for the Web

Note: To complete this assignment, you will be required to use the Data Files for Students. Visit solutions.cengage.com/ctdownloads for detailed instructions or contact your instructor for information about accessing the required files.

Instructions: Start Photoshop and perform the customization steps found on pages PS 6 through PS 11. Open the Make It Right 1-1 Young Stars file in the Chapter 01 folder from the Data Files for Students and save it on your storage device as Make It Right 1-1 Young Stars Edited in the PSD file format.

Members of your Astronomy Club have selected the Young Stars photo (Figure 1–91 on the next page) for the club's website. You are tasked with editing the photo to focus more clearly on the cluster of stars and its trailing dust blanket, and then optimizing the photo for the web.

Continued >

Make It Right *continued*

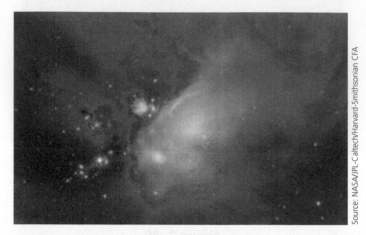

Figure 1–91

View the photo in different screen modes and at different magnifications.

Use the Crop Tool's Golden Spiral overlay to crop the photo to change its focal point and resave it. Then save the photo for the web as Make-It-Right-1-1-Young-Stars-for-web.

In the Labs

Design and/or create a project using the guidelines, concepts, and skills presented in this chapter. Labs are listed in order of increasing difficulty.

Lab 1: **Cropping a Photo and Adding a Smooth Border**

Problem: A gardening club has accepted your flower photo to publish in its upcoming brochure, but the club would like you to crop the photo more, add a smooth border, and resize it. The edited photo is displayed in Figure 1–92.

Figure 1–92

Note: To complete this assignment, you will be required to use the Data Files for Students. Visit solutions.cengage.com/ctdownloads for detailed instructions or contact your instructor for information about accessing the required files.

Instructions: Perform the following tasks:

1. Start Photoshop.

2. Tap or click Window on the application bar, tap or click Workspace, and then tap or click Essentials (Default). Repeat the process and tap or click Reset Essentials to reset the Essentials workspace.

3. Select the second button on the Tools panel to reset the Tools panel.

4. Press and hold or right-click the Rectangular Marquee Tool icon on the options bar and then tap or click 'Reset All Tools' to reset the options bar. Tap or click the OK button.

5. Press the D key to select the default colors. If black is not over white at the bottom of the Tools panel, tap or click the 'Switch Foreground and Background Colors' button.

6. Open the file, Lab 1-1 Flowers, from the Chapter 01 folder of the Data Files for Students or from a location specified by your instructor.

7. Tap or click Save As on the File menu, and then type the new file name, Lab 1-1 Flowers Edited. Navigate to your storage location, if necessary. Tap or click the Format button and choose PSD format. Tap or click the Save button.

8. Use the Magnification box to zoom the photo to 25% magnification, if necessary.

9. If the rulers do not appear, press CTRL+R to view the rulers.

10. Select the Crop Tool. Tap or click the photo to display the rule of thirds grid. SHIFT+drag the lower-right cropping handle until the middle of the flower cluster is positioned at the upper-right intersection of the rule of thirds grid.

11. Press the ENTER key. If your crop does not seem correct, tap or click the Undo command on the Edit menu and repeat Step 10.

12. Select another tool so the cropping handles no longer are displayed.

13. Save the photo again by pressing CTRL+S.

14. Press CTRL+A to select all of the photo. Tap or click Select on the Application bar, tap or click Modify to display the Modify submenu, and then tap or click Border to display the Border Selection dialog box. Type **100** in the Width box and then tap or click the OK button.

15. Display the Modify submenu again, and tap or click Smooth. Type **50** in the Smooth Radius box, and then tap or click the OK button to create a second marquee with smoothed corners.

16. If white is not the foreground color, press the X key to switch the foreground and background colors. Tap or click Edit on the Application bar and then tap or click Stroke. Type **100** in the Width box. Tap or click the Inside option button in the Location area. Tap or click the OK button to stroke the selection. Press CTRL+D to deselect.

17. Tap or click the Image Size command on the Image menu. When the Image Size dialog box is displayed, in the Document Size area, type **4** in the Width box. Tap or click the OK button.

18. Press CTRL+S to save the file again.

19. Use the Print One Copy command on the File menu to print a copy of the photo.

20. Close the file and quit Photoshop.

21. Send the photo as an e-mail attachment to your instructor, or submit it in the format specified by your instructor.

Continued >

In the Labs *continued*

Lab 2: **To Fill a Border**

Problem: The local hockey team is preparing a flyer to advertise its next game. The marketing department would like you to take one of the pictures from the last game and crop it to show just the face-off players and the official. Because the flyer will be printed on white paper, you should create a white border so the photo blends into the background and adds to the ice rink effect. The edited photo is displayed in Figure 1–93.

Courtesy of Joy Starks

Figure 1–93

Note: To complete this assignment, you will be required to use the Data Files for Students. Visit solutions.cengage.com/ctdownloads for detailed instructions or contact your instructor for information about accessing the required files.

Instructions: Perform the following tasks:

1. Start Photoshop. Perform the customization steps found on pages PS 6 through PS 11.

2. Open the file, Lab 1-2 Hockey, from the Chapter 01 folder of the Data Files for Students or from a location specified by your instructor.

3. Use the Save As command on the File menu to save the file on your storage device with the name, Lab 1-2 Hockey Edited, in the PSD format.

4. Tap or click the Zoom Tool button on the Tools panel. Tap or click the official to center the photo in the display. Zoom as necessary so you can make precise edits.

5. Crop the picture to display only the official and the two hockey players ready for the face-off. The vertical line of the hockey stick and the visual line of the official should be positioned using the rule of thirds.

6. Select a different tool so the cropping handles no longer are displayed.

7. Save the photo again with the same name.

8. Close the file and open it again using the Open Recent submenu.

9. Press CTRL+A to select all of the photo.

10. To create the border, do the following:

    a. On the Select menu, tap or click Modify, and then tap or click Border.

    b. When the Border Selection dialog box is displayed, type **100** in the Width box. Tap or click the OK button.

    c. On the Select menu, open the Modify submenu, and tap or click Smooth.

d. When the Smooth Selection dialog box is displayed, type **50** in the Sample Radius box to smooth the corners. Tap or click the OK button.

e. Press SHIFT+F5 to access the Fill command.

f. When the Fill dialog box is displayed, tap or click the Use button and then tap or click White in the list.

g. Tap or click the Mode button and then tap or click Normal in the list, if necessary.

h. If necessary, type **100** in the Opacity box. Tap or click the OK button.

i. Press CTRL+D to deselect the border.

11. Save the photo again.

12. Use the Print One Copy command on the File menu to print a copy of the photo.

13. Close the document window and quit Photoshop.

14. Submit the assignment in the format specified by your instructor.

Lab 3: **Preparing a Photo for the Web**

Problem: You decide to sell you dresser online. You need to crop the photo and then save it as a web graphic. The edited photo is displayed in Figure 1–94.

Note: To complete this assignment, you will be required to use the Data Files for Students. Visit solutions.cengage.com/ctdownloads for detailed instructions or contact your instructor for information about accessing the required files.

Instructions: Perform the following tasks:
Start Photoshop. Perform the customization steps found on pages PS 6 through PS 11. Open the file, Lab 1-3 Dresser, from the Chapter 01 folder of the Data Files for Students. Save the file in the PSD format with the name Lab 1-3 Dresser Edited. Resize the photo to 500 pixels wide. Search Photoshop Help for help related to optimization. Read about optimizing for the web. Print a copy of the help topic and then close the Adobe Help window.

Use the Save for Web dialog box to view the 4-Up tab. Choose the best-looking preview. Select the connection speed of your Internet connection. Save the web version of the photo using the name, Lab-1-3-Dresser-for-web. For extra credit, upload the web version to a web server. See your instructor for ways to submit this assignment.

Courtesy of Katie Starks

Figure 1–94

Cases and Places

Apply your creative thinking and problem-solving skills to design
and implement a solution.

Note: To complete this assignment, you will be required to use the Data Files for Students.
Visit solutions.cengage.com/ctdownloads for detailed instructions or contact your instructor for
information about accessing the required files.

1: Cropping and Straightening a Photo

Academic

You are writing a paper for your Sociology class about the calming effects of owning pets. As
examples, you are using photos of several pets, including a parrot. Open the file Case 1-1 Parrot
from the Chapter 01 folder of the Data Files for Students. Save the photo on your storage device as
Case 1-1 Parrot Edited, using the PSD format. Select the Crop Tool. Using the rule of thirds, and
the information in the chapter, crop the photo to focus on the bird. Use the Image Size dialog box
and an appropriate resampling algorithm to create a photo approximately three inches wide. Save
the photo again and print a copy for your instructor.

2: Creating a Photo for a Social Networking Site

Personal

You would like to place a photo of your recent tubing adventure on your social networking page.
The photo you have is of two people. You need to crop out the other person who is tubing. After
starting Photoshop and resetting the workspace, select the photo, Case 1-2 Tubing, from the
Chapter 01 folder of the Data Files for Students. Save the photo on your storage device as Case 1-2
Tubing Edited, using the PSD format. Crop the photo to remove one of the inner tubes, keeping in
mind the rule of thirds, the golden rectangle, and the direction of the action. Save the photo for the
web and upload it to Facebook or another social networking site as directed by your instructor.

3: Creating a Photo for a Brochure

Professional

You are an intern with an event planning business. The company is planning to send out a tri-fold
brochure about local churches and chapels used for weddings. The photo named Case 1-3 Chapel
is located in the Chapter 01 folder of the Data Files for Students. Save the photo on your storage
device as Case 1-3 Chapel Edited, using the PSD format. Resize the photo to be 3.5 inches wide.
Create a black border of 10 pixels. Save the file again and print a copy for your instructor.

Ps   File   Edit   Image   Layer   Type   Select   Filter   3D   View   Window   Help

Adobe **Photoshop CC**   Feather: 0 px   Anti-alias   Style: Normal   Width: Height: Refine Edge...

2 | Using Selection Tools and Shortcut Keys

Objectives

You will have mastered the material in this chapter when you can:

- Explain the terms layout, perspective, and storyboard

- Describe selection tools

- Select objects using marquee tools

- Move, duplicate, scale, and flip selections

- Use grids, guides, and snapping

- Employ lasso tools

- Use the History panel

- Refine edges to adjust selections

- Select objects using the Quick Selection and Magic Wand Tools

- Add, subtract, and intersect selections

- Save an image as a PDF file

- Use, create, and test new keyboard shortcuts

Ps File Edit Image Layer Type Select Filter 3D View Window Help

Adobe **Photoshop CC** Feather: 0 px   Anti-alias   Style: Normal   Width: Height: Refine Edge...

2 | Using Selection Tools and Shortcut Keys

Introduction

In Chapter 1, you learned about the Photoshop interface as well as navigation and zooming techniques. You cropped and resized a photo, added a border and text, and saved the photo for both web and print media. You learned about online help, along with opening, saving, and printing photos. This chapter continues to emphasize those topics and presents some new ones.

Recall that when you make a selection, you are specifying or isolating an area of your photo for editing. By selecting specific areas, you can edit and apply special effects to portions of your image, while leaving the unselected areas untouched. The new topics covered in this chapter include the marquee tools used to select rectangular or elliptical areas, the lasso tools used to select freeform segments or shapes, and the Quick Selection and Magic Wand Tools used to select consistently colored areas. You will learn how to use the Move Tool to move, duplicate, scale, and flip selections. Finally, you will save to a PDF file and create a new keyboard shortcut.

Project — Promotional Graphic

An advertisement, or ad, is a form of communication that promotes a product or service to a potential customer. An advertisement tries to persuade consumers to purchase a product or service. An advertisement typically has a single message directed toward a target audience.

A graphic designed for advertising, sometimes called an **advertising piece**, needs to catch the customer's eye and entice him or her to purchase the product. A clear graphic with strong contrast, item repetition, and visual lines tells the story and enhances text that might be added later. Chapter 2 creates a promotional graphic or advertising piece for a menu. You will begin with the image in Figure 2–1a that shows individual desserts. You then will manipulate the image by selecting, editing, and moving the objects to produce a more attractive layout, creating Figure 2–1b for use in the menu.

Overview

As you read this chapter, you will learn how to create the promotional graphic shown in Figure 2–1b by performing these general tasks:

- Select portions of the photo.
- Move, duplicate, scale, and flip selections.
- Refine edges of selections.
- Retrace editing steps using the History panel.
- Eliminate white space in and among objects in selected areas.
- Save the photo as a PDF file.
- Create a new shortcut key.

(a)

(b)

Figure 2–1

iStock.com/jcphoto, courtesy of Fred Starks

General Project Guidelines

Plan Ahead

When editing a photo, the actions you perform and decisions you make will affect the appearance and characteristics of the finished product. As you edit a photo, such as the one shown in Figure 2–1a, you should follow these general guidelines:

1. **Choose the correct tool.** When you need to copy and paste portions of your photo, consider carefully which Photoshop selection tool to use. You want the procedure to be efficient and produce a clear image. Keep in mind the shape and background of the photo you plan to copy, as well as your expertise with various tools.

2. **Plan your duplications.** Use a storyboard or make a list of the items you plan to duplicate. Then decide whether it will be an exact duplication or a manipulated one, called a **transformed copy**. The decision depends on the visual effect you want to achieve and the customer requirements.

3. **Use grids and guides.** When you are working with exact measurements, close cropping and moving, or just want to align things easily, use grids and guides to display nonprinting lines across the document window. Use the Photoshop snapping function to align selections. Visual estimations of size and location are easier to perceive when using these guides.

4. **Create files in portable formats.** You might have to distribute your artwork in a variety of formats depending on its use. Portability is an important consideration. It usually is safe to begin work in the Photoshop PSD format and then use the Save As command or Print command to convert your work to the PDF format. PDF files are platform and software independent.

When necessary, more specific details concerning the above guidelines are presented at appropriate points in the chapter. The chapter also will identify the actions performed and decisions made regarding these guidelines during the creation of the edited photo shown in Figure 2–1b.

Creating a Promotional Graphic

Figure 2–2 illustrates the design decisions made to create the dessert graphic. An attractive layout using multiple objects is a good marketing strategy; such a piece can encourage the viewer both visually and subconsciously to purchase more than one item. **Layout** refers to placing visual elements into a pleasing and understandable arrangement; in the dessert menu graphic, the layout is suggestive of how the product or products might look on a table. Advertising artists and product designers try to create a layout that is appealing, and in this case, appetizing.

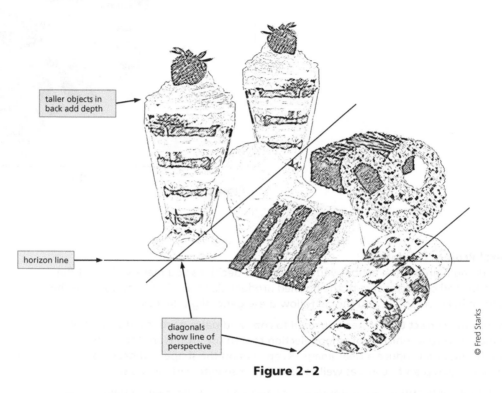

taller objects in
back add depth

horizon line

diagonals
show line of
perspective

© Fred Starks

Figure 2–2

From a design point of view, creating visual diagonal lines creates perspective. **Perspective** is the technique photographers, designers, and artists use to create the illusion of three dimensions on a flat or two-dimensional surface. Perspective is a means of fooling the eye by making it appear as if there is depth or receding space in an image. Adjusting the sizes and juxtaposing the objects creates asymmetrical balance and visual tension between the featured products. For example, in Figure 2–2, the height of the parfaits lead the viewer's eye to the background, as does the diagonal alignment of smaller items in front of the larger ones.

The **horizon line** in perspective drawing is a virtual horizontal line across the picture. The placement of the horizon line determines from where the viewer seems to be looking, such as down from a high place or up from close to the ground. In the dessert graphic, the horizon line runs across the lower-middle of the drawing.

Using white space, or non-image area, is effective in directing the viewer to notice what is important. The desserts grouped this way are framed, in a sense, by the white space.

This dessert layout also helps other members of the design team when it is time to make decisions about type placement. The group of items can be shifted up or down, as one image, to accommodate the layout and text, including future font sizes, placement, title, description, and price information. Recall that the rule of thirds offers a useful means to make effective layouts for images and text.

Designing a preliminary layout sketch, similar to Figure 2–2, to help you make choices about layout, placement, size, perspective, and spacing, is referred to as creating a **storyboard** or **rough**.

To Start Photoshop

If you are stepping through this project on a computer and you want your screen to match the figures in this book, then you should change your computer's resolution to 1366 × 768 and reset the panels, tools, and colors. For more information about how to change the resolution on your computer and other advanced Photoshop settings, read the Editing Preferences Appendix.

The following steps, which assume Windows 8 is running, start Photoshop based on a typical installation. You may need to ask your instructor how to start Photoshop for your system.

1 With Windows 8 running, scroll to display the Adobe Photoshop CC tile on the Start screen.

2 Tap or click the Adobe Photoshop CC tile to run the Photoshop app.

3 After a few moments, when the Photoshop window appears, if the window is not maximized, tap or click the Maximize button next to the Close button on the Application bar to maximize the window.

To Reset the Workspace

As discussed in Chapter 1, it is helpful to reset the workspace so that the tools and panels appear in their default positions. The following steps select the Essentials workspace.

1 Tap or click the workspace switcher on the options bar to display the list and then tap or click Essentials to select the default workspace panels.

2 Tap or click the workspace switcher on the options bar again, to display the list and then tap or click Reset Essentials to restore the workspace to its default settings and reposition any panels that might have been moved by previous users.

To Reset the Tools and the Options Bar

Recall that the Tools panel and the options bar retain their settings from previous Photoshop sessions. The following steps select the Rectangular Marquee Tool and reset all tool settings in the options bar.

1 If the tools in the Tools panel appear in two columns, tap or click the double arrow at the top of the Tools panel.

2 If necessary, tap or click the 'Rectangular Marquee Tool' button on the Tools panel to select it.

3 On the options bar, press and hold or right-click the Rectangular Marquee Tool icon to display the context menu, and then tap or click 'Reset All Tools'. When Photoshop displays a confirmation dialog box, tap or click the OK button to restore the tools to their default settings.

To Set the Interface and Default Colors

Recall that Photoshop retains the interface color scheme, as well as the foreground and background colors from session to session. The following steps set the interface to Medium Gray and the foreground and background colors to black over white.

1 Tap or click Edit on the Application bar to display the Edit menu. Tap or click Preferences and then tap or click Interface on the Preferences submenu to display the Preferences dialog box.

2 If necessary, tap or click the third button, Medium Gray, to change the interface color scheme.

3 Tap or click the OK button to close the Preferences dialog box.

4 Tap or click the 'Default Foreground and Background Colors' button on the Tools panel to set the default colors to black and white. If black is not over white on the Tools panel, tap or click the 'Switch Foreground and Background Colors' button.

To Open a File

To open a file in Photoshop, it must be stored as a digital file on your computer system or on an external storage device. The photos used in this book are included in the Data Files for Students. Visit solutions.cengage.com /ctdownloads for detailed instructions or contact your instructor for information about accessing the required files.

The following steps open the file, Desserts, from the Photoshop Chapter 02 folder in the Documents folder of Windows 8. The location of your file may differ.

1 Tap or click File on the Application bar to display the File menu, and then tap or click Open on the File menu to display the Open dialog box.

2 If necessary, tap or click the arrow next to Libraries or This PC in the Navigation pane to display the inclusive folders.

3 Tap or click the Documents location to display a list of the available folders and files.

4 Double-tap or double-click the desired folder to display its contents (in this case, the Photoshop folder).

5 Double-tap or double-click the Chapter 02 folder to display its contents.

6 Tap or click the file, Desserts, to select the file to be opened.

7 Tap or click the Open button to open the file. If the magnification box on the status bar does not display 12.5%, select the value in the box and then type **12.5** to match Figure 2–3.

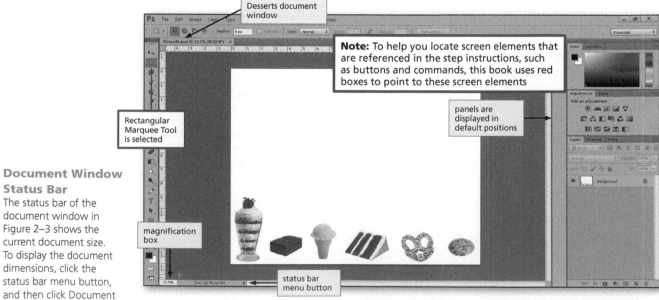

Desserts document window

Note: To help you locate screen elements that are referenced in the step instructions, such as buttons and commands, this book uses red boxes to point to these screen elements

Rectangular Marquee Tool is selected

panels are displayed in default positions

magnification box

status bar menu button

Figure 2–3

For a detailed example of this procedure using the Mac operating system, refer to the For Mac Users Appendix.

To View Rulers

The following steps display the rulers in the document window to facilitate making precise measurements.

1 If the rulers are not shown on the top and left sides of the document window, press CTRL+R to display the rulers in the workspace.

2 If necessary, press and hold or right-click the horizontal ruler, and then tap or click Inches on the context menu to display the rulers in inches.

To Save a Photo

Even though you have yet to edit the photo, it is a good practice to save the file on your personal storage device early in the process. The following steps save the file with the name Desserts Edited in a new folder named Chapter 02. Make sure your storage device is connected to your computer, if necessary.

1 Tap or click File on the Application bar to display the File menu and then tap or click Save As to display the Save As dialog box.

2 Type **Desserts Edited** in the File name text box to change the file name. Do not press the ENTER key after typing the file name.

3 Navigate to your storage location (or the Creative Cloud Files location) by using the Navigation pane or the Previous Locations box arrow to select that drive as the new save location.

4 Tap or click the New folder button on the Save As dialog box toolbar to create a new folder on the selected storage device.

5 When the new folder appears, type **Chapter 02** to change the name of the folder, and then press the ENTER key. Double-tap or double-click the new folder to open it.

6 If necessary, tap or click the 'Save as type' button to display the list of available file formats, and then tap or click Photoshop (*.PSD, *.PDD) in the list to select the file type.

7 Tap or click the Save button to save the document on the selected drive, in the new folder, and with the new file name.

BTW

The View Menu
The View menu has many commands to help you use the Photoshop interface, besides choosing among five different zoom levels; you also can view and create guides and slices and change the snapping features. The Extras command on the View menu shows nonprinting guides, grids, selection edges, slices, and text baselines that help you select, move, or edit objects. You can enable or disable any combination of Extras without affecting the image.

Choose the correct tool.
When you need to copy, paste, or move portions of your photo, consider carefully which selection tool to use. You want the procedure to be efficient and produce a clear image. Keep in mind the following as you choose a selection tool:

- The shape of the selection
- The background around the selection
- The contrast between the selection and its surroundings
- The proximity of the selection to other objects
- Your expertise in using the tool
- The availability of other pointing devices, such as a graphics tablet
- The destination of the paste

Plan Ahead

The Marquee Tools

The **marquee tools** allow you to draw a marquee that selects a portion of the document window. Marquee tools are useful when the part of an image or photo that you want to select fits into a rectangular or an elliptical shape. Photoshop has four marquee tools that appear in a context menu when you press and hold the mouse button, press and hold the touch screen, or when you right-click the tool. Recall that Photoshop offers the added flexibility of selecting a tool with a single letter shortcut key. Pressing the M key activates the current marquee tool.

The Rectangular Marquee Tool is the default marquee tool that selects a rectangular or square portion of the image or photo. The Elliptical Marquee Tool allows you to select an ellipsis, oval, or circular area.

Dragging with the Rectangular or Elliptical Marquee Tools creates a marquee drawn from a corner. If you press the SHIFT key while dragging a marquee, Photoshop constrains the proportions of the shape, creating a perfect square or circle. If you press the ALT key while drawing a selection, Photoshop creates the marquee from the center. Pressing SHIFT+ALT starts from the center and constrains the proportions.

The Single Row Marquee Tool allows you to select a single row of pixels. The Single Column Marquee Tool allows you to select a single column of pixels. A single tap or click in the document window then creates the selection. Because a single row or column of pixels is so small, it is easier to use these two marquee tools at higher magnifications.

Table 2–1 describes the four marquee tools.

Table 2–1 The Marquee Tools			
Tool	**Purpose**	**Shortcut**	**Button**
Rectangular Marquee	Selects a rectangular or square portion of the document window	M SHIFT+M toggles to Elliptical Marquee	
Elliptical Marquee	Selects an elliptical, oval, or circular portion of the document window	M SHIFT+M toggles to Rectangular Marquee	
Single Row Marquee	Selects a single row of pixels in the document window	(none)	
Single Column Marquee	Selects a single column of pixels in the document window	(none)	

The options bar associated with each of the marquee tools contains many buttons and settings to draw well-placed marquees (Figure 2–4). The options bar displays an icon for the chosen marquee on the left, followed by the Tool Preset picker. The Tool Preset picker allows you to save and reuse toolbar settings.

The next four buttons to the right adjust the selection. The New selection button allows you to start a new marquee. The resulting pointer appears as a plus sign in the document window.

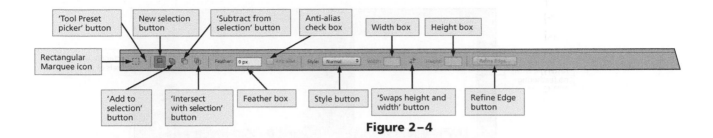

Figure 2–4

The 'Add to selection' button draws a rectangle or ellipsis and adds it to any current selection. The 'Add to selection' button is useful for selecting the extra corners of an L-shaped object or for shapes that do not fit within a single rectangle or ellipsis. To activate the 'Add to selection' button, you can tap or click it on the options bar, or press and hold the SHIFT key while dragging a second selection. When adding to a selection, the pointer changes to a crosshair with a plus sign.

The 'Subtract from selection' button allows you to deselect or remove a portion of an existing selection. The area within the new rectangle or ellipsis is removed from the original selection. It is useful for removing block portions of the background around oddly shaped images, or for deselecting ornamentation in an object. To activate the 'Subtract from selection' button, you can tap or click it on the options bar, or press and hold the ALT key while dragging a second selection. When subtracting from a selection, the pointer changes to a crosshair with a minus sign.

The 'Intersect with selection' button allows you to draw a second rectangle or ellipsis across a portion of the previously selected area, resulting in a selection border around only the area in which the two selections overlap. To activate the 'Intersect with selection' button, you tap or click it on the options bar, or hold down the SHIFT and ALT keys while dragging a second selection. When creating an intersection, the pointer changes to a crosshair with an X.

To the right of the selection buttons, the options bar displays a Feather box. **Feathering** softens the edges of the selection. In traditional photography, feathering is called **vignetting,** which creates a soft-edged border around an image that blends into the background. Photographers use feathering in wedding photos, or when they want a haloed effect. The width of the feather is measured in pixels. When using the Elliptical Marquee Tool, you also can specify blending by selecting the Anti-alias check box. **Anti-aliasing** softens the block-like, staircase look of rounded edges. Figure 2–5 on the next page shows a rectangle with no feathering, one with 10 pixels of feathering, an ellipsis with no anti-aliasing, and one created with a check mark in the Anti-alias check box.

When using the Rectangular Marquee Tool or the Elliptical Marquee Tool, you can tap or click the Style button (Figure 2–4) to choose how the size of the marquee selection is determined. A Normal style sets the selection marquee proportions by dragging. A Fixed Ratio style sets a height-to-width ratio using decimal values. For example, to draw a marquee twice as wide as it is high, enter **2** for the width and **1** for the height, and then drag in the photo. A Fixed Size style allows you to specify exact pixel values for the marquee's height and width. Photoshop enables the Width box and Height box when you choose a style other than Normal. A button between the two boxes swaps the values, if desired.

Sometimes you need to make subtle changes to a selection marquee. For example, if the border or edge of a selection seems to be jagged or hazy, or if the colors at the edge of a selection bleed slightly across the marquee, you can use the Refine Edge button. When tapped or clicked, it opens a dialog box in which you can increase or decrease the radius of the marquee, change the contrast, and smooth the selection border.

BTW

Single Row and Single Column Marquee Tools
To create interesting backgrounds, wallpapers, and color ribbons using the Single Row or Single Column Marquee tools, choose a colorful photo and create a single row or single column marquee. Press CTRL+T to display the bounding box. Then drag the sizing handles until the selection fills the document window.

BTW

Anti-Aliasing
Anti-aliasing is available for the Elliptical Marquee Tool, the Lasso Tool, the Polygonal Lasso Tool, the Magnetic Lasso Tool, and the Magic Wand Tool. You must specify this option before applying these tools. Once a selection is created, you cannot add anti-aliasing.

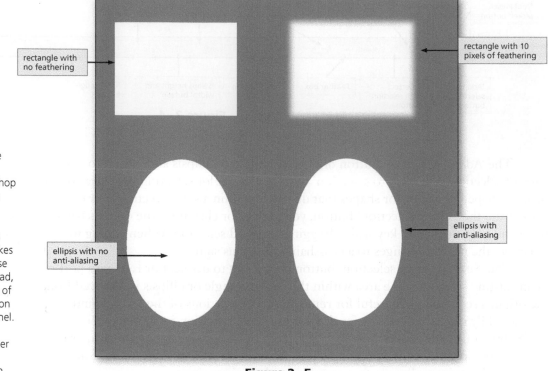

rectangle with
no feathering

rectangle with 10
pixels of feathering

ellipsis with no
anti-aliasing

ellipsis with
anti-aliasing

Figure 2–5

The Tool Preset Picker
Most tools display a Tool Preset picker on the options bar. When you click the button, Photoshop displays a list of settings used during the current Photoshop session or previously saved options bar settings. The list makes it easier to save and reuse tool settings. You can load, edit, and create libraries of tool presets in conjunction with the Tool Presets panel. To choose a tool preset, click the Tool Preset picker in the options bar, and then select a preset from the list.

Once you have drawn a marquee, you can choose from other options for further manipulation of the selected area. Pressing and holding or right-clicking a selection displays a context menu that provides access to many other useful commands such as deselecting, reselecting, or selecting the **inverse**, which means selecting everything in the image outside of the current selection. The context menu also enables you to create layers, apply color fills and strokes, and make other changes that you will learn about in future chapters.

If you make a mistake or change your mind when drawing a marquee, you can do one of three things:

1. If you want to start over, and the New selection button is selected on the options bar, you can tap or click somewhere else in the document window to deselect the marquee, and then simply draw a new marquee. Deselecting also is available as a command on the Select menu and on the context menu. The shortcut for deselecting is CTRL+D.

2. If you have already drawn the marquee but want to move or reposition it, and the New selection button is selected on the options bar, you can drag the selection to the new location.

3. If you want to reposition while you are creating the marquee, do not release the mouse button. Press and hold the SPACEBAR key, drag the marquee to the new location, and then release the SPACEBAR key. At that point, you can continue dragging to finish drawing the marquee. Repositioning in this manner can be done while using any of the four selection adjustment buttons on the options bar.

Selecting the Inverse
Sometimes it is easier to select the area around the desired object rather than the object, because of color changes or fuzzy borders. If you select everything except the desired object, you then can tap or click Inverse on the Select menu to invert the selection.

To Use the Rectangular Marquee Tool

The following step selects the parfait in the lower-left corner of the Desserts Edited image using the Rectangular Marquee Tool.

- With the Rectangular Marquee Tool selected on the Tools panel, drag to draw a rectangle around the parfait in the lower-left corner to create a marquee selection. Drag close to the parfait itself, as shown in Figure 2–6.

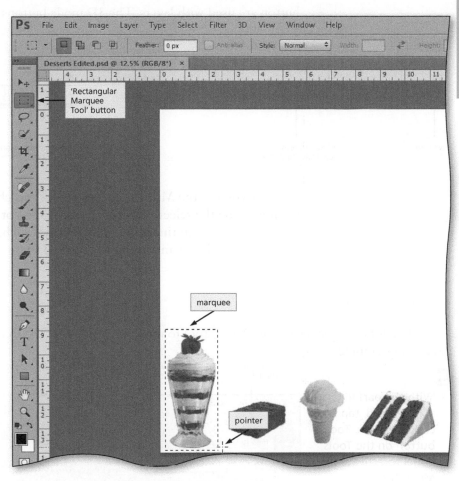

Figure 2–6

Experiment

- Practice drawing rectangular and elliptical marquees. Press SHIFT+M to switch between the two. SHIFT+drag to look at the effects. Press and hold the SPACEBAR key while you drag to reposition the current marquee. When you are finished, press CTRL+D to deselect, and then redraw a rectangle around the parfait.

Q&A

What was the black box that appeared as I created the marquee?
That box is the position indicator, which shows you exactly where you are in the image.

Other Ways

1. Press M or SHIFT+M until Rectangular Marquee Tool is active, drag selection

The Move Tool

The Move Tool on the Photoshop Tools panel allows you to move or make other changes to selections. Activating the Move Tool by tapping or clicking the Move Tool button, or by pressing the V key, enables you to move the selection contents by dragging in the document window. When you first use the Move Tool, the pointer displays a black arrowhead with scissors. To move the selection in a straight line, press and hold the SHIFT key while dragging. If you press and hold the ALT key while dragging, you duplicate or move only a copy of the selected area, effectively copying and pasting the selection. While duplicating, the pointer changes to a black arrowhead with a white arrowhead behind it.

When you move selections, you need to be careful about overlapping images. As you will learn in Chapter 3, Photoshop might layer or overlap portions of images when you move them. While that sometimes is preferred when creating collages or composite images, it is undesirable if an important object is obscured. Close tracing while creating selections and careful placement of moved selections from back to front will prevent unwanted layering.

BTW

Show Position Values
You can change the location of the transformation or position values indicator by pressing CTRL+K to open the Preferences dialog box. On the left, tap or click Interface, and then tap or click the Show Transformation Values button to display a list of locations.

The Move Tool options bar displays tools to help define the scope of the move (Figure 2–7). Later, as you learn about layers, you will use the Auto-Select check box and the 'Select group or layer' button to select layer groupings or single layers. The 'Show Transform Controls' check box causes Photoshop to display transformation controls on the selection. The align and distribute buttons and the Auto-Align Layers button are used with layers. The 3D mode buttons transform a 3-D selection.

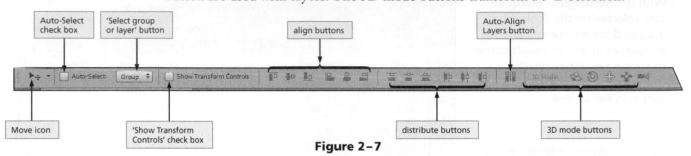

Figure 2–7

As you use the Move Tool throughout this chapter, be careful to position your pointer inside the selection before moving. Do not try to move a selection by dragging its border; at certain times, dragging the border changes the shape of the marquee. If you drag a border by mistake, press the ESC key.

To Use the Move Tool

The following steps use the Move Tool to move the parfait up and to the right to start building the advertising graphic.

1

- With the parfait still selected, tap or click the Move Tool button on the Tools panel to activate the Move Tool.

- If necessary, on the options bar, tap or click the Auto-Select check box so it does not display a check mark. If necessary, tap or click the 'Show Transform Controls' check box so it does not display a check mark (Figure 2–8).

Q&A Are there any other tools nested with the Move Tool?
No, the Move Tool does not have a context menu. Tools with a context menu display a small black rectangle in the lower-right corner.

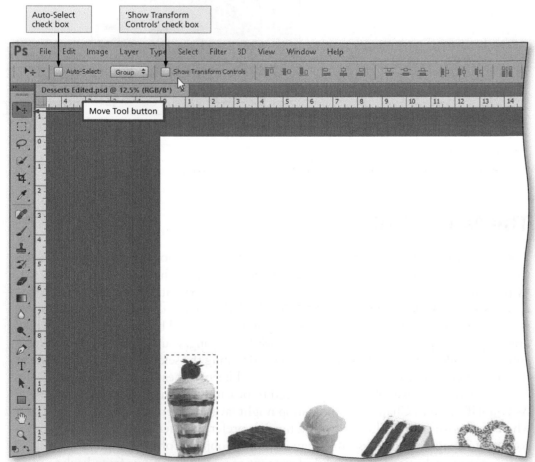

Figure 2–8

2

- Position your pointer over the selection (in this case, the parfait), within the marquee. Drag the selection to a position in the upper-center portion of the photo as shown in Figure 2–9. Do not press any other keys.

Q&A My document window shows a black square. What did I do wrong?
It is possible that another user changed the default colors on your system. Press CTRL+Z to undo the move. Press the D key to select the default foreground and background colors. If black is not on top at the bottom of the Tools panel, press the X key to exchange the black and white colors.

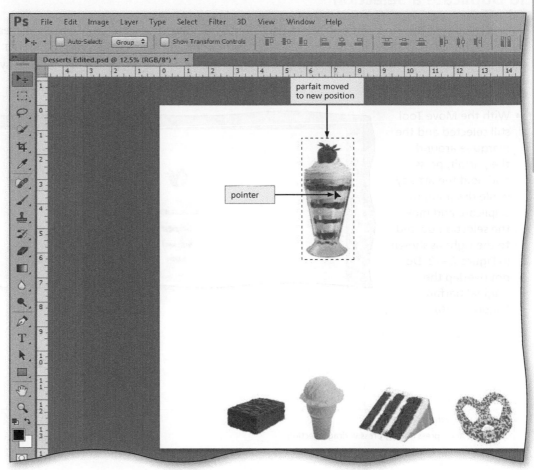

Figure 2–9

Other Ways

1. Press V, drag selection

Plan your duplications.

Creating a storyboard, either by hand or by using software, allows you to plan your image and make decisions about copies and placement. Some graphic artists annotate each copy in the storyboard with information about size, shape, location, and the tool they plan to use (Figure 2–2 on page PS 76). For example, when you paste or drag a new copy of an image into a photo, you have two choices. You can keep the copy as an exact duplicate, or you can transform the copy. The choice depends on the visual effect you want to achieve and the customer requirements. Notating those requirements on your storyboard ahead of time will facilitate creating your image.

Use an exact copy of a logo or a border to create a tiled background. Commercial applications sometimes use duplications to represent growth; or several duplications beside each other can emphasize a brand. Sometimes artists will duplicate an item several times when creating a quick sketch or a rough draft. Across photos, exact duplicates maintain consistency and product identification.

Transforming a copy or section provides additional flexibility and diversity. You might want to create the illusion of multiple, different items to promote sales. Scaling, skewing, warping, and distorting provide interest and differentiation, and sometimes can correct lens errors. Flipping, rotating, or changing the perspective of the copy adds visual excitement to reproductions and creates the illusion of three dimensions.

Plan Ahead

BTW

Nudging
To move a selection by one pixel, press an ARROW key rather than drag, in a move process called **nudging**. Using the SHIFT+ARROW key combination will nudge the selection by 10 pixels.

To Duplicate a Selection

Recall that pressing and holding the ALT key while dragging with the Move Tool creates a copy, or duplicates, the selection. SHIFT+dragging moves the selection in a straight line. Using both the SHIFT and ALT keys while dragging duplicates and moves the copy in a straight line. The following step creates a copy of the parfait.

- With the Move Tool still selected and the marquee around the parfait, press and hold the ALT key while dragging to duplicate and move the selection up and to the right as shown in Figure 2–10. Do not overlap the original parfait (Figure 2–10).

Figure 2–10

Q&A Could I just use the Copy and Paste commands?
Yes, however those commands create a new layer in the photo and increase the file size.

Other Ways

1. Press V, ALT+drag selection
2. Press CTRL+C, press CTRL+V, press V, drag selection

To Resize a Selection

To assist with creating perspective and adding depth in the image, you will resize the copy of the parfait to be smaller, so that it appears further in the distance. When you tap or click the 'Show Transform Controls' check box on the Move Tool options bar, Photoshop displays a bounding box with sizing handles. A **sizing handle** appears as a small square on the corners and sides of a selection. To resize, you simply drag one of the sizing handles. To resize proportionally, SHIFT+drag one of the sizing handles. When you change the size of a selection, it is called **scaling**.

The following steps resize the selection.

- On the Move Tool options bar, tap or click the 'Show Transform Controls' check box so that it displays a check mark (Figure 2–11).

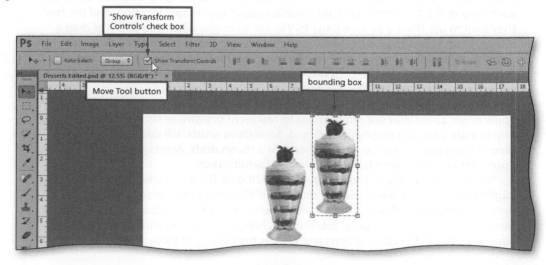

Figure 2–11

2

- SHIFT+drag the upper-right sizing handle toward the middle of the selection to reduce the size of the selection to approximately 85% as shown on the options bar (Figure 2–12).

Q&A

Why did the options bar change?
The options bar changed to the Transform options bar — an options bar not associated with any one specific tool. You will learn more about the Transform options bar in a later chapter.

How do I estimate 85%?
You can drag until the Transform options bar displays approximately 85% in the W and H boxes.

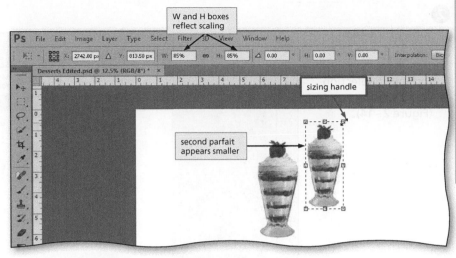

Figure 2–12

Other Ways

1. Press CTRL+T, drag sizing handle
2. Press CTRL+T, enter height and width on options bar

To Flip a Selection

The following steps horizontally flip the copy of the parfait, so that it looks slightly different and more like a second parfait.

1

- With the selection still displayed, tap or click Edit on the Application bar and then tap or click Transform to display the Transform submenu (Figure 2–13).

🔍 **Experiment**

- Tap or click other choices on the Transform submenu and see how the selection changes in the document window. After each transformation, press CTRL+Z to undo the change. When you are finished, tap or click Edit on the Application bar and then tap or click Transform again.

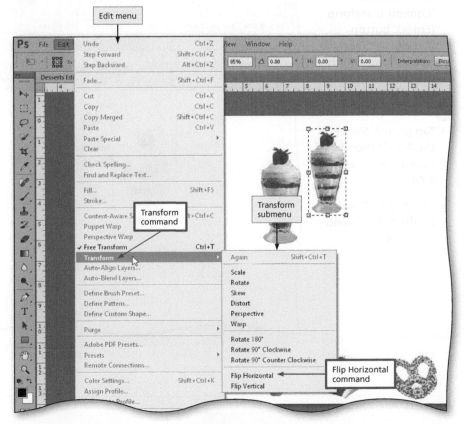

Figure 2–13

- Tap or click Flip Horizontal on the Transform submenu to flip the selection horizontally (Figure 2–14).

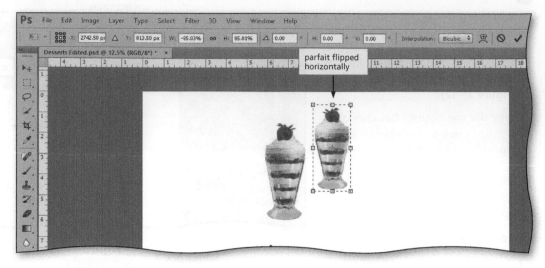

Figure 2–14

Other Ways

1. Press CTRL+T, press and hold or right-click selection, tap or click Flip Horizontal

To Commit the Selection Changes and Deselect

The following steps will **commit**, or confirm, the changes to the selection, and deselect the parfait. Recall that deselecting removes the marquee in the photo.

- Tap or click the 'Commit transform (Enter)' button (Figure 2–15) on the options bar to finish the flip.

- Tap or click Select on the Application bar to display the Select menu.

- Tap or click Deselect on the Select menu to deselect.

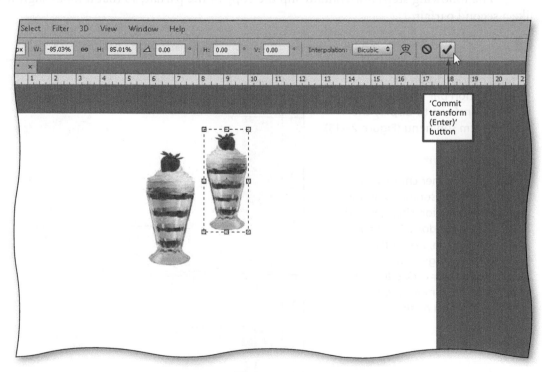

Figure 2–15

Other Ways

1. Press ENTER key, press CTRL+D

To Save using a Shortcut Key

The following step saves the image again, with the same file name, using a shortcut key.

① Press CTRL+S to save the Desserts Edited file with the same name.

Break Point: If you wish to take a break, this is a good place to do so. Quit Photoshop by pressing CTRL+Q. To resume at a later time, start Photoshop, open the file called Desserts Edited, and continue following the steps from this location forward.

Grids, Guides, and Snapping

Photoshop can show a **grid** of lines that appears as an overlay on the image. The grid is useful for laying out elements symmetrically or positioning them precisely. The grid can appear as nonprinting lines or as dots. To display the grid, tap or click Show on the View menu and then tap or click Grid.

Use grids and guides.
Showing grids in your document window gives you multiple horizontal and vertical lines with which you can align selections, copies, and new images. Grids also can help you match and adjust sizes and perspective.

Create guides when you have an exact margin, location, or size in mind. Because selections will snap to guides, you easily can create an upper-left corner to use as a boundary when you move and copy. Grids and guides do not print and are turned on and off easily.

Plan Ahead

A **guide** is a nonprinting ruler line or dashed line that graphic designers use to align objects or mark key measurements. To create a guide, you turn on the ruler display and then drag from the horizontal ruler at the top of the document window or from the vertical ruler at the left side of the document window. When you release the drag, a light, blue-green line appears across the image.

Table 2–2 displays various ways to manipulate guides.

BTW
Viewing and Clearing Guides
Guides are file-dependent, which means the guides you create stay with the photo or graphic, even if you turn off the display. They do not appear if you open a different file. If you want to remove the guide from a certain file permanently, use the Clear Guides command on the View menu.

Table 2–2 Manipulating Guides

Action	Steps
Change color and style	Double-tap or double-click guide.
Clear all guides	On the View menu, tap or click Clear Guides.
Convert between horizontal and vertical guide	Select the Move Tool, ALT+tap or ALT+CLICK guide.
Create	Drag from ruler into document window or, on the View menu, tap or click New Guide, and then enter the orientation and position.
Lock in place	On the View menu, tap or click Lock Guides.
Move	Select the Move Tool, and then drag the guide to a new location.
Remove	Select the Move Tool, and then drag the guide to the ruler.
Snap guide to ruler tick	SHIFT+drag the ruler.
Turn on/off display	On the Application bar, tap or click View, and then tap or click Extras, or, on the View menu, tap or click Show, and then tap or click Guides; or press CTRL+SEMICOLON (;).

BTW
Guides and Grids
You can change the color or style of guides and grids. On the Edit menu, point to Preferences, and then click Guides, Grid, & Slices.

© Cengage Learning

Displaying Extras
On the View menu is an Extras command with which you can show or hide selection edges, guides, target paths, slices, annotations, layer borders, and smart guides. You also can use CTRL+H to show or hide those items.

The term **snapping** refers to the ability of objects to attach to, or automatically align with, a grid or guide. For example, if you select an object and begin to move it, as you get close to a guide, the object's selection border will attach itself to the guide. It is not a permanent attachment. If you do not want to leave the object there, simply keep dragging. To turn on or off snapping, tap or click Snap on the View menu.

In a later chapter, you will learn about smart guides that automatically appear when you draw a shape or move a layer. Smart guides further help align shapes, slices, selections, and layers. The Editing Preferences Appendix describes how to set guide and grid preferences using the Edit menu.

To Display a Grid

The following steps display the grid.

1

- On the Application bar, tap or click View to display the View menu, and then tap or click Show to display the Show submenu (Figure 2–16).

Q&A What do the check marks mean on the View menu?
A check mark indicates that the feature is turned on or enabled. For example, the Snap command displays a check mark, which means objects will snap to grids and guides.

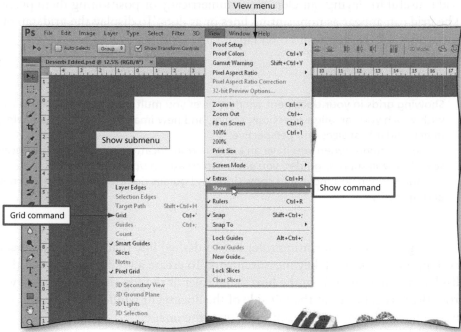

Figure 2–16

2

- Tap or click the Grid command to display the grid (Figure 2–17).

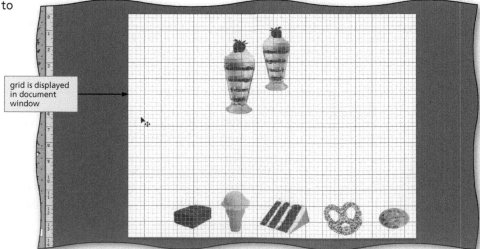

Figure 2–17

Other Ways

1. Press CTRL+APOSTROPHE (')

To Turn Off the Grid Display

The display of a grid is a **toggle**, which means that you turn it off in the same manner that you turned it on; in this case, with the same command.

1 On the Application bar, tap or click View to display the View menu, and then tap or click Show to display the Show submenu.

2 Tap or click Grid to remove the check mark from the menu and to remove the grid from the display.

To Create a Guide

The following steps create a guide to help you position other desserts, on the same horizontal plane later in the chapter.

1

- Position the pointer in the horizontal ruler at the top of the document window.

- Drag down to create a guide, and stop at the bottom of the left parfait (Figure 2–18).

Q&A What is the black box that appears as I drag?
It is a position indicator or tip that shows the location as you drag.

2

- Release the drag to place the guide.

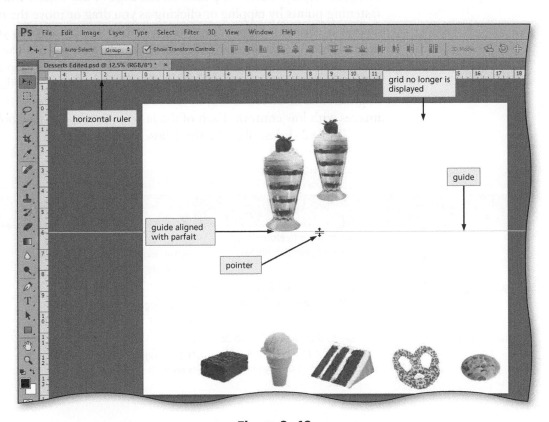

Figure 2–18

Other Ways

1. To show or hide guides, tap or click Show on View menu, tap or click Guides	2. To create guide, on View menu tap or click New Guide, enter value, tap or click OK button	3. To show or hide guides, press CTRL+SEMICOLON (;)

The Lasso Tools

The **lasso tools** draw freehand selection borders around objects. The lasso tools provide more flexibility than the marquee tools with their standardized shapes, and, as you will see, the lasso tools may be more suitable than the Quick Selection Tool when the object is close in color to the background. Photoshop provides three kinds of lasso tools. The first is the default Lasso Tool, which allows you to create a selection by dragging around any object in the document window. When you release the drag, Photoshop connects the selection border to the point where you began dragging, finishing the loop. The Lasso Tool is useful for a quick, rough selection.

BTW

Deleting Selections
You can delete a selection by pressing the DELETE key on the keyboard. Photoshop will display a Fill dialog box. Click the OK button. If you delete by accident, press CTRL+Z to bring the selection back.

The Polygonal Lasso Tool is similar to the Lasso Tool in that it draws irregular shapes in the image; however, the Polygonal Lasso Tool uses straight line segments. To use the Polygonal Lasso Tool, choose the tool, tap or click in the document window, and then move (rather than drag) in straight lines, tapping or clicking each time you turn a corner. When you get back to the beginning of the polygon, tap or click at the connection point to complete the loop; or, double-tap or double-click to have Photoshop complete the selection.

The Magnetic Lasso Tool allows you to tap or click close to the edge of the object you want to select. The Magnetic Lasso Tool tries to find the edge of the object by looking for the nearest color change. It then attaches the marquee to the pixel on the edge of the color change. As you move the pointer, the Magnetic Lasso Tool follows that color change with a magnetic attraction. The Magnetic Lasso Tool's marquee displays fastening points on the edge of the object. You can create more fastening points by tapping or clicking as you drag or move the mouse, to force a change in direction or to adjust the magnetic attraction. When you get all the way around the object, you tap or click at the connection point to complete the loop, or double-tap or double-click to have Photoshop connect the loop for you. Because the Magnetic Lasso Tool looks for changes in color to define the edges of an object, it might not be an effective tool to create selections in images with a busy background or images with low contrast. Each of the lasso tools displays its icon as the pointer.

Table 2–3 describes the three lasso tools.

Table 2–3 The Lasso Tools			
Tool	**Purpose**	**Shortcut**	**Button**
Lasso	Used to draw freeform loops, creating a selection border	L SHIFT+L toggles through all three lasso tools	
Polygonal Lasso	Used to draw straight lines, creating segments of a selection border	L SHIFT+L toggles through all three lasso tools	
Magnetic Lasso	Used to draw a selection border that snaps to the edge of contrasting color areas in the image	L SHIFT+L toggles through all three lasso tools	

© Cengage Learning

Each of the lasso tools displays an options bar similar to the marquee options bar, with buttons to add to, subtract from, and intersect with the selection; the ability to feather the border; and, an Anti-alias check box to smooth the borders of a selection (Figure 2–19). Unique to the Magnetic Lasso Tool options bar, however, is a Contrast box to enter the **contrast**, or sensitivity of color that Photoshop evaluates in making the selection path. A higher value detects only edges that contrast sharply with their surroundings; a lower value detects lower-contrast edges. The Width box causes the Magnetic Lasso Tool to detect edges only within the specified distance from the pointer. A Frequency box allows you to specify the rate at which the lasso sets fastening points. A higher value anchors the selection border in place more quickly. A tablet pressure button on the right changes the pen width when using a graphic drawing tablet instead of a mouse.

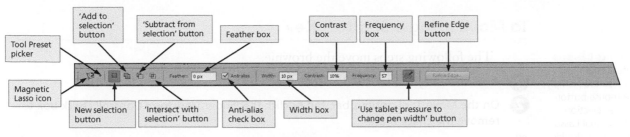

Figure 2–19

To Select using the Lasso Tool

The following steps select the brownie by dragging to draw a rough circle around it with the Lasso Tool.

1

- Press and hold or right-click the Lasso Tool button on the Tools panel to display the context menu (Figure 2–20).

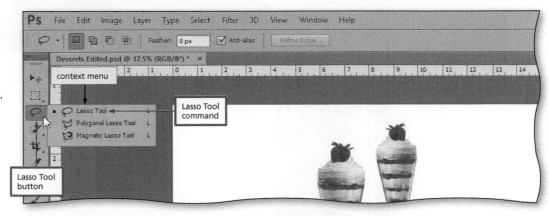

Figure 2–20

2

- Tap or click Lasso Tool to activate the Lasso Tool.

- If necessary, on the options bar, tap or click the New selection button.

- Using the tip of the black arrow on the pointer, drag around the brownie, as close to the edges as possible (Figure 2–21).

Q&A Can I reposition the starting point if I make a mistake?
Yes. Press CTRL+D to deselect, and then start again.

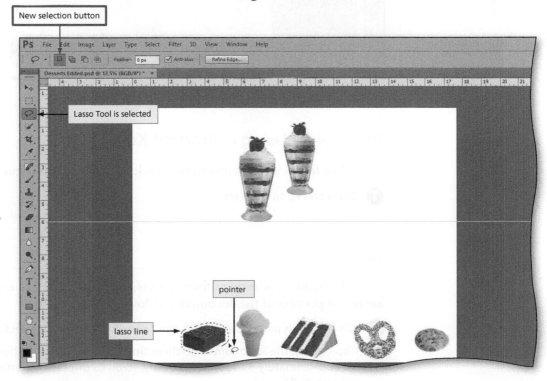

Figure 2–21

Other Ways

1. Press L or SHIFT+L until Lasso Tool is active, drag in photo

To Move using a Shortcut Key

Completing Lassos
To complete a selection using the Lasso tool, simply release the mouse button. To complete a selection using the Polygonal Lasso or Magnetic Lasso, double-click. Alternatively, you can move the mouse pointer close to the starting point. When a small circle appears on the edge of the mouse pointer, single-click to complete the lasso.

The following steps move the brownie.

1 Press the v key to activate the Move Tool.

2 On the Move Tool options bar, tap or click the 'Show Transform Control' check box to remove the check mark.

3 Drag the selection to the right of the parfaits, as shown in Figure 2–22. Do not overlap the parfait.

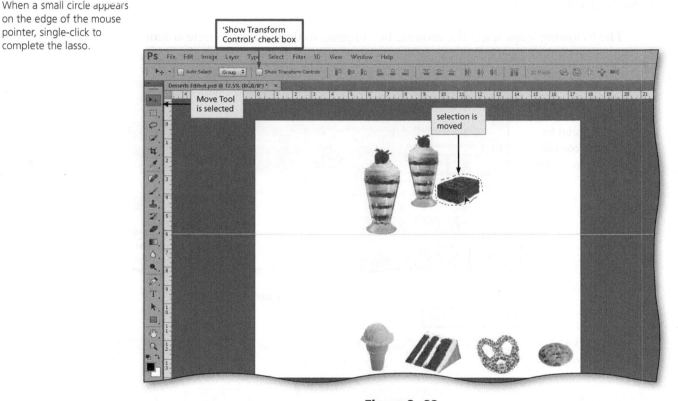

Figure 2–22

To Deselect Using a Shortcut Key

The following step deselects the selection using a shortcut key.

1 Press CTRL+D to deselect.

To Zoom

To facilitate selecting other desserts, the following steps zoom in on the lower-left portion of the document window.

1 On the Tools panel, tap or click the Zoom Tool button to select the tool.

2 Tap or click the ice cream cone three times to zoom that portion of the window to approximately 33.33%. If necessary, scroll to display the entire ice cream cone (Figure 2–23).

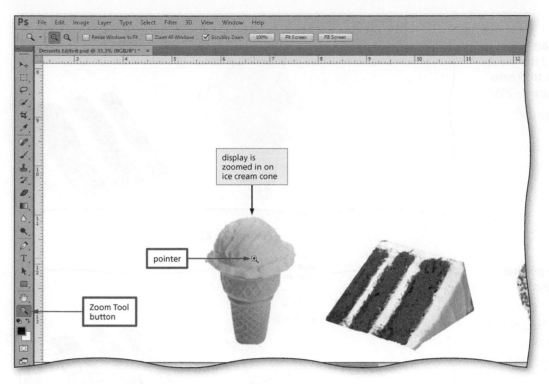

Figure 2–23

To Select using the Magnetic Lasso Tool

The following steps use the Magnetic Lasso Tool to select the ice cream cone. Recall that the Magnetic Lasso Tool selects by finding the edge of a contrasting color and creating fastening points.

1

- Press and hold or right-click the current lasso tool button, and then tap or click 'Magnetic Lasso Tool' to select it from the context menu.

- If necessary, on the options bar, tap or click the New selection button to select the tool.

- Tap or click the upper-left area of the ice cream to start the selection (Figure 2–24).

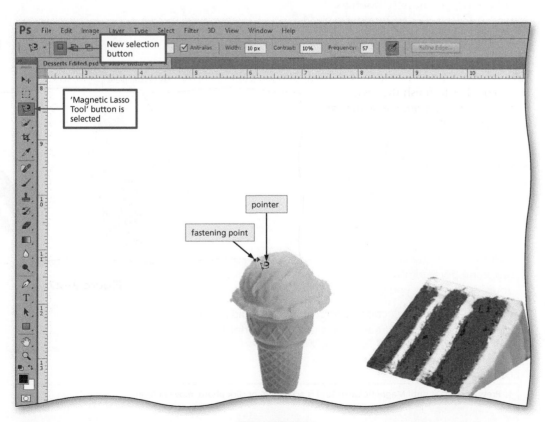

Figure 2–24

2

- Move, rather than drag, the pointer slowly around the top of the ice cream cone to create fastening points (Figure 2–25).

Q&A How do I correct a mistake?
As you use the Magnetic Lasso Tool, if you make a mistake, press the ESC key and begin again.

Figure 2–25

3

- Continue moving the pointer around the edge of the ice cream cone.

- When you get to the beginning again, move near the first fastening point until a small circle appears (Figure 2–26).

Q&A What is the purpose of the small circle?
When the pointer moves close to where you started the lasso, Photoshop displays a small circle, which means you can tap or single-click to complete the lasso. Otherwise, you have to double-tap or double-click to complete the lasso.

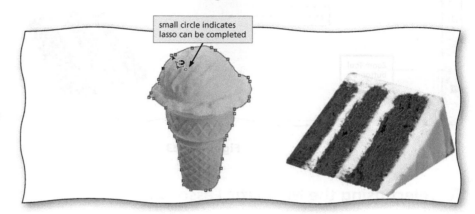

Figure 2–26

4

- Tap or click to finish the lasso. The flashing marquee will appear (Figure 2–27).

Q&A My flashing marquee did not appear. What did I do wrong?
You might not have been exactly on the beginning fastening point when you tapped or clicked. Press the ESC key and start again. If you continue to have trouble positioning on the beginning fastening point, double-tap or double-click when you get close.

Figure 2–27

When I clicked, the selection disappeared. What did I do wrong?
If your selection disappears, press CTRL+Z to undo; the selection then should appear as shown in Figure 2–27.

Other Ways

1. Press L or SHIFT+L until Magnetic Lasso Tool is active, tap or click photo, move pointer

To Zoom Out

The following steps zoom out in preparation for moving the ice cream cone.

1 Tap or click the Zoom Tool button on the Tools panel to activate the Zoom Tool.

2 ALT+tap or ALT+click twice to zoom out to approximately 16.67%.

To Snap a Selection to the Guide

The following steps move the selection, snapping it to the guide.

1

- Press the v key to activate the Move Tool.

- Slowly drag the selection to a location in front of the tall desserts until the bottom of the selection snaps to the guide (Figure 2–28).

2

- Press CTRL+D to deselect.

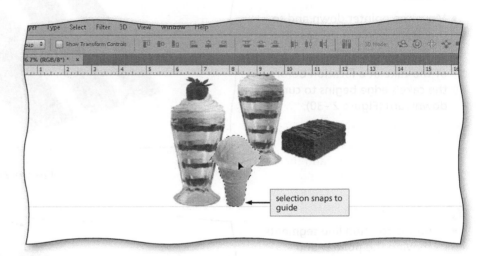

selection snaps to guide

Figure 2–28

Other Ways

1. To turn on or off snapping, tap or click View on Application bar, tap or click Snap
2. To turn on or off snapping, press SHIFT+CTRL+SEMICOLON (;)

To Select using the Polygonal Lasso Tool

The following steps select the slice of cake by drawing lines around it with the Polygonal Lasso Tool.

1

- Press the z key to activate the Zoom Tool, and then tap or click the slice of cake three times to zoom in to approximately 50%. Scroll the document window as necessary to display all of the cake.

- Press and hold or right-click the Lasso Tool button on the Tools panel to display the context menu.

- Tap or click 'Polygonal Lasso Tool' to activate the lasso.

- If necessary, on the options bar, tap or click the New selection button (Figure 2–29).

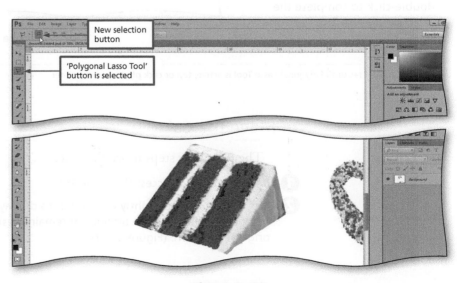

New selection button

'Polygonal Lasso Tool' button is selected

Figure 2–29

Experiment

- Practice using the Polygonal Lasso Tool to draw a triangle by doing the following: in a blank area of the photo, tap or click to begin; move the pointer to the right; and then tap or click to create one side. Move the pointer up, and then tap or click to create a second side. Move the pointer to the beginning point, and then tap or click to complete the lasso. When you are finished experimenting, press CTRL+D to deselect.

❷

- Using the tip of the black arrow on the pointer, tap or click the top of the slice of cake on the left side.

- Move the pointer down and to the right to create the first line.

- Tap or click the upper-right corner of the cake at a location before the cake's edge begins to curve downward (Figure 2–30).

◄ Q&A ► Can I reposition the starting point if I make a mistake?
Yes. Press the ESC key and then start again.

Figure 2–30

❸

- Continue creating line segments by moving the pointer and tapping or clicking each time you need to change direction.

- When you complete the lines all the way around the dessert, move the pointer until a small circle is visible, and then tap or click the circle to complete the selection. If you do not see the small circle, double-tap or double-click to complete the selection (Figure 2–31).

Figure 2–31

Other Ways

1. Press L or SHIFT+L until Polygonal Lasso Tool is active, tap or click photo, move pointer

To Move the Cake

The following steps move the cake.

❶ Press the v key to access the Move Tool.

❷ Move the selection slightly up and left to display any remaining pixels of the cake left behind as a shadow. The amount of remaining shadow may differ depending on the original selection. (Figure 2–32).

Figure 2–32

The History Panel

The History panel appears when you tap or click the History button on the vertical dock of minimized panels. The History panel records each step, called a **state**, as you edit a photo (Figure 2–33). Photoshop displays the initial state of the document at the top of the panel. Each time you apply a change to an image, Photoshop adds the new state of that image to the bottom of the panel. Each state lists the name of the tool or command used to change the image.

BTW

The History Panel
The History panel will list a Duplicate state when you use the ALT key to copy a selection. The word Paste will appear next to the state when you use the Copy and Paste commands from the keyboard or from the menu. The Copy command alone does not affect how the image looks; it merely sends a copy to the system Clipboard. Therefore, it does not appear as a state.

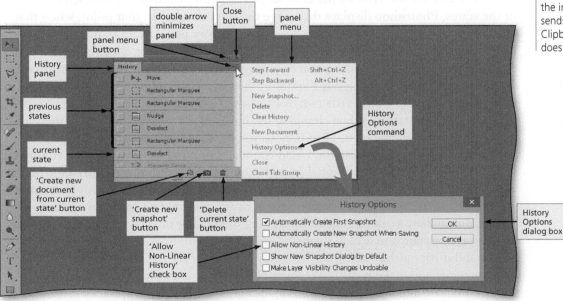

Figure 2–33

Like the Navigator panel that you learned about in Chapter 1, the History panel also has a panel menu where you can clear all states, change the history settings, or dock the panel. Buttons on the History panel status bar allow you to create a new document from a state, save the selected state, or delete it. The panel can be minimized by tapping or clicking the History button on the vertical dock or by tapping or clicking the double arrow at the top of the panel. To redisplay a minimized History panel, tap or click the History button on the vertical dock, or choose it from the Window menu.

To Display the History Panel

The following step displays the History panel.

1

- Tap or click the History button on the vertical dock of minimized panels (Figure 2–34).

Q&A

Can I see more history states? Yes. Drag the scroll box on the right of History panel to view more states. To resize the History panel, drag the lower right corner of the panel.

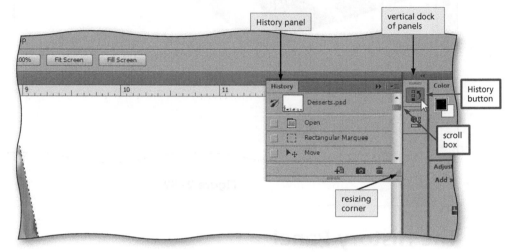

Figure 2–34

Other Ways

1. On Window menu, tap or click History

BTW

Moving Among History Panel States
Photoshop uses many function keys to move easily among the states in the History panel. To step forward, press SHIFT+CTRL+Z. To step backward, press CTRL+ALT+Z. You also can use the History panel menu to step forward and backward.

Using the History Panel

You can use the History panel in several different ways. When you select one of the states, Photoshop displays the image the way it looked at that point, when that change first was applied. Some users access the History panel to undo mistakes. Others use it to try out or experiment with different edits. By tapping or clicking a state, you can view the state temporarily or start working again from that point. You can step forward and backward through the states in the History panel by tapping or clicking them, or by pressing CTRL+SHIFT+Z or CTRL+ALT+Z, respectively.

Selecting a state and then changing the image in any way eliminates all the states in the History panel that came after it; however, if you select a state and change the image by accident, you can use the Undo command or CTRL+Z to restore the eliminated states. If you select the Allow Non-Linear History check box in the History Options dialog box (Figure 2–33 on the previous page), deleting a state deletes only that state.

You can use the History panel to jump to any recent state of the image created during the current working session by tapping or clicking the state. Alternatively, you also can give a state a new name, called a **snapshot**. Naming a snapshot identifies a state and distinguishes it from other states. Snapshots are stored at the top of the History panel and make it easy to compare effects. For example, you can take a snapshot before and after a series of transformations. Then, by tapping or clicking the snapshots in the History panel, you can see the total effect, or choose the before snapshot and start over. To create a snapshot, press and hold or right-click the state and then tap or click New Snapshot on the context menu, or tap or click the 'Create new snapshot' button on the History panel status bar. Snapshots are not saved with the image; closing an image deletes its snapshots.

Not all steps appear in the History panel. For instance, changes to panels, color settings, actions, and preferences are not displayed in the History panel because they are not changes to a particular image.

By default, the History panel lists the previous 20 states. You can change the number of remembered states by changing a preference setting. (See the Editing Preferences Appendix.) Photoshop deletes older states automatically to free more memory. Once you close and reopen the document, all states and snapshots from the last working session are cleared from the panel.

To Undo Changes using the History Panel

Notice in Figure 2–32 on page PS 99 that a shadow appears in the previous location of the cake. This shadow, or ghost shadow, sometimes occurs when using any of the selection tools, especially when fringe pixels are faded – those pixels were not included in the selection marquee. Therefore, you need to return to the previous state and try again. The following step uses the History Panel to undo the Move command.

1

- If necessary, scroll down in the History panel to display the last few states.

- Tap or click the Polygonal Lasso state in the History panel to go back one step and undo the move (Figure 2–35). Do not press any other keys.

Q&A Could I have pressed CTRL+Z to undo the move?
Yes, if you only need to undo one step, pressing CTRL+Z will work. If you need to go back more than one step, you can press CTRL+ALT+Z or use the History panel.

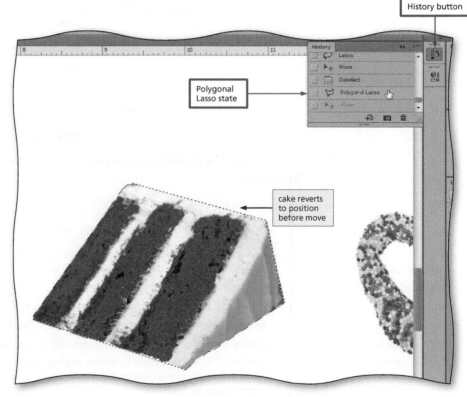

History button

Polygonal Lasso state

cake reverts to position before move

Figure 2–35

To Minimize the History Panel

Recall in Chapter 1 that you minimized the Navigator panel by tapping or clicking the double arrow at the top of the panel. You also can minimize a panel by tapping or clicking the panel button on the vertical dock, as demonstrated in the following step.

1 Tap or click the History button to minimize the panel.

Refining Edges

Each of the selection tools has a Refine Edge button located on its options bar. Tapping or clicking the Refine Edge button displays a dialog box where you can make choices about improving selections with jagged edges, soft transitions, hazy borders, or fine details, improving the quality of a selection's edges. Additionally, it allows you to view the selection on different backgrounds to facilitate editing (Figure 2–36).

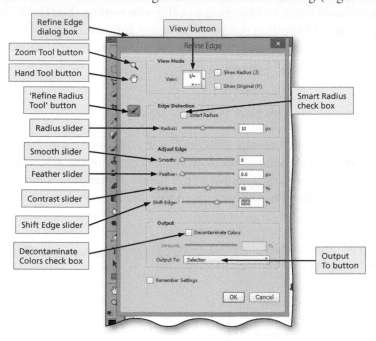

Figure 2–36

Table 2–4 displays some of the controls in the Refine Edge dialog box and their functions.

Table 2–4 Controls and Buttons in the Refine Edge Dialog Box

Control or Button	Function
View button	Allows you to choose the background of the selection and show the radius, original, or both views
Smart Radius check box	Adjusts the radius edges automatically
Radius slider	Adjusts the size of the selection boundary by pixels to increase or decrease the edge refinement.
Smooth slider	Reduces irregular areas in the selection boundary to create a smoother outline with values from 0 to 100 pixels
Feather slider	Softens the edges of the selection for blending into backgrounds using values from 0 to 250 pixels
Contrast slider	Sharpens the selection edges to remove any hazy or extraneous pixels, sometimes called fuzzy artifacts or noise; increasing the contrast percentage can remove excessive noise near selection edges caused by a high radius setting
Shift Edge slider	Moves soft-edged borders, helping remove or include background colors from selection edges
Decontaminate Colors check box	Replaces fringe color
Output To button	Sets the output to a mask, layer, or new document
Remember Settings check box	Saves all settings in the dialog box for use on another selection
Zoom Tool button	Zooms selection in or out
Hand Tool button	Moves portion of the document window that is displayed
'Refine Radius Tool' button	Precisely adjusts the border area in which edge refinement occurs; pressing SHIFT+E toggles to the 'Erase Refinements Tool' button
'Erase Refinements Tool' button	Precisely adjusts the border area in which edge refinement occurs; pressing SHIFT+E toggles to the 'Refine Radius Tool' button

The various settings in the Refine Edge dialog box take practice to use intuitively. The more experience you have adjusting the settings, the more comfortable you will feel with the controls. To improve selections for images on a contrasting background, you should first increase the radius and then increase the contrast to sharpen the edges. For grayscale images or selections where the colors of the object and the background are similar, try smoothing first, then feathering. For all selections, you might need to adjust the Shift Edge slider.

To Refine Edges

The following steps refine the edge of the selection to eliminate the shadow.

1

- On the Tools panel, tap or click the 'Polygonal Lasso Tool' button to return to the Polygonal Lasso Tool (Figure 2–37).

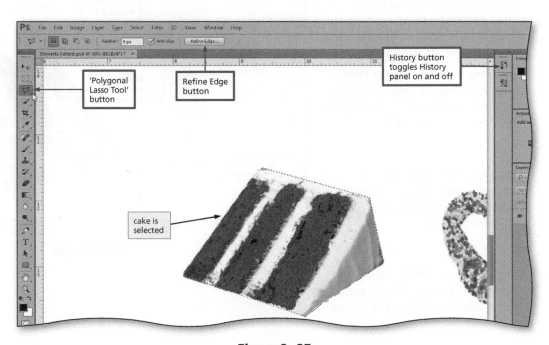

Figure 2–37

2

- On the 'Polygonal Lasso Tool' options bar, tap or click the Refine Edge button to display the Refine Edge dialog box.

- If necessary, drag the title bar of the dialog box slightly away from the piece of cake so all of the cake is visible.

- In the Refine Edge dialog box, tap or click the View button to display the views (Figure 2–38).

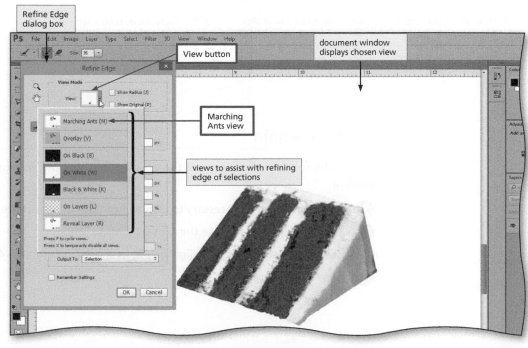

Figure 2–38

Experiment

- One at a time, tap or click each of the views and notice how the background of the document window changes.

3

- Double-tap or double-click Marching Ants to view the selection as a marquee.

- Drag the Radius slider until the Radius box displays approximately 10 pixels to increase the edge refinement of the selection.

- Drag the Contrast slider until the Contrast box displays 50% to increase the contrast between the selection and its surrounding.

- Drag the Shift Edge slider until the percentage is approximately 35% to include more pixels in the selection (Figure 2–39).

Experiment

- Drag the Shift Edge slider to various percentages and watch how the selection changes. Return the slider to 35%.

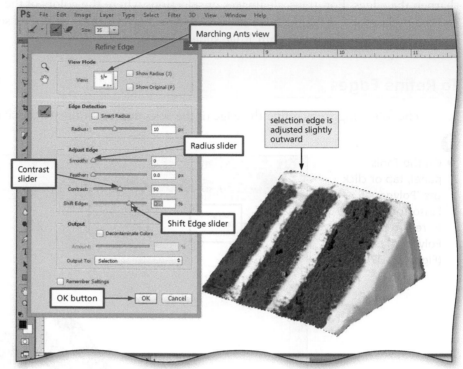

Figure 2–39

4

- Tap or click the OK button in the Refine Edge dialog box to apply the changes and close the dialog box.

Other Ways

1. Press and hold or right-click selection, tap or click Refine Edge, choose settings, tap or click OK button

2. On Select menu, tap or click Refine Edge, choose settings, tap or click OK button

3. Press ALT+CTRL+R, choose settings, tap or click OK button

To Move Again

The following steps move the cake again, this time without leaving behind a shadow.

1 Zoom and scroll as necessary to display both the cake and the ice cream cone.

2 Press the v key to activate the Move Tool.

3 Drag the selection up and slightly left, as shown in Figure 2–40.

4 Press CTRL+D to deselect.

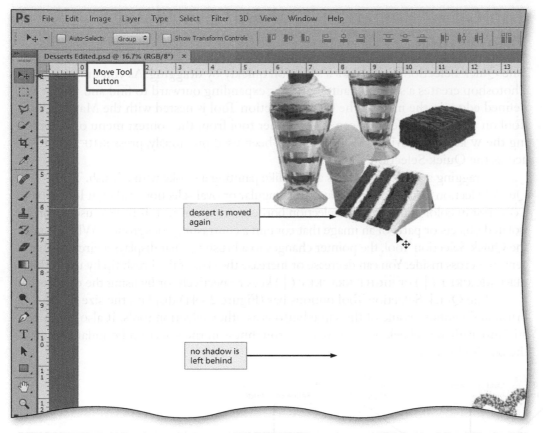

Figure 2–40

The Grow and Similar Commands

Another way to increase the size of a selection without using the Refine Edge dialog box is to use the Grow command on the Select menu. The Grow command will increase, or grow, the selection border to include all adjacent pixels falling within the tolerance range as specified on the options bar of most selection tools. **Tolerance** refers to color range of selected pixels. A low value selects colors very similar to the selection edge. A higher value selects a broader range of colors. Choosing the Grow command more than once will increase the selection in increments. Similar to refining the edge, the Grow command helps to avoid leaving behind a shadow when you move the selection.

The Similar command, also on the Select menu, adds to the selection by including pixels that fall within the tolerance range throughout the image, rather than just those in adjacent pixels.

To Save Again

The following step saves the image again, with the same file name.

1 Press CTRL+S to save the Desserts Edited file with the same name.

Break Point: If you wish to take a break, this is a good place to do so. Quit Photoshop by pressing CTRL+Q. To resume at a later time, start Photoshop, open the file called Desserts Edited, and continue following the steps from this location forward.

The Quick Selection Tool and the Magic Wand Tool

Anti-Aliasing
The Anti-alias check box smooths the jagged edges of a selection by softening the color transition between edge pixels and background pixels. Although anti-aliasing is useful when cutting, copying, and pasting selections to create composite images, it might leave behind a shadow after cutting or moving a selection.

The Quick Selection Tool draws a selection quickly by dragging. As you drag, Photoshop creates a selection automatically, expanding outward to find and follow the defined edges in the image. The Quick Selection Tool is nested with the Magic Wand Tool on the Tools panel. You can access either tool from the context menu or by pressing the w key; if the Magic Wand Tool has been used previously, press SHIFT+W to access the Quick Selection Tool.

Dragging a quick selection is almost like painting a stroke with a brush. The Quick Selection Tool does not create a rectangular or oval selection; rather, it looks for a contrast in color and aligns the selection border to that contrast. It is most useful for isolated objects or parts of an image that contain a contrasting background. When using the Quick Selection Tool, the pointer changes to a brush tip that displays a circle with a centered cross inside. You can decrease or increase the size of the brush tip by using the LEFT BRACKET ([ ) or RIGHT BRACKET ( ]) keys respectively, or by using the options bar.

The Quick Selection Tool options bar (Figure 2–41) displays the size of the brush and contains some of the same buttons as other selection tools. It also contains an Auto-Enhance check box that reduces roughness in the selection boundary when the box is checked.

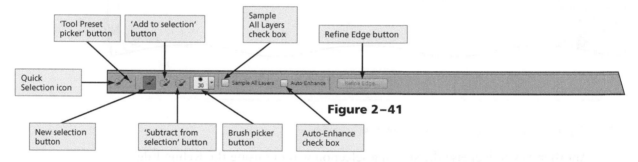

Figure 2–41

Embedded with the Quick Selection Tool, the Magic Wand Tool lets you select a consistently colored area with a single tap or click. For example, if you wanted to select the blue sky in an image, tapping or clicking with the Magic Wand Tool would select it automatically, no matter what the shape of the blue area. When you tap or click the image, Photoshop selects every pixel that contains the same or similar colors as the location you tapped or clicked. The Magic Wand Tool pointer appears as a small line with a starburst on the end, similar to a magic wand.

The Magic Wand Tool options bar (Figure 2–42) contains the same selection adjustment buttons as the marquee tools, including the ability to create a new selection, add to or subtract from a selection, and intersect selections. The Magic Wand Tool options bar also has a Tolerance box that allows you to enter a value that determines the similarity or difference in the color of the selected pixels. Recall that a low tolerance value selects the few colors that are very similar to the pixel you tap or click; a higher value selects a broader range of colors.

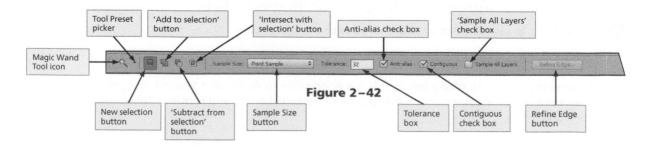

Figure 2–42

When checked, the Contiguous check box selects only adjacent areas with the same color. Otherwise, Photoshop selects all pixels in the entire image that use the same color. Finally, the Sample All Layers check box selects colors using data from all visible layers. Otherwise, the Magic Wand Tool selects colors from the active layer only. You will learn about layers in a future chapter.

Besides using the options bar, the Magic Wand Tool can be used with many shortcut keys. Holding the SHIFT key while tapping or clicking adds to a Magic Wand Tool selection. Holding the ALT key while tapping or clicking subtracts from the selection. Holding the CTRL key while dragging with the Magic Wand Tool moves the selection. If you want to narrow the scope of the Magic Wand Tool, create a selection first.

To Isolate the Pretzel

The following steps select the pretzel area in preparation for using the Magic Wand Tool.

1 Zoom in on the pretzel and scroll as necessary.

2 Tap or click the 'Rectangular Marquee Tool' button on the Tools panel to select it.

3 If necessary, on the options bar, tap or click the New selection button.

4 Drag around the pretzel to select the general area (Figure 2–43).

BTW

Cutting and Pasting
Just as you do in other applications, you can use the Cut, Copy, and Paste commands from the Edit menu or shortcut keys to make changes to selections. Unless you predefine a selection area by dragging a marquee, the Paste command pastes to the center of the document window. Both the commands and the shortcut keys create a new layer when they copy or paste.

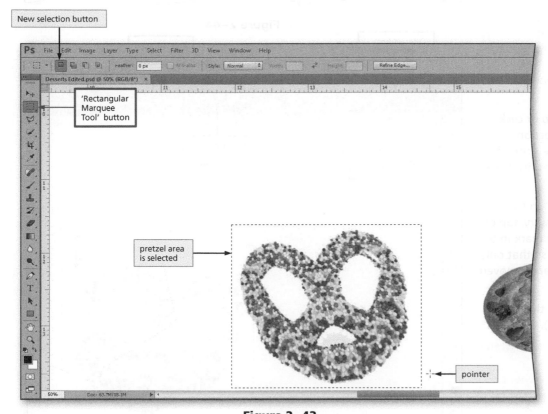

Figure 2–43

To Subtract from a Selection using the Magic Wand Tool

The following steps use the Magic Wand Tool to eliminate the white around and within the pretzel selection, leaving only the pretzel itself inside the marquee. Recall that the Magic Wand Tool selects, or in the case of subtraction, deselects all area consistent with the color at the location of the tap or click.

- With the pretzel still selected, press and hold or right-click the 'Quick Selection Tool' button on the Tools panel to display the context menu (Figure 2–44).

Q&A
Could I press the w key to choose the Magic Wand Tool?
Yes, if the Magic Wand Tool appears on the Tools panel, you can press the w key to activate it; however, if the Quick Selection Tool appears on the Tools panel, you have to press SHIFT+W.

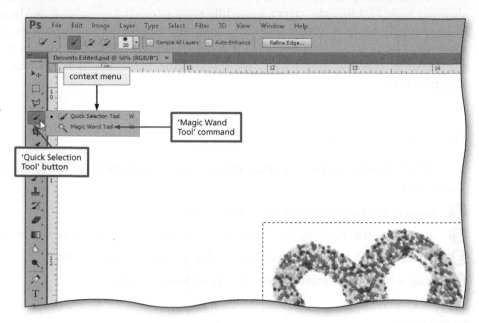

Figure 2–44

- Tap or click 'Magic Wand Tool' to activate it.

- On the options bar, tap or click the 'Subtract from selection' button. Tap or click the Anti-alias check box so it does not display a check mark.

- If necessary, type 32 in the Tolerance box. If necessary, tap or click to display a check mark in the Contiguous check box so that only the contiguous pixels are removed from the selection.

- Move the pointer into the selection (Figure 2–45).

Q&A
What is the minus sign next to the pointer?
The minus sign appears whenever you choose to subtract from a selection. A plus sign would indicate an addition to the selection, and an X indicates an intersection. Photoshop displays these signs so you do not have to glance up at the options bar to see which button you are using while you drag the selection.

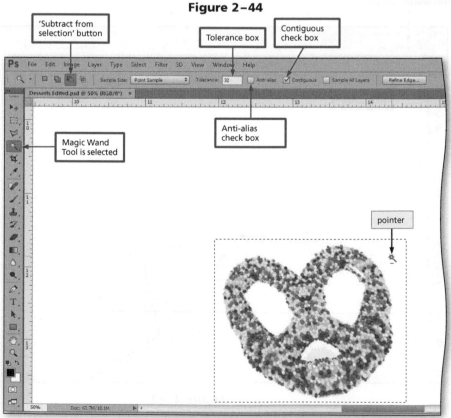

Figure 2–45

3

- Using the tip of the Magic Wand Tool pointer, tap or click the white space outside of the pretzel itself, but still within the selection, in order to remove the white color from the selection (Figure 2–46).

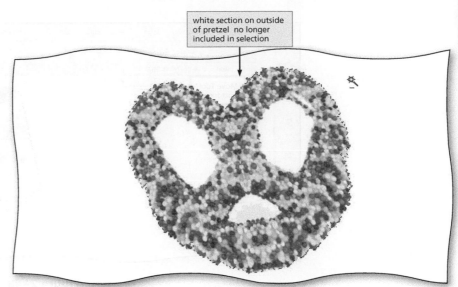

white section on outside of pretzel no longer included in selection

Figure 2–46

4

- One at a time, tap or click each of the three white, inner portions of the pretzel to subtract them from the selection (Figure 2–47).

Q&A Could I have removed the Contiguous check mark and just clicked the white area to remove all white areas?
Yes, but doing so would remove incorrect pixels because there is some white on the pretzel itself. It was better to remove the contiguous white spaces around and within the pretzel.

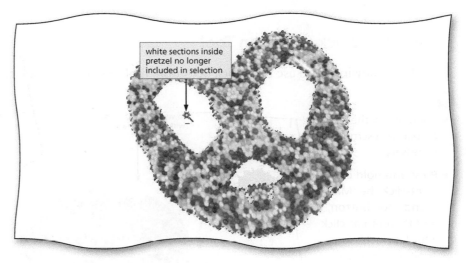

white sections inside pretzel no longer included in selection

Figure 2–47

Other Ways

1. Select Magic Wand Tool, press and hold or right-click photo, tap or click 'Subtract from selection'
2. Select Magic Wand Tool, ALT+TAP OR ALT+CLICK selection
3. Press W or SHIFT+W until Magic Wand Tool is active, tap or click 'Subtract from selection' button, tap or click selection

To Refine the Edge and Move the Pretzel

The following steps refine the selection by shifting the edge. You then will move the pretzel.

1 On the options bar, tap or click the Refine Edge button to display the Refine Edge dialog box.

2 Drag the Shift Edge slider to 30%.

3 Tap or click the OK button to close the dialog box.

4 Zoom and scroll as necessary to view both the pretzel and the brownie.

5 Activate the Move Tool.

6 Drag the pretzel to a location in front of the brownie, as shown in Figure 2–48 on the next page.

7 Deselect.

BTW

Resizing
Photoshop allows you to apply some transformations to entire images or photos, rather than just selections. For example, you can change the size of the photo or rotate the image using the Image menu. You then can enter dimensions or rotation percentages on the submenu and subsequent dialog boxes.

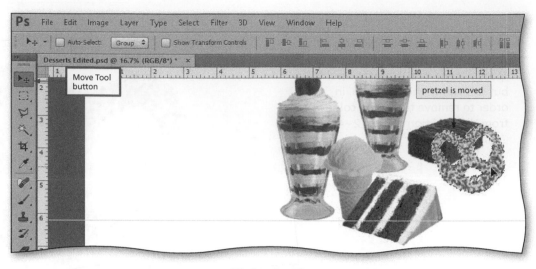

Figure 2–48

To Use the Quick Selection Tool

The following steps use the Quick Selection Tool to select the cookie.

1

- Zoom in on the cookie and scroll as necessary.

- Press and hold or right-click the 'Magic Wand Tool' button, and then tap or click 'Quick Selection Tool' to select the Quick Selection Tool.

- On the options bar, tap or click the New selection button, if necessary.

- If necessary, tap or click the Auto-Enhance check box so it displays a check mark (Figure 2–49).

Figure 2–49

Q&A What does the Auto-Enhance feature do?
Auto-Enhance reduces the block-like edges in the selection border and adjusts the selection further toward the edges of the image.

2

- Move the pointer to the upper-left corner of the cookie, and then slowly drag down and right to select the entire cookie (Figure 2–50).

Q&A

What should I do if I make a mistake with the Quick Selection Tool?

If you make a mistake and want to start over, you can deselect by pressing CTRL+D, and then begin again.

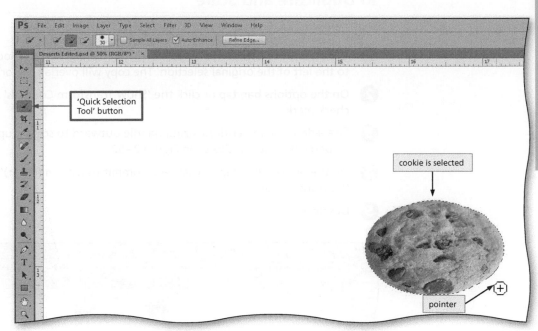

Figure 2–50

Experiment

- Practice resizing the pointer by using the LEFT BRACKET ([) key to decrease the size or the RIGHT BRACKET (]) key to increase the size.

Other Ways

1. Press and hold or right-click Magic Wand Tool, tap or click 'Quick Selection Tool', drag to select
2. Press W or SHIFT+W until Quick Selection Tool is active, drag to select

To Move the Cookie

The following steps move the cookie.

1 Zoom and scroll as necessary to display both the cookie and the group of desserts.

2 Activate the Move Tool.

3 Drag the selection to a location in front and to the right of the group of desserts, as shown in Figure 2–51. Do not deselect.

Figure 2–51

To Duplicate and Scale

The following steps create a larger copy of the cookie.

① With the Move Tool still selected, ALT+drag the selection to a location slightly down and to the left of the original selection. The copy will overlap the original cookie slightly.

② On the options bar, tap or click the 'Show Transform Controls' check box to display a check mark.

③ SHIFT+drag the lower-right sizing handle outward to scale it up approximately 10 percent larger, as shown in Figure 2–52.

④ On the options bar, tap or click the 'Commit transform (Enter)' button to accept the transformation.

⑤ Deselect.

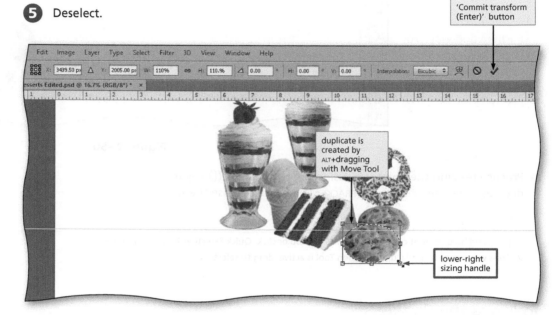

Figure 2–52

To Reselect

When you deselect on purpose or by accident, you can return to the previous selection by using the Reselect command. The following steps reselect the copy of the cookie.

①

- Tap or click Select on the Application bar to display the Select menu (Figure 2–53).

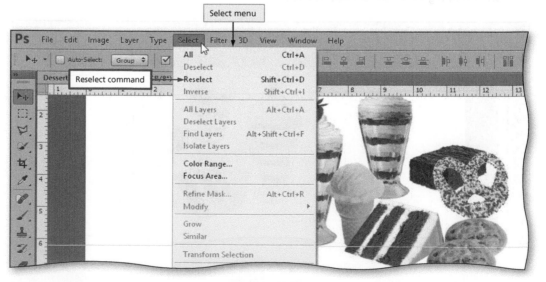

Figure 2–53

2

- Tap or click Reselect to display the previous selection (Figure 2–54).

Figure 2–54

Other Ways

1. Press SHIFT+CTRL+D

To Rotate

The following steps rotate the cookie to differentiate it slightly from the previous cookie.

1

- With the cookie reselected, tap or click Edit on the application bar to display the Edit menu.

- Tap or click Transform to display the Transform submenu (Figure 2–55).

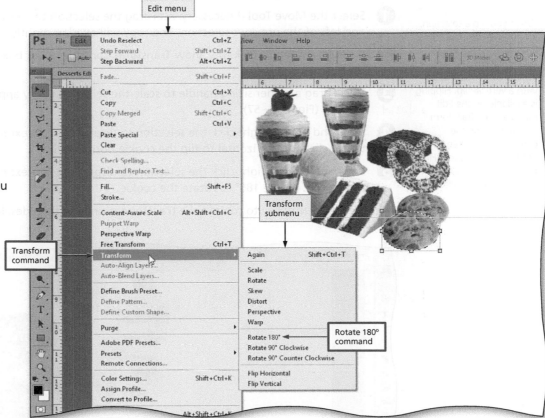

Figure 2–55

2

- Tap or click Rotate 180° to rotate the selection 180 degrees (Figure 2–56).

Figure 2–56

Other Ways

1. Press CTRL+T, press and hold or right-click selection, tap or click Rotate 180°

To Create, Scale, Flip, and Rotate Another Copy

The following steps create another copy of the cookie.

BTW

Flipping Selections
When you flip a selection, Photoshop creates a mirror image with a horizontal flip, or an upside-down version of the selection with a vertical flip. Flipping is available on the Edit menu and its Transform submenu or on the context menu when you right-click a selection. Flip transformations do not have to be committed.

1 Select the Move Tool if necessary. ALT+drag the selection to a location slightly down and left of the previous selection. The copy will overlap slightly.

2 If necessary, tap or click the 'Show Transform Controls' check box to display a check mark.

3 SHIFT+drag a corner sizing handle to scale the selection up by approximately 10 percent (Figure 2–57).

4 Press and hold or right-click the selection to display the context menu, and then tap or click Flip Horizontal to flip the cookie horizontally.

5 Press and hold or right-click the selection to display the context menu, and then tap or click Rotate 180° to rotate the cookie.

6 Press the ENTER key to commit the transformation, and then deselect.

Figure 2–57

To Fit Screen

In moving around the screen in this project, you have zoomed and scrolled many times. The following step uses the Fit Screen button on the Zoom Tool options bar to display the entire document window.

- Select the Zoom Tool.

- Tap or click the Fit Screen button on the Zoom Tool options bar to display the entire image in the document window. The exact placement of your desserts might differ (Figure 2–58).

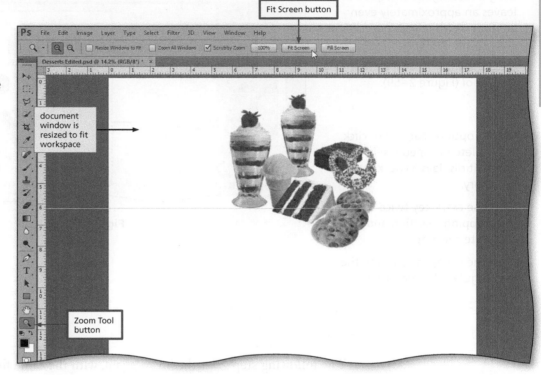

Fit Screen button

document window is resized to fit workspace

Zoom Tool button

Figure 2–58

Other Ways

1. On View menu, tap or click 'Fit on Screen'
2. Press CTRL+0 (zero)

To Turn Off Guides using a Shortcut Key

The following step turns off the display of the green ruler guide.

1 Press CTRL+SEMICOLON (;) to turn off the display of guides.

To Crop from a Selection

Finally, you will crop the graphic to center the desserts, including a minimal amount of border space. In Chapter 1, you activated the Crop Tool and then adjusted the size of the selection. In the steps on the next page, you will select first, and then crop.

● Press the M key to select the Rectangular Marquee Tool.

● Drag a rectangular marquee that leaves an approximately even amount of white space on all four sides of the desserts.

● Press the C key to activate the Crop Tool (Figure 2–59).

● On the options bar, tap or click the 'Delete Cropped Pixels' check box so it displays a check mark, if necessary.

● Press the ENTER key twice to accept the cropping selection and to complete the crop.

● Press the M key to return to the Rectangular Marquee Tool.

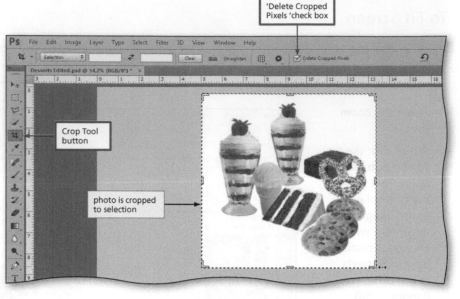

Figure 2–59

To Save Again

The following step saves the image again, with the same file name, using a shortcut key.

1 Press CTRL+S to save the Desserts Edited file with the same name.

Break Point: If you wish to take a break, this is a good place to do so. Quit Photoshop by pressing CTRL+Q. To resume at a later time, start Photoshop, open the file named Desserts Edited, and continue following the steps from this location forward.

Creating PDF Files

The final step is to create a PDF file of the promotional graphic for document exchange. **PDF** stands for **Portable Document Format**, a flexible file format based on the PostScript imaging model that is compatible across platforms and applications. PDF files accurately display and preserve fonts, page layouts, and graphics. There are two ways to create a PDF file in Photoshop. First, you can save the file in the PDF format. Alternatively, you can use the Print command to create the PDF format, allowing you to make some changes to the settings before saving.

Plan
Ahead

Create files in portable formats.
You might need to distribute your artwork in a variety of formats for customers, print shops, webmasters, and e-mail attachments. The format you choose depends on how you will use the file, but portability is always a consideration. The document might need to be used with various operating systems, monitor resolutions, computing environments, and servers.

It is a good idea to discuss with your client the types of formats he or she might need. It usually is safe to begin work in the Photoshop PSD format and then use the Save as command or Print command to convert the files. PDF is a portable format that is readable by anyone on the web with a free reader. The PDF format is platform and software independent. Commonly, PDF files are virus free and safe as e-mail attachments.

To Save a Photo in the PDF Format

The following steps save the photo in the PDF format for ease of distribution.

1

- Tap or click File on the Application bar, and then tap or click Save As to display the Save As dialog box.

- Tap or click the 'Save as type' button to display the various formats you can use to save Photoshop files (Figure 2–60).

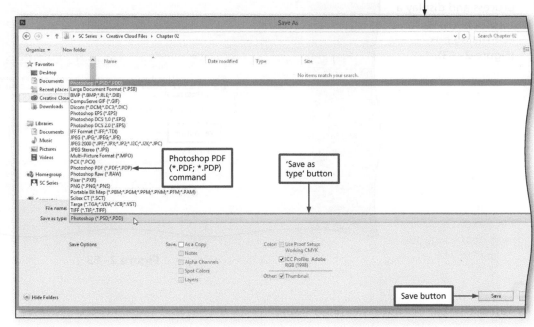

Figure 2–60

2

- Tap or click Photoshop PDF (*.PDF;*.PDP) in the list to select the PDF format, and then tap or click the Save button to display the Adobe Photoshop CC 2014 dialog box to continue saving process (Figure 2–61).

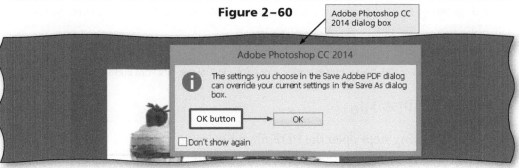

Figure 2–61

3

- Tap or click the OK button to display the Save Adobe PDF dialog box (Figure 2–62).

Q&A The Save Adobe PDF dialog box did not appear. What happened?
If you have multiple windows open on your system, the dialog box might be behind some of the other windows. In that case, minimize the other windows until the dialog box appears.

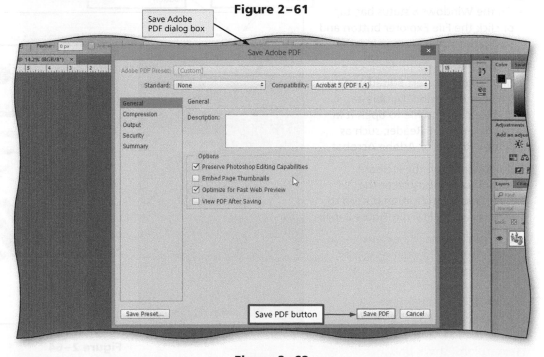

Figure 2–62

4

- Tap or click the Save PDF button to continue the saving process and display a second Save Adobe PDF dialog box (Figure 2–63).

Q&A

Will the PDF version have the same name?
Yes. After you save the file, you will see the name Desserts Edited.pdf on the document window tab because Photoshop can edit PDF files directly. The file also can be viewed with Adobe Acrobat or any PDF reader.

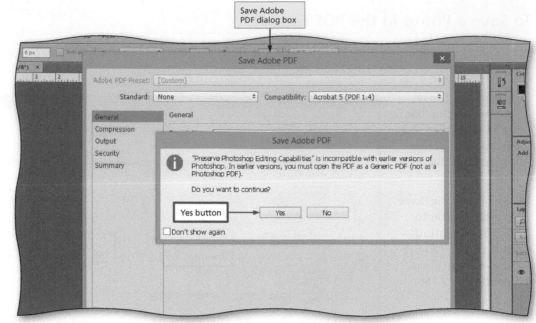

Figure 2–63

5

- Tap or click the Yes button to finish saving.

 For a detailed example of this procedure using the Mac operating system, refer to the For Mac Users Appendix.

Other Ways

1. Press CTRL+P, tap or click Printer button, tap or click Adobe PDF, tap or click Print button

To View the PDF File

The following steps open the PDF file for viewing.

1

- On the Windows 8 status bar, tap or click the File Explorer button and navigate to your storage location.

- In the Chapter 02 folder, locate the file named, Dessert Edited, with the .pdf extension. Double-tap or double-click the file to open it in the default PDF Reader, such as Adobe Reader or Adobe Acrobat.

- If necessary, use the Increase Magnification button or the Decrease Magnification button to view the entire PDF file (Figure 2–64).

Q&A

I cannot see the file extensions in the Chapter 02 folder. How can I turn them on?
In the File Explorer window, tap or click the View tab on the ribbon, and then tap or click to display a check mark in the 'File name extensions' check box.

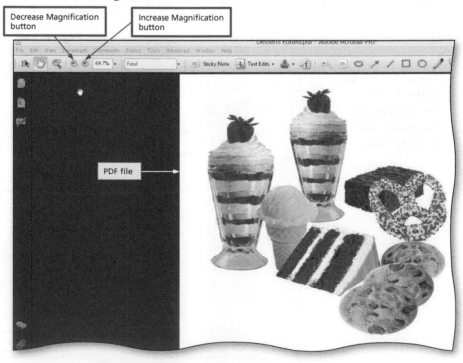

Figure 2–64

To Close a Photo without Quitting Photoshop

Recall that when you are finished editing a photo or file, you should close it to help save system resources. You can close a photo after you have saved it and continue working in Photoshop. The following steps close the Desserts Edited.pdf file without quitting Photoshop.

1 Tap or click the Close button on the document window tab to close the Desserts Edited.pdf file.

2 If Photoshop displays a dialog box, tap or click the No button to ignore the changes since the last time you saved the photo.

Keyboard Shortcuts

Recall that a **keyboard shortcut**, or **shortcut key**, is a way to activate menu or tool commands using the keyboard rather than by tapping or clicking. For example, pressing the L key on the keyboard immediately selects the current lasso tool without having to move your pointer away from working in the image. Shortcuts that combine two keystrokes are common as well, such as the use of CTRL+A to select an entire image. Shortcuts are useful when you do not want to take the time to traverse the menu system or when you are making precise edits and selections with the mouse and do not want to go back to any of the panels to change tools or settings. A Quick Reference summary describing Photoshop's keyboard shortcuts is included in the back of the book.

While many keyboard shortcuts already exist in Photoshop, there might be times when additional shortcuts would be useful. For instance, the Single Row and Single Column Marquee Tools have no shortcut key. If you frequently use those tools, adding the Single Row and Single Column Marquee Tools to the M keyboard shortcut might be helpful. Photoshop allows users to create, customize, and save keyboard shortcuts in one of three areas: menus, panels, or tools. When you create keyboard shortcuts, you can add them to Photoshop's default settings, save them in a personalized set for retrieval in future editing sessions, or delete them from your system.

Creating a Keyboard Shortcut

To create a new keyboard shortcut, Photoshop provides a dialog box interface, which is accessible from the Edit menu. Using that dialog box, you can select one of the three shortcut areas. Then you can assign a shortcut key or combination of keys. For menu commands, your shortcut keystrokes must include a combination of the CTRL key or a function key followed by a single keyboard character. When creating shortcuts for tools, you must use a single alphabetic character. To avoid conflicting duplications, Photoshop immediately warns you if you have chosen a keyboard shortcut that already is in use by the program.

BTW

Photoshop Help
The best way to become familiar with Photoshop Help is to use it. The Photoshop Help Appendix includes detailed information about Photoshop Help and exercises that will help you gain confidence in using it.

To Create a New Keyboard Shortcut

In the following steps, you will create a shortcut to display the Essentials workspace. Although that command is accessible on the Window menu, a shortcut would save time when you need to choose the workspace.

1

- Tap or click Edit on the Application bar to display the Edit menu, and then tap or click Keyboard Shortcuts to display the Keyboard Shortcuts and Menus dialog box.

- If necessary, tap or click the Shortcuts For button, and then tap or click Application Menus in the list.

- In the Application Menu Command list, scroll down, and then tap or click the triangle to the left of the Window command to display the list of Window menu commands (Figure 2–65).

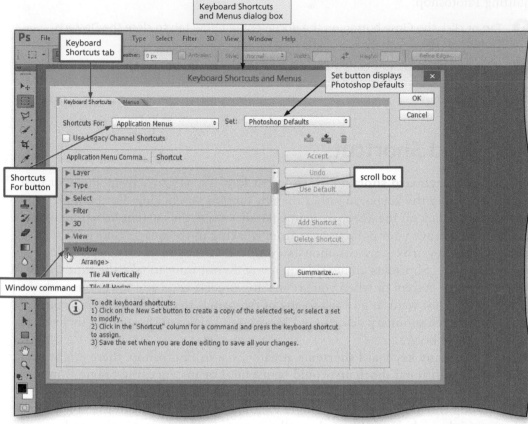

Figure 2–65

2

- Scroll down to display Workspace under the Window menu commands, and then tap or click Essentials (Default) to display a shortcut key box (Figure 2–66).

Q&A How are the buttons at the top of the dialog box used?
The 'Save all changes to the current set of shortcuts' button allows you to name the set for future retrieval. The 'Create a new set based on the current set of shortcuts' button creates a copy of the current keyboard shortcut settings. The 'Delete the current set of shortcuts' button deletes the set.

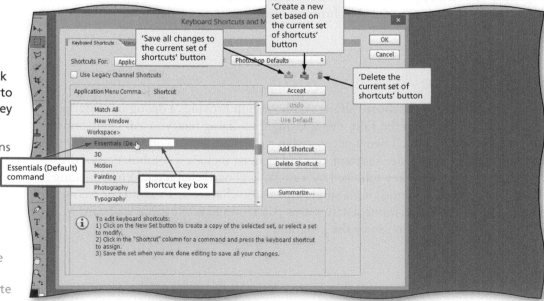

Figure 2–66

3

• Press the F12 key to enter a new shortcut keystroke for the Essentials (Default) command (Figure 2–67).

Q&A How can I find out which shortcuts keys still are available? When you tap or click the Summarize button, Photoshop creates a webpage with all of the keyboard shortcuts in the set. You can save that file on your system or print it.

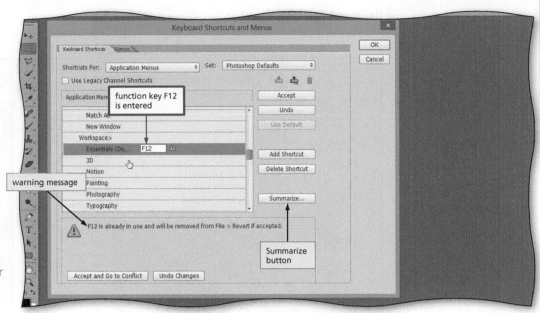

Figure 2–67

4

• Because Photoshop warns you that the F12 key already is being used as a shortcut for a different command, press CTRL+COMMA (,) to enter a new shortcut (Figure 2–68).

5

• Tap or click the Accept button to set the shortcut key.

• Tap or click the OK button to close the dialog box.

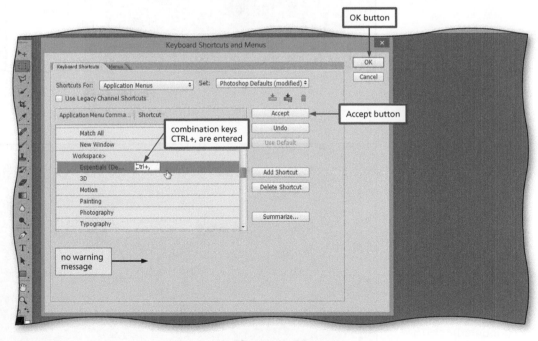

Figure 2–68

Other Ways

1. Press ALT+SHIFT+CTRL+K, edit settings, tap or click OK button

To Test a New Keyboard Shortcut

The next steps test the new keyboard shortcut.

1

• Tap or click Window on the Application bar, and then tap or click Workspace to verify the shortcut key assignment (Figure 2–69).

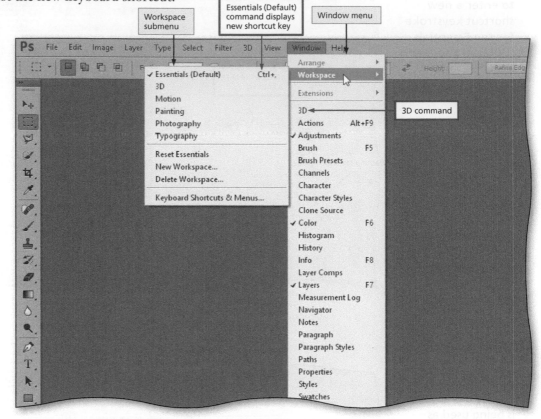

Figure 2–69

2

• Tap or click the 3D command to change to the 3D workspace (Figure 2–70).

Q&A Will the new shortcut become permanent?
The new shortcut will be saved on your system in the Photoshop Defaults (modified) set. That set will be in effect the next time you start Photoshop. If you want to remove it, you can edit that specific shortcut, or delete the set by tapping or clicking the 'Delete the current set of shortcuts' button.

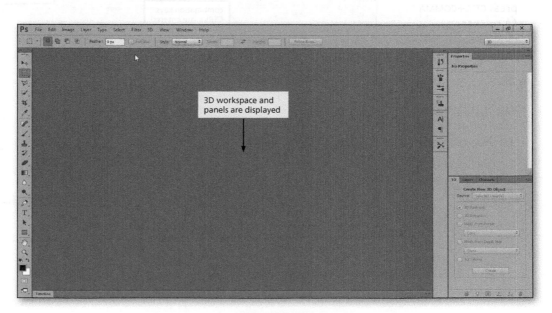

Figure 2–70

3

- Press CTRL+COMMA (,) to test the shortcut, and display the Essentials workspace again (Figure 2–71).

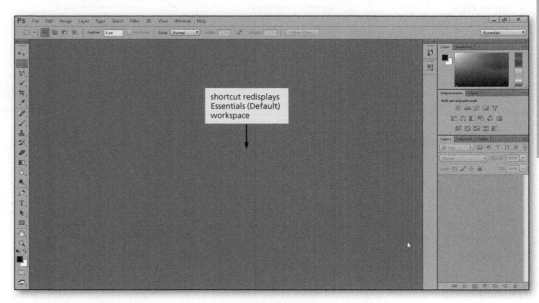

shortcut redisplays Essentials (Default) workspace

Figure 2–71

To Return to the Default Settings for Keyboard Shortcuts

It is a good idea, especially in a lab situation, to reset the keyboard shortcuts to their default settings. The following steps restore the default shortcut keys.

1

- On the Application bar, tap or click Edit, and then tap or click Keyboard Shortcuts to display the Keyboard Shortcuts and Menus dialog box.
- On the Keyboard Shortcuts tab, tap or click the Set button to display the list (Figure 2–72).

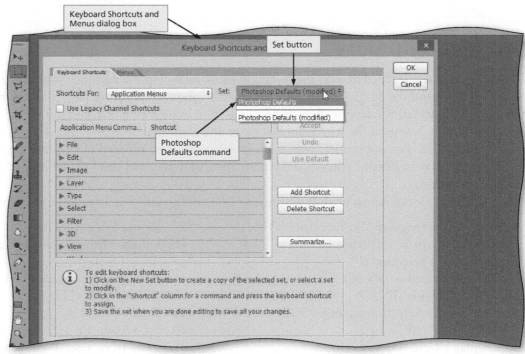

Keyboard Shortcuts and Menus dialog box

Set button

Photoshop Defaults command

Figure 2–72

- Tap or click Photoshop Defaults to choose the default settings for shortcuts (Figure 2–73).

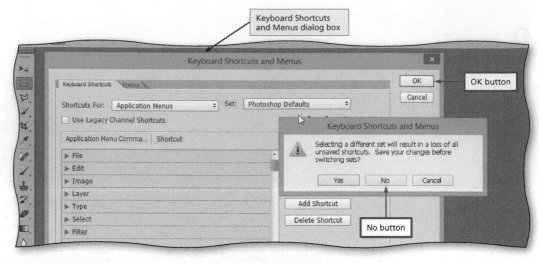

Keyboard Shortcuts and Menus dialog box

OK button

No button

Figure 2–73

- When Photoshop displays a message asking if you want to save your changes, tap or click the No button so your previous changes are not saved.

- In the Keyboard Shortcuts and Menus dialog box, tap or click the OK button to close the dialog box.

To Quit Photoshop using a Shortcut Key

The following step quits Photoshop and returns control to Windows.

1 Press CTRL+Q to quit Photoshop.

Chapter Summary

In this chapter, you learned how to use selection tools, including the marquee tools, the lasso tools, the Quick Selection Tool, and the Magic Wand Tool. You learned about the History panel and its states. You worked with the 'Subtract from selection' command, the Refine Edge dialog box, and the Grow command to edit the selection border. You used the Move Tool to move and copy selections and scaled them. Each of the tools and commands had its own options bar with settings to control how the tool or command worked. You used a guide to help align objects. Finally, you saved the photo as a PDF file, and you learned how to create and test a new keyboard shortcut.

The items listed below include all the new Photoshop skills you have learned in this chapter:

1. Use the Rectangular Marquee Tool (PS 83)
2. Use the Move Tool (PS 84)
3. Duplicate a Selection (PS 86)
4. Resize a Selection (PS 86)
5. Flip a Selection (PS 87)
6. Commit the Selection Changes and Deselect (PS 88)
7. Display a Grid (PS 90)
8. Create a Guide (PS 91)
9. Select using the Lasso Tool (PS 93)
10. Select using the Magnetic Lasso Tool (PS 95)
11. Snap a Selection to the Guide (PS 97)
12. Select using the Polygonal Lasso Tool (PS 97)
13. Display the History Panel (PS 100)
14. Undo Changes Using the History Panel (PS 101)
15. Refine Edges (PS 103)
16. Subtract from a Selection using the Magic Wand Tool (PS 108)
17. Use the Quick Selection Tool (PS 110)
18. Reselect (PS 112)
19. Rotate (PS 113)
20. Fit Screen (PS 115)
21. Crop from a Selection (PS 115)
22. Save a Photo in the PDF Format (PS 117)
23. View the PDF File (PS 118)
24. Create a New Keyboard Shortcut (PS 120)
25. Test a New Keyboard Shortcut (PS 122)
26. Return to the Default Settings for Keyboard Shortcuts (PS 123)

Apply Your Knowledge

Reinforce the skills and apply the concepts you learned in this chapter.

Moving Selections

Note: To complete this assignment, you will be required to use the Data Files for Students. Visit solutions.cengage.com/ctdownloads for detailed instructions or contact your instructor for information about accessing the required files.

Instructions: Start Photoshop and perform the customization steps found on pages PS 6 through PS 11. Open the Apply 2-1 Storage Devices file in the Chapter 02 folder from the Data Files for Students. Save the file on your storage device, in the PSD file format, with the name, Apply 2-1 Storage Devices Edited.

You will create a collage of computer external storage devices. First, you will select individual items from within the photo, and then you will move them so that the finished design looks like Figure 2–74.

Courtesy of Joy Starks

Figure 2–74

Perform the following tasks:

1. Select the Rectangular Marquee Tool. Draw a rectangle around the tape drives in the lower-left corner of the graphic. Select the Magic Wand Tool, and then tap or click the 'Subtract from selection' button on the options bar. Tap or click the Contiguous check box so it does not display a check mark. Tap or click the white area inside the selection to remove it. Press the v key to access the Move Tool. Use the Move Tool to move the selection to the lower-left corner of the monitor as shown in Figure 2–74.

Continued >

Apply Your Knowledge *continued*

2. Press SHIFT+M to select the Elliptical Marquee Tool. SHIFT+drag a circle around the CD image in the upper-right corner of the graphic. As you select it, if you need to move the circle, press the SPACEBAR key as you drag. If you have extraneous white space around the selection, press the w key to select the Magic Wand Tool. With the 'Subtract from selection' button selected on the options bar, tap or click the white area outside the CD to remove it. Use the Move Tool to move the selection to the center of the monitor as shown in Figure 2–74 on the previous page.

3. Table 2-5 displays the rest of the necessary selections in order, to build the collage from the back to the front. Zoom in on each storage device and scroll as necessary to assist in your selection techniques. In all cases, after you move the selection, if a shadow remains, press CTRL+Z to undo the move and then use the Grow Command on the Select menu to include more pixels. Use Figure 2–74 as a guide for placement.

Table 2–5 Selections and Techniques to Finish the Collage		
Storage Device	**Tool**	**Hint**
Red external hard drive	Magnetic Lasso Tool	Use Refine Edges button to help avoid leaving shadow behind as you move.
Zip disk with red and white label	Polygonal Lasso Tool	As you drag, tap or click to change direction.
Black 5¼ inch floppy disk	Magic Wand Tool	Use the 'Add to Selection' button and set the Tolerance level to 32. Select the Contiguous check box, and then tap or click the black area, gray area, and white area in the disk. Use the Grow command on the Select menu to increase the selection.
Punched card	Polygonal Lasso Tool	As you drag, tap or click to change direction.
Cassette tape	Quick Selection Tool	Use the Magic Wand Tool to remove the white from the center.
Tan 3½ inch floppy disk	Rectangular Marquee Tool	If some white remains at the corner, use the Magic Wand tool and the 'Subtract from Selection' button to remove it.
Red flash drive	Magnetic Lasso Tool	Use Refine Edges button to help avoid leaving shadow behind as you move.

© Cengage Learning

4. Save the Apply 2-1 Storage Devices Edited file, and then close Photoshop.

5. Submit the assignment in the format specified by your instructor.

Extend Your Knowledge

Extend the skills you learned in this chapter and experiment with new skills. You may need to use Help to complete the assignment.

Separating Objects from the Background

Note: To complete this assignment, you will be required to use the Data Files for Students. Visit solutions.cengage.com/ctdownloads for detailed instructions or contact your instructor for information about accessing the required files.

Instructions: Start Photoshop and perform the customization steps found on pages PS 6 through PS 11. Open the Extend 2-1 Flowers file in the Chapter 02 folder from the Data Files for Students and save it, in the PSD format, as Extend 2-1 Flowers Edited.

The original flower image displays the flowers in their natural settings, with various colors in the background. After moving the frame and making a copy, you will select the flowers while preventing background colors from straying into the selection. Finally, you will position each flower in front of a frame, as shown in Figure 2–75.

Figure 2–75

Continued >

Extend Your Knowledge *continued*

Perform the following tasks:

1. Use the Elliptical Marquee Tool to select the oval frame. (*Hint:* For more careful placement, while dragging to create the selection, you can press the SPACEBAR key to adjust the location of the drag and then release it to continue drawing the marquee.) Be careful to select only the frame, and eliminate any white around the edge of the selection using the Magic Wand Tool and the 'Subtract from selection' button.

2. Drag the selection to a location below the left side of the word, Flowers. Do not be concerned if you leave behind a slight shadow. On the Move Tool options bar, if necessary, tap or click the 'Show Transform Controls' check box to display a check mark in. SHIFT+drag a corner sizing handle to scale the selection approximately 10 percent bigger. (*Hint*: You also can increase the selection to 110 percent in both the Width and Height boxes.) Press the ENTER key to commit the transformation.

3. With the frame still selected, SHIFT+ALT+drag to create a duplicate and place it to the right of the original. (*Hint:* Recall that using the SHIFT key keeps the duplicate aligned with the original.)

4. Use appropriate selection tools to select the upper flower and its stem. (*Hint:* Use the Magic Wand Tool with a tolerance setting of 50 to select the contiguous pink and then add to the selection using other tools.) Tap or click the 'Intersect with selection' button to combine selected areas, if necessary. Do not include the background.

5. To ensure that the selection does not have any stray pixels around its border, use the Refine Edge dialog box to refine the edge by increasing the radius to 7 px.

6. As you create the selection, if necessary, press CTRL+ALT+Z to step back through the editing history and return the image to an earlier state.

7. Move the selected flower onto the left frame and resize as necessary.

8. Repeat Steps 4 through 7 for the lower flower and the right frame. If you make an error, display the History panel and then tap or click a previous state.

9. Crop the image to include only the word, Flowers, and the two framed flowers. Save the changes.

10. Use the Magic Wand Tool to select the blue color in the word, Flowers. (*Hint:* To select all of the letters, remove the check mark in the Contiguous box.) If parts of the image other than the word, Flowers, appear within the marquee, use the 'Subtract from selection' button to remove them.

11. Use Photoshop Help to investigate how to soften the edges of selections. Use the Refine Edge dialog box to soften the edges. Expand the selection and feather the edges.

12. Use Photoshop Help to investigate how to stroke a selection or layer with color. With the letters selected, use the Stroke command on the Edit menu to display the Stroke dialog box. Stroke the selection with a white color, 5 pixels wide, on the outside of the selection.

13. Save your changes, close the file, and then quit Photoshop. Send the revised photo to your instructor as an e-mail attachment.

Make It Right

Analyze a project and correct all errors and/or improve the design.

Correcting an Error in a Photo

Note: To complete this assignment, you will be required to use the Data Files for Students. Visit solutions.cengage.com/ctdownloads for detailed instructions or contact your instructor for information about accessing the required files.

Instructions: Start Photoshop and perform the customization steps found on pages PS 6 through PS 11. Open the Make It Right 2-1 Balloons file in the Chapter 02 folder from the Data Files for Students and save it as Make It Right 2-1 Balloons Edited in the PSD format.

A coworker has made an error when trying to create a duplicate of the balloon (Figure 2–76). The duplicate on the right included some blue sky around the balloon, which overlaps the balloon on the left. In addition, the balloon on the left should be bigger and in front so that it appears closer in the picture. To fix the error, you will select the right balloon and create a bigger copy.

Use selection tools as necessary, along with the 'Add to Selection' and 'Subtract from selection' buttons, to select only the right balloon, with no blue sky around it. Refine the edge. ALT+drag with the Move Tool to create a duplicate, which will become the new left balloon. Place the duplicate over the original left balloon. (*Hint:* the duplicate will overlap the right balloon slightly, but will not create an error because you removed the blue sky around the selection.) Display the transform controls and scale the selection to be approximately 10 percent bigger.

Save the project again. Submit the revised document in the format specified by your instructor.

Figure 2–76

In the Labs

Design and/or create a project using the guidelines, concepts, and skills presented in this chapter. Labs are listed in order of increasing difficulty.

Lab 1: **Using Keyboard Shortcuts to Create a Logo**

Note: To complete this assignment, you will be required to use the Data Files for Students. Visit solutions.cengage.com/ctdownloads for detailed instructions or contact your instructor for information about accessing the required files.

Problem: You are an intern with the Parks and Recreation department for the city. They are planning to create T-shirts for their summer youth program. Your supervisor has provided a file with some individual graphics about activities in the park. You are to arrange the graphics to form the logo shown in Figure 2–77. He reminds you that the T-shirt manufacturer needs a PDF file.

Instructions: Perform the following tasks:

1. Start Photoshop. Set the default workspace and reset all tools and colors.
2. Press CTRL+O to open the Lab 2-1 Park T-shirt file from the Chapter 02 folder of the Data Files for Students, or from a location specified by your instructor.
3. Press SHIFT+CTRL+S to display the Save As dialog box. Save the file on your storage device with the name, Lab 2-1 Park T-shirt Edited.
4. If the photo does not appear at 25% magnification, press CTRL+PLUS SIGN (+) or CTRL+ HYPHEN (–) to zoom in or out as necessary.
5. Drag from the horizontal ruler to create a guide at 3.25 inches, which you will use to align the graphics.

Courtesy of Joy Starks

Figure 2–77

6. To select and move the kite:

   a. Press SHIFT+L until the Polygonal Lasso Tool is selected. On the options bar, tap or click the New selection button, if necessary.

   b. Tap or click a corner of the kite to start the selection. Continue tapping or clicking corners to create straight line segments around the kite. When you are finished, double-tap or double-click to finish the selection.

   c. On the Select menu, tap or click Grow to expand the selection slightly.

   d. Press the V key to access the Move Tool. Drag the kite to a location in front of the red circle, snapping the bottom of the kite to the ruler guide.

   e. Press CTRL+D to deselect.

7. To select and move the bat:

   a. Press SHIFT+L until the Lasso Tool is selected. On the options bar, tap or click the New selection button, if necessary.

   b. Drag to create a selection around the bat.

   c. Press SHIFT+W until the Magic Wand Tool is selected.

   d. ALT+tap or ALT+click the white area around the bat, within the selection, to remove the white area.

   e. Activate the Move Tool. Drag the bat to a location in front of the kite, as shown in Figure 2–77, snapping the bottom of the bat to the ruler guide.

   f. Deselect.

8. To select and move the ball:

   a. Press SHIFT+M until the Elliptical Marquee Tool is selected. On the options bar, tap or click the New selection button, if necessary.

   b. SHIFT+drag to create a circular selection around the ball. Avoid including any white space around the ball. If necessary, press the SPACEBAR key while dragging to position the selection marquee.

   c. Activate the Move Tool and then drag the ball to a location in front of the kite as shown in Figure 2–77, snapping the ball to the ruler guide.

   d. If you make a mistake while selecting or moving the ball, tap or click the History button on the vertical docking of panels to display the History panel. Tap or click a previous state and begin to select or move again.

   e. Deselect.

9. To select and move the remote control airplane:

   a. Press the Z key to activate the Zoom Tool, and then tap or click the airplane several times to zoom in.

   b. Press SHIFT+L until the Magnetic Lasso Tool is selected. On the options bar, tap or click the New selection button, if necessary.

   c. Tap or click a corner of the airplane. Slowly move the pointer around the airplane, creating fasteners along the edge. Tap or click at each corner to create an extra fastener. When you get close to the beginning fastener, move your pointer until a small circle appears, and then tap or click to complete the lasso.

   d. On the options bar, tap or click the Refine Edge button to display the Refine Edge dialog box. Drag the Shift Edge slider to 75%, and then tap or click the OK button to close the dialog box.

Continued >

In the Labs *continued*

   e. Press the z key and then ALT+tap or ALT+click to zoom out as necessary. Scroll to display the red circle and the remote control airplane.

   f. Activate the Move Tool and then drag the airplane to a location in front of the kite and bat, as shown in Figure 2–77 on page PS 130.

   h. Deselect.

10. To select and move the tennis racquet:

   a. Press CTRL+PLUS SIGN (+) several times to zoom in on the racquet, scrolling as necessary.

   b. Press SHIFT+W until the Quick Selection Tool is selected. On the options bar, tap or click the New selection button, if necessary.

   c. Slowly drag from the handle, upward, to create a selection around the racquet. If you make a mistake, deselect and begin again.

   d. Press SHIFT+W until the Magic Wand Tool is selected. On the options bar, select the value in the Tolerance box and then type 10 to replace it. If necessary, tap or click to remove the check mark in the Contiguous check box.

   e. ALT+tap or ALT+click a white area within the selection. Be careful not to tap or click the strings of the racquet.

   f. Press CTRL+HYPHEN (-) to zoom out as necessary.

   g. Activate the Move Tool and then drag the racquet to a location in front of the kite as shown in Figure 2–77, snapping the bottom of the racquet to the ruler guide.

   h. Deselect.

11. Press CTRL+S to save the file with the same name. If Photoshop displays a Photoshop Format Options dialog box, tap or click the OK button.

12. To crop:

   a. Press SHIFT+M until the Rectangular Marquee Tool is selected.

   b. SHIFT+drag around the red circle to create a square selection.

   c. Press the c key to crop. On the options bar, if necessary, tap or click the Delete Cropped Pixels check box so it displays a check mark. Press the ENTER key twice to crop the selection.

13. To create the PDF file:

   a. Press SHIFT+CTRL+S to open the Save as dialog box.

   b. Tap or click the 'Save as type' button and then tap or click Photoshop PDF (*.PDF;*.PDP) in the list to select the PDF format.

   c. Tap or click the Save button to continue the saving process, saving the file with the same name.

   d. When Photoshop displays a dialog box, tap or click the OK button to display the Save Adobe PDF dialog box. Tap or click the Save PDF button to continue the saving process.

   e. When Photoshop displays the second Save Adobe PDF dialog box, tap or click the Yes button to finish saving.

14. Quit Photoshop by pressing CTRL+Q.

15. Send the PDF file as an e-mail attachment to your instructor, or submit it in the format specified by your instructor.

Lab 2: **Creating a Newsletter Heading**

Note: To complete this assignment, you will be required to use the Data Files for Students. Visit solutions.cengage.com/ctdownloads for detailed instructions or contact your instructor for information about accessing the required files.

Problem: A local church wants to change the heading for their newsletter, to create a kind of mirror image of the words. The edited graphic is shown in Figure 2–78.

Instructions: Perform the following tasks:

1. Start Photoshop. Set the default workspace and reset all tools.
2. Open the file, Lab 2-2 Newsletter Heading, from the Chapter 02 folder of the Data Files for Students, or from a location specified by your instructor.
3. Use the Save As command to save the file on your storage device with the name Lab 2-2 Newsletter Heading Edited.
4. Use the Rectangular Marquee Tool to draw a rectangle around the text. Use the Magic Wand Tool and the 'Subtract from selection' button to remove all of the white from the selection.
5. To duplicate the selection, select the Move Tool and then ALT+drag a copy just below the original.
6. To rotate the selection, tap or click Edit on the Application bar, tap or click Transform on the Edit menu, and then tap or click Rotate 180°.
7. To flip the selection, tap or click Edit on the application bar, tap or click Transform on the Edit menu, and then tap or click Flip Horizontal.
8. Select the Move Tool, and then press and hold the CTRL key while you use the ARROW keys to nudge the selection close to the original as shown in Figure 2–78.
9. Deselect and then save the file again.
10. Quit Photoshop and then submit the document in the format specified by your instructor.

Figure 2–78

Continued >

In the Labs *continued*

Lab 3: **Creating a Money Graphic**

Note: To complete this assignment, you will be required to use the Data Files for Students. Visit solutions.cengage.com/ctdownloads for detailed instructions or contact your instructor for information about accessing the required files.

Problem: Your local bank is starting an initiative to encourage children to open a savings account using their loose change. The bank would like a before and after picture showing how money can grow with interest.

Instructions: Perform the following tasks:

1. Start Photoshop. Set the default workspace and reset all tools.

2. Open the file, Lab 2-3 Coins, from the Chapter 02 folder of the Data Files for Students, or from a location specified by your instructor.

3. Use the Save As command to save the file on your storage device with the name Lab 2-3 Coins Edited.

4. Use the Elliptical Marquee Tool to select the quarter. (*Hint:* While dragging, if your selection marquee does not match the quarter exactly, press and hold the SPACEBAR key to move the selection.) Once the quarter is selected, ALT+drag to create several duplicate copies. As you create the duplicates, display the transform controls on the options bar, and then press and hold or right-click the selection to display the context menu. Use the context menu commands to rotate and flip in different ways.

5. Use the Magnetic Lasso Tool to select the dime. ALT+drag to create several duplicate copies. As you create the duplicates, use the transform control sizing handle to move, scale, and drag a corner to create a slight distortion.

6. Use the Quick Selection Tool to select the nickel. ALT+drag to create several duplicate copies. As you create the duplicates, use the transform controls to change some of the copies.

7. Use the Magic Wand Tool to select the penny. Create several copies. Your document should resemble Figure 2–79.

8. Save the file again, and submit it in the format specified by your instructor.

Figure 2–79

Cases and Places

Apply your creative thinking and problem-solving skills to design and implement a solution.

Note: To complete this assignment, you will be required to use the Data Files for Students. Visit solutions.cengage.com/ctdownloads for detailed instructions or contact your instructor for information about accessing the required files.

1: Design a Poster for the Computer Lab

Academic

The computer lab at your school wants a poster reminding students to save their work often. The department chair has asked you to create a graphic of a computer mouse that seems to be eating data. He has taken a picture of a mouse from the lab and started the poster for you. A file named Case 2-1 Poster is located in the Chapter 02 folder of the Data Files for Students. Start Photoshop and use the selection tools to select the mouse. Flip the mouse horizontally. Then, using the 'Subtract from selection' button, remove the white part around the selection. Also, remove the dark gray bottom portion of the mouse from the selection. With the top portion of the mouse selected, warp the selection up and away from the bottom part of the mouse to simulate an open mouth. Move the selection close to the 0 and 1 data pattern. Save a copy of the poster as a PDF and send it as an e-mail attachment to your instructor.

2: Create a New Shortcut

Personal

You have decided to create a new keyboard shortcut for the 'Reset All Tools' command, rather than having to move the mouse to the options bar, press and hold or right-click, and then choose 'Reset All Tools'. Because other family members work on your computer system, you would like to save the new shortcut in a separate set for your personal use. You also would like to see a complete listing of the Photoshop shortcuts for your system. Access the Keyboard Shortcuts and Menus dialog box. Tap or click the Shortcuts For button, and then tap or click Panel Menus in the list. Scroll down and double-tap or double-click Tool Presets, and then tap or click 'Reset All Tools' in the list. Enter the shortcut, CTRL+SLASH (/). Tap or click the 'Create a new set based on the current set of shortcuts' button, and save the shortcuts with your name. Tap or click the Summarize button and save the summary as My Shortcut Summary. When the summary appears in the browser, print a copy for your records.

3: Create a Grocery Store Flyer

Professional

You have been hired to create an advertisement for a grocery store flyer about citrus fruits that are on sale. Search the web for samples of fruit displays, noting the ones that look most appealing. A file named Case 2-3 Fruits is located in the Chapter 02 folder of the Data Files for Students. Start Photoshop and reset the workspace, tools, and colors. Use selection tools to select the various fruits and move them into an attractive display. Create duplicates of fruits and resize the copies as necessary. Keep in mind the horizon line and perspective.

3 | Working with Layers

Objectives

You will have mastered the material in this chapter when you can:

- Use the Layers panel and change options
- Create a layer via cut
- Rename layers and set identification colors
- Hide, view, and rearrange layers
- Arrange and consolidate document windows
- Create a new layer from another image or selection
- Duplicate layers and create layer groups
- Transform selections and layers

- Use the Eraser, Magic Eraser, and Background Eraser Tools
- Create layer masks
- Make level adjustments and opacity changes
- Apply adjustments using the Adjustments panel
- Add a layer style
- Use the Paste Special commands
- Flatten a composite image

Ps File Edit Image Layer Type Select Filter 3D View Window Help

Adobe **Photoshop CC**   Feather: 0 px   Anti-alias   Style: Normal ▾   Width: Height: Refine Edge...

3 | Working with Layers

Introduction

Whether it is adding a new person to a photograph, combining artistic effects from different genres, or creating 3D animation, the concept of layers in Photoshop allows you to work on one element of an image without disturbing the others. You might think of layers as sheets of clear film stacked on top of one another. You can see through transparent areas of a layer to the layers below. The nontransparent, or opaque, areas of a layer are solid, and they obscure the content of the layers beneath. You can change the composition of an image by changing the order and attributes of layers. In addition, special features, such as adjustment layers, layer masks, fill layers, and layer styles, allow you to create sophisticated effects.

Graphic designers use layers, along with other tools in Photoshop, to create **composite** images that combine or merge multiple images and drawings to create a new image, also referred to as a **montage**. Composite images illustrate the power of Photoshop to prepare documents for businesses, advertising, marketing, and media artwork. Composite images such as navigation bars can be created in Photoshop and used on the web along with layered buttons, graphics, and background images.

Project — Planning a Laptop Lab

Chapter 3 uses Photoshop to create a composite image from several photographs by using layers. Specifically, it begins with a photo of an empty room (Figure 3–1a) and creates a composite image by inserting layers of furniture, monitors, a podium, a smart board, and other pieces to create a complete lab design (Figure 3–1b). The enhancements will show how the lab will look when furnished. Carpeting will replace the current floor and an accent wall will be added. Finally, adjustment layers will give the lab eye appeal.

Overview

As you read this chapter, you will learn how to create the composite room shown in Figure 3–1b by performing these general tasks:

- Create a layer via cut.
- Insert layers from new images.
- Use the eraser tools.
- Add a layer mask.
- Create layer adjustments, layer groups, and apply layer styles.
- Use specialized paste commands.
- Flatten the image.
- Save the photo with and without layers.

(a)

(b)

Figure 3–1

General Project Guidelines

When editing a photo, the actions you perform and decisions you make will affect the appearance and characteristics of the finished product. As you edit a photo, such as the one shown in Figure 3–1, you should follow these general guidelines:

1. **Gather your photos and plan your layers.** The graphics you choose should convey the overall message of your composite image. Choose high-quality photos with similar lighting characteristics. Create an ordered list of the layers you plan to include. Select images that are consistent with the visual effect you want to achieve as well as with customer requirements.

2. **Evaluate the best way to move outside images into the composite.** Sometimes it is easier to create a selection first and move the selection into the composite image as a layer. Other times, you may want to bring in the entire image and then erase or mask portions of the image. Once the layer exists, choose the correct tool for making edits and erasures.

3. **Create layer adjustments.** Fine-tune your layers by creating layer adjustments. Look at each layer and evaluate how it fits into the background scene. Experiment with different adjustment tools until the layer looks just right. Decide whether to use destructive or nondestructive edits. Keep in mind the standard tonal dimensions of brightness, saturation, and hue.

4. **Edit layer styles.** Add variety to your layers by including layer styles such as shadow, glow, emboss, bevel, overlay, and stroke. Make sure the layer style does not overwhelm the overall image or detract from previous layer adjustments.

When necessary, more specific details concerning the above guidelines are presented at appropriate points in the chapter. The chapter also will identify the actions performed and decisions made regarding these guidelines during the creation of the edited photo shown in Figure 3–1.

Creating a Composite

Creating a composite with visual layers is a powerful effect. Photographers sometimes try to achieve this effect by using a sharp focus on objects in the foreground against an out-of-focus background. Others stage their photos with three layers of visual action. For example, at a baseball game, a person in the stands (foreground) may be observing a close call at first base (middle ground), while outfielders watch from afar (background). When those kinds of photographic techniques cannot be achieved with a camera, graphic artists use **composition techniques,** the layering of images and actions. Not only can you make realistic changes to parts of a photo, but you also can add additional images and control their placement, blending, and special effects. In addition, you can make changes to a layer, independent of the layer itself, which is extremely helpful in composite production.

Simple layers can be used to incorporate new objects or new people. Layer effects create adjustments, add blending modes, or edit the coloring, fill, and opacity of the layer. Masks conceal or reveal part of a layer. Most of the layering techniques are **nondestructive,** which means that no pixels in the background are changed in the process; the effect is applied over the image or layer to create the change. Adding layers increases the file size of a Photoshop document, but that increase is justified by the value and flexibility layers provide. When you are finished working with layers, you can flatten the Photoshop document to reduce the file size. You will learn about flattening later in this chapter.

The steps in this chapter create a composite image with layers, layer groups, layer effects, adjustments, and masks.

To Start Photoshop

If you are stepping through this project on a computer and you want your screen to match the figures in this book, then you should change your computer's resolution to 1366 × 768 and reset the panels, tools, and colors. For more information about how to change the resolution on your computer and other advanced Photoshop settings, read the Editing Preferences Appendix.

The following steps, which assume Windows 8 is running, start Photoshop based on a typical installation. You may need to ask your instructor how to start Photoshop for your system.

1 With Windows 8 running, scroll to display the Adobe Photoshop CC tile on the Start screen.

2 Tap or click the Adobe Photoshop CC tile to run the Photoshop app.

3 After a few moments, when the Photoshop window appears, if the window is not maximized, tap or click the Maximize button next to the Close button on the Application bar to maximize the window.

To Reset the Workspace

As discussed in Chapter 1, it is helpful to reset the workspace so that the tools and panels appear in their default positions. The following steps select the Essentials workspace.

1 Tap or click the workspace switcher on the options bar to display the list and then tap or click Essentials to select the default workspace panels.

2 Tap or click the workspace switcher on the options bar again to display the list and then tap or click Reset Essentials to restore the workspace to its default settings and reposition any panels that might have been moved by previous users.

To Reset the Tools and the Options Bar

Recall that the Tools panel and the options bar retain their settings from previous Photoshop sessions. The following steps select the Rectangular Marquee Tool and reset all tool settings in the options bar.

1 If the tools in the Tools panel appear in two columns, tap or click the double arrow at the top of the Tools panel.

2 If necessary, tap or click the 'Rectangular Marquee Tool' button on the Tools panel to select it.

3 On the options bar, press and hold or right-click the 'Rectangular Marquee Tool' icon to display the context menu, and then tap or click 'Reset All Tools'. When Photoshop displays a confirmation dialog box, tap or click the OK button to restore the tools to their default settings.

To Set the Interface and Default Colors

Recall that Photoshop retains the interface color scheme, as well as the foreground and background colors, from session to session. The following steps set the interface to Medium Gray and the foreground and background colors to black over white.

1 Tap or click Edit on the Application bar to display the Edit menu. Tap or click Preferences and then tap or click Interface on the Preferences submenu to display the Preferences dialog box.

2 If necessary, tap or click the third button, Medium Gray, to change the interface color scheme.

3 Tap or click the OK button to close the Preferences dialog box.

4 Tap or click the 'Default Foreground and Background Colors' button on the Tools panel to set the default colors to black and white. If black is not over white on the Tools panel, tap or click the 'Switch Foreground and Background Colors' button.

BTW

Open and Save Locations
The Data Files for Students often are located on common drives in electronic classrooms, which is why this book uses separate locations for the data files versus the edited files you create in the chapters. Thus, the first set of save instructions directs you to create a new folder to organize your files on your personal storage device.

To Open a File

To open a file in Photoshop, it must be stored as a digital file on your computer system or on an external storage device. The photos used in this book are included in the in Data Files for Students. Visit solutions.cengage.com/ctdownloads for detailed instructions or contact your instructor for information about accessing the required files.

The following steps open the file, Laptop Lab, from the Photoshop Chapter 03 folder in the Documents folder of Windows 8. The location of your file may differ.

1 Tap or click File on the Application bar to display the File menu, and then tap or click Open on the File menu to display the Open dialog box.

2 If necessary, tap or click the arrow next to Libraries, or This PC, in the Navigation pane to display the folders.

3 Tap or click the Documents location to display a list of the available folders and files.

4 Double-tap or double-click the desired folder to display its contents (in this case, the Photoshop folder).

5 Double-tap or double-click the Chapter 03 folder to display its contents.

6 Double-tap or double-click the file, Laptop Lab, to open the file.

7 Double-tap or double-click the magnification box on the document window status bar, type **3 0** and then press the ENTER key to change the magnification (Figure 3–2).

BTW

The View Menu
The View menu has many commands to help you use the Photoshop interface, besides choosing among five different zoom levels; you also can view and create guides and slices and change the snapping features. The Extras command on the View menu shows nonprinting guides, grids, selection edges, slices, and text baselines that help you select, move, or edit objects. You can enable or disable any combination of Extras without affecting the image.

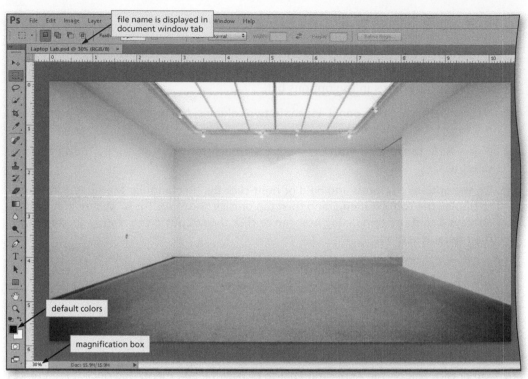

Figure 3–2

For a detailed example of this procedure using the Mac operating system, refer to the For Mac Users Appendix.

To View Rulers

The following steps display the rulers in the document window to facilitate making precise measurements.

1. If the rulers are not shown on the top and left sides of the document window, press CTRL+R to display the rulers in the workspace.

2. If necessary, press and hold or right-click the horizontal ruler and then tap or click Inches on the context menu to display the rulers in inches.

To Save a Photo

Even though you have yet to edit the photo, it is a good practice to save the file on your personal storage device early in the process. The following steps save the file with the name Laptop Lab Edited in a new folder named Chapter 03. Make sure your storage device is connected to your computer, if necessary.

1. Tap or click File on the Application bar to display the File menu and then tap or click Save As to display the Save As dialog box.

2. Type **Laptop Lab Edited** in the File name text box to change the file name. Do not press the ENTER key after typing the file name.

3. Navigate to your storage location (or the Creative Cloud Files location) by using the Navigation pane or the Previous Locations box arrow to select that drive as the new save location.

4. Tap or click the New folder button on the Save As dialog box toolbar to create a new folder on the selected storage device.

5 When the new folder appears, type `Chapter 03` to change the name of the folder, and then press the ENTER key. Double-tap or double-click the new folder to open it.

6 If necessary, tap or click the 'Save as type' button to display the list of available file formats, and then tap or click Photoshop (*.PSD; *.PDD) in the list to select the file type.

7 Tap or click the Save button to save the document on the selected drive, in the new folder, and with the new file name.

MAC For a detailed example of this procedure using the Mac operating system, refer to the For Mac Users Appendix.

Composites with Layers

Photoshop has many tools to help create composite images, photomontages, and collages. Recall that a composite, or composite image, is one that combines multiple photographs or images to display in a single combined file. Graphic artists use the newer term, **photomontage**, to refer to both the process and the result of creating a composite from photos.

Gather your photos and plan your layers.
One of the keys to successful image compositions is finding the best source material with similar lighting situations and tonal qualities. Choose high-quality photos and images that convey your overall message. Make sure you have permission to use the images if they are not original photographs taken by you or provided to you by a colleague or client. Obtain several versions of the same photo, if possible, including photos from different angles and with different lighting situations. Make two copies of each photo and store one as a backup. Crop unwanted portions of the photos before adding them as new layers.

Plan Ahead

BTW

Layer Comps
Graphic artists often create multiple versions, or compositions, of their work. A **layer comp** is a single view of the page layout with specific visible layers and attributes. You can use layer comps to demo versions of your composition to customers or colleagues, or simply to jump back and forth between different views and layers of your document. Similar to the History panel's snapshot, a layer comp takes a picture of the composite, using the Layers panel to show a particular stage of development.

Layers

One of the most powerful tools in Photoshop is layering. A **layer** is a section within a Photoshop document that you can manipulate independently from the rest of the document. Layers can be stacked one on top of the other, resembling sheets of clear film, to form a composite image. You can perform countless actions associated with layers. You will learn some in this chapter, and more in each subsequent chapter.

Layers have been used by business and industry for years. Cartoonists create layers of physical transparencies to help with animation. The medical field uses overlays to illustrate anatomical features. Virtual simulations use layers to display processes. With Photoshop, layers are easy to create and export for these kinds of applications.

Recall that you used selections in Chapter 2 to move, copy, flip, and scale portions of a photo. Layers can perform all of the same functions performed by selecting, while providing added features. The most powerful feature of layers is the ability to revisit a portion of the image to make further changes, even after deselecting. Layers can be created, copied, deleted, displayed, hidden, merged, locked, grouped, repositioned, and flattened. Layers can be composed of images, patterns, text, shapes, colors, or filters. You can use layers to apply special effects, correct or colorize pictures, repair damaged photos, or import text elements. In previous chapters, you worked with images in a flat, single layer called the **Background layer**. In this chapter, you will create, name, and manipulate multiple layers on top of the Background layer.

BTW

Layer Comps vs. History Snapshots
Layer comps include the visibility, position, and appearance of layers, not the edited steps. In addition, layer comps are saved with the document, whereas History panel snapshots are not. You can export layer comps to separate graphic or PDF files for easy distribution.

Many layer manipulations are performed using the Layers panel, which lists all the layers, groups, and layer effects in an image (Figure 3–3). Each time you insert a layer onto an image, the new layer is added above the current layer, or to the top of the panel. The default display of a layer on the Layers panel includes a visibility icon, a thumbnail of the layer, and the layer's name. To the right of the layer's name, a locking icon or other special effect notations might appear.

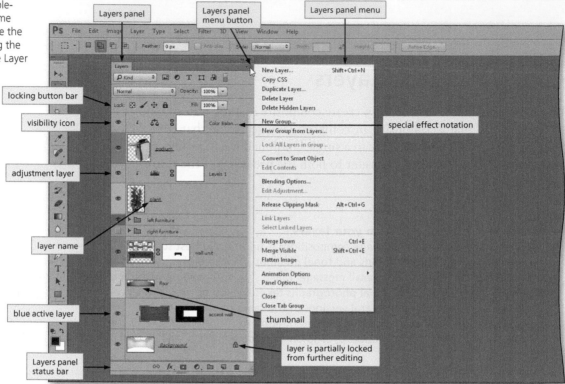

Figure 3–3

Photoshop allows you to **lock** three different components of layers on the locking button bar. From left to right: the 'Lock transparent pixels' button confines editing to opaque layer portions. The 'Lock image pixels' button prevents modification of the layer's pixels using paint tools. The Lock position button prevents the layer from being moved. The Lock all button enables all of the three ways of locking the layer. A lock icon appears to the right of the name on the Layers panel on locked layers.

The Layers panel is used in several different manners: to show and hide layers, create new layers, and work with groups of layers. You can access additional commands and attributes by tapping or clicking the Layers panel menu button, or by pressing and holding or right-clicking a layer. The Layers panel defines how layers interact. As you use the buttons and boxes on the Layers panel, each will be explained.

Although Photoshop allows background editing, as you have done in previous chapters, the Background layer cannot be moved, nor can its transparency be changed. In other words, the Background layer fills the document window, and there is no layer behind the background. Partially locked by default, the Background layer displays a hollow lock icon (Figure 3–3). If you want to convert the Background layer into a fully editable layer, double-tap or double-click the layer on the Layers panel, and then tap or click the OK button in the New Layer dialog box.

When working with layers, it is important to make sure you know which layer you are editing by looking at the active layer on the Layers panel or by looking at the layer name, appended to the file name on the document window tab. Many other layer commands appear on the Layer menu, including those for making adjustments to the layer, creating layer masks, grouping layers, and other editing and placement commands.

To Change Layers Panel Options

The Panel Options command, accessible from the Layers panel menu, allows you to change the view and size of the thumbnail related to each layer. A thumbnail displays a small preview of the layer on the Layers panel. The Panel Options dialog box allows you to choose small, medium, large, or no thumbnails. The following steps select a medium-sized thumbnail.

- Tap or click the Layers panel menu button to display the Layers panel menu (Figure 3–4).

Q&A Do I have to display thumbnails?
No, but displaying a thumbnail of each layer allows you to see easily what the layer looks like and helps you to be more efficient when editing a layer. To improve performance and save screen space, however, some Photoshop users choose not to display thumbnails.

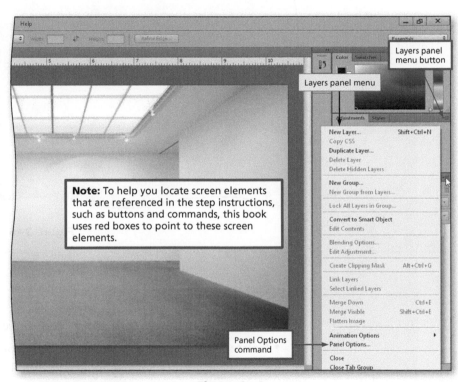

Figure 3–4

- Tap or click Panel Options on the menu to display the Layers Panel Options dialog box.

- Tap or click the medium thumbnail to select it.

- Tap or click the Layer Bounds option button to change the look and feel of the Layers panel (Figure 3–5).

Q&A How does the Layer Bounds option change the interface?
The Layer Bounds option causes the Layers panel to display only the layer, restricting the thumbnail to the object's pixels on the layer.

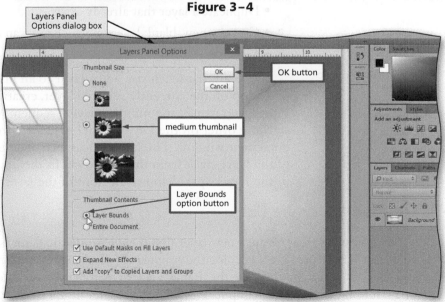

Figure 3–5

3

- Tap or click the OK button to close the Layers Panel Options dialog box (Figure 3–6).

Q&A Should I see a difference on the Layers panel? Yes. Unless a previous user had changed it already, the size of the thumbnail should have changed on the Layers panel. Layer bounds will not appear until you create a layer other than the Background layer.

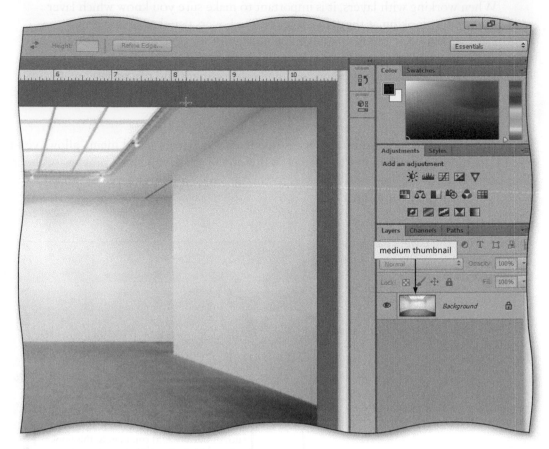

Figure 3–6

Creating New Layers

There are several ways to create a new layer. You can:

- Isolate a portion of the image and then cut or make a layer copy.
- Create a new layer by copying from a different image.
- Duplicate a layer that already exists.
- Create a new, blank layer on which you can draw or paint.
- Create text.

Recall that when you add a layer to an image, a new layer appears above, or on top of, the currently selected layer, creating a **stacking order**. By default, Photoshop names and numbers layers sequentially; however, you can rearrange the stacking order on the Layers panel to change the appearance of the image in the document window. The final appearance of an edited Photoshop document is a view of the layer stack from the top down. In the document window, the layers at the top of the Layers panel appear in front of the layers at the bottom of the panel.

To Create a Layer via Cut

The following steps create a new layer that includes only the floor. Isolating the floor allows for replacing it with different surfaces, while keeping the original if you change your mind. You will use the Quick Selection Tool to select the area and then use the 'Layer Via Cut' command to isolate the floor from the rest of the photo, creating a new layer. You will manipulate the new layer later in the chapter.

1

- On the Tools panel, tap or click the 'Quick Selection Tool'. If the 'Magic Wand Tool' is selected, press SHIFT+W to toggle to the 'Quick Selection Tool'.

- If necessary, tap or click the New selection button on the options bar to start a new selection.

- In the photo, drag slowly from the upper-left corner of the floor to the lower-right corner of the photo to select only the floor (Figure 3–7).

Q&A Why did Photoshop change to the 'Add to selection' button on the options bar?
Once you create a new selection, the most common task is to add more to the selection, so Photoshop selects that button automatically. If you want to start over, you can tap or click the New selection button again.

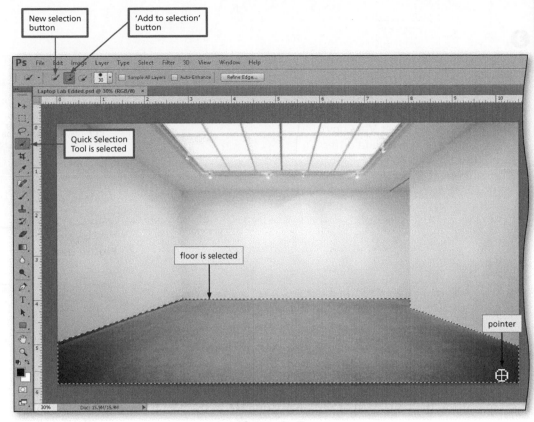

Figure 3–7

2

- Press and hold or right-click the selection to display the context menu (Figure 3–8).

Q&A Could I use the New Layer command?
No. The New Layer command creates a blank layer.

Experiment

- Press and hold or right-click the selection, tap or click Select Inverse and see how the selection marquee changes. Press CTRL+Z to under the Select Inverse command.

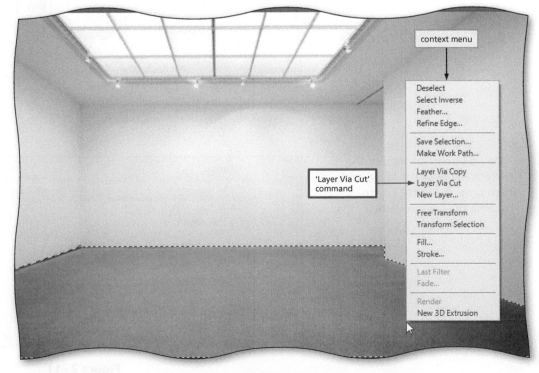

Figure 3–8

- Tap or click 'Layer Via Cut' on the context menu to create the new layer (Figure 3–9).

Q&A What is the difference between Layer Via Cut and Layer Via Copy? The Layer Via Cut command differs from the Layer Via Copy command in that it removes the selection from the background. Future edits to the Background, such as changing the color or lighting, will not affect the cut layer.

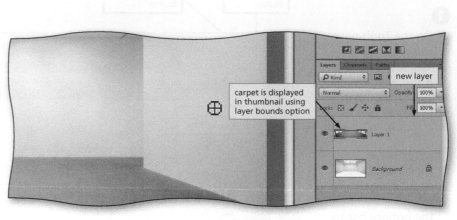

Figure 3–9

Other Ways

1. Create selection; on Layer menu, tap or click New, tap or click 'Layer Via Cut'
2. Create selection, press SHIFT+CTRL+J

To Rename a Layer

It is a good practice to give each layer a unique name so you can identify it more easily. The name of the active layer appears on the Layers panel and on the title bar of the document window. The following steps rename a layer.

- On the Layers panel, double-tap or double-click the name of the layer you want to rename, in this case Layer 1 (Figure 3–10).

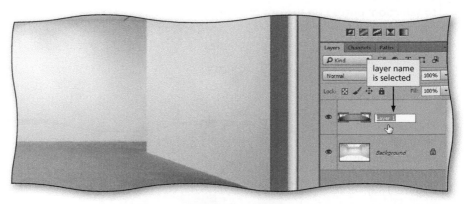

Figure 3–10

- Type **floor** to replace the current name of the layer, and then press the ENTER key to rename the layer (Figure 3–11).

Q&A Should I use lowercase letters for layer names?
It is helpful to do so; that way, you do not confuse file names with layer names.

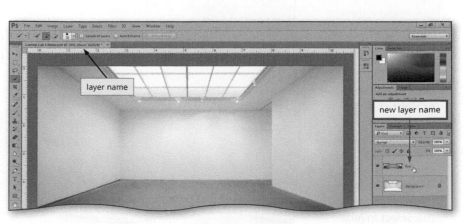

Figure 3–11

Other Ways

1. On Layer menu, tap or click Rename Layer, enter new name, press ENTER key

To Assign a Color to a Layer

Photoshop allows you to give each layer its own color identification. Assigning a color helps you recognize relationships among layers. For example, if two of your layers display objects in the sky, you might assign those two layers a blue identification color so you quickly could see which layers were related to the sky. The color appears around the visibility icon on the left side of the layer. The following steps assign a color to a layer.

1

• Press and hold or right-click the floor layer on the Layers panel to display its context menu (Figure 3–12).

Q&A Does it make any difference exactly where I press and hold or right-click?
No. You can press and hold or right-click anywhere on the layer. If you tap or click the area around the visibility icon, Photoshop displays a shorter context menu with only color and hide/show options.

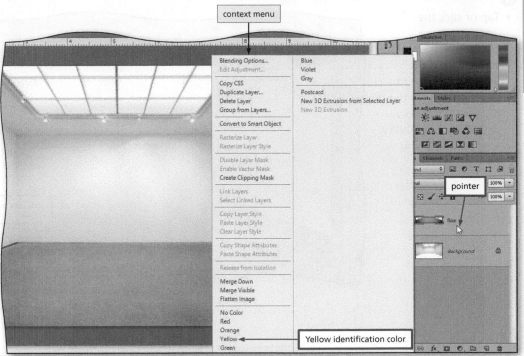

Figure 3–12

2

• Tap or click Yellow in the list to choose a yellow identification color (Figure 3–13).

Q&A What is the purpose of the Kind button on the Layers panel?
When you tap or click the Kind button, you can choose the specific kinds of layers you want to see, by name, effect, color, or selection, among others.

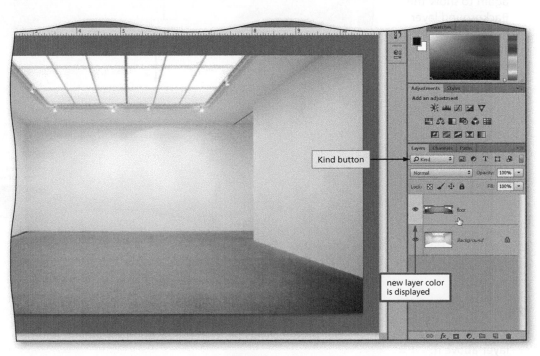

Figure 3–13

Other Ways

1. Press and hold or right-click visibility area, tap or click color

To Hide and Show a Layer

Sometimes you want to hide a layer to view other layers and make editing decisions. The visibility icon, which looks like an eye, is part of the 'Indicates layer visibility' button that toggles the visibility of the layer on and off. The following steps hide and show the Background layer.

- Tap or click the 'Indicates layer visibility' button to the left of the Background layer to hide the layer in the document window and hide the visibility icon (Figure 3–14).

Q&A What is the checkerboard effect in the background?
The checkerboard effect represents blank portions of the document window that are transparent.

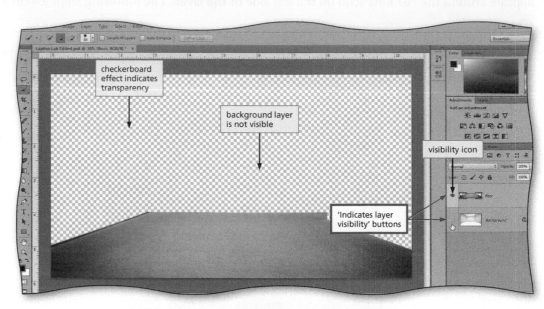

Figure 3–14

- Tap or click the 'Indicates layer visibility' button again to show the Background layer in the document window and display the visibility icon (Figure 3–15).

Q&A What is the white area on the Background layer thumbnail?
When you cut or delete from a locked layer, such as the Background layer, the default background color shows through; in this case, it is the default white color.
Because other layers will eclipse the white, you do not have to remove it.

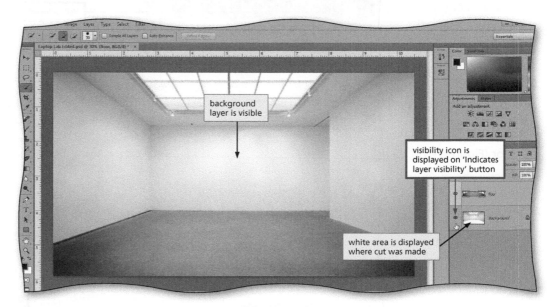

Figure 3–15

- If necessary, select the floor layer on the Layers panel in preparation for adding another layer above it.

Other Ways

1. Press and hold or right-click visibility icon, tap or click 'Hide this layer' or 'Show this layer'

2. On Layer menu, tap or click Hide Layers or Show Layers

Creating a Layer from Another Image

When you create composite images, you might want to create layers from other images. It is important to choose images that closely match or complement color, lighting, size, and perspective if you want your image to look natural. While you can adjust disparate images to improve how well they match, it is easier to start with as close a match as possible, ideally with similar lighting situations and tonal qualities.

Evaluate the best way to move outside images into the composite.
If the desired portion of the outside image is a shape that is selected easily, such as a rectangle, oval or polygon, then select and copy it. Paste it in the composite image to create a layer. If the desired portion of the outside image is not easy to select, drag the entire image into the composite, creating a layer. Then, use eraser tools to eliminate the unwanted portion of the layer. That way, you have not changed the original image, should you need to return to it later.

Plan Ahead

Many sources exist for composite images, and they come in many different file types and sizes. For example, you can use your own digital photos, scanned images, images from royalty-free websites, or you can draw your own.

The basic process of creating a new layer from another image involves opening a second image, selecting the area you want to use, and then moving it to the original photo in a drag-and-drop or cut-and-paste fashion. Once the layer exists in the destination photo, you might need to do some editing to remove portions of the layer, to resize it, or to make tonal adjustments.

BTW

Hiding and Showing Multiple Layers
To view only one layer in the document window, ALT+click the visibility icon for the layer you want to view. Pressing ALT+click again restores the previous visibility settings. Show or hide all other layers by selecting Show/Hide all other layers from the visibility icon's context menu. To hide or view several contiguous layers, drag through the eye column.

To Open a Second Image

To add a set of desks as a layer to the Laptop Lab Edited image, you will need to open a new file, Desks, from the Data Files for Students. Visit solutions.cengage.com /ctdownloads for detailed instructions or contact your instructor for information about accessing the required files. The following steps open the Desks file, which is stored in the TIFF format.

① Press CTRL+O to display the Open dialog box.

② In the Open dialog box, if necessary, tap or click the Previous Locations box arrow, and then navigate to the Chapter 03 folder of the Data Files for Students or a location specified by your instructor.

③ Double-tap or double-click the file named Desks to open it (Figure 3–16).

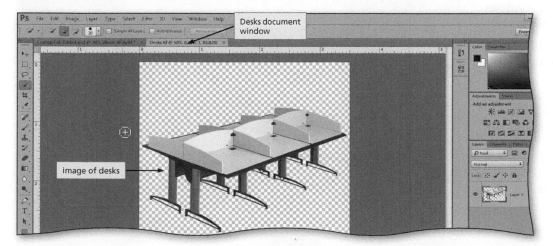

Figure 3–16

2-up vs. Tile
When you click Window on the Application bar, the Arrange submenu displays the 2-up Horizontally command, which arranges the more recently opened window on top. The Tile All Horizontally command puts the new window on the bottom.

Displaying Multiple Files

Photoshop offers many different ways to arrange and view document windows when more than one file is open. You also can create a custom workspace by moving and manipulating document windows manually.

For example, you might want to display two document windows, horizontally or vertically, in order to drag and drop from one image to another. You might want to compare different versions or views of photos, beside each other in the document window. Or, when creating a panorama, you might want to preview how certain photos will look, side by side.

When you are finished viewing multiple document windows in the workspace, you can **consolidate** them, or view only one window at a time.

To Arrange the Document Windows

The following steps display the Laptop Lab Edited and Desks windows beside each other using the Arrange submenu on the Window menu.

1

- On the Application bar, tap or click Window and then tap or click Arrange to display the Arrange submenu (Figure 3–17).

Q&A Why are some of the arrangements grayed out?
Because you have only two document windows open, the only arrangements enabled are the ones that display two windows.

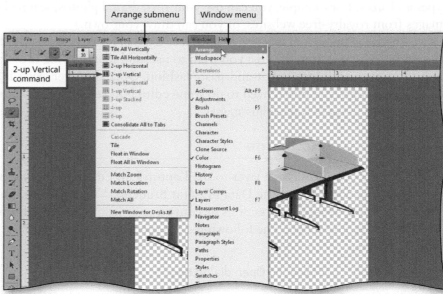

Figure 3–17

2

- Tap or click 2-up Vertical on the submenu to display the windows beside each other (Figure 3–18).

Q&A What is the difference between 2-up Vertical and Tile All Vertically?
When you have only two document windows open, there is no difference. If you have more than two document windows open, Tile All Vertically will display all the windows; 2-up Vertical will display only the two most recently used document windows.

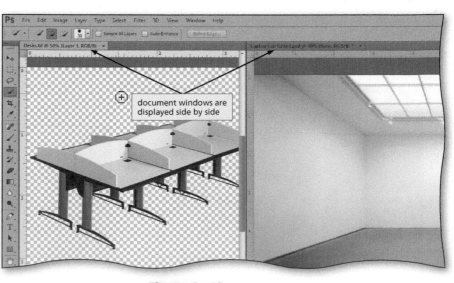

Figure 3–18

To Create a Layer by Dragging an Entire Image

When you drag a selection from one document window to the other, Photoshop creates a new layer in the destination document window, above the currently selected layer. If you want to include the entire image from the source window, use the Move Tool to drag from any location in the source window to the destination window. Dragging between document windows is an automatic duplication rather than a true move out of one window and into the other. The original source image remains unchanged.

The following step moves the entire image from the source window, Desks, to the destination window, Laptop Lab Edited.

1

- Press the V key to activate the Move Tool.

- Drag the Desks image into the Laptop Lab Edited window and drop it in the room (Figure 3–19).

Q&A

Why do the desks appear so much bigger in the original document window?
The desks are the same size; the magnification of the windows is different. Your magnifications may differ.

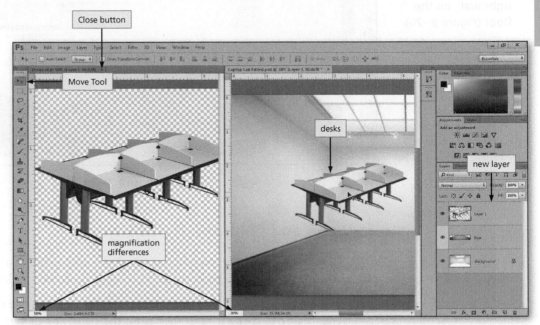

Figure 3–19

Other Ways

1. In source window, press CTRL+A, on Edit menu tap or click Copy, in destination window, on Edit menu, tap or click Paste

To Close the Desks Document Window

Because you are finished with the Desks image, the following step closes the Desks window.

1 Tap or click the Close button on the Desks document window tab. If Photoshop asks you to save the file again, tap or click the No button.

To Move a Layer in the Document Window

If there is no marquee selection, the Move Tool moves the entire active layer as you drag. The step on the next page moves the desks to a new location.

1

- With the new layer still selected on the Layers panel, and the Move Tool still selected on the Tools panel, drag the desks to a position along the right wall, on the floor (Figure 3–20).

Q&A

Is it acceptable for some of the desk to disappear off the edge of the document window? Yes. Your goal is to make it look as natural as possible, as if it is sitting on the floor.

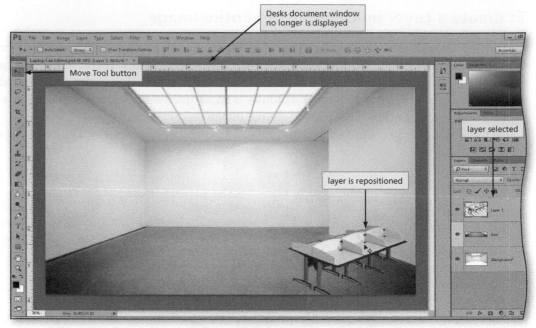

Figure 3–20

To Name and Color the Desks Layer

The following steps rename the new layer and assign it a color. Later in the chapter, you will copy the layer to create a set of desks on the left.

1 On the Layers panel, double-tap or double-click the name of the layer, Layer 1. Type **right desks** and then press the ENTER key to name the layer.

2 Press and hold or right-click the layer to display the context menu, and then tap or click Blue in the list to choose a blue identification color (Figure 3–21).

Consolidate Windows
Sometimes, after viewing multiple document windows, you may want to view only one window at a time. In that case, right-click the tab at the top of the document window to display the context menu, and then click Consolidate All to Here to view that document window alone. The Arrange submenu has a 'Consolidate all to Tabs' command which has the same effect.

Figure 3–21

To Save the File

Because you have created layers and made changes to the image, it is a good idea to save the file again. The following step saves the file again.

1 Press CTRL+S to save the Laptop Lab Edited file with the same name. If Photoshop displays a dialog box about compatibility, tap or click the OK button.

Break Point: If you wish to take a break, this is a good place to do so. Quit Photoshop by pressing CTRL+Q. To resume at a later time, start Photoshop, open the file named Laptop Lab Edited, and continue following the steps from this location forward.

Creating a Layer by Dragging a Selection

Sometimes you do not want to move an entire image from one window to another. When you want to move only a part of an image, you create a selection as you learned in Chapter 2, and then move the selection to the destination window. Once the selection exists in the destination window, you might need to do some editing, such as scaling, erasing, adjusting, or duplicating the layer.

To Open the Monitor Image

The following steps open a file named Monitor.

1 Press CTRL+O to display the Open dialog box.

2 If necessary, navigate to the Chapter 03 folder of the Data Files for Students, or a location specified by your instructor.

3 Double-tap or double-click the file named Monitor to open it.

To Select the Monitor

When adding the Monitor image to the Laptop Lab Edited image, you will not need the surrounding wall. The following steps select the monitor using the Rectangular Marquee Tool.

1 If necessary, press and hold or right-click the current marquee tool and then tap or click 'Rectangular Marquee Tool' on the context menu to select it.

2 If necessary, tap or click the New selection button on the options bar to start a new selection.

3 Drag around the monitor. Avoid including the wall in the selection. If you make a mistake while selecting, press the ESC key and then begin again (Figure 3–22).

BTW

Layer Selection
Sometimes a menu or panel will cover the Layers panel, or a layer may be scrolled out of sight. You always can identify which layer you are working with by looking at the document window tab. The name of the current layer appears in parentheses.

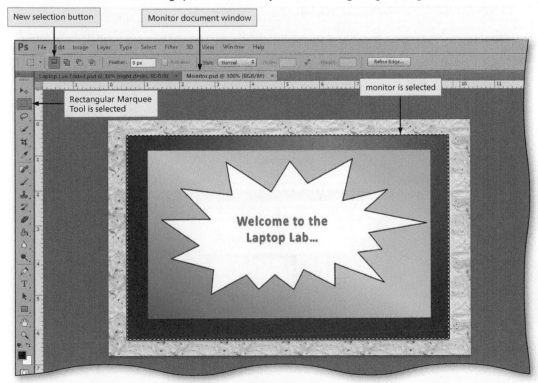

Figure 3–22

To Create a Layer by Dragging a Selection

The following steps move the selection. To facilitate dragging the selection between windows, you will view the windows above and below one another.

• On the Application bar, tap or click Window, tap or click Arrange to display the submenu, and tap or click the 2-up Horizontal command to display the windows above and below one another (Figure 3–23).

Q&A My windows were reversed. Did I do something wrong? No. Depending on previously opened files, the monitor might appear at the bottom. You can still drag and drop.

document windows appear above and below one another

Figure 3–23

Experiment

• Open a third file and then try some of the other configurations on the Arrange submenu. When you are done, close the third file. Repeat Step 1.

• Press the v key to activate the Move Tool.

• Drag the selection and drop it in the Laptop Lab Edited window (Figure 3–24).

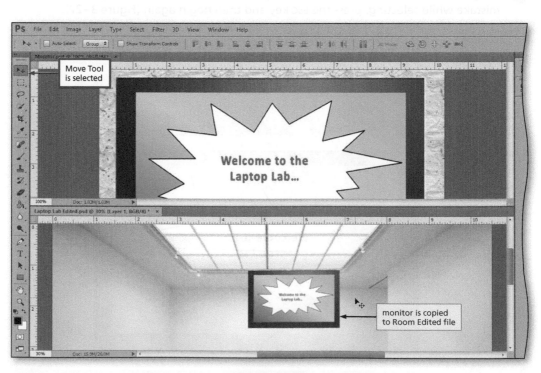

Move Tool is selected

monitor is copied to Room Edited file

Figure 3–24

Other Ways

1. In source window, create selection, on Edit menu, tap or click Copy, in destination window, on Edit menu, tap or click Paste

2. In source window, create selection, press CTRL+C, in destination window, press CTRL+V

To Close the Monitor Window

The next step closes the Monitor window.

1 Tap or click the Close button on the Monitor document window tab. If Photoshop displays a dialog box asking if you want to save the changes, tap or click the No button.

To Name and Assign a Color to the Monitor Layer

The following steps rename the new layer and assign an identification color.

1 Double-tap or double-click the name, Layer 1, on the Layers panel and then type **right monitor** and press the ENTER key to rename the layer.

2 Press and hold or right-click the layer and then tap or click Blue to assign an identification color.

To Position the Monitor Layer

The following steps move the monitor to a location above the desks.

1 Press the V key to active the Move Tool, if necessary.

2 Drag the monitor to a location above the desks, as shown in Figure 3–25.

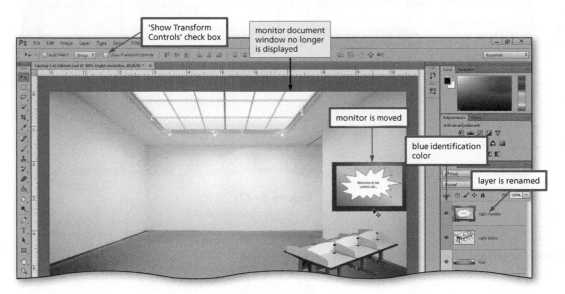

Figure 3–25

To Duplicate a Layer

When you duplicate a layer, a new layer is added to the Layers panel and a copy of the layer appears over the original in the document window. The steps on the next page duplicate the right monitor layer, and rename it using the Layers panel.

BTW

Smart Objects
You can convert a layer into a smart object, which is a nondestructive layer that does not change the original pixels. They are useful for warping, scaling, or rotating both raster and vector graphic layers. To convert a layer into a smart object, right-click the layer, and then click 'Convert to Smart Object' on the context menu.

- On the Layers panel, press and hold or right-click the right monitor layer to display the context menu (Figure 3–26).

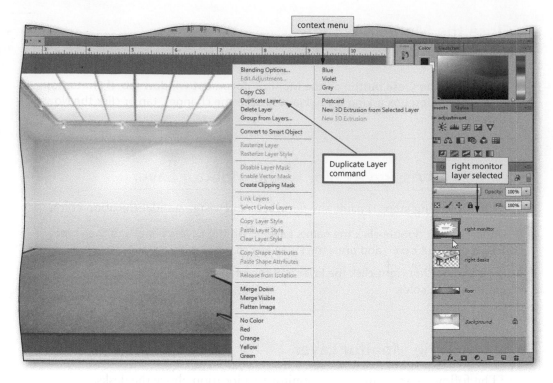

Figure 3–26

- Tap or click Duplicate Layer on the menu to display the Duplicate Layer dialog box.

- Type **left monitor** in the As box to replace the layer name (Figure 3–27).

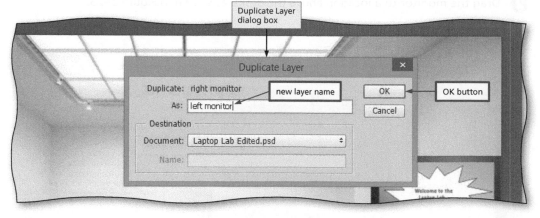

Figure 3–27

- Tap or click the OK button to duplicate the layer.

- Press and hold or right-click the new layer and change the layer color to Red.

To Align a Layer using Smart Guides

When you move layers or create shapes within the document window, Photoshop displays **smart guides** that appear as nonprinting pink lines that float at the top, middle, and bottom, of the layer to help you align. As you align multiple layers, Photoshop displays **reference measurement guides**, which appear as pink boxes similar to the black position indicators you learned about previously. The reference measurement guides display the distance between objects or the distance to the edge of the canvas. At any time, you can display smart guides and reference measurement guides by pressing the CTRL key (or the CMD key on a Mac) and hovering over a layer in the document window. If you do not have a mouse, you can CTRL+TAP the edge of the layer. You can toggle the display of smart guides using the View menu and the Show submenu.

The following steps move the left monitor layer and align it using smart guides.

- If necessary, select the Move Tool.

- In the document window, drag the monitor to the left as shown in Figure 3–28. Do not release the drag in order to view the smart guides.

2

- Release the drag to position the layer.

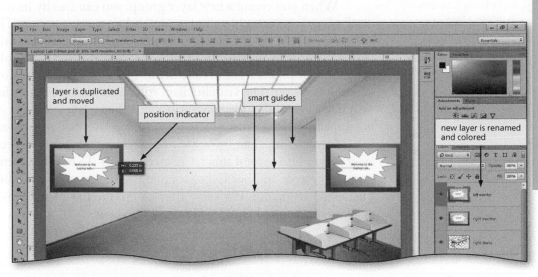

Figure 3–28

To Duplicate Another Layer

The following steps duplicate the right desk layer.

1 On the Layers panel, press and hold or right-click the right desk layer, and then tap or click Duplicate Layer to display the Duplicate Layer dialog box.

2 Type **left desks** in the As box to replace the layer name.

3 Tap or click the OK button to duplicate the layer.

4 On the Layers panel, change the left desks layer color to Red.

5 With the Move Tool still selected, move the duplicate layer to the left side of the Laptop Lab Edited window.

6 Press the CTRL key and hover over the left desks to display the reference measurement guides (Figure 3–29).

BTW

Show Transformation Values
You can change the location of the position indicator by pressing CTRL+K to open the Preferences dialog box. On the left, tap or click Interface, and then tap or click the 'Show Transformation Values' button to display a list of locations.

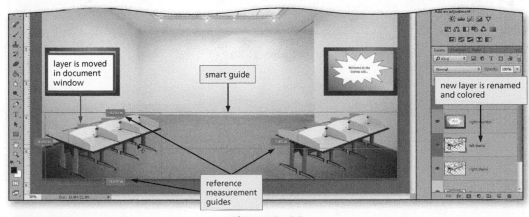

Figure 3–29

Layer Groups

A **layer group** is a named folder on the Layers panel that is used to contain a collection of layers. You can create layers within the folder or select existing layers and move them into the folder. The number of additional layers, layer effects, and layer groups is limited only by the computer's memory capacity. The New Group command creates an empty group. The 'New Group from Layers' command creates a group and places the selected layers in it.

Deleting Layers
To delete a layer permanently, right-click the layer name and then click Delete Layer on the context menu, or activate the layer and press the DELETE key.

When you create a new layer group, you can specify its name, its identifying color on the Layers panel, a blending mode, and an opacity setting. The settings apply to all layers created in, or moved into, the group. A layer group is displayed on the panel with a folder icon, and with a triangle that points down to reveal the individual layers in the group, or points right to hide them. The folder icon does not affect the document window, however. The visibility icon still determines whether the layer group is hidden or is displayed in the document window. When a layer or layer group is hidden, it does not appear in the document window. Hidden layers do not appear on printed copies.

Layer groups can be nested. This is helpful when you need to subdivide a large layer group into several smaller related groups. To nest layer groups, drag a layer group on top of another layer group in the Layers panel. To undo the nesting, drag the nested group out. Pay close attention to the Layers panel as you drag; Photoshop displays borders to help identify the drop zones.

To Create a Layer Group from Layers

You will create two layer groups for the Laptop Lab Edited document: one to hold the furniture on the right side of the classroom and one to hold the furniture on the left. The following steps select the blue layers and then create a group using those layers.

1

- Tap or click the right monitor layer in the Layers panel to select it.

- CTRL+tap or CTRL+click the right desks layer to add it to the selection.

- Press and hold or right-click the selected layers to display the context menu (Figure 3–30).

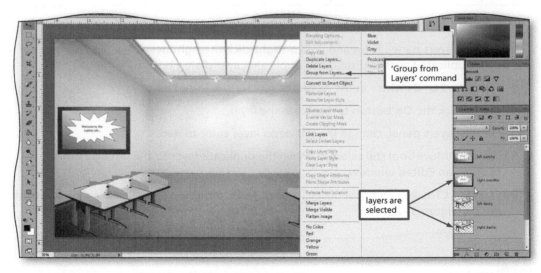

Figure 3–30

2

- Tap or click 'Group from Layers' to display the New Group from Layers dialog box.

- Type **right furniture** in the Name text box. Tap or click the Color button, and then tap or click Blue in the list to change the color for the new layer group (Figure 3–31).

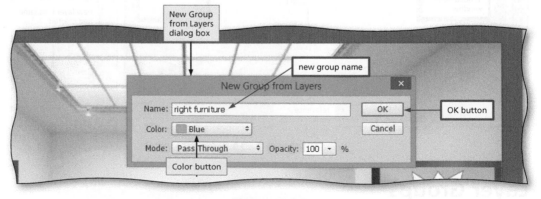

Figure 3–31

Q&A What does Pass Through mean on the Mode button?

Pass Through is the default blending mode for layer groups and means the group will have no blending properties of its own.

3

- Tap or click the OK button to create the new layer group (Figure 3–32).

4

- Repeat Steps 1 through 3 with the left monitor layer and the left desks layer to create a new layer group named left furniture. Color the layer Red.

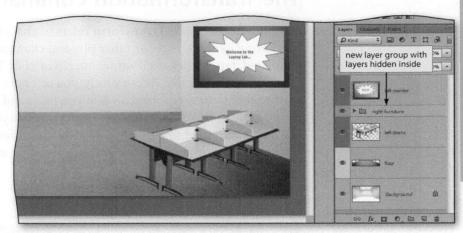

Figure 3–32

Other Ways

1. Select layers, drag selected layers to folder icon on Layers panel status bar

2. Select layers, tap or click Layer on Application bar, tap or click Group Layers

3. Select layers, press CTRL+G

TO CREATE A NEW EMPTY LAYER GROUP

If you wanted to create a new empty layer group, you would perform the following steps.

1. Display the Layers panel menu and then tap or click New Group.

2. Assign a name to the new group. Assign a color, and then tap or click the OK button to create the first new empty group.

To Open the Layer Group

The following step opens one of the new layer groups.

1

- On the Layers panel, tap or click the triangle next to the left furniture layer group to see the layers in the layer group (Figure 3–33).

Experiment

- Tap or click the triangle again to close the layer group. Tap or click the visibility icon to hide the layer group. When you are finished, make the group visible, and open it.

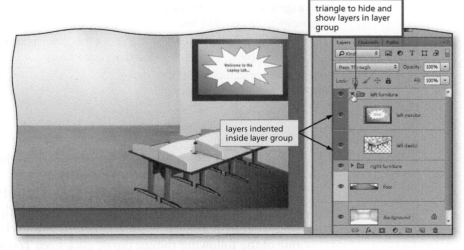

Figure 3–33

The Transformation Commands

In Photoshop, the word **transform** refers to changing the appearance of a selection by altering its shape, size, or other physical characteristics. To choose a transformation command, tap or click the Edit menu, tap or click Transform, and then tap or click the desired transformation. Alternatively, you can tap or click Transform Selection on the context menu that is displayed when you press and hold or right-click a selection.

Table 3–1 lists the types of transformations you can perform on a selection, the techniques used to perform a particular transformation, and the result of the transformation. Many of the commands also appear on the context menu.

Table 3–1 Transformation Commands

Using the Menu (Edit |Transform)	Using the Mouse or Stylus (Free Transform)	Using the Transform Options Bar	Result
Scale	Drag a sizing handle on the bounding box. SHIFT+drag to scale proportionately. ALT+drag to scale opposite sides at the same time.	To scale numerically, enter percentages in the Width and Height boxes, shown as W and H, on the options bar. Tap or click the Link icon to maintain the aspect ratio.	Selection is displayed at a different size.
Rotate 180° Rotate 90° CW Rotate 90° CCW (CW stands for clockwise. CCW stands for counterclockwise.)	Move the pointer outside the bounding box border. It becomes a curved, two-headed arrow. Drag in the direction you want to rotate. SHIFT+drag to constrain the rotation to 15° increments.	In the Set Rotation box, shown as a compass on the options bar, type a positive number for clockwise rotation or a negative number for counterclockwise rotation.	Selection is rotated or revolved around the reference point.
Skew	Press and hold or right-click selection and then tap or click Skew. Drag a side of the bounding box. ALT+drag to skew both vertically and horizontally.	To skew numerically, enter decimal values in the horizontal skew and vertical skew boxes, shown as H and V on the options bar.	Selection is tilted or slanted either horizontally or vertically.
Distort	Press and hold or right-click selection and then tap or click Distort. Drag a corner sizing handle to stretch the bounding box.	Enter new numbers in the location, size, rotation, and skew boxes.	Selection is larger on one edge than on the others.
Perspective	Press and hold or right-click selection and then tap or click Perspective. Drag a corner sizing handle to apply perspective to the bounding box.	Enter new numbers in the size, rotation, and skew boxes.	The selection appears larger on one edge than on the others, giving the larger edge the appearance of being closer to the viewer.
Warp	When the warp mesh is displayed, drag any line or point.	Tap or click the Custom button. Tap or click a custom warp.	Selection is reshaped with a bulge, arch, warped corner, or twist.
Flip Horizontal Flip Vertical	Press and hold or right-click selection and then tap or click appropriate Flip command	N/A	Selection is turned upside down or mirrored.

© Cengage Learning

Figure 3–34 displays the monitor used in this chapter, in its original state and with various transformation effects applied.

Transform is not a tool on the Tools panel; Photoshop displays a Transform options bar that contains boxes and buttons to help you with your transformation (Figure 3–35). To display the Transform options bar, create a selection and then do one of the following things: tap or click Free Transform on the Edit menu, tap or click a sizing handle, or press CTRL+T. Recall that if you are using the Move Tool, you also can tap or click the 'Show Transform Controls' check box. As you start to transform, Photoshop displays the Transform options bar.

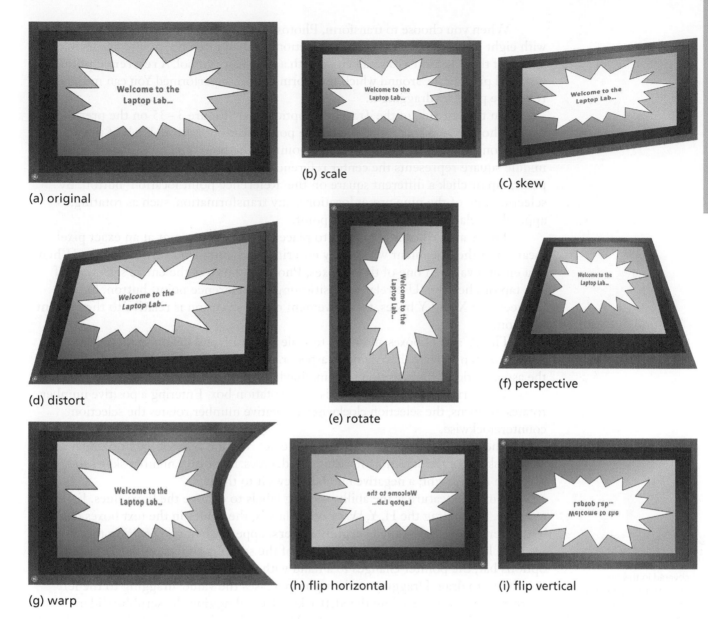

(a) original

(b) scale

(c) skew

(d) distort

(e) rotate

(f) perspective

(g) warp

(h) flip horizontal

(i) flip vertical

Figure 3–34

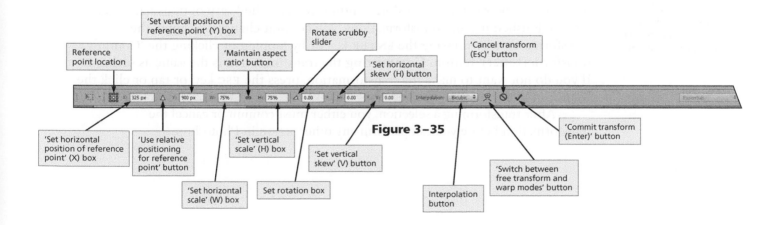

Figure 3–35

Reference point location

'Set vertical position of reference point' (Y) box

'Maintain aspect ratio' button

Rotate scrubby slider

'Set horizontal skew' (H) button

'Cancel transform (Esc)' button

'Commit transform (Enter)' button

'Set horizontal position of reference point' (X) box

'Use relative positioning for reference point' button

'Set vertical scale' (H) box

'Set vertical skew' (V) button

'Switch between free transform and warp modes' button

'Set horizontal scale' (W) box

Set rotation box

Interpolation button

When you choose to transform, Photoshop displays a **bounding box**, or border with eight sizing handles around the selection. A small reference point appears in the center of the selection as a small circle with a crosshair symbol. A **reference point** is a fixed pivot point around which transformations are performed You can move a reference point by dragging it.

On the left side of the Transform options bar (Figure 3–35 on the previous page), Photoshop displays the 'Reference point location' button. Each of the nine squares on the button corresponds to a point on the bounding box. The default middle square represents the center reference point. To select a different reference point, tap or click a different square on the 'Reference point location' button. By selecting one of the nine preset locations, any transformation, such as rotating, is applied in relation to that reference point.

The X and Y boxes allow you to place the reference point at an exact pixel location in the document window by entering horizontal and vertical values. When you enter a value in one of those boxes, Photoshop moves the entire selection. If you tap or click the 'Use relative positioning for reference point' button, located between the X and Y boxes, the movement of the selection is relative to the current location.

The W and H boxes allow you to scale the width and height of the selection. When you tap or click the 'Maintain aspect ratio' button between the W and H boxes, the aspect ratio of the selection is maintained.

To the right of the scale boxes is a Set rotation box. Entering a positive number rotates, or turns, the selection clockwise; a negative number rotates the selection counterclockwise.

The H and V boxes, to the right of the Set rotation box, set the horizontal and vertical skews of the selection, measured in degrees. A positive number skews the selection to the right; a negative number skews it to the left.

A unique feature is the ability to drag labels to change the box values. For example, if you drag the H, Y, W, or other labels, the values in the text boxes change. The interactive labels, called **scrubby sliders,** appear when you position the pointer over the label. When you tap or click any of the scrubby sliders on the Transform options bar, the pointer changes to a hand with a double-headed arrow, indicating the ability to drag. Dragging to the right increases the value; dragging to the left decreases the value. Holding the SHIFT key while dragging the scrubby slider accelerates the change by a factor of 10. Many options bars and panels use scrubby sliders.

On the far right of the Transform options bar are three buttons. The first one switches between the Transform options bar and the Warp options bar. After you are finished making transformations, you commit changes, or apply the transformations by pressing the ENTER key or by tapping or clicking the 'Commit transform (Enter)' button. **Committing** the transformation is the same as saving it. If you do not want to make the transformation, press the ESC key, or tap or click the 'Cancel transform (Esc)' button.

After transforming a selection, you either must commit or cancel the transformation before you can perform any other action in Photoshop.

BTW

Quick Reference
For a table that lists how to complete the tasks covered in this book using touch gestures, the mouse, the Application bar menu, shortcut menu, and keyboard, see the Quick Reference Summary at the back of this book, or visit the Quick Reference resource on the Student Companion Site located on www.cengagebrain.com.

To Transform by Placing and Scaling

The following step moves the left furniture layer by entering new coordinates on the options bar. The layer also is scaled down to 75%.

- Within the left furniture layer group, tap or click the left monitor layer to select it.

- Press CTRL+T to display the bounding box and the Transform options bar.

- On the options bar, drag to select the text in the X box. Type 3 2 5 in the X box to place the left side of the layer.

- Press the TAB key to move to the Y box and then type 9 0 0 as the new top location.

- Press the TAB key and then type 7 5 in the W box. Press the TAB key and then type 7 5 in the H box (Figure 3–36).

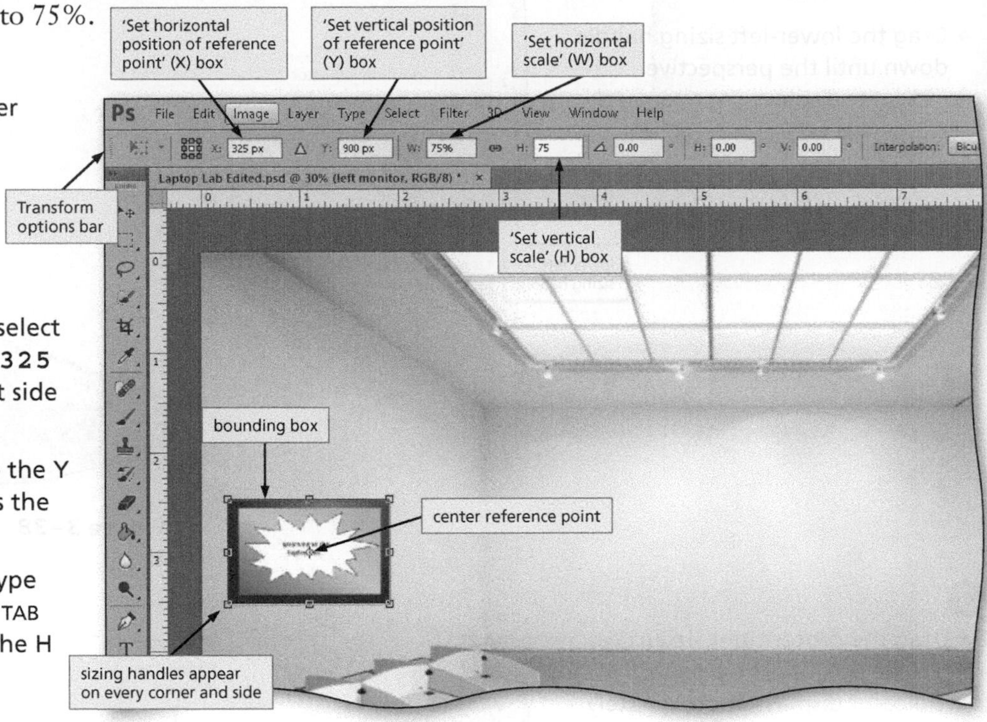

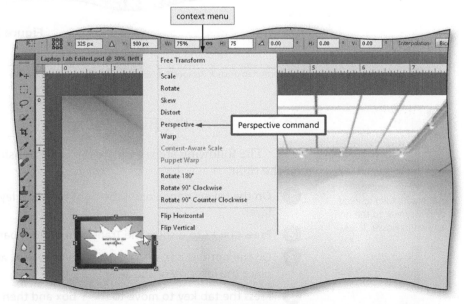

'Set horizontal position of reference point' (X) box

'Set vertical position of reference point' (Y) box

'Set horizontal scale' (W) box

'Set vertical scale' (H) box

Transform options bar

bounding box

center reference point

sizing handles appear on every corner and side

Figure 3–36

Other Ways

1. To display Transform options bar, tap or click Edit on Application bar, tap or click Free Transform

2. To place, drag bounding box

3. To scale, drag corner sizing handle

To Transform by Changing the Perspective

The following steps change the perspective of the layer to make the monitor appear more natural in the setting. Recall that adjusting the perspective causes one side of a selection or layer to be larger, thus appearing closer to the viewer.

- Press and hold or right-click the selection to display the context menu with the list of transformations (Figure 3–37).

Q&A When should I use skew rather than perspective?
You should use skew when you want to tilt or slant the layer horizontally or vertically. Use perspective when you want part of the selection to appear closer or further away in the setting.

context menu

Free Transform
Scale
Rotate
Skew
Distort
Perspective ◄———— Perspective command
Warp
Content-Aware Scale
Puppet Warp

Rotate 180°
Rotate 90° Clockwise
Rotate 90° Counter Clockwise

Flip Horizontal
Flip Vertical

Figure 3–37

2

- Tap or click Perspective on the context menu.

- Drag the lower-left sizing handle down until the perspective indicator displays approximately 6.5 degrees (Figure 3–38).

Figure 3–38

3

- Drag the center-right sizing handle up until the perspective indicator displays approximately -10 degrees (Figure 3–39).

4

- Press the ENTER key to commit the transformation.

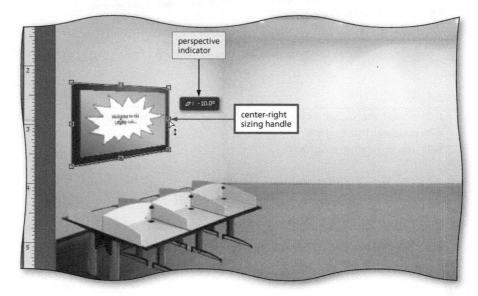

Figure 3–39

Other Ways

1. On Edit menu, tap or click Transform, tap or click Perspective, drag bounding box sizing handle

---

BTW

Rotating
When the bounding box is displayed, you can rotate the selection by dragging just outside of the corner. The pointer changes to a double-headed, curved arrow similar to the one shown in Figure 3–39.

To Transform the Right Monitor

The following steps emulate the same transformation process with the monitor on the right.

1 On the Layers panel, open the right furniture layer group and select the right monitor layer.

2 Press CTRL+T to display the Transform options bar.

3 On the options bar, select the text in the X box and type **2780** in the X box to place the left side of the layer.

4 Press the tab key to move to the Y box and then type **900** as the new top location.

5 Press the TAB key and then type 7 5 in the W box. Press the TAB key and then type 7 5 in the H box.

6 Press and hold or right-click the selection to display the context menu with the list of transformations, and then tap or click Perspective on the context menu.

7 Drag the lower-right sizing handle down until the perspective indicator displays approximately -6.5 degrees.

8 Drag the center-left sizing handle up until the perspective indicator displays approximately 10 degrees.

9 Press the ENTER key to commit the transformation (Figure 3–40).

Figure 3–40

To Transform by Flipping and Skewing

The following steps flip the left desks layer horizontally and skew the layer to slant it vertically in the scene. Recall that adjusting the skewing tilts the selection or layer, based on an axis to create the illusion of a slant. For example, when you skew a square (using a center sizing handle in Photoshop), it becomes a parallelogram.

1

- On the Layers panel, tap or click the left desks layer to select it.

- Press CTRL+T to display the bounding box and the Transform options bar.

- Press and hold or right-click the selection, and then tap or click Flip Horizontal on the context menu.

- Press and hold or right-click the selection again (Figure 3–41).

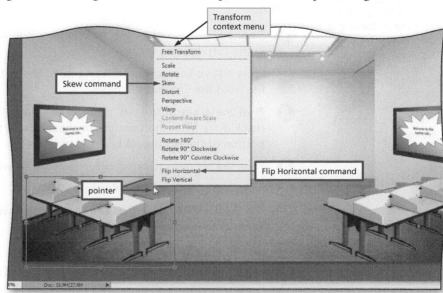

Figure 3–41

2

- Tap or click Skew on the context menu.

- Drag the center-right sizing handle down until the skew indicator displays 3.0 (Figure 3–42).

3

- Press the ENTER key to commit the transformation.

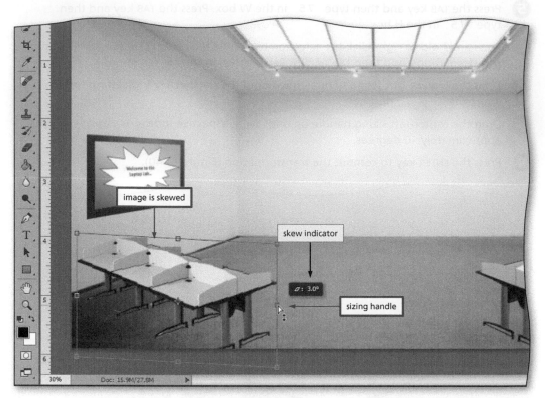

image is skewed

skew indicator

sizing handle

Figure 3–42

Other Ways

1. To flip horizontal, type -100 in W box on options bar	2. To flip horizontal, tap or click Edit on the Application bar, tap or click Transform, tap or click Flip Horizontal	3. To skew, enter new skewing degrees in V box on options bar	4. To skew, tap or click Edit on the Application bar, tap or click Transform, tap or click Skew, drag sizing handle

To Create a Layer by Copying and Pasting

The following steps use shortcut keys to create the chair layer by copying and pasting.

1 On the Layers panel, select the right monitor layer, so that the new layer will appear in the correct layer group.

2 Press CTRL+O to open a file. Navigate to the Data Files for Students and open the Chair file from the Chapter 03 folder.

3 Press the W key or SHIFT+W to select the Magic Wand Tool. Tap or click to remove the check mark from the Contiguous check box on the options bar. Tap or click the white portion of the document window to select it.

4 Press SHIFT+CTRL+I to select the inverse of the white (the chair).

5 Press CTRL+C to copy the selection.

6 Tap or click the Laptop Lab Edited document window tab to activate the window. Press CTRL+V to paste the selection.

7 On the Layers panel, rename the layer, chair.

8 Close the Chair document window (Figure 3–43).

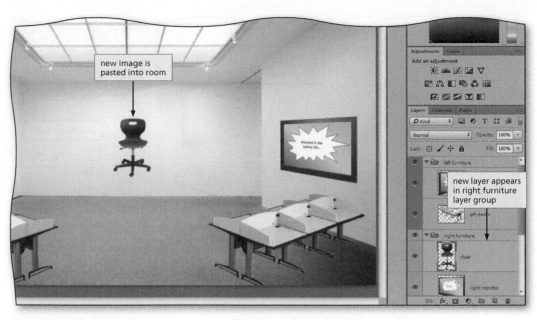

Figure 3–43

To Reorder Layers

The following step moves the chair layer below the right desks layer in order to place the chair behind the desk.

①

- On the Layers panel, drag the chair layer down, to a position below the right desks layer (Figure 3–44).

Q&A Why am I moving the chair below the desk?
The chair should appear behind the desk in the document window. Items in back appear below front objects on the Layers panel.

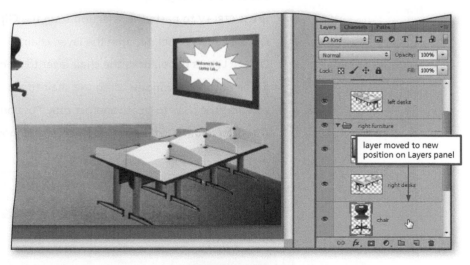

Figure 3–44

To Position and Duplicate the Chair

The following steps position the chair and create two more copies.

① Activate the Move Tool.

② In the document window, drag the chair to a position at the left side of the right desk.

③ ALT+drag the chair to create another copy. Position the chair in the middle of the right desks.

④ ALT+drag another copy to create a chair on the right side.

⑤ Scroll the Layers panel as necessary to view the copies (Figure 3–45 on the next page).

original chair and
two copies positioned
at right desk

two copied layers

Figure 3–45

To Create More Chairs

The following steps create more chairs.

1 On the Layers panel, select the left monitor layer, so that the new layer will appear in the correct layer group.

2 Press CTRL+V to paste the selection from the Clipboard.

3 On the Layers panel, rename the layer, chair.

4 On the Layers panel, drag the chair layer to a position below the left desks layer.

5 In the document window, drag the chair to a position at the left side of the left desk.

6 ALT+drag the chair to create another copy. Position the chair in the middle of the left desks.

7 ALT+drag another copy to create a chair and move it to the right side (Figure 3–46).

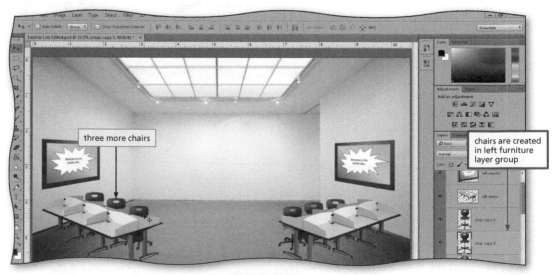

three more chairs

chairs are created
in left furniture
layer group

Figure 3–46

To Create Chairs Facing the Other Way

The following steps create layers of a chair facing the other way and position them in front of the desks.

1 On the Layers panel, select the left desks layer, so that the new layer will appear in the correct layer group.

2 Press CTRL+O to open a file. Navigate to the Data Files for Students and open the Chair Back file from the Chapter 03 folder.

3 Select the Magic Wand tool. Tap or click the white portion of the document window.

4 Press SHIFT+CTRL+I to select the inverse, and then press CTRL+C to copy the selection.

5 Select the Laptop Lab Edited document window, and then press CTRL+V to paste the selection.

6 Close the Chair Back document window.

7 Rename the new layer, chair back.

8 Select the Move Tool. Drag the chair to a position at the left side of the left desk. ALT+drag two more copies and position them.

9 On the Layers panel, scroll as necessary to select the right desks layer and then press CTRL+V to paste the selection from the clipboard. Name the new layer, chair back.

10 Position the layer and make two more copies as shown in Figure 3–47.

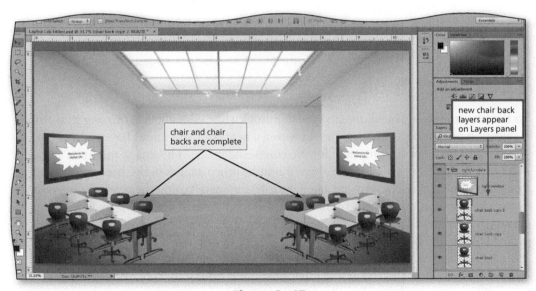

chair and chair backs are complete

new chair back layers appear on Layers panel

Figure 3–47

To Hide Layers in the Layer Groups

The following steps hide the layers in the layer group folders.

1 On the Layers panel, tap or click the triangle next to the right furniture layer group hide the layers.

2 Tap or click the triangle next to the left furniture layer group to hide the layers.

3 Tap or click the left furniture layer to select it, so future additions to the composite will appear above that layer group.

BTW

JPG File Type
The Podium image is stored as JPG file. Recall that JPG stands for Joint Photographic Experts Group and is the file type typically generated by digital cameras. JPG format supports many different color modes. JPG retains all color information in an RGB image, unlike the GIF format.

To Open the Podium Image and Create a Podium Layer

The following steps open a file named Podium and move it into the Laptop Lab Edited composite image.

1 Open the Podium file from the Chapter 03 folder of the Data Files for Students, or a location specified by your instructor.

2 On the Application bar, tap or click Window, tap or click Arrange, and then tap or click 2-up Vertical to display the windows beside one another.

3 With the Podium window still active, select the Move Tool button and then drag the entire podium image and drop it in the Laptop Lab Edited window. Dropping it in the upper portion of the window will allow easier editing.

4 Rename the layer podium and assign a violet identification color to the layer.

5 Close the Podium document window. If Photoshop displays a dialog box asking if you want to save the changes, tap or click the No button.

To Save the File

The following step saves the file again.

1 Press CTRL+S to save the Laptop Lab Edited file with the same name.

Break Point: If you wish to take a break, this is a good place to do so. Quit Photoshop by pressing CTRL+Q. To resume at a later time, start Photoshop, open the file named Laptop Lab Edited, and continue following the steps from this location forward.

The Eraser Tools

BTW

Saving Files
Photoshop displays an asterisk (*) on the document window tab to denote changes have been made to the file (Figure 3–49). Once you save the file, the asterisk no longer is displayed.

In the monitor layer, you eliminated the monitor's white edges before moving it by using a selection technique. At other times, however, a new layer still might have extra color or objects that are not appropriate for the composite image. The image might be shaped oddly, making selecting tedious, or there might be other images in the background that come along with the selection and are not easily eliminated using the marquee selection technique you used previously. In those cases, dragging the image into a layer and then erasing part of that layer gives you more freedom and control over how the layer appears.

On the Tools panel, when you press and hold or right-click the Eraser Tool button, Photoshop displays the three eraser tools. To alternate among the three eraser tools, press SHIFT+E. To access the eraser tools after using a different tool, press the E key.

The eraser tools are described in Table 3–2.

Table 3–2 Eraser Tools

Tool	Purpose	Shortcut	Button
Eraser Tool	Erases pixels beneath the cursor or brush tip	E SHIFT+E toggles through all three eraser tools	
Background Eraser Tool	Erases sample color from the center of the brush	E SHIFT+E toggles through all three eraser tools	
Magic Eraser Tool	Erases all similarly colored pixels	E SHIFT+E toggles through all three eraser tools	

© Cengage Learning

When using the eraser tools, it is best to erase small portions at a time. That way each erasure is a separate state on the History panel. If you make mistakes, you can tap or click earlier states on the panel. Small erasures also can be undone. To undo an erasure, press CTRL+Z, or tap or click Edit on the Application bar, and then tap or click Undo Eraser.

Using the Eraser Tool

The Eraser Tool changes pixels in the image as you drag through them. On most layers, the Eraser Tool simply erases the pixels or changes them to transparent, revealing the layer beneath. On a locked layer, such as the Background layer, the Eraser Tool changes the pixels to the current background color.

The Eraser Tool options bar (Figure 3–48) displays a Mode button in which you can choose one of three shapes for erasure: brush, block, and pen. The brush mode gives you the most flexibility in size, and many different brush tips are available. The default brush tip is a circle. Block mode is a hard-edged, fixed-sized square with no options for changing the opacity or flow; however, it does give you quick access to a square to erase straight lines and corners. The pencil mode is similar to the brush mode, except that the pencil does not spread as much into adjacent pixels.

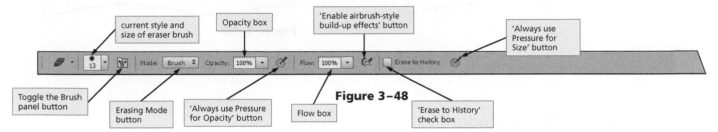

Figure 3–48

Opacity refers to the level at which you can see through a color to reveal the layer beneath it. When using the eraser tools, an opacity setting of 100% completely erases pixels. A lower opacity makes the layer more transparent. The Flow box specifies how quickly the erasure is performed. In addition, you can erase to a saved state or snapshot in the History panel. Other buttons change the eraser based on tablet pressure.

As you erase with the brush shape, the RIGHT BRACKET ( ]) and LEFT BRACKET ([ ) keys increase and decrease the size of the eraser, respectively.

To Erase using the Eraser Tool

The following steps erase the area around the podium using the Eraser Tool.

- Press the Z key to select the Zoom Tool, and then tap or click the podium several times to zoom to 66.67%.

- Press the E key to select the Eraser Tool button on the Tools panel.

- In the document window, drag across a portion of the layer above the podium to erase it. Do not drag across the podium (Figure 3–49).

Q&A How should I position the Eraser Tool pointer?
By default, the Eraser Tool pointer appears as a circle. When you tap, click, or drag, Photoshop erases everything within the circle. You can change the size of the pointer using the bracket keys.

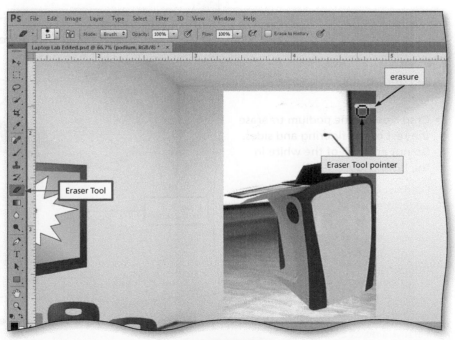

Figure 3–49

2

- Press the RIGHT BRACKET (]) key several times to increase the size of your eraser.

- Erase more of the area around the podium. Do not erase completely along the very edge of the podium (Figure 3–50).

 Experiment

- Drag a short erasure over the podium that creates an error. Then press CTRL+Z to undo the erasure.

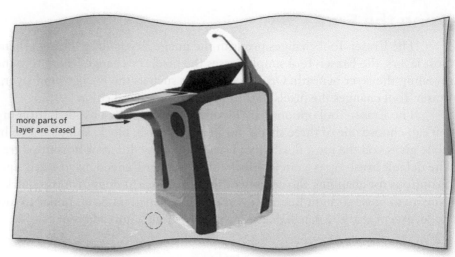

Figure 3–50

Other Ways

1. Press E or SHIFT+E until Eraser Tool is selected, tap or click image

To Erase using the Block Mode

The following steps erase more of the podium using a block pointer.

1

- Tap or click the Erasing Mode button on the options bar to display its list (Figure 3–51).

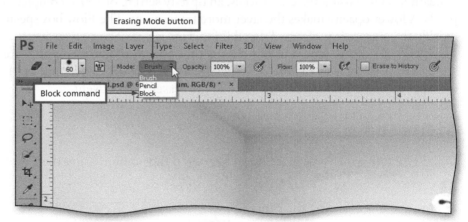

Figure 3–51

2

- Tap or click Block to choose a block pointer.

- Drag close to the podium to erase the rest of the flooring and sides. Do not erase all of the white in the layer (Figure 3–52).

Q&A I cannot get close enough to the edge to erase. What should I do? You can zoom in to erase more closely, or use the Pencil and Brush modes as necessary. However, the block pointer will remain the same size. You can press and hold the SHIFT key while dragging to create a straight horizontal or vertical line of erasure.

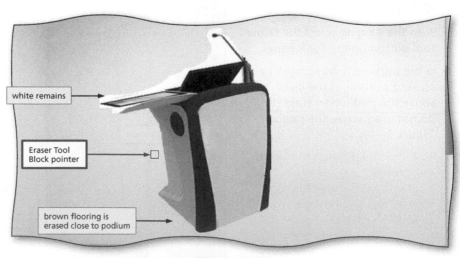

Figure 3–52

Using the Magic Eraser Tool

The Magic Eraser Tool erases all similarly colored pixels with one tap or click. The Magic Eraser Tool options bar (Figure 3–53) gives you the choice of erasing contiguous or noncontiguous pixels and allows you to enter a tolerance value to define the range of erasable color. A lower tolerance erases pixels within a range of color values very similar to the pixel you tap or click. A higher tolerance erases pixels within a broader range. Recall that the Anti-alias check box creates a smooth edge that can apply to both selecting and erasing. As with the Eraser Tool options bar, an Opacity box allows you to specify the depth of the erasure.

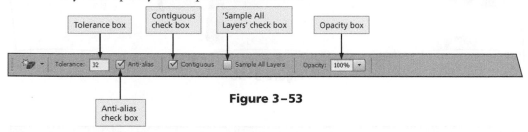

Figure 3–53

To Erase using the Magic Eraser Tool

The following steps use the Magic Eraser Tool to remove the white background from the podium layer.

①

- Press and hold or right-click the Eraser Tool button on the Tools panel to display the context menu (Figure 3–54).

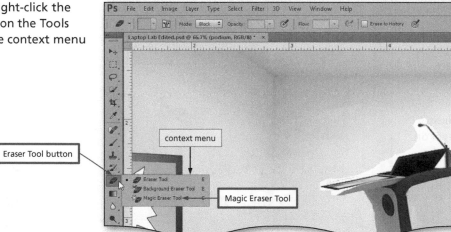

Figure 3–54

②

- Tap or click 'Magic Eraser Tool' to select it.

- If necessary, tap or click the Anti-alias check box so it displays a check mark.

- Tap or click the Contiguous check box so it does not display a check mark.

- Move the pointer into the document window (Figure 3–55).

Q&A Why do I need to remove the Contiguous check mark?
You want to erase all occurrences of the color, even those that are not connected continuously, such as those in between the microphone and the monitor on the podium.

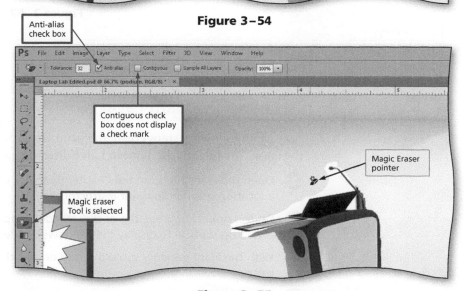

Figure 3–55

③

- Tap or click the white area to remove all the white in the layer (Figure 3–56).

Q&A How should I position the Magic Eraser Tool pointer?
Position the lower-left tip of the eraser over the pixel color to erase.

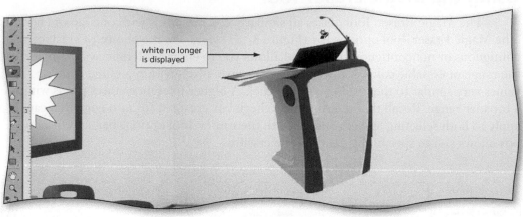

white no longer is displayed

Figure 3–56

④

- If any other parts of the podium background need to be erased, choose the appropriate eraser tool and erase them.

- Press CTRL+0 (ZERO) to fit the image in the document window.

- Using the Move Tool, move the podium to the floor level on the left side of the room as shown in Figure 3–57.

Move Tool button

podium moved to floor

Figure 3–57

Other Ways

1. Press E or SHIFT+E until Magic Eraser Tool is selected, choose settings, tap or click image

To Create the Plant Layer

The following steps create the plant layer, by opening the file and then moving the entire image into the Laptop Lab Edited document window.

① Open the Plant file from the Chapter 03 folder of the Data Files for Students, or from a location specified by your instructor.

② On the Application bar, tap or click Window, tap or click Arrange, and then tap or click 2-up Vertical to display the windows beside each other.

③ With the Plant window still active, tap or click the Move Tool button on the Tools panel, if necessary.

④ Drag the entire plant image and drop it in the Laptop Lab Edited window.

5 Close the Plant document window. If Photoshop displays a dialog box asking if you want to save the changes, tap or click the No button.

6 Rename the layer, plant, and assign a green identification color to the layer (Figure 3–58).

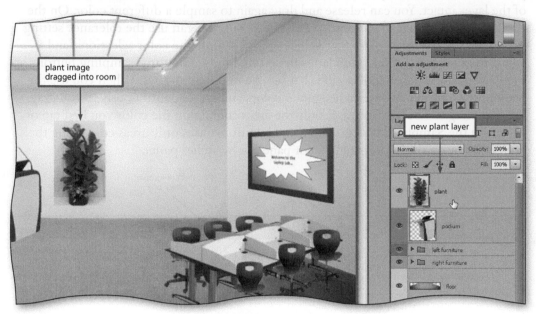

Figure 3–58

To Display Only the Current Layer

Some users find it easier to erase in a layer when only that layer appears in the document window. The following step hides all but the current layer using the visibility icon.

1

- On the Layers panel, ALT+tap or ALT+click the plant layer visibility icon, so only the plant is displayed.

- Zoom to 100%. If necessary, scroll the document window so that the entire plant is visible (Figure 3–59).

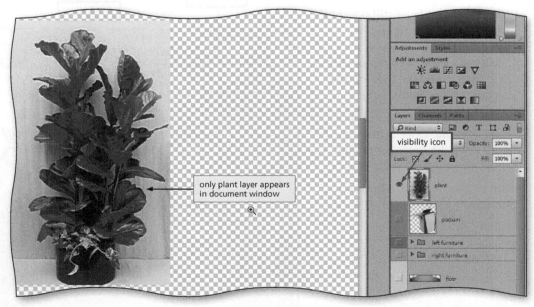

Figure 3–59

The Background Eraser Tool
The Background Eraser Tool samples the hot spot and then, as you drag, it deletes that color wherever it appears inside the brush. The Background Eraser Tool overrides the lock transparency setting of a layer.

Using the Background Eraser Tool

The Background Eraser Tool erases the background while maintaining the edges of an object in the foreground, based on a set color that you choose for the background. The Background Eraser Tool samples the color in the center of the pointer, called the **hot spot**. As you drag, the tool erases that color, leaving the rest of the layer intact. You can release and drag again to sample a different color. On the Background Eraser Tool options bar (Figure 3–60), you can use the tolerance setting to control the range of colors that will be erased, sample the color selections, and adjust the sharpness of the boundaries by setting limits. The three sampling buttons on the Background Eraser Tool options bar sample in different ways. When you use the Sampling: Continuous button, it samples colors and erases continuously as you drag, the Sampling: Once button erases only the areas containing the color you first tap or click, and the Sampling: Background Swatch button erases only areas containing the current color on the Tools panel, Color panel, or Swatches panel.

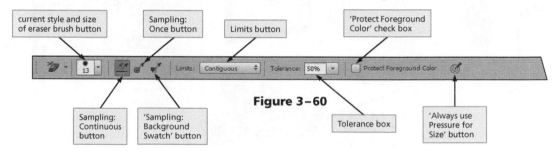

Figure 3–60

To Erase using the Background Eraser Tool

The following steps use the Background Eraser Tool to remove the paneling from behind the plant. If you make a mistake while erasing, select the previous state on the History panel or press CTRL+Z and begin erasing again. Using the Background Eraser Tool with a touch screen is difficult. If you do not have a mouse or stylus, consider increasing the Windows scaling to at least 200%. (See the Editing Preferences Appendix.)

- With the plant layer still selected, press and hold or right-click the Eraser Tool button on the Tools panel and then tap or click 'Background Eraser Tool' on the context menu to select the tool.

- On the options bar, tap or click the Sampling: Once button to erase only the areas containing the color you first tap or click.

- Tap or click the Limits button to display its list (Figure 3–61).

Q&A

What does Discontiguous mean?
Discontiguous refers to noncontiguous pixels, or pixels of the same color that are not physically located together. In the plant layer, parts of the brown panel appear behind the plant and are not adjacent pixels to the other brown paneling pixels.

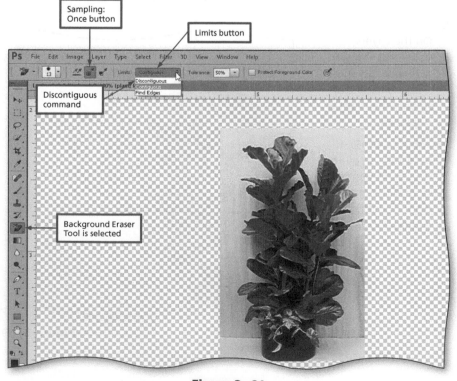

Figure 3–61

2

- Tap or click Discontiguous to choose the setting.

- Move the pointer to the document window, and then press the RIGHT BRACKET (]) key several times to increase the size of the eraser, if necessary.

- Position the center of the pointer directly over a portion of the image outside of the plant.

- Tap or click and then hold. Drag across the layer, including the plant, to erase some of the background (Figure 3–62).

Q&A What is the purpose of the 'Protect Foreground Color' check box?
When checked, the Protect Foreground Color check box gives you even more control of the background erasing by protecting whatever color shows as the foreground color on the Tools panel. When colors are very similar, you can ALT+tap or ALT+click the color you want to keep (making it the foreground color), and then hold and drag the color you want to erase.

Figure 3–62

3

- Position the pointer directly over another portion of the background that remains.

- Tap or click and hold. Drag to erase the rest of the background.

- If some of the paneling remains, reduce the Tolerance setting to approximately 25 and continue erasing in the same style (Figure 3–63).

Q&A How can I make cleaner erasures?
Effectively using the various eraser tools, along with their modes and settings, takes a lot of practice. Some people like to use selection tools and then delete. Others change the tolerance. Of the three eraser tools, the Background Eraser tool is the most difficult to use. Look at your erasures at various magnifications. Some minor imperfections will never been noticed.

Figure 3–63

Other Ways

1. Press E or SHIFT+E until Background Eraser Tool is selected, set options, tap or click document

To Position the Plant Layer

The following steps erase the rest of the background and resize the plant layer.

1 ALT+tap or ALT+click the visibility icon for the plant layer to display all of the layers.

2 Press CTRL+0 (ZERO) to fit the image in the document window.

3 On the Layers panel, drag the plant layer to a location below the podium layer.

4 Select the Move Tool. In the document window, drag the plant to a location just behind the podium (Figure 3–64).

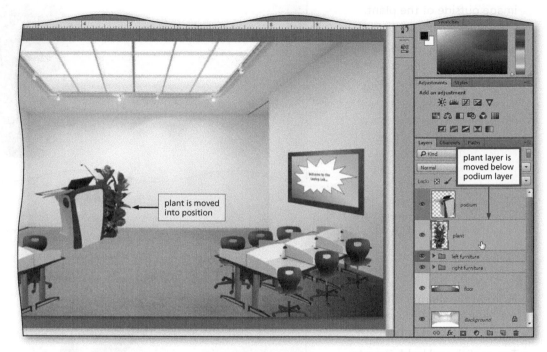

plant layer is moved below podium layer

plant is moved into position

Figure 3–64

Layer Masks

Another way to edit layers is by creating a mask. A **mask** is an overlay that hides portions of a layer; it also can protect areas of the layer from inadvertent editing. For example, in a graphic of an exotic animal, you might want to mask all of the area except the animal, rather than permanently delete the background. Or, if you wanted to layer a musical score over the top of a piano graphic, you could mask the edges of the paper so the notes look like they blend into the piano. A mask does not alter the layer as the Eraser Tool does; it merely overlays a template to conceal a portion of the layer. That way, if you change your mind and need to display more of the layer, you can. Nothing has been erased permanently. With the Eraser Tool, you would have to delete the layer, open a backup copy, recreate the layer, and then begin to edit again. With masks, you simply edit the mask.

Photoshop provides two types of masks. **Layer masks** or **pixel masks** are resolution-dependent bitmap images, created with the painting or selection tools. **Vector masks** are resolution independent, created with a pen or shape tool. In this chapter, you will create a layer mask using selection and painting techniques.

When you add a mask, a layer mask thumbnail appears on the Layers panel in **grayscale**, which means each pixel in the mask uses a single shade of gray on a scale

Default Colors and Layer Masks
When you apply a mask to a layer, or select a previously created mask on the Layers panel, Photoshop automatically inverts the default colors. White is used to reveal portions of the mask. Black is used to hide portions of the mask. Double-check the colors in the lower portion of the Tools panel when working with masks.

from black to white. When selecting the layer mask thumbnail, the default colors change to white over black and the eraser tools are inactive. To mask, you paint on the layer with black. If you change your mind and want to unmask, you paint with white. Painting with gray displays various levels of transparency in the layer.

To Open the Wall Unit File

The following steps open the Wall Unit file in preparation for creating a layer mask. You then use a copy and paste process to place the wall unit in the room.

1 On the Layers panel, select the floor layer, so that the wall unit will appear behind other layers.

2 Open the file named Wall Unit from the Chapter 03 folder of the Data Files for Students or from a location specified by your instructor.

3 With the Wall Unit window active, press CTRL+A to select all, and then press CTRL+C to copy the entire image.

4 Tap or click the Laptop Lab Edited document window tab to make the window active. Press CTRL+V to paste the copied image from the Clipboard.

5 Use the Move Tool to move the pasted image to a location just right of the podium, as shown in Figure 3–65.

6 Name the new layer, wall unit, and color the layer Gray.

7 Close the Wall Unit document window.

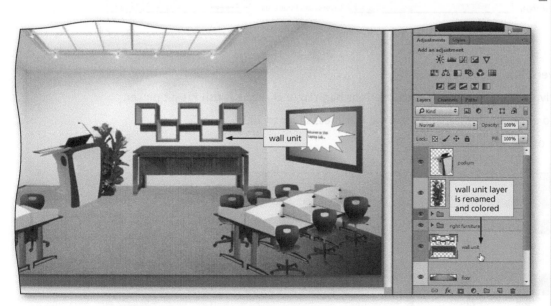

Figure 3–65

To Create a Layer Mask

The following steps mask the work table in the wall unit layer to reveal only the shelves. That way, potential decorators can see what the room would look like with and without the work table. As you create the layer mask, you will use the Brush Tool to brush over the parts of the image to mask. You will learn more about the Brush Tool and its settings in a future chapter.

❶

- If necessary, press the D key to choose the default colors. If white appears over black on the Tools panel, press the X key to exchange the foreground and background colors.

- With the wall unit layer selected, press CTRL+1 (ONE) to zoom to 100 percent.

- Tap or click the 'Add layer mask' button on the Layers panel status bar to create a layer mask and automatically reverse the colors (Figure 3–66).

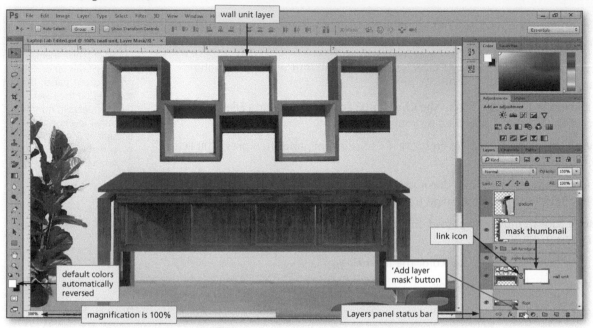

Figure 3–66

❷

- Press the X key to reverse the colors.

- Press the B key to activate the Brush Tool. On the options bar, tap or click the Brush Preset picker.

- Drag the Size slider to approximately 75 px. Drag the Hardness slider to 100%.

- Drag across a portion of the worktable (Figure 3–67).

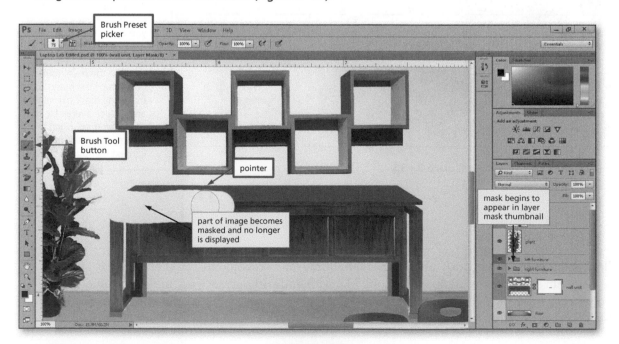

Figure 3–67

3
- Continue dragging to mask the entire worktable (Figure 3–68).

Q&A

Did I erase the worktable?
No, you still can see the worktable in the layer thumbnail on the Layers panel. You only masked it out of view.

Why does the layer mask use a brush tip pointer?
Layer masks use painting techniques to mask out portions of the image.

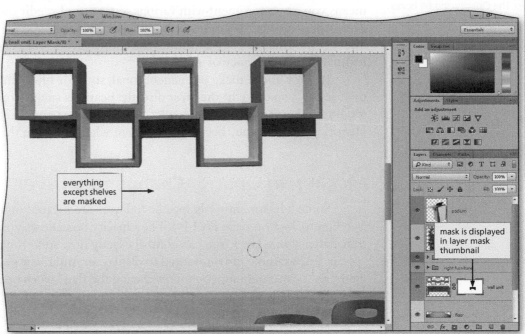

Figure 3–68

TO CORRECT A MASKING ERROR

If you make a mistake while painting on a layer mask, you would perform the following steps.

1. Press the x key to switch the foreground and background colors so you are painting with white, which restores the image.
2. Drag across the masking error portion of the image to unmask it.

Fine-Tuning Layers

Sometimes layers need special adjustments to better fit into their new surroundings in the document window. This fine-tuning usually involves **tonal adjustments** that affect the color, lighting, opacity, level, or fill; **style adjustments** such as special effects or blends; or **filter adjustments** that let you apply grains, tiles, or patterns. With the correct adjustment, a layer can be made to look like it was an original part of the image, maintaining a consistency of appearance for the overall composite image.

BTW

Moving Masks
To move the mask, first click the link icon on the Layers panel to unlink the mask from the layer. Select the Move Tool. Then, in the document window, drag the layer to reposition it. When the mask is positioned correctly, click between the layer and layer mask on the Layers panel to relink them.

Create layer adjustments.
Layer adjustments allow you to fine-tune your layers. Evaluate layers to see if a change in levels, brightness, saturation, or hue would help them to fit more naturally into the background scene. Use nondestructive edits when possible, so that if you are not satisfied with the adjustment, you can remove it.

Plan Ahead

When you do not want to alter the pixels in an image permanently, you can create an extra layer in which to make changes while preserving the original pixels. An **adjustment layer** is a new layer added to the image to affect a large-scale tonal change. You can create adjustment layers for the entire composite image or just a specific layer.

Panel Boxes
The Opacity and Fill boxes can be changed in one of three ways. You can drag the scrubby slider label. When you click the box arrow, a pop-up slider is displayed to adjust the percentage. You also can type a percentage in either box.

Adjustment layers have several advantages. They are nondestructive, which means you can experiment with various settings and reedit the adjustment layer at any time. Adjustment layers reduce the amount of damage you do to an image by making direct edits. You can copy adjustments to other layers and images, saving time and maintaining consistency of appearance.

If you want to make permanent tonal, style, or filter changes to the pixels themselves, you can edit the layer directly. Features such as opacity, fill, and blending modes can be changed on the Layers panel. These changes can be undone using the History panel, but they become permanent when you save the image.

Making an Opacity Change to a Layer

Some adjustment tools specific to layers are located on the Layers panel (see Figure 3–3 on page PS 144). The Opacity box allows you to change the opacity or transparency of a layer. You can control exactly how solid the objects on a specific layer appear. For example, if you wanted to display an American flag superimposed over a memorial or monument, you might change the flag layer's opacity to 50 percent. The monument easily would be visible through the flag.

The Fill box changes the fill of a layer's opacity as well, but it only changes the pixels in the layer rather than changing any applied layer styles or blending modes. Adjusting the fill percentage sometimes is called changing the **interior opacity**. If you have no layer styles or blending modes, you can use either the Opacity or Fill box.

The Blending mode button displays a list of blending modes for the selected layer or layers. **Blending modes** define how an object interacts with other objects, such as the Background layer.

To Make an Opacity Change to a Layer

The following step lightens the plant by lowering the opacity slightly, to make it fit better in the room design.

1

- Zoom to display the plant in the document window at 100% magnification.

- On the Layers panel, tap or click to select the plant layer.

- On the Layers panel, tap or click the word, Opacity, and then drag the scrubby slider to the left until the Opacity box displays 85% to lower the opacity (Figure 3–69).

Experiment

- Tap or click the Blending mode button and choose a blending mode such as Hard Light or Linear Burn. Experiment with other blending modes. When you are done, tap or click the Blending mode button and then tap or click Normal in the list.

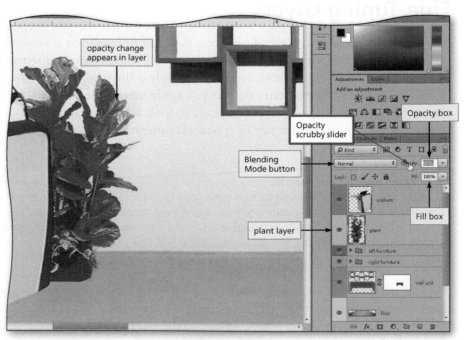

Figure 3–69

To Save the File

Many edits have been made to the layers in the composite image. The following step saves the file again.

1 Press CTRL+S to save the Laptop Lab Edited file with the same name.

> **Break Point:** If you wish to take a break, this is a good place to do so. Quit Photoshop by pressing CTRL+Q. To resume at a later time, start Photoshop, open the file named Laptop Lab Edited, and continue following the steps from this location forward.

Adjustments and Properties

Tools that nondestructively adjust image color, lighting, and shading are located on the Adjustments panel (Figure 3–70).

Tapping or clicking an **adjustment icon**, or preset, also displays the Properties panel and its settings for the specific adjustment, including channel selectors, eyedroppers, sliders, and input boxes, among others. Buttons on the Properties panel status bar allow you to specify visibility, delete the adjustment, or create a **clip** that applies the adjustment to a layer rather than the entire image.

Some adjustments also can display their settings using a dialog box, if accessed from outside the Adjustments panel with a shortcut key or a menu command. Table 3–3 on the next page displays a list of the adjustments available on the Adjustments panel. Many of the adjustments also are available through the Adjustments panel menu (Figure 3–70), through the Layers menu on the application bar, or through a button on the Layers panel.

BTW

Image Adjustments
If you choose adjustments from the Image menu, the adjustment is made to the current layer in a destructive process. Use the Layer menu instead

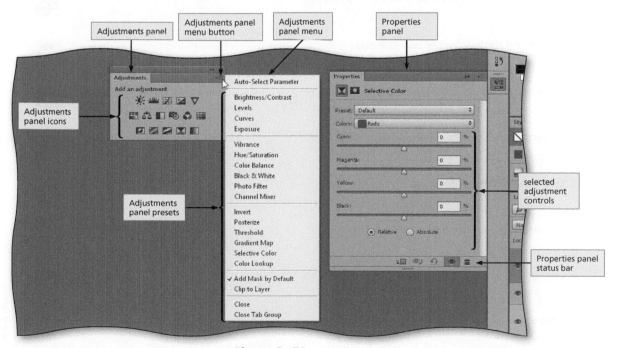

Figure 3–70

Adjustments create a layer above the selected layer on the Layers panel, and can be duplicated and then moved, to apply to other layers or even moved into other images.

Table 3–3 Adjustments Panel Icons

Adjustment	Description	Shortcut (if available)	Icon
Brightness/Contrast	Changes general brightness (shadows and highlights) and overall contrast (tonal range)		
Levels	Adjusts color balance for shadows, midtones, highlights, and color channels	CTRL+L	
Curves	Adjusts individual points in the tonal range of black to white	CTRL+M	
Exposure	Changes exposure, which adjusts the highlights; changes offset, which darkens the shadows and midtones; changes gamma, which adjusts the midtones		
Vibrance	Adjusts vibrance and color saturation settings so shifting to primary colors, or clipping, is minimized		
Hue/Saturation	Changes hue, saturation, and lightness of entire image or specific colors	CTRL+U	
Color Balance	Adjusts the overall midtone of colors in an image	CTRL+B	
Black & White	Converts a color image to grayscale	ALT+SHIFT+CTRL+B	
Photo Filter	Simulates effects of using a filter in front of a camera lens		
Channel Mixer	Modifies and adjusts individual color channels		
Color Lookup	Remaps every color using a lookup table or predetermined style		
Invert	Converts every color to its inverse or opposite	CTRL+I	
Posterize	Specifies the number of tonal levels in each channel		
Threshold	Converts images to high-contrast black and white		
Selective Color	Changes the mixture of colors in each of the primary color components		
Gradient Map	Maps colors to a specified gradient fill		

Level Adjustments

A **level adjustment** is one way to make tonal changes to shadows, midtones, and highlights. A **shadow** is a darkened shade in an image. A **midtone**, also called **gamma**, is the midpoint gray between shadows and highlights. A **highlight** is a portion of an image that is strongly illuminated and may appear as the lightest or whitest part of the image. To change levels, Photoshop uses black, gray, and white sliders to adjust any or all of the three tonal input levels. A **histogram**, or frequency distribution bar chart, indicates the amount of color in the tonal ranges. When adjusting levels using the histogram, a general guideline is to drag the black-and-white sliders to the first indication, or outlier, of strong tonal change in the histogram. Then, experiment with the gray slider to change the intensity value of the middle range of gray tones without dramatically altering the highlights and shadows. Becoming skilled at adjusting levels takes practice. Furthermore, adjustments are subjective; the impact of some effects is a matter of opinion.

BTW

Other Level Adjustments
The three eyedroppers in the Levels area allow you to select the values for shadow, midtone, and highlight from the image itself. To do so, click the eyedropper and then click the location in the image that you want to use. Once selected, that color becomes the slider value.

To Create a Levels Adjustment Layer

Earlier you made an opacity change to the plant layer to reduce its overall density; however, it is still dark and not very green. The following steps adjust the levels to create more contrast between the dark and light tones in the plant, bringing out the green color.

1

- With the plant layer still selected, tap or click the Levels icon on the Adjustments panel to display the Levels settings and options on the Properties panel.

- Tap or click the 'Clip to Layer' button on the Properties panel status bar to adjust only the plant layer (Figure 3–71).

Experiment

- At the top of the Properties panel, tap or click the Preset button to view the various preset Levels adjustments. One at a time, tap or click several to see the changes in the plant. When you are finished, tap or click the Preset button again, and then tap or click Default.

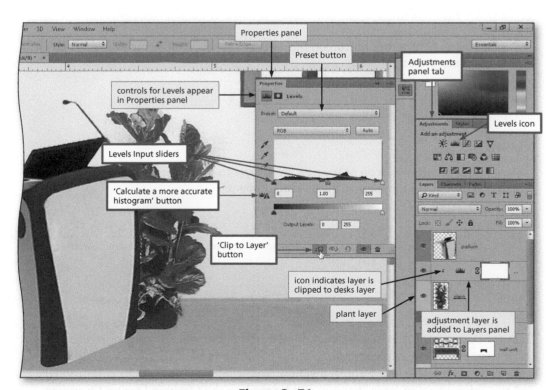

Figure 3–71

②

- Tap or click the 'Calculate a more accurate histogram' button to make the level change more visible.

- Below the histogram display, drag the white Levels Input slider to approximately 218, aligning it with the major increase on the right side of the histogram to adjust the highlights.

- Drag the gray Levels Input slider to 1.10 to adjust the midtone colors (Figure 3–72).

Q&A My visible changes were at different levels. Did I do something wrong?

No, your histogram might differ, depending on your previous erasures.

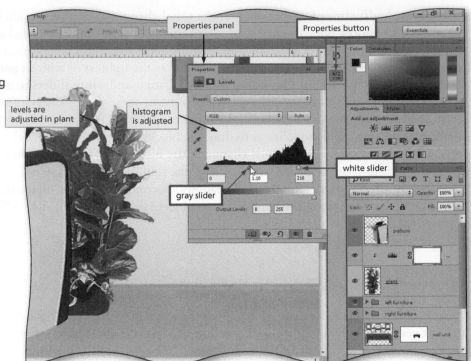

Figure 3–72

③

- Tap or click the Properties button on the vertical dock to collapse the Properties panel and complete the adjustment.

Q&A Did the Layers panel change?

Yes, you will see an extra layer created just above the plants layer, with a clipping symbol to imply the relationship (Figure 3–72).

⌕ Experiment

- Tap or click the visibility icon of the new levels layer to notice the change in the plant. Tap or click it again to redisplay the level adjustment.

Other Ways
1. On Layer menu, tap or click New Adjustment Layer, tap or click Levels, tap or click OK button, adjust levels

Color Balance

Another way to adjust a layer or image is to change the color balance. A **Color Balance** adjustment changes the overall mixture of colors in an image for generalized color correction. The associated Properties panel contains sliders for three different color spectrums: cyan, magenta, and yellow. You will learn more about color models and the color wheel in later chapters and by reading the Graphic Design Overview Appendix.

BTW

Color Modes
The color mode of an image appears on the document window tab. You will learn more about color modes in a later chapter.

To Adjust the Color Balance

The following steps adjust the color balance of the podium so it more closely matches the color of the desks in the room.

①

- Select the podium layer.

- Tap or click the Color Balance icon on the Adjustments panel.

- Tap or click the 'Clip to Layer' button on the Properties panel status bar to adjust only the selected layer.

- Drag the Yellow slider to -60 to adjust the yellow colors in the podium (Figure 3–73).

 Experiment

- Drag the sliders to view the effect of cyan, magenta, and yellow settings on the layer. When you are done experimenting, drag the sliders to the settings shown in Figure 3–73.

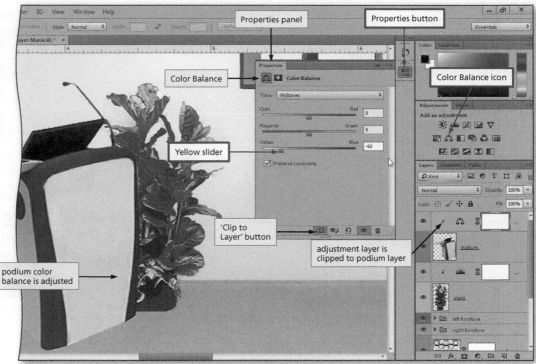

Figure 3–73

②

- Tap or click the Properties button on the vertical dock to collapse the Properties panel and complete the adjustment.

Other Ways

1. On Layer menu, tap or click New Adjustment Layer, tap or click Color Balance, tap or click OK button, edit settings

Brightness and Contrast

Brightness refers to color luminance or intensity of a light source, perceived as lightness or darkness in an image. Photoshop measures brightness on a sliding scale from –150 to +150. Negative numbers move the brightness toward black. Positive numbers compress the highlights and expand the shadows. For example, the layer might be an image photographed on a cloudy day; conversely, the image might appear overexposed by having been too close to a photographer's flash. Either way, editing the brightness might enhance the image.

Contrast is the difference between the lightest and darkest tones in an image, involving mainly the midtones. When you increase contrast, the middle-to-dark areas become darker, and the middle-to-light areas become lighter. High-contrast images contain few color variations between the lightest and darkest parts of the image; low-contrast images contain more tonal gradations.

To Adjust the Brightness and Contrast

The steps on the next page edit the brightness and contrast of the Background layer to reduce the brightness or glare in the room, this time creating the adjustment layer using the Layers panel.

1

- Press CTRL+0 (ZERO) to fit the image on the screen
- Scroll in the Layers panel as necessary to select the Background layer.
- On the Layers panel status bar, tap or click the 'Create new fill or adjustment layer' button to display the list of adjustments (Figure 3–74).

Q&A What is the difference between clicking the Brightness/ Contrast button on the Adjustments panel and clicking the 'Create new fill or adjustment layer' button?

There is no difference when adjusting the brightness or contrast. The list of adjustments accessed from the Layers panel includes a few more settings than the Adjustments panel.

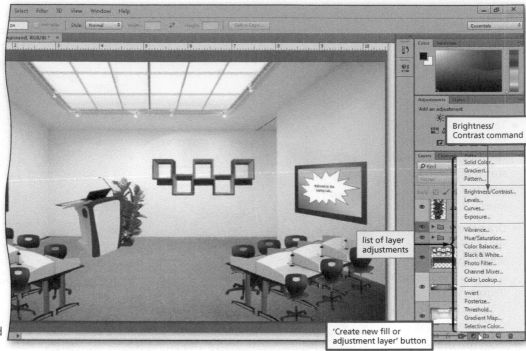

Figure 3–74

2

- Tap or click Brightness/Contrast in the list to display the settings on the Properties panel.
- Tap or click the 'Clip to Layer' button on the Properties panel status bar to adjust only the Background layer.
- Drag the Brightness slider to -20 to reduce the brightness or glare in the room (Figure 3–75).

Experiment

- Drag the sliders to various locations and note how the document window changes. When you are finished, drag the Brightness slider to -20 and the Contrast slider to 0.

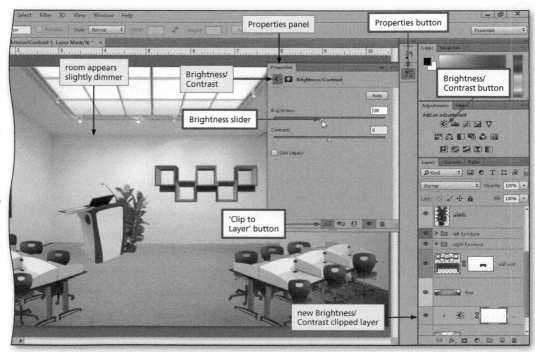

Figure 3–75

3

- Collapse the Properties panel.

Other Ways

1. On Adjustments panel, tap or click Brightness/Contrast icon, adjust settings

2. On Layer menu, tap or click New Adjustment Layer, tap or click Brightness/ Contrast, tap or click OK, adjust settings

Layer Styles

Similar to a layer adjustment, a **layer style** is applied to a layer rather than changing the layer's actual pixels. Layer styles, or layer effects, alter the appearance of the layer by adding depth, shadow, shading, texture, or overlay. A layer can display multiple styles or effects.

> **Edit layer styles.**
> Layer styles add dimension, texture, and definition to your layers. Styles such as shadow, glow, emboss, bevel, overlay, and stroke commonly distinguish the layer rather than making it fit in. Choose the settings carefully and think about direction, angle, distance, and spread. Make sure the layer style does not overwhelm the overall image or detract from previous layer adjustments.

Plan Ahead

Table 3–4 lists the layer styles.

Table 3–4 Layer Styles

Style	Description
Drop Shadow	Creates a shadow behind the layer
Inner Shadow	Creates a shadow inside the edges of the layer
Inner Glow	Adds a glow around the inside edge of the layer
Outer Glow	Adds a glow around the outside edge of the layer
Bevel and Emboss	Adds highlights, contour, texture, and shading to a layer
Satin	Applies interior shading to create a satin finish
Color Overlay	Adds a color over the layer
Gradient Overlay	Inserts a gradient in front of the layer
Pattern Overlay	Fills the layer with a pattern
Stroke	Outlines the layer with a color, gradient, or pattern

© Cengage Learning

BTW

Styles vs. Adjustments
Layer styles are special effects such as shadows, glows, and overlays. Styles appear attached to a layer on the Layers panel. An adjustment applies color, level, and tonal changes on its on layer.

Each of the layer styles has its own set of options and properties that appear in a dialog box. Table 3–5 describes some of the layer style options. The options apply to many of the styles.

Table 3–5 Layer Style Options

Option	Description
Angle	Sets a degree value for the lighting angle at which the effect is applied
Anti-alias	Blends the edge pixels of a contour or gloss contour
Blend Mode	Determines how a layer style blends with its underlying layers
Color	Assigns the color of a shadow, glow, or highlight
Contour	Allows you to create rings of transparency such as gradients, fades, beveling and embossing, and sculpting
Depth	Sets the depth of a bevel or pattern
Distance	Specifies the offset distance for a shadow or satin effect
Fill Type	Sets the content of a stroke
Global Light	Allows you to set an angle to simulate the direction of the light
Gloss Contour	Creates a glossy, metallic appearance on a bevel or emboss effect
Gradient	Indicates the gradient of a layer effect
Highlight or Shadow Mode	Specifies the blending mode of a bevel or emboss highlight or shadow
Jitter	Varies the color and opacity of a gradient
Layer Knocks Out Drop Shadow	Controls the drop shadow's visibility in a semitransparent layer

BTW

Hide Layer Styles
If you want to hide the notation of the Layer styles on the Layers panel, click the click the 'Reveals layer effects in the panel' button. To redisplay the style, click the button again.

BTW

Delete Layer Styles
If you want to delete a layer style, right-click the layer style, and then click Clear Layer Style on the context menu.

Continued

Table 3–5 Layer Style Options (continued)	
Option	Description
Noise	Assigns the number of random elements in the opacity of a glow or shadow
Opacity	Sets the opacity or transparency
Pattern	Specifies the pattern
Position	Sets the position of a stroke
Range	Controls which portion or range of the glow is targeted for the contour
Size	Specifies the amount of blur or the size of the shadow
Soften	Blurs the results of shading to reduce unwanted artifacts
Source	Specifies the source for an inner glow
Style	Specifies the style of a bevel or emboss

BTW

Bevels
A bevel adds depth to an image by creating an angle between an edge and a shadow that softens the look. A bevel increases the 3D look of an image.

When a layer has a style applied to it, an fx icon appears to the right of the layer's name on the Layers panel (Figure 3–78). You can expand or collapse the layer style on the Layers panel to view all of the applied effects and edit them when changing the style.

To Apply a Bevel Layer Style

The following steps apply a layer style to the monitors. You will create an inner bevel to give the monitor more depth.

1
- On the Layers panel, open the right furniture layer group and select the right monitor layer.

- Tap or click the 'Add a layer style' button on the Layers panel status bar to display the menu (Figure 3–76).

Q&A

Will I see much change in the document window? It depends on the magnification – at larger magnifications, you will see more change. The printed image will display more depth in the monitor.

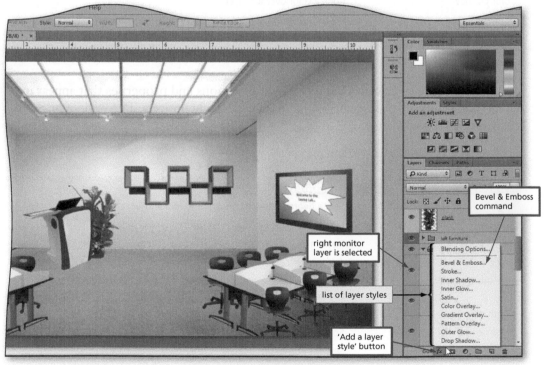

Figure 3–76

2

- Tap or click Bevel & Emboss to display the Layer Style dialog box.

- In the Layer Style dialog box, enter **120** in the Depth box to increase the strength of the shading.

- Enter **15** in the Size box to increase the size of the Bevel (Figure 3–77).

3

- Tap or click the OK button to close the Layer Style dialog box and thus apply the layer style.

Experiment

- To view the difference that the adjustment has made, press CTRL+Z to undo the step and then press CTRL+Z again to redo the step.

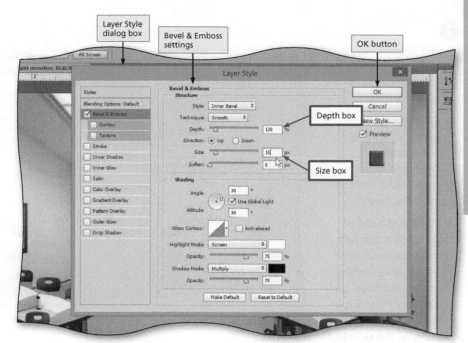

Figure 3–77

Other Ways

1. On Layer menu, tap or click Layer Style, tap or click desired style, edit settings in Layer Style dialog box, tap or click OK button

To Copy a Layer Style

The following steps copy the layer style to the other monitor.

1

- On the Layers panel, press and hold or right-click the right monitor layer style to display the context menu (Figure 3–78).

Q&A
My context menu looks different. Did I do something wrong?
No, depending on exactly where you tapped or clicked you may see more or fewer commands on the context menu.

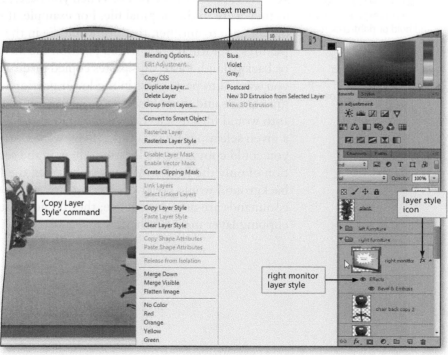

Figure 3–78

②

- Tap or click 'Copy Layer Style' to copy the layer style to the Clipboard.

- On the Layers panel, open the left furniture's layer group and then select the left monitor layer.

- Press and hold or right-click the left monitor layer to display the context menu and then tap or click 'Paste Layer Style' to apply the style to the selected layer (Figure 3–79).

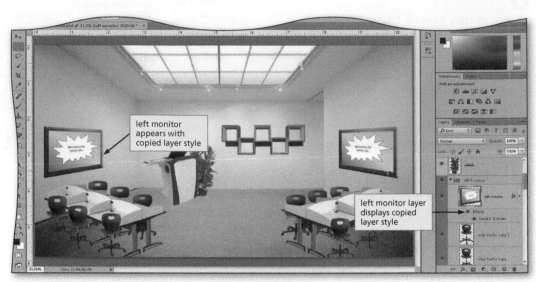

Figure 3–79

Specialized Paste Commands

BTW

Copying and Moving Layer Styles

To copy a layer style, press and hold or right-click the source layer and then tap or click 'Copy Layer Style' on the context menu. Press and hold or right-click the destination layer and then tap or click 'Paste Layer Style'. To move a layer style, drag the fx icon from one layer to another on the Layers panel.

In this and previous chapters you have used traditional copy and paste methods to copy images across documents and within documents. You also have copied and pasted layers and layer styles. Photoshop has three specialized paste commands to assist you with bringing in outside selections: Paste in Place, Paste Into and Paste Outside. Paste in Place pastes the copied pixels and remembers the horizontal and vertical location of the pixels. When you paste, the pixels appear in the exact location as they were in the original file. For example, if you were pasting a bird in flight from one picture to another, the bird would be in the exact same part of the sky on both pictures. A normal paste would position the bird in the middle of the selected layer or background. Paste Into pastes copied pixels into a given selection. For example, if you wanted to paste grass in the lower portion of a picture only, you would copy the grass pixels and then, in your new file, select the ground or dirt in the picture. Paste Into would fill the selection. Paste Outside copies the pixels to everywhere outside of a given selection. For example, if you wanted to show a person in an exotic location, you could copy a scenic location; then, in the second image, you would create a selection of only the person. When you selected the Paste Outside command, the scenic background would cover everything else except the person. The specialized paste commands are non-destructive; they do not destroy any other pixels. They create a clipping layer mask on the Layers panel.

To Paste Into

The following steps open a file named carpeting, copy it, and then use the Paste Into command to paste it into the Laptop Lab Edited image, in place of the gray flooring.

1

- Open the file named Carpeting from the Chapter 03 folder of the Data Files for Students.

- Press CTRL+A to select all of the carpeting. Press CTRL+C to copy.

- Return to the Laptop Lab Edited file. On the Layers panel, tap or click the visibility icon to hide the floor layer, and then select the Background layer.

- Use the Magic Wand Tool, with the Contiguous check box checked, to select the white portion of the background layer.

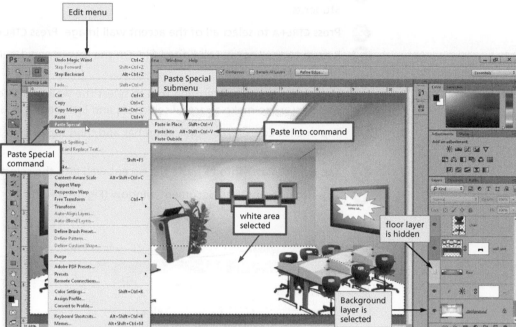

Figure 3–80

- Tap or click Edit on the Application bar and then tap or click Paste Special to display the submenu (Figure 3–80).

2

- Tap or click Paste Into to paste the carpeting pixels into the selection.

- Close the Carpeting document window (Figure 3–81).

Q&A

Could I have dragged the carpeting from one window to the other?

Dragging the carpeting would copy the pixels from one window to

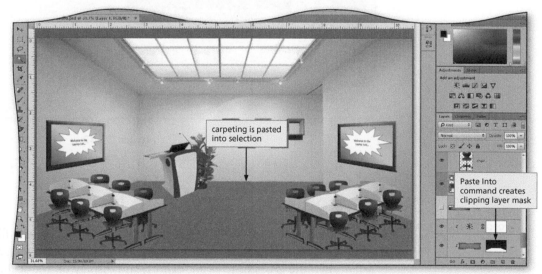

Figure 3–81

another, but the carpeting would not have filled the floor automatically. You would have had a lot of editing and cropping to do.

Other Ways

1. Copy pixels, create selection, press ALT+SHIFT+CTRL+V

To Paste Into Again

The following steps copy and paste pixels to create an accent wall.

1 Open the file named, Accent Wall from the Chapter 03 folder of the Data Files for Students.

2 Press CTRL+A to select all of the accent wall image. Press CTRL+C to copy it.

3 Return to the Laptop Lab Edited file. On the Layers panel, select the Background layer, if necessary.

4 Use the Rectangular Marquee Tool to select the wall in the center of the image. Zoom as necessary to make a careful selection, and include the entire wall.

5 Tap or click Edit on the Application bar and then tap or click Paste Special to display the submenu.

6 Tap or click Paste Into to paste the accent wall into the selection.

7 Close the Accent Wall document window (Figure 3–82).

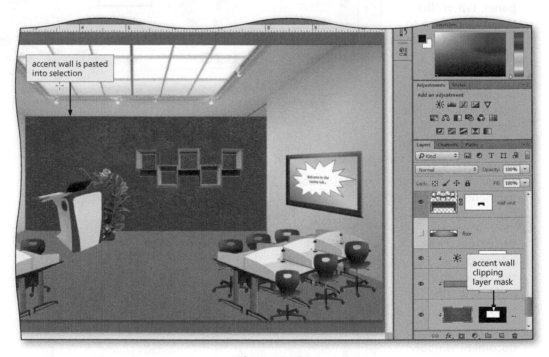

Figure 3–82

Certification
BTW

The Adobe Certified Expert (ACE) program provides an opportunity for you to obtain a valuable industry credential — proof that you have the Photoshop CC skills required by employers. For more information, visit the Certification resource on the Student Companion Site located on www.cengagebrain.com.

Flattening a Composite Image

When you **flatten** a composite image, Photoshop reduces the file size by merging all visible layers into the background, discarding hidden layers, and applying masks. A flattened file is easier to print, export, and display on the web. It is a good practice, however, to save the layered version in PSD format before flattening, in case you want to make further changes to the file. It is very important to remember that once a file is flattened and saved, no changes can be made to individual layers. If you flatten an image and then change your mind, if the file still is open, you can tap or click the previous state on the History panel to restore all of the layers.

If you want to save each layer as a separate file, tap or click File on the Application bar, tap or click Scripts, and then tap or click Export Layers to Files. This script is useful if you think you might want to use your layers in other composite images.

The Layer menu displays a Flatten Image command and has many of the same choices as the Layers panel menu. The choice of which to use is a matter of personal preference and the location of your pointer at the time. After saving the composite image, you will use the Layer menu to flatten the visible layers. Finally, you will save the flattened file in TIFF format with the name, Laptop Lab TIFF.

To Save the Composite Image Before Flattening

The following step saves the Laptop Lab Edited image with its layers.

1 Press CTRL+S to save the Laptop Lab Edited file with the same name.

To Flatten a Composite Image

The following steps use the Layer menu to flatten the composite image.

1

- Tap or click Layer on the Application bar to display the Layer menu (Figure 3–83).

Q&A What is the difference between flatten and merge?
The Merge command flattens specific layers together. The Flatten command uses all of the layers and merges into a Background layer.

Figure 3–83

2

• Tap or click Flatten Image on the Layer menu to combine all of the layers. If Photoshop displays a dialog box asking you to discard the hidden layers, tap or click the OK button (Figure 3–84).

image appears without layers

Figure 3–84

Other Ways

1. Press and hold or right-click any layer, tap or click Flatten Image
2. Tap or click Layers panel menu button, tap or click Flatten Image

To Save a File in the TIFF Format

The following steps save the flattened image as a TIFF file.

1 Tap or click File on the Application bar and then tap or click Save As.

2 When the Save As dialog box is displayed, type **Laptop Lab TIFF** in the File name text box. Do not press the ENTER key after typing the file name.

3 Tap or click the Format button and then tap or click TIFF (*.TIF; *TIFF) in the list.

4 Tap or click the Save button in the Save As dialog box.

5 When Photoshop displays the TIFF Options dialog box, tap or click the OK button to finish saving the file.

To Print the Laptop Lab TIFF Image

The following steps print a copy of the Laptop Lab TIFF image on the default printer. If you are unsure which printer is set as your default, use the Print command rather than the Print one Copy command so you can choose your printer.

1 Ready the printer according to the printer instructions.

2 Tap or click File on the Application bar and then tap or click 'Print One Copy' on the File menu to print the image on the default printer.

To Close the Document Window and Quit Photoshop

The final steps close the document window and quit Photoshop.

1 Tap or click the Close button on the document window tab.

2 If Photoshop displays a dialog box, tap or click the No button to ignore the changes since the last time you saved the photo.

3 Quit Photoshop.

BTW

Flash Cards
The Student Companion Site has interactive flash cards of the important concepts in each chapter. For detailed instructions about accessing available resources, visit solutions. cengage.com/ctdownloads or contact your instructor for information about the flash cards.

Chapter Summary

In virtually designing a computer lab, you gained a broad knowledge of Photoshop's layering capabilities. First, you were introduced to the concept of layers. You created a layer via cut, a layer from another image, and a layer from a selection, using the Layers panel to set options, select, rename, color, view, and hide layers. You then used the eraser tools to erase unneeded portions of a layer. You learned how to hide portions of layers and fine-tune layers with layer masks, adjustments, and styles. Finally, you used the Paste Into command to add carpeting and an accent wall into the composite image. The file was flattened and saved in the TIFF format.

The items listed below include all the new Photoshop skills you have learned in this chapter:

1. Change Layers Panel Options (PS 145)
2. Create a Layer via Cut (PS 146)
3. Rename a Layer (PS 148)
4. Assign a Color to a Layer (PS 149)
5. Hide and Show a Layer (PS 150)
6. Arrange the Document Windows (PS 153)
7. Create a Layer by Dragging an Entire Image (PS 154)
8. Move a Layer in the Document Window (PS 154)
9. Create a Layer by Dragging a Selection (PS 157)
10. Duplicate a Layer (PS 159)
11. Align a Layer using Smart Guides (PS 160)
12. Create a New Empty Layer Group (PS 161)
13. Create a Layer Group from Layers (PS 162)
14. Create a New Empty Layer Group (PS 163)
15. Open the Layer Group (PS 163)
16. Transform by Placing and Scaling (PS 167)
17. Transform by Changing the Perspective (PS 167)
18. Transform by Flipping and Skewing (PS 169)
19. Reorder Layers (PS 171)
20. Erase using the Eraser Tool (PS 175)
21. Erase using the Block Mode (PS 176)
22. Erase using the Magic Eraser Tool (PS 177)
23. Display Only the Current Layer (PS 179)
24. Erase using the Background Eraser Tool (PS 180)
25. Correct a Masking Error (PS 183)
26. Create a Layer Mask (PS 184)
27. Correct a Masking Error (PS 185)
28. Make an Opacity Change to a Layer (PS 186)
29. Create a Levels Adjustment Layer (PS 187)
30. Adjust the Color Balance (PS 191)
31. Adjust the Brightness and Contrast (PS 192)
32. Apply a Bevel Layer Style (PS 194)
33. Copy a Layer Style (PS 195)
34. Paste Into (PS 197)
35. Flatten a Composite Image (PS 199)

Apply Your Knowledge

Reinforce the skills and apply the concepts you learned in this chapter.

Creating Layers

Note: To complete this assignment, you will be required to use the Data Files for Students. Visit solutions.cengage.com/ctdownloads for detailed instructions or contact your instructor for information about accessing the required files.

Instructions: Start Photoshop and perform the customization steps found on pages PS 6 through PS 11. Open the Apply 3-1 House file from the Chapter 03 folder of the Data Files for Students. The purpose of this exercise is to create a composite image of what a new house might look like with landscaping. The edited photo is displayed in Figure 3–85 on the next page.

Continued >

Apply Your Knowledge *continued*

Courtesy of Fred Starks

Figure 3–85

Perform the following tasks:

1. Press SHIFT+CTRL+S to open the Save As dialog box. Enter the name, **Apply 3-1 House Composite**, and save in your storage location in the PSD format. Table 3–6 lists the other files, layer names, identification colors, and manipulations that you will use in this assignment.

Table 3–6 Landscaping Files and Layers

File Name	Layer Name	Layer Color	Layer Manipulations
Apply 3-1 House	Background		
Apply 3-1 Flowerbed	flowerbed	Red	Drag and drop image.
Apply 3-1 Tree	tree	Violet	Drag entire image and then use eraser tools.
Apply 3-1 Bush	bush	Orange	Use shortcut keys to copy and paste image. Add layer mask to remove pot.
Apply 3-1 Lion	lion	Gray	Copy and paste image. Add a layer style.
Apply 3-1 Clouds	sky	Blue	Paste into selection. Add an adjustment layer.
Apply 3-1 Grass	grass	Green	Paste into selection. Add an adjustment layer.

© Cengage Learning

2. To create the flowerbed layer:
   a. Press CTRL+O to display the Open dialog box. Navigate to the Data Files for Students and then double-tap or double-click the file named Apply 3-1 Flowerbed to open it.
   b. On the Application bar, tap or click Window, tap or click Arrange, and then tap or click 2-up Horizontal to arrange the document windows.
   c. Select the Move Tool. Drag the flowerbed image into the Apply 3-1 House Composite document window. Close the Apply 3-1 Flowerbed file.
   d. Name and color the layer as directed in Table 3-6.
   e. Resize the flowerbed and position it as shown in Figure 3–85.

3. To create the tree layer:

   a. Press CTRL+O to display the Open dialog box. Navigate to the Data Files for Students and open the file named Apply 3-1 Tree.

   b. On the Application bar, tap or click Window, tap or click Arrange to display the Arrange submenu, and then tap or click 2-up Horizontal to arrange the document windows.

   c. Select the Move Tool, if necessary. Drag the entire tree image into the Apply 3-1 House Composite document window. (*Hint:* no selection is necessary.) Close the Apply 3-1 Tree file.

   d. Name and color the layer as directed in Table 3-6.

   e. Select the Magic Eraser Tool. On the options bar, tap or click to remove the check box in the Contiguous check box. In the document window, tap or click the blue sky and the clouds.

   f. Select the Eraser Tool. Erase the grass and bushes. Use the LEFT BRACKET ([) or RIGHT BRACKET (]) keys to adjust the size of the eraser. (*Hint:* do not erase within the branches of the tree.) Zoom as necessary.

   g. Select the Background Eraser Tool. On the options bar, tap or click the Sampling: Once button. If necessary, tap or click the Limits button and then choose Discontiguous. Type 24 in the Tolerance box. In the document window, press and hold over the remaining grass that displays among the lower branches of the tree. Drag to erase.

   h. Resize the tree, if necessary, by pressing CTRL+T and SHIFT+dragging a corner sizing handle. Position the tree as shown in Figure 3–85.

4. To create the bush layers:

   a. Open the file named Apply 3-1 Bush.

   b. Use the Magic Wand tool to select the contiguous white area. Press SHIFT+CTRL+I to select the inverse. Press CTRL+C to copy the bush and its pot. Close the Apply 3-1 Bush file.

   c. In the Apply 3-1 House Composite window, press CTRL+V to insert the copied image.

   d. Name and color the layer.

   e. On the Layers panel status bar, tap or click the 'Add layer mask' button. Press the B key to activate the brush. Drag to mask the pot. Use the LEFT BRACKET ([) or RIGHT BRACKET (]) keys to adjust the size of the brush.

   f. Press CTRL+T to display the transformation bounding box. SHIFT+drag a corner sizing handle until the bush is approximately .5 inches wide. Press the ENTER key to commit the transformation.

   g. Position the bush layer as shown in Figure 3–85. CTRL+drag to create another copy and position it as shown in Figure 3–85.

5. To create the lion layers:

   a. Open the file named Apply 3-1 Lion. Press CTRL+A to select the entire image. Press CTRL+C to copy the image to the Clipboard. Paste the image into the Apply 3-1 House Composite document window. Close the Apply 3-1 Lion file.

   b. Name and color the layer.

   c. On the Layers panel status bar, tap or click the 'Add a layer style' button, and then tap or click Drop Shadow. In the Layer Style dialog box, drag the Distance slider to 5. Drag the Size slider to 5.

   d. Resize the lion, if necessary, and position it as shown in Figure 3–85. ALT+drag to create another copy and position it as shown in Figure 3–85.

Continued >

Apply Your Knowledge *continued*

6. To create the clouds:

   a. Open the file named Apply 3-1 Clouds. Select all and copy. Close the Apply 3-1 Clouds file.

   b. In the Apply 3-1 House Composite, ALT+tap or ALT+click the visibility icon on the Background layer to hide all of the other layers.

   c. Select the Magic Wand Tool. On the options bar, tap or click the 'Add to selection' button. Change the Tolerance setting to 15. If necessary, tap or click to display a check mark in the Contiguous check box. Tap or click the sky to select it. If any portion of the sky is not in the selection, tap or click it.

   d. Tap or click Edit on the Application bar, tap or click Paste Special, and then tap or click Paste Into to paste the clouds into the sky layer.

   e. On the Adjustments panel, tap or click the Levels icon and then tap or click the 'Clip to Layer' button. Adjust the gray slider to 2.76 to match the highest point in the histogram. Adjust the white slider to approximately 153 so that the sky better fits the scene.

   f. Tap or click the Properties button in the vertical dock to collapse the panel.

   g. Name and color the layer.

7. To create the grass layer:

   a. Open the file named Apply 3-1 Grass. Select all and copy. Close the file.

   b. If necessary, in the Apply 3-1 Composite document, ALT+tap or ALT+click the Background layer visibility icon to hide all the layers except the Background layer. Select the Background layer. Select the Quick Selection Tool. Carefully select only the three areas of dirt in the picture. If you make a mistake, press CTRL+Z and select again.

   c. With the dirt still selected in the document window, tap or click the visibility icon on the grass layer, and tap or click the grass layer itself. Use the Paste Special command, Paste Into, to insert the grass into the selection.

   d. Name and color the layer.

8. Save the file again by pressing CTRL+S.

9. On the Layers panel, tap or click the Layers panel menu button to display the menu. Tap or click Flatten Image on the menu to flatten all of the layers.

10. Press SHIFT+CTRL+S to open the Save As dialog box. Type **Apply 3-1 House Complete** in the Name box. Tap or click the Format button and then tap or click TIFF in the list. Tap or click the Save button. If Photoshop displays a dialog box, tap or click the OK button.

11. Turn in a hard copy of the photo to your instructor.

12. Quit Photoshop.

Extend Your Knowledge

Extend the skills you learned in this chapter and experiment with new skills. You may need to use Help to complete the assignment.

Exploring Layer Comps

Note: To complete this assignment, you will be required to use the Data Files for Students. Visit solutions.cengage.com/ctdownloads for detailed instructions or contact your instructor for information about accessing the required files.

Instructions: Start Photoshop and perform the customization steps found on pages PS 6 through PS 11. Open the file Extend 3-1 Marketing Graphic from the Chapter 03 folder of the Data Files for Students.

The purpose of this exercise is to create layer comps of a product box for client evaluation. The current graphic has layers for the background, inside, and outside of the box. You are to insert the trophy graphic and scale it to fit the box, then create layer comps showing the inside and the outside. The edited photo is shown in Figure 3–86.

Perform the following tasks:

1. Save the file with the name, Extend 3-1 Marketing Graphic Composite, on your storage location, in the PSD format.

2. Show and hide the various layers using the visibility icon to gain familiarity with the graphic.

3. Make the Background layer and inside layer visible; hide all other layers. Select the inside layer.

4. Open the Extend 3-1 Trophy file from the Chapter 03 folder of the Data Files for Students. Arrange the windows side by side.

5. Use the Move Tool to drag the trophy from its own window into the Extend 3-1 Marketing Graphic Composite document window. Scale the trophy to fit in the box. Make the outside layer visible and make sure the trophy can be seen through the opening in the outer box. Name the layer, trophy.

6. Make the front panel layer visible and select it. At the top of the Layers panel, adjust the Fill setting so the layer looks more transparent, as if it were plastic.

7. Make the gleam layer visible. Adjust the Opacity and Fill settings as necessary to make the layer more transparent as shown in Figure 3–86. Save the file.

8. Use Photoshop Help to learn about layer comps. Also read the BTW boxes on pages PS 143 and PS 144. Open the Layer Comps panel and create the layer comps described in Table 3–7.

9. Save the file again.

10. For extra credit, copy the trophy layer and scale it to approximately 30 percent of its original size. In the Layers panel, move the trophy layer copy above the outside layer. Position the trophy in the lower-middle portion of the box. Warp the layer to make it wrap around the corner of the box. Create a layer comp named Complete with Wrapped Logo and include all layers.

11. Submit this assignment in the format specified by your instructor.

Figure 3–86

Continued >

Extend Your Knowledge *continued*

Table 3–7 Marketing Graphic Layer Comps	
Layer Comp Name	**Visible Layers**
Empty Box	Background, inside
Inner Box with Trophy	Background, inside, trophy
Outer Box with Trophy	Background, inside, trophy, outside, shadow
Complete Graphic	All layers

© Cengage Learning

Make It Right

Analyze a project and correct all errors and/or improve the design.

Correcting Layer Errors

Note: To complete this assignment, you will be required to use the Data Files for Students. Visit solutions.cengage.com/ctdownloads for detailed instructions or contact your instructor for information about accessing the required files.

Instructions: Start Photoshop and perform the customization steps found on pages PS 6 through PS 11. Open the Make It Right 3-1 Park file from the Chapter 03 folder of the Data Files for Students. The photo has layers that are invisible, layers that need transformation, and layers that need to be moved, trimmed, and adjusted for levels (Figure 3–87).

Perform the following tasks:
Save the file on your storage device in the PSD format with the name, Make It Right 3-1 Park Composite. For each invisible layer, reveal the layer, correct any order problem by dragging the layer to an appropriate position on the Layers panel, erase or mask parts of the layer as necessary, and move the layer to a logical position in the document window.

　　Use the Adjustments panel and tools such as Levels, Brightness/Contrast, and Hue/ Saturation to create adjustment layers. (*Hint:* be sure to tap or click the 'Clip to Layer' button on the Adjustments panel status bar, so the adjustment will apply to that layer only.) Make any other adjustments or layer style changes that you deem necessary. Save the file again and submit it in the format specified by your instructor.

Figure 3–87

Courtesy of Fred Starks

In the Labs

Design and/or create a project using the guidelines, concepts, and skills presented in this chapter. Labs are listed in order of increasing difficulty.

Lab 1: Creating Layer Groups and Adjustments

Note: To complete this assignment, you will be required to use the Data Files for Students. Visit solutions.cengage.com/ctdownloads for detailed instructions or contact your instructor for information about accessing the required files.

Problem: Your friend has started a picture collage of his past three vacations, but he needs your help in organizing the layers adding some special effects. The final result is displayed in Figure 3–88.

Instructions: Perform the following tasks:

1. Start Photoshop. Set the default workspace, default colors, and reset all tools.

2. Open the file named Lab 3-1 Vacation Collage from the Chapter 03 folder of the Data Files for Students.

3. Tap or click View on the Application bar and then tap or click 'Fit on Screen' to view the entire image at the largest possible magnification.

4. Tap or click the Save As command on the File menu. Type **Lab 3-1 Vacation Collage Complete** as the file name. If necessary, tap or click the Format button and then tap or click PSD in the list. Browse to your storage location. Tap or click the Save button. If Photoshop displays a Format Options dialog box, tap or click the OK button.

5. On the Layers panel, tap or click the Florida flamingos layer. CTRL+tap or CTRL+click the Florida palm tree layer. CTRL+tap or CTRL+click the Florida park layer. Tap or click the Layers panel menu button and then tap or click the 'New Group from Layers' command. Name the layer group Florida and use a blue identification color.

6. On the Layers panel, tap or click the Arizona scene layer. CTRL+tap or CTRL+click the other two Arizona layers. Tap or click the Layers panel menu button and then tap or click the 'New Group from Layers' command. Name the layer group Arizona and use a violet identification color.

Courtesy of Fred Starks and David Reneau

Continued >

Figure 3–88

In the Labs *continued*

7. Create a final layer group from the three Indiana layers, using a green identification color.

8. On the Layers panel, tap or click the Indiana layer group. On the Adjustments panel, tap or click the Black and White adjustment. In the adjustment status bar, tap or click the 'Clip to Layer' button. Accept all of the default values. Tap or click the Properties button to close the adjustment.

9. On the Layers panel, tap or click the Florida layer group. Tap or click the 'Add a layer style' button on the Layers panel status bar, and then tap or click Stroke. When the Layer Style dialog box is displayed, type **8** in the Size box, and then tap or click the OK button.

10. On the Layers panel, tap or click the Arizona layer group. Drag the Opacity scrubby slider to 75%.

11. When you are satisfied with your layers and adjustments, save the file again.

12. Submit the assignment in the format specified by your instructor.

Lab 2: Transforming Layers

Note: To complete this assignment, you will be required to use the Data Files for Students. Visit solutions.cengage.com/ctdownloads for detailed instructions or contact your instructor for information about accessing the required files.

Problem: Your graphics design teacher has asked you to create a document that she can use in her beginning classes to illustrate the various transformation effects, similar to Figure 3–34 on page PS 163. She has provided you with a file that contains a layer of flowers. You are to create the document with images as shown in Figure 3–89.

Instructions: Perform the following tasks:

1. Start Photoshop. Perform the customization steps found on pages PS 6 through PS 11.

2. Open the Lab 3-2 Handout from the Chapter 03 folder of the Data Files for Students and save it in your storage location with the file name Lab 3-2 Handout Composite.

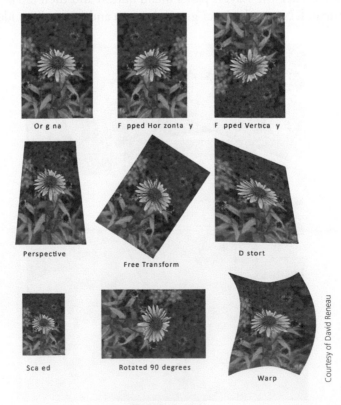

Courtesy of David Reneau

Figure 3–89

3. Tap or click the original flowers layer. Select the Move Tool. In the document window, ALT+drag to create a copy next to the original.

4. Press CTRL+T to display the transformation bounding box. Press and hold or right-click the selection to display the context menu. Tap or click Flip Horizontal. Rename the layer, flowers flip horizontally.

5. Tap or click the text layer, named Original. Select the Move Tool. In the document window, ALT+drag to create a copy and position it under the flipped flowers.

6. Press the T key to activate the Horizontal Text Tool. Tap or click the copied text, and then press CTRL+A to select all of the text. Type **Flipped Horizontally** to replace the text. If necessary, resize the text box so the text fits on one line.

7. Repeat Steps 3 through 6 to create the flowers flipped vertically.

8. Repeat Steps 3 through 6 to create the flowers using the Perspective transformation.

9. Repeat Steps 3 through 6 to create the flowers using the Free Transform command on the selection's context menu.

10. Repeat Steps 3 through 6 to create the flowers using the Distort transformation.

11. Repeat Steps 3 through 6 to create the flowers scaled smaller.

12. Repeat Steps 3 through 6 to create the flowers rotated 90 degrees.

13. Repeat Steps 3 through 6 to create the flowers using the Warp transformation. Drag several points during the warp process. Your warp does not have to match Figure 3–89.

14. Save the composite file again with all the layers.

15. See your instructor for ways to submit this assignment and then quit Photoshop.

Lab 3: **Creating a Contest Entry with Layers**

Note: To complete this assignment, you will be required to use the Data Files for Students. Visit solutions.cengage.com/ctdownloads for detailed instructions or contact your instructor for information about accessing the required files.

Problem: You would like to enter your hamster in a creative pet photo contest. You decide to use Photoshop's layering capabilities to dress up your hamster, as shown in Figure 3–90.

Instructions: Perform the following tasks:

Start Photoshop. Perform the customization steps found on pages PS 6 through PS 11. Open the file Lab 3-3 Hamster from the Chapter 03 folder of the Data Files for Students. Rename the file, Lab 3-3 Hamster Composite and save it as a PSD file in your storage location.

Figure 3–90

Continued >

In the Labs *continued*

Open the Lab 3-3 Pipe file, arrange the windows, and then drag a copy to the Lab 3-3 Hamster Composite window. Set the layer properties (name and color). Close the Lab 3-3 Pipe document window. Remove the background around the pipe. Scale and position the layer as necessary. Adjust the perspective. Repeat the process for the Lab 3-3 Magnifying Glass file. Reposition the layers as necessary.

Repeat the process for the Lab 3-3 Hat file, scaling the layer as necessary, and place it on top of the hamster's head. Select the right third (back) of the hat and create a layer via cut. On the Layers panel, set the properties and move the back of hat layer, below the hamster layer, so that part of the hat appears behind the hamster's ear.

Make any other adjustments to the layers that you feel would enhance the photo. When you are satisfied with your layers, save the image again. Flatten the image, save it as a TIFF file, and submit a copy to your instructor.

Cases and Places

Apply your creative thinking and problem-solving skills to design and implement a solution.

Note: To complete this assignment, you will be required to use the Data Files for Students. Visit solutions.cengage.com/ctdownloads for detailed instructions or contact your instructor for information about accessing the required files.

1: Create a Graphic with Opacity Changes

Academic

Earlier in this chapter, a suggestion was made to create a flag with 50 percent opacity superimposed over a memorial. Open the files named Case 3-1 Memorial and Case 3-1 Flag, located in the Chapter 03 folder of the Data Files for Students. (Alternately, locate or take a photo of a memorial in your city or a building on your campus. If necessary, obtain permission to use a digital photo or scan the image.) Arrange the windows. Select only the flag and then drag it as a new layer into the memorial photo. Resize the layer to fit across the memorial. Change the flag opacity to 50 percent. Make other corrections as necessary. Save the composite photo and print a copy. Save the file in the TIFF format with the file name Case 3-1 Memorial with Flag.

2: Creating Layers and Effects

Personal

You decide to recreate the Desserts graphic from Chapter 2, this time using layers. Open the photo named Desserts from the Chapter 02 folder in the Data Files for Students. One at a time, select each dessert, and then use the 'Layer via Cut' command to create each dessert on its on layer. Use the eraser tools as necessary. Name and color each layer appropriately. Add a clipped layer adjustment or layer style to each layer to improve the way it looks. If your instructor asks you to do so, write a short paragraph about why you chose each adjustment or style. In the document window, move the layers to create a group for an advertisement. Adjust the front-to-back layering using the Layers panel. Do not flatten. Save the file as Case 3-2 Desserts Edited.

3: Create a Greeting Card Graphic with Masking

Professional

You have been hired as an intern with a greeting card company. You were given several photos to use in preparing holiday cards. The file named Case 3-3 Santa Scene is located in the Chapter 03 folder of the Data Files for Students. You want to use only the figure of Santa Claus on the front of a card. Save the photo in the PSD format on your storage device as Case 3-3 Santa Layered. Create a rectangular marquee selection around the figure. Use the 'Layer Via Cut' command and name the new layer, Santa. Hide the background. Create a layer mask, painting with black to display only the figure. Print the photo with the background hidden.

Ps File Edit Image Layer Type Select Filter 3D View Window Help

Adobe **Photoshop CC** Feather: 0 px   Anti-alias   Style: Normal   Width: Height: Refine Edge...

4 | Drawing and Painting with Color

Objectives

You will have mastered the material in this chapter when you can:

- Create a Photoshop document from scratch using the Painting workspace
- Differentiate between color modes
- Apply gradients using the Gradient Tool
- Create smart objects
- Select colors using the Swatches panel
- Paint and draw using Photoshop brushes
- Adjust the hardness and diameter settings of brushes

- Append brush libraries
- Use a Color Picker dialog box
- Differentiate among the shape tools, modes, and settings
- Create a shape
- Sample colors with the Eyedropper Tool
- Format text with advanced character features
- Change spacing between paragraphs

Ps File Edit Image Layer Type Select Filter 3D View Window Help

Adobe **Photoshop CC** Feather: 0 px Anti-alias Style: Normal Width: Height: Refine Edge...

4 | Drawing and Painting with Color

Introduction

In both academic and business environments, you will be called upon to create graphics from scratch using the tools and techniques available in Photoshop. While many sources of graphics, such as clip art and stock photos, are widely available, some are copyrighted, rights-controlled, or expensive to buy. Others have to be edited so extensively that it might be easier to start from scratch. Still others simply do not fit the particular circumstances for the required project. By creating an original graphic, you solve many of the problems that result when attempting to use ready-made images. Using basic design principles and the vast array of drawing tools available in Photoshop, along with an input device such as a graphics tablet or stylus, the kinds of graphics you can create are unlimited.

Another way to design graphics is to start from scratch and add images that are digital photographs or scans. That way, your image has the best of both worlds — combining the texture and lines of drawing with the realism of actual photographs. In Photoshop, working from scratch to create an image or illustration is more successful when the subject is conceptual, imaginative, less formal, or open to interpretation. Beginning with a digital photo is better when the subject is living, tangible, for sale, or more formal; photography does not risk loss of meaning through interpretation. Regardless of the approach you choose, you need to know how to use the drawing and painting tools in Photoshop.

Project — Creating a Poster

Chapter 4 uses Photoshop to create a science poster for an elementary-level classroom. The poster incorporates brush strokes, text, a gradient, a graphic, and other shapes. The completed image appears in Figure 4–1. Nearly all posters, magazines, and catalogs on the market today are full-color, and are printed using a four-color process (CMYK) that provides bright color shades and an eye-catching look. CMYK is an acronym for the four-color process used in printing: cyan, magenta, yellow, and black. You will use colors from the CMYK color mode.

Posters commonly are placed on a wall or used outdoors in large venues, so it is important to use large text. People sometimes see posters while driving or walking by; therefore, eye-catching graphics and straight-to-the-point messages are essential.

Overview

As you read this chapter, you will learn how to create the poster shown in Figure 4–1 by performing these general tasks:

- Create a new file, starting with a blank canvas.
- Apply a gradient background.

Figure 4–1

- Choose colors using a variety of tools and dialog boxes.
- Combine real images with drawn images.
- Use brushes to draw and paint.
- Create shapes.
- Format characters and paragraphs with advanced features.

General Project Guidelines

When editing a photo, the actions you perform and decisions you make will affect the appearance and characteristics of the finished product. As you create a poster, such as the one shown in Figure 4–1, you should follow these general guidelines:

1. **Plan your layout and gather necessary photos.** As you plan your layout of original graphics, create the storyboard and the graphic from the back to the front. Decide on the background first, then layers, followed by foreground objects or text. The graphics you choose should convey the overall message, incorporating high-quality photos with similar lighting characteristics. Keep in mind the customer requirements. For professional-looking graphics, adhere to the general principles of alignment, contrast, repetition, and proximity.

Plan Ahead

Continued >

Converting Between Modes
In Photoshop, you easily can convert from one color mode to another using the Mode command on the Image menu. As you choose a new color mode, Photoshop will inform you of any problems converting the image.

2. **Choose colors purposefully.** Consider the cost of full-color printing, paper, shelf life, and customer requirements when choosing your colors. **Shelf life** refers to how long the publication remains useful and nondated. Try to repeat colors that already exist in incorporated images. Some clients already may have colors that help brand their publications. Consult with the client and print shops for the correct color numbers and the plan for printing. Unless you need a rainbow special effect, limit your colors to two or three on a contrasting background.

3. **Use predefined shapes for tangible objects.** Use shapes rather than freehand drawings when you are trying to create a graphic that represents a tangible object. Shapes allow you to maintain straight lines, create even corners, use constrained proportions, and edit curves. Except when intentionally creating a randomized pattern, try to align shapes with something else in the graphic, or parallel to the edge of the publication.

4. **Design your brush strokes.** Photoshop brushes imitate the actions of artistic paintbrushes. By varying the settings, such as tip shape, hardness, and so on, you can add creative effects to your work.

5. **Use type wisely.** Although many graphics include type or text as a means to educate and inform, text often becomes a creative element itself in the design. The first rule of type is to choose a font that is easy to read. No matter how creative the font style is, if the customer cannot make out the words, the message fails. Avoid using more than two different fonts on the same page or graphic. As a second font, use either the same font at a different size or a highly contrasting font. Keep similar text components in proximity to each other. For example, do not split the address, telephone number, and webpage address onto different parts of the page. Use a stroke of color around the text for a more distinctive look that stands out.

When necessary, more specific details concerning the preceding guidelines are presented at appropriate points in the chapter. The chapter also will identify the actions performed and decisions made regarding these guidelines during the creation of the edited composite image in Figure 4–1 on the previous page.

Composite Images
Photoshop documents that combine drawing and painting effects with photographs and other elements are sometimes called composite images, or comps.

Indexed Color
When converting to Indexed color, Photoshop builds a **color lookup table (CLUT)**, which stores and indexes the colors in the image. If a color in the original image does not appear in the table, Photoshop chooses the closest one, or dithers the available colors, to simulate the color. Indexed color mode therefore limits the panel of colors to reduce file size yet maintain visual quality.

Creating a New File

In this chapter, you will create a new Photoshop document starting with a blank canvas. Photoshop allows you to customize the attributes of file name, image size, resolution, color mode, and background when creating a new document image. Alternatively, Photoshop provides several groups of attributes that are preset. The new image size can be set in pixels, inches, or centimeters, among other units. You can set the width and height independently. When setting the resolution of an image, you specify the number of **pixels per inch** (**ppi**), or **pixels per centimeter** (**ppc**), on the printed page.

A **color mode**, or **color method**, determines the number of colors and combinations of colors used to display and print the image. Each color mode incorporates a numerical method called a **color model** or **color space** to describe the color. Photoshop bases its color modes on the color models that are commonly used when publishing images. Color modes also directly affect the file size of an image. As you will learn in this chapter, choosing a color mode determines which Photoshop tools and file formats are available.

When choosing a color mode, you must take into consideration many factors, including purpose, printing options, file size, number of colors, and layers that may be flattened in later conversions between color modes. Common color modes include RGB, CMYK, Lab, Indexed, and Grayscale, among others. See the Graphic Design Overview Appendix for more details about each of the color modes.

RGB (red, green, blue) is an additive color mode because its colors are created by adding together different wavelengths of light in various intensities. Also called **24-bit color**, RGB color mode is used typically for images that are reproduced on monitors, projectors, slides, transparencies, and the web.

CMYK (cyan, magenta, yellow, black) is a subtractive color mode because its colors are created when light strikes an object or image and the wavelengths are absorbed. Also called the **four-color process**, the CMYK color mode is used by most desktop printers and commercial printing businesses.

A **gamut**, or **color gamut**, is the range of printed or displayed colors. The color gamut on your monitor might not be the same as on your printer. For example, the RGB color mode displays a wider range of discernible colors than does CMYK. When you print an RGB image from your monitor, it must be reproduced with CMYK inks on your printer. The gamut of reproducible ink colors is smaller than what we see with our eyes, and any color that cannot be printed is referred to as **out of gamut**. In Photoshop, you will see an out of gamut warning if you select colors that have to be converted from RGB to CMYK.

Once you choose a color mode, you also can set a bit depth. The **bit depth**, also called **pixel depth** or **color depth**, measures how much color information is available for displaying or printing each pixel in an image. The word **bit** stands for binary digit. A bit depth of eight means that Photoshop assigns eight binary settings for each color.

Photoshop's **color management system (CMS)** translates colors from the color space of one device into a device-independent color space. The process is called **color mapping** or **gamut mapping**.

To Start Photoshop

If you are stepping through this project on a computer and you want your screen to match the figures in this book, then you should change your computer's resolution to 1366 × 768 and reset the panels, tools, and colors. For more information about how to change the resolution on your computer and other advanced Photoshop settings, read the Editing Preferences Appendix.

The following steps, which assume Windows 8 is running, start Photoshop based on a typical installation. You may need to ask your instructor how to start Photoshop for your system.

1 With Windows 8 running, scroll to display the Adobe Photoshop CC tile on the Start screen.

2 Tap or click the Adobe Photoshop CC tile to run the Photoshop app.

3 After a few moments, when the Photoshop window appears, if the window is not maximized, tap or click the Maximize button next to the Close button on the Application bar to maximize the window.

BTW

Lab Color
Three basic parameters make up the Lab color mode. First, the lightness of the color is measured from 0 (indicating black) to 100 (indicating white). The second parameter represents the color's position between magenta and green — negative values indicate green, whereas positive values indicate magenta. Finally, the third parameter indicates a color's position between yellow and blue — negative values indicate blue, whereas positive values indicate yellow.

To Reset the Tools and the Options Bar

Recall that the Tools panel and the options bar retain their settings from previous Photoshop sessions. The following steps select the Rectangular Marquee Tool and reset all tool settings in the options bar.

1 If the tools on the Tools panel appear in two columns, tap or click the double arrow at the top of the Tools panel.

2 Tap or click the 'Rectangular Marquee Tool' button on the Tools panel to select it.

3 On the options bar, press and hold or right-click the 'Rectangular Marquee Tool' icon to display the context menu, and then tap or click 'Reset All Tools'. When Photoshop displays a confirmation dialog box, tap or click the OK button to restore the tools to their default settings.

To Set the Interface and Default Colors

Recall that Photoshop retains the interface color scheme, as well as the foreground and background colors from session to session. The following steps set the interface to Medium Gray and reset foreground and background colors.

1 Tap or click Edit on the Application bar to display the Edit menu. Tap or click Preferences and then tap or click Interface on the Preferences submenu to display the Preferences dialog box.

2 If necessary, tap or click the third button, Medium Gray, to change the interface color.

3 Tap or click the OK button to close the Preferences dialog box.

4 Press the D key to set the default colors to black and white. If black is not over white on the Tools panel, press the X key.

To Select the Painting Workspace

The Painting workspace displays the Brush Presets, Swatches, and Layers panels, open and on top of their panel groupings. Later in the chapter, this workspace will be helpful when choosing brushes and colors. The following steps select the Painting workspace.

1

• Tap or click the workspace switcher on the Application bar, to display the list of stored workspaces (Figure 4–2).

Experiment

• Tap or click different workspaces to see how the panels and layout change. When you are finished, display the list again.

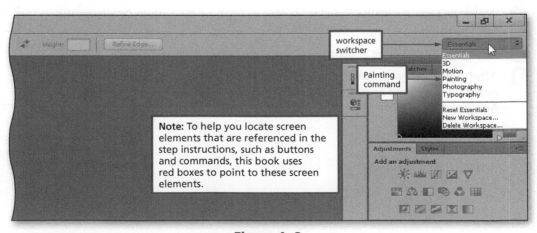

Figure 4–2

2

- Tap or click Painting on the Workspace switcher menu to choose the Painting workspace (Figure 4–3).

Q&A What kind of changes will I notice in the workspace?
You should see a different set of panels along the right side of the workspace.

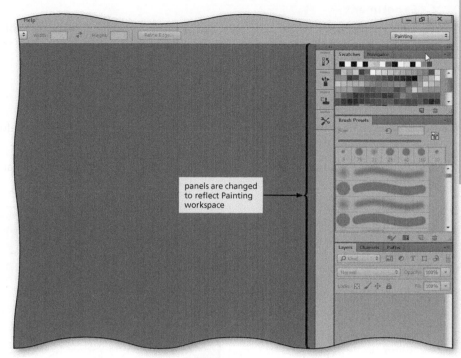

panels are changed to reflect Painting workspace

Figure 4–3

Other Ways

1. Tap or click Window on Application bar, tap or click Workspace, tap or click Painting

To Start a New Photoshop File

In a real business situation, the printing of the poster would be outsourced to a print shop for printing on paper that is 24 × 36 inches; therefore, you will use that size canvas. Because the graphic will be printed professionally, rather than used on the web, the color mode will be CMYK and the bit depth will be 8. The resolution will be 150 pixels per inch (ppi). Recall that resolution refers to the number of pixels per inch, printed on a page or displayed on a monitor. The background will be transparent at the beginning of the design process.

The following steps use the New command on the File menu and set the attributes for a new document image.

1

- Tap or click File on the Application bar, and then tap or click New to display the New dialog box.

- Type **Poster** in the Name box to replace the default name.

- If necessary, tap or click the Preset button, and then tap or click Custom in the list.

- Tap or click the Width button to display the list of units (Figure 4–4).

Q&A My settings are different. Did I do something wrong?
No, your settings might differ. Photoshop imports the settings from the last copy function performed on your system, in case you want to create a new file from something you copied to the Clipboard.

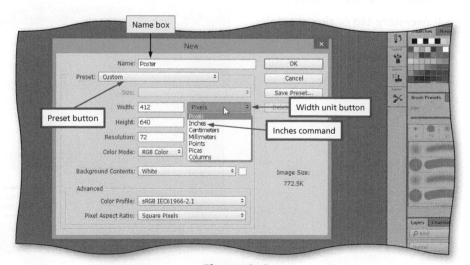

Figure 4–4

Ⓟ **Experiment**

- Tap or click the Preset button, and then tap or click one of the preset sizes. Notice how the width, height, and other settings change. When you are finished, tap or click the Preset button, and then tap or click Custom.

2

- Tap or click Inches in the list to select Inches as the unit of measure.

- Double-tap or double-click the Width box, and then type 24 to enter a value of 24 inches wide.

- Double-tap or double-click the Height box, and then type 36 to enter a value of 36 inches high.

- Double-tap or double-click the value in the Resolution box, and then type 150 to enter the resolution.

- Tap or click the Color Mode button to display its list (Figure 4–5).

Q&A Why are we using 150 in the resolution box?

At higher resolutions, the file size becomes very large, without adding very much quality. For example, if you change the resolution to 300, this poster file size would be more than 300 megabytes.

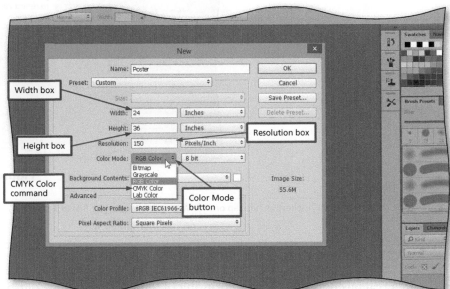

Figure 4–5

3

- Tap or click CMYK Color in the list to choose the CMYK Color mode.

- If necessary, tap or click the Color Mode unit button, and then tap or click 8 bit in the list.

- Tap or click the Background Contents button to display the available backgrounds (Figure 4–6).

Q&A My screen shows Advanced settings. Do I need to edit those settings?

No. The Advanced Options area displays settings for color profile and aspect ratios. You will leave those at their default values.

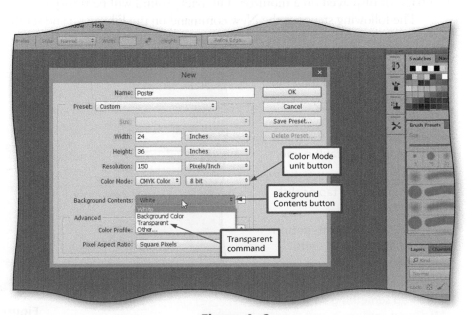

Figure 4–6

4

- Tap or click Transparent in the list to set the background to transparent (Figure 4–7).

What does the Save Preset button do?
Once you choose a color mode, Photoshop displays an approximate image size on the right side of the New dialog box, based on your settings. If you find that you commonly use those specific settings, you could tap or click the Save Preset button and give your collection of attributes a name. In future sessions, you then could choose the preset from a list.

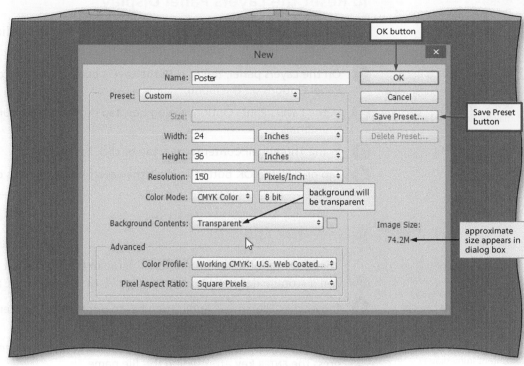

Figure 4–7

5

- Tap or click the OK button to close the dialog box.

- If the rulers do not appear in the document window, press CTRL+R.

- Press CTRL+0 (ZERO) to fit the image on the screen (Figure 4–8).

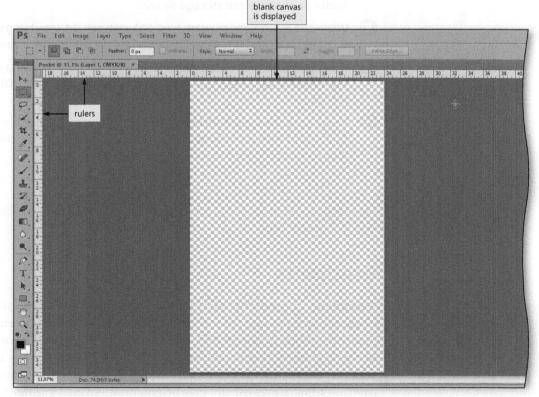

Figure 4–8

Other Ways

1. Press CTRL+N, set attributes, tap or click OK button

BTW
Image Sizes
The larger the dimensions of your publication, the larger the file size. Photoshop imposes no limit to the size of your publication, except for its ability to fit on your storage device. System resources may be slower in larger documents.

To Reset the Layers Panel Display

The following steps set the Layers panel to display medium thumbnails and layer bounds, which matches the figures in this chapter.

① On the Layers panel, tap or click the Layers panel menu button, and then tap or click Panel Options on the menu.

② In the Layers Panel Options dialog box, tap or click the option button for the medium thumbnail.

③ In the Thumbnail Contents area, tap or click Layer Bounds.

④ Tap or click the OK button to close the Layers Panel Options dialog box.

To Save the File

Background Layer
When you start a new file with transparency, the Background Layer is replaced with Layer 1 and the layer is not locked, so you can begin to create content immediately.

Even though the document has a name in the document window tab, it is not saved on a storage device. The next steps save the file with the name Poster Edited.

① Tap or click File on the Application bar to display the File menu and then tap or click Save As to display the Save As dialog box.

② Type **Poster Edited** in the File name text box to change the file name. Do not press the ENTER key after typing the file name.

③ Navigate to your storage location (or the Creative Cloud Files location) by using the Navigation pane or the Previous Locations box arrow to select that drive as the new save location.

④ Tap or click the New folder button on the Save As dialog box toolbar to create a new folder on the selected storage device.

⑤ When the new folder appears, type **Chapter 04** to change the name of the folder, and then press the ENTER key. Double-tap or double-click the new folder to open it.

⑥ If necessary, tap or click the 'Save as type' button to display the list of available file formats, and then tap or click Photoshop (*.PSD;*.PDD) in the list to select the file type.

⑦ Tap or click the Save button to save the document on the selected drive, in the new folder, and with the new file name. If Photoshop displays a dialog box reminding you about maximizing compatibility, tap or click the OK button.

MAC For a detailed example of this procedure using the Mac operating system, refer to the For Mac Users Appendix.

Gradients

Gradient Colors
Gradients work best with RGB or CMYK colors. The Gradient Tool cannot be used with the Bitmap or Index color modes.

A **gradient**, or **gradient fill**, is a graphic effect consisting of a smooth blend, change, or transition from one color to another. Although there is potential for overuse with gradients, subtle gradients add depth and texture to a graphic or webpage. Shade-to-shade gradients sometimes seem elegant and emotive. They can emulate how light strikes real-world surfaces. Vertical gradients help the eyes to move further down the page. Graphic artists usually save bright, multi-striped gradients for smaller portions of a page, such as a heading, or when they intentionally want to overwhelm the viewer. Figure 4–9 shows examples of different gradient styles.

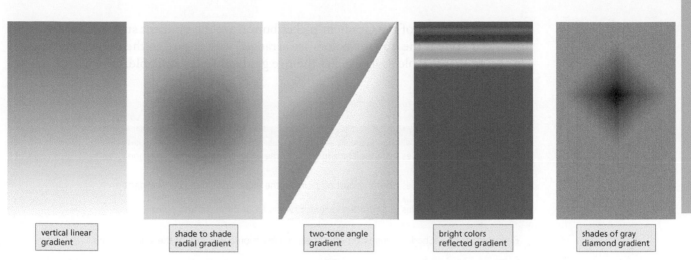

| vertical linear gradient | shade to shade radial gradient | two-tone angle gradient | bright colors reflected gradient | shades of gray diamond gradient |

Figure 4–9

Plan your layout and gather necessary photos.
Recall that a storyboard is a preliminary layout sketch used to help plan graphics placement, size, perspective, and spacing. Using a storyboard allows you to create an original graphic from the back to the front.

- As you start the graphic, fill the background with color, unless the graphic will become part of another publication.

- For busy foregrounds, keep the background simple; consider using only one color. If text will be used, keep in mind that anything in the darker half of the color spectrum will need light text and vice versa.

- Use black backgrounds sparingly — they are most effective for starkness and special effects.

- For extra depth or perspective, consider using a gradient. A gradient can create depth, add visual interest, or highlight a portion of an image. Use colors that will match colors in your graphic or those desired by the customer. The direction of the gradient should either lead viewers toward a specific focal point or entice them to turn the page.

Plan Ahead

BTW

Gradient Directions
You can create a gradient at any straight line, angle, or position. If you start and end in the extreme corners of the frame, the gradient appears across the entire area. To leave the corners solid and start the gradient more toward the center, drag an end closer to the middle of the area. To constrain the line angle to a multiple of 45°, hold down the SHIFT key as you drag.

Typically used as a graduated blend between two colors, the direction of a gradient transition can be top to bottom, bottom to top, side to side, or a variety of other shapes and diagonals. You can apply gradients to the entire image or a selected portion of an image. Photoshop offers many preset gradient fills, or you can create your own using the Gradient Tool. To create a gradient, tap or click the Gradient Tool button on the Tools panel. If you press and hold or right-click the Gradient Tool button, its context menu includes the Gradient Tool, the Paint Bucket Tool, and the 3D Material Drop Tool.

When you select the Gradient Tool, the Gradient Tool options bar (Figure 4–10) allows you to set the style, blending mode, and other attributes for the gradient fill.

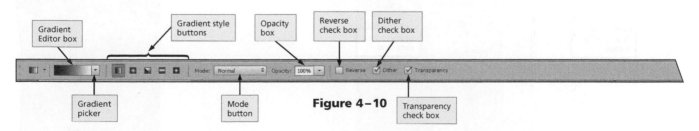

Figure 4–10

When you tap or click the Gradient Editor box, Photoshop displays the Gradient Editor dialog box, commonly called the **Gradient Editor**. It allows you to fine-tune and define a new gradient by modifying a copy of an existing gradient or preset, or by choosing colors to create a new blend.

To the right of the Gradient picker button are the gradient styles or shades. A **gradient style** is the way the colors are arranged with regard to the reflection of light in the gradient. Table 4–1 displays the five gradient styles available.

Table 4–1 Gradient Styles	
Gradient	**Style**
Linear	Shades from the starting point to the ending point in a straight line
Radial	Shades from the starting point to the ending point in a circular pattern
Angle	Shades in a counterclockwise sweep around the starting point
Reflected	Shades using symmetric linear gradients on either side of the starting point
Diamond	Shades from the starting point outward in a diamond pattern — the ending point defines one corner of the diamond

© Cengage Learning

The Mode button controls how the colors of the gradient affect the pixels in the image. Some modes apply full color; others randomize, calculate, darken, or lighten to create specific effects. You will learn more about modes in a future chapter.

Further right on the Gradient options bar, Photoshop includes an Opacity box to set the percentage of opacity, a Reverse check box to reverse the order of colors in the gradient fill, a Dither check box to create a smoother blend with less banding, and a Transparency check box to create a transparency mask for the gradient fill.

To Select the Gradient Tool and Style

To create a gradient in the poster, you will select the Gradient Tool and then choose a gradient style from the options bar, in the following steps.

1

- Press and hold or right-click the Gradient Tool button or the 'Paint Bucket Tool' button on the Tools panel to display the context menu (Figure 4–11).

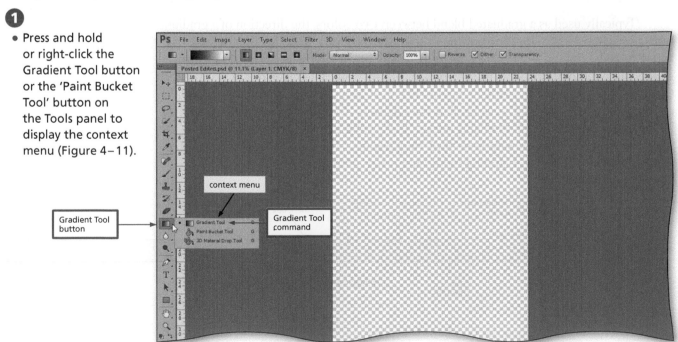

Figure 4–11

2

- Tap or click Gradient Tool to select it.

- On the Gradient options bar, tap or click the Linear Gradient button to select the gradient style (Figure 4–12).

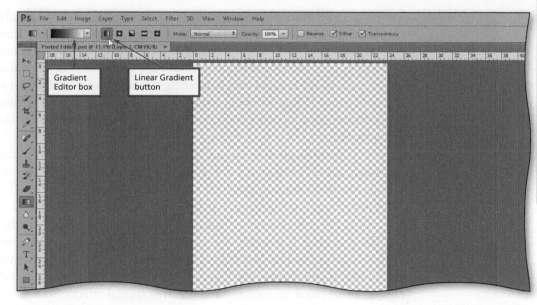

Figure 4–12

Other Ways

1. Press G or SHIFT+G, choose gradient options

Gradient Presets

When you tap or click the Gradient Editor button on the options bar, Photoshop displays the Gradient Editor dialog box (Figure 4–13). In the Gradient Editor dialog box, the Presets area includes 16 predefined gradients called **presets** and a menu button. When clicked, the menu button displays choices for thumbnail size and other gradient presets. Photoshop has 10 sets or **libraries** of additional gradients to create a wide variety of special fill effects. When you choose one of the additional sets, Photoshop will ask if you want to replace or append the new gradient library. The Presets menu button also displays a Reset Gradients command, which changes the presets back to the default list.

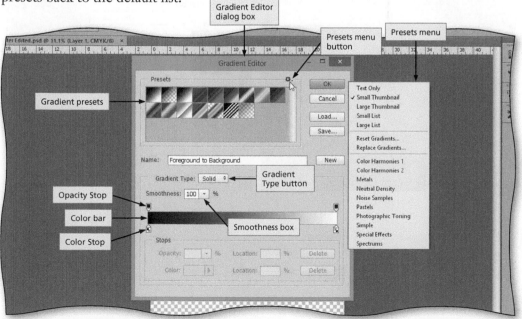

Figure 4–13

The **smoothness** setting is a percentage determining the smoothness of the transition between color bands. A setting of 100% indicates an equally weighted transition in color pixels. When you use lower transition values, the gradient colors will appear more pixelated, with abrupt transitions in the color bands. This effect is even more evident when creating gradients of nonadjacent colors in the color spectrum. When working with a noise gradient, the Smoothness box becomes a Roughness box that indicates how vividly the colors transition between one another.

A **solid gradient** is one that uses the color spectrum to transition the gradient from one color to another. If you choose a solid gradient, Opacity Stop buttons appear above the Color bar, and Color Stop buttons appear below it. Tapping or clicking a Color Stop button opens a dialog box in which you can choose a new color. If you adjust the colors, a small diamond, called the Color Midpoint button, appears below the color bar. It indicates the place in the gradient where the display is an even mix of the starting and ending colors. By placing Color Stop buttons very close together in the Gradient Editor, you can reduce the gradient effect and produce strong, distinct bands of color for exciting and creative special effects.

A **noise gradient** is a gradient that contains randomly distributed color specks within the range of colors that you specify. If you choose a noise gradient, the color bar is adjusted by dragging sliders. Noise gradients also display options for restricting color, setting the transparency, and randomizing the colors.

When you want to identify or edit a gradient color, Photoshop displays a Color Picker dialog box, shown in Figure 4–14. The Color Picker dialog box, also generically called the **Color Picker**, includes a clickable color field and color bar. Text boxes allow you to identify color model numbers. In addition, the Color Picker displays the original color and a preview of any change. Color Pickers appear when you tap or click a Color box on any panel or options bar, or when you tap or click a Color Stop button.

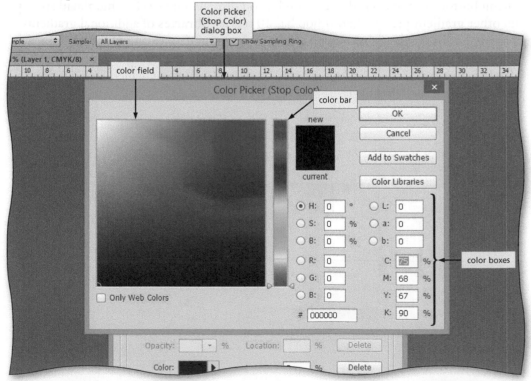

Figure 4–14

To Edit the Gradient

The following steps use the Gradient Editor to choose a gradient preset for the poster.

1

- On the options bar, tap or click the Gradient Editor box (see Figure 4–11) to display the Gradient Editor dialog box.

- Tap or click the first preset, 'Foreground to Background' to select it (Figure 4–15).

 Experiment

- Tap or click each of the various presets in the Gradient Editor dialog box, and watch how the color settings vary. When you are finished, tap or click the 'Foreground to Background' preset again.

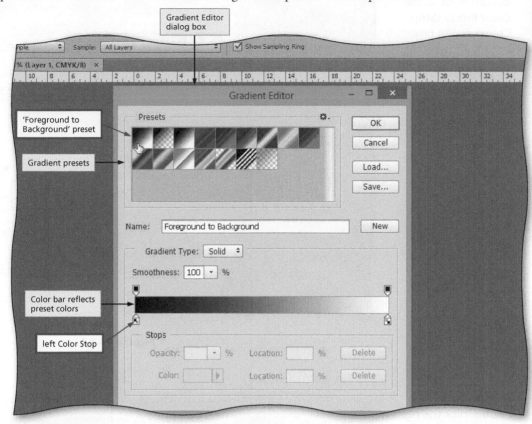

Figure 4–15

2

- Double-tap or double-click the left Color Stop button to open the Color Picker (Stop Color) dialog box.

 Experiment

- Tap or click the color field to change the color and the color values. Tap or click the color slider to watch the colors change.

- In the hexadecimal # box, type **f7ffe5** to choose a pale green color (Figure 4–16).

Q&A | What does the hexadecimal color code mean?

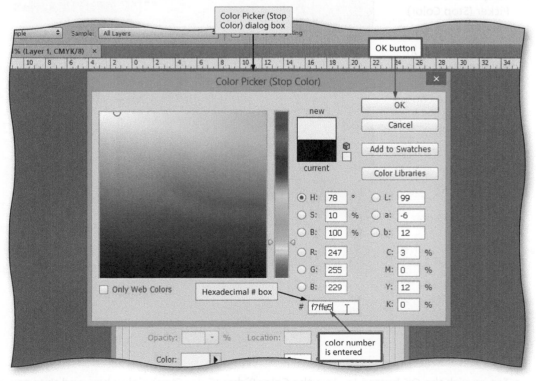

Figure 4–16

Hexadecimal color codes are three pairs of digits using the Base 16 numbering system of 0-9 and then a-f; each pair represents a shade or tint of a primary color. The combination of digits can create up to 16 million different colors.

● Tap or click the OK button to close the Color Picker (Stop Color) dialog box.

● Drag the left Color Stop button to approximately **4 5** as displayed in the Location box (Figure 4–17).

Q&A What does the location number represent?

In this case, the pale green color will continue through the first 45 percent of the overall gradient before it starts to change.

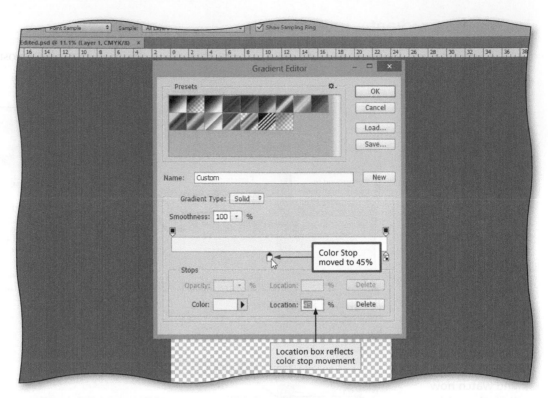

Figure 4–17

● Double-tap or double-click the right Color Stop button to open the Color Picker (Stop Color) dialog box again.

● Select any value in the hexadecimal # box, and then type **8 7 6 a 4 9** to choose a brown color (Figure 4–18).

Q&A How do I find other hexadecimal values that represent colors?

Use a web search engine, such as Google, to search for the words, hexadecimal color values, or, color converter. Many websites display a color wheel, sliders, or converters to help you identify color numbers.

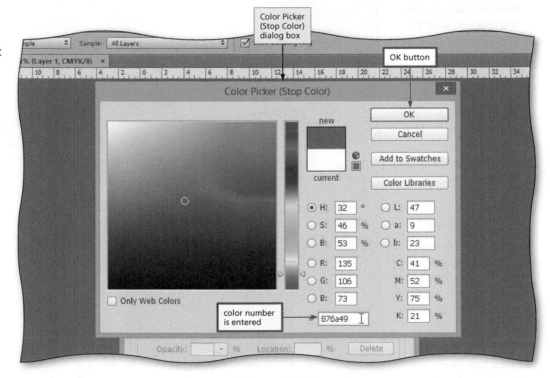

Figure 4–18

● Tap or click the OK button to close the Color Picker (Color Stop) dialog box, and then tap or click the OK button to close the Gradient Editor dialog box.

To Draw the Gradient

The final step in creating a gradient background for the poster is to draw or apply the gradient. To apply the gradient, you drag in the image or selected area, beginning at the point where you want the base color to begin. For linear and radial gradients, you drag in the direction of the desired transition — the rate of transition is dependent on the settings in the Gradient Editor dialog box, as well as on the Transform options bar. The following steps create a diagonal gradient.

- In the document window, drag from a location in the upper-left corner of the canvas, down and right diagonally, to the lower-right corner. Do not release the drag (Figure 4–19).

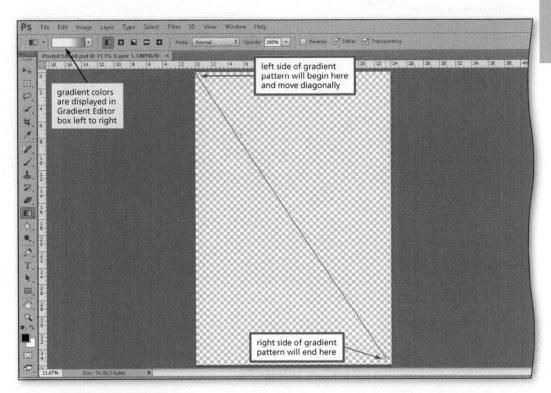

Figure 4–19

2

- Release the mouse button to apply the gradient (Figure 4–20).

Experiment

- Tap or click another style button on the Gradient options bar. Drag in the document window to display a different style gradient. Press CTRL+Z to return to the gradient shown in Figure 4–20.

Figure 4–20

To Set Layer Properties

The following steps name the layer and set its identification color.

1 Double-tap or double-click the name of the layer, Layer 1, on the Layers panel. Type `gradient background` and then press the ENTER key to replace the name.

2 Press and hold or right-click the layer, and then tap or click Blue in the list to change the layer's identification color (Figure 4–21).

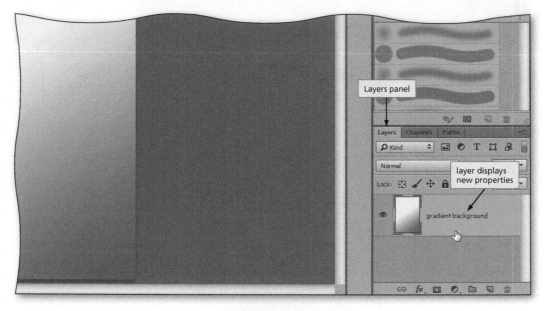

Figure 4–21

Smart Objects

Recall from Chapter 3 that you inserted new images into a document by opening a second file and using various copy, paste, and edit techniques. That insertion became a new layer, independent of its source file; the layer allowed full editing. A **smart object** is a layer that does not allow direct editing, but provides the advantage that it can be resized and transformed without pixelation. You can create a smart object by embedding a new image, linking a new image, or converting a traditional layer.

Embedding an image places a copy of the new image as a smart object layer into your current file. If you make transformations such as resizing or skewing, you do not lose any pixels. It is easy to undo any transformations to the embedded layer, even after closing and reopening the file. Transformations on an embedded smart object do not affect the actual original picture. Additionally, when you embed a smart object from a nonnative file format, such as vector artwork from Adobe Illustrator or Adobe InDesign, Photoshop transforms the image information into a format it can recognize without altering the native data. The disadvantage of embedding is that the overall file size is increased because a copy of the new image is saved with the current file. An embedded layer displays an embedded icon on the Layers panel that looks like a file within a file.

Linking an image displays a linked copy of the new image as a smart object layer in the current file but the file size does not increase. If you (or another user) edits the original version of the linked image, you can update your linked smart object. If both files are open during the editing process, the update happens immediately. Linking is new to Photoshop CC, and a linked layer allows you to edit the smart object and choose to update all of the linked instances automatically by double-tapping or double-clicking the smart object icon on the Layers panel. A linked layer displays a chain link icon on the Layers panel.

A third way to create a smart object is to **convert** a traditional layer. If you press and hold or right-click a traditional layer, Photoshop displays a 'Convert to Smart Object' command on the context menu. Converting to a smart object gives you nondestructive transformation abilities on that layer, and displays an embedded icon on the Layers panel.

Deciding which way to create a layer or smart object layer depends on how you intend to use the file. For instance, you might have a company logo that is used on many publications and documents. A traditional copy and paste of the logo would create a layer that might pixelate if it were resized. An embedded image would not pixelate, but if the company logo changed, the logo would have to be embedded again. A linked image would not pixelate and would update automatically; therefore, it might be the best choice for a company logo.

A smart object layer preserves the image with all of its original characteristics, separately from any filters, masks, edits, or styles. When editing a smart object, you cannot perform operations that alter pixel data — such as painting, dodging, burning, or cloning. However, because a smart object is similar to a file within a file, resizing keeps the maximum resolution and allows the same transformations as a traditional layer such as skewing, warping, rotating flipping, and so on. Smart objects display a bounding box with solid handles in the document window to assist with transformations. In a later chapter, you will learn how to use smart objects with filters, for additional nondestructive editing.

To Create a Smart Object using the Place Linked Command

The following steps use the Place Linked command to embed an image within the poster file as a smart object. That way, you can resize the image without losing any resolution. The image is stored in the Data Files for Students. Visit solutions.cengage.com/ctdownloads for detailed instructions or contact your instructor for information about accessing the required files.

- Tap or click File on the Application bar to display the File menu (Figure 4–22).

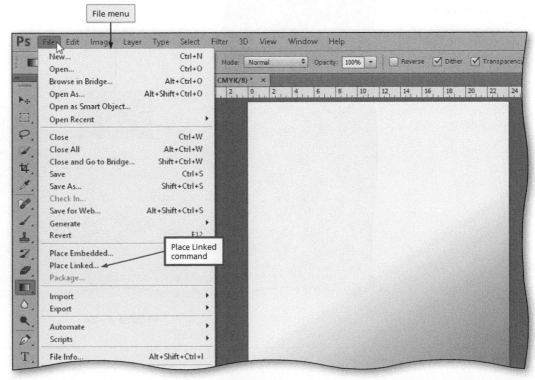

Figure 4–22

2

- Tap or click Place Linked to display the Place Linked dialog box.

- Tap or click the Previous Locations box arrow to display the list of available locations, and then navigate to the Photoshop Data Files for Students.

- Double-tap or double-click the Chapter 04 folder to open it.

- Tap or click the file named Grasshopper to select it (Figure 4–23).

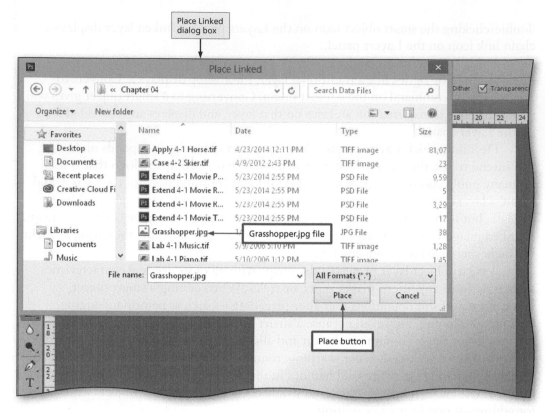

Figure 4–23

3

- Tap or click the Place button to place the image into the current file (Figure 4–24).

Q&A What changed on the Layers panel? The new layer automatically takes on the name of the document with which it is linked, in this case, Grasshopper.

Figure 4–24

Other Ways

1. ALT+drag image from one window to another

To Transform the Smart Object

The following steps reposition and resize the smart object.

1

- On the Transform options bar, select the value in the X box and then type `1725` to change the horizontal position of the reference point.

- Press the TAB key to move to the next box. Type `1670` in the Y box to change the horizontal position of the reference point.

- Press the TAB key, and then type `500` in the W box to change the width of the linked layer.

- Press the TAB key, and then type `500` in the H box to change the height of the linked layer (Figure 4–25).

Q&A Could I drag a handle to resize the placed image?
Yes, you can SHIFT+drag a handle to maintain proportions. Photoshop also displays a small, floating, black box noting the location as you drag.

What happens to the part of the image that is off the canvas?
That part of the image will not print, but is saved in case you decide to resize the picture later.

Figure 4–25

2

- If necessary, tap or click the 'Commit transform (Enter)' button on the options bar to finish the transformation and hide the bounding box.

- Press and hold or right-click the new layer to display its context menu, and then tap or click Green in the list to set an identification color for the Grasshopper layer (Figure 4–26).

Experiment

- On the Layers panel, double-tap or double-click the layer thumbnail to open the image file itself. Tap or click the Close button on the document tab to close the image file and return to the original file.

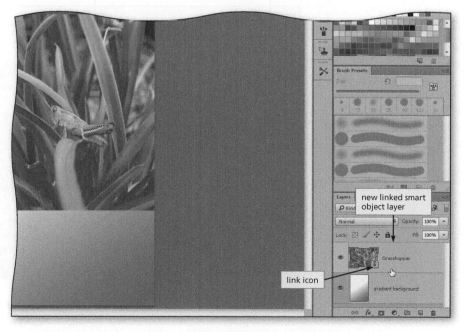

Figure 4–26

Other Ways

1. To move, drag border
2. To scale proportionally, SHIFT+drag handle

To Save Again

The following step saves the poster again, with the same file name.

1. Press CTRL+S to save the Poster Edited file with the same name.

Break Point: If you wish to take a break, this is a good place to do so. Quit Photoshop by pressing CTRL+Q. To resume at a later time, start Photoshop, open the file called Poster Edited, and continue following the steps from this location forward.

Sampling Colors

BTW

Color Sampler Tool
If you right-click the Eyedropper Tool button on the Tools panel, you can choose the Color Sampler Tool from the context menu. Tapping or clicking with the Color Sampler Tool displays the color mode values in the Info panel. You can select up to four color samples per image.

The Eyedropper Tool samples an existing color in a graphic or panel to assign a new foreground or background color. When you tap or click a color using the Eyedropper Tool, Photoshop sets a new foreground color on the Tools panel and Color panel. When you ALT+click a color, Photoshop sets a new background color.

The Eyedropper Tool options bar (Figure 4–27) allows you to change the sample size and create a color sample from the active image or from anywhere else in the Photoshop window. The Sample Size button list contains several choices. The default size, Point Sample, samples the precise color of the pixel you click. The other sample sizes, such as 3 by 3 Average and 5 by 5 Average, sample the color of the pixel, where you tap or click along with the surrounding pixels, and then calculate an average color value of the area. The **sampling ring** is a large circle of color that appears when you click a location with the Eyedropper Tool. The top half of the ring represents the color being sampled and the bottom half represents the existing foreground color. The sampling ring provides a large visual aid when color matching is important. Sampling a color ensures that you will match the color without having to enter color values or make selections in other dialog boxes or panels.

BTW

Info Panel
The Info panel displays information about the color values beneath the pointer and other useful information depending on the tool that you use. For example, the Info panel can tell you if the color you are using will not print in certain color modes. To view the Info panel, click Info on the Window menu, or press the F8 key.

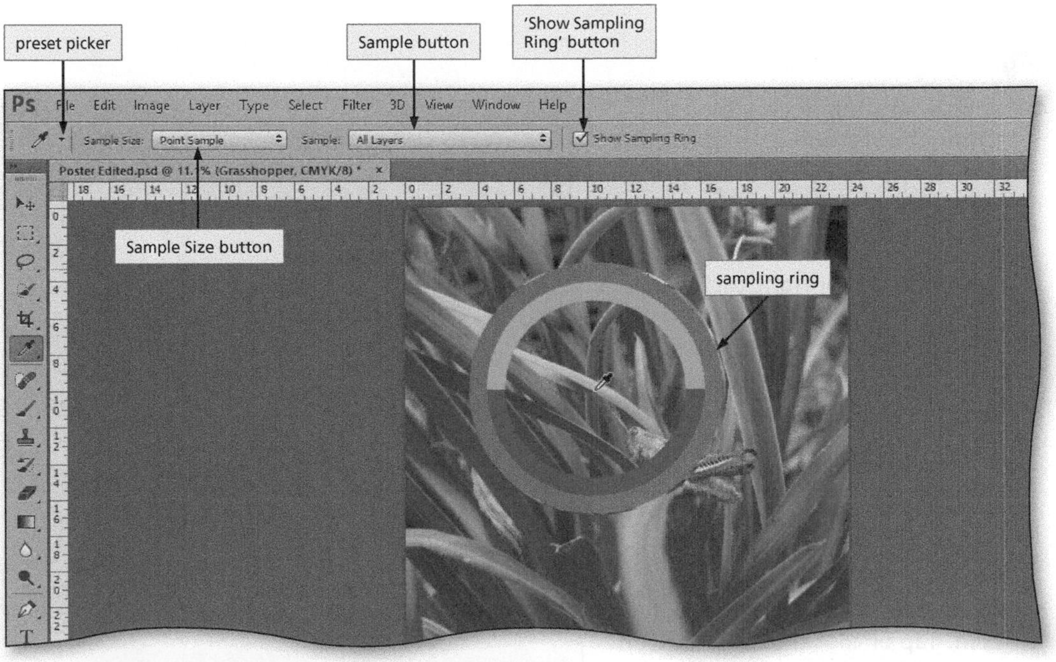

Figure 4–27

Other tools grouped with the Eyedropper Tool are the 3D Material Eyedropper Tool, the Color Sampler Tool, the Ruler Tool, the Note Tool, and the Count Tool. You will learn more about these tools in later chapters.

To Use the Eyedropper Tool

The following steps select the Eyedropper Tool and then sample the brown color from the picture for use in an upcoming shape. Using a color from the picture maintains color consistency in all parts of the poster.

1

- On the Tools panel, press and hold or right-click the Eyedropper Tool button to display its context menu (Figure 4–28).

Q&A   What is the difference between the Eyedropper Tool and the Color Sampler Tool?
The Eyedropper Tool picks up the color and displays it at the bottom of the Tools panel. The Color Sampler Tool only displays information about the color in an Info panel.

Figure 4–28

2

- Tap or click Eyedropper Tool to select it.

- Move the pointer into the document window and then tap or click the dark brown color in the grass to set a new foreground color (Figure 4–29).

Q&A   Why did my Eyedropper Tool set the background color instead of the foreground color?
Someone might have reversed your foreground and background colors. To fix the problem, press the F6 key to display the Color panel and then tap or click the 'Set foreground color' button, which appears as a square color swatch on the left side of the panel.

Figure 4–29

Other Ways

1. Press I or SHIFT+I, tap or click color

Shapes

One of the more creative uses for Photoshop is drawing shapes. A **shape** is a specific figure or form that can be drawn or inserted into an image. A shape is usually a **vector object** or **vector shape**, which means it does not lose its sharp lines or anti-aliasing if it is resized or reshaped. A vector object is made up of lines and curves defined by mathematical vectors or formulas. Photoshop provides five standard shapes as tools on the Tools panel: rectangle, rounded rectangle, ellipse, polygon, and line. The Custom Shape Tool offers a variety of custom shapes, and the ability to create new shapes using a path. A path is a kind of vector shape that you will learn about in a later chapter.

Plan Ahead

> **Use predefined shapes for tangible objects.**
> If your goal is to create a graphic that the viewer will recognize right away, start with a predefined shape. This approach is a necessity if you do not have a drawing tablet or if your artistic skills are limited. Shapes allow you to maintain straight lines, even corners, constrained proportions, and consistent curves. To create unique graphics, shapes can be scaled, distorted, skewed, warped, shadowed, and combined in many ways. Using shapes does not limit your creativity, however. Try experimenting with combinations and transformations of shapes to create graphics with perspective, horizon lines, and alignment.

The Shape Tool options bar (Figure 4–30) contains buttons to choose shape styles, fills, strokes, sizes, and colors. If you select a custom shape, the options bar displays a Shape box, allowing you to choose from a panel of customized shapes and append new libraries of shapes. Besides the traditional shapes of lines, rectangles, and an ellipse, you can create freeform shapes, equilateral polygons, rounded rectangles, and custom shapes.

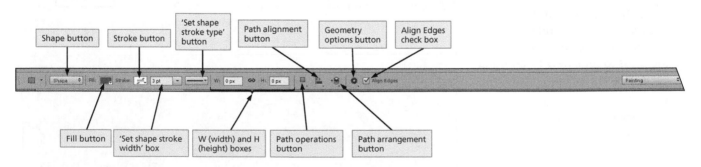

Figure 4–30

Shape Layers
When you choose Shape on the Shape button menu, Photoshop creates a shape layer. A **shape layer** is a vector object that occupies its own layer. Because shape layers are moved, resized, aligned, and distributed easily, they are useful for creating web graphics. You can draw multiple shapes on a single layer.

When you tap or click either the Fill or Stroke boxes on the options bar, Photoshop displays a pop-up panel. **Pop-up panels** provide easy access to available options for many tools, such as brushes, stamps, gradients, patterns, healing tools, and shapes. You can customize pop-up panels by renaming and deleting items and by loading, saving, and replacing libraries or sets of options. You also can change the display of a pop-up panel using the menu button, to view items by their names, as thumbnail icons, or with both names and icons.

After making selections on the options bar, you either can drag to create the shape in the document window, or click to display a Create dialog box with additional size options. Photoshop also displays the Live Shape Properties panel when creating a shape, which you can use to edit further the fill, stroke, stroke width, actual width, and height, among other settings. The panel also provides a way to adjust the corner radius. At the bottom of the panel are buttons to combine, subtract, intersect, and exclude multiple shapes.

On each shape options bar, a Geometry options button displays context sensitive settings for each of the shapes. Table 4–2 displays the geometry options, the shape or shapes with which they are associated, and a description of their functions.

BTW

Resizing Shapes
To resize a shape, press CTRL+T to display the shape's bounding box. Resize the shape by dragging the sizing handles, then press the ENTER key.

Table 4–2 Geometry Options for Shapes

Options	Applicable Shape(s)	Description
Arrowheads, Width, Length, Concavity	Line	Adds arrowheads to a line, specifies the proportions of the arrowhead as a percentage of the line width, specifies concavity value defining the amount of curvature on the widest part of the arrowhead
Circle	Ellipse	Constrains to a circle
Curve Fit	Freeform Pen	Controls how sensitive the final path is to the movement of the mouse or stylus based on a value between 0.5 and 10.0 pixels — a higher value creates a simpler path with fewer anchor points
Proportional or Defined Proportions	Rectangle, Rounded Rectangle, Ellipse, Custom Shape	Renders proportional shape based on the values you enter in the W (width) and H (height) boxes
Defined Size	Custom Shape	Renders a custom shape based on the size specifications
Fixed Size	Rectangle, Rounded Rectangle, Ellipse, Custom Shape	Renders a fixed size based on the values you enter in the W (width) and H (height) boxes
From Center	Rectangle, Rounded Rectangle, Ellipse Custom Shape	Renders the shape from the center
Magnetic	Freeform Pen	Draws a path that snaps to the edges of defined areas, allowing the user to define the range and sensitivity of the snapping behavior, as well as the complexity of the resulting path
Pen Pressure	Freeform Pen	When working with a stylus tablet, an increase in pen pressure causes the width to decrease
Radius	Rounded Rectangle, Polygon	For rounded rectangles, specifies the corner radius; for polygons, specifies the distance from the center of a polygon to the outer points
Rubber Band	Pen	Previews path segments as you draw
Sides	Polygon	Specifies the number of sides in a polygon
Smooth Corners or Smooth Indents	Polygon	Renders the shape with smooth corners or indents
Snap to Pixels	Rectangle, Rounded Rectangle	Snaps edges of a rectangle or rounded rectangle to the pixel boundaries
Square	Rectangle, Rounded Rectangle	Constrains to a square
Star	Polygon	Creates a star from the specified radius — a 50% setting creates points that are half the total radius of the star; a larger value creates sharper, thinner points; a smaller value creates fuller points
Unconstrained	Rectangle, Rounded Rectangle, Ellipse, Custom Shape	Does not constrain shapes

© Cengage Learning

To Create a Rectangle

The following steps use the Rectangle Tool to create a box in the poster. You will then modify the corners of the rectangle, add a stroke to give the shape definition, and then duplicate the rectangle to serve as the check boxes at the bottom of the poster.

- Press and hold or right-click the Shape Tool on the Tools panel to display its context menu (Figure 4–31).

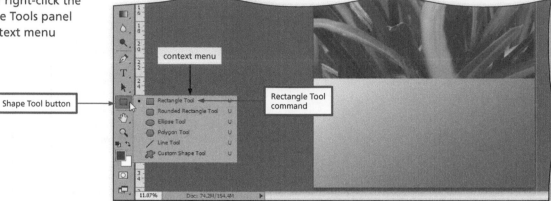

Figure 4–31

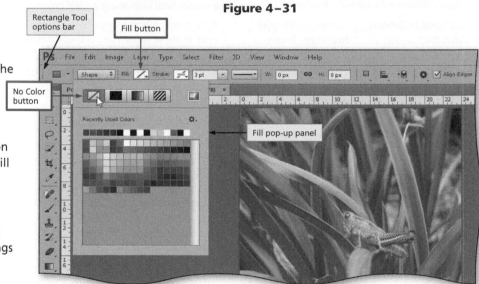

- Tap or click Rectangle Tool to select the tool and to display the Shape Tools options bar.
- Tap or click the Fill button to display the Fill pop-up panel.
- Tap or click the No Color button to create a rectangle with no fill color (Figure 4–32).

 **Experiment**

- Tap or click the Fill panel menu button to view the panel settings and choices.

Figure 4–32

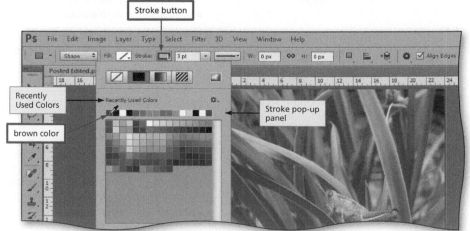

- Tap or click the Stroke button to display the Stroke pop-up panel.
- Tap or click the first color, brown, in the list of Recently Used Colors as the stroke color (Figure 4–33).

 **Experiment**

- Tap or click the Geometry options button to view the options for rectangles.

Figure 4–33

• Select the value in the 'Set shape
  stroke width' box, and then
  type **18** to replace the value
  (Figure 4–34).

Q&A Why does the value 18 represent?
The number 18 will create a
stroke width of 18 pixels. Because
the rectangle has no fill color, 18
pixels of brown will appear on all
four sides of the shape.

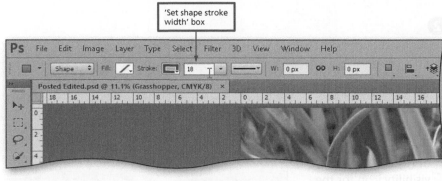

Figure 4–34

• In the document window,
  SHIFT+drag to create a square in
  the lower portion of the canvas,
  approximately 2 inches square
  (Figure 4–35).

Q&A Why should I hold down the SHIFT
key while dragging?
SHIFT+dragging constrains the
proportions when creating shapes,
and causes the Rectangle Tool to
create a square.

Figure 4–35

Other Ways

1. Press U or SHIFT+U, adjust options bar settings

To Use the Live Shape Properties Panel

The default value for rectangular shapes is to display a square corner. The following steps use the Live
Shape Properties panel, to round the corners slightly.

①

• In the lower portion of the Live
  Shape Properties panel, select
  the value in the 'Top left corner
  radius' box.

• Type **36** and then press the
  ENTER key to change the value
  (Figure 4–36).

Q&A Why did the value in all four
corner boxes change?
The default value is for all four
corners to be linked and change
identically for consistent corners.
If you wanted one corner to be
rounded differently, you would tap
or click the Link button to cancel
the link and then enter individual
values for the four corners.

Figure 4–36

2

- Tap or click the Properties button on the vertical dock to close the Live Shape Properties panel.

- On the Layers panel, press and hold or right-click the visibility icon for the Rectangle 1 layer, and then tap or click Orange in the list to change the layer's identification color (Figure 4–37).

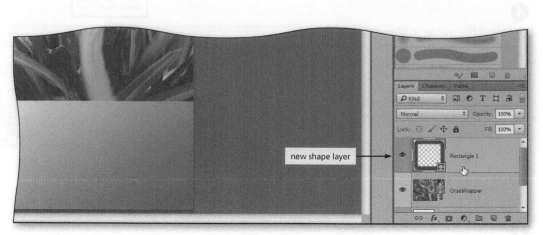

Figure 4–37

To Duplicate a Shape Layer

The following steps duplicate the Rectangle 1 layer, twice, to create a total of three check boxes.

1 Select the Move Tool.

2 In the document window, ALT+drag to create a copy of the shape and place it approximately .8 inches below the original as shown in the pink smart guide.

3 ALT+drag another copy and place it below the previous copy as shown in Figure 4–38.

Figure 4–38

Custom Shapes

Table 4–3 explains the process for creating some common shapes that are not immediately available on the Tools panel; however, the kinds of shapes you can create by combining settings is almost endless.

Table 4–3 How to Create Common Shapes

Shape	Directions
Circle	Use the Oval Tool and SHIFT+drag in the document window to create a circle.
Diamond	Use the Polygon Tool and enter 4 in the Sides box on the options bar. Drag straight down in the document window.
Heart	Use the Custom Shape Tool and choose a heart using the Custom Shape picker.
Parallelogram	Use the Rectangle Tool and drag in the document window to create a rectangle. Press CTRL+T to access transformations. Press and hold or right-click the rectangle and then tap or click Perspective on the context menu. Drag the upper-middle sizing handle to the right or left.
Right Triangle	Use the Rectangle Tool and SHIFT+drag in the document window to create a square. Select the Delete Anchor Point Tool on the Tools panel, and then tap or click on one corner of the square.
Square	Use the Rectangle Tool and SHIFT+drag in the document window to create a square.
Star	Use the Polygon Tool and enter the desired number of points on the star in the Sides box on the options bar. Tap or click the Geometry options button on the options bar, and then tap or click Stars.
Triangle	Use the Polygon Tool and enter 3 in the Sides box on the options bar.

© Cengage Learning

To Save Again

The following step saves the poster again, with the same file name.

 Press CTRL+S to save the Poster Edited file with the same name.

Break Point: If you wish to take a break, this is a good place to do so. Quit Photoshop by pressing CTRL+Q. To resume at a later time, start Photoshop, open the file called Poster Edited, and continue following the steps from this location forward.

Painting with Brushes

The brush tools change the color of pixels in an image by painting. The Brush and Pencil tools work like their traditional counterparts, applying color with strokes. The Color Replacement Tool replaces a selected color with a new color. The History Brush Tool paints a copy of the selected state or snapshot into the current image or layer. The Art History Brush Tool paints with stylized strokes that simulate the look of different paint styles, using a selected state or snapshot. The Mixer Brush Tool simulates realistic painting techniques, such as blending canvas colors and varying paint wetness. By specifying how each tool applies or modifies the color, you can create an endless number of possibilities. You can apply color gradually, with soft or hard edges, with small or large brush tips, and with various brush dynamics and blending properties, as well as by using brushes of different shapes. You even can simulate spraying paint with an airbrush.

In the next section, you first will choose a color from the Swatches panel and create a new layer for the check mark. Then, you will select the Brush Tool, edit the Brush settings, and finally draw the check mark on the new layer. You will repeat the process for a second brush stroke using a wet brush tip to create a shaded grassy header across the top of the graphic.

The Swatches Panel

The Swatches panel stores colors for repeated use (Figure 4–39). To choose a foreground color, tap or click a color in the Swatches panel. To choose a background color, CTRL+click a color in the Swatches panel. The Swatches panel menu allows you to add more color libraries, or change the settings of the current panel for different projects.

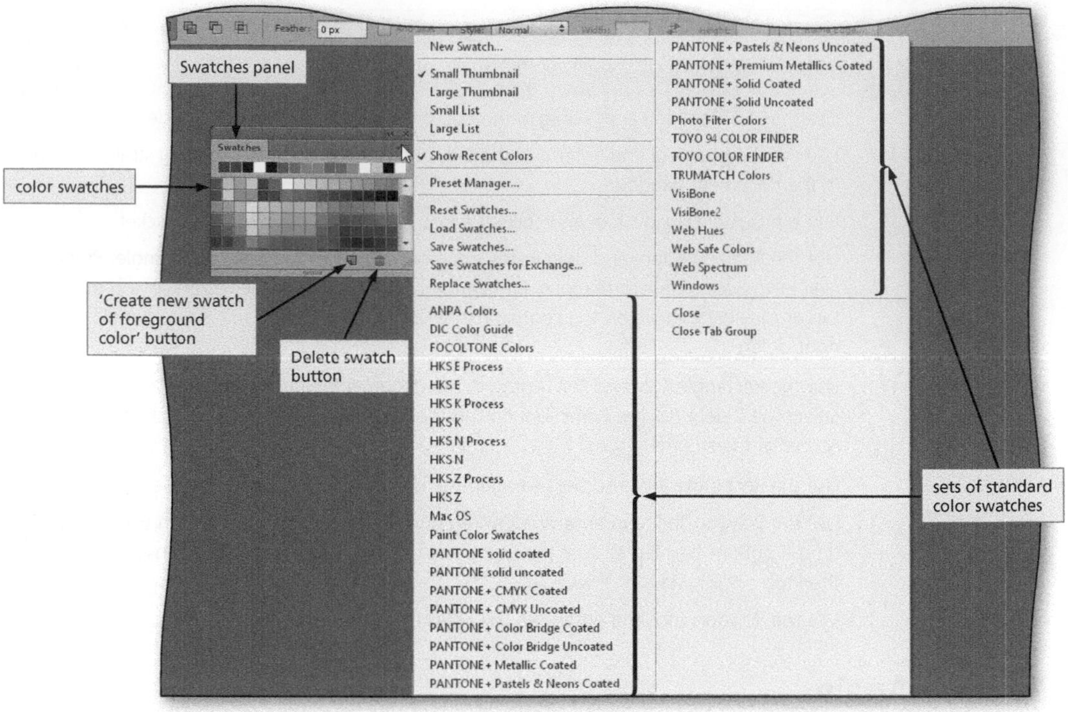

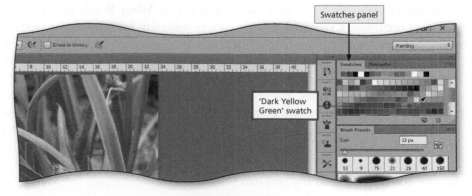

Figure 4–39

Choose colors purposefully.
Choose two or three colors that fit with your client's colors or that match a color that already exists in an image in your layout. Limiting the number of colors creates a stronger brand or identity. The main color should be the one that viewers will remember when they look away. Colors two and three should either contrast or complement the main color to balance the design. Complementary colors create gray, white, or black when mixed in proper proportions, or are found opposite one another on a standard color wheel.

To Choose a Color on the Swatches Panel

The following step chooses a foreground color using the Swatches panel. You will use the color later as you create the check marks.

1

- On the Swatches panel, tap or click the color 'Dark Yellow Green' to change the foreground color. The order of your swatches may differ (Figure 4–40).

Q&A Why did my pointer change to an eyedropper?
The Swatches panel is one of the dialog boxes and panels that allow you to sample colors. Anytime you are sampling, the pointer will display an eyedropper.

 **Experiment**

- Point to various colors on the Swatches panel to display their tool tip names.

Figure 4–40

To Create a New Layer

The following steps create a new layer on which to draw the check mark, just above the background layer.

1 Press SHIFT+CTRL+N to create a new layer.

2 In the New Layer dialog box, type `check mark` for the name.

3 Tap or click the Color box arrow, and then tap or click Yellow to change the layer's identification color.

4 Tap or click the OK button to close the New Layer dialog box and display the new layer on the Layers panel.

The Brush Tool

The Brush Tool paints the current foreground color on an image with strokes of color as you drag. When you tap or click the Brush Tool button on the Tools panel, the Brush options bar appears (Figure 4–41).

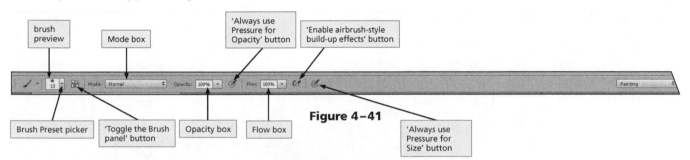

Figure 4–41

The Brush Preset picker button is used to display the pop-up panel with the current set of brush tips and settings, such as brush size and hardness. Next to the Brush Preset picker is the 'Toggle the Brush panel' button, which shows and hides the Brush panel. The Mode box arrow displays brush blending modes when clicked, and the Opacity box allows you to specify the degree of transparency. Entering a value in the Flow box specifies how quickly the paint is applied. A lower number applies paint more slowly. The airbrush button enables airbrush capabilities.

In addition to the options bar, several panels used with brushes help you choose and adjust brush settings. Each panel has a button menu to change the size of the thumbnail previews, to create, choose, or append new brushes, as well as reset options. Table 4–4 lists the panels and their respective purposes.

BTW

Related Tools
The Pencil and Color Replacement Tools are related closely to the Brush Tool. The only difference between the Pencil and Brush Tool is that the Brush Tool paints with an anti-aliased or smooth edge, and the Pencil Tool draws with an aliased or rough edge. The Color Replacement Tool replaces specific colors when you paint over a targeted color with a corrective color.

Table 4–4 Panels Used with Brushes

Panel	Access	Contents	Purpose
Brush panel	Window menu | Brush or F5 or Toggle the Brush panel button	Paint options, brush settings, brush tip shapes, stroke preview	To select or modify a brush or to design custom brushes
Brush Presets panel	Window menu | Brush Presets or Painting Workspace	Brush tip and stroke preview, size settings	To choose a preset brush and adjust its size
Brush Preset pop-up panel	Brush Preset picker on Brush options bar	Brush tip preview, size setting, hardness settings	A small panel to quickly choose or verify a brush preset using the options bar

Plan
Ahead

Design your brush strokes.
When choosing a brush tip, keep in mind the basic shape of your brush strokes or marks. Use the Brush panel to choose a Brush Preset or Brush Tip shape. Consider the brush shape you want to use such as round, square, or patterned. Think about the density or thickness you wish to see in the brush stroke, as indicated in black, gray, and white in the brush tip preview. Finally think about the style before choosing a brush tip. Many brushes are points (flat, blunt, rounded, or angled); others are brushed, spattered, or stroked with various edges.

Once you have chosen a brush tip, adjust settings for the beginning, middle, and end of the brush stroke. For the beginning, choose an appropriate tip, color, shape, rotation, hardness, spacing, and diameter. For the middle of the stroke, set the shape dynamics, such as pen pressure and tilt, texture, flow, brush edge, distortion, noise, and scattering. For the end of the brush stroke, set the fading effect.

BTW

Brush Tips
A brush tip has specific characteristics such as size, shape, and hardness. When you use the Brush Tool, the tip creates the shape that paints in the document window.

To Select the Brush Tool and a Brush Tip

The following steps select the Brush Tool on the Tools panel and a Chalk brush tip.

 ❶

- Press and hold or right-click the current brush tool on the Tools panel to display the context menu (Figure 4–42).

Figure 4–42

❷

- On the context menu, tap or click Brush Tool in the list to select it and to display the Brush options bar.

- Tap or click the Brush Preset picker to display the Brush Preset pop-up panel.

- Scroll in the presets area as necessary, and then tap or click the Dry Brush 39 preset.

- Drag the diameter slider to approximately 84 (Figure 4–43).

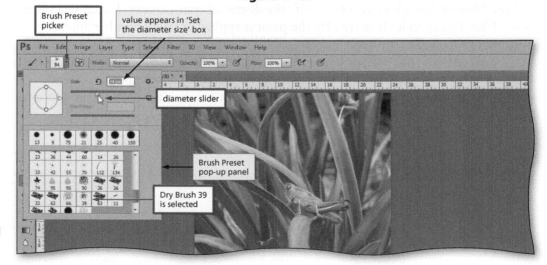

Figure 4–43

Other Ways

1. To choose Brush Tool, press B, or SHIFT+B

To Draw with the Brush Tool

The following steps draw with the brush tool to create a check mark.

❶

- On the status bar, type **33.33** in the magnification box and scroll as necessary to display the rectangles in the document window.

- With the Brush tool still selected, draw a check mark across the first rectangle (Figure 4–44).

Q&A My check mark does not look good. Can I redo it?

Yes. Press CTRL+Z to undo and try again. You also can tap or click on the top left, then SHIFT+tap or SHIFT+click the bottom center to create a straight brush stroke for the left side of the check mark.

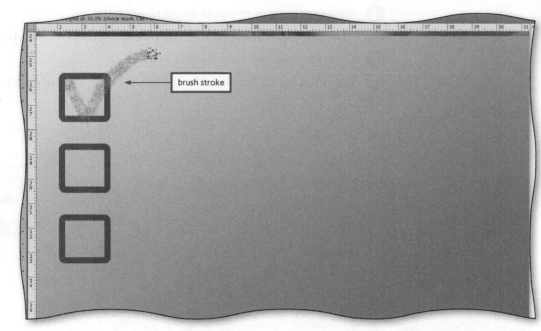

brush stroke

Figure 4–44

❷

- Press the V key to select the Move Tool, and then ALT+drag to create another checkmark and drag it over the second rectangle.

- ALT+drag again to create a third check mark (Figure 4–45).

Q&A Could I just draw another check mark instead of copying the first one?

Yes, but copying keeps all three of the check marks exactly the same.

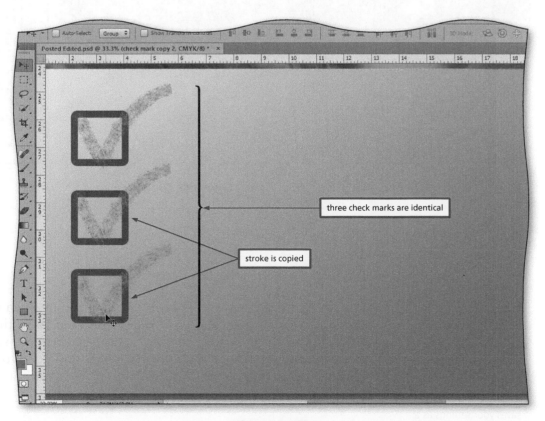

three check marks are identical

stroke is copied

Figure 4–45

To Create a Layer for the Header

The following steps scroll to the top of the poster and create a layer for an advanced brush stroke to create a grassy header.

1 Press SHIFT+CTRL+N to create a new layer.

2 Name the layer, grassy header and choose a Violet identification color.

3 Close the New Layer dialog box.

4 Zoom to 25% and scroll to the top of the poster (Figure 4–46).

Figure 4–46

BTW

Saving Brush Settings

If you change the size, shape, or hardness of a preset brush, the change is temporary; the next time you choose that brush, it reverts to its original settings. If you use a certain brush tip and characteristics often, you might use the New Brush preset command on the Brush panel menu, which saves your settings as a named brush tip.

The Brush Presets Panel

The Brush Presets panel is displayed automatically when using the Painting workspace. It allows you quickly to choose a brush and size without covering any of your workspace (Figure 4–47). Buttons on the panel help you set the size of the brush, create new brushes, and perform other functions. In addition to the basic brush tips, Photoshop has 15 other libraries of brush tips that you can append to the panel using the Brush Presets panel menu.

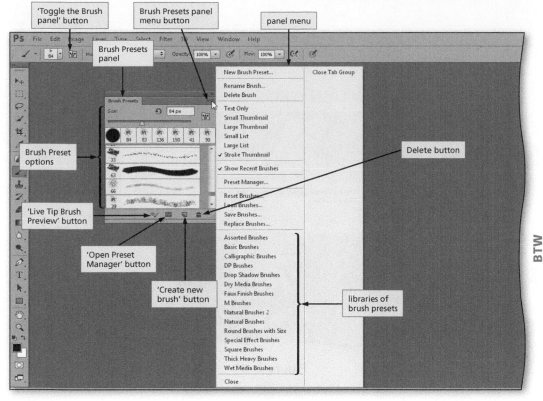

Figure 4–47

The Preset Manager
The Preset Manager helps you manage the libraries of preset brushes, gradients, styles, custom shapes, patterns, and other tools. Use it to change the current set of preset items or create new libraries. The Preset Manager lists new presets all in one place for easy access. To use the Preset Manager, tap or click Preset Manager on the Edit menu.

To Append a Brush Library

The following steps append a brush library using the Brush Presets panel.

1

- Press the B key to select the Brush Tool. Press the D key to reset the default colors.

- Tap or click the Brush Presets panel menu button to display its menu (Figure 4–48).

Figure 4–48

2

• Tap or click 'Wet Media Brushes' to choose the library and to start the append process (Figure 4–49).

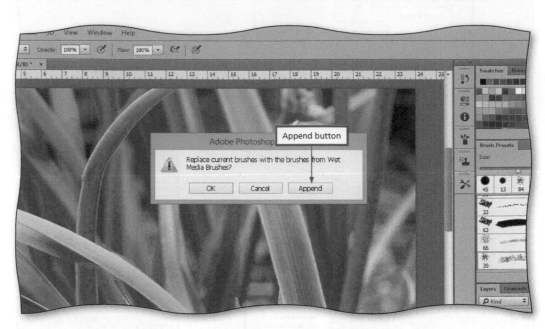

Figure 4–49

3

• Tap or click the Append button to append the brushes to the panel list.

• Scroll down through the new brushes and then tap or click 'Paintbrush Tool Texture Comb' brush; ensure that you select the brush with a size of 95 (Figure 4–50).

Figure 4–50

Other Ways

1. Press and hold or right-click document window, choose brush, edit settings

2. On options bar, tap or click Brush Preset picker button, choose brush, edit settings

BTW

Choosing Brushes
Sometimes it is confusing whether to use the Brush Preset picker, the Brush panel, or the Brush Presets panel to choose a brush. Normally, you should choose the tool that is closer to your current location. However, if you want to customize the brush, use the Brush panel.

The Brush Panel

The Brush panel (Figure 4–51) displays settings such as brush tips, painting characteristics, angles, and spacing, among others. To display the Brush panel, you can tap or click the 'Toggle the Brush' panel button on the Brush options bar, tap or click Brush on the Window menu, tap or click the Brush panel button on the vertical dock, or press the F5 key. The Brush panel menu button displays a list of available commands.

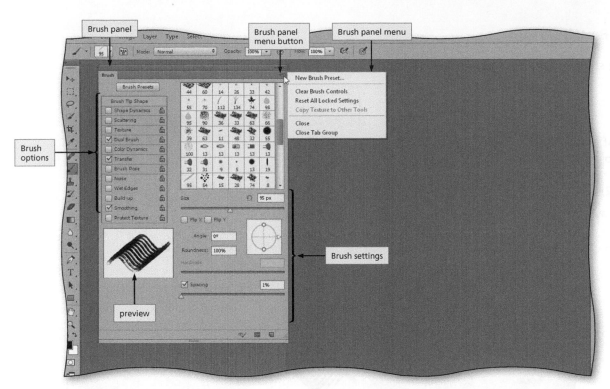

Figure 4–51

The Brush panel allows you to customize preset brush tips. For example, you can set the diameter, which scales the size of the brush tip. The **brush size** is the diameter of the brush tip measured in pixels. The flip boxes change the direction of the brush tip on the specified axis. For example, a brush tip that displays a leaf image with the stem down would display the leaf with the stem up if the Flip X check box were checked. **Brush angle** is a measurement of degrees of flat rotation. Positive numbers rotate the brush tip counterclockwise; negative numbers rotate the brush tip clockwise. For example, a brush tip of a raindrop with the pointed end straight up would point left if rotated 90 degrees, counterclockwise. The **roundness** percentage specifies the ratio between the brush's short and long axes. Adjusting the roundness makes the brush tip appear to rotate on its vertical axis in a 3D fashion. A value of 100% indicates a full view or circular brush tip. A value of 0% indicates a sideways view or linear brush tip as if you were painting with a wide brush turned on its side. Values between 0% and 100% represent partial view or elliptical brush tips. For example, a star brush tip set at 50% roundness creates a star that tips backward from the top. Additionally, several settings, such as the angle, rotation, roundness, or height, can be changed by dragging in the visual setting box.

The Spacing slider controls the **spacing** or distance between the brush marks in a stroke. The lower the percentage, the closer together the brush tips are within the stroke. For example, a snowflake brush tip set at 1% spacing would display a snowflake shape connected to another snowflake shape. Higher percentages — up to 1000% — space the brush tips farther apart as you drag. For example, a spacing value of 200% would create snowflakes all across the brush stroke with some space in between each one. When the Spacing check box is deselected, the speed at which you drag or paint determines the spacing.

Solid brush tips have a hardness setting that indicates the amount of anti-aliasing for the Brush Tool. **Hardness** is a percentage value indicating how solid the edge of the brush stroke appears.

BTW | **Brush Sets**
Sometimes you might want a unique or distinctive brush that is not among the many brush tips available in Photoshop. In that case, you can purchase the design or create it from scratch. Brush tip files have the extension ABR and are available for purchase on the web.

BTW | **The Restore Sample Size Button**
When selecting brush tip shapes on the Brush panel, if you change the diameter of a brush tip, Photoshop might display a Restore Sample Size button. The Restore Sample Size button allows you to reset the brush tip back to its default size.

BTW | **Brush Preset Previews**
When you click the Brush Preset picker, your previews might appear as thumbnails, as lists, or as text only. You can choose the preview style on the Brush Presets panel.

To Display the Brush Panel

The following step displays the Brush panel.

1

- Tap or click the Brush button on the vertical dock of collapsed panels to display the Brush panel (Figure 4–52).

Q&A

What is the best way to access the Brush panel?

The best way is the way that seems efficient or natural to you. If your pointer happens to be near the menu, perhaps tapping or clicking Brush on the Window menu might be the best way. If you commonly use function keys, pressing the F5 key may seem most natural.

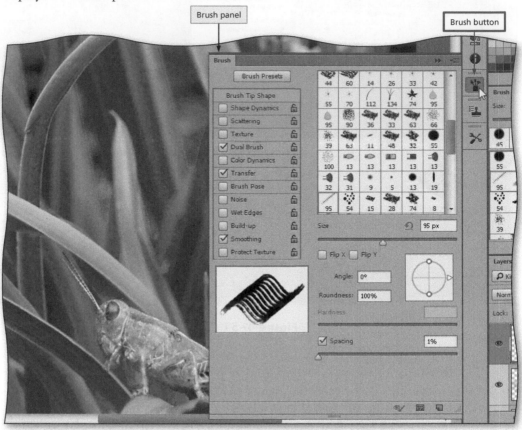

Figure 4–52

Other Ways

1. On Window menu, tap or click Brush
2. Tap or click 'Toggle the Brush panel' button
3. Press F5

Brush Options

When you choose a Brush option, settings specific to that option appear on the Brush panel. Table 4–5 displays some of the options not previously mentioned, along with their settings and descriptions.

Table 4–5 Brush Options

Option	Setting	Description
Shape Dynamics	Jitter, Initial Direction, Direction	Specifies how the size, angle, or roundness of brush marks vary in a stroke
	Fade	Fades the size of brush marks between the initial diameter and the minimum diameter in the specified number of steps
	Pen Pressure, Pen Tilt, Stylus Wheel, Rotation	Available only with graphic tablets — varies the size of brush marks between the initial diameter and the minimum diameter based on the pen pressure, pen tilt, position of the pen thumbwheel, or rotation of the pen
Scattering	Scatter	Specifies how brush marks are distributed in a stroke — if the Both Axes check box is selected, brush marks are distributed in a radial direction; if the Both Axes check box is deselected, brush marks are distributed perpendicular to the stroke path
	Count	Specifies the number of brush marks applied at each spacing interval

Continued

Table 4–5 Brush Options *(continued)*

Option	Setting	Description
Texture	Invert	Used for patterns — inverts the high and low points in the texture based on the tones in the pattern
	Scale	Specifies the scale of the pattern
	Depth	Specifies how deeply the paint penetrates into the texture
Dual Brush	Mode	Sets a blending mode to use when combining brush marks from the primary tip and the dual tip
Color Dynamics	Hue, Saturation, Brightness, Purity	Specifies a percentage by which the hue, saturation, or brightness of the paint can vary in a stroke
Transfer	Opacity Jitter and Control	Specifies how the opacity of paint varies in a brush stroke
	Flow Jitter and Control	Specifies how the flow of paint varies in a brush stroke
Noise		Adds additional randomness to individual brush tips
Wet Edges		Causes paint to build up along the edges of the brush stroke, creating a watercolor effect
Airbrush		Applies gradual tones to an image, simulating traditional airbrush techniques
Smoothing		Produces smoother curves in brush strokes
Protect Texture		Applies the same pattern and scale to all brush presets that have a texture

To Set Brush Options

The following steps use the Brush panel to edit the settings and options.

1

- On the Brush panel, select the value in the 'Set the brush diameter' box and then type **735** to set the diameter.

- Drag the arrow in the 'Set the brush angle and roundness' icon to change the angle to approximately 46%.

- Drag either of the circles in 'Set the brush angle and roundness' icon to change the roundness to approximately 50% (Figure 4–53).

Q&A I cannot drag to the exact sizes. Is there another way to size the brush?
You can select the text in the Diameter, Angle, and Roundness boxes and then type the exact size.

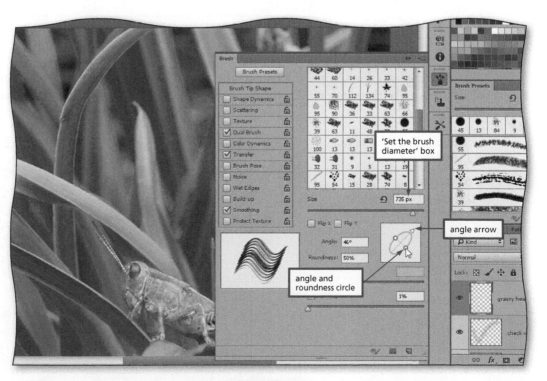

Figure 4–53

2

- In the list of options, tap or click the Wet Edges check box to display the check mark and emphasize the edges of the brush stroke.

- Double-tap or double-click the Texture option to display the Texture settings.

- Set the Scale to 252%, the Brightness to -100, and the Contrast to 0 (zero) (Figure 4–54).

Q&A Should any other check boxes be selected?

No. Tap or click to remove any other check boxes, so your check boxes match Figure 4–53.

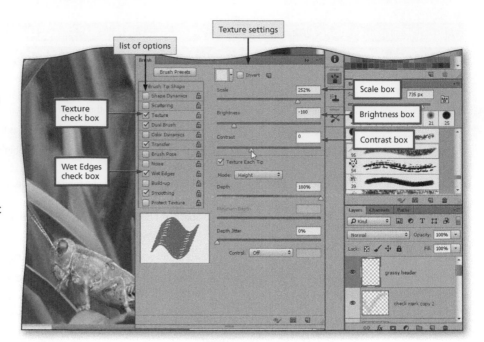

Figure 4–54

To Collapse the Brush Panel

The following step collapses the Brush panel.

1 Tap or click the Brush button on the vertical dock of panels to collapse the Brush panel.

To Create the Grassy Header

The following step drags in the document window to create the grassy header. Remember that if you make a mistake, or do not like the result while creating a brush stroke, press CTRL+Z to undo, and then begin again.

1

- On the Options bar, change the Opacity to 35%.

- Slowly drag from right to left across the top of the image as shown in Figure 4–55.

Q&A If I wanted to change the size of the brush, is there an easy way other than getting back into the Brush panel?

Yes. As you did with the Eraser Tool, press the LEFT BRACKET ([) key to reduce the size of the brush. Press the RIGHT BRACKET (]) key to enlarge the size of the brush.

Experiment

- On the options bar, tap or click the 'Enable airbrush-style build-up effects' button on the options bar. In a remote place on the document window, press and hold the mouse button for several seconds to build up ink. Experiment with drawing a stroke. When you are finished, press CTRL+Z to undo the stroke. Tap or click the 'Enable airbrush-style build-up effects' button again to turn it off.

Figure 4–55

To Save Again

The following step saves the image again, with the same file name.

 Press CTRL+S to save the Poster Edited file with the same name.

Break Point: If you wish to take a break, this is a good place to do so. Quit Photoshop by pressing CTRL+Q. To resume at a later time, start Photoshop, open the file called Poster Edited, and continue following the steps from this location forward.

Use type wisely.
Make purposeful decisions about your type styles and typefaces, including the font family, font size, font style, direction, color, spacing, and stroking.

- When combining font families on the same page, chose fonts that contrast in style, weight, and form. For example, if one typeface is tall and thin, choose a contrasting one that is short and thick – and vice versa. Fonts that are too similar appear to be design errors.

- A font or typeface defines the appearance and shape of the letters, numbers, and special characters used in text. The fonts you use create the look, feel, and style of your graphic publications.

- Be consistent about using the same font style for similar purposes, such as bold for emphasis.

- Look for the stress or slant of where the typeface displays wider versus thinner lines within the same letter, or serifs on lowercase letters.

- Examine text for places where kerning, tracking, or leading might lead to increased legibility or contrast.

- For a more historical, retro, formal, or literary look and feel, use a **serif** font. Serif means flourish, and indicates that the letters will contain small intersecting lines, sometimes called appendages, at the end of characters.

- For a more modern feel, use **sans serif,** which means without flourish, and displays in block-like letters without appendages.

- If you use different sizes of the same font family, choose sizes that deliberately are different — not close in size. Do not use more than three sizes of the same font on the same page.

- Use strokes or outlines around the lettering when the text has high priority in the graphic, and you want a distinctive look. White strokes make dark text stand out; conversely, black strokes around light-colored text help delineate the text and make it stand out.

Formatting Type

Graphic designers use the term, **type,** to refer to the mathematically defined shapes of letters, numbers, and symbols in a typeface or font family. The terms, type, text, and copy have become interchangeable with the advent of desktop publishing; however, Photoshop uses the word, type, when referring to the various tools that manipulate text. **Typography** is a more over-arching term for the style and appearance of type. In Photoshop, the Character panel and the Paragraph panel contain the tools and settings for creating a range of type styles.

The Character Panel

Besides the basic text and style buttons and boxes shown on text tool options bars, Photoshop provides a set of extended type tools in the Character panel (Figure 4–56). You access the Character panel through the 'Toggle the Character and Paragraph panels' button, located on the text options bar. The Character panel and

BTW

Graphics Tablet
Dragging, without using the SHIFT key, creates strokes of color that may include corners, curves, and arcs. Graphic designers who create many freehand brush strokes sometimes use a graphics tablet, which is an input device that uses a stylus, or specialized mouse, to draw on a tablet surface.

BTW

Adjusting Text
To adjust the size of the text bounding box, drag the sizing handles. Later, if you need to edit the text, you select the layer and select the type tool. The pointer then becomes a cursor when positioned over the text.

the options bar contain some of the same tools; the Character panel also has tools for character spacing, special effects, ligatures, language, and anti-aliasing methods. The Character panel menu button displays many of the same commands and provides the capability to reset all value boxes so fractional settings can be used.

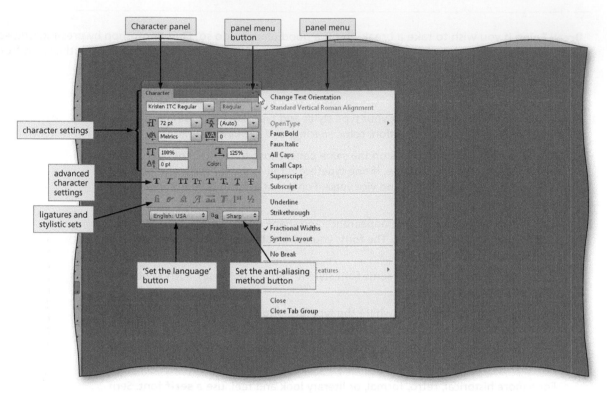

Figure 4–56

You will learn more about type and text in future chapters; however, of special interest to the effects in the poster are the letter spacing tools of scaling, tracking, kerning, leading, and baseline shift.

Scaling, the process of shrinking or stretching text, changes the width of individual characters. **Tracking**, on the other hand, refers to the adjustment of the general spacing between characters. Tracking text compensates for the spacing irregularities caused when you make text much bigger or much smaller. For example, smaller type is easier to read when it has been tracked loosely. Tracking both maintains the original height and width of the characters and overrides adjustments made by justification or bounding box changes.

Kerning is a special form of tracking related to pairs of adjacent characters that can appear too far apart. For instance, certain letters such as T, V, W, and Y, often need kerning when they are preceded or followed by a, e, i, o, or u. The word Tom typed in a large font might create too much space between the letters T and o. Tapping or clicking between the letters and then adjusting the kerning would make the word more readable.

Leading, also called line spacing, refers to the amount of vertical spacing between lines of type; the term originates from the pre-computer practice of adding lead to create space between lines of metal type characters.

Baseline shift controls the distance of type from its original baseline, either raising or lowering the selected type.

To Scale Text

The following steps scale text horizontally to create a text header for the poster.

1

- On the Swatches panel, tap or click 'Pastel Pea Green' (first color on the third row).

- On the Tools panel, select the Horizontal Type Tool.

- On the options bar, tap or click the 'Toggle the Character and Paragraph panels' button to display the Character panel (Figure 4–57).

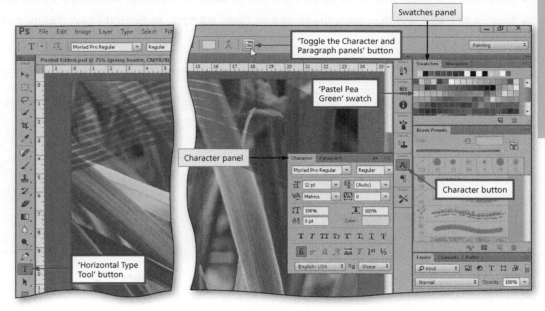

Figure 4–57

2

- Select the text in 'Set the font family' box, and then type **Kristen ITC Regular** or a similar font.

- Select the text in the 'Set the font size' box and then type **72** to replace it.

- Select the text in the Horizontally scale box and then type **125** to enlarge the scaling.

- If necessary, tap or click the 'Set the anti-aliasing method' button, and then choose Sharp in the list (Figure 4–58).

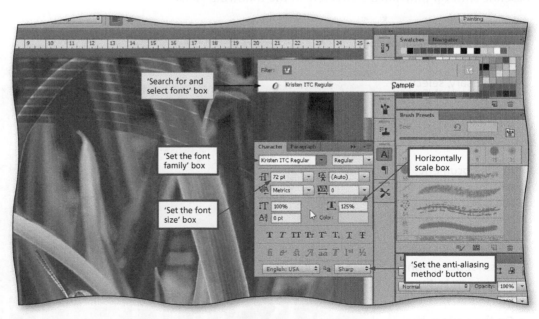

Figure 4–58

Q&A

What is the new box that appears above the Character panel?

The box is the same box that appears when you use the 'Search for and select fonts' button on the options bar. The Kristen ITC Regular is from Adobe Typekit, a set of fancy fonts now integrated with Photoshop CC.

• Tap or click the Character button in the vertical dock to hide the Character panel.

• Drag to create a text box in the upper-right corner of the image, approximately 7 inches wide and 3 inches tall.

• Type **ANIMAL** and then press the ENTER key. Type **FACTS** to finish the text (Figure 4–59).

4

• On the options bar, tap or click the 'Commit any current edits' button to finish the text layer.

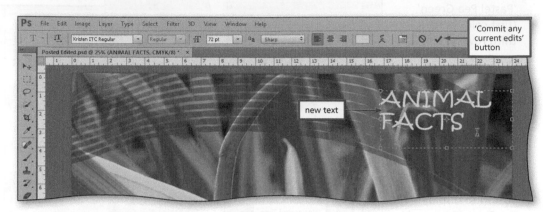

Figure 4–59

To Create Text with a Baseline Shift

As you create the words across the middle of the poster, you will use the Character Style panel to create a baseline shift on individual characters in the following steps.

• Scroll to the middle of the poster.

• If necessary, select the Horizontal Type Tool. On the options bar, tap or click the Center text button.

• In the document window, starting at the left margin, drag a text box approximately 2.5 inches high across the bottom of the grasshopper graphic continuing to the right side.

• On the options bar, tap or click the 'Toggle the Character and Paragraph panels' button to display the Character panel

Figure 4–60

• Change the font to Baskerville Old Face Regular, or a similar font, and change the font size to 174. Tap or click the 'Set the anti-aliasing method' button, and then choose Strong in the list

• If necessary, tap or click the text box and type **GRASSHOPPERS** to enter the text (Figure 4–60).

Q&A My text wrapped to two lines. Did I do something wrong?
You might have used a slightly different font style. Select the text and reduce the font size until GRASSHOPPERS appears on one line.

- Drag across the letter H to select it.
- On the Character panel, select the text in the 'Set the baseline shift' box. Type **144** to change the baseline for the letter (Figure 4–61).

Q&A What does 144 represent?
The number is a **point** value, abbreviated as **pt**. At 72 points per vertical inch, the letter will be 2 inches higher than the other letters.

Figure 4–61

- Drag across the letter O to select it.
- On the Character panel, select the text in the 'Set the baseline shift' box. Type **120** and then press the ENTER key to change the baseline on the letter.
- Using the same technique, change the first P to **84**, the second P to **36** (Figure 4–62)

④

- On the options bar, tap or click the 'Commit any current edits' button to finish the text layer.

Figure 4–62

Other Ways

1. Press SHIFT+ALT+DOWN ARROW or press SHIFT+ALT+UP ARROW

To Create a Drop Shadow on the Text

Recall that you used layer styles to stroke text in Chapter 1. And you created layer styles in Chapter 3. By using a **layer style**, you can keep the effect separate from the rest of the layer, which allows you to copy, remove, or change the effect. The following steps create a drop shadow on the GRASSHOPPERS text.

1 With the GRASSHOPPERS layer still selected, tap or click the 'Add a layer style' button at the bottom of the Layers panel. Tap or click Drop Shadow in the list.

2 In the Layer Style dialog box, change the opacity to 40 and change the angle to -124. Change the distance to 26, the spread to 65, and the size to 5 (Figure 4–63).

3 Tap or click the OK button to apply the shadow.

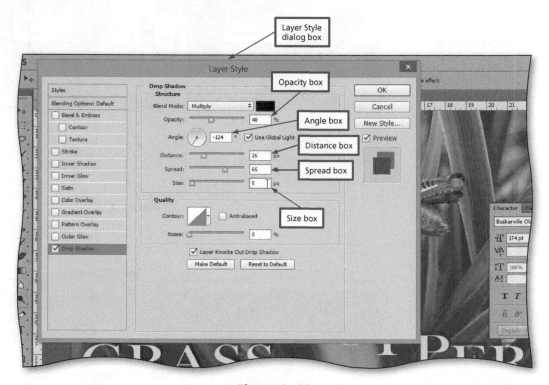

Figure 4–63

The Paragraph Panel

The Paragraph panel (Figure 4–64) contains buttons to change the formatting of columns and paragraphs, also called text blocks. Unique to the Paragraph panel are settings to change the justification for paragraphs, indent margins and first lines, and change the spacing above and below paragraphs. The panel's menu button displays other commands to change settings, including access to the Hyphenation dialog box where you can be very specific about how and when hyphenation occurs. You also can edit the way Photoshop indents paragraphs and adjusts the line spacing, which is the vertical spacing before and after paragraphs.

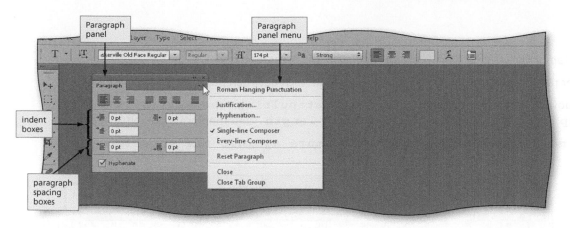

Figure 4–64

To Use the Paragraph Panel

The following steps set a specific spacing between paragraphs as you enter text in the lower part of the poster.

1

- Scroll to the lower portion of the poster.
- On the Swatches panel, tap or click the brown color in the list of previously used colors.
- If necessary, select the Horizontal Type Tool. On the options bar, tap or click the 'Left align text' button to set the type alignment.
- In the document window, to the right of the check boxes and check marks, drag to create a text box approximately, 17 inches wide and 10 inches tall.
- On the Character panel, change the font size to 48 and change the baseline shift to 0 (zero) (Figure 4–65).

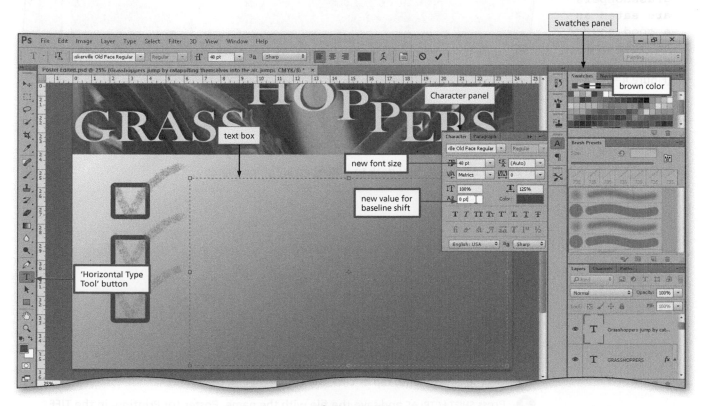

Figure 4–65

②
- On the vertical dock, tap or click the Paragraph button to display the Paragraph panel.
- In the 'Add space after paragraph' box, type `24` to leave one-half inch between paragraphs.
- In the document window, type `Grasshoppers jump by catapulting themselves into the air, jumping up to 20 times their own body length.` and then press the ENTER key.
- Type `They make noise by rubbing the hind femurs against the forewings or abdomen, or by snapping their wings in flight.` and then press the ENTER key.
- Type `Many species are adapted to green fields and forests, and blend in well there to avoid predators. Some change color depending on their environment. In certain countries, grasshoppers are eaten as a good source of protein.` to finish the text (Figure 4–66).

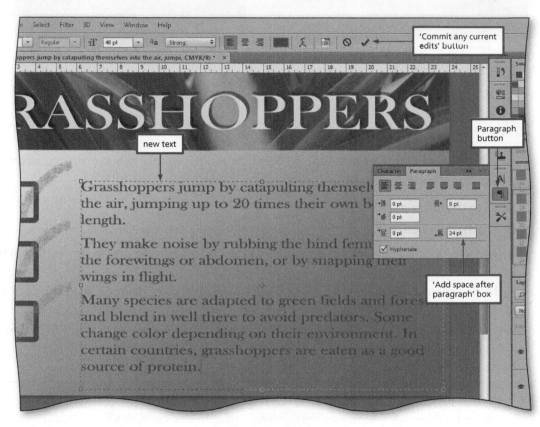

Figure 4–66

③
- Tap or click the 'Commit any current edits' button on the options bar to accept the text.
- Tap or click the Paragraph button on the vertical dock to hide the Paragraph panel.

To Save the File

The poster is complete. You will save the file once again before flattening the layers.

① Press SHIFT+S and save the file with the same name.

To Flatten and Save the File

The following steps flatten the image and save it as a TIFF file.

① On the Layer menu, tap or click the Flatten Image command.

② Press SHIFT+CTRL+S and save the file with the name, Poster for Printing, in the TIFF format. When Photoshop displays the TIFF Options dialog box, tap or click the OK button to finish saving the file.

To Print the Poster

The following steps print the poster.

1 Prepare the printer according to the printer instructions.

2 Tap or click File on the Application bar, and then tap or click Print to display the Photoshop Print Settings dialog box.

3 If necessary, tap or click the Printer box arrow and then select your printer from the list. Scroll as necessary to check the 'Scale to Fit Media' check box (Figure 4–67).

4 In the Print dialog box, tap or click the Print button to start the printing process. If your system displays a second Print dialog box or a Print Settings dialog box, unique to your printer, tap or click its Print button.

5 When the printer stops, retrieve the hard copy of the poster.

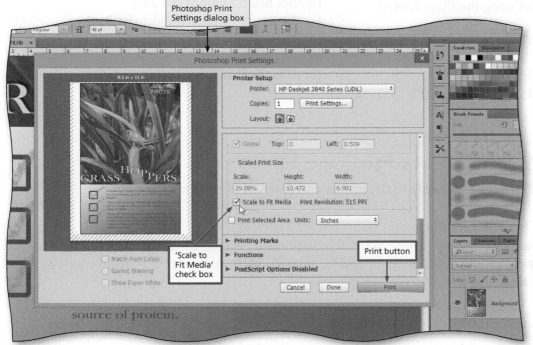

Figure 4–67

To Close the Document Window and Quit Photoshop

The final step is to close the document window and quit Photoshop.

1 Press CTRL+Q to close the document window and quit Photoshop.

Chapter Summary

You used many tools and panels in the Painting workspace as you created the poster in this chapter. You started a new file from scratch and used the Gradient Tool to create a colorful backdrop. You linked a graphic. After using the Eyedropper Tool to select a color, you created a rectangle shape to use as a checkbox. You chose a color using the Swatches panel and selected a brush to create a checkmark. You then appended a brush library and used a different brush tip to draw a header. You used advanced character and paragraph techniques as you added text to the poster. Finally, you flattened the image and saved the file.

The items listed below include all the new Photoshop skills you have learned in this chapter:

1. Select the Painting Workspace (PS 214)
2. Start a New Photoshop File (PS 215)
3. Select the Gradient Tool and Style (PS 220)
4. Edit the Gradient (PS 223)
5. Draw the Gradient (PS 225)
6. Create a Smart Object using the Place Linked Command (PS 227)
7. Transform the Smart Object (PS 229)
8. Use the Eyedropper Tool (PS 231)
9. Create a Rectangle (PS 234)
10. Use the Live Shape Properties Panel (PS 235)
11. Choose a Color on the Swatches Panel (PS 238)
12. Select the Brush Tool and a Brush Tip (PS 240)
13. Draw with the Brush Tool (PS 241)
14. Append a Brush Library (PS 243)
15. Display the Brush Panel (PS 246)
16. Set Brush Options (PS 247)
17. Create the Grassy Header (PS 248)
18. Scale Text (PS 251)
19. Create Text with a Baseline Shift (PS 252)
20. Use the Paragraph Panel (PS 255)

Apply Your Knowledge

Reinforce the skills and apply the concepts you learned in this chapter.

Creating a Magazine Cover

Note: To complete this assignment, you will be required to use the Data Files for Students. Visit solutions.cengage.com/ctdownloads for detailed instructions or contact your instructor for information about accessing the required files.

Instructions: Start Photoshop and perform the customization steps found on pages PS 6 through PS 11. You will create the magazine cover shown in Figure 4–68.

Perform the following tasks:
1. Use the New command on the File menu to create a canvas named Magazine Cover, measuring 7 inches wide by 9 inches high. Use a resolution of 72 and an 8-bit CMYK Color mode. Set the background contents to Transparent.

2. Use the Place Linked command to place the image named Apply 4-1 Horse, located in the Chapter 04 folder of the Data Files for Students, as a smart object. Resize the placed object to fill the canvas. Color the new layer green.

3. Select the Eyedropper Tool. Sample a dark blue color from the sky.

4. Select the Rectangle Tool. In the document window, drag to create a rectangle, approximately 5.5 inches wide and 2 inches tall. Press CTRL+T to display the transform bounding box. Move the pointer just outside of the rectangle and rotate it 45 degrees counterclockwise. Drag the rectangle to the lower-right corner as shown in Figure 4–68. (*Hint:* some of the rectangle will run over the edge of the canvas.) Color the new layer blue.

FREE RANGE

$3.99 August 2015

LOYAL COMPANION SPECIAL
The Best Dogs in America

© Source: Library of Congress, courtesy of Mike Flaherty

Figure 4–68

5. Press SHIFT+CTRL+N to create a new layer, named stars. Color the new layer violet. Press the D key to revert to the default colors. Press the X key to exchange the foreground and background colors.

6. Select the Brush Tool. On the options bar, tap or click the Brush Preset picker to display the pop-up panel. Select the brush named, 'Watercolor Spatter Fine Drops.' Reduce the size to 12.

7. With the stars layer still selected on the Layers panel, move the pointer into the document window. Tap or click the top of the rectangle at the right margin. Move the pointer to the upper-left corner of the rectangle (at the bottom margin). SHIFT+tap or SHIFT+click to create a straight line brush stroke across the top of the rectangle. Repeat the process for the bottom of the rectangle, as shown in Figure 4–67.

8. Select the Horizontal Type Tool. On the options bar, tap or click the Center text button. Tap or click the 'Toggle the Character and Paragraph panels' button to display the Character panel. Choose the Corbel font or a similar font in your list. Set the font style to Bold and the font size to 20. If necessary, tap or click the Faux Bold button and the Underline button to deselect them on the Character panel.

Continued >

Apply Your Knowledge *continued*

9. Drag in the document window to create a text box approximately 4.5 inches wide and 1.5 inches tall. Type **LOYAL COMPANION SPECIAL** and then press the ENTER key. Tap or click to turn off the Underline on the Character panel, and then type **The Best Dogs in America** to finish the text. On the options bar, tap or click the 'Commit any current edits' button to close the text box. If necessary, resize the text box so that the text fits. To do so: press CTRL+T, SHIFT+drag a sizing handle, and then tap or click the 'Commit any current edits' button on the options bar.

10. Press CTRL+T to display the bounding box and rotate the text 45 degrees counterclockwise. Move the text to the location shown in Figure 4–68 on the previous page.

11. Press the x key to exchange the foreground and background colors. Select the 'Horizontal Type Tool'. On the options bar, tap or click the 'Left align text' button. In the document window, draw a large text box across the top of the canvas, approximately 1.5 inches tall. On the Character panel, change the font to Imprint MT Shadow or a similar font. Change the font size to 72. Type **FREE RANGE** to finish the text.

12. Create a third text box in the upper-right corner below the title text box, as shown in Figure 4–68. Use the Imprint MT Shadow font and a size of 24. Type **$3.99 August 2015** to finish the text.

13. Color all of the text layers yellow.

14. Save the file with the name Apply 4-1 Magazine Cover on your storage device.

15. Flatten the file and save it the name Apply 4-1 Magazine Cover for Print in the TIFF format. Submit the files in the format specified by your instructor.

Extend Your Knowledge

Extend the skills you learned in this chapter and experiment with new skills. You may need to use Help to complete the assignment.

Creating a Promotional Movie Poster

Note: To complete this assignment, you will be required to use the Data Files for Students. Visit solutions.cengage.com/ctdownloads for detailed instructions or contact your instructor for information about accessing the required files.

Instructions: Start Photoshop and perform the customization steps found on pages PS 6 through PS 11. Open the Extend 4-1 Movie Poster file from the Chapter 04 folder of the Data Files for Students. The purpose of this exercise is to create a composite photo with various components, similar to Figure 4–69, and to create both a PSD and TIFF version of the final composition.

Perform the following tasks:

1. Save the image on your storage location as a PSD file, with the file name Extend 4-1 Movie Poster Edited.

2. To create a gradient at the top of the photo:
   a. Create a new layer named, sky.
   b. With the new layer selected, use the Rectangular Marquee Tool to create a selection that includes the top half of the canvas, down to the horizon line in the photo. Make sure your selection includes all of the document window, horizontally.

Courtesy of Kevin Marshall

Figure 4–69

c. Select the Gradient Tool and its Linear Gradient style. Tap or click the Gradient Editor box to display the Gradient Editor dialog box. Tap or click the left Color Stop button and sample a dark blue in the photo. Tap or click the right Color Stop button and sample a light blue from the photo. (*Hint*: you might have to drag the dialog boxes out of the way to sample the colors.) Close the Gradient Editor dialog box.

d. SHIFT+drag from the top of the selection to the bottom of the section to create a linear gradient.

3. To create a gradient at the bottom of the photo:

a. Create a new layer named, footer.

b. With the new layer selected, use the Rectangular Marquee Tool to create a selection that includes the bottom 2 inches of the photo. Again, make sure your selection includes all of the document window, horizontally.

c. Select the Gradient Tool and its Linear Gradient style. Tap or click the Gradient Editor box to display the Gradient Editor. Choose the second preset, named Foreground to Transparent. Close the Gradient Editor dialog box.

d. SHIFT+drag from the bottom of the selection to the top of the section to create a linear gradient.

Continued >

Extend Your Knowledge *continued*

4. To insert the placeholder text:

   a. Open the Extend 4-1 Movie Text file and arrange the two document windows side by side.

   b. Use the Move Tool to drag the text into the Extend 4-1 Movie Poster Edited window and position it in the lower part of the photo, as shown in Figure 4–69 on the previous page.

   c. Close the Extend 4-1 Movie Text file.

5. To insert the movie rating text:

   a. Open the Extend 4-1 Movie Rating file and arrange the two document windows side by side.

   b. Use the Move Tool to drag the rating into the Extend 4-1 Movie Poster Edited window and position it below the placeholder text, as shown in Figure 4–69.

   c. Close the Extend 4-1 Movie Rating file.

6. Use Photoshop Help to read about stylistic alternatives and contextual alternatives.

7. To create the movie title text:

   a. Press the D key to set the default colors. Press the X key to exchange the foreground and background colors.

   b. Display the Character panel. Set the font to Consolas. Set the font size to 100, and set the horizontal scale to 85%. If necessary, tap or click the Contextual Alternates button to select it and tap or click the Stylistic Alternates button to select it. Drag a text box completely across the top of the canvas, approximately 1.75 inches tall. Type **The Big City** in the text box. On the options bar, tap or click the 'Commit any current edits' button.

   c. On the Layers panel, tap or click the 'Add a layer style' button, and then tap or click Stroke. When Photoshop displays the Layer Style dialog box, tap or click the Color button, and then choose a dark blue color. Tap or click the OK button to add a stroke to the title.

8. To create movie subtitle text:

   a. Using the Horizontal Type Tool again, with the same font, set the font size to 30. Drag a text box below the title and to the right. Type **A MOVIE ABOUT THE CITY** in the text box.

9. To add the movie reel image:

   a. Tap or click File on the Application bar, and then tap or click Place Embedded. Browse to the file named Extend 4-1 Movie Reel and select it. Tap or click the Place button and then position the movie reel image as shown in Figure 4–69. Press the ENTER key to finish the place.

10. Save the file again and then flatten the image.

11. Press SHIFT+CTRL+S to open the Save As dialog box. Type **Extend 4-1 Movie Poster Complete** in the Name box. Tap or click the 'Save as type' button, and then tap or click TIFF in the list. Tap or click the Save button. When Photoshop displays the TIFF Options dialog box, tap or click the OK button to finish saving the file.

12. Submit the file in the format specified by your instructor.

Make It Right

Analyze a project and correct all errors and/or improve the design.

Correcting a Cell Phone Ad

Note: To complete this assignment, you will be required to use the Data Files for Students. Visit solutions.cengage.com/ctdownloads for detailed instructions or contact your instructor for information about accessing the required files.

Instructions: Start Photoshop and perform the customization steps found on pages PS 6 through PS 11. Open the Make It Right 4-1 Cell Phone file from the Chapter 04 folder of the Data Files for Students. The file contains an ad for the Super Chrome 2020 cell phone (Figure 4–70). The client thinks that it is too bland. You are to improve the look of the ad with gradients and brushes.

Perform the following tasks:

1. On the violet background layer, create a radial gradient with shades of purple, from the upper-right to the lower-left, so the radial appears around the cell phone.
2. Add a radial gradient with shades of green from left to right to the shape in the green layer.
3. Add a radial gradient with shades of blue from top to bottom to the shape in the blue layer.
4. On the Layers panel, CTRL+click the super chrome layer thumbnail to select its content. Apply the Chrome preset gradient in a linear style from top to bottom.
5. Repeat Step 4 for the 2020 layer.
6. For a final touch, use the 'Add a layer style' button to add a bevel and a drop shadow to help set the text layers apart from the blue background. Use the default settings for both layer styles.
7. Save the file as Make It Right 4-1 Cell Phone Edited.

Figure 4–70

In the Labs

Design and/or create a publication using the guidelines, concepts, and skills presented in this chapter. Labs are listed in order of increasing difficulty.

Lab 1: **Creating a Concert Flyer**

Note: To complete this assignment, you will be required to use the Data Files for Students. Visit solutions.cengage.com/ctdownloads for detailed instructions or contact your instructor for information about accessing the required files.

Problem: The Music Department at your college wants to advertise an upcoming piano concert. The chair has heard you are studying Photoshop, and he would like you to create a flyer for him. He plans to have the flyers professionally printed, and therefore he wants a high resolution, CMYK file to submit to the publisher. He has sent you a picture of a piano, a scan of some piano music, and instructions for the text. You need to put it all together, adding a gradient background and inserting a shape. A sample solution is shown in Figure 4–71.

Courtesy of Joy Starks

Figure 4–71

Instructions: Perform the following tasks:

1. Start Photoshop. Set the default workspace, default colors, and reset all tools. On the File menu, click New. Set the size to 8.5 inches by 11 inches. Set the color mode to CMYK 8-bit, and the resolution to 300. Set the background to transparent.
2. Tap or click the Save As command on the File menu. Browse to your storage device. Name the file, Lab 4-1 Piano Concert Flyer and save it in the PSD format.
3. Rename Layer 1, gradient.
4. Press the G key to activate the Gradient Tool. If the Paint Bucket Tool is active, press SHIFT+G to toggle to the Gradient Tool.

5. On the Gradient options bar, tap or click the Linear Gradient button, and then tap or click the Gradient Editor box. When Photoshop displays the Gradient Editor dialog box, tap or click the Foreground to Background preset. Tap or click the Gradient Type box arrow, and then tap or click Solid. Double-tap or double-click the Smoothness box and then type **100**.

6. Below the color bar, double-tap or double-click the right Color Stop button. When the Color Picker (Stop Color) dialog box is displayed, tap or click red on the color bar and then tap or click a bright red in the color field. Tap or click the OK button.

7. Below the color bar, double-tap or double-click the right Color Stop button. When the Color Picker (Stop Color) dialog box is displayed, tap or click purple on the color bar and then tap or click a medium purple in the color panel. Tap or click the OK button.

8. Tap or click the OK button in the Gradient Editor dialog box. Draw a gradient by dragging from the upper-right corner of the page in the document window to the lower-left corner. (*Hint:* if you do not like the result and want to redo the gradient, press CTRL+Z to undo the step. Set your options and drag again.)

9. On the File menu, tap or click Place Embedded. Navigate to the Data Files for Students and the Chapter 04 folder. Double-tap or double-click the Lab 4-1 Music file. When the music is displayed in the document window, move the music to the upper-left corner of the canvas. If necessary, press CTRL+T to display the transform options bar, and then tap or click the 'Switch between the free transform and warp modes' button. One at a time, drag each of the handles on the right side of the graphic to the right. Use Figure 4–70 as a guide. Tap or click the 'Commit transform (Enter)' button to finish the warp. Color the layer blue.

10. On the File menu, tap or click Place Linked. Navigate to the Data Files for Students and the Chapter 04 folder. Double-tap or double-click the Lab 4-1 Piano file. If Photoshop asks to place the file, tap or click the Yes button. When the piano is displayed in the document window, SHIFT+drag a corner sizing handle to increase the size by approximately 25%. Move the piano to the lower-right corner of the canvas. On the options bar, tap or click the 'Commit transform (Enter)' button to finish the link. Color the layer green.

11. Create a new layer named stars with a yellow identification color.

12. On the Swatches panel, select the 'Pastel Yellow Orange' swatch.

13. To append a new brush set and choose a star brush:

   a. Select the Brush Tool.

   b. On the options bar, tap or click the 'Brush Preset picker' to display the pop-up panel. Tap or click the pop-up panel menu, and then tap or click the Assorted Brushes. When Photoshop displays a dialog box, tap or click the Append button.

   c. Scroll through the brush tips in the pop-up panel and select the Star - Large 19 brush.

   d. Tap or click the 'Toggle the Brush panel' button to display the Brush panel. Change the size to 80 and the spacing to 125. Tap or click the Brush button on the vertical dock to hide the Brush Panel.

   e. Drag to create rows of stars as shown in Figure 4–70. Tap or click other locations to add extra stars.

14. To create the text:

   a. Select the Horizontal Type Tool. If necessary, on the options bar, tap or click the 'Left align text' button.

   b. Tap or click the Character button on the vertical dock to display the Character panel. Choose the Gabriola Regular font at size 36. Change the horizontal Scale to 85%. Change the leading to 5. Change the anti-aliasing to Strong.

Continued >

In the Labs *continued*

   c. Tap or click the Paragraph tab to display the Paragraph panel. Change the spacing after paragraph to 28.

   d. In the document window, drag a text box in the lower-left corner of the flyer, approximately 3 inches wide and 2.5 inches tall. Type `All Beethoven` and then press the ENTER key. Type `Sunday, Oct. 18` and then press the ENTER key. Type `Lilly Hall` and then press the ENTER key. Type `3:00 p.m.` and then press the ENTER key. Type `Senior Piano Majors` to finish the text.

   e. On the options bar, tap or click the 'Commit any current edits' button. Change the layer color to orange.

15. Save the file.

16. On the Layer menu, tap or click Flatten Image. Save the flattened image as Lab 4-1 Piano Concert Flyer for Print in the TIFF format.

17. Quit Photoshop. E-mail the flattened file, as an attachment, to your instructor.

Lab 2: Creating a Web Graphic from Scratch

Problem: You have been asked to create a graphic to place on the paper-recycling box in your computer lab (Figure 4–72).

Instructions: Perform the following tasks:

1. Start Photoshop. Set the default workspace and reset all tools.

2. Tap or click New on the File menu. When the New dialog box is displayed, start with a blank page named Recycle Sign that is 8.5 by 11 inches with a white background and a resolution of 300 pixels per inch.

3. Choose the Custom Shape Tool. Tap or click the Shape box on the Shape options bar. When the panel is displayed, tap or click the menu button and then tap or click Symbols in the list. Tap or click to Append the Symbols to the current set. Scroll to display the recycling logo and tap or click it.

Figure 4–72

4. Tap or click the Fill box on the Shape option bar and select a dark green color.

5. Drag to create a recycling logo that fills the page.

6. Add the text, Paper Only in the middle of the recycling logo. Use a large italic font, such as Lucida Handwriting. Use the Character panel to change the baseline shift for the letters a, p, and e, as shown in Figure 4-72.

7. Print the sign on a color printer. Save the file with the name, Lab 4-2 Recycle Sign in the PSD format, and submit it as specified by your instructor.

Lab 3: **Creating a Flyer**

Problem: A local bowling alley has asked you to create a simple image with the words, Bowl-O-Rama, above a colorful bowling ball. The address should appear below the bowling ball. A sample solution is displayed in Figure 4–73.

Instructions: Perform the following tasks:

1. Start Photoshop. Set the default workspace and reset all tools and colors. Create a new Photoshop file named Lab 4-3 Bowling Flyer and save it to your storage location. The new file should be approximately 8.5 inches wide by 5.5 inches high. Choose a resolution of 150 and use RGB, 8 bit for the color mode.

2. On the Background layer, create a radial gradient with shades of purple. Drag in the canvas from the middle to the upper-right corner. Create a new layer named ground. Select the lower half of the canvas and create a second linear gradient as shown in Figure 4–73. (*Hint:* the Reverse check box on the options bar should not display a check mark.) Create a new layer named shadow, and draw a large circle in the middle of the canvas. (*Hint:* use the Elliptical Marquee Tool and the SHIFT key.) Add a radial gradient using the Foreground to Transparent preset.

Figure 4–73

Continued >

In the Labs *continued*

3. In a new layer, use the Ellipse tool to create the bowling ball. (*Hint:* on the options bar, tap or click the Fill button, and then choose Gradient on the pop-up panel, choose a gray to white gradient as shown in Figure 4–73 on the previous page. Create the finger holes on the bowling ball using shapes. (*Hint:* reset the default colors to black over white.)

4. Create the upper text using a typeface similar to Cooper Std, and a large size font. (*Hint:* tap or click the 'Create warped text' button on the options bar and then tap or click the Style button. Choose the Arc style.) Add the lower text. Create the stars in their own layer using an appropriate brush to make a star pattern randomly across the top of the background.

5. Save the image again, flatten it, and then save it in the TIFF format with the file name, Lab 4-3 Bowling Flyer Complete. Submit it in the format specified by your instructor.

Cases and Places

Apply your creative thinking and problem-solving skills to design and implement a solution.

Note: To complete this assignment, you will be required to use the Data Files for Students. Visit solutions.cengage.com/ctdownloads for detailed instructions or contact your instructor for information about accessing the required files.

1: Create a Character Style

Academic

The Computer Information Technology (CIT) department has asked you to design a stylized font that they can use on all graphics and letterhead. Use the Character panel and create a font that includes your choice of a font family, size, color, faux bold, faux italics, and all caps. Name the character style, CIT. Use the style to create a sample for your instructor.

2: Create a Snow Scene

Personal

Create a new image that is 8 inches wide and 4 inches tall with a medium blue background. Use the RGB color scheme and set the resolution to 72 pixels per inch. Select white from the Swatches panel. Append the Assorted brush presets, if necessary. Select the snowflake 20 preset. Tap or click to create individual snowflakes all around the upper portion of the canvas. Select the texture 6, size 32 brush preset and drag to create a bed of snow across the bottom, creating a hill on the right. Use the Place command to insert an image of a skier on the hill. The skier image, Case 4-2 Skier, is stored in the Data Files for Students. Use the Ornament 3 brush tip, rotated 90 degrees with a size of 15 pt, to create black small lines at the end of the skis to simulate movement.

3: Create a Special Effects Storyboard

Professional

You are in charge of special effects for a small movie production company. You need to plan a storyboard of special effects for an upcoming action movie. Decide on a theme for your movie. Create a new document that is 11 inches × 8.5 inches. Copy several digital or electronic images onto your blank canvas. Use painting and drawing tools to add at least four of the following special effects to each of the real images: flames, lightning bolts, explosions, tattoos, jet streams, rocket flares, spider webs, sunbursts, or some other effect of your choosing. Save the file and submit it as directed by your instructor.

5 | Enhancing and Repairing Photos

Objectives

You will have mastered the material in this chapter when you can:

- Discuss technical tips for digital cameras and scanners
- Repair documents with aging damage
- Change the Image Mode
- Use the Dodge, Burn, and Sponge Tools
- Make curve corrections
- Employ Content-Aware technology
- Create new layers for editing and viewing corrections
- Lock transparent pixels

- Use the Clone Stamp Tool
- Correct damage using the healing tools
- Remove or correct lens errors, angle errors, and perspective distortions
- Create a hue and saturation adjustment layer
- Apply blending modes
- Enhance a photo using the Blur, Sharpen, and Smudge Tools

Ps File Edit Image Layer Type Select Filter 3D View Window Help

Adobe **Photoshop CC**   Feather: 0 px   ☐ Anti-alias   Style: Normal ↕   Width: ⇄   Height: Refine Edge...

5 | Enhancing and Repairing Photos

Introduction

Repairing and enhancing photos is an important skill for people such as graphic designers, restoration experts, and professional photographers. It is a useful skill for the amateur photographer as well. Many families have old photographs that have been damaged over time, and most people have taken a red-eye photo, a photo that is too light or dark, or one in which the subject is tilted. Freelance photographers, genealogists, family historians, and proud parents all use Photoshop to restore, correct, and improve their photographs.

It is impossible to make every photo look perfect — even with graphic-editing software. Graphics professionals know that a camera lacks the flexibility to rival reality — the tonal range of color is too small. Digital cameras or digital creations cannot reproduce the large number of spectrum colors visible to the human eye. Therefore, enhancing and repairing photos is both an art and a science. Using the digital tools available in Photoshop, you can employ technology to make reparative and restorative changes. Artistically, you need a strong sense of color and design.

Restoring original documents is a highly skilled art. It takes education, research, and years of practice. When dealing with documents of great value, or when dealing with materials in advanced stages of deterioration, you should consult a professional conservator or restoration service. Many restorers, however, choose to electronically renovate original documents using digital copies. If the document can be scanned or photographed, the original does not have to be disturbed. Photoshop has many tools to help repair and enhance documents.

Project — Enhancing and Repairing Photos

Chapter 5 uses Photoshop to enhance and repair several photographs and documents. A yellowed baptism certificate needs to be repaired and the fold lines removed. A vacation picture has a missing edge and needs to have people added to the scene. An antique photo contains damage. A photo of an airplane needs to have a tourist removed from the background. A photo containing a building needs a perspective correction. A photo of a train is improved with blending. Finally, a photo of a boy in a crowd is enhanced with blending and sharpening. The before and after photos are illustrated in Figure 5–1.

Courtesy of Fredrick and Laura Starks

building straightened and keystone distortion repaired

Courtesy of Amanda Brodkin; courtesy of David Reneau

torn edge repaired and couple added to scene

Courtesy of David Reneau

blending mode brings out details

Courtesy of Fred Starks

tourist removed from scene

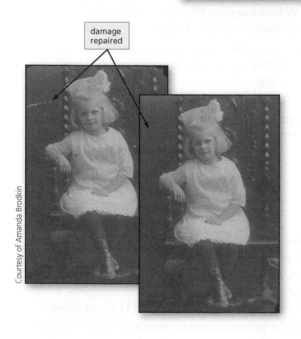

Courtesy of Amanda Brodkin

damage repaired

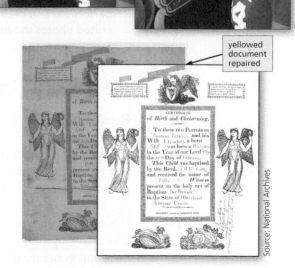

Courtesy of Amanda Brodkin

crowd smudged

yellowed document repaired

Source: National Archives

Figure 5–1

Overview

As you read this chapter, you will learn how to enhance and repair the images shown in Figure 5–1 on the previous page by performing these general tasks:

- Remove yellowing.
- Fix dark spots in a photo.
- Repair tears and blemishes.
- Recompose missing portions of a document.
- Correct using tonal curves.
- Clone images.
- Correct lens errors and distortions.
- Apply blending modes.
- Use smudging for artistic effect.
- Sharpen images.

Plan Ahead

> **General Project Guidelines**
>
> When editing a photo, the actions you perform and decisions you make will affect the appearance and characteristics of the finished product. As you edit photos, such as the ones shown in Figure 5–1, you should follow these general guidelines:
>
> 1. **Create a high-resolution digital image.** When repairing a printed photo or document, the scanning technique is the most important step in enhancing and repairing the image. Scan using the highest resolution possible with the correct settings. Other image sources may include digital cameras and graphics from the web. Always work on a copy of the original scan, or create a corrections layer.
>
> 2. **Heal specific defects.** Remove defects such as yellowing, blemishes, tears, and red-eye to improve legibility and clarity. Restoration professionals attempt to recreate the original look and feel of old documents and photos.
>
> 3. **Use Content-Aware techniques for repairs and retouching.** When portions of an image are missing or damaged, the Content-Aware techniques in Photoshop can reproduce them with amazing results. With the various fills, tools, and modes associated with Content-Aware, it is important to use the right tool for the job.
>
> 4. **Correct lens errors.** The final touch is to correct any lens errors. You can correct distortion, angles, blurs, vignetting, perspective errors, keystone distortions, barrel distortions, chromatic aberrations, and scaling.
>
> When necessary, more specific details concerning the preceding guidelines are presented at appropriate points in the chapter. The chapter also will identify the actions performed and decisions made regarding these guidelines during the creation of the edited photos shown in Figure 5–1.

Gathering Images

Recall that a variety of pictures and documents can be imported into Photoshop in different ways. Pictures taken using old photograph-generating devices, such as tintypes, daguerreotypes, and stereographic cameras, as well as those taken with film and instant print cameras, must be scanned using a digital scanner. Many photo-processing services can digitize any type of film onto a photo CD or DVD. Modern digital cameras use simple software to transfer pictures directly into computer systems. Documents and personal papers can be scanned in as images; or, if they are typewritten and easily legible, some scanners can produce digital text files. However, no matter how you generate the image, starting with a high-quality, high-resolution copy is an important step in enhancing and repairing photos and documents.

Plan
Ahead

Create a high-resolution digital image.
You can acquire images from a variety of sources:

- Scanners: Considerations that affect the outcome of a scanned image include color, size, and resolution settings of the scanner and the desired file type. When converting an original image to a digital copy, some loss of resolution is inevitable, so you should try to minimize that loss by using correct scanner settings.

- Digital cameras and cell phones: You can transfer images directly from a digital camera's storage medium to a file or import them into Photoshop, avoiding any loss of resolution. Use the highest possible image file settings.

- Web: Images downloaded from the web or sent by e-mail sometimes need enhancement or repair. Make sure you have the legal rights to use the image.

Scanners

A scanner is a peripheral hardware device that scans photos, documents, or even 3D objects, in an optical manner, converting the result to a digital image. Table 5–1 presents some simple tips for using digital scanners that will produce better results. In addition, you should review your scanner documentation carefully.

Table 5–1 Scanner Tips	
Issue	**Tip**
File Type and Mode	Most scanners have a range of settings optimized for various types of documents. Scanners make automatic anti-aliasing adjustments and tonal changes based on the file type you choose. Use the closest possible settings to your original. For example, if you have a text-only document, do not use a setting related to color photos; use the black-and-white or grayscale setting.
Multiple Scans	Do not assume that your first scan is the one you will use. Try scanning with various file types and settings, and at different sizes. Look at a black-and-white scan even if color was your first choice. Keep in mind your final use of the image.
Placement	Place the photo in the upper-left corner of the scanner bed. Align the long side of the original with the long side of the scanner. Use the scanner's preview capability so that the scanner will determine the size and location of the photograph. Use scanner settings to select the exact size rather than the entire scanner bed when possible. After a preview scan, if available, a scaling feature such as Scale to Fit page will produce a bigger copy.
Quality	Always choose the best resolution when scanning an image for use in Photoshop, keeping in mind that an image with higher resolution requires more disk space to store and may be slower to edit and print. Image resolution is a compromise between image quality and file size.
Resolution	The scanner's resolution is a measure of how many dots per inch are scanned. Higher-resolution images can reproduce greater detail and subtler color transitions than lower-resolution images because of the density of the pixels in the images. High-quality images often look good at any print size.
Shading	To maintain the background shading, especially in color, select a setting related to text with pictures rather than just text. A text-only setting can create a picture area that appears as a solid black rectangle.
Size	Use the largest original you can. For instance, scanning an 8 × 10-inch photo rather than a 4 × 6-inch photo will produce a higher-quality 24-inch poster. Use a reduce or enlarge setting only when absolutely necessary. Keep in mind that, when you print a copy, most printers need at least 1/4-inch margin. A printed copy produced from a scan may lose its edges if the original is the exact size as the paper.
Text	Most scanners have a text or drawing setting, which is appropriate only if your original document contains black-and-white areas, text, or other solid areas, such as signatures, clip art, line drawings, maps, or blueprints. If you use this setting for a photograph or picture that also contains gray areas, the result may be unsatisfactory.
Tone	If the copy appears too light or too dark, or just appears as solid black, make sure that you have selected the correct file type for the original you are using. Look for darken and lighten settings that might be adjusted.

BTW

Camera Raw Files
Working with camera raw files allows maximum control for settings such as white balance, tonal range, contrast, color saturation, and sharpening, similar to how photo processors try to fix photos taken by traditional film, reprocessing the negative with different shades and tints. Photoshop displays a special dialog box when working with camera raw photos.

Digital Cameras

The popularity of digital cameras and cell phones with cameras has reduced dramatically the need for the intermediate step of scanning. Images can be transferred from the camera's storage medium to a file or imported directly into Photoshop. A digital camera's resolution is measured in megapixels, or millions of dots per inch. It is not uncommon for a digital camera to create photos with eight or more megapixels. Typically, a digital camera processes the pixels using a 24-bit color scheme in the RGB color mode, creating a JPG file. Many photographers prefer to use a feature called Camera Raw, available with advanced digital cameras. **Camera Raw** files are captured with a wider range of colors, and provide minimal in-camera processing. This allows photographers to condense color image information later. Certain digital cameras export images using Windows Image Acquisition (WIA) support. When you use WIA, Photoshop works with Windows and your digital camera or scanner software to import images directly into Photoshop.

Table 5–2 presents some simple tips about digital cameras that will produce better results when working with Photoshop. Again, carefully review your camera's documentation.

BTW

Image Resolution
Image resolution is a compromise between image quality and file size. Resolution is measured by the number of dots per linear inch on a hard copy, or the number of pixels across and down on a display screen. A digital image's file size is proportional to its resolution. In other words, if you increase the resolution, the file size increases. And, if you decrease the resolution, the file size decreases. You should try to optimize images to produce the highest quality image at the lowest file size, making sure that you find a good compromise.

Table 5–2 Digital Camera Tips

Issue	Tip
File Type	If possible, set the camera to save files in its own raw file format. The Adobe website has a list of cameras supported by Photoshop.
Quality	Use high-capacity memory cards and higher megapixel counts to take more images at a much higher resolution. Use the highest-quality compression setting as well.
Storage	Copy images from the camera to a storage device before editing them in Photoshop. Adobe Bridge can read from most media cards, or you can use the software that comes with your camera.
Lighting and Speed	Experiment with the correlation between light and shutter speeds. Most of the newer digital cameras can take many pictures in a short amount of time, avoiding the shutter lag problem — the delay that occurs between pressing the shutter release button and the actual moment the picture is taken.
Balance	Changing your white balance setting from auto to cloudy when shooting outdoors creates a filtered, richer color, increasing the reds and yellows.
Filters	If possible, use a polarizing filter for landscapes and outdoor shooting. It reduces glare and unwanted reflections. Polarized shots have richer, more saturated colors, especially in the sky. You also can use sunglasses in front of the lens to reduce glare. When shooting through glass, use an infinity focus setting.
Flash	When shooting pictures of people or detailed subjects, use the flash — even outdoors. If available, use the camera's fill flash or flash on mode. That way, the camera exposes the background first and then adds just enough light to illuminate your subject. Keep in mind that most flash mechanisms only have a range of approximately 10 feet.
Settings	When possible, use a plain background, look at your subject in a straight, level manner, and move in as close as possible. Consider the rule of thirds when taking photographs. For busy backgrounds, if your camera has a focus lock feature, center the subject, and push the shutter button halfway down to focus on the subject. Then, move the camera horizontally or vertically away from the center before pressing the shutter button all the way down.
Motion	For moving objects use a fast shutter speed.

© Cengage Learning

Web Graphics

A vast source of images and documents can be found on the web. The advantage in using web graphics is the fact that the pictures and documents already are digitized, so you do not have to manipulate or scan them; neither do you lose any resolution when transferring them to your computer system. The disadvantage of using web graphics is related to ownership issues. You must obtain permission to use images you download from the web unless the image is free and unrestricted. You need to scrutinize carefully any websites that advertise free graphics. Some cannot be used for business purposes, for reproductions, or for resale. Some illegitimate sites that advertise free downloads also may embed spyware on your system.

Starting and Customizing Photoshop

The following steps start Photoshop and reset the tools, options bar, colors, and interface.

To Start Photoshop

If you are stepping through this project on a computer and you want your screen to match the figures in this book, then you should change your computer's resolution to 1366 × 768 and reset the panels, tools, and colors. For more information about how to change the resolution on your computer and other advanced Photoshop settings, read the Editing Preferences Appendix.

The following steps, which assume Windows 8 is running, start Photoshop based on a typical installation. You may need to ask your instructor how to start Photoshop for your system.

1 With Windows 8 running, scroll to display the Adobe Photoshop CC tile on the Start screen.

2 Tap or click the Adobe Photoshop CC tile to run the Photoshop app.

3 After a few moments, when the Photoshop window appears, if the window is not maximized, tap or click the Maximize button next to the Close button on the Application bar to maximize the window.

To Set the Workspace

The Photography workspace has panels to help you repair photos and tonal adjustments, such as the Histogram panel and the Clone Source panel. The following steps select the Photography workspace.

1 Tap or click the workspace switcher on the options bar to display the list and then tap or click Photography to select the default Photography panels.

2 Tap or click the workspace switcher on the options bar again, to display the list and then tap or click Reset Photography to restore the workspace to its default settings and reposition any panels that might have been moved by previous users.

To Reset the Tools and the Options Bar

Recall that the Tools panel and the options bar retain their settings from previous Photoshop sessions. The following steps select the Rectangular Marquee Tool and reset all tool settings in the options bar.

1 If the tools in the Tools panel appear in two columns, tap or click the double arrow at the top of the Tools panel.

2 If necessary, tap or click the 'Rectangular Marquee Tool' button on the Tools panel to select it.

3 On the options bar, press and hold or right-click the Rectangular Marquee Tool icon to display the context menu, and then tap or click 'Reset All Tools'. When Photoshop displays a confirmation dialog box, tap or click the OK button to restore the tools to their default settings.

To Set the Interface and Default Colors

Recall that Photoshop retains the interface color scheme, as well as the foreground and background colors from session to session. The following steps set the interface to Medium Gray and the foreground and background colors to black over white.

1 Tap or click Edit on the Application bar to display the Edit menu. Tap or click Preferences and then tap or click Interface on the Preferences submenu to display the Preferences dialog box.

2 If necessary, tap or click the third button, Medium Gray, to change the interface color scheme.

3 Tap or click the OK button to close the Preferences dialog box.

4 Tap or click the 'Default Foreground and Background Colors' button on the Tools panel to set the default colors to black and white. If black is not over white on the Tools panel, tap or click the 'Switch Foreground and Background Colors' button.

Restoring Documents

Antique documents, such as licenses, records, letters, and other forms of paper, have some unique aging characteristics that photographs typically do not have. Common document paper is an organic substance composed of cellulose plant fibers that deteriorates faster than professional photo paper. Rapid deterioration results from the use of production acids that break down the fibers, weakening the paper. Acid deterioration commonly is accompanied by a yellow discoloration caused by the alum-resin sizing agents. High temperatures and moisture compound the problem. Even now, unless the paper is designated as acid-free, archival quality, or permanent, its expected useful life is less than 50 years.

**Plan
Ahead**

Heal specific defects.
Defects in photos and documents that are not related to user or lens errors may include the following:

- Physical tears, ragged edges, or missing portions
- Fading due to exposure to light
- Light or dark spots due to aging
- Creasing caused by folding
- Natural aging of paper

It is helpful to make a list of the specific repairs you plan to apply. Create a corrections layer so you can use portions, textures, and colors from the original document for the repairs. Repair smaller areas first. Consider making separate layers for each large repair. Do not be afraid to experiment until the repair is perfect.

Other types of damage include dry and brittle creases caused by folding or rolling documents; brown spots from water stains or fungus, called **foxing**; brown edges due to airborne pollutants; and the fading of colors caused by light damage, as well as mold, bacteria, improper storage effects, and deterioration caused by animal or insect damage. Handwritten portions of documents are particularly vulnerable. Ink and pencil exposed to significant amounts of sunlight can fade dramatically.

Repairing damage using the Photoshop restoration tools can require some trial and error. Many of the tools work in similar ways, and you might find it more intuitive to use one tool rather than another. It also is possible that in correcting one error, you create another. In this case, use CTRL+Z to undo the last step, or work your way back through the History panel. The effectiveness or obviousness of a repair is subjective, so be willing to experiment to achieve the desired results. The more you work with the Photoshop repair tools, the more proficient you will become with them.

BTW

Converting to Black and White
Photoshop has many ways to convert color images to black and white, including image modes, adjustment layers, and blending modes. You will learn more about converting images to black and white in a later chapter.

To Open the Baptism Certificate File

The first image you will edit is a scan of an old baptism certificate. Many times, old documents are scanned and then repaired so details can be seen and the text can be read clearly. Museums often place a corrected copy next to the original.

You will use restorative techniques to correct the discoloration, remove dark spots, and clean up the decorative border. To complete this assignment, you will be required to use the Data Files for Students. Visit solutions.cengage.com/ctdownloads for detailed instructions or contact your instructor for information about accessing the required files. The following steps open the Baptism Certificate file from the Data Files for Students.

1 Press CTRL+O to display the Open dialog box.

2 Open the Baptism Certificate file from the Chapter 05 folder of the Data Files for Students or from a location specified by your instructor.

3 Press CTRL+0 (ZERO) to maximize the magnification. Press CTRL+R to display the rulers if necessary (Figure 5–2 on the next page).

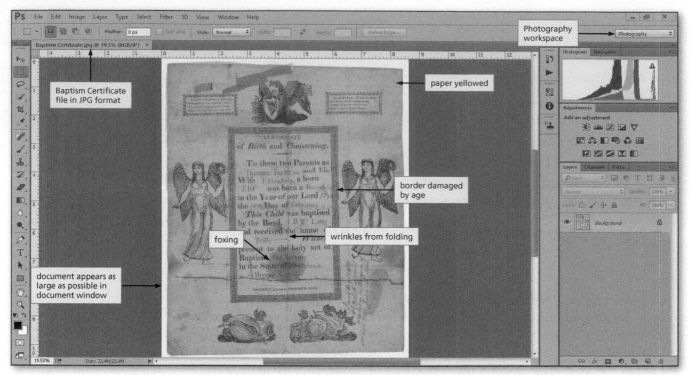

Figure 5–2

Q&A Why is my magnification different?
The magnification is related to your monitor's resolution. If you press CTRL+0 (zero), Photoshop will adjust the magnification to fill your particular workspace.

To Save the Baptism Certificate Repaired File

BTW

The Photoshop Window
The chapters in this book begin with the Photoshop window appearing as it did at the initial installation of the software. Your Photoshop window might look different depending on your screen resolution and other Photoshop settings.

When repairing photos, it is important to save the original file and your edited file separately; that way, you can also go back to the original and future scans will be unnecessary. The following steps save the Baptism Certificate file with a new name in the PSD format.

1 Tap or click File on the Application bar to display the File menu and then tap or click Save As to display the Save As dialog box.

2 Type **Baptism Certificate Repaired** in the File name text box to change the file name. Do not press the ENTER key after typing the file name.

3 Navigate to your storage location (or the Creative Cloud Files location) by using the Navigation pane or the Previous Locations box arrow to select that drive as the new save location.

4 Tap or click the New folder button on the Save As dialog box toolbar to create a new folder on the selected storage device.

5 When the new folder appears, type **Chapter 05** to change the name of the folder, and then press the ENTER key. Double-tap or double-click the new folder to open it.

6 If necessary, tap or click the 'Save as type' button to display the list of available file formats, and then tap or click Photoshop (*.PSD;*.PDD) in the list to select the file type.

7 Tap or click the Save button to save the document on the selected drive, in the new folder, and with the new file name.

For a detailed example of this procedure using the Mac operating system, refer to the For Mac Users Appendix.

To Straighten and Crop

The following steps begin the document repair by straightening the scan and cropping the white background. Recall that the Crop Tool has a Straighten button on its options bar.

1 Select the Crop Tool.

2 Drag the cropping handles to eliminate most of the white around the edge of the image.

3 On the options bar, tap or click the Straighten button. Drag across a horizontal line in the image, such as the border around the center text (Figure 5–3).

4 Press the ENTER key to complete the crop.

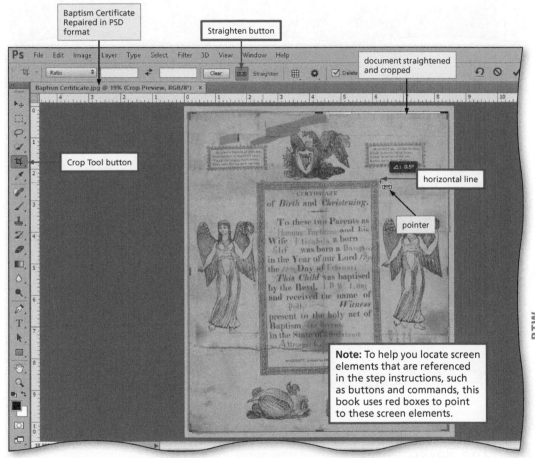

Figure 5–3

To Convert to Grayscale

The steps on the next page remove all discoloration from the image by converting it to Grayscale mode. When Photoshop converts an image with color to grayscale, it discards all color information in the original image. The luminosity of the original pixels is represented by shades of gray in the converted pixels.

1

- Tap or click Image on the Application bar. Tap or click Mode to display the Mode submenu (Figure 5–4).

Q&A Should I make these changes on a duplicate layer?
No, the process of converting to Grayscale mode changes all layers. If you had a duplicate layer for corrections, Photoshop would require you to merge before converting to grayscale.

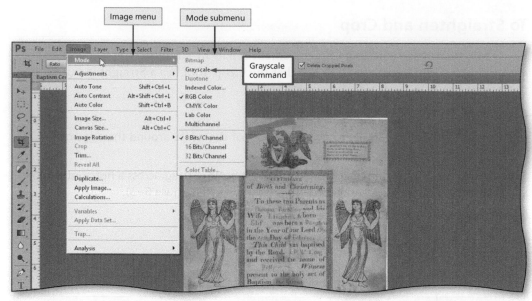

Figure 5–4

2

- Tap or click Grayscale to remove all color. If Photoshop asks if you want to discard all color information, tap or click the Discard button (Figure 5–5).

Q&A Is this a destructive process?
Yes; however, you can reopen the original file from the Data Files for Students should you need it.

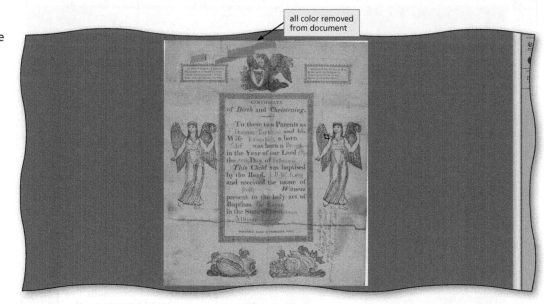

Figure 5–5

To Create a Layer from the Background

The Background layer is locked for direct editing. The following steps change the Background layer into a fully editable layer.

1

- On the Layers panel, press and hold or right-click the Background layer to display the context menu (Figure 5–6).

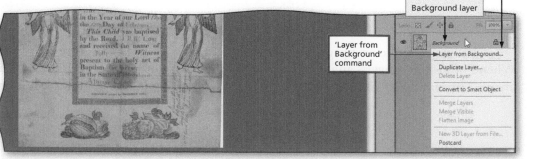

Figure 5–6

- Tap or click 'Layer from Background' to display the New Layer dialog box.

- Type **corrections** in the Name box to name the layer.

- Tap or click the Color button, and then tap or click Red in the list to set the identification color (Figure 5–7).

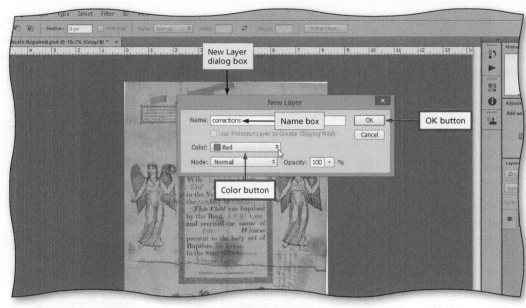

- Tap or click the OK button to create the layer.

Figure 5–7

Other Ways

1. Double-tap or double-click Background layer, enter new name (New Layer dialog box), tap or click OK button

2. On Layer menu, tap or click New, tap or click Layer from Background, enter new name (New Layer dialog box), tap or click OK button

---

The Histogram Panel

Recall that a histogram illustrates how pixels in an image are distributed by graphing the number of pixels at each color intensity level. You adjusted image levels in an earlier chapter. At any time, you can view the tonal characteristics of an image using the Histogram panel (Figure 5–8). The histogram shows detail in the shadows, midtones, and highlights. The Histogram panel can help you identify the tonal range, determine appropriate tonal corrections, or even determine if the image has enough detail to make a good correction. A low tonal range, also called a **key type**, has detail concentrated in shadows, a high tonal range has detail concentrated in highlights, and an average tonal range has detail concentrated in midtones. An image with full tonal range has some pixels in all areas.

BTW

Quick Reference
For a table that lists how to complete the tasks covered in this book using touch gestures, the mouse, the Application bar menus, shortcut menu, and keyboard, see the Quick Reference Summary at the back of this book, or visit the Quick Reference resource on the Student Companion Site located on www.cengagebrain.com.

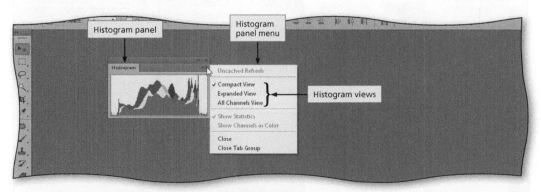

Figure 5–8

By default, the histogram displays the tonal range of the entire image; however, you can make a selection and view the histogram of just that selection. In addition to the Histogram panel, you can view a histogram using the Levels and Curves Adjustment panels. The Histogram panel can be displayed in several different views, and with or without statistics.

To Edit Curves

The **curve** of an image is a measure of the brightness value. Adjusting the curve is changing or remapping those brightness values. Similar to the Levels adjustment you learned about in a previous chapter, the Curves adjustment allows you to make very precise adjustments throughout the tonal range of an image, from shadows to highlights. The following steps create an adjustment layer and edit the curves.

1

- On the Adjustments panel, tap or click the Curves icon to display Curves on the Properties panel.

- If necessary, drag the resizing handle down to display the Input and Output percentages (Figure 5–9).

- Tap or click the 'Calculate a more accurate histogram' button to make sure the histogram reflects the most current edits in the file.

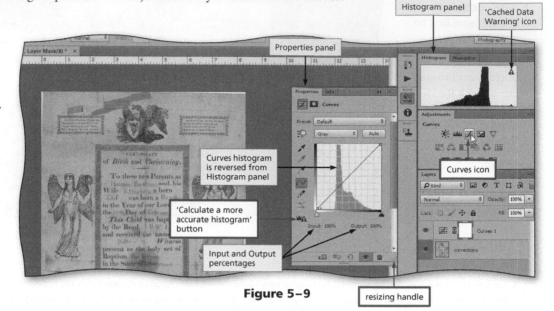

Figure 5–9

Q&A The histogram is reversed from what shows in the Histogram panel. Did I do something wrong?

No. The Histogram panel is still displaying the tonal range of the original RGB image, which displays dark to light. The Curves Adjustment panel is displaying the grayscale mode, from light to dark.

2

- Drag the white point slider to the right until most of the gray background is removed from the document. The exact position of your slider may differ.

- Drag the black point slider to the left to remove the glare (Figure 5–10).

Q&A How do I make a curve decision?
Designers usually move the sliders inward, to the first spike in the histogram, and then adjust the curve line. You want to balance the photo to bring out the details.

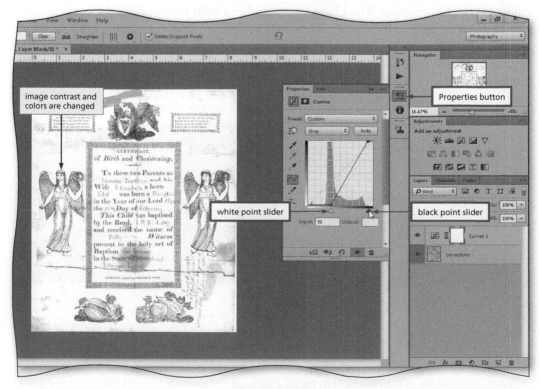

Figure 5–10

- Collapse the Properties panel by tapping or clicking the Properties button on the vertical dock of panels.

Other Ways

1. On Layer menu, tap or click New Adjustment Layer, tap or click Curves, tap or click OK, edit settings

2. On Layers panel, tap or click 'Create new fill or adjustment layer' button, tap or click Curves, edit settings

To Edit the Curve Line on a Selection

The following steps use the curve line on a selection to reduce the appearance of the damage in the document.

- Tap or click the corrections layer on the Layers panel. Zoom to the center of the publication.

- Press and hold or right-click the 'Rectangular Marquee Tool' button on the options panel and then tap or click 'Elliptical Marquee Tool' to select the tool.

- SHIFT+drag to create a circle over the damaged portion as shown in Figure 5–11. If necessary, adjust the selection to better fit around the damage.

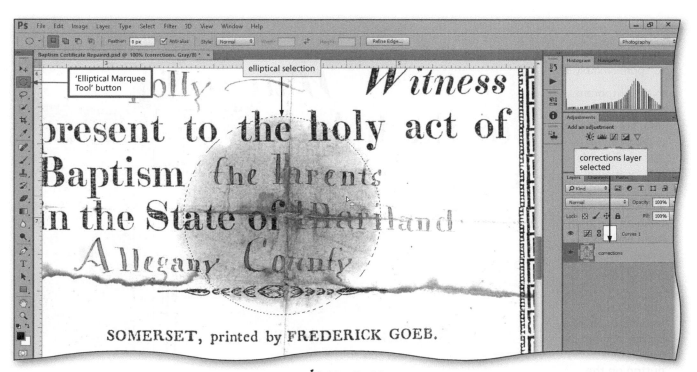

Figure 5–11

2

- On the Adjustments panel, tap or click the Curves Adjustment icon to display Curves on the Properties panel (Figure 5–12).

- Tap or click the 'Calculate a more accurate histogram' button to make sure the histogram reflects the most current edits in the file.

Q&A

What is the new notation on the Layers panel?
A curve adjustment on a selection creates a layer mask on the Layers panel.

Figure 5–12

3

- Drag the white slider to approximately 34.

- In the histogram, drag the curve line until the damage is reduced, but the text is still visible — to a location of approximately 74 in the upper-right quadrant for both Input and Output values (Figure 5–13).

4

- Collapse the Properties panel by tapping or clicking the Properties button on the vertical dock of panels.

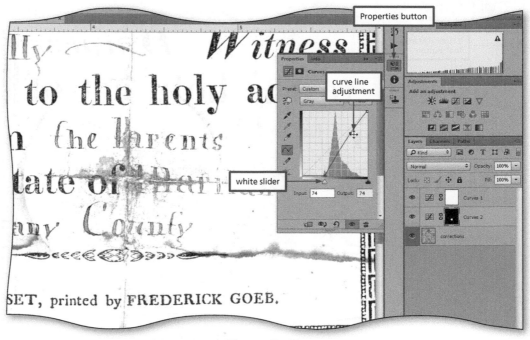

Figure 5–13

To Lock Transparent Pixels

The following step locks the transparent pixels of the image so that erasing any dark spots will result in a white area rather than a transparent area.

- Select the corrections layer.
- Tap or click the 'Lock transparent pixels' button on the Layers panel to lock the pixels (Figure 5–14).

Figure 5–14

To Use the Eraser Tool

The following steps erase the dark spots in the center of the document using the Eraser Tool.

1 On the Tools panel, press and hold or right-click the current eraser tool, and then tap or click Eraser Tool to select it.

2 Use the LEFT BRACKET ([) or RIGHT BRACKET (]) keys to adjust the size of the eraser brush. With short strokes, drag the remaining dark spots in the center of the document, avoiding the text and dark areas that are part of the baptism certificate itself. If you make a mistake, press CTRL+Z to undo. The erasures do not have to be perfect (Figure 5–15).

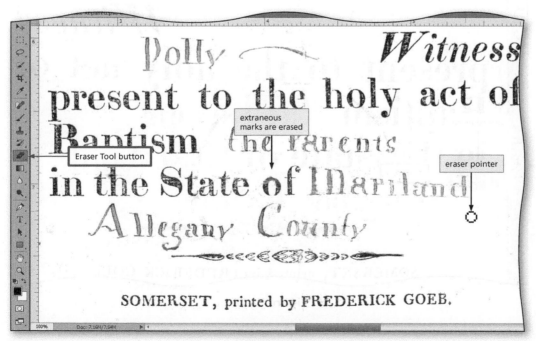

Figure 5–15

The Dodge, Burn, and Sponge Tools

The Dodge Tool is used to lighten areas of an image. The Burn Tool does just the opposite; it darkens areas of an image. Both tools are based on a technique of traditional photography, regulating exposure on specific areas of a print. Photographers reduce exposure to lighten an isolated area on the print, which is called **dodging**. Increasing the exposure to darken areas on a print is called **burning**. Another tool, the Sponge Tool, subtly changes the color saturation of an area, increasing or decreasing the amount of color by a flow percentage.

An Exposure box on the options bar (Figure 5–16) allows you to specify a percentage of dodging or burning. The default value is 50%. A higher percentage in the Exposure box increases the effect (for example, while using the Dodge Tool, a higher exposure results in greater lightening of the image), while a lower percentage reduces it. The Dodge, Burn, and Sponge Tools have similar options bars.

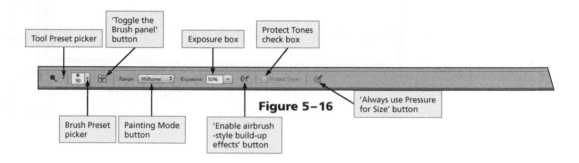

Figure 5–16

To Darken using the Burn Tool

The following steps darken the light text in the center of the document using the Burn Tool.

1

- Press and hold or right-click the Dodge Tool button to display the context menu (Figure 5–17).

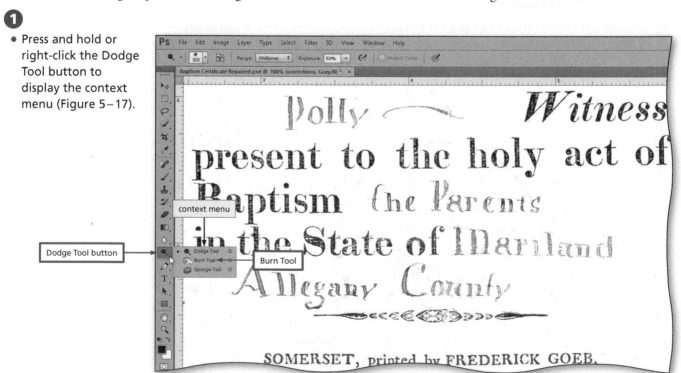

Figure 5–17

2

- Tap or click Burn Tool to select it.

- If your pointer does not appear as a circle, tap or click the Preset picker on the options bar, and then choose a circular brush.

- If necessary, tap or click the Painting Mode button on the options bar and then tap or click Midtones.

- Select the text in the Exposure box, and then type 25 to reduce the exposure, thus reducing the burn effect slightly.

Figure 5–18

- Use the RIGHT BRACKET (]) key or the LEFT BRACKET ([) key to adjust the size of the brush tip so that it is just larger than the light text.

- Tap or click several times on the light text to burn it, enhancing the contrast (Figure 5–18).

Q&A My edits created more dark spots on the publication. What should I do?
Press CTRL+Z to undo and then reduce the size of your brush to cover one character of text. You also can reduce the exposure setting. If you still create unwanted dark spots, erase them.

Other Ways

1. Press O or SHIFT+O, adjust brush size, tap or click imperfection

To Lighten using the Dodge Tool

The following steps use the Dodge Tool to lighten some dark places in the certificate.

1

- Zoom out to view the entire page.

- Press and hold or right-click the Burn Tool button to display the context menu, and then tap or click Dodge Tool to select it.

- Use the LEFT BRACKET ([) key or the RIGHT BRACKET (]) key to change the size of the brush tip so that it is just larger than the dark spot in the lower-left corner of certificate.

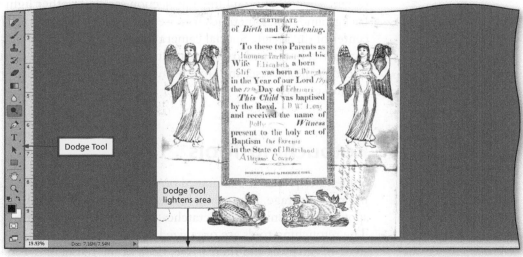

Figure 5–19

- Tap or click several times to dodge the selection (Figure 5–19).

2

• Repeat Step 1 for other dark places in the certificate. Do not remove the traces of the ribbon at the top of the certificate. Do not try to fix areas within the decorative border around the text or the dark crease mark; you will fix those in the next steps (Figure 5–20).

other dark spots are removed

Figure 5–20

Other Ways

1. Press O or SHIFT+O, adjust brush size, tap or click imperfection

Vignetting

Vignetting is a change of an image's brightness at the edges compared to the center. Vignetting usually is an unintended effect, such as the halo effect that occurs when photographing a projection screen or other light source against a dark background, but sometimes it is used as a creative effect to draw attention to the center of the image. Special camera filters and post-processing procedures can create a vignette, but you also can create it using Photoshop by creating an oval selection, selecting the inverse, and then burning. You will work with vignetting in the end-of-chapter exercises.

Retouching Tools

Sometimes photos are damaged or worn from excessive use, age, physical damage, or improper storage. Photoshop has several **retouching tools** that help you touch up spots, tears, wrinkles, and scratches, as well as **recomposing** portions of the image. The retouching tools are organized in the middle of the Tools panel. Table 5–3 lists some of the tools and their usage. Each of the retouching tools will be explained further as it is used.

Table 5–3 Retouching Tools

Tool	Use	Button
Blur Tool	Blurs small portions of the image	
Burn Tool	Darkens areas in an image	
Content-Aware Move Tool	Moves or extends a selection to a new area and then integrates texture, lighting, transparency, and shading to create new content	
Dodge Tool	Lightens areas in an image	
Healing Brush Tool	Removes and repairs imperfections by first taking a sample from another place in the image and then painting an area to match the texture, lighting, transparency, and shading of the sampled pixels to the pixels being healed	
Patch Tool	Repairs imperfections in a selected area of an image by copying a sample or pattern taken from another part of the image — commonly used for larger areas and does not allow brush size selection as with the Healing Brush Tool	
Red Eye Tool	Removes the red tint from all contiguous cells	
Sharpen Tool	Sharpens small portions of an image	
Smudge Tool	Simulates the effect you see when you drag a finger through wet paint	
Sponge Tool	Changes the color saturation of an area	
Spot Healing Brush Tool	Removes blemishes and imperfections by sampling pixels around the spot and then paints with matching texture, lighting, transparency, and shading	

© Cengage Learning

The first set of retouching tools includes five healing or restoration tools to correct imperfections in photos and images. The Spot Healing Brush Tool, the Healing Brush Tool, the Patch Tool, the Content-Aware Move Tool, and the Red Eye Tool are used to make specific kinds of repairs to blemishes, tears, holes, and red-eye problems. As you work with some of these tools, you will create a corrections layer for each photo in order to protect the original. By creating a corrections layer, or multiple corrections layers, it is easy to compare the original to the corrections and see the difference you have made by showing and hiding various layers. A corrections layer also protects the original in case you want to start again.

BTW

Certification
The Adobe Certified Expert (ACE) program provides an opportunity for you to obtain a valuable industry credential — proof that you have the Photoshop CC skills required by employers. For more information, visit the Certification resource on the Student Companion Site located on www.cengagebrain.com.

The Patch Tool

The Patch Tool lets you repair imperfections within a selected area using pixels from another area or by using a pattern. The Patch Tool is more than just a copy-and-paste mechanism, however. The Patch Tool matches the texture, shading, and lighting of the pixels. When repairing with pixels from the image, select a small area to produce the best results. The Patch Tool can sample pixels from the same image, from a different image, or from a chosen pattern. In Content-Aware mode, the options bar changes slightly, and the Patch Tool requires you to drag around the damaged area to create a selection. You then move that selection to a location that contains the pixels you want to use as a patch. As you drag to move the selection, Photoshop displays a preview of what the repair will look like. When you release the mouse button, the original selected area is replaced. In Normal mode, the Patch Tool options bar displays settings for the source and destination of the patch, as well as options to adjust the selection or use a pattern to make the patch repair (Figure 5–21).

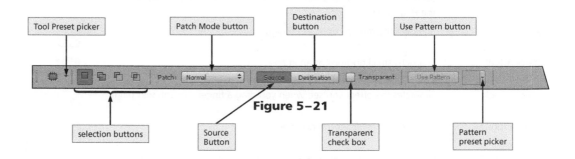

Figure 5–21

To Patch Areas

The following steps use the Patch Tool to patch missing portions and clean up other portions of the border around the text in the certificate.

1

- Zoom to 100% and then scroll to the lower-left side of the border, where a dark line runs through the border.

- Press and hold or right-click the 'Spot Healing Brush Tool' button to display the context menu (Figure 5–22).

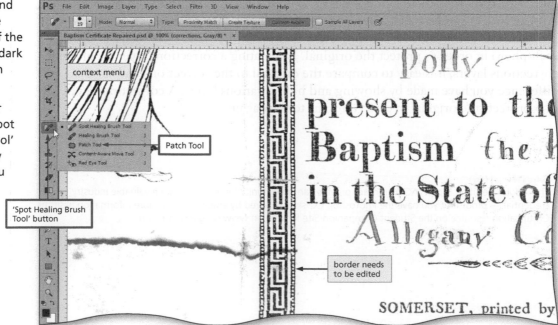

Figure 5–22

2

- Tap or click Patch Tool in the list.

- On the options bar, tap or click the New selection button, if necessary.

- Tap or click the Source button to identify the location to patch.

- Draw around the damaged area to select it (Figure 5–23).

Q&A Should I see a change?
No. The correction will not take place until you drag the selection down to an undamaged portion of the image.

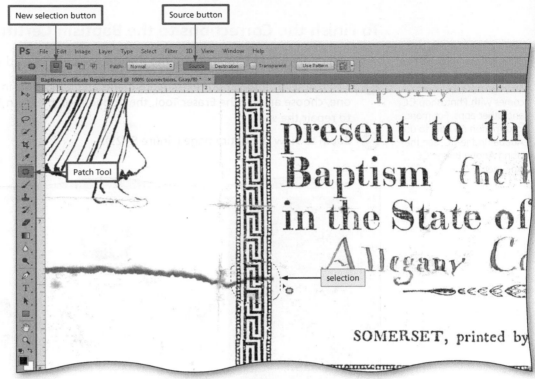

Figure 5–23

3

- Drag the selection straight down to an undamaged area of the border to repair the original location. Do not release the drag (Figure 5–24).

Q&A How do I choose where to drag the selection?
Look for an area in the photo that has undamaged pixels of the same color, pattern, or texture. When you drag the damage to that area, the Patch Tool will repair the original location using pixels from the destination of the drag.

Figure 5–24

4

- Make sure the pattern matches, adjusting the placement of the patch as needed by dragging it, and then release the drag.

- Press CTRL+D to remove the selection and display the patch.

- Repair other areas of the border in the same manner.

Other Ways

1. Press J or SHIFT+J, tap or click Source button, drag area, tap or click Destination button, drag area

To Finish the Corrections to the Baptism Certificate

The following steps clean up the remaining portions of the certificate.

1 Zoom and scroll to various extraneous marks and dark spots in the certificate. For each one, choose among the Eraser Tool, the Dodge Tool, the Burn Tool, or the Patch Tool to repair the spots.

2 Zoom to view the entire page (Figure 5–25).

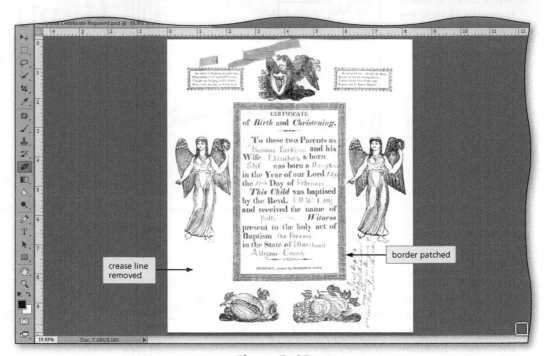

Figure 5–25

To Save and Close the Baptism Certificate Repaired File

The following steps save the file again and close it.

1 Press CTRL+S to save the file again. If Photoshop displays a dialog box, tap or click the OK button.

2 Press CTRL+W to close the file without quitting Photoshop.

Break Point: If you wish to take a break, this is a good place to do so. Press CTRL+Q to quit Photoshop. To resume at a later time, start Photoshop, and continue following the steps from this location forward.

The Spot Healing Brush Tool

The Spot Healing Brush Tool removes blemishes and imperfections by sampling pixels around the spot. Used for small spots, Photoshop paints in the image with matching texture, lighting, transparency, shading, shadows, and edges. The Spot Healing Brush Tool options bar (Figure 5–26) contains settings for the blending mode of the repair and the sampling methods. Recall that sampling occurs when Photoshop stores the pixel values of a selected spot or area. The Proximity method uses the pixels around the edge of the selection as a sample in order to fill in the selection. The Create Texture method uses pixels within the selection to replicate the texture. The Content-Aware method uses an algorithm to compare nearby image content to fill the selection realistically.

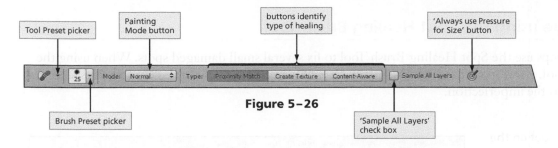

Figure 5–26

In the next steps, you will open a file, save it with a new name, and create a corrections layer in preparation for using the Spot Healing Brush Tool.

To Open the Girl Image and Save It with a Different Name

The following steps open the Girl image from the Data Files for Students. Visit solutions.cengage.com/ctdownloads for detailed instructions or contact your instructor for information about accessing the required files.

1 Open the file named Girl from the Chapter 05 folder of the Data Files for Students, or from a location specified by your instructor.

2 Press SHIFT+CTRL+S to open the Save As dialog box, and then navigate to your preferred storage location and the Chapter 05 folder you created earlier.

3 Save the file in the PSD format using the name, `Girl Repaired`.

To Create a Corrections Layer in the Girl Repaired File

The following steps create a corrections layer.

1 On the Layers panel, press and hold or right-click the Background layer and then tap or click Duplicate Layer on the context menu.

2 When Photoshop displays the Duplicate Layer dialog box, type `corrections` in the As box and then tap or click the OK button to create the corrections layer.

3 Press and hold or right-click the visibility icon on the corrections layer, and then tap or click Red to assign an identification color (Figure 5–27).

BTW

The Create Texture Button
When contrasting tones or colors are near the area to be repaired, the Create Texture option creates a healing stroke by sampling the pixels inside the selection brush, not just the ones near the edges.

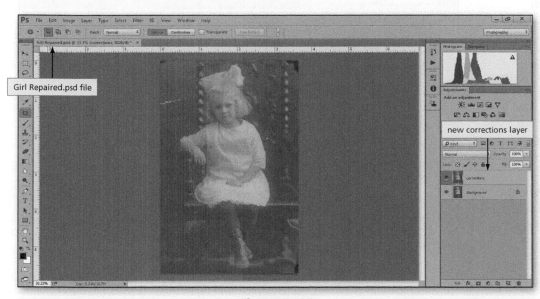

Figure 5–27

To Repair Damage using the Spot Healing Brush Tool

The following steps use the Spot Healing Brush Tool to fix several small damaged spots. When using the Spot Healing Brush Tool, it is important to use the smallest possible brush tip so that the sample comes from the area directly adjacent to the imperfection.

1

- Zoom in to the black spot on the girl's dress.

- Press and hold or right-click the current healing tool on the Tools panel and then tap or click 'Spot Healing Brush Tool' in the list to select it.

- If necessary on the options bar, tap or click the Mode button, and then tap or click Normal.

- Tap or click the Content-Aware button, if necessary, to select it.

- In the document window, move the pointer to the dark spot on the dress.

- Press the LEFT BRACKET ([) key or the RIGHT BRACKET (]) key until the brush tip is slightly larger than the spot (Figure 5–28).

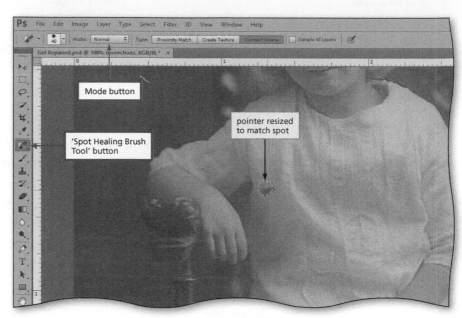

Figure 5–28

Q&A What other modes are there besides Normal?
If you tap or click the button, you can see there are several choices. The Replace mode, for example, preserves the noise, film grain, and texture at the edges. You will learn about other blending modes later in the chapter.

2

- Tap or click the spot and then move the pointer away to view the results (Figure 5–29).

Q&A Why does my correction look different?
The size or position of your pointer may have been different, or the color settings on your monitor may be slightly different. If you do not like the result, press CTRL+Z and then try it again.

3

- Repeat Steps 2 and 3 to repair other spots on the wall and the chair. Do not correct the tear on the left.

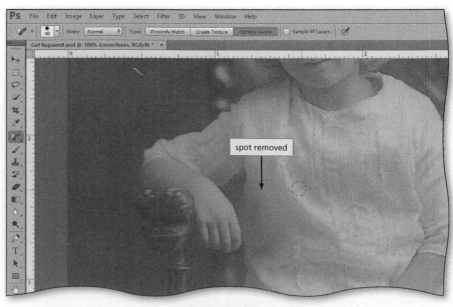

Figure 5–29

Other Ways

1. Press J or SHIFT+J, adjust brush size, tap or click imperfection

The Healing Brush Tool

The Healing Brush Tool is suited for larger areas such as creases, tears, or wrinkles. Whereas the Spot Healing Brush Tool samples the surrounding pixels automatically, the Healing Brush Tool requires you to choose a sample area first, as you did with the Background Eraser Tool in a previous chapter. When using the Healing Brush Tool, the Brush Preset picker allows you to set specific characteristics of the brush. On the options bar, you also can choose to use a tablet pen. The Mode box allows you to choose one of several blending modes, or choose to replace the pixels to preserve the grain and texture at the edges of the brush stroke. Additionally, the Healing Brush Tool options bar has an Aligned setting to sample pixels continuously without losing the current sampling point, even if you release the mouse button.

To Sample and Paint using the Healing Brush Tool

The following steps use the Healing Brush Tool to fix the tear on the left side of the photo.

1

- Scroll to the tear in the upper-left portion of the photo.

- Press and hold or right-click the 'Spot Healing Brush Tool' button to display the context menu, and then tap or click 'Healing Brush Tool' in the list.

- Tap or click the Aligned check box so it displays a check mark.

- Move the pointer into the document window and use the BRACKET keys to resize the pointer so it is slightly bigger than the edges of the tear (Figure 5–30).

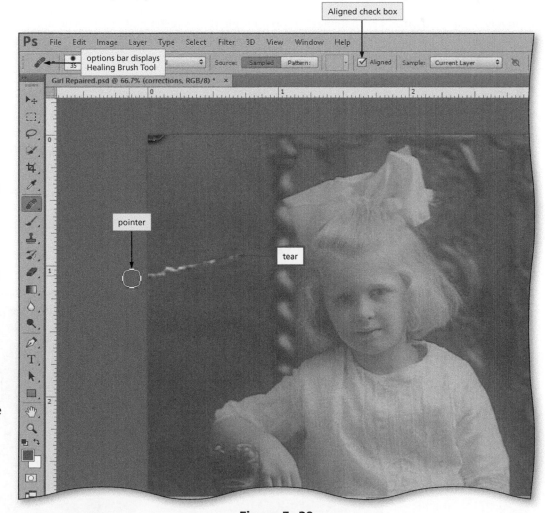

Figure 5–30

2

- To sample the pixels, ALT+tap or ALT+click above the tear, approximately ½ inch.

- Using short, horizontal strokes, drag across a short section of the tear to repair the damage. Resample if necessary (Figure 5–31).

Q&A How can I make my corrections look better?
A certain amount of document repair

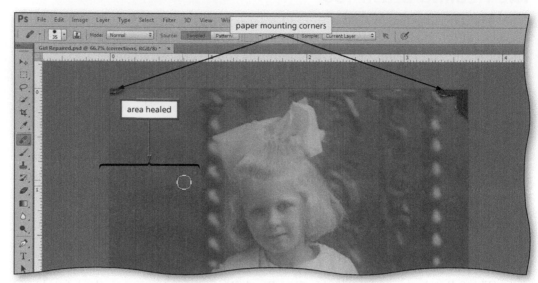

Figure 5–31

involves trial and error–and patience! Using multiple repair techniques, such as healing, patching, cloning, and Content-Aware, creates better results. Zooming in or resampling frequently also generates better corrections. You will improve with more practice.

3

- Repeat Step 2 to remove the old paper photo mounting corners.

Other Ways

1. Press J or SHIFT+J, ALT+tap or ALT+click sample, drag flawed areas

To View Corrections

The following step compares the original layer with the corrections layer.

1

- ALT+tap or ALT+click the visibility icon on the Background layer to view the original image before corrections (Figure 5–32).

- ALT+tap or ALT+click the visibility icon on the corrections layer to view corrections again.

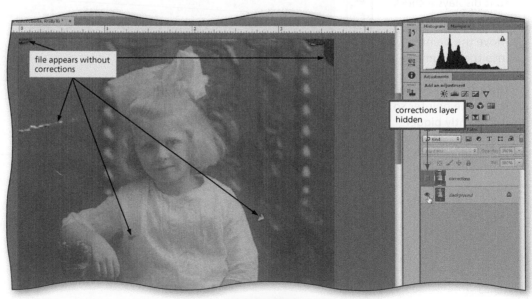

Figure 5–32

To Save and Close the Girl Repaired File

The following step saves the file again and closes it.

 Save and close the file without quitting Photoshop.

The Red Eye Tool

In photographs, **red-eye** is a red appearance in the pupils of the subject's eyes. Red-eye occurs in flash photography when the flash of a camera is bright enough to cause a reflection off the retina. Red-eye can be avoided by moving the flash farther away from the lens or by using a more modern camera that has a red-eye reduction feature. In those cameras, the flash goes off twice — once before the picture is taken and then again to take the picture. The first flash causes the pupils to contract, which significantly reduces the red-eye.

Red-eye can be corrected in Photoshop using a specialized tool designed specifically for this problem. The Red Eye Tool removes red-eye in flash photos by recoloring all contiguous red pixels. The Red Eye Tool options bar has settings to change the pupil size and the darken amount. The Red Eye Tool can be used only on photos in the RGB and Lab color formats. It does not work in the CMYK color mode.

BTW

Red-Eye
The amount of red light emerging from the pupil of the eye depends on the amount of melanin in the layers behind the retina. This amount varies strongly between individuals. People with blue eyes have relatively low melanin in the interior surface of the eye, and thus show a much stronger red-eye effect than people with brown eyes. The same holds true for animals.

Content-Aware

Content-Aware is a texture synthesis technology used to edit and repair photos. You have used Content-Aware features with the Patch Tool, however, you also can use this feature with the Content-Aware Move Tool or by itself with the Fill command. Using mathematical algorithms, Content-Aware fills the selection with similar nearby content to replicate a portion of an image. Content-Aware reconstructs a texture based on data sampled from around the area. Texture synthesis is used in computer graphics, digital image editing, 3D computer graphics, and post-production of films.

Use Content-Aware techniques for repairs and retouching.
When portions of an image are missing or damaged, the Content-Aware techniques in Photoshop can reproduce them with amazing results. You can use Content-Aware to fill in portions of an image that are missing, either because the photo was damaged or because the original photo contained an error, or you can remove portions of an image such as a spot on a camera lens or an object that should not be in the scene.

Plan Ahead

The Content-Aware Move Tool

The Content-Aware Move Tool moves or extends portions of an image using Content-Aware algorithms. The options bar for the Content-Aware Move Tool displays tools for creating selections and choosing a mode and an adaptation (Figure 5–33 on the next page). The Move mode replaces both the source and destination area, integrating texture, lighting, transparency, and shading to create new content. The Extend mode replaces only the destination area, similar to a copy command, but with Content-Aware technology. The Extend mode continues an edge or pattern, rather than fills it. Adaptation options control how closely the new area reflects existing image patterns using a range of numbers, structure, and color.

BTW

Red Eye Tool Options Bar
The Red Eye Tool options bar displays options for the pupil size and percentage of darkening. The labels are scrubby sliders.

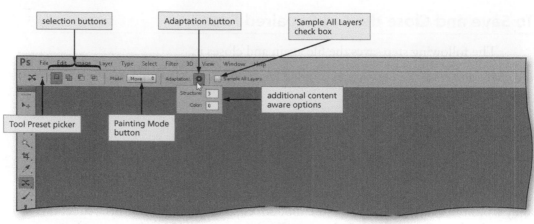

Figure 5–33

BTW

The Content-Aware Button
The Content-Aware button works in the same way as the Fill command. It compares nearby image content to fill the selection using an algorithm, maintaining key details such as shadows and object edges.

To Open the B17 Image and Save It with a Different Name

The following steps open the B17 image from the Data Files for Students. Visit solutions.cengage.com/ctdownloads for detailed instructions or contact your instructor for information about accessing the required files.

1 Open the file named B17 from the Chapter 05 folder of the Data Files for Students, or from a location specified by your instructor.

2 Use the Save As command to save the file on your preferred storage device in the PSD format using the name, **B17 Repaired**.

BTW

Layer from Background
The 'Layer from Background' command renames the background layer in an image and unlocks it. The Duplicate Layer command creates a second, unlocked layer with a copy of the background. Use the latter when you want to maintain the original background layer.

To Create a Corrections Layer in the B17 Repaired File

The following steps create a corrections layer.

1 On the Layers panel, press and hold or right-click the Background layer and then tap or click Duplicate Layer on the context menu.

2 When Photoshop displays the Duplicate Layer dialog box, type **corrections** in the As box and then tap or click the OK button to create the corrections layer.

3 Press and hold or right-click the visibility icon on the corrections layer, and then tap or click Red to assign an identification color (Figure 5–34).

Figure 5–34

To Use the Content-Aware Move Tool

The following steps use the Content-Aware Move Tool in Move mode to remove a person from the scene.

1

- Zoom in on the person in the scene.

- On the Tools panel, press and hold or right-click the current healing brush tool, and then tap or click 'Content-Aware Move Tool' to select the tool.

- On the options bar, tap or click the New selection button, if necessary. Tap or click the Mode button and then tap or click Move in the list, if necessary. Deselect the 'Sample All Layers' check box if necessary.

- In the photo, drag an area to the right of the person, approximately the same size and shape to create a selection (Figure 5–35).

 Q&A What is the purpose of the 'Sample All Layers' check box?
When you are using many layers with varying colors and textures in the same part of the image, checking the box will cause the selection to sample all layers as it makes the correction.

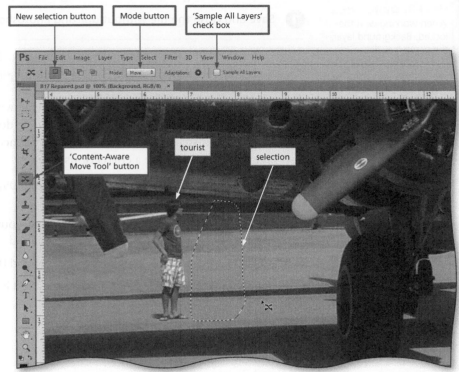

New selection button   Mode button   'Sample All Layers' check box

'Content-Aware Move Tool' button   tourist   selection

Figure 5–35

2

- Drag the selection over the top of the person and watch while Photoshop creates the new portion of the image (Figure 5–36).

 Q&A My selection was too small to replace all of the person. What should I do?
You can undo by pressing CTRL+Z, or you can create another selection and drag it over the remaining portion of the person.

3

- Press CTRL+D to deselect.

- Tap or click the visibility icon on the corrections layer to look at your correction. If it does not look good, tap or click the visibility icon on the corrections layer, and then select and drag a new area over the top of the correction.

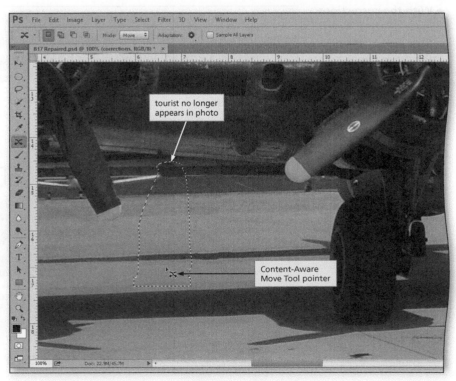

tourist no longer appears in photo

Content-Aware Move Tool pointer

Figure 5–36

Other Ways

1. Press J or SHIFT+J, create selection in sample area, drag selection to error

To Save and Close the B17 Repaired File

BTW

Content-Aware and the Fill Dialog Box
When working with the locked, Background layer, the DELETE key does not immediately delete a selection to transparency. Photoshop will display the Fill dialog box, offering to fill the selection with a Content-Aware texture or a color. If you are not on the Background layer, you must use the Fill command on the Edit menu.

The following steps save the file again and close it.

 Save and close the file without quitting Photoshop.

To Prepare the Vacation Spot File for Corrections

The following step opens a scanned image with a missing edge from the Data Files for Students. Visit solutions.cengage.com/ctdownloads for detailed instructions or contact your instructor for information about accessing the required files. The steps also save the file and create a corrections layer.

1 Open the Vacation Spot file from the Chapter 05 folder of the Data Files for Students or a location specified by your instructor.

2 Use the Save As command to save the file on your preferred storage device in the PSD format using the name, Vacation Spot Repaired.

3 Press CTRL+J to create a copy of the Background layer

4 Rename the layer, corrections, and assign a red identification color.

To Fill using Content-Aware

The Fill command fills a selection with colors, patterns, or by using Content-Aware. The Fill dialog box also allows you to choose different blending modes. The following steps fill in a portion of an image using Content-Aware with the Fill command.

1

- With the corrections layer selected, select the Lasso Tool on the Tools panel.

- Drag to create a marquee around the torn corner. Include a small amount of the picture itself in the lasso (Figure 5–37).

Q&A

Could I have used the Magic Wand Tool to select only the white area?
Yes, but if you include a bit of the edge around the white area, Photoshop has more information with which to create a better Content-Aware fill.

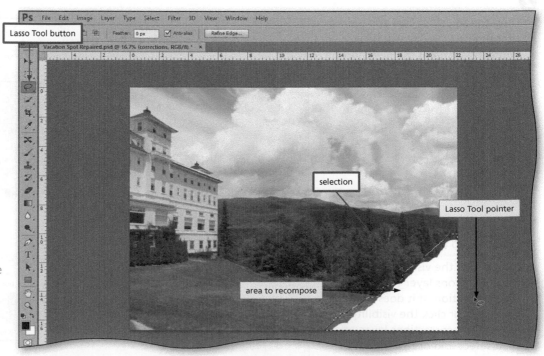

Figure 5–37

2

- Tap or click Edit on the Application bar to display the menu (Figure 5–38).

Could I use the DELETE key rather than fill?

If you were on a Background layer, the DELETE key would open the Fill dialog box; otherwise, the DELETE key erases pixels.

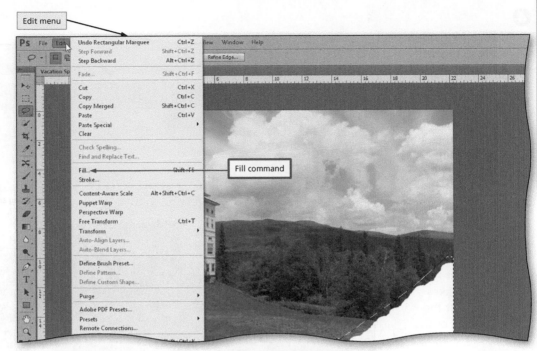

Figure 5–38

3

- Tap or click Fill on the Edit menu to display the Fill dialog box.

- Tap or click the Use button to display its list (Figure 5–39).

What do the Pattern and History commands do?

The Pattern command will display a box to choose from a list of Photoshop-created patterns or patterns you have saved. If you choose History in the Use list, Photoshop will fill the selected area with a selected snapshot from the History panel.

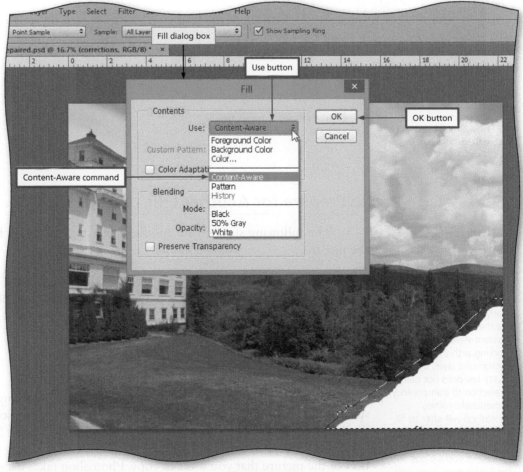

Figure 5–39

4

- Tap or click Content-Aware in the list.

- Tap or click the OK button to fill the selection, thereby replacing the missing portion of the photo (Figure 5–40).

Q&A My fill does not look like the one in the book. What did I do wrong?

You probably did nothing wrong. The Content-Aware algorithm takes into account the exact pixels of the selection, and, to some extent, creates the solution a bit differently each time. Press CTRL+Z to undo. Reselect, and then try again.

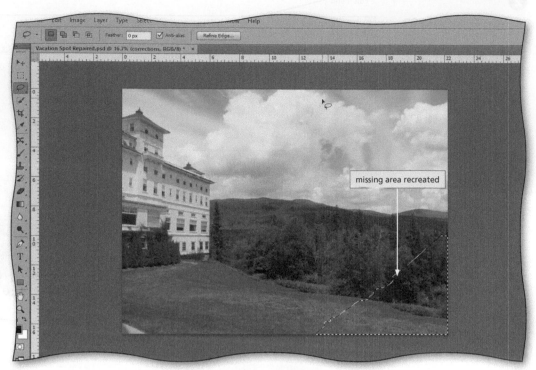

Figure 5–40

5

- Press CTRL+D to deselect.

Other Ways	
1. On selection context menu, tap or click Fill, edit settings, tap or click OK button	2. Press SHIFT+F5, edit settings, tap or click OK button

To Prepare for Another Edit

The following steps create another layer in preparation for cloning a couple into the picture.

1 Press SHIFT+CTRL+N to create a new layer.

2 Name the new layer, couple, and use a blue identification color.

The Clone Stamp Tool

The Clone Stamp Tool reproduces portions of an image, changing the pixels in a specific area. Whereas the Content-Aware tool emulates the scene, the Clone Stamp Tool makes an exact copy. After tapping or clicking the Clone Stamp Tool button on the Tools panel, you press and hold the ALT key while tapping or clicking the portion of the picture that you want to copy. Photoshop takes a **sample** of the image, remembering where you tapped or clicked. You then move the pointer to the position where you want to create the copy. As you drag with the brush, the image is applied.

Each stroke of the tool applies more of the sample. The Clone Stamp Tool is useful for duplicating specific parts of an object or correcting defects in an image. You can clone from image to image, or clone locations within the same document window. Photoshop cloning has been used famously to insert people into important photos, as well as to clone members missing from family photos.

The Clone Source panel (Figure 5–41) panel has options to rotate or scale the sample, or specify the size and orientation. The scaling feature especially is useful if you want the clone to be a different size than the original. In addition, the Clone Source panel makes it easy to create variegated patterns using multiple sources. You can create up to five different clone sources to select the one you need quickly, without resampling each time. For example, if you are using the Clone Stamp Tool to repair several minor imperfections in an old photo, you can select your various samples first, and then use the sources as needed. The Clone Source panel also helps you create unique clones positioned at different angles and perspectives from the original.

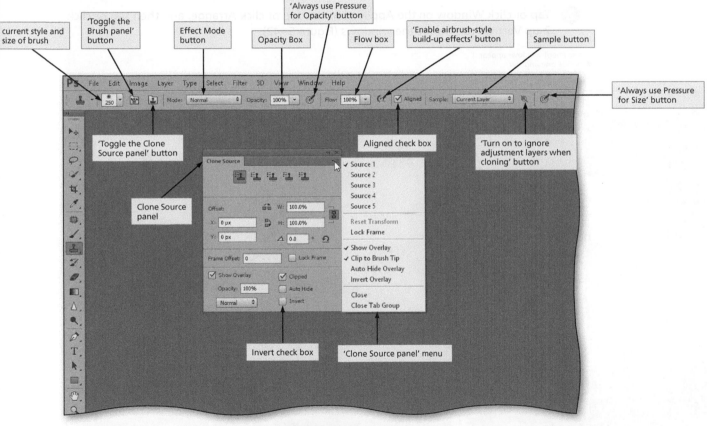

Figure 5–41

The Clone Stamp Tool options bar (Figure 5–41) displays some of the same settings that you used with layer masks, along with an Aligned check box and Sample button. When you align, the sample point is not reset if you start dragging in a new location; in other words, the sampling moves to a relative point in the original image. Otherwise, the sample point begins again as you start a new clone. The default value is to sample only the current layer or background. When you select All Layers in the Sample box, the clone displays all layers. One restriction when using the Clone Stamp Tool from one image to another is that both images have to be in the same color mode, such as RGB or CMYK. The color mode of an image appears on the document window tab. You will learn more about color modes in a later chapter.

Grouped with the Clone Stamp Tool, a second kind of stamp, the Pattern Stamp Tool, allows you to paint with a pattern chosen from Photoshop's pattern library. A **pattern** is a repeated or tiled image, used to fill a layer or selection. On the Pattern Stamp Tool options bar, a Pattern picker displays installed patterns. You can import additional patterns into the Pattern picker pop-up panel.

To Prepare Files for Cloning

As you prepare to clone, the following steps open the Couple file from the Data Files for Students, and then arrange the two photos side by side. Visit solutions. cengage.com/ctdownloads for detailed instructions or contact your instructor for information about accessing the required files.

1 Open the Couple file from the Chapter 05 folder of the Data Files for Students or from a location specified by your instructor.

2 Tap or click Window on the Application bar, tap or click Arrange, and then tap or click 2-up Vertical to arrange the windows (Figure 5–42).

Figure 5–42

To Create a Clone

The following steps use the Clone Stamp Tool and panel to sample the Couple image and then clone it to the Vacation Spot Repaired image.

1

• Tap or click the Clone Source button on the vertical dock to display the Clone Source panel.

• On the Clone Source panel, select the value in the W box and then type 75 to create a clone smaller than the original.

- Tap or click the Invert check box to remove its check mark, if necessary.
- On the Tools panel, press and hold or right-click the 'Clone Stamp Tool' button to display its context menu (Figure 5–43).

Figure 5–43

Q&A | What is the difference between the Healing Brush Tool and the Clone Tool?
The Healing Brush Tool does not create an exact copy. It samples the texture, color, and grain of the source and then applies that to the destination, matching the destination surrounding pixels as much as possible. Cloning creates an exact copy.

2

- Tap or click 'Clone Stamp Tool' to select it.
- On the options bar, tap or click the Aligned check box so it displays a check mark, if necessary.
- Tap or click the Couple document window tab to make it active.
- ALT+tap or ALT+click the lower-left edge of the girl to select the sampling point (Figure 5–44).

Q&A | How do I know if I indicated the clone source correctly?
As you ALT+tap or ALT+click, the Clone Stamp Tool displays a crosshair pointer and the Clone Source panel displays the source of the clone.

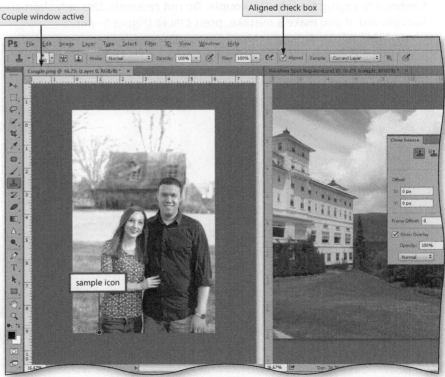

Figure 5–44

3

- Tap or click the Clone Source button on the vertical dock to collapse the panel.
- Tap or click the Vacation Spot Repaired document window tab to make it active, and scroll to the right side of the photo.
- Press the RIGHT BRACKET (]) key to increase the size of the pointer to approximately 250 as shown on the options bar.
- Drag across the bottom of the Vacation Spot Repaired image to create the first stroke of the clone (Figure 5–45).

Figure 5–45

4

- Continue dragging to clone the couple. Do not resample. Use only short strokes and clone only the couple, not the background. If you make a mistake, press CTRL+Z (Figure 5–46).

Figure 5–46

Other Ways

1. Press S or SHIFT+S, ALT+tap or ALT+click sample, drag clone

Close the Couple Window

The following step closes the Couple window.

1 Tap or click the Close button on the Couple document window tab. If Photoshop asks if you want to save changes to the document, tap or click the No button. Do not close the Vacation Spot Repaired document window.

Hue and Saturation

Another way to adjust a layer or image is to change the hue or saturation. **Hue** is the shade of a color in an image. **Saturation** is the intensity of a hue and is highly dependent on the chosen color model, but in general, pastels have low saturation, and bright colors have high saturation. **Lightness** is related to the brightness of a color or color space, measured by adding white to increase the lightness and black to decrease it. You will learn more about color models and the color wheel in later chapters and by reading the Graphic Design Overview Appendix.

To Adjust the Hue and Saturation

Your goal in the following steps is to make the couple fit in the scene more naturally, by adjusting the hue and saturation of the couple layer. As you use the Hue and Saturation sliders, drag slowly and watch for the subtle matching of sunlight, color, and depth.

1
- With the couple layer selected, tap or click the Hue/Saturation icon on the Adjustments panel.

- Tap or click the 'Clip to Layer' button on the Properties panel status bar to adjust only the selected layer.

- Drag the Saturation slider to -15. Drag the Lightness slider to -24 (Figure 5–47).

 Experiment
- Drag the sliders to view the effect of hue and saturation settings to the layer. When you are done experimenting, drag the sliders to the settings listed in the step.

2
- Collapse the Properties panel.

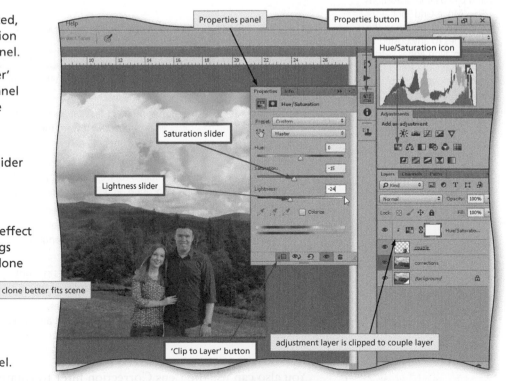

Figure 5–47

Other Ways

1. Select layer, press CTRL+U, drag sliders, tap or click OK button

2. On Layer menu, tap or click New Adjustment Layer, tap or click Hue/Saturation, edit settings

To Save and Close the Vacation Spot Repaired File

The following steps save the file again and close it.

 Save and close the file without quitting Photoshop.

Break Point: If you wish to take a break, this is a good place to do so. Press CTRL+Q to quit Photoshop. To resume at a later time, start Photoshop, and continue following the steps from this location forward.

Lens Correction Tools

Many kinds of photographic errors can be corrected in Photoshop. The most common mistakes include lens flaws, focus errors, distortions, camera shake, unintended angle errors, chromatic aberrations, and perspective errors. Every photographer has made an error from time to time.

Plan Ahead

> **Correct lens errors.**
> While digital cameras help you correct many user and lighting errors, some **lens correction** is necessary from time to time. If you have a photo that has lens errors, correct these errors after making any color, sharpening, cropping, or healing corrections.

The Lens Correction Dialog Box
The 'Remove Distortion Tool' button corrects barrel and pincushion distortions. The 'Move Grid Tool' button is used to drag the grid lines to any position to help align edges within the image. The Hand Tool button moves or scrolls images that are more than 100 percent magnified.

Table 5–4 describes some typical errors and correction methods using the Lens Correction filter.

Table 5–4 Kinds of Distortions

Type of Error	Description	Correction Method
Angle error	An image is crooked or tilted in the photograph	Rotate image
Barrel distortion	A lens defect that causes straight lines to bow out toward the edges of the image	Decrease the barrel effect by negatively removing distortion
Chromatic aberration	Appears as a color fringe along the edges of objects caused by the lens focusing on different colors of light	Increase or decrease the red/cyan fringe or blue/yellow fringe in different planes
Keystone distortion	Wider top or bottom effect that occurs when an object is photographed from an angle or perspective	Correct vertical and/or horizontal perspective error
Pincushion distortion	A lens defect that causes straight lines to bend inward	Decrease the pincushion effect by positively removing distortion
Vignette distortion	A defect where the edges, especially the corners, of an image are darker than the center	Lighten or darken the amount of color at the four corners based on a midpoint in the image

© Cengage Learning

You also can use the Lens Correction filter to rotate an image or fix image perspective caused by vertical or horizontal camera tilt. The filter's image grid makes these adjustments more easily and more accurately than using a transform command. You will learn about correcting a camera shake in a future chapter.

Angle and Perspective Errors

Although you can use the Crop Tool and warp grids to transform and correct the perspective in an image, the Lens Correction dialog box has the added advantages of allowing very precise measurements and other ways to correct errors. This is useful particularly when working with photos that contain keystone distortion. **Keystone distortion** in perspective occurs when an object is photographed from an angle. For example, if you take a picture of a tall building from ground level, the edges of the building appear closer to each other at the top than they do at the bottom. Keystone distortions can be corrected by changing the vertical or horizontal perspective in the photo. Angle errors occur when the camera is tilted to the left or right, making objects in the photo appear slanted.

After correcting keystone and angle errors, it is sometimes necessary to straighten and scale the image to regain any edges that were clipped by the correction. You also might need to fill in transparent edges created by changing the angle. The Lens Correction dialog box (Figure 5–48) has boxes, sliders, and buttons for correcting the distortions and repairing damage created by the correction.

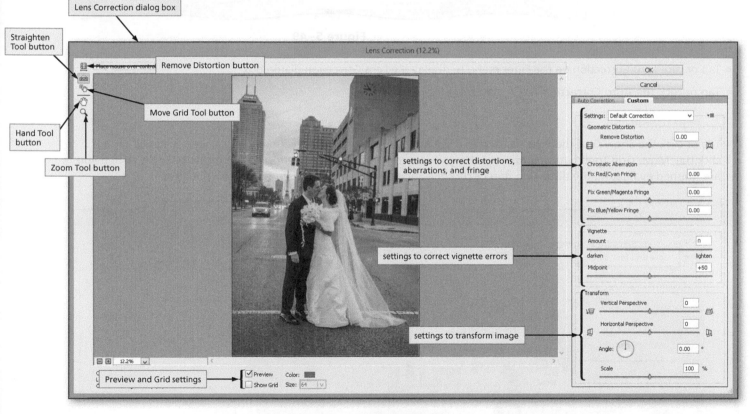

Figure 5–48

To Open the Wedding File and Save it with a Different Name

The next photo to correct is a wedding photo with lens errors. The following steps open a file named Wedding from the Data Files for Students. Visit solutions. cengage.com/ctdownloads for detailed instructions or contact your instructor for information about accessing the required files.

1 Open the file named Wedding from the Chapter 05 folder of the Data Files for Students.

2 Use the Save As command to save the file on your preferred storage device in the PSD format using the name, Wedding Repaired.

To Display the Lens Correction Dialog Box

The following steps display the Lens Correction dialog box. Because lens corrections must be performed on a single, unlocked layer, Photoshop adjusts the layer for you.

1

- Tap or click Filter on the Application bar to display the Filter menu (Figure 5–49).

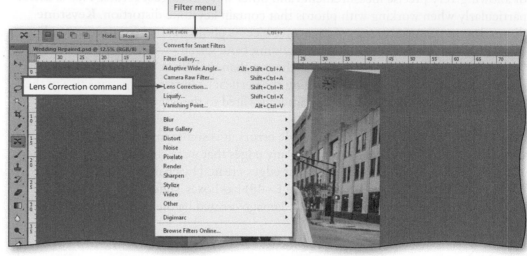

Figure 5–49

2

- Tap or click Lens Correction on the Filter menu to display the Lens Correction dialog box.
- Tap or click the Auto Correction tab, if necessary (Figure 5–50).

Experiment

- Tap or click the Show Grid check box to obtain a visual cue on how much correction you will need to apply. Tap or click the 'Move Grid Tool' button and move the grid so a corner aligns with the top corner of the building. When you are finished evaluating the distortion, tap or click the Show Grid check box again to turn off the grid.

Figure 5–50

Other Ways

1. Press SHIFT+CTRL+R

To Straighten the Photo

To straighten the photo, the following steps use the Straighten Tool in the Lens Correction dialog box.

 1

- If necessary, tap or click the Straighten Tool button to select it.

- Drag vertically across something in the photo that should be straight, such as the building on the left. Do not release the mouse button so you can see the line and readjust as necessary (Figure 5–51).

Q&A What if my adjustment causes part of my image to disappear?
If that happens, tap or click the Cancel button and open the Lens Correction dialog box again. Drag shorter strokes. You do not have to drag across the entire image to straighten it.

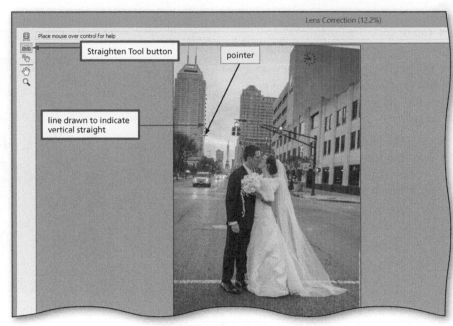

Figure 5–51

 2

- Release the mouse button to straighten the photo vertically (Figure 5–52).

⊘ Experiment

- Drag at different angles and watch the image change. When you are finished, drag in the image in a straight line, left to right and top to bottom.

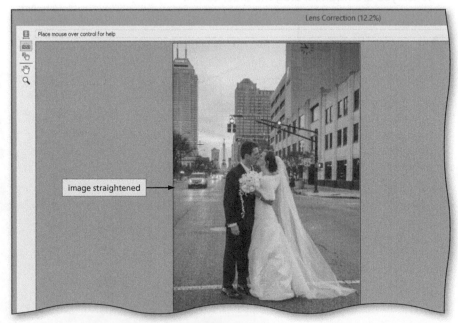

Figure 5–52

 **Other Ways**

1. Tap or click Custom tab (Lens Correction dialog bog), drag Angle icon

To Correct Distortions

The following steps correct the slight keystone distortion in the photo. You also will scale the photo to make sure you include all of the image.

1

- Tap or click the Custom tab to display the correction settings.

- Double-tap or double-click the Vertical Perspective box, and type -15 to remove the keystone distortion.

- Drag the Scale slider to the left until the top of the building is visible; the value will be approximately 90% (Figure 5–53).

 Q&A How do negative values affect the vertical perspective?
A negative value in the Vertical Perspective box brings the top of the picture closer, such as when shooting up from the base of a tall building.

Experiment

- Drag the Vertical Perspective slider back and forth to watch the perspective change in the preview. When you are finished, drag the slider to -15.

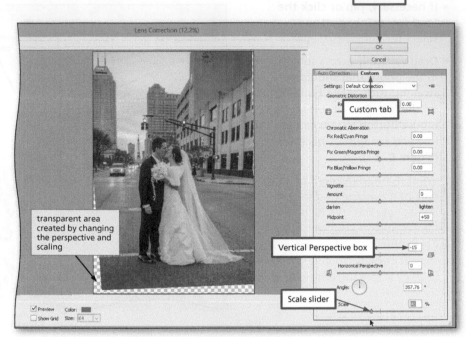

Figure 5–53

2

- Tap or click the OK button to close the Lens Correction dialog box.

- Use the Lasso Tool to select any remaining transparent area, and then press SHIFT+F5 to fill the area using Content-Aware technology (Figure 5–54).

Q&A Why did I have transparent areas in the image?
When you correct distortions, Photoshop often has to reduce one side or end of the photo to align the image.

Figure 5–54

Other Ways

1. Tap or click Remove Distortion button in Lens Corrections dialog box, drag document window

To Save and Close the Wedding Repaired File

The following step saves the file again and closes it.

 Save and close the file without quitting Photoshop.

Blending Modes

Blending modes define how an object interacts with other objects, specifically with respect to tonal adjustments. In previous chapters, you used a blending mode such as opacity to edit a layer's transparency. The Mode box appears in the options bar of many tools, as well as on several panels in Photoshop. Typically, it displays a list of blending modes to change how pixels in the image are affected by a color. The default blending mode is Normal, which sometimes is called the **threshold**. Each blending mode works differently, depending on the tool. For example, if you select the Gradient Tool, the blending mode changes how the gradient recolors the pixels as the colors change from one shade to another. The combination of these blending modes with the other settings on the options bar creates an almost infinite number of possibilities.

Experimenting with the blending modes can give you a better feel for how they work. Photoshop Help has sample images of each of the blending modes. Table 5–5 describes some of the blending modes. As you look through the list, keep in mind that the **base color** is the original color in the image. The **blend color** is the color being applied with the painting or editing tool. The **result color** is the color resulting from the blend. Not all of the blending modes appear on every mode list.

Extending the Edges
When you alter the angle or perspective in a photo, using the Lens Correction dialog box, you commonly move the edges of the photo, leaving transparency along the edge of the original rectangular shape of the image. Using the Edge button, Photoshop offer choices about how to fill those transparent areas.

Table 5–5 Blending Modes	
Blending Mode	**Description**
Normal	Paints each pixel to make it the result color
Dissolve	Used in conjunction with opacity to paint each pixel randomly with the result color
Behind	Paints each pixel in the transparent part of a layer — the Transparency check box must be deselected
Darken	Result color becomes the darker of either the base or blend color — pixels lighter than the blend color are replaced, and pixels darker than the blend color do not change
Multiply	Multiplies the base color by the blend color, resulting in a darker color
Color Burn	Darkens the base color to reflect the blend color by increasing the contrast
Linear Burn	Darkens the base color to reflect the blend color by decreasing the brightness
Darker Color	Result color is the lower value of the base or blend colors
Lighten	Result color becomes the lighter of either the base or blend color — pixels darker than the blend color are replaced, and pixels lighter than the blend color do not change
Screen	Multiplies the inverse of the blend and base colors, resulting in a lighter color
Color Dodge	Brightens the base color to reflect the blend color by decreasing the contrast
Linear Dodge (Add)	Brightens the base color to reflect the blend color by increasing the brightness
Lighter Color	The result color is the higher value of the base or blend colors
Overlay	Preserves the highlights and shadows of the base color as it is mixed with the blend color to reflect the lightness or darkness of the base color
Soft Light	Darkens or lightens the colors depending on the blend color — the effect is similar to shining a diffused spotlight on the image
Hard Light	Multiplies or screens the colors depending on the blend color — the effect is similar to shining a harsh spotlight on the image
Vivid Light	Burns or dodges the colors by increasing or decreasing the contrast depending on the blend color
Linear Light	Burns or dodges the colors by decreasing or increasing the brightness depending on the blend color
Pin Light	Replaces the colors depending on the blend color, creating a special effect

Continues

Table 5–5 Blending Modes *(Continued)*

Hard Mix	Changes all pixels to primary colors by adjusting the RGB values
Difference	Looks at the color information in each channel and subtracts either the blend color from the base color, or the base color from the blend color, depending on which has the greater brightness value; blending with white inverts the base color values; blending with black produces no change
Exclusion	Creates an effect similar to, but lower in contrast than, the Difference blending mode
Hue	Creates a result color with the luminance and saturation of the base color, and the hue of the blend color
Saturation	Creates a result color with the luminance and hue of the base color, and the saturation of the blend color
Color	Creates a result color with the luminance of the base color, and the hue and saturation of the blend color
Luminosity	Creates a result color with the hue and saturation of the base color and the luminance of the blend color

© Cengage Learning

To Prepare the Train File

The next photo to correct is a train in which some parts are dark and the details are not discernible. The following steps open a file named Train from the Data Files for Students. Visit solutions.cengage.com/ctdownloads for detailed instructions or contact your instructor for information about accessing the required files. You also will save the file and create a corrections layer.

1 Open the file named Train from the Chapter 05 folder of the Data Files for Students.

2 Use the Save As command to save the file on your preferred storage device in the PSD format using the name, Train Repaired.

3 Press CTRL+J to create a copy of the Background layer.

4 Rename the layer, corrections, and assign a red identification color (Figure 5–55).

Figure 5–55

To Apply a Blending Mode

The following steps apply a blending mode to the corrections layer.

1

- With the corrections layer selected, tap or click the Blending mode button on the Layers panel to display the list (Figure 5–56).

Q&A Are there shortcut keys for the blending modes?

Yes, nearly every blending mode has a shortcut key beginning with the SHIFT and ALT keys. Photoshop Help has a complete list. Additionally in Chapter 2, you learned how to create a complete listing of the shortcut keys, which includes the blending modes.

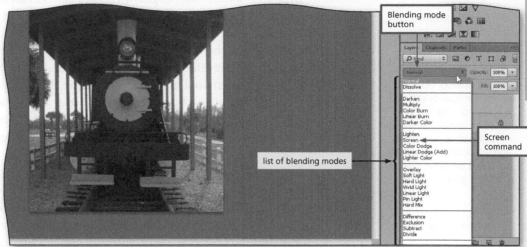

Figure 5–56

2

- Tap or click Screen to set the layer's blending mode to Screen (Figure 5–57).

Q&A How does the Screen blending mode work?

The Screen blending mode multiplies the inverse of the blend and base colors, resulting in a lighter color. It is a good mode for correcting exposure in photos that are too dark.

Figure 5–57

To Save and Close the Train Repaired File

The following step saves the file again and closes it.

1 Save and close the file without quitting Photoshop.

Break Point: If you wish to take a break, this is a good place to do so. Press CTRL+Q to quit Photoshop. To resume at a later time, start Photoshop, and continue following the steps from this location forward.

The Blur, Sharpen, and Smudge Tools

A final set of tools used to help enhance, restore, and create special effects include the Blur, Sharpen, and Smudge Tools.

The Blur Tool softens hard edges or reduces detail in an image when you drag in the selection or image, by decreasing the color contrast between adjacent pixels. The Blur Tool is used for very subtle changes in small areas. If you are working on a high-resolution image, then the effect of the Blur Tool can be very slight; zooming in on a portion of the photo helps you notice the effect. The options bar includes settings for brush size, mode, and strength. The Sharpen Tool is the opposite of the Blur Tool. It increases contrast along edges to add sharpness. The more you paint over an area with the tool, the greater the sharpen effect. The Smudge Tool picks up color where the stroke begins and pushes it in the direction you drag. The effect is much like finger painting.

To Prepare the Boy File for Corrections

You will use the Smudge Tool to smudge the background of a photo, and then sharpen the face. The following steps open a file named Boy from the Data Files for Students. Visit solutions.cengage.com/ctdownloads for detailed instructions or contact your instructor for information about accessing the required files. The steps then save the file and create a corrections layer.

1. Open the file named Boy from the Chapter 05 folder of the Data Files for Students.

2. Use the Save As command to save the file on your preferred storage device in the PSD format using the name, Boy Repaired.

3. Press CTRL+J to create a copy of the Background layer

4. Rename the layer, corrections, and assign a red identification color (Figure 5–58).

Figure 5–58

To Smudge

The following steps use the Smudge Tool to create an artistic swirl in the Boy image, and lessen the appearance of the crowd in the background.

- Use the Quick Selection Tool to select the crowd background in the photo.
- On the Tools panel, press and hold or right-click the Blur Tool button to display the context menu (Figure 5–59).

Figure 5–59

- Tap or click Smudge Tool to select it.
- On the options bar, change the Strength to 25%.
- Click the selection, if necessary, and then press the RIGHT BRACKET (]) key to increase the size of the brush until the options bar displays 300 for the brush size.
- With short strokes, drag several different directions in the image to create smudges. Each smudge will take several seconds to appear (Figure 5–60).

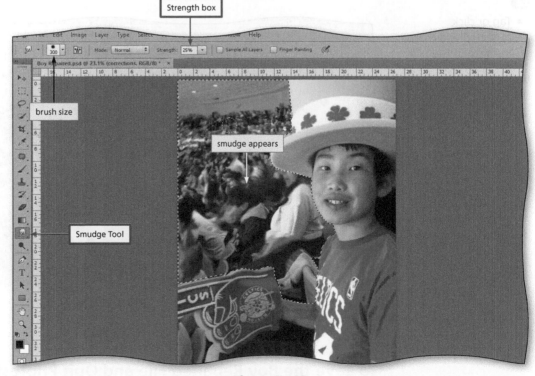

Figure 5–60

Q&A | How do I use the Smudge Tool's options bar?
The Smudge Tool's Strength setting modifies the power of the smudge. Setting the Strength to 100% erases nearly all of the existing color. A Strength setting of 25% will give the appearance of trying to smudge dried paint. The Finger Painting check box mimics dipping your finger in the paint color before performing the smudge.

- Deselect.

To Use the Sharpen Tool

The following steps sharpen the face of the boy to make it stand out.

1

- Press and hold or right-click the Smudge Tool and then tap or click Sharpen Tool to select it.

- Adjust the size the Sharpen Tool brush using the BRACKET keys until the brush completely surrounds the face of the boy (Figure 5–61).

Figure 5–61

2

- Tap or click repeatedly to sharpen the face of the boy (Figure 5–62).

  Experiment

- Tap or click the visibility icon on the corrections layer to see the effect of your editing versus the original Background layer. Tap or click it again to turn on the visibility of the corrections.

Figure 5–62

To Save the Boy Repaired File and Quit Photoshop

The final steps are to save the file again and quit Photoshop.

1 Save the file again.

2 Press CTRL+Q to quit Photoshop.

Chapter Summary

To repair and enhance photos, you used healing tools, tools that repaired damage; tools to lighten, darken, straighten, and align; and tools to create artistic effects. You first removed yellowing from a document and used a Curves adjustment to bring it into better focus. You then repaired scratches and damage to a black-and-white photo. You used Content-Aware to fill in a missing portion of a picture and replace another portion. Using the Dodge, Burn, and Sponge Tools, you varied the shading and intensity of selected areas of an image. You used the Lens Correction dialog box to correct a keystone distortion, and you used a blending mode to lighten a photo of a train. Finally, you used the Sharpen and Smudge Tools to enhance a photo artistically.

The items listed below include all the new Photoshop skills you have learned in this chapter:

1. Convert to Grayscale (PS 279)
2. Create a Layer from the Background (PS 280)
3. Edit Curves (PS 282)
4. Edit the Curve Line on a Selection (PS 283)
5. Lock Transparent Pixels (PS 285)
6. Darken using the Burn Tool (PS 286)
7. Lighten using the Dodge Tool (PS 287)
8. Patch Areas (PS 290)
9. Repair Damage using the Spot Healing Brush Tool (PS 294)
10. Sample and Paint using the Healing Brush Tool (PS 295)
11. View Corrections (PS 296)
12. Use the Content-Aware Move Tool (PS 299)
13. Fill using Content-Aware (PS 300)
14. Create a Clone (PS 304)
15. Adjust the Hue and Saturation (PS 307)
16. Display the Lens Correction Dialog Box (PS 310)
17. Straighten the Photo (PS 311)
18. Correct Distortions (PS 312)
19. Apply a Blending Mode (PS 315)
20. Smudge (PS 317)
21. Use the Sharpen Tool (PS 318)

Apply Your Knowledge

Reinforce the skills and apply the concepts you learned in this chapter.

Enhancing an Old Document for the Web

Note: To complete this assignment, you will be required to us the Data FIles for Students. Visit solutions.cengage.com/ctdownloads for detailed instructions or contact your instructor for information about accessing the required files.

Instructions: Start Photoshop and perform the customization steps found on pages PS 6 through PS 11. Open the Apply 5-1 Birth Certificate file from the Chapter 05 folder of the Data Files for Students. The purpose of this exercise is to make corrections to a scan of an old birth certificate and enhance it for use on a family history website. The edited file is shown in Figure 5–63 on the next page.

Perform the following tasks:
1. Use the Save As command to save the image on your storage device as a PSD file, with the file name, Apply 5-1 Birth Certificate Repaired.
2. Use the Crop Tool to straighten the image and crop some of the white around the edges of the scan. Try to keep the same amount of room on each side of the decorative border.
3. Use the Image menu and the Mode submenu to change the image to the Grayscale mode.
4. On the Layers panel, press and hold or right-click the Background layer to display the context menu. Tap or click 'Layer from Background' to display the New Layer dialog box. Type **corrections** in the Name box to name the layer. Tap or click the Color button, and then tap or click Red in the list to set the identification color. Tap or click the OK button to create the layer.
5. On the Adjustments panel, tap or click the Curves icon to display Curves on the Properties panel. Tap or click the 'Calculate a more accurate histogram' button to make sure the histogram reflects the most current edits in the file. Drag the white point slider to the right until most of the gray background is removed from the document. Collapse the panel.
6. On the Layers panel, select the corrections layer, and then tap or click the 'Lock Transparent Pixels' button. Hide the Background layer.

Continued >

Apply Your Knowledge *continued*

7. Select the corrections layer. Use the Eraser Tool to erase all of the area outside of the decorative border.

8. Select the Burn Tool. On the options bar, tap or click the Painting Mode button and select Highlights. Change the Exposure to 25%. Drag over any light text in the image.

9. To repair the upper-left corner of the border:

   a. Select the Rectangular Marquee Tool.

   b. Drag a marquee around the upper-right corner of the decorative border, approximately .6 inches square.

   c. Press CTRL+C to copy the corner. Press CTRL+V to paste a copy of the corner, creating a new layer. Name the layer, corner, and color it green.

   d. Press CTRL+T to show the transform box. Press and hold or right-click the selection and then tap or click Flip Horizontal to flip the corner. Move the corner into place in the upper-left corner of the border. (*Hint:* use the ARROW keys to nudge the corner into perfect alignment.)

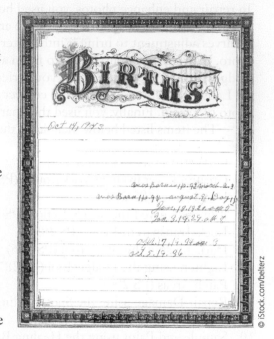

Figure 5–63

   e. Tap or click the 'Commit transform (Enter)' button on the options bar.

10. To patch the center-left side of the border:

    a. Select the corrections layer.

    b. Select the Patch Tool.

    c. Drag a selection around the damaged portion of the border on the left side. Try not to include areas inside the border.

    d. Drag down, to patch in a straight line. When the patch looks good, release the drag.

11. Erase, patch, or fix any other major imperfections.

12. Press CTRL+S to save the file again. If Photoshop displays an options dialog box, tap or click the OK button.

13. Flatten the image; and, when Photoshop asks, discard the hidden layer.

14. Tap or click File on the Application bar, and then tap or click the Save for Web command. When the Save for Web dialog box is displayed, tap or click the 4-Up tab, if necessary, and then tap or click the best preview for your system. Tap or click the Save button. When the Save Optimized As dialog box is displayed, tap or click the Format button, and then choose HTML only. Save the image on your storage device. Photoshop will fill in the name, Apply-5-1-Birth-Certificate-Repaired, for you.

15. Submit the assignment in the format specified by your instructor.

Extend Your Knowledge

Extend the skills you learned in this chapter and experiment with new skills. You may need to use Help to complete the assignment.

Using Content-Aware Tools and Cloning

Note: To complete this assignment, you will be required to us the Data Files for Students. Visit solutions.cengage.com/ctdownloads for detailed instructions or contact your instructor for information about accessing the required files.

Instructions: Start Photoshop and perform the customization steps found on pages PS 6 through PS 11. Open the Extend 5-1 Building file from the Chapter 05 folder of the Data Files for Students. The purpose of this exercise is to replace the graffiti on the side of the building with brickwork and a window, using Content-Aware techniques, cloning, and the Vanishing Point command in Photoshop CC. The finished image is displayed in Figure 5–64.

Courtesy of Kevin Marshall

Figure 5–64

Perform the following tasks:

1. Start Photoshop. Select the Essentials workspace and default colors, and reset all tools.

2. Save the image on your storage device as a PSD file, with the file name Extend 5-1 Building Complete.

3. To create a corrections layer:

   a. Press CTRL+J to create a second layer. Name the layer corrections and use a red identification color.

4. To recompose the missing portion of the photo:

   a. Create a selection marquee around the white area.

   b. Press SHIFT+F5 to display the Fill dialog box. Use Content-Aware mode to fill in the missing portion.

5. Press SHIFT+CTRL+R to display the Lens Correction dialog box. On the Custom tab, change the Vertical Perspective to -5. Change the Horizontal Perspective to +5. Scale to 97%. Close the dialog box.

6. Select the transparent areas and again use the Fill dialog box to recompose the area.

7. Use Help to read about the Vanishing Points and then make the following corrections:

   a. With the corrections layer selected, tap or click Filter on the Application bar, and then tap or click Vanishing Point to display the Vanishing Point dialog box.

   b. On the left, tap or click the 'Create Plane Tool' to specify the angles in the image. In the image window, tap or click the four corners of the brickwork on the front of the building. Do not include the soffit, roofing, or side of the building.

   c. On the top, tap or click the Heal button and then tap or click On to blend the edits with the color, lighting, and shading of surrounding pixels.

   d. On the left, tap or click the Stamp Tool. ALT+tap or ALT+click at the upper-left corner of the top window to sample the area. Move the pointer to a location at the room, above the lower-right window. Drag to clone the window.

   e. Sample again to repair the irregularities in the brick as necessary.

   f. Tap or click OK to close the dialog box.

8. Lighten dark areas.

9. Save the file again and submit the assignment in the format specified by your instructor.

10. Quit Photoshop.

Make It Right

Analyze a project and correct all errors and/or improve the design.

Correcting Red-Eye

Note: To complete this assignment, you will be required to us the Data Files for Students. Visit solutions.cengage.com/ctdownloads for detailed instructions or contact your instructor for information about accessing the required files.

Continued >

STUDENT ASSIGNMENTS

Make It Right *continued*

Instructions: Start Photoshop and perform the customization steps found on pages PS 6 through PS 11. Open the Make It Right 5-1 file from the Chapter 05 folder of the Data Files for Students. A friend of yours would like you to correct the red-eye and blemishes on a picture of her nephew (Figure 5–65).

Courtesy of Amanda Brodkin

Figure 5–65

Perform the following tasks:
Using the techniques you learned in the chapter, make the following corrections.

1. Save the file with the name Make It Right 5-1 Repaired, in the PSD format, on your storage device.

2. Create a Layer from Background, named corrections.

3. Select the 'Red Eye Tool'. On the options bar, change the pupil size to 20%, since this is a child. Change the darken amount to 24%. Click each pupil to correct the red-eye.

4. Use the Spot Healing Brush to eliminate the small spots on the face and near the lip.

5. Create a Hue and Saturation adjustment layer clipped to the corrections layer. Use a Hue setting of 6 and a Saturation setting of -14.

6. View the corrections versus the original on the Layers panel and Save the file again.

In the Labs

Design and/or create a document using the guidelines, concepts, and skills presented in this chapter. Labs are listed in order of increasing difficulty.

Lab 1: **Restoring with Curves**

Note: To complete this assignment, you will be required to use the Data Files for Students. Visit solutions.cengage.com/ctdownloads for detailed instructions or contact your instructor for information about accessing the required files.

Problem: You would like to enhance a photo from Chicago in the 1930s and print several copies. The repaired photo is shown in Figure 5–66.

Instructions: Perform the following tasks:

1. Start Photoshop. Select the Essentials workspace and then reset the workspace, all tools, and colors.

2. Open the file Lab 5-1 Chicago from the Chapter 05 folder of the Data Files for Students.

3. Tap or click the Save As command on the File menu. Type **Lab 5-1 Chicago Repaired** as the file name. Save the file in the PSD format on your Storage device.

4. Tap or click Image on the Application bar, tap or click Mode, and then tap or click Grayscale to remove the yellowing in the photo.

5. Press CTRL+J to duplicate the Background layer and name it, corrections.

6. Tap or click Curves on the Adjustment panel. When Photoshop displays the Curves Adjustment panel, drag the white slider to approximately 10, to brighten the image without losing the background. Drag the black slider to approximately 90 to reduce the glare. Drag the curves line slightly down and right until the picture looks better.

7. Select the Dodge Tool. Drag across the chrome pin striping below the car windows to brighten them.

8. Zoom in on the spare tire. To repair the bright spot on the edge of the hold-down clamp, select the 'Clone Stamp Tool'. ALT+tap or ALT+click an area to the right of the bright spot that

includes where the dark and light colors meet. Change the size of the pointer to be slightly larger than the bright spot, and then position the pointer until the pattern matches. Tap or click to correct.

9. Make any other repairs you feel are necessary. Turn off and on the visibility of the corrections and Background layers to notice the difference between the original and the corrections.

10. Save the image again. Flatten the layers. Save the image with the file name Lab 5-1 Chicago Final in the TIFF format, and then print a copy for your instructor.

Courtesy of Fred Starks

Figure 5–66

Lab 2: **Creating a Vignette**

Note: To complete this assignment, you will be required to use the Data Files for Students. Visit solutions.cengage.com/ctdownloads for detailed instructions or contact your instructor for information about accessing the required files.

Problem: The local historical society would like you to create a vignette around the picture of a sailor from World War II. After your edits, the photo should appear as shown in Figure 5–67.

Instructions: Perform the following tasks:

1. Start Photoshop. Select the Essentials workspace and then reset all tools, colors, and the workspace.

2. Open the Lab 5-2 Sailor file from the Chapter 05 folder of the Data Files for Students. Save the file on your Storage device storage device as Lab 5-2 Sailor Repaired in the PSD format.

3. Use the Lens Correction dialog box to straighten the photo vertically. Use the line of the nose as a guide.

4. Create a corrections layer, and then choose the Spot Healing Brush Tool and repair any blemishes or damaged areas of the photo.

5. Create a Curves adjustment to bring out the features of the sailor's face.

6. To create the vignette:

   a. Use the Elliptical Marquee Tool to draw selection oval around the sailor's face.

   b. Use the Dodge Tool to lighten the selection.

   c. On the Select menu tap or click Inverse.

   d. Use the Burn Tool to darken the selection.

7. Experiment with different blending modes using Table 5-5 on page PS 315 as a guide. Apply the one you like best.

8. Save the file again. Submit the assignment in the format specified by your instructor.

Courtesy of Donna Reneau

Figure 5–67

Lab 3: **Fixing Chromatic Aberrations**

Note: To complete this assignment, you will be required to use the Data Files for Students. Visit solutions.cengage.com/ctdownloads for detailed instructions or contact your instructor for information about accessing the required files.

Problem: A photographer at the bird sanctuary discovered a rare bird in some branches near the road; however, he had to take the picture fast, without adjusting his lens. He wants to submit the picture to the sanctuary's Hall of Fame, but would like you to correct a few things. After your repairs, the photo should appear as shown in Figure 5–68.

Continued >

In the Labs *continued*

Instructions: Perform the following tasks:
Start Photoshop and perform the customization steps
found on pages PS 6 through PS 10. Open the file Lab
5-3 Bird from the Data Files for Students. Save the file
as Lab 5-3 Bird Repaired.psd on your storage device.

Open the Lens Correction dialog box. Tap or
click the Custom tab, and then adjust the Chromatic
Aberration sliders. Use cloning techniques or Content-Aware techniques to remove the shadows on the
bird's beak. Use the Dodge, Burn, and Sharpen tools
to highlight the bird. Make any other adjustments
you feel necessary. Save the image again.

Courtesy of David Reneau

Figure 5–68

Cases and Places

Apply your creative thinking and problem solving skills to design and implement a solution.

Note: To complete these assignments, you may be required to use the Data Files for Students.
Visit www.cengage.com/ct/studentdownload for detailed instructions or contact your instructor
for information about accessing the required files.

Create a Clean Photo for a Slide Show

Academic
On a recent vacation, you took pictures of several monuments along the Lewis and Clark trail.
You want to use a photo of a memorial in a slide show for your history class, but the picture you
took has a trash can and light pole in the background. It also is a bit crooked. Open the Case 5-1
Memorial file that is located in the Chapter 05 folder of the Data Files for Students. Use the Lens
Correction tool to straighten the photo. Use the Content-Aware Move Tool in Extend mode to fill
in any resulting transparent edges. Use Content-Aware techniques to remove the unwanted background objects from the image. Save the file as Case 5-1 Memorial Repaired in the PSD format.

Correcting Photographer Errors

Personal
You friend is getting married and wants to post a picture of the church on social media. The picture
he gives you has some lens issues. You decide to fix it for him. Start Photoshop and then reset all the
defaults. Open the Case 5-2 Church photo that is located in the Chapter 05 folder of the Data Files
for Students. Save the photo with the name Case 5-2 Church Repaired, in the PSD format. Use the
Lens Correction dialog box to straighten the photo, both vertically and horizontally. Fix the vertical
perspective error. Scale the photo as necessary so that the crosses at the top of the church are still
visible. Close the Lens Correction dialog box. Use the Content-Aware Move Tool and the Extend
mode to fill in any areas left around the edge of the crop. Use the Sharpen Tool to bring out fine
features around the door. Save the photo again and submit an electronic copy to your instructor.

Creating a Signature File

Professional
You need to create a signature that you can place on various electronic documents, including PDF
files. Sign your name on a piece of paper and scan it using a high resolution of black and white (or
use the Case 5-3 Signature file included in the Chapter 05 folder of the Data Files for Students).
Create a Layer From Background. Remove all of the white and extraneous marks. Lock the layer
for transparency. Use the Burn Tool to darken the signature. Save the file with the name, Case 5-3
Signature Transparent as a PSD file.

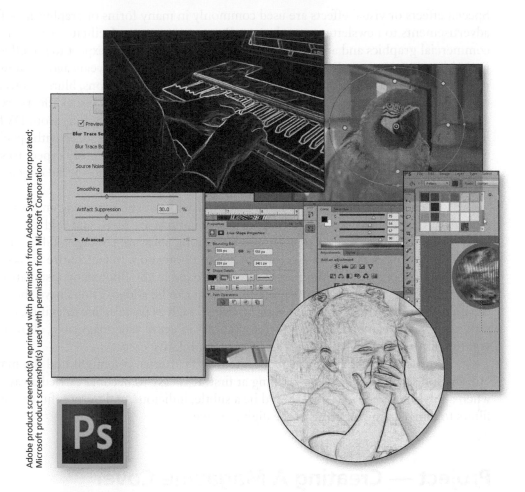

6 | Applying Filters and Patterns

Objectives

You will have mastered the material in this chapter when you can:

- Adjust the Color Panel
- Describe the categories of filters in Photoshop
- Reduce camera shake
- Use the Filter Gallery to create special effects
- Apply Water Color and Glowing Edges filters
- Describe and use Blur filters
- Create a shape clipping mask
- Define a pattern
- Fill with the Paint Bucket Tool
- Create knockout text
- Add an outer glow
- Generate image assets
- Explain the terms knockout, trapping, surprinting, and misregistration
- Print a hard proof

Ps   File   Edit   Image   Layer   Type   Select   Filter   3D   View   Window   Help

Adobe **Photoshop CC**   Feather: 0 px   Anti-alias   Style: Normal   Width   Height   Refine Edge...

6 | Applying Filters and Patterns

Introduction

Special effects or visual effects are used commonly in many forms of graphic art – from advertisements to newsletters to webpages. Because computers facilitate nearly all commercial graphics and animation, many clients and customers expect to see effects in their creative designs. Effects that seemed rare and unusual 20 years ago are now the norm. Special effects visually spice up static graphics with distortions, blurs, contour alterations, color manipulations, and applied overlays. Imaginative visual effects create a customized, attention-grabbing appearance, and are used in everything from DVD liners to billboards. It is not unusual for people to design branding logos with special effects for use in business and social media. Most people subconsciously expect to see fancy, stimulating graphics in every advertisement; indeed, when no special effects are included, some may interpret the graphic as retro or even boring.

The entertainment industry has led the way with artistic rendering and advanced animation techniques. Specialized graphic manipulations are saved and sold as downloadable filters for most popular graphic editing software packages. Filters are the most common way to create special effects in Photoshop. In fact, entire books have been written about the vast number of filters included in the Photoshop installation, along with the thousands of third-party filters that can be added. Filters have the capability to mimic many traditional forms of art, such as pastels, line drawings, or watercolors. You can blend, blur, or warp graphics in every way imaginable, allowing you to enliven commercial artwork in-house with relative ease.

In this chapter, as you learn about filters and patterns, you might find the many options and settings to be overwhelming at first. It is easy to become carried away when applying filters. Your goal should be a subtle, judicious, and purposeful use of filters to enhance the meaning of the digital image.

Project — Creating A Magazine Cover

Chapter 6 uses Photoshop to create a cover for a magazine. The magazine cover incorporates graphics, color, shapes, knockout text, and patterns. Photoshop filters are applied to the various images on the cover. The large image is sharpened to reduce the effect of camera shake. From top to bottom, the smaller images use Spin Blur, Watercolor, and Glowing Edges filters. A pattern adds visual interest to the background area of the upper text. Knockout text brings the night skyline up into the overall scene. The completed image is displayed in Figure 6–1.

Figure 6-1

Courtesy of Mike Flaherty.

Overview

As you read this chapter, you will learn how to create the images shown in Figure 6-1 by performing these general tasks:

- Create a background and add images.
- Apply filters.
- Use a pattern.
- Place pictures in a circle shape and stroke.
- Create knockout text.
- Generate image assets.
- Print a hard proof.

**Plan
Ahead**

General Project Guidelines

When editing a photo, the actions you perform and decisions you make will affect the appearance and characteristics of the finished product. As you edit a photo, such as the one shown in Figure 6–1 on the previous page, you should follow these general guidelines:

1. **Plan your use of filters.** Think about your purpose in using filters. Is it for correction or decoration? Are you trying to create a special effect or does the filter enhance the purpose of the image? Decide whether a filter is appropriate for the entire image or just a part. If you are working on a business photo, consult with the client, and offer him or her many examples or layer comps. After creating a new layer so the filter will be nondestructive, make sure you label the filter layer with the type and settings so you can remember what you did.

2. **Use special effects purposefully.** Plan your special effects to serve a purpose and fit with other parts of your image. When you want to draw attention to images or parts of images, use strokes, borders, patterns, and clipping shapes based on colors, textures, and shapes in the image itself.

3. **Avoid color printing problems.** In commercial printing, the speed of the printer and possible shifts in the paper may make some colors run together, creating spreads of blended color; or, the printer may leave small missed areas between very close objects or layers. Use knock out techniques and correct alignment to avoid color printing problems.

4. **Consult with printing professionals.** As design specialists create and modify artwork, they routinely consult with printing professionals to help plan the best method to produce projects. Print professionals have expertise on paper, color management systems, file transfer, output devices, and the way those devices interpret and process color and type information.

Starting and Customizing Photoshop

The following steps start Photoshop, and reset the default workspace, tools, colors, and Layer panel options.

To Start Photoshop

If you are stepping through this project on a computer and you want your screen to match the figures in this book, then you should change your computer's resolution to 1366 × 768 and reset the panels, tools, and colors. For more information about how to change the resolution on your computer and other advanced Photoshop settings, read the Editing Preferences Appendix.

The following steps, which assume Windows 8 is running, start Photoshop based on a typical installation. You may need to ask your instructor how to start Photoshop for your system.

1 With Windows 8 running, scroll to display the Adobe Photoshop CC tile on the Start screen.

2 Tap or click the Adobe Photoshop CC tile to run the Photoshop app.

3 After a few moments, when the Photoshop window appears, if the window is not maximized, tap or click the Maximize button next to the Close button on the Application bar to maximize the window.

To Reset the Workspace

As discussed in Chapter 1, it is helpful to reset the workspace so that the tools and panels appear in their default positions. The following steps select the Essentials workspace.

1 Tap or click the workspace switcher on the options bar to display the list and then tap or click Essentials to select the default workspace panels.

2 Tap or click the workspace switcher on the options bar again, to display the list and then tap or click Reset Essentials to restore the workspace to its default settings and reposition any panels that might have been moved by previous users.

To Reset the Tools and the Options Bar

Recall that the Tools panel and the options bar retain their settings from previous Photoshop sessions. The following steps select the Rectangular Marquee Tool and reset all tool settings in the options bar.

1 If the tools in the Tools panel appear in two columns, tap or click the double arrow at the top of the Tools panel.

2 If necessary, tap or click the 'Rectangular Marquee Tool' button on the Tools panel to select it.

3 On the options bar, press and hold or right-click the 'Rectangular Marquee Tool' icon to display the context menu, and then tap or click 'Reset All Tools'. When Photoshop displays a confirmation dialog box, tap or click the OK button to restore the tools to their default settings.

To Set the Interface and Default Colors

Recall that Photoshop retains the interface color scheme, as well as the foreground and background colors, from session to session. The following steps set the interface to Medium Gray and the foreground and background colors to black over white.

1 Tap or click Edit on the Application bar to display the Edit menu. Tap or click Preferences and then tap or click Interface on the Preferences submenu to display the Preferences dialog box.

2 If necessary, tap or click the third button, Medium Gray, to change the interface color scheme.

3 Tap or click the OK button to close the Preferences dialog box.

4 Tap or click the 'Default Foreground and Background Colors' button on the Tools panel to set the default colors to black and white. If black is not over white on the Tools panel, tap or click the 'Switch Foreground and Background Colors' button.

To Create a Blank Canvas

Because you are working with a magazine medium that prints to the edge of the paper, you will create a blank canvas 8.5 inches wide × 10.75 inches high, which is a common magazine size. Nearly all magazines on the market today are full-color magazines, and are printed using a four-color process (CMYK), providing bright color

BTW

Spot Colors
Occasionally a fifth color is added to magazine covers to match an exact brand color or to add a specialized finish or sheen, such as metallic. Adding a fifth spot color is more expensive, but sometimes is desired. Consult a printing specialist for color samples, because the distinctive sheens are difficult to emulate on a computer screen, as the RGB color display has no mechanism for indicating metallic or fluorescent colors.

shades and an eye-catching look. However, more filter effects are available for RGB images, so the following steps create the image in RGB and later convert it to CMYK.

① Press CTRL+N to open the New dialog box. Type **Magazine Cover** in the Name box.

② Tap or click the Width unit button, and then tap or click Inches, if necessary.

③ Set the width to 8.5 and the height to 10.75 to apply standard magazine measurements.

④ Set the resolution to 300, and set the Color Mode to RGB, 8 bit.

⑤ If necessary, tap or click the Background Contents button, and then tap or click Transparent in the list (Figure 6–2).

⑥ Tap or click the OK button to create the transparent canvas.

⑦ If the rulers do not appear in the document window, press CTRL+R.

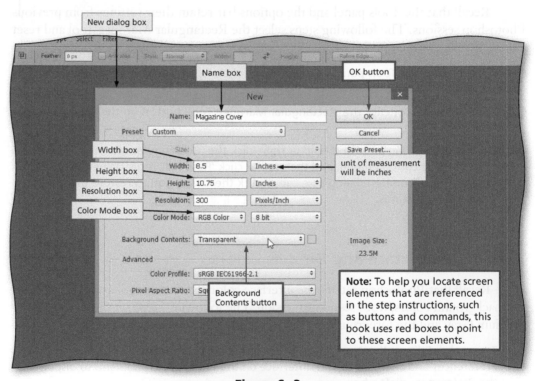

Figure 6–2

To Reset the Layers Panel Display

The following steps set the Layers panel to display medium thumbnails and Layer Bounds, which matches the figures in this chapter.

① On the Layers panel, tap or click the Layers panel menu button, and then tap or click Panel Options on the menu.

② In the Layer Panel Options dialog box, tap or click the option button for the medium thumbnail.

③ In the Thumbnail Contents area, tap or click Layer Bounds.

④ Tap or click the OK button to close the Layer Panel Options dialog box.

To Save the File

Even though the document has a name in the document window tab, it is not saved on a storage device. The next steps save the file in a new folder.

1 Tap or click File on the Application bar to display the File menu and then tap or click Save As to display the Save As dialog box. If necessary, type **Magazine Cover** in the File name box.

2 Navigate to your storage location (or the Creative Cloud Files location) by using the Navigation pane or the Previous Locations box arrow to select that drive as the new save location.

3 Tap or click the New folder button on the Save As dialog box toolbar to create a new folder on the selected storage device.

4 When the new folder appears, type **Chapter 06** to change the name of the folder, and then press the ENTER key. Double-tap or double-click the new folder to open it.

5 If necessary, tap or click the 'Save as type' button to display the list of available file formats, and then tap or click Photoshop (*.PSD; *.PDD) in the list to select the file type.

6 Tap or click the Save button to save the document on the selected drive, in the new folder, and with the new file name. If Photoshop displays a dialog box reminding you about maximizing compatibility, tap or click the OK button.

BTW

File Management
Adobe Bridge CC is a file management tool that comes with Photoshop CC and other apps. For more information on how to use Adobe Bridge CC, see the Using Adobe Bridge CC Appendix.

MAC For a detailed example of this procedure using the Mac operating system, refer to the For Mac Users Appendix.

To Edit Layers

The following steps assign a name and an identification color to the existing layer in preparation for the first image.

1 Double-tap or double-click the name, Layer 1, on the Layers panel, type **background,** and then press the ENTER key to rename the layer.

2 Press and hold or right-click the layer and choose an orange identification color (Figure 6–3).

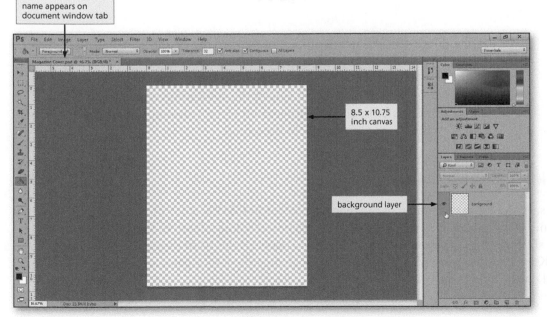

Figure 6–3

The Color Panel

Photoshop has many different ways to select or specify colors for use in the document window. You specify colors when you use paint, gradient, or fill tools. Previously you used the Color picker dialog box to choose colors. Some other ways include using the Color panel, the Swatches panel, the Eyedropper Tool, the Color Replacement Tool, and the Info panel.

A convenient way to select and edit colors is to use the Color panel (Figure 6–4). In its default view, the Color panel displays a hue cube. You can click anywhere in the cube or on the horizontal **color bar** or **ramp**. Other views display sliders and numeric color values for the current foreground and background colors, with a color bar across the bottom. Using the sliders in the Color panel, you can edit the foreground and background colors using different color modes. The Color panel menu allows you to change the color mode, change the displayed sliders, copy the color, or close the panel.

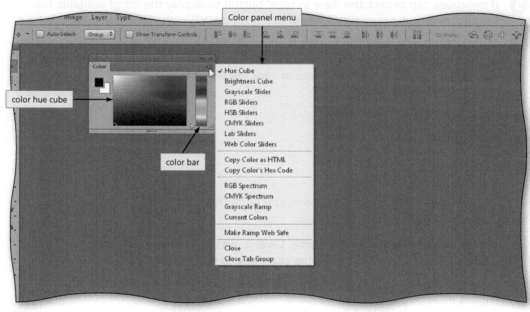

Hiding and Showing the Color Panel
If the Color Panel currently is displayed, pressing the F6 key hides the panel. Pressing it again displays the panel.

Figure 6–4

A triangle with an exclamation point appears to the left of the color hue cube if you choose an out-of-gamut color. Recall that gamut refers to the range of available colors in any specific color mode. If you are working on a document destined for the web, a small cube appears above the left side of the color ramp when you choose a color that is not web-safe. To correct either color error, you simply click the error icon; Photoshop will choose the closet color in the gamut.

To Change the Sliders on the Color Panel

Because you will save the ultimate version of the magazine cover in CMYK color mode, changing the sliders on the Color panel will help you determine whether your chosen colors adhere to the color mode. In addition, using CMYK sliders will help you resolve any difference between the RGB display colors on your monitor and the CMYK inks on the printer. The following steps change the Color panel to reflect CMYK colors in the sliders and on the color bar.

1

- Tap or click the Color panel menu button to display its menu (Figure 6–5).

Q&A What is a spectrum? The spectrum is the range of colors displayed in the color ramp. To make sure your colors are in the correct mode, both the sliders and the spectrum should be set identically, in this case, to CMYK.

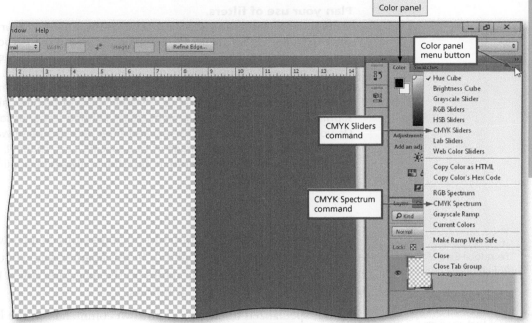

Figure 6–5

2

- Tap or click CMYK Sliders to change the sliders in the Color panel (Figure 6–6).

Q&A Did Photoshop select the CMYK Spectrum command on the panel menu? Yes, when switching from the Hue Cube, the spectrum is selected automatically.

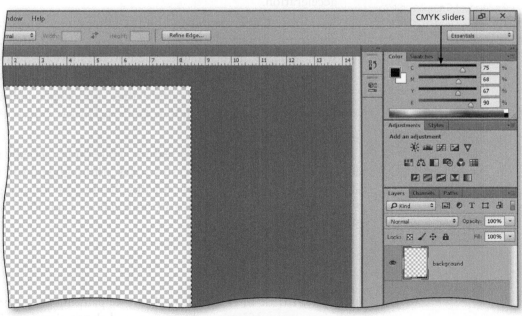

Figure 6–6

Filters

A **filter** is a special effect that changes the look of your image or selection by altering the pixels either by manipulating their physical location or by applying a color change. Filters can mimic traditional photographic filters, which are pieces of colored glass or gelatin placed over the lens to change the photo's appearance, or they can be more complex, creating advanced artistic effects.

Plan
Ahead

Plan your use of filters.
Some filters in Photoshop help you perform restorations on your photos. Others alter color to create sophisticated color rendering or alter pixels purposefully to distort. The possibilities are endless. It is a good idea to look through the lists of filters in this chapter or use Photoshop Help to get ideas on what is available. Remember: your usage of filters should be driven by the purpose of the photo. For example, you might use a filter to simulate the appearance of stained glass or texture paintings to portray a sophisticated artistic tone. You might create lighting scenarios to create what-if images. Or, you simply might want to use a water filter on a picture of water. Most filters can be applied either to the entire image or to a specific layer, channel, or selection. Filters can be used for correction or decoration, but should always be applied to a non-destructive layer with correct labeling.

BTW

Certification
The Adobe Certified Expert (ACE) program provides an opportunity for you to obtain a valuable industry credential — proof that you have the Photoshop CC skills required by employers. For more information, visit the Certification resource on the Student Companion Site located on www. cengagebrain.com.

You used a Lens Correction filter in a previous chapter when you corrected perspective and straightened a photo. In this chapter, you will use additional filters to change the appearance of the graphics on the magazine cover. Filters are displayed in three ways on the Filter menu, as follows:

- Four specialized filters have their own commands on the Filter menu and display their own dialog box interface and buttons. These include the Adaptive Wide Angle, Lens Correction, Liquefy, and Vanishing Point filters. Some of these specialized filters require a video card that can perform graphic processor acceleration.

- The Filter Gallery command on the Filter menu categorizes standard filters into six groups: Artistic, Brush Strokes, Distort, Sketch, Stylize, and Texture. As you will learn later in this chapter, the Filter Gallery has its own interface and settings.

- Other filter commands appear only in submenus on the Filter menu. Rather than using the Filter Gallery interface, these filters open individual dialog boxes in the following categories: Blur, Blur Gallery, Distort, Noise, Pixelate, Render, Sharpen, Stylize, Video, and Other.

Some filters alter color or texture, while others actually rearrange the pixels or recreate the image with new brush strokes. Although you will not use all of the filter categories in the magazine cover for this chapter, the following sections provide a general description of each category and a table of specific filters and their adjustable settings.

Artistic Filters

The Artistic filters (Table 6–1) create painting and artistic effects, adding a certain amount of texture, dimension, and abstraction to an image. The Artistic filters replicate traditional media effects such as grain patterns, oils, watercolors, charcoals, pastels, line drawings, neon shading, and sponges. Artistic filters are used in typography, commercial art, and personal art expression.

Table 6–1 Artistic Filters

Artistic Filter	Description	Adjustable Settings
Colored Pencil	Redraws to simulate colored pencils on a solid background to create a crosshatched effect.	Pencil Width Stroke Pressure Paper Brightness
Cutout	Redraws to simulate roughly cut pieces of colored paper, such as a collage or a screen print.	Number of Levels Edge Simplicity Edge Fidelity
Dry Brush	Uses a dry brush technique on all edges and reduces the range of color.	Brush Size Brush Detail Texture
Film Grain	Applies a film grain pattern to shadow tones and midtones with a smoother pattern to lighter areas; helps to unify diverse elements in an image.	Grain Highlight Area Intensity
Fresco	Repaints using coarse, short, and rounded daubs.	Brush Size Brush Detail Texture
Neon Glow	Inserts various types of glows to objects in the image.	Glow Size Glow Brightness Glow Color
Paint Daubs	Redraws to simulate an oil painting.	Brush Size Sharpness Brush Type
Palette Knife	Reduces detail to simulate a thinly painted canvas, revealing underlying textures.	Stroke Size Stroke Detail Softness
Plastic Wrap	Redraws the image as if it were coated in shiny plastic.	Highlight Strength Detail Smoothness
Poster Edges	Reduces the number of colors in an image and draws black lines on edges.	Edge Thickness Edge Intensity Posterization
Rough Pastels	Applies strokes of chalk, pastel-like color on a textured background; appears thicker in brighter colors.	Stroke Length Stroke Detail Texture Scaling Relief Light Invert
Smudge Stick	Uses short diagonal strokes to smudge or smear darker parts of the image; lighter areas become brighter with a spotty texture and less detail.	Stroke Length Highlight Area Intensity
Sponge	Creates textured areas of contrasting color that simulate the effect of sponge painting.	Brush Size Definition Smoothness
Underpainting	Creates a textured background, and then paints the image over the background to create a paler, softer version; commonly used in conjunction with other filters.	Brush Size Texture Coverage Texture Scaling Relief Light Invert
Watercolor	Creates a watercolor style that flattens yet brightens color; the greater the detail, the more realistic the image will appear.	Brush Detail Shadow Intensity Texture

BTW

Smudge Stick Filter
The Smudge Stick filter redraws the image using short diagonal strokes to smudge or smear darker parts of the image; lighter areas become brighter with a spotty texture and less detail. The Stroke Length setting controls the length of each diagonal, the Highlight Area setting brightens lighter areas in the photo, and the Intensity setting allows you to adjust the highlight.

Blur Filters

The Blur filters (Table 6–2) soften or smooth an image by locating defined edges, lines, and shadows, adding together the color value, and then averaging the pixels to create a new value. Commonly used for retouching, most of the Blur filters allow you to specify the radius of affected pixels. You can blur the background to draw attention to foreground objects, create dreamlike scenes and portraits, or add visual movement to an image.

Quick Reference
For a table that lists how to complete the tasks covered in this book using touch gestures, the mouse, the Application bar menus, shortcut menu, and keyboard, see the Quick Reference Summary at the back of this book, or visit the Quick Reference resource on the Student Companion Site located on www.cengagebrain.com.

Table 6–2 Blur Filters

Blur Filter	Description	Adjustable Settings
Average	Creates a smooth look by averaging the pixels in the entire selection or image to create a new replacement color.	None
Blur Blur More	Eliminates extraneous noise in areas with strong color transitions by averaging pixels.	None
Box Blur	Averages the pixel color values of all neighboring pixels to create special effects; the larger the radius setting, the greater the blur.	Radius
Gaussian Blur	Blurs using a weighted average to add low-frequency detail that produces a hazy effect.	Radius
Lens Blur	Applies a blur with a narrower depth of field so that some objects in the image stay in focus and others are blurred.	Depth Map Iris Special Highlights Noise
Motion Blur	Blurs in a specified direction and at a specified intensity or distance.	Angle Distance
Radial Blur	Simulates the blur of a zooming or rotating camera.	Amount Blur Method Quality
Shape Blur	Blurs in a specified pattern or shape.	Radius Shape
Smart Blur	Blurs with precise settings.	Radius Threshold Quality Mode
Surface Blur	Blurs an image while preserving edges.	Radius Threshold

© Cengage Learning

Blur Gallery Filters

The Blur Gallery filters (Table 6–3) create distinct photographic blurs using multiple fields of blur control. The controls overlay the image and provide live preview with finely tuned sliders and adjustment handles. The last two filters in the list appear as panels when you choose one of the other Blur Gallery filters.

Table 6–3 Blur Gallery Filters

Blur Gallery Filter	Description	Adjustable Settings
Field	Creates one or more areas of focus in the image, blurring the background by changing pixels.	Blur
Iris	Adds focus points to simulate depth of field, allowing you to alter the size, shape, transition and amount of blur using on-screen graphic controls.	Blur

Table 6–3 Blur Gallery Filters *(continued)*

Blur Gallery Filter	Description	Adjustable Settings
Tilt-Shift	Blurs with a gradient effect by placing multiple pins with different blur amounts, or by aligning one or more planes.	Blur Distortion Symmetric Distortion
Path Blur	Creates motion blurs along path using handles in live preview.	Speed Taper Cantered Edit Blur Shapes
Spin Blur	Creates a radial-style blur measured in degrees; in live preview, you can alter the ellipse size and shape.	Blur Angle
Blur Effects panel	Similar to camera shake reduction, Blur Effects filters control the appearance of out-of-focus or blurred parts.	Light Bokeh Bokeh Color Light Range
Motion Blur Effects panel	Creates a multiple strobe/flash effect.	Strobe Strength Strobe Flashes

© Cengage Learning

Brush Strokes Filters

The Brush Strokes Filters (Table 6–4) paint with an artistic impression using different brush and ink stroke effects. Many of the filters allow you to set smoothness, sharpness, and intensity. Graphic artists use the Brush Strokes Filters to achieve natural or traditional media effects.

Table 6–4 Brush Strokes Filters

Brush Stroke Filter	Description	Adjustable Settings
Accented Edges	Accentuates edges based on a brightness control.	Edge Width Edge Brightness Smoothness
Angled Strokes	Creates brush strokes at opposite angles.	Direction Balance Stroke Length Sharpness
Crosshatch	Preserves details while adding pencil hatching texture.	Stroke Length Sharpness Strength
Dark Strokes	Paints dark areas with short, dark strokes, and light areas with long, white strokes.	Balance Black Intensity White Intensity
Ink Outlines	Redraws with fine narrow lines, creating a strong edge effect similar to an ink outline.	Stroke Length Dark Intensity Light Intensity
Spatter	Simulates an airbrush, creating an exaggerated spatter and ripple effect.	Spray Radius Smoothness
Sprayed Strokes	Repaints using dominant colors, with angled, sprayed strokes in specific directions.	Stroke Length Spray Radius Stroke Direction
Sumi-e	Creates soft, blurred edges with full ink blacks and uses a saturated brush style similar to Japanese rice paper painting.	Stroke Width Stroke Pressure Contrast

© Cengage Learning

BTW

Editing Filters
If you are using smart filters, they appear in the Layers panel as a layer effect. To edit the opacity and blending mode of each smart filter, click the layer effect button and then right-click the smart filter setting. The context menu will allow you to edit the filter with adjustments such as blending, shadows, highlights, and opacity. When using multiple smart filters, you can move them up or down to apply in sequence, over or under one another.

Distort Filters

The Distort filters (Table 6–5) reshape images not by recoloring pixels, but by moving pixels in a geometric fashion to create 3-D effects and reshaping effects. Some of the distort filters purposefully add noise or altering effects to the image, while others correct the same kinds of problems. Distortion is used in advertising to give an emotional, comical, or exaggerated dimension for product recognition, or to express shape, size, and spatial relations. Some of the Distort filters are in the Filter Gallery; others open in their own dialog boxes from the Distort submenu.

BTW

Diffuse Glow Filter
The Diffuse Glow is a soft diffusion filter that adds see-through white noise and a glow that fades from the center. The Graininess setting adds noise to the layer. The Glow Amount controls the intensity of the glow effect, with higher values resulting in more glow. The Clear Amount controls the intensity of the portions of the filter not involved in the glow effect.

BTW

Perspective Warp
Another way to distort and image is the new Perspective Warp in Photoshop CC. You will learn more about Perspective Warp in a later chapter.

Table 6–5 Distort Filters

Distort Filter	Description	Adjustable Settings
Diffuse Glow (Filter Gallery)	A soft diffusion filter that adds see-through white noise; glow fades from the center.	Graininess Glow Amount Clear Amount
Displace	Distorts using a displacement map.	Horizontal Scale Vertical Scale Displacement Map Undefined Areas
Glass (Filter Gallery)	Distorts as if viewed through glass.	Distortion Smoothness Texture Scaling Invert
Ocean Ripple (Filter Gallery)	Ripples the surface randomly as if underwater.	Ripple Size Ripple Magnitude
Pinch	Squeezes from the center.	Amount
Polar Coordinates	Toggles between rectangular and polar coordinates simulating a mirrored cylinder.	Rectangular to Polar Polar to Rectangular
Ripple	Redraws with ripples.	Amount Size
Shear	Distorts or warps along a line.	Undefined Areas
Spherize	Creates a spherical distortion.	Amount Mode
Twirl	Rotates, creating a twirl pattern.	Angle
Wave	Precisely redraws with ripples.	Number of Generators Wavelength Amplitude Scale Type Undefined Areas
ZigZag	Distorts radially, with reversals from center.	Amount Ridges Style

© Cengage Learning

Noise Filters

Noise is a term that refers to hazy, grainy, or extraneous pixels as well as flecks of random color distributed through a background. Noise also can refer to variation in brightness or color information. The Noise filters (Table 6–6) add or remove noise and help blend a selection into the surrounding pixels. Noise filters can create unusual textures or remove problem areas, such as dust and scratches.

Table 6–6 Noise Filters

Noise Filter	Description	Adjustable Settings
Add Noise	Applies random pixels to an image, simulating the effect of high-speed film photography.	Amount Distribution Monochromatic
Despeckle	Detects edges of color in an image and blurs all of the selection except those edges.	None
Dust & Scratches	Reduces noise by changing dissimilar pixels.	Radius Threshold
Median	Reduces noise by blending the brightness of pixels within a selection, useful for eliminating or reducing the effect of motion on an image.	Radius
Reduce Noise	Reduces noise while preserving edges based on user settings.	Strength Preserve Details Reduce Color Noise Sharpen Details Remove JPEG Artifact

© Cengage Learning

Pixelate Filters

The Pixelate filters (Table 6–7) redraw an image or selection by joining, grouping, or clustering pixels of similar color values into cells defined by the tolerance settings. The cells become blocks, rectangles, circles, or dots of color, creating an impression of looking at an image through a powerful magnifying glass. Many of the Pixelate filters replicate artistic movement styles such as pointillism, divisionism, or stippling.

Table 6–7 Pixelate Filters

Pixelate Filter	Description	Adjustable Settings
Color Halftone	Replaces rectangular areas with circles of halftone screening on each color channel.	Max. Radius Screen Angles (Degrees)
Crystallize	Creates a solid color polygon shape by clustering pixels.	Cell Size
Facet	Creates solid color by clustering similarly colored pixels; commonly used to remove color noise and specks.	None
Fragment	Draws four copies of pixels and then averages the values and offsets them, creating a hazy blur.	None
Mezzotint	Randomizes black-and-white areas or color areas, creating pixilation according to the chosen type.	Type
Mosaic	Creates solid-colored, square blocks based on original pixel colors.	Cell Size
Pointillize	Randomizes foreground colors and creates dots similar to pointillism; background simulates a canvas texture.	Cell Size

© Cengage Learning

Render Filters

In publishing, graphic design, and image editing, the term **render** simply means to create an artistic change. In Photoshop, rendering is used as a means to create a drawing or painting that is represented by discrete pixels, especially in perspective. The Render filters (Table 6–8 on the next page) create cloud patterns, texture fills, 3D shapes, refraction patterns, and simulated light reflections in an image. The Render effects are on the Filter menu. During rendering, image data on the active layer is replaced, so it is best to use the commands on layer copies rather than on the original.

Lighting Effects
The Lighting Effects command on the Render submenu displays a dialog box that contains numerous settings to create an almost endless number of effects. **Lighting styles** have to do with the number of light sources in the lighting effect, and their color, intensity, direction, and focus. A **light type** specifies the direction and distance of the perceived light. Properties such as Gloss, Material Exposure and Ambience affect the reflection and quantity of the perceived light source.

Table 6–8 Render Filters

Render Filter	Description	Adjustable Settings
Clouds	Creates a soft cloud pattern using random values that vary between the foreground and the background colors.	None
Difference Clouds	Same as Clouds filter except the filter blends with existing pixels.	None
Fibers	Generates the look of woven fibers using the foreground and background colors.	Variance Strength Randomize
Lens Flare	Simulates camera lens refraction caused by bright lights.	Brightness Lens Type
Lighting Effects	Produces various lighting effects using settings.	Style Light Type Properties Texture Channel

© Cengage Learning

Sharpen Filters

Recall that sharpening means to emphasize the transitions between light and dark objects in your image. The Sharpen filters (Table 6–9) focus blurred images by increasing the contrast of adjacent pixels.

Table 6–9 Sharpen Filters

Sharpen Filter	Description	Adjustable Settings
Shake Reduction	Reduce blurring caused by camera motion, errors in focal length or slow shutter speeds.	Blur Trace Bounds Source Noise Smoothing Artifact suppression Show Blur Estimation Regions
Sharpen	Focuses a selection to improve its clarity.	None
Sharpen Edges	Sharpens edges but preserves smoothness of the image.	None
Sharpen More	Applies a stronger sharpening effect than the Sharpen filter.	None
Smart Sharpen	Sharpens the parts of the image where significant color changes occur, with more control using the settings.	Brightness Lens Type
Unsharp Mask	Adjusts the contrast of edge detail, producing lighter and darker edges.	Style Light Type Properties Texture Channel

© Cengage Learning

Sketch Filters

The Sketch filters (Table 6–10) add texture and changes in color, creating artistic 3-D effects and hand-drawn looks. Many of the filters mimic sketch media used for loosely executed freehand drawing, not intended as a finished work. The Sketch filters use many techniques, including overlapping lines, dry media imitation, pencil, pen, and watercolor simulations. Most of the Sketch filters convert the image to black and white; however, they can be applied to individual channels to create interesting color combinations in the composite.

Table 6–10 Sketch Filters

Sketch Filter	Description	Adjustable Settings
Bas Relief	Accents surface variations with carving-like strokes; dark areas use the foreground color, and light areas use the background color.	Detail Smoothness Light
Chalk & Charcoal	Simulates a coarse chalk sketch with black diagonal charcoal lines in the foreground.	Charcoal Area Chalk Area Stroke Pressure
Charcoal	Redraws with a smudged, posterized effect using diagonal strokes; a charcoal color is used on the foreground, while the background simulates paper.	Charcoal Thickness Detail Light/Dark Balance
Chrome	Creates a polished metallic surface.	Detail Smoothness
Conté Crayon	Simulates the Conté style with textured crayon-like, chalk strokes.	Foreground Level Background Level Texture Scaling Relief Light Invert
Graphic Pen	Redraws using thin, linear ink strokes for the foreground color, and uses background color to simulate paper.	Stroke Length Light/Dark Balance Stroke Direction
Halftone Pattern	A halftone screen effect that maintains a continuous range of tones, consisting of dots that control how much ink is deposited at a specific location.	Size Contrast Pattern Type
Note Paper	Replicates handmade paper with dark areas masked out to reveal background colors.	Image Balance Graininess Relief
Photocopy	Creates a photocopy effect.	Detail Darkness
Plaster	Simulates molded plaster, with dark areas raised, and light areas recessed.	Image Balance Smoothness Light
Reticulation	Distorts similar to film emulsion patterns in negatives caused by extreme changes of temperature or acidity and alkalinity during processing.	Density Foreground Level Background Level
Stamp	Simulates a rubber or wooden stamp version.	Light/Dark Balance Smoothness
Torn Edges	Redraws to look like ragged, torn pieces of paper.	Image Balance Smoothness Contrast
Water Paper	Daubs with color, imitating fibrous, damp paper.	Fiber Length Brightness Contrast

© Cengage Learning

BTW

Filters and RAM
Some filters are created using your system's random access memory (RAM). When applied to a high-resolution image, your system may slow down. If several applications are running, you may get a low memory warning message. To reduce the strain on your system's memory, you can experiment with filters on small portions of an image, apply filters to individual channels instead of the entire image, or use the Purge command on the Edit menu to remove your previous history states. Closing other running applications also will increase available RAM.

Stylize Filters

The Stylize filters (Table 6–11 on the next page) displace pixels and heighten contrast in an image or selection, producing an impressionistic, painting-like effect. Graphic artists use the Stylize filters to create unique and interesting effects and accents to artwork. Several of the Stylize filters accent edges of contrast in the image, which then can be inverted to highlight the image inside the outlines. Some of the Stylize filters are in the Filter Gallery; others open in their own dialog boxes from the Stylize submenu.

BTW

Glowing Edges Filter
The Glowing Edges filter adds a neon glow to obvious edges in the images. Photoshop looks for strong color change to define an edge. Three settings are adjusted when using the Glowing Edges filter. The Edge Width setting increases or decreases the thickness of the edge lines. The Edge Brightness setting adjusts the contrast between the edges and the background. Finally, the Smoothness setting softens the color change between the edges and the background.

Table 6–11 Stylize Filters

Stylize Filter	Description	Adjustable Settings
Diffuse	Softens focus by rearranging pixels randomly or by dark and light settings.	Mode
Emboss	Converts fill color to gray and traces the edges to create raised or stamped effects.	Angle Height Amount
Extrude	Adds a 3-D texture based on specific settings.	Type Size Depth
Find Edges	Outlines edges with dark lines against a white background for a thickly outlined, coloring book effect.	None
Glowing Edges (Filter Gallery)	Adds a neon glow to edges.	Edge Width Edge Brightness Smoothness
Solarize	Creates a photographic light exposure tint.	None
Tiles	Creates a series of offset blocks with tiled edges.	Number Of Tiles Maximum Offset Fill Empty Area With
Trace Contour	Outlines transition areas in each channel, creating a contour map effect.	Level Edge
Wind	Redraws using small horizontal lines to create a windblown effect.	Method Direction

© Cengage Learning

Texture Filters

The Texture filters (Table 6–12) add substance or depth to an image by simulating a texture or organic representation. Graphic artists use the Texture filters to add a 3-D effect or to apply a segmented style to photos.

Table 6–12 Texture Filters

Texture Filter	Description	Adjustable Settings
Craquelure	Creates an embossing effect with a network of cracks on a plaster-like background.	Crack Spacing Crack Depth Crack Brightness
Grain	Simulates different types of graininess.	Intensity Contrast Grain Type
Mosaic Tiles	Creates small tiles with grout.	Tile Size Grout Width Lighten Grout
Patchwork	Redraws with randomly filled squares replicating highlights and shadows.	Square Size Relief
Stained Glass	Repaints using random, five-sided, polygonal shapes to emulate stained glass.	Cell Size Border Thickness Light Intensity
Texturizer	Applies selected texture with settings.	Texture Scaling Relief Light Invert

© Cengage Learning

Specialized Filters

Each of the four specialized filters is displayed its own interface dialog box. The Adaptive Wide Angle filter allows you to correct perspective errors and straighten curves and lines in photos taken with a fisheye or wide-angle lens, with settings for scale. In many cases, the filter will recognize the kind of camera lens used to take the photo and correct the errors automatically. You also can make manual corrections for the Adaptive Wide Angle filter such as changing the scale, focal length, and calibration.

You previously learned about the Lens Correction filter that fixes common lens flaws such as keystone, barrel, and pincushion distortion; it also corrects chromatic aberration and vignetting. The Vanishing Point filter which you may have used in the previous chapter, also corrects perspective errors but in a different way. The Vanishing Point filter allows you to specify a plane, such as a road, building, wall, or other rectangular portion of the image. Then, the edits you make, such as painting, healing, copying, and transforming, are performed in the perspective of the plane. The results are more realistic because the edits are properly oriented and scaled to the perspective planes.

The fourth specialized filter, the Liquify filter, lets you distort an image by pushing, pulling, or rotating any area of an image. The Liquify filter is a powerful tool for retouching images as well as for creating artistic effects. The Liquify filter has its own dialog box and tools panel with distortion tools such as Forward Way, which pushes and twirls pixels just as you might do while finger painting, and Pucker and Bloat tools used to push and pull pixels toward and way from the center, respectively. Other settings edit the brush, reconstruct the image, set the mask, and change the view.

Some of the specialized filters require a video card that can perform graphics processor acceleration. Computer video cards with **graphics processor acceleration** contain their own processor to boost performance. Also called GPU-accelerated features, these filters use the graphic card's processor to free up the computer's processor to execute other commands. If your video card cannot process the filter, Photoshop will display an error message. In that case, you might have to upgrade your video card. You can check your graphic processor acceleration by pressing CTRL+K to open Photoshop preferences. Tap or click Performance on the left. If your video card cannot handle graphics processor acceleration, the Use Graphics Processor check box will be grayed out.

The following sections focus on specific filters used in this project. You will use other filters in future chapters.

BTW

Adding Filters
You can download many new filters from various websites. When you find one, make sure the file is legal to copy. Copy the downloaded filter file to the Adobe Photoshop CC Plug-ins folder. You then should be able to see the new filter on the Filter menu.

To Insert the Space Needle Graphic

The first graphic to insert is the main graphic on the magazine cover. To complete this assignment, you will be required to use the Data Files for Students. Visit solutions.cengage.com/ctdownloads for detailed instructions or contact your instructor for information about accessing the required files. The following steps copy and paste the image into the Magazine Cover.

1. Open the file named Space Needle from the Chapter 06 folder of the Data Files for Students.

2. Press CTRL+A to select the entire image and then press CTRL+C to copy the selection.

3. Close the Space Needle window to return to the Magazine Cover file.

4. Press SHIFT+CTRL+N to create a new layer, and then tap or click the OK button in the New Layer dialog box.

5. Press CTRL+V to paste the copy into the new layer.

6. Rename the layer, Space Needle, and use a Violet identification color (Figure 6–7 on the next page).

Figure 6–7

Camera Shake Reduction

Every photographer has taken a blurry picture due to moving the camera. A new feature in Photoshop CC automatically can reduce image blurring caused by camera shake. The Shake Reduction filter, which is one of the Sharpen filters, reduces blurring not only due to various types of motion: linear, rotational, zigzag, etc., but also from incorrect focal length or slow shutter speed. The Shake Reduction dialog box has tools to help fine-tune corrections (Figure 6–8).

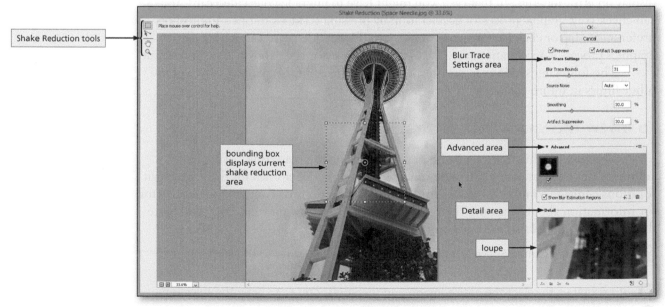

Figure 6–8

Because different regions of the image may have different blurs, Photoshop allows you to select a region, called a **blur trace**, with different extents of blurring. The Blur Trace settings include sliders to adjust the Blur Trace Bounds, Source Noise, Smoothing, and Artifact Suppression. Recall that noise describes randomly distributed color specks or graininess in the image. **Artifacts** are the blocky edges that may appear when adjusting pixels.

The Advanced area of the Shake Reduction dialog box allows you to create and save multiple blur traces. The Detail area contains the **loupe** or interactive magnifying window, that you can drag over the image to position the shake reduction region.

To Reduce Camera Shake

The Space Needle image has some blur, especially in the lower section of the image. The following steps use the Shake Reduction filter dialog box to remove the blur.

- Tap or click Filter on the Application bar to display the Filter menu.

- Tap or click Sharpen to display the Sharpen submenu (Figure 6–9).

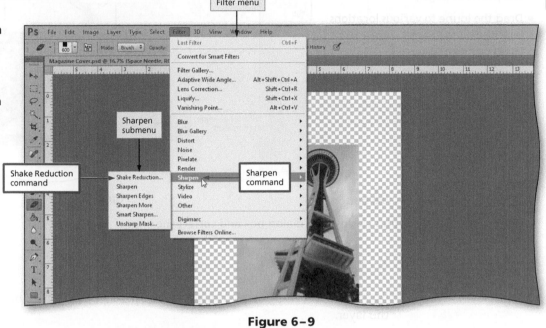

Figure 6–9

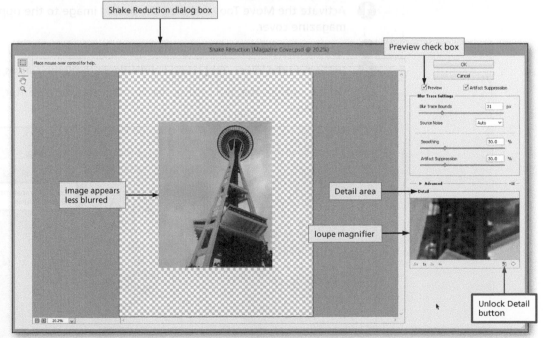

Figure 6–10

- Tap or click Shake Reduction to display the Shake Reduction dialog box and reduce the blur (Figure 6–10).

Experiment

- Tap or click the Preview check box several times to see the before and after results of the shake reduction.

Q&A My image has a yellow warning triangle. Did I do something wrong?
No. Your graphics card might not be able to reproduce the correction in the dialog box; however, it will be performed on the image. Point to the triangle to see the message in the box at the top of the screen. The triangle may disappear after a few moments.

To Examine using a Loupe

The following steps examine portions of the image using the loupe in the Detail area of the Shake Reduction dialog box. When using the loupe, Photoshop displays an 'Enhance at loupe location' icon that you can tap or click to update the correction.

 ❶

- Tap or click the Unlock Detail button on the status bar of the Detail section. (See Figure 6-10 on the previous page.)

- Drag the loupe to various locations over the image to get a preview of the corrections (Figure 6–11).

Q&A
Should I click the 'Enhance at loupe location' icon?
You can, if you think there is a place on the image that needs some more shake reduction. You can press CTRL+Z if you do not like the result.

❷

- Tap or click the loupe's Close button.

- Tap or click the OK button to close the dialog box and correct the image.

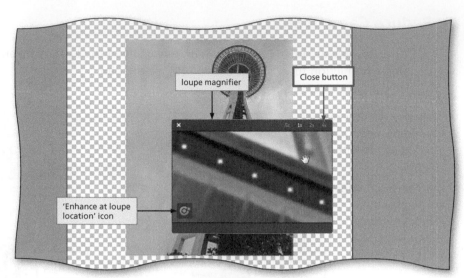

Figure 6–11

To Resize the Space Needle Image

The following steps transform the Space Needle image by moving and resizing the layer.

❶ Activate the Move Tool and drag the pasted image to the upper-left corner of the magazine cover.

❷ Press CTRL+T to display the transformation handles.

❸ SHIFT+drag the lower-right sizing handle down to fill the canvas, as shown in Figure 6–12.

❹ On the options bar, tap or click the 'Commit transform (Enter)' button to finish placing the image.

Figure 6–12

To Insert More Graphics

The following steps copy and place four more images from the Data Files for Students into the Magazine Cover file. Visit solutions.cengage.com/ctdownloads for detailed instructions or contact your instructor for information about accessing the required files.

① Open the file named Skyline from the Chapter 06 folder of the Data Files for Students.

② Press CTRL+A to select the entire image and then press CTRL+C to copy the selection.

③ Close the Skyline window to return to the Magazine Cover file.

④ Press CTRL+V to paste the copy into the Magazine Cover canvas.

⑤ Rename the layer, skyline, and use a gray identification color.

⑥ Repeat steps 1 through 5 to insert the following three files — Keyboard, Food, Aquarium — one at a time. Rename the layers appropriately, and use your choice of identification colors (Figure 6–13).

⑦ Tap or click the visibility icon on each of the four layers other than the background and Space Needle layers to hide them temporarily.

Figure 6–13

To Save the File

After adding many layers and applying a filter, it is a good time to save the file again in the following step.

① Press CTRL+S. If Photoshop displays a dialog box, tap or click the OK button.

Break Point: If you wish to take a break, this is a good place to do so. Press CTRL+Q to quit Photoshop. To resume at a later time, start Photoshop, open the file named Magazine Cover, and continue following the steps from this location forward.

The Filter Gallery

BTW

Filter Gallery Dialog Box
The Filter Gallery dialog box is displayed with thumbnails of many of the Photoshop filters, and a preview that is updated when settings are changed.

The Filter Gallery lets you apply filters cumulatively and apply individual filters more than once. With thumbnail examples of the filters organized into folders, the Filter Gallery previews the effect that the filter will have on your image. You can use the Filter Gallery to make appropriate choices, rearrange filters, and change individual settings to achieve the desired special effect.

By default, filters change the pixels in a layer, and therefore are considered destructive; however, you can use the Convert for Smart Filters command to convert your layers into smart objects that make the filter editable. Recall that smart objects are layers that preserve the source content of an image with all its original characteristics, separately from any filters, edits, or styles. Smart Objects enable you to perform nondestructive editing to the layer. A filter added to a smart object is called a **smart filter**. Smart filters add to the size of the file on your storage device but offer the luxury of keeping the pixels in the original layer – in case you want to make further edits. Smart filters also allow you to adjust or delete filter settings. Smart filters retain the name of the filter used and its filter settings, even when those may have been reset by you or another user. A smart filter therefore is a substitute for creating a copy of the layer on which to apply filters, and renaming it to include the filter name and settings.

Not all filters are included in the Filter Gallery. Those filters with adjustable settings that are not in the Filter Gallery present their own preview when selected from the menu system. Photoshop Help also has many visual examples of the various filters.

To Create a Smart Filter

In the following steps, you will use the Convert for Smart Filters command to make layer changes editable.

- On the Layers panel, tap or click the food layer visibility icon to show the layer, and select the food layer.

- Tap or click Filter on the Application bar to display the Filter menu (Figure 6–14).

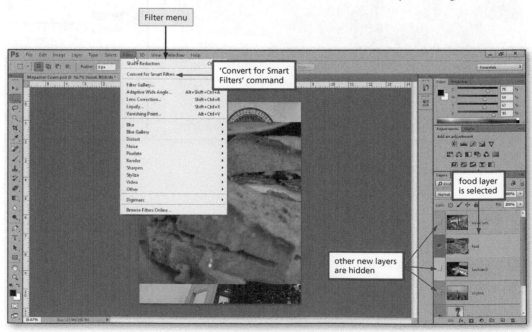

Figure 6–14

2

- Tap or click 'Convert for Smart Filters' to display a confirmation dialog box (Figure 6–15).

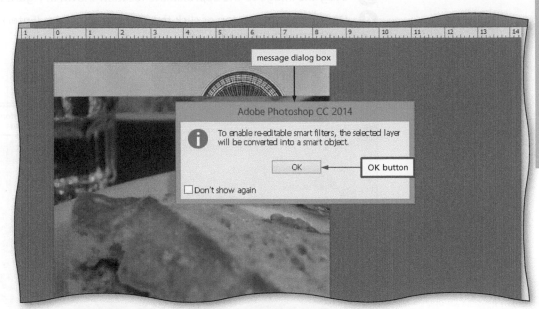

Figure 6–15

3

- Tap or click the OK button to create an adjustable smart filter (Figure 6–16).

Q&A Should I see any difference?
Yes. The smart object icon is added to the layer on the layer's panel.

Figure 6–16

Other Ways

1. Press and hold or right-click layer, tap or click Convert to Smart Object

To Transform the Food Layer

The following steps resize the food layer and position in the scene.

1 Press CTRL+T to display the transformation handles. Notice that some if the image runs off the canvas.

2 On the options bar, select the text in the W box and then type 20% to reduce the width of the image. Press the TAB key and then type 20% to reduce the height.

Combining Filters
You can create many interesting effects by combining filters as well as applying them more than once. The only restrictions are that filters cannot be applied to Bitmap or Index color images, and some filters will only work on 8-bit or RGB images.

③ Drag the image to the approximate location shown in Figure 6–17.

④ On the options bar, tap or click the 'Commit transform (Enter)' button to finish transforming the image.

Figure 6–17

To Apply a Watercolor Smart Filter

Using the Filter Gallery, you will apply the Watercolor filter, which is an Artistic filter, to the food layer in the following steps. The Watercolor filter changes the image to look like a watercolor painting by flattening color change edges and brightening within colors.

①

• Tap or click Filter on the Application bar to display the Filter menu (Figure 6–18).

Q&A
What is the command at the top of the menu?
The first command on the Filter menu is always the most recent filter activity you have performed; that way, if you want to apply the same filter to various images, you do not have to perform all the steps again and remember the settings.

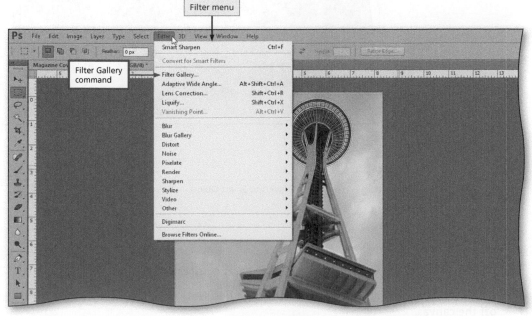

Figure 6–18

2

- Tap or click Filter Gallery to display the Filter Gallery dialog box.

- If necessary, tap or click the Zoom in or Zoom out button until the entire food image is displayed in the preview.

- If more than one filter is displayed in the list of filter effects, tap or click the 'Delete effect layer' button (Figure 6–19).

Q&A What does the 'New effect layer' button do in the Filter Gallery?

Tapping or clicking the 'New effect layer' button between each filter selection allows you to apply multiple filters to the same image.

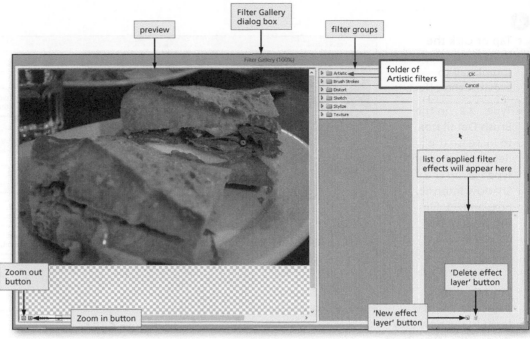

Figure 6–19

3

- Tap or click Artistic in the list of filter groups to open the folder. Tap or click any other open folders to close them (Figure 6–20).

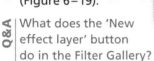 **Experiment**

- One at a time, tap or click each Artistic filter to view its effect on the image.

Figure 6–20

4

- Tap or click the Watercolor thumbnail to preview the effect.

- Type **12** in the Brush Detail box to increase the detail. If necessary, type **1** in the Shadow Intensity box, and **1** in the Texture box (Figure 6–21).

 Experiment

- Drag the three sliders back and forth to see how they change the layer. Reset them to 12, 1, and 1 when you are done experimenting.

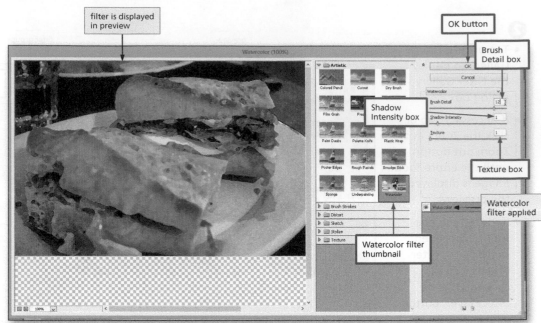

Figure 6–21

5

- Tap or click the OK button to apply the Watercolor filter to the food layer (Figure 6–22).

Figure 6–22

To Prepare the Keyboard Layer

The following steps show the keyboard layer, convert it to a smart filter, and transform it, as you did with the food layer.

1 On the Layers panel, tap or click the keyboard layer visibility icon to show the layer, and select the keyboard layer.

2 Tap or click Filter on the Application bar to display the Filter menu.

3 Tap or click 'Convert for Smart Filters' to display a confirmation dialog box.

4 Tap or click the OK button to create an adjustable smart filter.

5 Press CTRL+T to display the transformation handles. Notice that some of the image runs off the canvas.

6 On the options bar, select the text in the W box and then type 20% to reduce the width of the image. Press the TAB key and then type 20% to reduce the height.

7 Drag the image to the approximate location shown in Figure 6–23.

8 On the options bar, tap or click the 'Commit transform (Enter)' button to finish transforming the image.

Figure 6–23

To Apply a Glowing Edges Smart Filter

You will apply the Glowing Edges filter to the keyboard layer in the steps on the next page. Upon opening the keyboard layer in the Filter Gallery, the gallery will display the previously used filter, in this case, Watercolor. The previous settings in the Filter Gallery will be replaced when you choose the Glowing Edges filter.

1

- With the keyboard layer still selected, tap or click Filter on the Application bar and then tap or click Filter Gallery to display the Filter Gallery dialog box. Adjust the size of the preview using the zoom buttons.

- If more than one filter is displayed in the list of filter effects, tap or click the 'Delete effect layer' button.

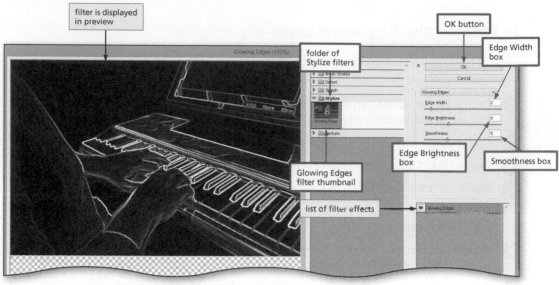

Figure 6–24

- Tap or click Artistic in the filter list to close the Artistic folder.

- Tap or click Stylize in the filter list to open the Stylize folder, and then tap or click the Glowing Edges thumbnail.

- Type 2 in the Edge Width box, 6 in the Edge Brightness and 5 in the Smoothness box (Figure 6–24).

Q&A I could not get the 'Delete effect layer' button to work. What did I do wrong?
The 'Delete effect layer' button only works when there is more than one filter in the list. You cannot delete the existing filter – you either can change the filter or cancel the operation.

2

- Tap or click the OK button to apply the Glowing Edges filter to the keyboard layer (Figure 6–25).

Q&A What if I decide not to apply a filter?
If you change your mind and do not want to apply any filters, tap or click the Cancel button. If the filter already has been applied, you press CTRL+Z. If it is a smart filter, you can delete the filter on the Layers panel. Simply press and hold or right-click the filter, and then tap or click 'Delete Smart Filter' on the context menu.

Figure 6–25

To Prepare the Aquarium Layer

The following steps prepare the aquarium layer for the addition of a blur filter.

1 On the Layers panel, tap or click the aquarium layer visibility icon to show the layer, and select the layer.

2 Tap or click Filter on the Application bar to display the Filter menu.

3 Tap or click 'Convert for Smart Filters' to display a confirmation dialog box.

4 Tap or click the OK button to create an adjustable smart filter.

5 Press CTRL+T to display the transformation handles.

6 On the options bar, select the text in the W box and then type **15%** to reduce the width of the image. Press the TAB key and then type **15%** to reduce the height.

7 Drag the image to the upper-left corner of the canvas, as shown in Figure 6–26.

8 On the options bar, tap or click the 'Commit transform (Enter)' button to finish transforming the image.

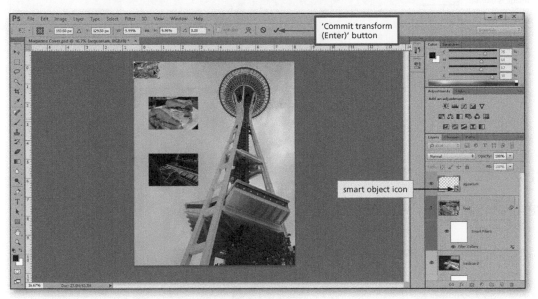

'Commit transform (Enter)' button

smart object icon

Figure 6–26

The Blur Filters

As with the Sharpen filters and the Shake Reduction filter, Blur filters and Blur Gallery filters are not a part of the Filter Gallery; rather they use the menu system to display a live preview and various panels.

Blur filters selectively blur portions of an image to create a stronger focus on the non-blurred portions. Selective blurring is common in movies and television, when the figure in the foreground slowly blurs to shift the focus to an object in the background. Each of the filters uses live preview bulleted center points to position the focus, as well as a wheel and slider controls to increase or decrease the blur.

Blur Gallery filters use live preview with rotation handles, a center point, and an adjustable diameter circle to adjust the blur, distortion, and Bokeh effect (Figure 6–27 on the next page). In photography, the **Bokeh effect** refers to the way the camera lens renders out-of-focus points of light, generated by differences in lens aberrations and aperture shapes.

BTW

Identifying Applied Filters
If you choose to add a filter to a layer other than a smart object layer, the filters do not appear on the Layers panel. In those cases, you should name any filtered layers with both the name of the filter and the numerical settings. For example, if your edits layer employs the Plastic Wrap filter, you might name it edits plastic wrap 8 8 11 so you could remember the filter and settings you used.

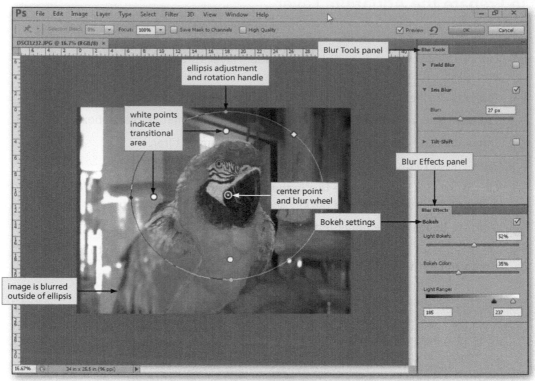

Figure 6–27

Filter Gallery Settings

Filter Gallery settings carry over each time you use the Filter Gallery. When you choose a new filter, the previous one is replaced. However, if more than one filter is displayed in the list of filter effects, and you do not want to use the filters, click the 'Delete effect layer' button.

To Apply a Spin Blur Filter

The following steps apply a Spin Blur filter to the aquarium layer.

1

- On the Layers panel, select the aquarium layer, if necessary.

- Press CTRL+1 (ONE) to zoom to 100% and then scroll as necessary to display the aquarium image on the canvas.

- Tap or click Filter on the Application bar and then tap or click Blur Gallery to display the submenu (Figure 6–28).

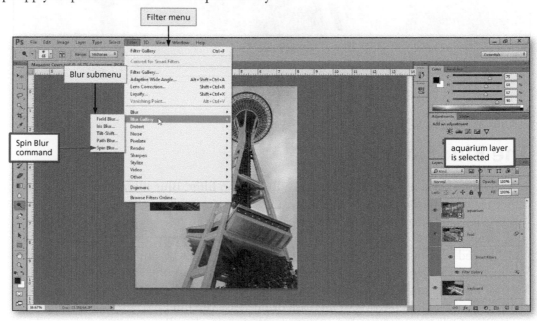

Figure 6–28

2

- Tap or click Spin Blur to display the Blur Tools panel and options bar (Figure 6–29).

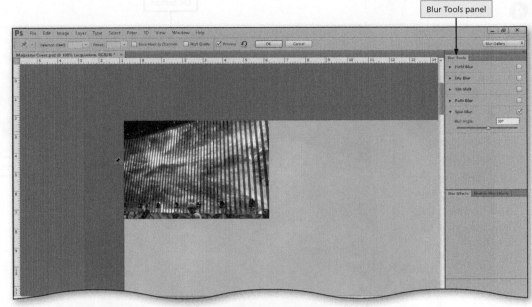

Figure 6–29

3

- Tap or click the center of the aquarium image to apply the blur (Figure 6–30).

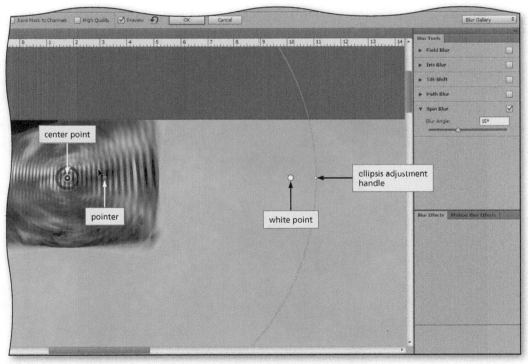

Figure 6–30

4

- On the Blur Tools panel, drag the Blur Angle slider to 5 to decrease the amount of blur (Figure 6–31).

 Experiment

- Experiment by dragging the white points to increase and decrease the transitional area of the blur.

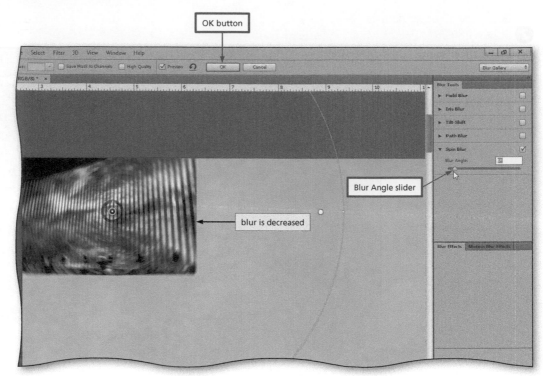

Figure 6–31

5

- On the options bar, tap or click the OK button to apply the filter (Figure 6–32).

Q&A Is it common for the blur to take a long time to appear?
Yes, as Photoshop has to change every pixel in the layer, it may take 15 seconds or longer for the image to appear blurred.

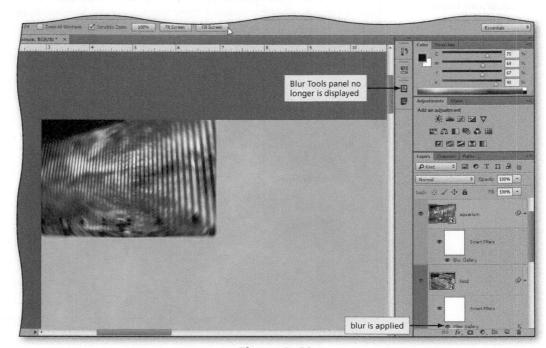

Figure 6–32

To Save the File

After adding several filters, it is a good time to save the file again in the following step.

1 Press CTRL+S. If Photoshop displays a dialog box, tap or click the OK button.

Break Point: If you wish to take a break, this is a good place to do so. Press CTRL+Q to quit Photoshop. To resume at a later time, start Photoshop, open the file called Magazine Cover, and continue following the steps from this location forward.

Special Effects

You have learned about using filters, strokes, and shapes to modify photographs; in addition, you can include masks, patterns, lines, and renderings to add variety, attraction, and appeal to your publications. Each of the small photos on the left side of the magazine cover will be masked in a circular pattern using a brown color from the Space Needle image. This will draw attention to the smaller images. You also will define a pattern and use it to create a background for text in the upper-left corner of the magazine cover.

Plan Ahead

Use special effects purposefully.
Avoid using special effects for their own sake, or just to dress up your image. Plan your special effects to serve a purpose and fit with other parts of your image. Special effects can add emphasis, introduce color or texture, or cover up raw edges or errors in an image. Use strokes, borders and clipping shapes to draw attention and delineate certain images or parts of the overall images. Design shapes that already are found within the pictures themselves. Reuse colors rather than create new ones. Define patterns from images and use them only as backgrounds to draw attention to portions of the overall concept.

To Use the Ellipse Tool

The following steps create a circular shape using the Ellipse Tool. A circle will echo the circular shape of the top of the Space Needle to better fit into the scene. The Ellipse Tool options bar allows you to fill, stroke, set the width and line style, as well as use other tools to work with paths. You will learn about paths in a later chapter.

- On the Layers panel, select the keyboard layer.

- Change the magnification setting to approximately 50% and scroll as necessary to view the keyboard image as well a part of the Space Needle.

- On the Tools panel, press and hold or right-click the current shape tool button (Figure 6–33).

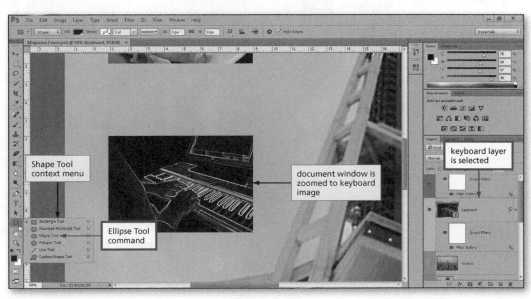

Figure 6–33

2

- Tap or click Ellipse Tool in the list to select it.

- On the options bar, tap or click the 'Set the shape fill type' button button to display the options (Figure 6–34).

Experiment

- One at a time, tap or click each of the four buttons across the top of the Fill panel to see the choices for No Color, Solid Color, Gradient, and Pattern.

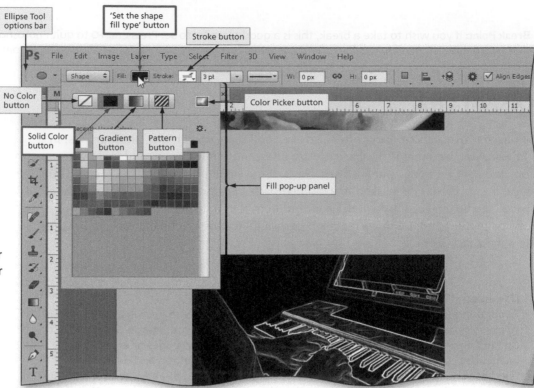

Figure 6–34

3

- Tap or click the Solid Color button to create a filled ellipse.

- On the options bar, tap or click the Stroke button to display the Stroke pop-up panel. Tap or click the Color Picker button to open the Color Picker (Stroke Color) dialog box (Figure 6–35).

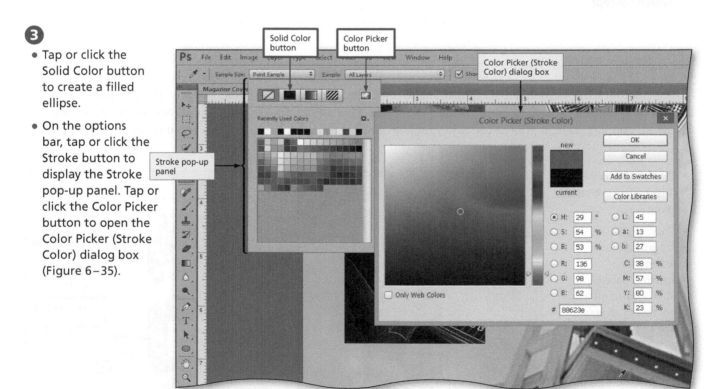

Figure 6–35

4

- Move the pointer into the document window, and then tap or click a medium brown color in the Space Needle to copy the color.

- If the color you choose displays an out-of-gamut warning triangle, click the warning to change the color to a CMYK acceptable shade of brown (Figure 6–36).

Q&A
Why did Photoshop change to the Eyedropper Tool?
Anytime a Color Picker dialog box is displayed, you have the options of using the hue cube, the color ramp, or the color number boxes to choose colors, as you have done in previous chapters. You also have the ability to copy colors, so Photoshop displays the Eyedropper Tool to allow you to copy any color from the image.

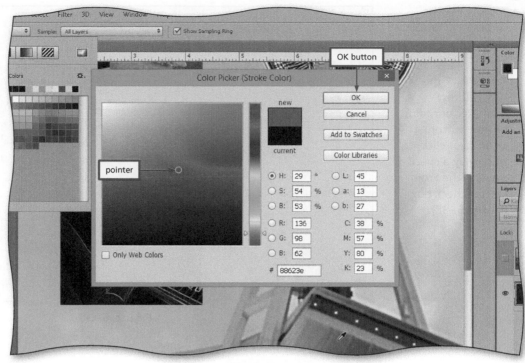

Figure 6–36

5

- Tap or click the OK button to close the Color Picker box and return to the Ellipse Tool.

- Select the text in the 'Set the shape stroke width' box, and then type 5 to set the width (Figure 6–37).

Q&A
What does the 'Set the shape stroke type' button do?
When you click the 'Set the shape stroke type' button, Photoshop displays a panel allowing you to choose solid lines, dotted lines, or corners for polygonal shapes.

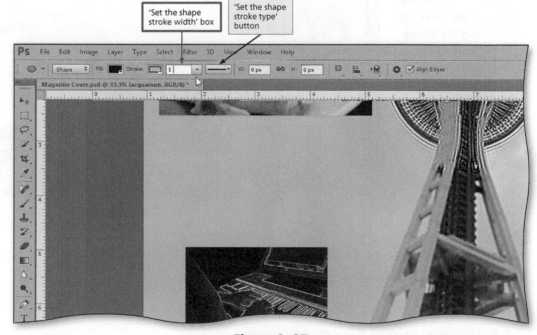

Figure 6–37

6

- Tap or click the Geometry Options button to display its panel.

- Tap or click the 'Circle (draw diameter or radius)' option button, and tap or click to display a check mark in the From Center check box (Figure 6–38).

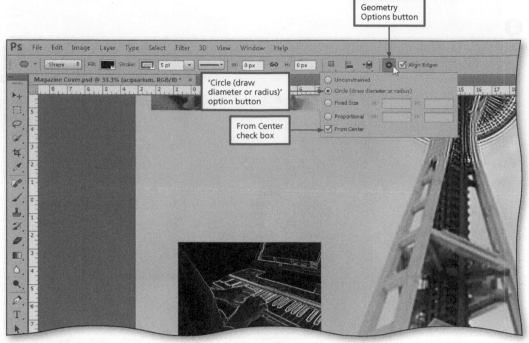

Figure 6–38

7

- In the document window, slowly drag a circle beginning in the center of the keyboard image. Because the stroke will cover the edges, you should make the circle slightly bigger than the image. As you drag, if you need to adjust the placement of the circle, press and hold the SPACEBAR key as you drag (Figure 6–39).

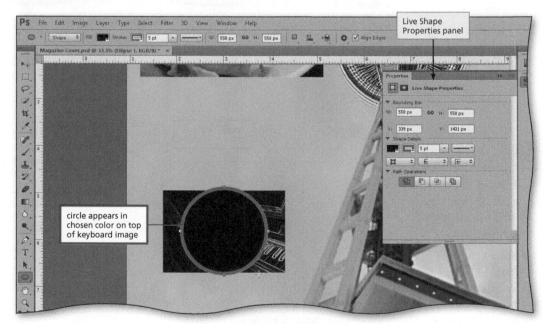

Figure 6–39

8

- Release the mouse button if necessary.

- Close the Live Shape Properties panel.

Other Ways

1. Press U or SHIFT+U, set options, drag in document window

To Create a Clipping Mask

In a previous chapter, you created a layer mask that eclipsed a portion of an image without destroying pixels. Those layer masks resided on the same layer as the image; you used a brush to create or remove the mask. A clipping mask is similar; however, it uses its own layer and can employ a variety of shapes or other images as the mask. You do not have to use a brush stroke.

Clipping masks are a good way to create a picture inside a shape. Just make sure that the picture resides above the shape on the Layers panel, and that you apply a clipping mask to the picture layer, as you do in the following steps.

1

- On the Layers panel, drag the Ellipse 1 layer below the keyboard layer.

- Press and hold or right-click the keyboard layer to display the context menu (Figure 6–40).

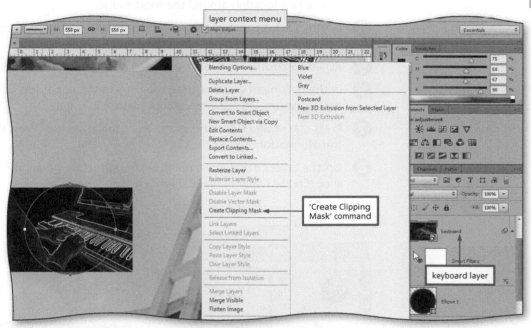

Figure 6–40

2

- Tap or click 'Create Clipping Mask' to clip the picture to the shape of the layer below it (Figure 6–41).

Figure 6–41

Other Ways

1. On Layer menu, tap or click 'Create Clipping Mask'
2. Press ALT+CTRL+G

To Create More Clipping Masks

To apply identical clipping masks to the food layer and the aquarium layer, you will duplicate the shape layer, and then create a clipping mask. The following steps create more clipping masks.

1 Zoom to fit the document window on the screen.

2 On the Layers panel, ALT+drag the Ellipse 1 layer to a location just below the food layer to create a copy.

3 Press the V key to activate the Move Tool. In the document window, drag the copied ellipse to a location around the food image.

4 On the Layers panel, press and hold or right-click the food layer, and then tap or click 'Create Clipping Mask' on the context menu.

5 ALT+drag another copy of the Ellipse layer to a location just below the aquarium layer.

6 In the document window, drag the copy to the upper-left corner of the image, near the aquarium. Do not worry about placing it exactly.

7 Press CTRL+T and resize the image to fit the aquarium. Press the ENTER key to finish the transformation.

8 On the Layers panel, press and hold or right-click the aquarium layer, and then tap or click 'Create Clipping Mask' (Figure 6–42).

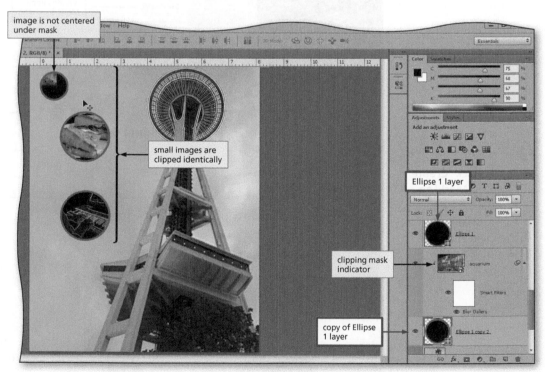

Figure 6–42

To Nudge

The following step repositions the aquarium clipping mask. When you use arrow keys to move very small distances, it is called nudging.

- On the Layers panel, select the Ellipse 1 copy 2 layer.

- Select the Move Tool, if necessary.

- Press the appropriate ARROW key, as necessary, to move the ellipse to a centered position within the clipped image (Figure 6–43).

Q&A My mask was already centered. Did I do something wrong? No, your images may have been centered well to begin with. You might need to nudge very little or not at all.

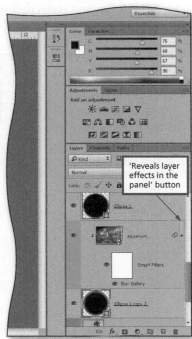

Figure 6–43

To Organize the Layers Panel

The following steps assign identification colors to the three new layers on the Layers panel, which will assist you in keeping the masks and images organized. You also will hide the layer effects.

1 Assign the Ellipse 1 layer the same identification color as the keyboard layer.

2 Assign the Ellipse 1 copy layer the same identification color as the food layer.

3 Assign the Ellipse 1 copy 2 layer the same identification color as the aquarium layer.

4 For each layer that displays layer effects, tap or click the 'Reveals layer effects in the panel' button (shown in Figure 6–43) to hide the effects.

Patterns

A **pattern** is an image that is tiled, or repeated, to fill a selection or a layer. Photoshop has libraries of preset patterns that can be loaded and used in any document. You can access the Pattern picker from the Layer Style dialog box or from the options bar associated with the Paint Bucket tool, the Pattern Stamp tool, the Healing Brush tool, and the Patch tool. Commands on the Pattern picker menu allow users to load, save, and manage pattern libraries. Recall that libraries associated with many kinds of presets — including gradients, brushes, styles, and custom shapes — also can be managed using the Preset Manager command on the Edit menu.

In Photoshop, you can use one of the preset patterns or you can create your own patterns and save them for use with different tools and commands. Photoshop gives you the ability to create a specific pattern, either from scratch or from another image. Alternatively, you can use the Pattern Maker Filter that generates a random pattern based on a selection or image.

To Define a Pattern

The following steps define a pattern using part of the Space Needle image.

● Zoom in on the top of the Space Needle.

● Use the Rectangular Marquee Tool to draw a selection around the pattern at the top of the Space Needle, as shown in Figure 6–44.

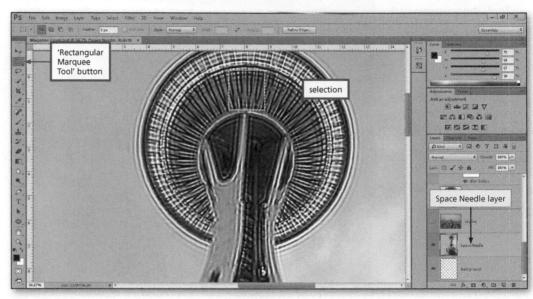

Figure 6–44

❷

● Tap or click Edit on the Application bar to display the menu (Figure 6–45).

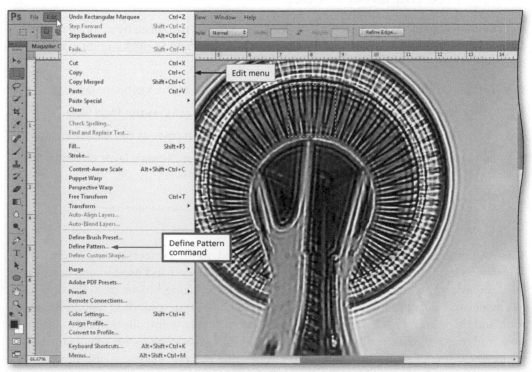

Figure 6–45

③

• Tap or click Define Pattern to display the Pattern Name dialog box.

• Type **Space Needle** in the Name box to name the pattern Figure 6–46).

Q&A Where will the new pattern be stored?
There is a Patterns folder created by the Photoshop installation. Your new pattern will be saved there, and will appear as a pattern thumbnail later in the chapter.

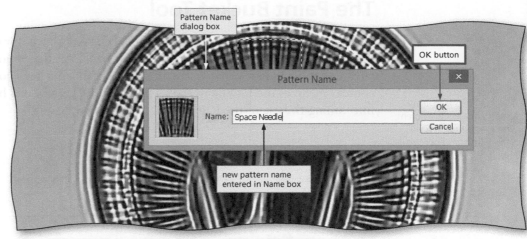

Figure 6–46

④

• Tap or click the OK button to close the Pattern Name dialog box.

To Create a New Layer and Selection

The next steps create a new layer and draw a selection in preparation for using the new pattern.

① On the Layers panel, select the Space Needle layer.

② Press SHIFT+CTRL+N to create a new layer. Name the layer, pattern, and use a yellow identification color.

③ Zoom in on the upper-left corner of the image.

④ Select the Rectangular Marquee Tool, if necessary, and draw a rectangle in the upper-left corner of the image, approximately 3 inches wide and 1.25 inches tall. The rectangle selection will overlap the aquarium (Figure 6-47).

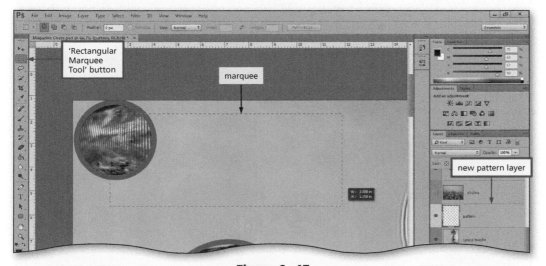

Figure 6–47

The Paint Bucket Tool

The Paint Bucket Tool fills adjacent, similar pixels with a color or pattern. To use the Paint Bucket Tool, you select it on the Tools panel, set the options, and then tap or click in the document window. Recall that the Paint Bucket Tool appears on the same context menu as the Gradient Tool. The Paint Bucket options bar displays choices for fine-tuning the use of the Paint Bucket Tool (Figure 6–48).

'Set source for fill area' button · Fill Mode button · Opacity box · Tolerance box · Contiguous check box · Pattern picker · Anti-alias check box · All Layers check box

Figure 6–48

By default, the Paint Bucket Tool uses the foreground color as its fill color, but you also can choose from a predefined pattern when filling. The Fill Mode, Opacity, and Tolerance boxes work the same way as they do for the Magic Wand Tool and the Eraser Tool. Recall that higher tolerance values fill a wider range of colors. The Contiguous check box allows you to fill all adjacent pixels of the same color within the tolerance. To fill pixels based on the merged color data from all visible layers, select the All Layers check box. The Paint Bucket Tool pointer displays a paint bucket. The tip of the paint coming out of the bucket is the fill location.

To Use the Paint Bucket Tool

The next steps create a new layer, and use the newly defined pattern with the Paint Bucket Tool to create a background for future text at the upper-left part of the magazine cover.

- Press and hold or right-click the Gradient Tool button on the Tools panel to display the context menu and then tap or click 'Paint Bucket Tool' to select it.

- On the options bar, tap or click the 'Set source for fill area' button to display the choices (Figure 6–49).

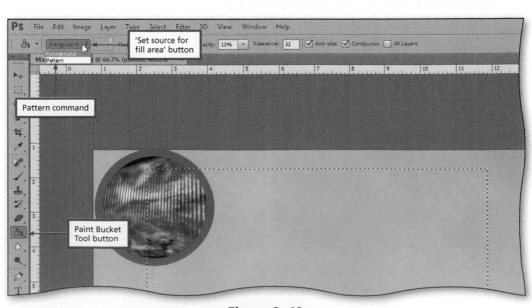

Figure 6–49

2

- Tap or click Pattern in the list to select it.

- Tap or click the Pattern picker to display its panel and then scroll to the bottom of the pattern thumbnails (Figure 6–50).

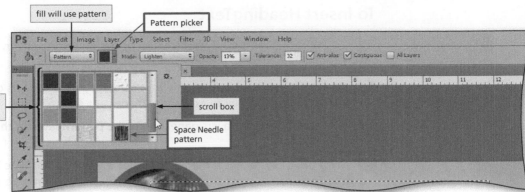

Figure 6–50

3

- Tap or click the Space Needle thumbnail to select it.

- In the document window, tap or click the selection to apply the pattern using the Paint Bucket Tool (Figure 6–51).

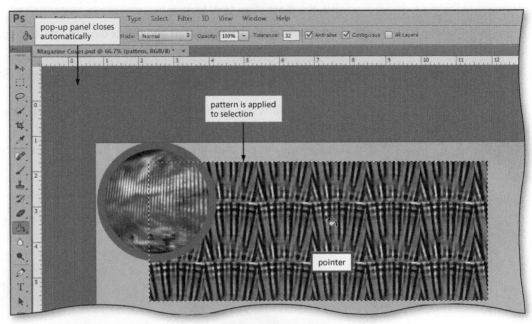

Figure 6–51

4

- On the Layers panel, tap or click the Blending Mode button, and then tap or click Soft Light to set the blending mode (Figure 6–52).

5

- Deselect.

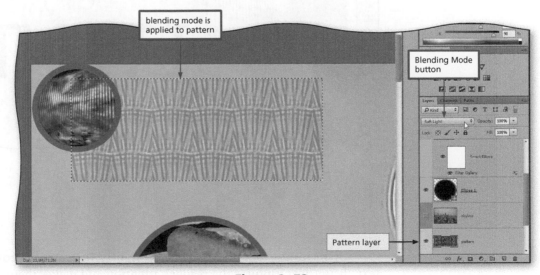

Figure 6–52

Other Ways

1. Press G or SHIFT+G, choose settings, tap or click document window

To Insert HeadingText

Two lines of text appear at the top of the magazine cover. The following steps insert the text.

① Press the D key to choose the default colors. If white appears over black on the Tools panel, press the X key to exchange the default colors.

② If necessary, on the Layers panel, select the pattern layer so the text layer will appear above it.

③ Press the T key to access the type tools. If the Horizontal Type Tool is not displayed on the Tools panel, press and hold or right-click the current type tool button, and then tap or click 'Horizontal Type Tool' in the list.

④ On the options bar, tap or click the 'Set the font family' box arrow and then choose the Gabriola Regular font or a similar font. Set the font size to 14. If necessary, tap or click the 'Left align text' button.

⑤ In the document window, drag a text box over the patterned area of the magazine cover, approximately 2.5 inches wide and 1.5 inch tall.

⑥ Type **This month's special calendar:** and then press the ENTER key three times.

⑦ On the options bar, change the font size to 60, and then type **EVENTS** to complete the text (Figure 6–53).

⑧ On the options bar, tap or click the 'Commit any current edits' button.

Figure 6–53

To Insert Teaser Text

Beneath the food and keyboard graphics, the magazine cover contains teaser text. Teaser text captures the reader's attention and makes them want to open the magazine to find out more. The following steps insert teaser text.

① On the Layers panel, select the keyboard layer so the text layer will appear above it. Zoom to display the entire page.

2 Press the T key to access the Horizontal Type Tool. On the options bar, if necessary, choose the **Gabriola Regular** font or a similar font. If necessary, set the font size to **36**. Tap or click the Center text button.

3 In the document window, drag a text box below the food picture, approximately 2.5 inches wide and 1 inch tall. Do not worry about the exact location; you will align the text box later.

4 Type **Where to eat** and then press the ENTER key.

5 On the options bar, change the font size to 24, and then type **pg. 18** to complete the text.

6 On the options bar, tap or click the 'Commit any current edits' button.

7 On the Layers panel, select the aquarium layer so the text layer will appear above it.

8 On the 'Horizontal Type Tool' options bar, change the font size to 36.

9 In the document window, drag a text box below the keyboard picture, approximately 2.5 inches wide and 1 inch tall. Do not worry about the exact location.

10 Type **Where to play** and then press the ENTER key.

11 On the options bar, change the font size to 24, and then type **pg. 23** to complete the text.

12 On the options bar, tap or click the 'Commit any current edits' button (Figure 6–54).

Figure 6–54

To Align and Distribute Layers

When you **align** layers, you make the edges, or the centers, line up with one another. When you **distribute** layers, you create equal distances between the edges or centers. The following step uses the Move Tool options bar to align layers.

- On the Layers panel, tap or click the food layer. Scroll as necessary and then SHIFT+tap or SHIFT+click the 'Where to play' layer to select all the inclusive layers.

- On the Tools panel, select the Move Tool to display the Move Tool options bar.

- Tap or click the 'Align horizontal centers' button to align the layers (Figure 6–55).

Figure 6–55

 Experiment

- One at a time, tap or click other align and distribute buttons on the options bar. After each one, press CTRL+Z to undo the change. When you are finished, tap or click the 'Align horizontal centers' button again.

Other Ways

1. On Layer menu, tap or click Align, choose alignment
2. On Layer menu, tap or click Distribute, choose distribution

To Save the File Again

The following step saves the file again.

1 Press CTRL+S. If Photoshop displays a dialog box, tap or click the OK button.

Break Point: If you wish to take a break, this is a good place to do so. Press CTRL+Q to quit Photoshop. To resume at a later time, start Photoshop, open the file named Magazine Cover, and continue following the steps from this location forward.

Knockouts and Trapping

In most printing media, when two objects of different colors overlap they create a **knockout** — the inks will not print on top of each other. At the point where the top layer overlaps the bottom one, the bottom one is not printed at all. In Photoshop, the Flatten Layers command automatically saves only the topmost color in overlapped layers, which creates the knockout for you. Sometimes that is not enough to prevent all of the problems caused by overlapping colors, however.

**Plan
Ahead**

Avoid color printing problems.
As you plan your graphic designs, consider the following ways to avoid color printing problems.

- Avoid putting colored objects too close together. Leave some white space between objects in your design or use black to stroke objects that overlap, or meet, with black outlines.

- Use common process colors when colors need to touch each other.

- For contiguous colors, use colors within 20% of each other in the CMYK color spectrum.

- Overprint black text using an overlay blending mode on type layers to cancel the knockout and force black ink to print on the background color.

When you print a hard copy using a desktop printer, the color is applied all at once; each color normally is printed where you expect it to be. In commercial printing, the printing device makes multiple passes over the paper. The speed of the printer and possible shifts in the paper may make some colors run together, creating spreads of blended color; or, the printer may leave small missed areas between very close objects or layers (Figure 6–56). Commercial printers use the term **misregistration** to describe those gaps in printing that are out of the printer's register or alignment. **Trapping** is a prepress activity of calculating an intentional compensation for the misregistration. Chokes and spreads are both methods of trapping. **Chokes** intentionally shrink an image to eliminate overprinting, and **spreads** intentionally overlap images to avoid gaps in the ink coverage where the base paper might show through.

Figure 6–56

When you cannot avoid placing colors close together, intentionally printing one layer of ink on top of another is called **overprinting**, or **surprinting**. Most service bureaus determine if trapping is needed in the overprinting process and can perform that prepress activity for you. It is not recommended you do this yourself, but if you need or want to do it, you will have to enter values in the Trap dialog box. The Trap command is on the Image menu. The service bureau, who understands its printing process best, is the ideal source for correctly gauging these values.

Photoshop's automatic settings use industry standard rules when applying a trap:

- White is knocked out automatically.

- All colors spread under black.

- Lighter colors spread under darker colors.

- Yellow spreads under cyan, magenta, and black.

- Pure cyan and pure magenta spread under each other equally. White graphics and text will not cause a problem because it will be knocked out to the paper color.

To Create Knockout Text

A special kind of knockout is knockout text, which knocks out or removes the color of the text to reveal the layer below. The shape of the text is retained so it looks like the letters are made from the layer or image below. Photoshop offers many ways to create a knockout, from layer styles to using the Horizontal Type Mask Tool. The following steps create knockout text using a clipping mask.

 1

- On the Layers panel, make the skyline layer visible and select it.

- Press CTRL+T and resize the image to fit at the bottom of the canvas (Figure 6–57).

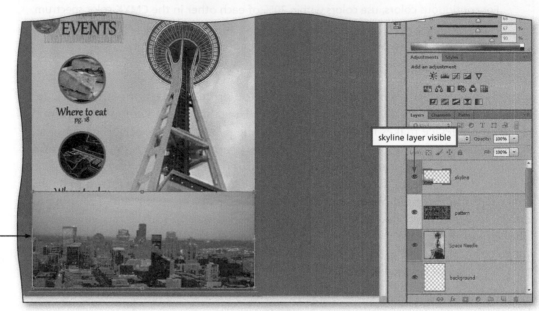

skyline layer transformed to fit at bottom of canvas

skyline layer visible

Figure 6–57

2

- Press the ENTER key to complete the transformation.

- On the Layers panel, use the context menu to duplicate the layer. Name the new layer, knockout.

- Hide the new knockout layer and select the skyline layer (Figure 6–58).

Q&A Why am I hiding the new layer?
Hiding the clipping layer allows you to create the text independently, keeping the picture out of the way until you need it.

new layer via copy is hidden

skyline layer is selected

Figure 6–58

3

- Select the 'Horizontal Type Tool'. On the options bar, change the font size to 200.

- In the document window, drag a text box across the bottom of the image approximately 2 inches tall.

- Type **Seattle** to insert the text.

- Drag across the text and then press ALT+RIGHT ARROW two times, to increase the tracking of the text (Figure 6–59).

Figure 6–59

4

- On the options bar, tap or click the 'Confirm any edits' button to close the text box.

- Press CTRL+T to display the Transform options bar and then type **-5** in the Set rotation box (Figure 6–60).

Q&A

Why did my text become thin? Sometimes with large-sized fonts, Photoshop will provide editing using the biggest possible space, so you can see how much room the text will take up. When you confirm the edits, the font family is applied.

Figure 6–60

5

- On the options bar, tap or click the 'Commit transform (Enter)' button to close the text box.

- On the Layers panel, hide the skyline panel and show the knockout layer.

- Press and hold or right-click the knockout layer, and then tap or click 'Create Clipping Mask' to knockout the letters (Figure 6–61).

Figure 6–61

To Add an Outer Glow

Another way to differentiate text, without changing the font family, is to add a layer style. Recall that layer styles are applied to a layer rather than changing the layer's actual pixels with a filter. Layer styles alter the appearance of the layer by adding depth, shadow, shading, texture, or overlay. To make the text stand out, the following steps add an Outer Glow layer style that contains some unique settings to tailor not only the color, opacity, and noise of the glow, but also to change the contour of the glow. The **contour** controls the shape or outline of the outer glow form.

1

- If necessary, select the Seattle text layer.

- Tap or click the 'Add a layer style' button on the Layers panel status bar. When Photoshop displays the context menu, tap or click Outer Glow to open the Layer Style dialog box.

- If necessary, drag the dialog box title bar to display more of the text.

- In the Structure area, tap or click the Blend Mode button to display the list (Figure 6–62).

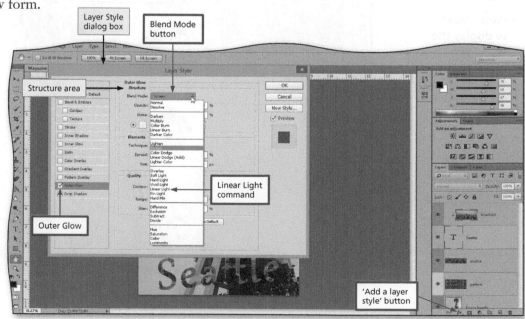

Figure 6–62

 How will changing the blending mode affect the characters in the text?

Because you chose Outer Glow, the blending mode will be applied around the edges of the characters, rather than to the characters themselves.

2

- Tap or click Linear Light to select the blending mode.

- If necessary, change the Opacity setting to 50%.

- Drag the Noise slider to 0% (Figure 6–63).

Q&A
What is the effect of the Linear Light blending mode?
Linear Light dodges light colors by increasing the brightness of the selected color – in this case the yellow color of the glow.

 Experiment

- Drag the Noise slider all the way to the right and notice the difference in the text. Drag the slider back to 0%.

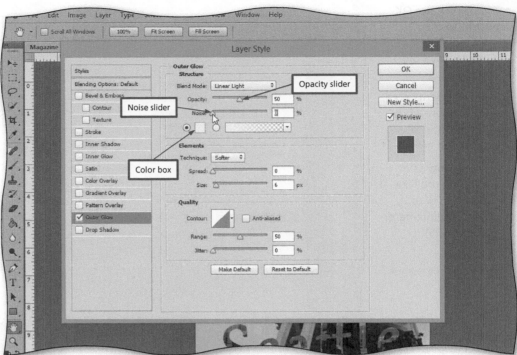

Figure 6–63

3

- Tap or click the Color box to display the Color Picker (Outer Glow Color) dialog box. Enter 13 in the C box, 43 in the M box, 91 in the Y box, and 1 in the K box to enter the CMYK color numbers for dark orange (Figure 6–64).

Q&A
Could I have chosen the color with the eyedropper tool?
Yes, the orange color appears in the skyline layer, but it is very small. Entering the color numbers might be easier.

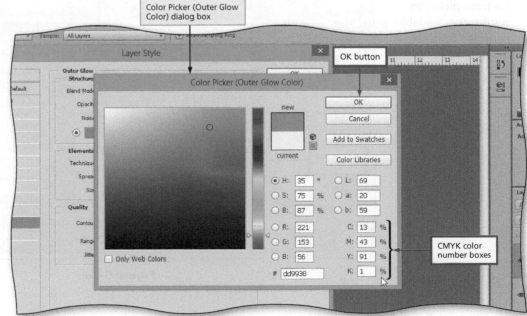

Figure 6–64

4

- Tap or click the OK button to close the Color Picker (Outer Glow Color) dialog box.

- In the Elements area, drag the Spread slider to 30% to expand the glow.

- In the Elements area, drag the Size slider to 15% to expand the diameter (Figure 6–65).

 What is the difference between Spread and Size?
Size changes the diameter of the setting, in this case the outer glow. Spread changes the diameter and blurs slightly.

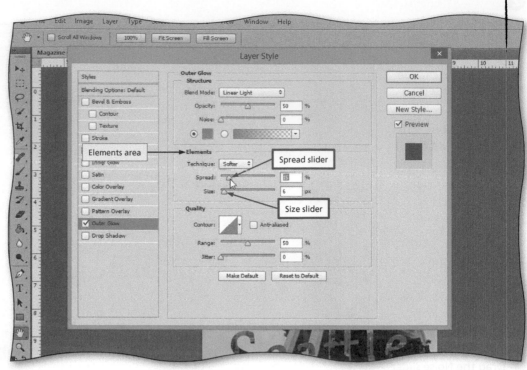

Figure 6–65

5

- Tap or click the Contour picker to display the available contours for the glow.

- Tap or click the Half Round contour to select it (Figure 6–66).

 Can I create my own contour?
Yes, if you tap or click the Contour box itself, Photoshop displays a Contour Editor dialog box where you can drag to edit the line of the contour.

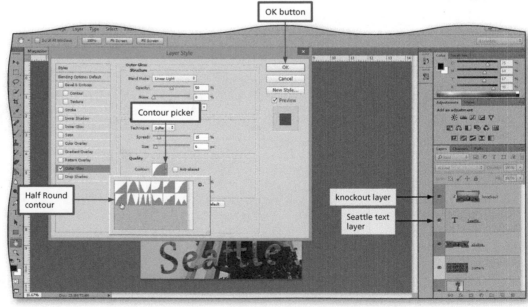

Figure 6–66

🔍 **Experiment**

- Tap or click each of the contours and notice the effect of the glow on the text. When you are finished, tap or click the Half Round contour again.

6

- Tap or click the OK button to close the dialog box and apply the glow.

To Convert to a Smart Object

The following steps convert the knockout and Seattle text layer into a smart object. Recall that converting layers to smart objects gives you nondestructive transformation abilities and displays an embedded icon on the Layers panel. In this case, converting the two layers into a smart object will secure the position of the knockout so you can move it easily in future steps.

1 Tap or click the knockout layer, and then CTRL+click the Seattle layer to select both layers.

2 Press and hold or right-click the selected layers, and then tap or click 'Convert to Smart Object' on the context menu (Figure 6–67).

Figure 6–67

To Edit the Skyline Layer

The following steps remove the sky from the skyline layer and make a brightness adjustment change to the layer. Recall that brightness refers to the tonal range of shadows and highlights in an image.

1 On the Layers panel, tap or click the visibility icon on the skyline layer to make it visible, and then select the layer.

2 Use the Rectangular Marquee Tool to select the area from the horizon upward. It will include the top of some buildings.

3 Press the DELETE key to delete the selection.

4 Deselect.

5 On the Adjustments panel, tap or click the Brightness/Contrast icon to display the Properties panel.

6 Tap or click the 'Clip to layer' button, and then drag the Brightness slider to -100 (Figure 6–68).

7 Minimize the Properties panel.

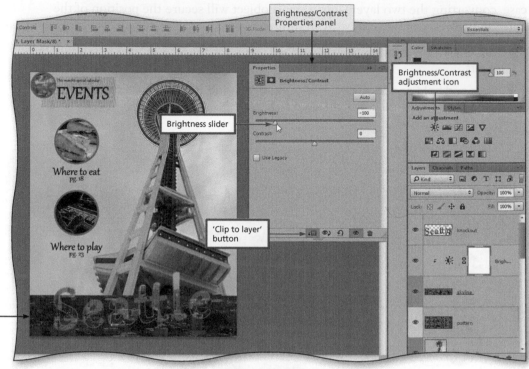

Figure 6–68

To Finish Text

The following steps finish the text in the magazine cover.

1 Select the knockout layer and select the Move Tool.

2 In the document window, drag the knockout upward, until approximately half of the uppercase S in Seattle appears above the skyline.

3 On the Color panel, enter the CMYK colors from the outer glow: 13 in the C box, 43 in the M box, 91 in the Y box, and 1 in the K box to choose the same dark orange color as the outer glow.

4 Select the Horizontal Type Tool. On the options bar, change the font size to 36, and then tap or click the 'Left align text' button.

5 In the document window, drag a text box in the lower-right corner of the canvas, approximately .75 inches tall and 2 inches wide.

6 Type **at night** to complete the text (Figure 6–69).

7 Tap or click the 'Confirm any current edits' button on the options bar.

8 On the Layers panel, change the identification colors as necessary to make filters and adjustments the same color as the layer to which they apply.

knockout text is moved up

new text

Figure 6–69

Generate Image Assets

You can convert any individual layer or layer group into its own image file using a process called **generating image assets**. Photoshop generates a JPG, PNG, or GIF image from the contents of a layer or layer group in a PSD file when you append a supported image format extension to a layer name or a layer group name. Generating image assets is useful particularly for reusing and repurposing images, as well as in multi-device web design projects. The generated assets are saved in a folder in the same location as the original PSD file.

To Generate Image Assets

Because you might want to use the filtered images in another publication, the following steps generate image assets.

1

- Tap or click File on the Application bar and then tap or click Generate to display the Generate submenu (Figure 6–70).

Q&A Can I make every layer a separate image?
Yes, the feature stays on in the file until you turn it off using the same command; however, in most images, you would not need to generate an image asset from every layer.

File menu

Generate submenu

Image Assets command

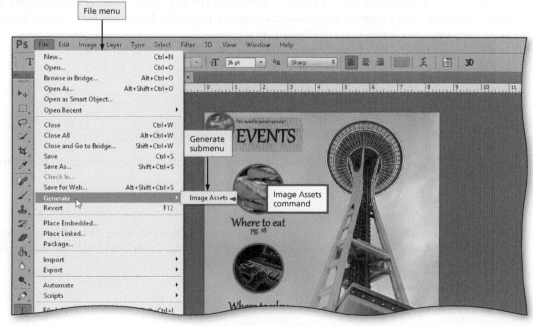

Figure 6–70

2

- Tap or click Image Assets to turn on the features.

- On the Layers panel, scroll as necessary and then double-click the name, food, in the food layer.

- Type **food .png** to add the file extension to the layer name (Figure 6–71).

Q&A

Can I specify the size of the asset?
Yes, you can change the layer name to something such as **200% food.gif** that would save the layer as a GIF file, double in size. Or, you can specify dimensions such as **500 × 500 food.jpeg**, which would create a JPG file of 500 pixels square.

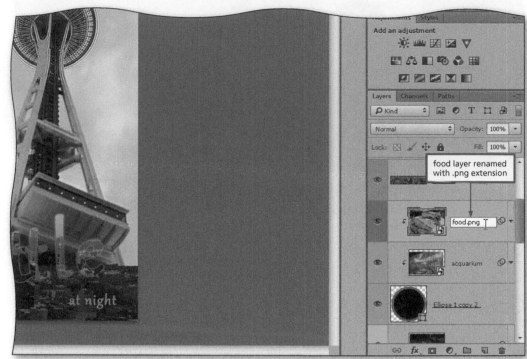

Figure 6–71

3

- Press the ENTER key to create the folder and the asset.

- Repeat the process for the keyboard layer, using the .png extension.

 **Experiment**

- Double-tap or double-click the File Explorer button on the Windows 8 taskbar and navigate to your storage location. Notice the new folder named, Magazine Cover-assets. Inside the folder are two images: food.png and keyboard.png.

To Save the File Again

The following step saves the file again.

1 Press CTRL+S. If Photoshop displays a dialog box, tap or click the OK button.

Break Point: If you wish to take a break, this is a good place to do so. Press CTRL+Q to quit Photoshop. To resume at a later time, start Photoshop, open the file named Magazine Cover, and continue following the steps from this location forward.

To Convert to the CMYK Color Mode

You used an RGB image as the basis for the magazine cover because more filter effects are available in RGB mode. Recall, however, that most paper printing is done using the CMYK color mode. So, as you chose new colors, you used the CMYK sliders and color boxes to make sure that your new colors will print correctly. The next step is to convert the entire image to CMYK and merge the layers. Recall that the color mode is changed using the Image menu. CMYK is the correct color mode for professional print jobs.

1 On the Image menu, tap or click Mode, and then tap or click CMYK Color (Figure 6–72).

2 When Photoshop displays a warning message about merging layers, tap or click the Merge button. If Photoshop displays a dialog box about conversion profiles, tap or click the OK button.

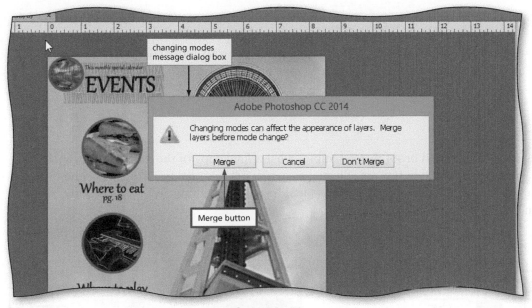

Figure 6–72

Proofs

A **proof** is a copy of a document that you can examine to check color, layout, spelling, and other details before printing the final copy. A hard proof simulates what your final output will look like on a printing press. Sometimes called a proof print or a match print, a **hard proof** is produced on an output device that is less expensive to operate than a printing press. Some ink-jet printers have the resolution necessary to produce inexpensive prints that can be used as hard proofs. Hard proofs need to fit on the page of the proof printer, so it sometimes is necessary to scale the proof. Alternatively, if you need to see a full-size proof, you may be able to tile or poster print the image, printing smaller portions of the image, each on its own sheet of paper, but at actual size. Be careful about judging color with a desktop printer. Less-expensive printers sometimes produce output that does not represent the screen color accurately. For example, lower quality printers can produce a blue hue that appears slightly purple; red hues sometimes appear orange. Users should be aware that the use of inferior printers could result in somewhat false or misleading output—sometimes indicating problems where none exists. Ask your service bureau about color matching.

Plan Ahead

> **Consult with printing professionals.**
> Printing professionals can help you make decisions about paper, color, type, and surprinting, trapping, knockouts and misregistration. Some print shops do professional proofreading, prepress activities, digital proofing, die-cutting, typesetting, binding, and a variety of other services. Digital typesetters, lithographers, and machine operators are the best source of information because they know the machinery, color management systems, and font libraries.

While a hard proof is a printed copy, a **soft proof** is a copy you look at on the screen. Soft proofs can be as simple as a preview or more complex when color adjustments and monitor calibrations take place.

To Print a Hard Proof

The next series of steps prints a hard proof that resembles what a final copy of the magazine cover should look like. Settings in the Print Preview dialog box are adjusted to match professional print settings. The quality of your hard proof will depend on your printer. Some printers handle color matching and overlays better than others do. See your instructor for exact settings.

1

• Tap or click View on the Application bar and then tap or click Proof Setup to display the submenu (Figure 6–73).

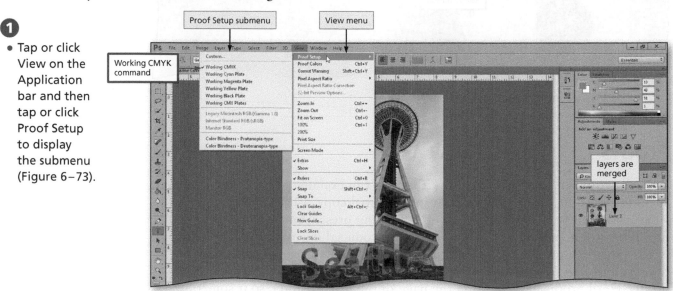

Figure 6–73

2

- If the Working CMYK command does not display a check mark, tap or click it.

- On the File menu, tap or click Print to display the Photoshop Print Settings dialog box.

- In the Color Management area, tap or click the Color Handling button and then tap or click 'Photoshop Manages Colors'.

- Tap or click the Normal Printing button and then tap or click Hard Proofing to choose the setting (Figure 6–74).

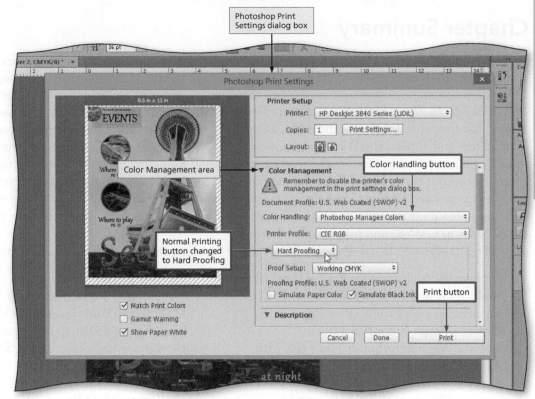

Figure 6–74

 Experiment

- Scroll to the Position and Size area, tap or click the 'Scale to Fit Media' check box to scale the image, and note the difference in the preview. Expand the Printing Marks area and tap or click the check boxes one at a time to see how they affect the preview. When you are finished, remove the check marks.

3

- Tap or click the Print button to print the hard proof.

To Save the File and Quit Photoshop

The magazine cover is complete. The final steps are to save the file and quit Photoshop.

1 Press SHIFT+CTRL+S to open the Save As dialog box.

2 Type **Magazine Cover CMYK** in the File name text box.

3 Tap or click the Save button. If Photoshop displays an options dialog box, tap or click the OK button.

4 Tap or click the Close button on the Photoshop application bar.

BTW

Flash Cards
The Student Companion Site has interactive flash cards of the important concepts in each chapter. Visit For detailed instructions about accessing available resources, visit solutions. cengage.com/ctdownloads or contact your instructor for information about the flash cards.

Chapter Summary

In this chapter, you created a magazine cover from scratch. After choosing CMYK sliders on the Color panel, you used the Reduce Camera Shake Filter to remove some of the blur from the main image. You learned that Photoshop contains a large number of filters that can be combined and edited to produce an endless number of special effects. Some of the filters manipulate the pixels geometrically while others change the color. Filters that specialize in strokes and edges analyze the image to produce effects only in certain areas. You created smart filters and applied the Watercolor, Glowing Edges, and Spin Bur filters. You created a pattern and used the Paint Bucket Tool to fill with the pattern. By creating a clipping mask, you put a picture inside a shape and created knockout text. Finally, you generated image assets and learned about misregistration, potential printing problems associated with objects being close to one another, and the value of consulting with a print service bureau to obtain information about printing details. With the magazine cover complete, you flattened the image, converted it to CMYK, and printed a hard proof.

The items listed below include all the new Photoshop skills you have learned in this chapter:

1. Change the Sliders on the Color Panel (PS 332)
2. Reduce Camera Shake (PS 345)
3. Examine using a Loupe (PS 346)
4. Create a Smart Filter (PS 348)
5. Apply a Watercolor Smart Filter (PS 350)
6. Apply a Glowing Edges Smart Filter (PS 353)
7. Apply a Spin Blur Filter (PS 356)
8. Use the Ellipse Tool (PS 359)
9. Create a Clipping Mask (PS 363)
10. Nudge (PS 365)
11. Define a Pattern (PS 366)
12. Use the Paint Bucket Tool (PS 368)
13. Align and Distribute Layers (PS 372)
14. Create Knockout Text (PS 374)
15. Add an Outer Glow (PS 376)
16. Generate Image Assets (PS 381)
17. Print a Hard Proof (PS 384)

Apply Your Knowledge

Reinforce the skills and apply the concepts you learned in this chapter.

Creating a Sign with Multiple Filters

Note: This assignment requires the Data Files for Students. Visit solutions.cengage.com /ctdownloads for detailed instructions or contact your instructor for information about accessing the required files.

Instructions: Start Photoshop and perform the customization steps found on pages PS 6 through PS 11. Open the Apply 6-1 Sign file from the Chapter 06 folder of the Data Files for Students. You will insert more pictures, apply filters, add clipping masks, define a pattern, and add text as shown in Figure 6–75.

Perform the following tasks:
1. Save the image on your storage device as a PSD file, with the file name Apply 6-1 Sign Complete.
2. Tap or click the 'Color panel menu' button to display its menu and then tap or click CMYK Sliders to change the sliders in the Color panel.
3. Select the snowmobile large layer. To correct the camera shake:
   a. Tap or click Filter on the Application bar, tap or click Sharpen, and then tap or click Shake Reduction to display the Shake Reduction dialog box and reduce the blur.
   b. Tap or click the Unlock Detail button on the status bar of the Detail section. Drag the loupe to various locations over the image to get a preview of the corrections. If any spots need further correction, tap or click the 'Enhance at loupe location' icon.
   c. Tap or click the OK button to close the dialog box.

Figure 6–75

4. To insert more pictures:

   a. Press CTRL+O to display the Open dialog box. Navigate to the Data Files for Students and open the file named, Apply 6-1 Snowmobile 1. Press CTRL+A to select the entire image. Press CTRL+C to copy the image. Return to the Apply 6-1 Sign image and press CTRL+V to paste the image.

   b. Using the Move Tool, drag the image to the right side of the canvas and position it in the lower-right corner. Resize the image to match Figure 6-75.

   c. Name the new layer, snowmobile 1, and add a violet identification color.

   d. On the Filter menu, tap or click 'Convert for Smart Filters'.

   e. Repeat Steps 4a through 4d to insert the Apply 6-1 Snowmobile 2 image, above snowmobile 1. Name the layer, snowmobile 2, and use a blue identification color.

   f. Repeat Steps 4a through 4d to insert the Apply 6-1 Snowmobile 3 image, above snowmobile 2. Name the layer, snowmobile 3, and use a green identification color.

5. To apply filters:

   a. Select the snowmobile 1 layer. Open the Filter gallery and choose the Texture filter named Mosaic Tiles. Change the Tile Size to 39, the Grout Width to 3, and the Lighten Grout to 9.

   b. Select the snowmobile 2 layer. Open the Filter gallery and choose the Artistic filter named Plastic Wrap. Change the Highlight Strength to 15, the Detail to 9, and the Smoothness to 7.

   c. Select the snowmobile 3 layer. Open the Filter gallery and choose the Stylize filter named Glowing Edges. Change the Edge Width to 2, the Edge Brightness to 6, and the Smoothness to 5.

Continued >

Apply Your Knowledge *continued*

6. To create the background pattern:

   a. Select the snowmobile large layer.

   b. Select the Rectangular Marquee Tool and draw a rectangle around the trees above the snowmobiler. On the Edit menu, tap or click Define Pattern. Name the pattern, trees. Deselect.

   c. Select the Paint Bucket Tool. On the options bar, tap or click the 'Set source for fill area' button, and then tap or click Pattern. Tap or click the pattern picker and scroll as necessary to select the trees pattern.

   d. Select the Background layer. Tap or click the white area of the canvas to fill it with the pattern.

7. To create the knockout shapes:

   a. Select the Polygon Tool on the Tools panel.

   b. On the options bar, tap or click the Fill button, and then tap or click the Solid Color button on the pop-up panel.

   c. Tap or click the Stroke button and then tap or click the Color Picker button on the pop-up panel. Move the Color Picker dialog box as necessary to tap or click a yellow color from the large snowmobile image. If the color you choose displays an out-of-gamut warning triangle in the dialog box or the Color panel, click the warning to change the color to a CMYK acceptable shade of yellow. Tap or click the OK button.

   d. Change the shape stroke width to 5. Change the number of sides to 3.

   e. Tap or click the Geometry Options button and then tap or click to select the Smooth Corners check box.

   f. In the document window, drag a large shape over the large snowmobile and rider. As you drag, point the triangular shape downward. Add an orange identification color to the shape layer on the Layers panel.

   g. On the Layers panel, press and hold or right-click the snowmobile large layer and then tap or click 'Create Clipping Mask.' Adjust the shape layer as necessary.

   h. On the Layers panel, ALT+drag a copy of the Polygon shape layer just below the snowmobile 1 layer. Change the identification color to violet to match the snowmobile 1 layer. Create a clipping mask on the snowmobile 1 layer. In the document window, drag the new shape layer to display around the snowmobile 1 image. Press CTRL+T and rotate the image so the triangle points upward as shown in Figure 6–75. Resize the shape layer as necessary. Repeat the process for the other two small images.

8. On the Layers panel, select all of the small images and shapes. Press the v key to display the Move Tool options bar. Use the 'Align horizontal centers' button to align the images and shapes.

9. Select the 'Horizontal Type Tool'. Tap or click the Color box and then use the eyedropper pointer to sample the yellow color. Use the Comic Sans MS Bold Italic font at a font size of 88. Drag a text box at the top of the sign, and enter the word `Snowmobile`. Stroke the text with 15 pixels of black (*Hint*: use the 'Add a layer style' button on the Layers panel.) Repeat the process for the text, Rentals, at the bottom of the sign.

10. Save the file and print a hard proof using the directions from the chapter.

Extend Your Knowledge

Extend the skills you learned in this chapter and experiment with new skills. You may need to use Help to complete the assignment.

Creating the Illusion of Flowing Water

Note: This assignment requires the Data Files for Students. Visit solutions.cengage.com /ctdownloads for detailed instructions or contact your instructor for information about accessing the required files.

Instructions: Start Photoshop and perform the customization steps found on pages PS 6 through PS 11. Open the Extend 6-1 Faucet file from the Chapter 06 folder of the Data Files for Students. The Beta Faucet Company needs you to finish an ad for a new line of faucets. You are to add the appearance of water flowing from the end of the faucet, as shown in Figure 6–76.

Perform the following tasks:

1. On the File menu, tap or click Save As. Save the image on your storage device as a PSD file, with the file name Extend 6-1 Faucet Edited. You will notice that several layers are not visible.

2. Tap or click the visibility icons next to the light blue and dark blue layers.

3. On the Tools panel, tap or click the 'Set foreground color' button to display the Color Picker dialog box. In the document window, tap or click the light blue color to select it. Tap or click the OK button to close the Color Picker dialog box.

4. Repeat Step 3 to assign the background color to the dark blue color in the document window.

5. Select the background layer. On the Tools panel, select the Gradient Tool and create a radial gradient from left to right across the middle of the document window. Press SHIFT+CTRL+N to create a new layer above the background layer and name it, dark rectangle.

6. If a green ruler guide does not appear in the document window, press CTRL+SEMICOLON(;). Use the Rectangular Marquee Tool to draw a rectangle enclosing the right side of the document window.

Figure 6–76

Continued >

Extend Your Knowledge *continued*

7. Press the D key to select the default colors. Fill this new selection by using the Fill shortcut keys, ALT+BACKSPACE.

8. Deselect the marquee by pressing CTRL+D.

9. On the Layers panel, change the opacity of the dark rectangle layer to 60%, creating a navy blue color.

10. Open the Extend 6-1 Single Faucet file from the Chapter 06 folder of the Data Files for Students.

11. Arrange the document windows side by side, and then move the faucet image into the Extend 6-1 Faucet Edited document window as shown in Figure 6–76 on the previous page. Close the Extend 6-1 Single Faucet document window.

12. Create a new layer below the faucet layer with the name, water.

13. With the water layer still selected, on the Filter menu, tap or click Render, and then tap or click Clouds.

14. On the Filter menu, tap or click Blur, and then tap or click Gaussian Blur. Set the radius to 6, and then close the Gaussian Blur dialog box.

15. On the Filter menu, tap or click Blur, and then tap or click Motion Blur. Enter the following settings, and then tap or click the OK button:

    a. Angle 90

    b. Distance 80

16. On the Filter menu, tap or click Filter Gallery, tap or click Artistic, and then tap or click Plastic Wrap. Apply the filter with the following settings:

    a. Highlight Strength: 15

    b. Detail: 10

    c. Smoothness: 10

17. On the Filter menu, tap or click Filter Gallery, tap or click Sketch, then tap or click Chrome. Apply the filter with the following settings:

    a. Detail: 0

    b. Smoothness: 8

18. On the Edit menu, tap or click Fade Filter Gallery. Set the Opacity to 100% and the Mode to Hard Light.

19. On the Edit menu, tap or click Transform, then tap or click Scale. On the options bar, set width to 30% while leaving the height at 100%. Press the ENTER key to commit the transformation.

20. On the Edit menu, tap or click Transform, and then tap or click Warp. Drag the anchor points to simulate a stream of running water and move the layer to a location below the faucet in the document window. Press the ENTER key to commit the transformation.

21. On the Layers panel, change the blending mode to Hard Light.

22. Tap or click the visibility icons for the rest of the layers to view the completed image.

23. Save the file as Extend 6-1 Faucet Complete and submit the assignment to your instructor in the specified format.

Make It Right

Analyze a document and correct all errors and/or improve the design.

Correcting Bokeh Errors

Note: This assignment requires the Data Files for Students. Visit solutions.cengage.com /ctdownloads for detailed instructions or contact your instructor for information about accessing the required files.

Instructions: Start Photoshop and perform the customization steps found on pages PS 6 through PS 11. Open the Make It Right 6-1 Butterfly file from the Chapter 06 folder of the Data Files for Students. The file contains an edits layer whose settings caused too high a distortion, as shown in Figure 6–77.

Figure 6–77

Perform the following tasks:

Delete the edits layer. Duplicate the background layer and name it corrections. With the corrections layer selected, use the Filter menu and the Blur Gallery submenu to access the Iris Blur. Adjust the focus ring to be a circle around the butterfly. Drag the center point as necessary. Use the following settings on the Blur Tools and Blur Effects panels:

    a. Set the Blur to 35 px.
    b. Set the Light Bokeh to 30%.
    c. Set the Bokeh Color to 0%.
    d. Drag the black Light Range slider to 150.
    e. Drag the white Light Range slider to 250.

      Save the image as a PSD file on your storage device with the name, Make It Right 6-1 Butterfly Corrected.

In the Labs

Design and/or create a document using the guidelines, concepts, and skills presented in this chapter. Labs are listed in order of increasing difficulty.

Lab 1: Creating Knockout Text from a Pattern

Note: This assignment requires the Data Files for Students. Visit solutions.cengage.com /ctdownloads for detailed instructions or contact your instructor for information about accessing the required files.

Problem: You are to create a welcome sign for a small museum that features the museum's front door. The completed poster is displayed in Figure 6–78.

Courtesy of Laura Starks

Figure 6–78

Instructions: Perform the following tasks:
1. Start Photoshop. Perform the customization steps found on pages PS 6 through PS 11.
2. Press CTRL+N to open the New dialog box. Name the file, Lab 6-1 Welcome Sign, with dimensions of 8.5 × 11 inches. Use a resolution of 72 in the RGB color mode. Choose a white background.
3. Use the Place Embedded command on the File menu to place the Lab 6-1 Doorway image in the lower center of the page as shown in Figure 6–78.
4. Use the Horizontal Type Tool to create the text at the top of the sign with the Elephant Regular font at size 111.
5. Press SHIFT+CTRL+N to create a new layer, named leaded glass.

6. Use the Rectangular Marquee Tool to select one of the leaded glass windows in the door. Tap or click Define Pattern on the Edit menu and name the pattern, leaded glass.

7. Select the Paint Bucket Tool on the Tools panel. On the options bar, tap or click the 'Set source for fill area' button and choose Pattern. Tap or click the pattern picker and scroll as necessary to choose the leaded glass pattern.

8. With the leaded glass layer selected, tap or click the canvas to fill the new layer with the pattern. On the Layers panel, press and hold or right-click the new layer and then tap or click 'Create Clipping Mask' to create the knockout text.

9. Use the Eyedropper Tool to sample the light gray color in the floor.

10. If necessary, select the Paint Bucket Tool on the Tools panel. On the options bar, tap or click the 'Set source for fill area' button and choose Foreground.

11. Select the Background layer and then tap or click the canvas to apply the light gray color.

12. Organize your layers with appropriate names and identification colors

13. Save the image with the name, Lab 6-1 Welcome Sign.

14. Print a hard proof using the directions from the chapter. See your instructor for ways to submit this assignment.

Lab 2: Creating a Coloring Page

Note: This assignment requires the Data Files for Students. Visit solutions.cengage.com /ctdownloads for detailed instructions or contact your instructor for information about accessing the required files.

Problem: You decide to take a picture of your niece and turn it into a coloring page for her. The resulting page is displayed in Figure 6–79.

Courtesy of David Reneau

Figure 6–79

Continued >

In the Labs *continued*

Instructions: Perform the following tasks:

1. Start Photoshop. Perform the customization steps found on pages PS 6 through PS 11.

2. Open the file named Lab 6-2 Girl from the Data Files for Students.

3. Save the file in the PSD format, with the name, Lab 6-2 Girl Complete.

4. Duplicate the Background layer and name it coloring book. On the Filter menu, convert the new layer to a smart filter layer.

5. On the Filter menu, tap or click Stylize, and then tap or click Find Edges to apply the filter.

6. Flatten the image.

7. On the Image menu, convert the image to the Grayscale Mode. If Photoshop displays a message about discarding the color information, tap or click the Discard button.

8. Save the file again.

9. Tap or click Print on the File menu. When Photoshop displays the Photoshop Print Settings dialog box, tap or click the 'Print paper in landscape orientation' button. Scroll to the Position and Size area. Tap or click the 'Scale to Fit Media' check box. Ready the printer. Tap or click the Print button and submit the printout to your instructor.

Lab 3: Fizzy Root Beer Advertisement

Note: This assignment requires the Data Files for Students. Visit solutions.cengage.com /ctdownloads for detailed instructions or contact your instructor for information about accessing the required files.

Problem: The Fizzy Root Beer Company has a new label and needs you to finish the design for their latest advertisement. They want the background to look like bubbles, but they do not have any close-ups of root beer bubbles for you to use. By combining several filters, you will create a bubbly background and add a spotlight effect as shown in Figure 6–80.

Figure 6–80

Instructions: Perform the following tasks:

Start Photoshop and perform the customization steps found on pages PS 6 through PS 11. Open the Lab 6-3 Fizzy file from the Data Files for Students.

Save the image on your storage device as a PSD file with the name Lab 6-3 Fizzy Edited.

Hide the label layer. Select the Background layer. Tap or click the D key to reset the default colors. On the Filter menu, tap or click Convert for Smart Filters. To simulate bubbles, apply the Render filter named Clouds. Apply the Stylize filter named Glowing Edges, setting the Edge width to 3, the Edge Brightness to 19, and the Smoothness to 15. Apply the Sketch filter named Plaster, setting the Image Balance to 16 and the Smoothness to 2.

Note: If your computer does not have a newer graphics card, you may not be able to complete the following step. In that case, do not complete the lighting effect instructions in this paragraph and skip to the next paragraph. To make the bubbles look like they are in liquid, add a lighting effect. On the Filter menu, tap or click Render, and then tap or click Lighting Effects. On the options bar, tap or click the Presets button and then choose Blue Omni for the style. In the preview, drag the ellipse handles to create a circle that encompasses the entire preview. Drag the center point to the lower-left corner of the preview. Tap or click the OK button to close the Lighting Effects dialog box.

Apply the Sketch filter named Chrome. Set the Detail to 8 and the Smoothness to 10.

To make the bubbles brown, tap or click the Hue/Saturation icon on the Adjustments panel. Select the Colorize check box so that it displays a check mark. Set the Hue to 22, the Saturation to 70, and the Lightness to –25. Tap or click the 'Clip to layer' button on the Adjustments panel status bar.

On the Layers panel, display the label layer. If you have a newer graphics card, add a spotlight filter to the label layer by tapping or clicking Render from the Filter menu, then tapping or clicking Lighting Effects. Select Flashlight as the Style and scale the light so that it covers the top and bottom of the label. Save the file again and submit it to your instructor in the specified format.

Cases and Places

Apply your creative thinking and problem solving skills to design and implement a solution.

Note: To complete these assignments, you may be required to use the Data Files for Students. Visit solutions.cengage.com/ctdownloads for detailed instructions or contact your instructor for information about accessing the required files.

1: Create a Surface Blur

Academic

The photo of your campus, taken from the roof of its tallest building, was taken on a very cloudy day. The school would like to use the picture on its website, but would prefer a brighter sky. Open the file named Case 6-1 Cityscape from the Chapter 06 folder of the Data Files for Students. Select the sky and create a layer via cut. Use the Color panel to select a very light blue foreground color. Use the Render Filter named Clouds to create clouds in the sky. Flatten the file and save it for the web in the gif format.

Continued >

Cases and Places *continued*

2: Create a T-shirt Logo

Personal

As a big racing fan, you would like to create an image of a checkered flag against the sky to put on a t-shirt. Open the file Case 6-2 Flag from the Data Files for Students. Use the Rectangular Marquee Tool to select the black and white squares. Define a pattern named racing. Delete the black and white squares. Use the Rectangular Marquee Tool again to create a rectangle approximately 5 inches wide and 3 inches tall. Select the Paint Bucket Tool. On the options bar set the source to Pattern, and then use the picker to choose the racing pattern. Fill the rectangle selection with the racing pattern. Erase any of edges that do not complete a full square. Press CTRL+T and then, on the options bar, choose the warp mode. On the top of the rectangle, drag the second handle from the left, down slightly to simulate the flag waving. On the bottom of the rectangle, drag the far right handle up slightly. Confirm the transformation. Make the pole layer visible and align it with the flag. Switch to the sky layer and make it visible. Use the Eyedropper Tool to sample the blue. Use the Render filter named Clouds to create a cloud-filled sky.

3: Using a Filter for Corrections

Professional

A professional photographer would like you to enhance a picture of a sunset with a filter. He plans to upload the picture to several social media sites. Specifically, he would like to reduce the JPG artifacts produced by his camera. Open the file named Case 6-3 Sunset from the Chapter 06 folder of the Data Files for Students. Duplicate the background and convert the layer into a smart filter. On the Filter menu, select the Noise filter named Reduce Noise. Drag the Preserve Details slider and the Sharpen Details slider to the right. Slowly drag the Reduce Color Noise slider to the left until you are happy with the result. Tap or click the OK button in the Reduce Noise dialog box and then save the file with the name, Case 6-3 Sunset Edited in the PSD format.

Ps File Edit Image Layer Type Select Filter 3D View Window Help

Adobe Photoshop CC   Feather: 0 px   ☐ Anti-alias   Style: Normal   ⬍   Width: ⇄   Height: Refine Edge...

7 | Creating Color Channels and Actions

Objectives

You will have mastered the material in this chapter when you can:

- Build a composite, master image
- View channel color separations
- Use the Channels panel to create alpha channels
- Use a brush in overlay mode to help define a selection
- Replace a color
- Create an image with a transparent background
- Use the Refine Mask Tool

- Warp text
- Create a new action set
- Record, save, edit, and play back an action
- Desaturate
- Create black-and-white, sepia, and duotone versions of an image
- Convert an RGB image to Lab color and then to CMYK
- List prepress activities
- Print color separations

Ps File Edit Image Layer Type Select Filter 3D View Window Help

Adobe **Photoshop CC** Feather: 0 px   Anti-alias   Style: Normal   Width: Height: Refine Edge...

7 | Creating Color Channels and Actions

Introduction

Photographers and graphic artists routinely create multiple versions of the same image. Creating a master version – along with versions for the web, for black-and-white advertising media, for color separations and tints, and for various color modes and sizes – allows for maximum repurposing. Multiple versions of photos are used commonly in advertising, photo cataloging, and on photo websites. Portrait studios produce and sell a wide assortment of special effect portraits, which require a variety of image versions. Creating a reusable graphic or logo adds flexibility for business publications.

Another timesaving tool is the ability to record a series of action steps as you work in Photoshop and play them back when needed. The saved recording, called a Photoshop action, is a powerful automation device. Tasks that you perform repeatedly, such as adding a logo to each publication, can be recorded and then played back with a single keystroke.

You will learn about channels, color changes, warping text, and actions as you work through this chapter.

Project — Campus Recycling Sign

Chapter 7 uses Photoshop to edit photographs for a campus recycling sign. First, you will hide the background and create a masked piece of artwork that can be dropped into other backgrounds and page layout applications. You will prepare images in different ways as you build the composite image. A black-and-white version of the sign will be created for campus newspaper placement. Sepia and tinted versions will provide visual variety and styling, such as retro or filtered special effects. You will style the advertisement and resize it with an automated action. Finally, the sign – complete with graphics and text – will be converted to the CMYK color model and printed with color separations. The images are shown in Figure 7–1.

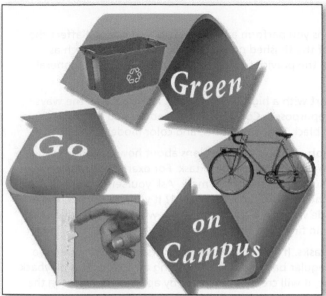

(a) full color

(c) sepia

(b) black and white

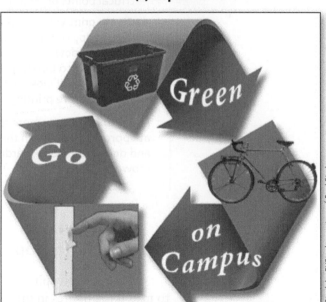

(d) duotone

iStock by EHStock; courtesy of Fred Starks

Figure 7–1

Overview

As you read this chapter, you will learn how to create the images shown in Figure 7–1 by performing these general tasks:

- Add an alpha channel.
- Hide the background to create a floating image.
- Create a graphic with transparency.
- Insert and warp text.
- Use action sets.
- Record and play back an action.
- Recolor images to produce black and white, sepia, and duotone versions.
- Print color separations.

Plan
Ahead

General Project Guidelines

When editing a photo, the actions you perform and decisions you make will affect the appearance and characteristics of the finished product. As you edit photos, such as the ones shown in Figure 7–1 on the previous page, you should follow these general guidelines:

1. **Plan your versions.** Always start with a high-quality photo. Anticipate all the ways the image might be used or repurposed. Consider client needs as you create versions, such as color, masked images, black and white, tints, and color modes.

2. **Choose the best tool for the job.** As you make decisions about how to edit your image, look at various ways to accomplish the same task. For example, compare using a simple delete command versus an alpha channel mask. Ask yourself if you will need to use the selection again. Is the background complicated? If you are considering a black-and-white version, decide whether a simple grayscale will be as effective as an adjustment layer where you can fine-tune the contrast.

3. **Record actions for repetitive tasks.** If you or your client have specialized, repetitive tasks that you perform on a regular basis, consider recording an action. This playback feature will not only save time, it will create consistency by applying revisions in the same way each time. Actions can give users flexibility by pausing for user decisions at critical points or by waiting for dialog box responses.

4. **Create print versions of artwork.** If you plan to print your artwork, convert and save a copy of it in the CMYK color mode. The RGB color mode, used for display on electronic devices such as computers and smartphones, is not suitable for printing. Converting to CMYK gives a better representation on the computer screen of how the image will look when printed. You then can make adjustments to the CMYK version before printing, if necessary.

When necessary, more specific details concerning the above guidelines are presented at appropriate points in the chapter. The chapter also will identify the actions performed and decisions made regarding these guidelines during the creation of the edited photos shown in Figure 7–1.

To Start Photoshop

If you are stepping through this project on a computer and you want your screen to match the figures in this book, then you should change your computer's resolution to 1366×768 and reset the panels, tools, and colors. For more information about how to change the resolution on your computer and other advanced Photoshop settings, read the Editing Preferences Appendix.

The following steps, which assume Windows 8 is running, start Photoshop based on a typical installation. You may need to ask your instructor how to start Photoshop for your system.

1 With Windows 8 running, scroll to display the Adobe Photoshop CC tile on the Start screen.

2 Tap or click the Adobe Photoshop CC tile to run the Photoshop app.

3 After a few moments, when the Photoshop window appears, if the window is not maximized, tap or click the Maximize button next to the Close button on the Application bar to maximize the window.

To Set the Workspace and the Layers Panel

The following steps select and reset the Essentials workspace, as well as setting options on the Layers panel.

1 Tap or click the workspace switcher on the options bar to display the list and then tap or click Essentials to select the default workspace panels.

2 Tap or click the workspace switcher on the options bar again, to display the list and then tap or click Reset Essentials to restore the workspace to its default settings and reposition any panels that might have been moved by previous users.

3 Tap or click the Layers panel menu button and then tap or click Panel Options. In the Panel Options dialog box, click the medium thumbnail, and tap or click to select the Layer Bounds options button.

To Reset the Tools and the Options Bar

Recall that the Tools panel and the options bar retain their settings from previous Photoshop sessions. The following steps select the Rectangular Marquee Tool and reset all tool settings in the options bar.

1 If the tools in the Tools panel appear in two columns, tap or click the double arrow at the top of the Tools panel.

2 If necessary, tap or click the 'Rectangular Marquee Tool' button on the Tools panel to select it.

3 On the options bar, press and hold or right-click the Rectangular Marquee Tool icon to display the context menu, and then tap or click 'Reset All Tools'. When Photoshop displays a confirmation dialog box, tap or click the OK button to restore the tools to their default settings.

To Set the Interface and Default Colors

Recall that Photoshop retains the interface color scheme, as well as the foreground and background colors from session to session. The following steps set the interface to Medium Gray and the foreground and background colors to black over white.

1 Tap or click Edit on the Application bar to display the Edit menu. Tap or click Preferences and then tap or click Interface on the Preferences submenu to display the Preferences dialog box.

2 If necessary, tap or click the third button, Medium Gray, to change the interface color scheme.

3 Tap or click the OK button to close the Preferences dialog box.

4 Tap or click the 'Default Foreground and Background Colors' button on the Tools panel to set the default colors to black and white. If black is not over white on the Tools panel, tap or click the 'Switch Foreground and Background Colors' button.

BTW

Photoshop Help
At anytime while using Photoshop, you can find answers to questions and display information about various topics through Photoshop Help. Used properly, this form of assistance can increase your productivity and reduce your frustrations by minimizing the time you spend learning how to use Photoshop. For instruction about Photoshop Help and exercises that will help you gain confidence in using it, read the Using Photoshop Help appendix.

Using Channels

BTW

Primary Colors
A primary color is one that cannot be created by mixing other colors in the gamut of a given color space. Traditionally, the colors red, yellow, and blue are considered primary colors.

The first version of the photo will be a floating image without a background. **Floating images** have a transparent background so they can be placed in front of other elements. Photoshop offers many ways to remove a background, including methods you have used before, such as using the Eraser Tool, layer masks, or editing selections. Another way to isolate and remove the background is to use Photoshop channels.

As you learned in previous chapters, digital images are made of many pixels, or tiny dots, each of which represents an abstract sample of color. Pixels use combinations of primary colors, or pigments. Recall that additive colors involve light emitted directly from a source. Subtractive colors absorb some wavelengths of light and reflect others. The two color modes RGB and CMYK are based respectively on the additive and subtractive primary colors.

BTW

Inverting Channels
If you need to swap the colors of a channel, you can press CTRL+I to invert the colors of the channel.

Each of the primary colors creates a channel in Photoshop. In an image, a **channel** consists all the pixels of the same color, identified using the color modes. An image from a digital camera will have a red, green, and blue channel, whereas a printed image will have a cyan, magenta, yellow, and black channel. Channels are used in Photoshop to separate and store information about an image's colors so that users can manipulate them. Traditionally, the term **color separations** refers to the process of separating image colors into individual films or pattern plates of cyan, magenta, yellow, and black in preparation for printing. Photoshop takes that process one step further by automatically creating the color separation anytime you convert a file to the CMYK color mode.

Photoshop creates channels automatically when you open a new image. The color mode you are using determines the number of color channels created. By default, bitmap, grayscale, duotone, and indexed-color images have one channel; RGB and Lab images have three, plus a composite; and CMYK images have four, plus a composite. You can add specialized channels to all image types except bitmap images.

BTW

The Channel Mixer
The Channel Mixer creates high-quality images by choosing the percentages from each color channel. It lends itself more toward artistic expression than for tasks related to simple restoration or technical graphics. Artists use the Channel Mixer to create a variety of tints, pastels, infrareds, and sepia tones.

In addition to the default color channels, extra channels — called alpha channels — are used for storing and editing selections as masks; spot color channels can be added to incorporate spot color plates for printing. A **spot color plate** is an extra part of the separation printing process that applies a single color to areas of the artwork. Alpha channels are described in detail later in this chapter.

Plan Ahead

> **Plan your versions.**
> Once you create a master image, you should plan for possible uses and versions. If you are creating a photo for a client or business, consider all the ways the image could be repurposed. **Repurposing** is using all or part of a photo for something other than its original purpose. Ask yourself these questions and create versions based on your needs:
>
> - Might the image need to be used with and without its background?
> - Will the image be used in more than one medium, such as web, newspaper, posters, flyers, and so on?
> - Might you need both a color and black-and-white version?
> - Would special tints, such as sepia or duotones, extend the possibilities for the image?
> - Could you use all or part of the photo in another composite image?
> - Can you save money by performing some prepress activities yourself?
> - How will you organize your versions for maximum use over time?

The Channels Panel

The Channels panel (Figure 7–2) is used to create and manage channels. The panel lists all channels in the image — the composite channel first, then each individual color channel, followed by any spot color channels, and finally any alpha channels. The **composite channel** shows what your image looks like with all of the colors turned on. The **individual channels** display the saturation of a single color using grayscale, because the colors themselves would be so bright and distracting it would be difficult to make use of the information. It is much easier to see a particular color's strength or **luminosity** when the color is represented in shades of gray. Because colors are made from light, white in the channel indicates areas where the color is at full strength, black indicates areas where it is weakest, and shades of gray represent everything in between. **Spot channels** are used in commercial printing to define certain areas in your image that should be printed with special premixed inks such as varnish, foil, or metallic ink. As you will learn, Alpha channels are grayscale representations of a temporary selection such as a quick mask or saved selection or path.

As in the Layers panel, the Channels panel displays a visibility icon and a thumbnail of each channel's contents. The visibility icon is useful for viewing specific colors in the document window, or to see how edits might affect a specific color.

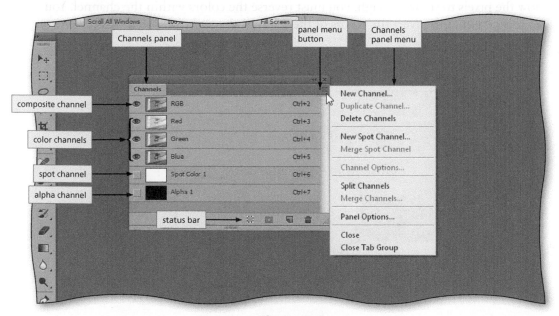

Figure 7–2

When you select one specific channel, it is displayed in grayscale in the document window by default. If more than one channel is selected, the document window displays the color combinations.

The Channels panel menu displays commands to create new channels, change the color overlay, or set other channel options.

RGB Channels

When you view a single RGB channel, pixels with a high concentration of the color indicated by the channel appear light, while pixels with a low concentration appear dark. For example, when viewing the red channel, areas of the original image that are red will appear almost white, and areas that do not contain red appear almost black.

Recall that the RGB color mode is an additive color mode. When the maximum amounts of red, green, and blue are combined, white is produced, which means that white areas of an image contain a high concentration of red, green, and blue. When minimal amounts of red, green, and blue are combined, black is produced. Therefore, black areas of an image contain very little red, green, or blue. For this reason, white areas of the original image will appear as white no matter which channel is viewed because those white pixels are produced by combining large amounts of red, green, and blue. Black areas of the original image will appear as black no matter which channel is viewed because those black pixels are produced by removing red, green, and blue and therefore have very little of any of the colors represented by the channels.

For example, when viewing in the green channel a picture of a white golf ball and a black hole on green grass, both the green grass and white ball appear as white because they have a high concentration of green. The black hole will appear as black because it has a low concentration of green. However, the same image when viewed in the red channel will look completely different. In the red and blue channels, only the white ball will be displayed as white. The green grass and black hole that both lack red and blue, will appear as dark gray (Figure 7–3).

Sometimes if you want to create a mask using channels, you will invert the white for strong color saturation versus the black for low color saturation. In that case, because the black areas will hide pixels when used as a mask while the white areas will allow the pixels to show through, you must reverse the colors within the channel. You can press CTRL+I to invert the colors of the selected channel.

all channels
are visible

grass appears dark in the red channel because it has very little red color information

grass appears light in the green channel because it has a lot of green color information

Figure 7–3

To Open a File

To open a file in Photoshop, it must be stored as a digital file on your computer system or on an external storage device. The photos used in this book are included in the in Data Files for Students. Visit solutions.cengage.com/ctdownloads for detailed instructions or contact your instructor for information about accessing the required files.

The following steps open the file, Light Switch, from the Photoshop Chapter 07 folder in the Documents folder of Windows 8. The location of your file may differ.

1 Tap or click File on the Application bar to display the File menu, and then tap or click Open on the File menu to display the Open dialog box.

2 If necessary, tap or click the arrow next to Libraries or This PC in the Navigation pane to display the folders.

3 Tap or click the Documents location to display a list of the available folders and files.

4 Double-tap or double-click the desired folder to display its contents (in this case, the Photoshop folder).

5 Double-tap or double-click the Chapter 07 folder to display its contents.

6 Double-tap or double-click the file, Light Switch, to open the file.

7 If necessary, change the magnification to 100%.

8 If the rulers are not shown on the top and left sides of the document window, press CTRL+R to display the rulers in the workspace.

> **BTW**
>
> **The Photoshop Window**
> The chapters in this book begin with the Photoshop window appearing as it did at the initial installation of the software. Your Photoshop window may look different depending on your screen resolution and other Photoshop settings.

 For a detailed example of this procedure using the Mac operating system, refer to the For Mac Users Appendix.

To View Channels

The following steps open the Channels panel and allow you to view individual channels. As you view each channel, the channel color will appear almost white; other colors will appear in shades of gray.

1
- Tap or click the Channels panel tab to access the Channels panel (Figure 7–4).

Experiment
- One at a time, tap or click each of the channels. Be sure to tap or click the channel thumbnail or name – do not tap or click the visibility icons. As you view each channel, look for strong contrast between the lightest and darkest colors in the image, which will make it easier to isolate parts of the image.

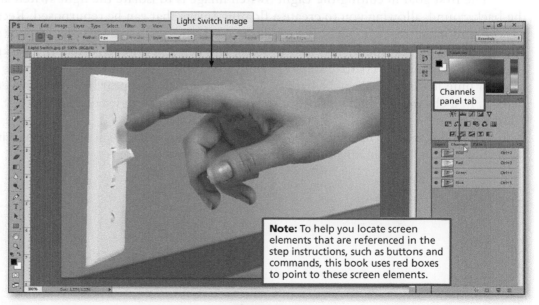

Figure 7–4

- Tap or click the Blue channel to view the channel displaying the most contrast between the light switch, hand, and background (Figure 7–5).

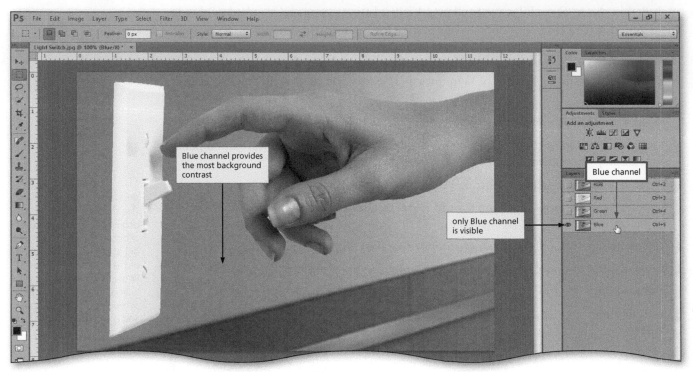

Figure 7–5

Other Ways

1. To display composite channel, press CTRL+2	2. To display first channel, press CTRL+3	3. To display second channel, press CTRL+4	4. To display third channel, press CTRL+5

To Select using a Channel

The first goal in editing the Light Switch image is to isolate the light switch and hand by removing the background, allowing you to create a floating image that can be repurposed. Recall that removing the background in an image involves isolating it in a selection area and then deleting or masking it. When you have a solid background, it is easy to select and delete. However, often, the background is busy or shaded, requiring more creative steps to remove it. Variegated colors, such as shades of green in grassy areas or blue in sky areas, may be hard to delete because they appear behind, between, and around other objects. In a channel, those kinds of backgrounds appear as a single color; thus, they are isolated and selected easily.

The following step uses the Magnetic Lasso Tool to select as much of the light switch and hand as possible in the Blue channel, eliminating the similarly colored background.

①

- Press and hold or right-click the Lasso Tool button on the Tools panel to display a context menu, and then tap or click Magnetic Lasso Tool.

- If necessary, tap or click the New selection button on the options bar.

- Tap or click the edge of the light switch and then drag carefully around both the light switch and the hand, staying close to the edges, to create a selection. The selection does not have to be perfect, as you will fix errors in the next steps.

- Tap or click the starting point close the selection (Figure 7–6).

Q&A Could I use the Magic Wand Tool or Quick Selection Tool to select the hand and light switch? Yes, you can use any of the selection tools, but it may be tedious to get the tolerance setting correct, especially because the hand and the wall are very close in color.

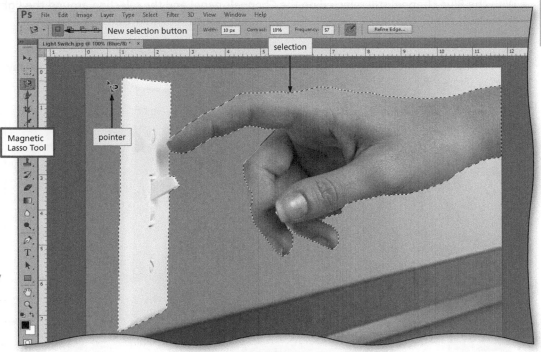

Figure 7–6

Alpha Channels

Photoshop provides a way to save selections. An **alpha channel,** or **alpha channel mask,** is a special channel that saves and loads selection marquees. When you create a new channel, by default it becomes an alpha channel. It is similar to a new layer or layer mask in that it is used to edit or mask parts of an image. Alpha channel masking can be performed on the Background layer, whereas masks created using the Layers panel cannot. Alpha channels selections exist independently of any particular layer — for that reason, storing selections as alpha channels creates more permanent masks than saving as layer masks. You can reuse the stored selections or even load them into another image. The Channel Options command on the Channels panel menu allows you to name the alpha channel and adjust settings related to editing.

Most commonly, alpha channels are used to isolate and protect areas of an image as you apply color changes, filters, or other effects to the rest of the image. Additionally, alpha channels are used for complex image editing, such as gradually applying color or filter effects to an image. For instance, viewing an alpha channel and the composite channel together allows you to see how changes made in the alpha channel relate to the entire image. When you display an alpha channel at the same time as a color channel, Photoshop lightly colors the area outside of the selection with a transparent color **overlay** in the document window. Light red is the default color for overlays. Overlays are visible only by using the Channels panel. They do not print. Viewing an overlay can help you determine areas you missed when creating the selection.

To Create an Alpha Channel from a Selection

When making an alpha channel, you either can create the channel first and then paint the selected area, or you can select the area first and then create the channel. The following step creates an alpha channel when a selection already has been made. You will use the 'Save selection as channel' button on the Channels panel status bar to create an alpha channel with colored overlay and adjustable opacity.

1
- With the Blue channel still selected on the Channels panel and the selection around the light switch and hand still active, tap or click the 'Save selection as channel' button to create an alpha channel.

- Deselect.

- Tap or click the 'Indicates channel visibility' button to left of the Alpha 1 channel to display its color overlay (Figure 7–7).

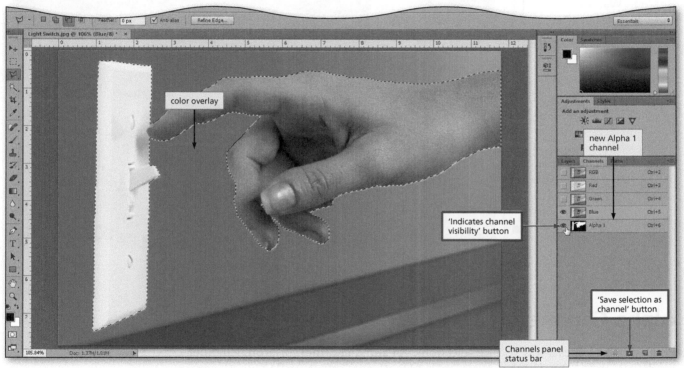

Figure 7–7

📖 **Experiment**
- Double-tap or double-click the Alpha 1 channel thumbnail and view the name, color, and opacity settings. Tap or click the OK button to close the dialog box.

Other Ways

1. On Channels panel status bar, ALT+click 'Create new channel' button	2. On Channel panel menu, tap or click New Channel, edit settings

To Edit an Alpha Channel

It is likely that after creating an initial selection and creating an alpha channel, you will need to edit the channel to modify the selection. It often is easiest to do this using the Brush Tool and painting with black or white, which are the colors used with masks and alpha channels. Recall that painting with white adds to the selection while painting with black subtracts from the selection. The following steps edit the selection to create what will become a good starting point for a mask. As you paint with black, the area you paint will turn red to match the red overlay.

①

- On the channels panel, tap or click the Alpha 1 channel to select it, if necessary. Be sure only the Blue and Alpha 1 channels are visible.

- Zoom in on any errors you made in the selection. In Figure 7–8, part of the finger is not in the selection, and there are some small white areas. Your errors might differ.

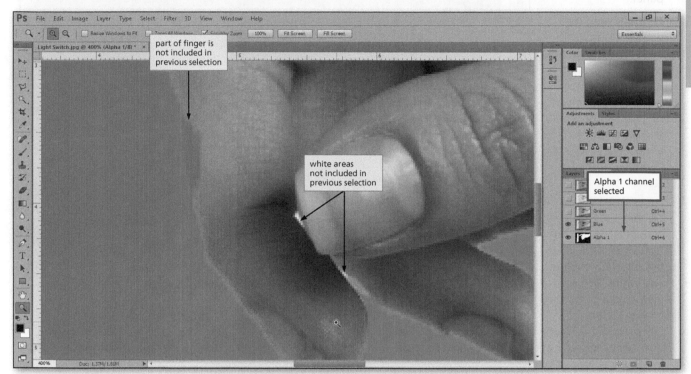

Figure 7–8

②

- Press the B key to select the Brush Tool.

- On the options bar, tap or click the Brush Preset picker to display the pop-up panel.

- Change the Size to 5 px.

- Change the Hardness to 100% (Figure 7–9).

Q&A Why am I setting the Hardness to 100%?
The high Hardness setting lets you paint with crisp edges rather than with feathered edges that create a fade.

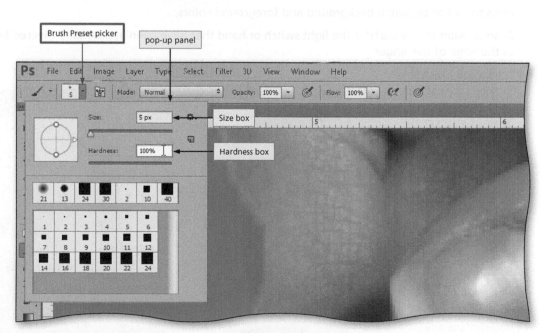

Figure 7–9

3

- Tap or click the Brush Preset picker button again to close the pop-up panel.

- Carefully drag the pointer over any areas that should not be in the selection, such as the white areas between the fingers. Adjust the size of the brush as necessary (Figure 7–10).

Experiment

- Tap or click the visibility icon on the Blue channel to view the selection in black and white. Zoom and scroll around the image. Take note of

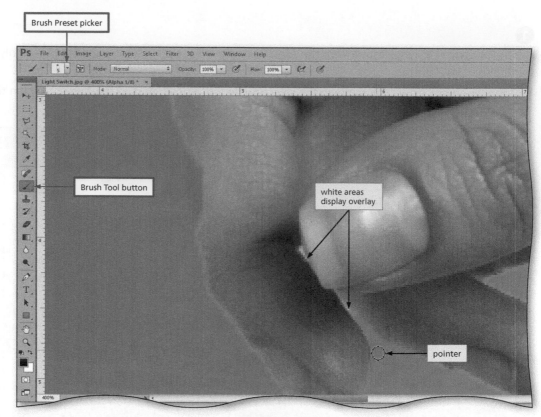

Figure 7–10

any parts of the image that should not be in the selection. Tap or click the visibility icon on the Blue channel again to display it. Tap or click the Alpha channel to select it, if necessary. Paint over any parts of the image that should not be in the selection.

4

- Press the X key to switch background and foreground colors.

- Drag to paint in any parts of the light switch or hand that have been accidentally covered by the red overlay, such as the edge of the finger.

- Adjust the brush size as necessary using the LEFT BRACKET ([) or RIGHT BRACKET (]) key as you paint, to get in to the smaller spaces and corners.

- Zoom and scroll as necessary to inspect the entire image and make corrections (Figure 7–11).

 Q&A

Can I make corrections any other way?

You can use any selection tool to make new selections on a channel and then fill them with black or white.

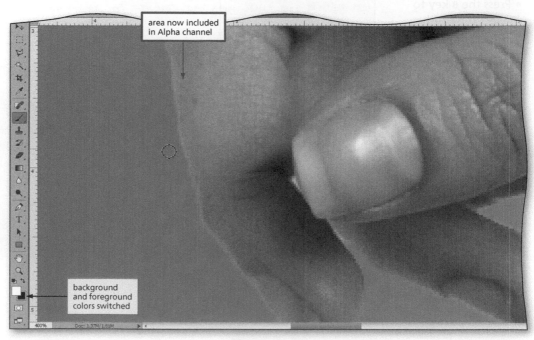

Figure 7–11

- Double-tap or double-click the channel name Alpha 1, type **selection** to rename the channel, and then press the ENTER key to save the new name (Figure 7–12).

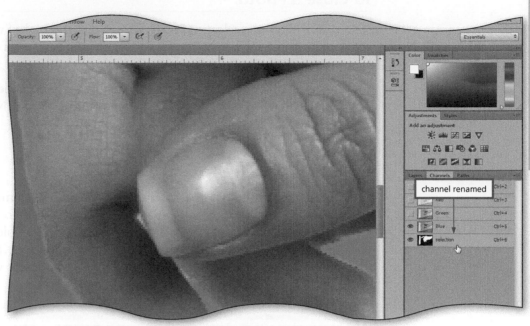

channel renamed

Figure 7–12

To Save a Photo with Channels

Because channels and saved selections cannot be saved using the JPG format, the following steps save the photo with the name Light Switch Selection in the Photoshop format in a new folder named Chapter 07.

BTW

Alpha Channels
Photoshop allows you to create and save multiple alpha channels. This is helpful because it lets you store multiple selections for later use.

1 Tap or click File on the Application bar to display the File menu and then tap or click Save As to display the Save As dialog box.

2 In the File name text box, type **Light Switch Selection** to rename the file. Do not press the ENTER key after typing the file name.

3 Navigate to your storage location (or the Creative Cloud Files location) by using the Navigation pane or the Previous Locations box arrow to select that drive as the new save location.

4 Tap or click the New folder button on the Save As dialog box toolbar to create a new folder on the selected storage device.

5 When the new folder appears, type **Chapter 07** to change the name of the folder, and then press the ENTER key. Double-tap or double-click the new folder to open it.

6 If necessary, tap or click the 'Save as type' button to display the list of available file formats, and then tap or click Photoshop (*.PSD;*.PDD) in the list to select the file type.

7 Tap or click the Save button to save the document on the selected drive, in the new folder, and with the new file name.

MAC For a detailed example of this procedure using the Mac operating system, refer to the For Mac Users Appendix.

To Close a Photo

You will use the selections you have saved in the Light Switch Selection file later when you copy image into to another document. For now, you are finished with the Light Switch Selection file. The following step closes the file.

1 Tap or click the Close button in the document tab to close the file but leave Photoshop open. If Photoshop asks you to save the file, tap or click the No button.

Brush Modes

You can use the Brush Tool in a variety of modes. The brush mode is a type of blending mode that defines how the pixels you create with the Brush Tool interact with the layers below the current layer. Recall that you learned about blending modes in a previous chapter. Table 7–1 lists a few common brush modes. The best way to learn the capabilities and effect of the brush modes is to experiment with them.

Table 7–1 Brush Modes	
Mode	**Use**
Normal	The default mode. Use when you want to paint normally.
Darken	Pixels combine to form a darker color than the painted colors or the original pixels. The texture of the original pixels is retained.
Lighten	Pixels combine to form a lighter color than the painted colors or the original pixels. The texture of the original pixels is retained.
Overlay	When used on a mask, light areas can be made lighter without affecting dark areas. Dark areas can be made darker without affecting light areas.
Color	The painted pixels resemble the brush color while retaining the texture of the original pixels.

Brush Overlay Mode

Using channels to create and fine-tune selections is an ideal way to isolate challenging selections, such as masking around hair, tree branches, or other small and thin objects that would be difficult to select with other tools. You have learned how to paint on an existing alpha channel with black and white to fine-tune a selection using the brush in its default normal mode. Using a brush in **overlay mode** allows you to make even finer selections. Painting with black makes dark areas darker without affecting light areas. Similarly, painting with white in overlay mode makes light areas lighter without affecting dark areas. This approach is ideal when working with the grayscale pixels in an alpha channel.

To Open the Recycle Bin File

The following steps open the file, Recycle Bin, from the Data Files for Students.

1 Open the file, Recycle Bin, from the Chapter 07 folder of the Data Files for Students.

2 When Photoshop displays the image in the document window, press CTRL+0 to fit the image in the window.

To Duplicate a Channel

Sometimes it is easier to create a selection by painting with the Brush Tool rather than by using a selection tool. To paint a selection, you should start with a new alpha channel to avoid painting directly on an existing color channel, which would permanently change the image's color information. The following steps create a new alpha channel by duplication.

- Display the Channels panel if necessary.
- Tap or click the Blue channel thumbnail to select the Blue channel, because it provides the most contrast between the recycle bin and its background.
- Press and hold or right-click the Blue channel to display its context menu (Figure 7–13).

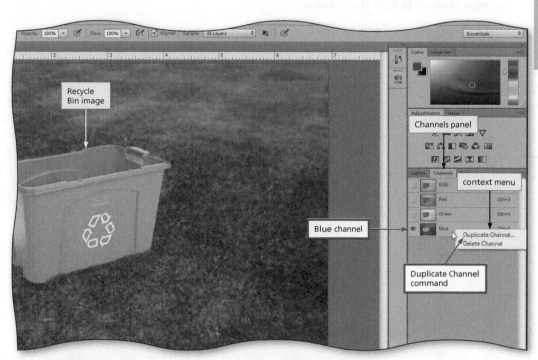

Figure 7–13

- Tap or click Duplicate Channel on the context menu to display the Duplicate Channel dialog box.
- In the As box, type **recycle bin** as the channel name (Figure 7–14).

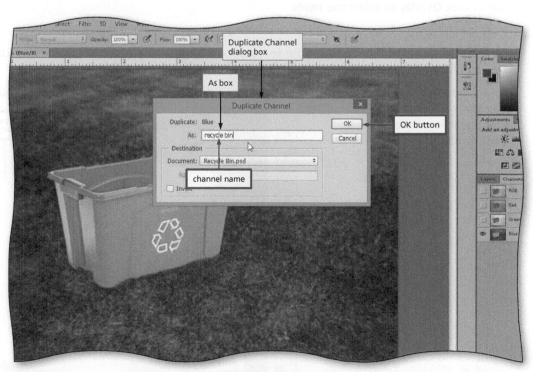

- Tap or click the OK button to close the Duplicate Channel dialog box.

Figure 7–14

To Paint in Brush Overlay Mode

The following steps use the Brush Tool's overlay mode to isolate the recycle bin, mask out the background, and retain the fine wisps of grass.

1

- On the Channels panel, display the Recycle Bin channel and tap or click the Indicates channel visibility button for the Blue channel to hide the channel.

- Tap or click the Brush Tool button.

- On the options bar, tap or click the Mode button to display the list of brush modes (Figure 7–15).

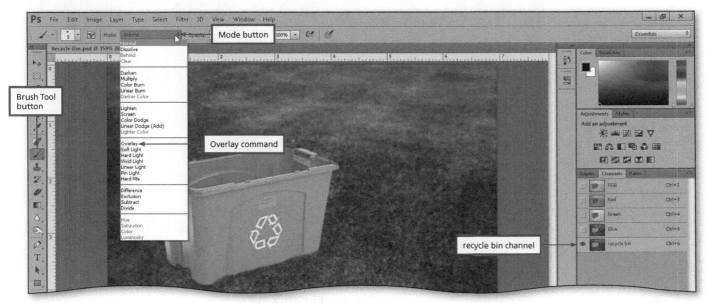

Figure 7–15

2

- Tap or click Overlay to select the mode.

- Press the LEFT BRACE ({) key several times to reduce the hardness of the brush, and adjust the size of the brush as necessary.

- If necessary, press the D key to reset the foreground/background colors, then press the x key so white is the foreground color.

- Point to the lower-left edge of the recycle bin, then drag to begin to paint it white. As you paint, drag slightly outside the body so the brush paints a little on the grass background.

- Continue until the entire recycle bin is white (Figure 7–16).

Q&A

Why do I need to reduce the hardness?
Using a soft-edged brush helps to retain the details of the wisps of grass. You can verify the hardness of your brush using the Brush Preset picker and its pop-up panel.

Why is the grass not turning white like the body?
In overlay mode, light areas turn white when painted with white, but darker areas remain relatively unaffected.

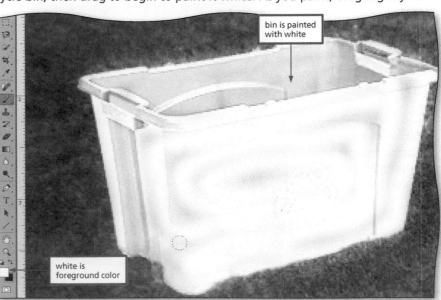

Figure 7–16

3

- Press the x key to reverse the colors, and set the foreground color to black.

- Drag the pointer over the grassy background, just around the recycle bin to paint a wide black area. Because you are in overlay mode, painting on the white parts will not affect them (Figure 7–17).

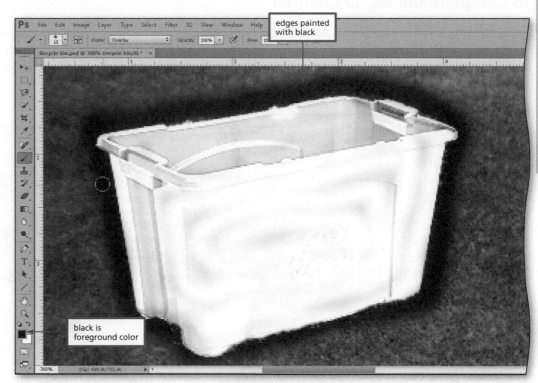

Figure 7–17

4

- Press the x key to reverse the colors and set the foreground color to white.

- Drag the wispy edges of the grass. Drag only once over the wisps, without dragging back and forth, to lightly paint them with white. It is OK if some of the edges remain gray instead of pure black or white (Figure 7–18).

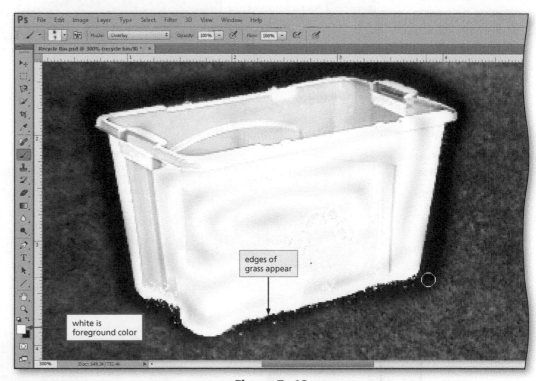

Figure 7–18

To Complete the Alpha Channel

Because you are creating a channel that can be used as a mask, the areas you want to hide must be completely black. Painting in brush overlay mode helps you define the edges of a difficult selection; however, for larger selections, such as the rest of the grassy background, using selection tools and the Fill command is easier. The next steps fill the rest of the channel with black

1

- Press the x key to change the foreground color back to black.

- Select the Magic Wand Tool.

- On the options bar, tap or click the 'Add to selection' button. Set the Tolerance to 50.

- Tap or click the recycle bin. If any part of the bin is not selected, tap or click it (Figure 7–19).

Q&A Could I have used the Magic Wand Tool to help me paint with white?
It would have been difficult to use the Magic Wand Tool to select the edges of the recycle bin in the grass. Painting with white created an easy way to select only the bin.

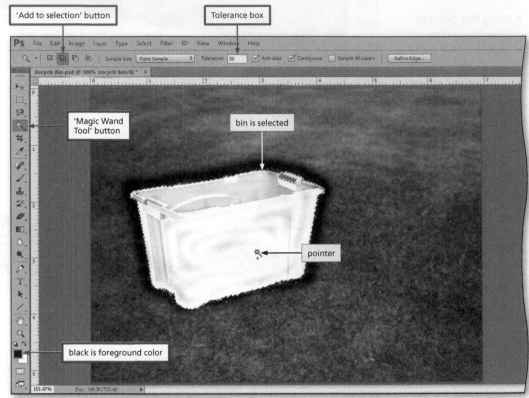

Figure 7–19

2

- Press SHIFT+CTRL+I to select the inverse.

- Press SHIFT+F5 to display the Fill dialog box.

- Tap or click the Use button and then tap or click Black to set the fill color (Figure 7–20).

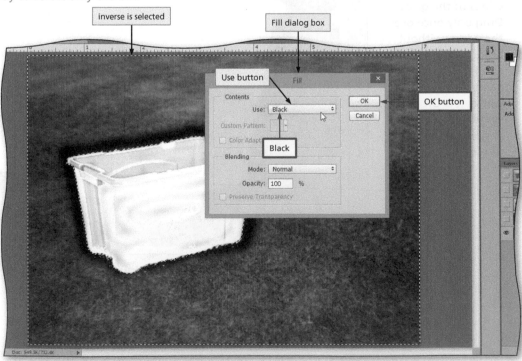

Figure 7–20

3
- Tap or click the OK button to fill the selection with black.
- Deselect (Figure 7–21).

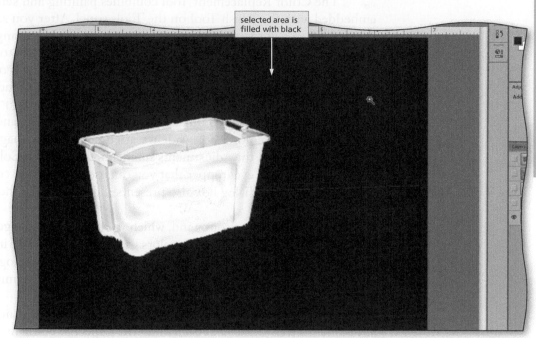

selected area is filled with black

Figure 7–21

To Save and Close the File

The following steps save the file with the name Recycle Bin Selection in the Photoshop format in the Chapter 07 folder.

1 On the File menu, tap or click Save As to display the Save As dialog box.

2 In the File name text box, type `Recycle Bin Selection` to rename the file. Do not press the ENTER key after typing the file name.

3 If necessary, navigate to your storage device and the Chapter 07 folder.

4 If necessary, tap or click the Format button and then tap or click Photoshop (*.PSD;*.PDD) in the list, if necessary.

5 Tap or click the Save button in the Save As dialog box to save the file with the new name in the Chapter 07 folder.

6 Press CTRL+W to close the file without quitting Photoshop.

Break Point: If you wish to take a break, this is a good place to do so. Press CTRL+Q to quite Photoshop. To resume at a later time, start Photoshop, open the file called Campus Recycling Sign, and continue following the steps from this location forward.

Replacing Colors

You can change or replace one color for another in several different ways. After making a selection of the part of the image you want to recolor, you can use tools that you have learned about already, including the Fill command, the Color Picker dialog box, the Swatches panel, a layer mask, or even the Colorize option on the Hue and Saturation adjustment panel. Unless you use a mask, replacing colors is a destructive process – pixels are changed. It is a good idea to create a duplicate layer or make sure you have a backup copy of your image before replacing colors.

The Color Replacement Tool combines painting and selection, and is embedded with the Brush Tool on the Tools panel. After you set the destination color, you can paint with the Color Replacement Tool to change all colors or only the color you click as a sample. Like the Background Eraser tool, once you create a sample, Photoshop will replace (rather than erase) only that color as you drag. The advantage of using the Color Replacement Tool is that it blends the color over the existing texture.

The Replace Color command exchanges one color for another, and is the fastest way to change one color that is widely scatted through the image. Located on the Image menu, within the Adjustments submenu, the Replace Color command displays a dialog box with an eyedropper that you can use to select the color or colors you want to change; the dialog box also presents sliders to adjust the hue, saturation and lightness.

The Match Color command, which works for RGB images only, matches colors in one layer or image with colors from another layer or image. Also on the Adjustments submenu, the Match Color command uses a dialog box to edit the luminance, color intensity, and fade. Use the Match Color command to replace colors with an exact match of another color.

Finally, a Selective Color adjustment uses the Adjustments panel to create an adjustment layer that corrects shading for a specific color in your image. Selective color correction changes the amount of process colors in each of the primary color components in an image. You can modify one color without changing any of the others. For example, you might want to increase the amount of green in all gray or neutral colors without changing parts of the image that already are green.

BTW

Layers and File Size
Using an adjustment layer adds to the file size of the image, however; it also demands more random access memory (RAM) from your computer.

In the following sections, you will open a bicycle image, change the blue color of the bicycle to orange using the Replace Color command, and create a transparent floating copy of the bicycle, in preparation for creating a composite image.

To Open the Bicycle Image

The following steps open the Bicycle image from the Data Files for Students, in preparation for replacing the color of the bicycle. Visit solutions.cengage.com/ctdownloads for detailed instructions or contact your instructor for information about accessing the required files.

1 Press CTRL+O to display the Open dialog box.

2 Navigate to the Data Files for Students and the Photoshop folder named Chapter 07.

3 Double-tap or double click the Bicycle file to open the image in Photoshop. Press CTRL+0 (zero) to fit the image in the window, if necessary.

To Replace a Color

The following steps use the Replace Color command to change the blue bicycle into an orange one. Trying to paint individual parts of the bicycle with the Brush Tool would be very tedious, as would dragging the very narrow areas with the Color Replacement Tool.

1

- Choose the default colors, with black over white on the Tools panel.

- Tap or click Image on the Application bar to display the Image menu, and then tap or click Adjustments to display the Adjustments submenu (Figure 7–22).

Q&A Is there a Replace Color icon on the Adjustments panel?
No. It only appears on the Adjustments submenu, and does not create a separate adjustment layer.

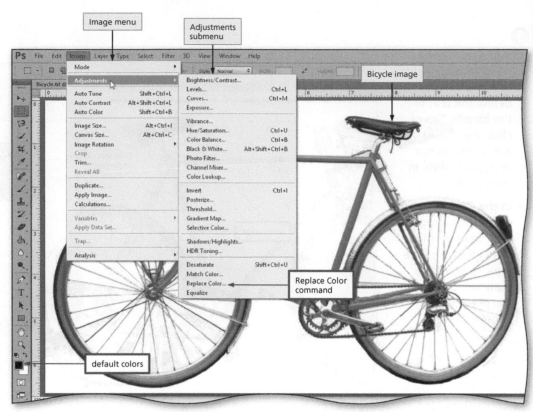

Figure 7–22

2

- Tap or click Replace Color to display the Replace Color dialog box.

- Drag the title bar of the dialog box to move the dialog box to the right, so it does not overlap any of the blue color in the bicycle.

- Tap or click the 'Add to Sample' button to select the eyedropper.

- Drag the Fuzziness slider to   0 (zero).

- If necessary, tap or click the Selection option button to assign the preview to display only the color change area (Figure 7–23).

Q&A Should I create a new layer for this recoloring?
You could; however, you will save these changes with a different name in a different location. You always could reopen the original file, if you need it.

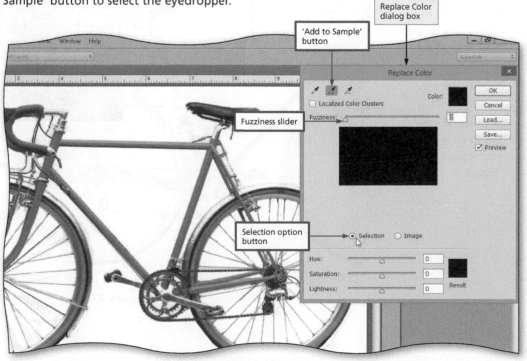

Figure 7–23

3

- In the document window, tap or click the blue vertical bar below the seat of the bicycle. Tap or click any other blue areas that do not appear as white in the preview.

- In the Replace Color dialog box, drag the Fuzziness slider until all of the blue area appears as a mask selection in the preview (Figure 7–24).

Q&A

How do I determine the amount of fuzziness?

You should drag the Fuzziness slider until all of the color you want to change appears white. Do not drag it so far that other colors in the image start to appear.

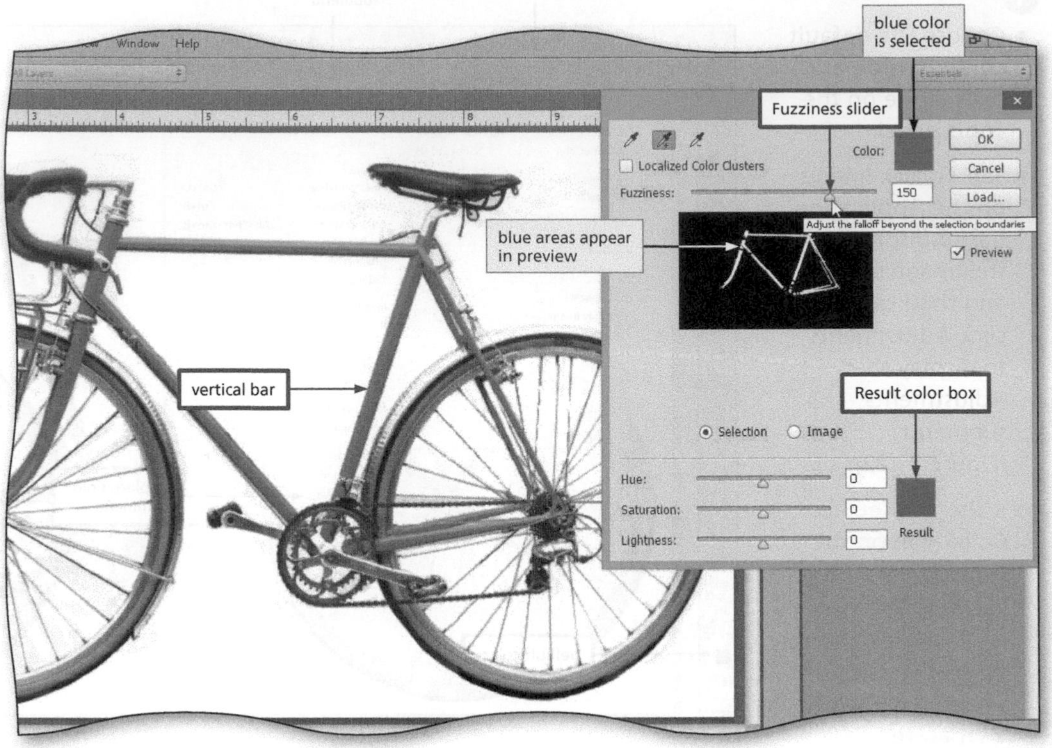

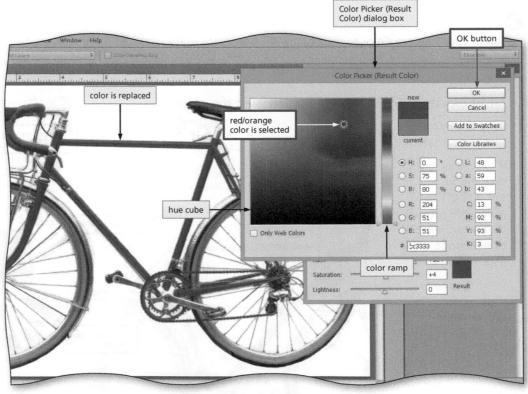

Figure 7–24

4

- Tap or click the Result color box to display the Color Picker (Result Color) dialog box. Drag the title bar of the dialog box so the bicycle is visible.

- In the color ramp, tap or click an orange color.

- In the hue cube, tap or click a bright red/orange (Figure 7–25).

Figure 7–25

- Tap or click the OK button to close the Color Picker (Result Color) dialog box.

- In the Replace Color dialog box, adjust the Hue, Saturation, and Lightness sliders to create a bright orange (Figure 7–26).

- Tap or click the OK button to close the Replace Color dialog box.

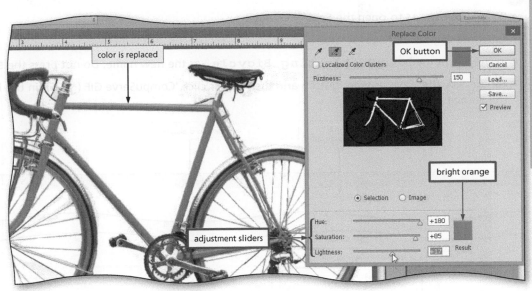

Figure 7–26

To Create a Transparent Background and Save

Many times, you may need a transparent, floating image to add to a composite or desktop publishing program. First, you must unlock the Background layer so you can erase the white. Then you need to make a decision on the file format in which to save. Both GIF and PNG formats support transparency easily and are portable across applications. Recall that the GIF format uses an Indexed Color mode, which means it will display a maximum of 256 colors. The advantage of GIF files is that they have a very small file size. PNG files use more space than GIF files, but can support RGB and other color modes. PNG reduces the jagged edges that may result in GIF formats. The following steps delete the background and save the file in the GIF format.

- On the Layers panel, tap or click the lock on the Background layer to unlock it.

- On the Tools panel, select the 'Magic Eraser Tool'. If necessary, remove the check mark from the Contiguous check box on the options bar.

- Tap or click the white area to erase it (Figure 7–27).

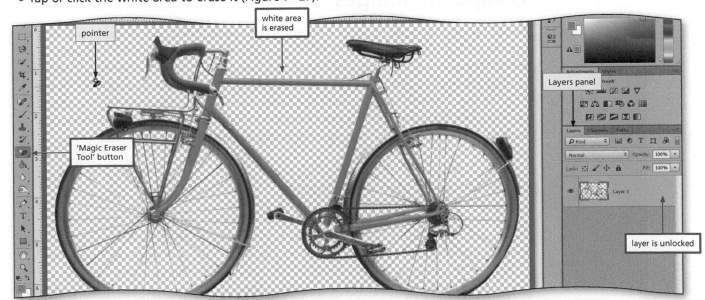

Figure 7–27

● Press SHIFT+CTRL+S to open the Save As dialog box.

● Navigate to your storage location.

● In the File name box, type **Floating Bicycle** as the new name. Do not press the ENTER key.

● Tap or click the 'Save as type' button and then tap or click 'CompuServe GIF (*.GIF)' in the list to choose the format (Figure 7–28).

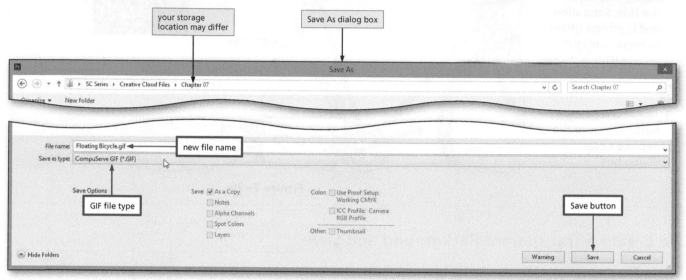

Figure 7–28

3

● Tap or click the Save button to close the dialog box.

● When Photoshop displays the Indexed Color dialog box, tap or click the OK button to accept the default settings.

● When Photoshop displays the GIF Options dialog box, tap or click the OK button to finishing saving the file.

● Press CTRL+W to close the file. When Photoshop asks you to save the original TIF file before closing, tap or click the No button.

Composite Images

Recall that a composite image is a Photoshop document that contains multiple images, usually on individual layers in the file. You have used many techniques to insert external images, such as drag and drop, copy, move, and place. Composite artists also employ channels, alpha channels, and masks to create new images and layers. In the next section, you will build a composite image by creating a layer mask from an alpha channel. You then will place an image for the background, load and move a selection from another image, and finally insert a floating image to create the composite.

To Build the Composite Image

The following steps open the Recycle Bin Selection file from your storage device, and then place a file named Recycle Symbol as a new layer. The Recycle Symbol file is located in the Data Files for Students. Visit solutions.cengage.com/ctdownloads for detailed instructions or contact your instructor for information about accessing the required files. You then will organize the layers and save the file on your storage device with the name Campus Recycling Sign.

① Open the Recycle Bin Selection file from your storage location.

② Tap or click the Layers panel tab to display the Layers panel.

③ On the File menu, tap or click Place Embedded to display the Place Embedded dialog box. Navigate to the Data Files for Students and double-tap or double-click the Recycle Symbol file to embed it. On the options bar, tap or click the 'Commit transform (Enter)' button to finish placing the file.

④ On the Layers panel, tap or click the lock symbol on the Background layer to unlock it. Rename the layer, bin.

⑤ Drag the Recycle Symbol layer below the bin layer.

⑥ Save the composite file in the PSD format on your storage device with the name, Campus Recycling Sign (Figure 7–29).

Figure 7–29

To Create a Layer Mask from an Alpha Channel

The following steps create a layer mask from the channel you created earlier. The mask is used to hide the grass background so only the recycle bin appears in the composite.

①

- Tap or click Select on the Application bar, and then tap or click Load Selection to display the Load Selection dialog box.

- Tap or click the Channel box arrow to display the list, and then select recycle bin to select the channel you created previously (Figure 7–30).

Q&A What does the Load Selection dialog box do?

Loading a selection is the same process as making a selection. Loading the channel as a selection selects the channel, displaying the dashed border visible around the recycle bin just as if you made a selection with a lasso tool.

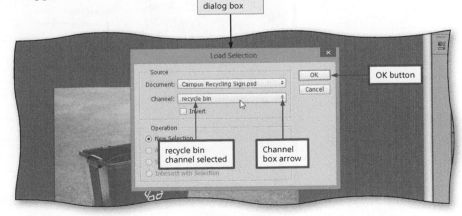

Figure 7–30

2

- Tap or click the OK button to load the selection.

- On the Layers panel, tap or click the bin layer to make it the active layer.

- On the Layers panel status bar, tap or click the 'Add layer mask' button to create a mask from the selection (Figure 7–31).

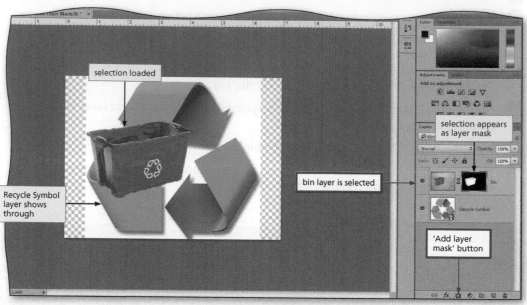

Figure 7–31

Refine Mask

It is unlikely that a mask selection in a difficult image, such as an object with grass or hair, will be perfect the first time. You can use Photoshop's Refine Mask Tool to adjust the edges of the mask to achieve better results (Figure 7–32). The Refine Mask Tool is available from the Select menu, but only when a mask thumbnail on the Layers panel is selected. Table 7–2 describes the options in the Refine Mask Tool and their uses.

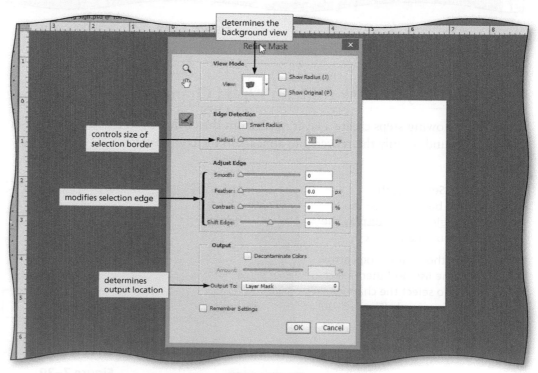

Figure 7–32

Option	Use
Table 7–2 Refine Mask Options	
View	Determines the background. For example, the masked layer can be shown on a white background, a black background, the underlying layers, or other choices. Choose the On Layers view to see how your masked layer interacts with the rest of the layers in the document.
Radius	Controls the size of the selection border where the edge refinement occurs.
Smooth	Smoothes the selection border, eliminating hills and valleys.
Feather	Blurs the transition between the selection and its surrounding pixels.
Contrast	Changes soft-edged transitions to be more or less abrupt.
Shift Edge	Removes unwanted background colors from soft selection edges. Negative values move the selection edges inward while positive values move the selection edges outward.
Decontaminate Colors	Replaces the color of the outermost pixels within a selection with fully selected pixels nearby. This helps reduce unwanted outlines around a selection.
Output	Determines whether the refined selection becomes a new mask on the current layer or a new layer with the mask applied.

To Use the Refine Mask Tool

The following steps use the Refine Mask Tool to remove the dark outline around the masked recycle bin, decontaminating the mask colors. You will export the edited improvements or refinement to a new layer that has the refined mask applied so that the original mask remains unaltered in case you need to start over.

- Tap or click the mask thumbnail on the bin layer to select it.

- Tap or click Select on the Application bar, and then tap or click Refine Mask to display the Refine Mask dialog box.

- Drag the dialog box title bar as necessary to display the recycle bin in the document window.

- Tap or click the View button to display the list of views (Figure 7–33).

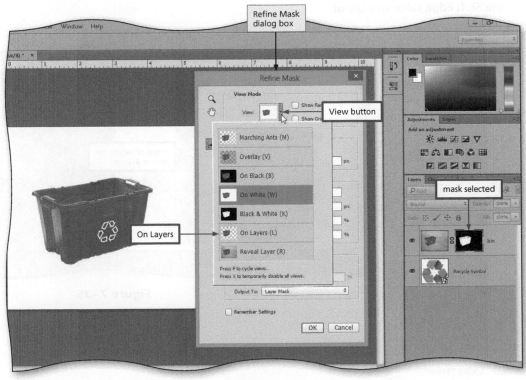

Figure 7–33

2

- Tap or click On Layers to select it. Tap or click the View box arrow again to close it.

- Drag the Radius slider to approximately 5.0 to increase the size of the selection border where the edge refinement occurs.

- Drag the Smooth slider to approximately 50 so the recycle bin image displays smoother edges.

- Drag the Contrast slider to approximately 50 to deepen the blue of the recycle bin image.

- Tap or click the Output To button to display its list (Figure 7–34).

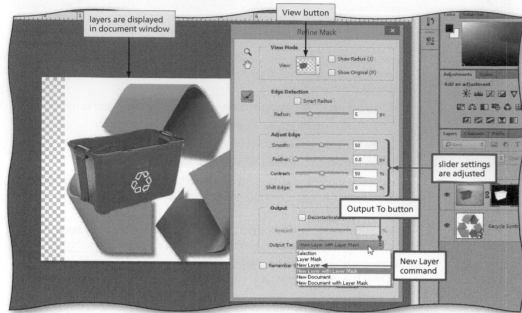

Figure 7–34

Experiment

- Drag the Shift Edge slider all the way to the left, and notice areas of the recycle bin turn invisible, looking like holes in the recycle bin. Try different values for the Shift Edge to see how the mask is affected. When you are finished, return the Shift Edge value to 0 (zero).

3

- Tap or click New Layer so that Photoshop creates a new layer with the refined mask applied.

- Tap or click the OK button to apply the refinement (Figure 7–35).

Q&A Should I delete the original bin layer because it has been hidden and no longer is being used?
No. It is best to leave the original recycle bin layer in the document because you have spent a lot of time creating the initial mask. This layer now acts as a backup in case you need start over and refine the mask again.

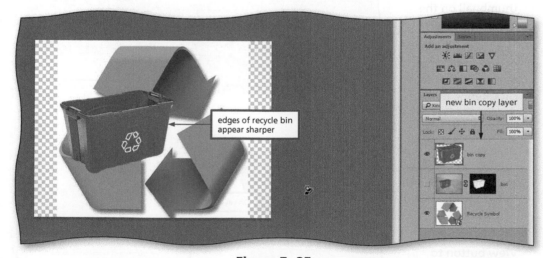

Figure 7–35

Experiment

- Hide the bin copy layer, and then make the bin layer visible to compare the refinement to the original. When you are finished, make the bin copy layer visible again, and hide the bin layer.

Other Ways

1. ALT+CTRL+R, choose settings, click OK button

To Move the Bin into Position

The following steps move the recycle bin into position.

1 If necessary, tap or click the bin copy layer on the Layers panel to select it.

2 Tap or click the Move Tool to select it and then press CTRL+T to display the bounding box.

3 SHIFT+drag a corner sizing handle to scale the bin to about 45% of its original size.

4 Move the bin to the left side of the top arrow as shown in Figure 7–36.

5 Press the ENTER key to commit the transformation and then press CTRL+S to save the changes.

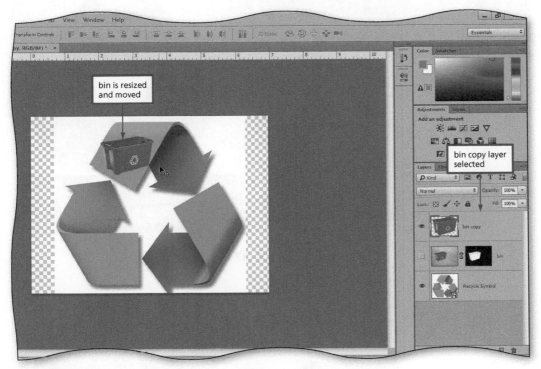

Figure 7–36

To Open and Arrange the Light Switch Selection File

The following steps open the Light Switch Selection file from your storage device and arrange the windows side by side so that layers can be copied easily between them.

1 Open the Light Switch Selection file from the Chapter 07 folder on your storage device.

2 On the Window menu, tap or click Arrange, and then tap or click 2-up Vertical to arrange the document windows side by side.

To Load and Move a Selection

The following steps load a selection from the alpha channel that you created earlier. You then will move only the selection as a floating object to the Campus Recycling Sign document window.

1

- With the Light Switch Selection document as the active document, tap or click Select on the Application bar, and then tap or click Load Selection to display the Load Selection dialog box.

- Tap or click the OK button to load the alpha channel as a selection (Figure 7–37).

Figure 7–37

2

- Select the Move Tool and drag the selection from one window to the other.

- Close the Light Switch Selection document window without saving.

- In the Campus Recycling sign document window, press CTRL+T. Resize the selection and move it as shown in Figure 7–38. Commit the transformation.

- Press CTRL+0 (ZERO) to fit the image on the screen.

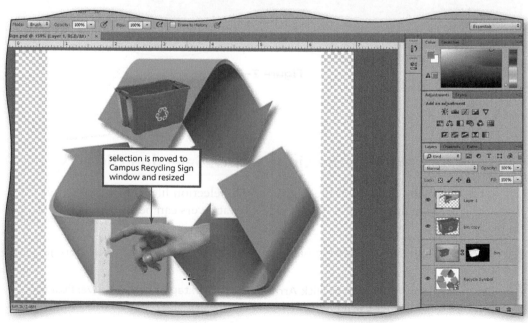

Figure 7–38

3

- Use the Eraser Tool in Block mode to erase the part of the hand that extends past the end of the lower-left arrow.

- Rename the layer, light switch (Figure 7–39).

Experiment

- Tap or click the Eraser Tool preset picker to display the pop-up panel. Tap or click the panel menu button and append the square brushes. Erase the edge with a square brush.

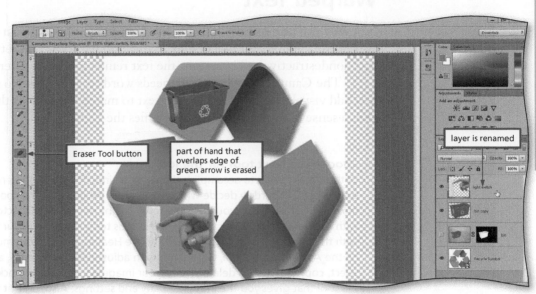

Figure 7–39

To Embed the Floating Bicycle

The following steps embed the Floating Bicycle image into the composite image.

1 On the File menu, tap or click Place Embedded to display the Place Embedded dialog box. Navigate to the Data Files for Students and double-tap or double-click the Floating Bicycle file to embed it. On the options bar, tap or click the 'Commit transform (Enter)' button to finish placing the file.

2 Rename the layer, bicycle.

3 Resize the layer and position it as shown in Figure 7–40.

4 Save the composite file again.

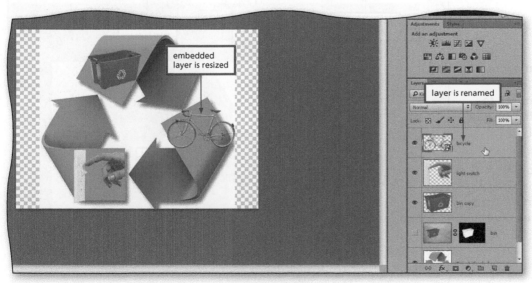

Figure 7–40

Warped Text

Not only can text provide information for people to read, but it also can provide visual appeal and add interest to a design. Photoshop has tools that let you bend and warp text nondestructively. This means the text remains editable after it has been warped.

The Campus Recycling sign needs words that are easy to read, but also words that add visual interest. Warping the text to match the flow of the recycling arrows adds a sense of movement that also unifies the scene.

Plan Ahead

Choose the best tool for the job.
With so many ways to accomplish the same or similar tasks (such as making a selection), sometimes it is hard to decide which tool to use. While using the tool with which you are most familiar may save you time, the result might not be as satisfactory as you could achieve with a different tool. Look through the various tools related to your task and experiment with the settings. For example, there are five Healing Brush tools, more than 20 adjustments on the Adjustments panel, two menus with adjustment commands, and countless ways to select, copy, move, and delete. Unless your image is just a quick mock-up or sketch, choose the tool that gives you the most flexibility and settings. Also, do not forget the detail edits. Adjustments and color toning are among the most important edits you can perform.

To Add Point Text

Recall that when you previously have inserted text, you first created a text box. Drawing a text box, sometimes called entering **paragraph type or area type**, allows you to insert text and use word-wrapping techniques. Alternatively, you can insert **point type** or **character type**, which does not need a text box prerequisite. When you enter point type, you simply click and start typing. Each line of type becomes independent; it does not wrap to the next line. Both paragraph type and point type create a type layer on the Layers panel.

The following steps insert point type.

- Press the D key to select the default colors. Press the X key to place white over black on the Tools panel.

- Press the T key to access the Horizontal Type Tool.

- In the options bar, set the font to Minion Pro Bold Italic or a similar font. Set the font size to 36. Tap or click the 'Left align text' button. Set the text color to white, if necessary.

- In the document window, tap or click the left recycling arrow, above and to the left of the light switch, as shown in Figure 7–41.

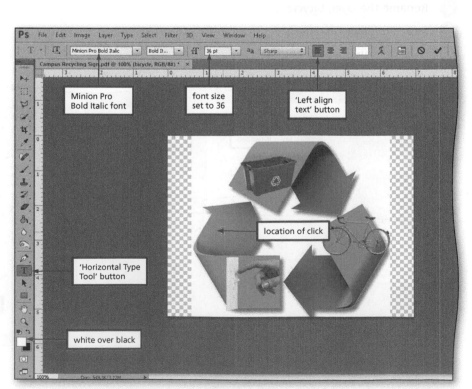

Figure 7–41

2

- Type **Go** to enter the first line of point type (Figure 7–42).

Q&A **What is the line that appears under the word, Go?**
The line is Photoshop's way of telling you that you are on a single path that will not wrap around.

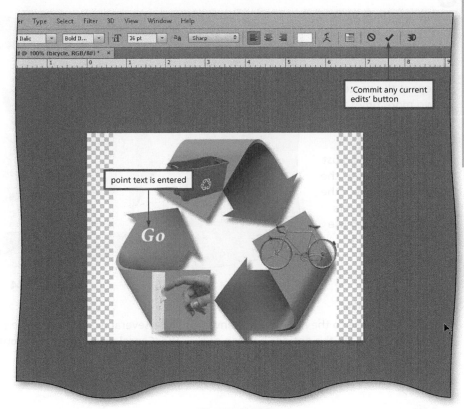

Figure 7–42

3

- Tap or click the 'Commit any current edits' button on the options bar.

- Tap or click the document window at a location to the right of the recycle bin and slightly down to create more point type.

- Type **Green** to enter the point type (Figure 7–43).

Q&A When should I use point type versus paragraph type?
If you are typing small amounts of text or single words, it is easier to click and type, creating point type. For larger amounts of text that needs to wrap or fill a vertical area, paragraph type is best.

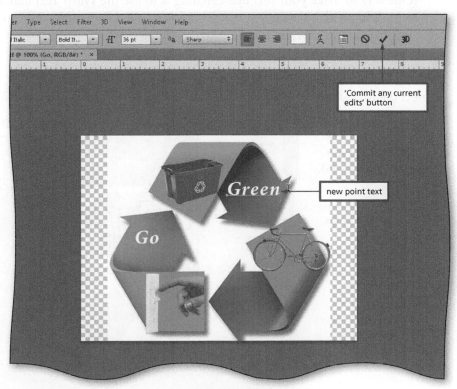

Figure 7–43

4
- Tap or click the 'Commit any current edits' button on the options bar.

- Repeat the process two more times to enter the text, **on** and **Campus**.

- If you need to adjust the placement of the point type, select the layer on the Layers panel, and then use the Move Tool to adjust the text layer (Figure 7–44).

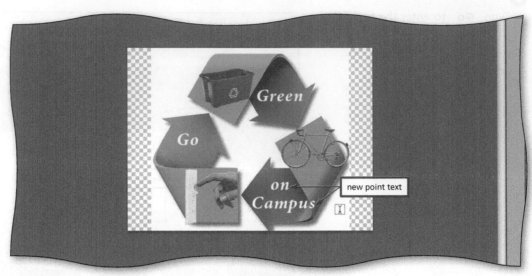

Figure 7–44

 **Experiment**

- Tap or click close to the edge of the canvas and type several words. Watch the text go off the edge of the page, as it does not wrap. On the options bar, tap or click the 'Cancel any current edits' button to cancel the insertion of the text.

To Warp Text

One way to make your text eye-catching is to use the Warp Text dialog box. Photoshop has 15 different warp styles, each with adjustable settings, to create an endless number of possibilities for warped text. The following steps create warped text.

- On the Layers panel, select the Go layer.

- Tap or click Type on the Application bar to display the Type menu (Figure 7–45).

Q&A
What are some other things I can do on the Type menu? You can display various type-related panels, change type settings like those on the options bar, rasterize and convert text, as well as set language options.

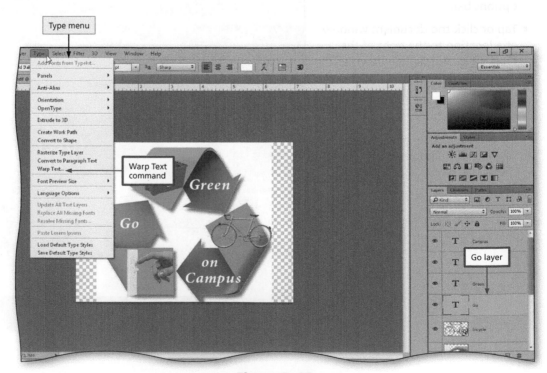

Figure 7–45

2

- Tap or click Warp Text to display the Warp Text dialog box.

- Tap or click the Style button to display the different warp styles (Figure 7–46).

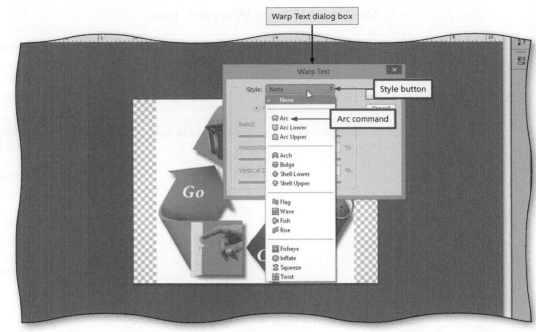

Figure 7–46

3

- Tap or click Arc in the list to choose an upward-pointing warp.

- Drag the Bend slider to 40 to adjust the bend of the text (Figure 7–47).

 Experiment

- Drag the Bend, Horizontal Distortion, and Vertical Distortion sliders to both the right and left, watching how they affect the text box. When you are finished, return Bend to +40, Horizontal Distortion to 0, and Vertical Distortion to 0.

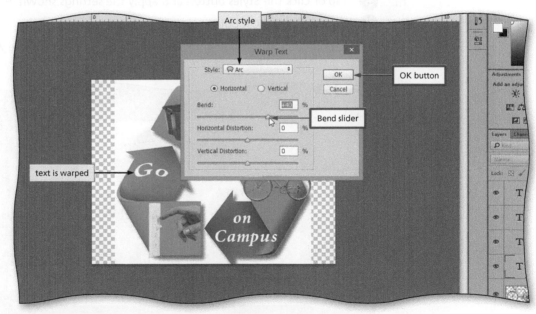

Figure 7–47

4

- Tap or click the OK button in the Warp Text dialog box to commit the changes.

- If necessary, use the Move Tool to adjust the placement of the text.

Other Ways

1. On options bar, tap or click 'Create warped text' button, choose settings, click OK button

To Create More Warped Text

Table 7–3 displays the settings you will use in the following steps to add warping to the other text layers in the sign.

Table 7–3 Warped Text Settings		
Layer	**Style**	**Setting**
Green	Arc Lower	Bend: 50 Horizontal Distortion: 0 Vertical Distortion: 0
on	Wave	Bend: 30 Horizontal Distortion: 0 Vertical Distortion: 0
Campus	Wave	Bend: 50 Horizontal Distortion: 0 Vertical Distortion: 0

1 One at a time, select a layer from Table 7–3.

2 On the options bar, tap or click the 'Create warped text' button to display the Warp Text dialog box.

3 Tap or click the Styles button and apply the settings shown in Table 7–3.

4 Tap or click the OK button to complete the warp.

5 Repeat Steps 1 through 4 for each of the three layers (Figure 7–48).

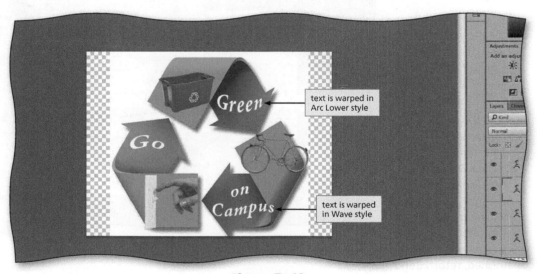

Figure 7–48

To Fine-Tune the Sign

The following steps make final adjustments to the image.

1 To change the levels of the bicycle image, select the bicycle layer. On the Adjustments panel, tap or click the Levels icon to display the Levels Properties panel. Set the black slider to approximately 100, the gray slider to 1, and the white slider to 155. On the Layers panel, press and hold or right-click the Levels 1 layer name, and then tap or click 'Create Clipping Mask' on the context menu.

2 To stroke the light switch layer, select the light switch layer, and then tap or press the 'Add a layer style' button on the Layers panel status bar. Tap or click Stroke. When Photoshop displays the Layer Style dialog box, set the Size to 1 px and the Opacity to 50%.

3 To add a glow to the recycle bin, select the bin copy layer, and then tap or press the 'Add a layer style' button on the Layers panel status bar. Tap or click Outer Glow. When Photoshop displays the Layer Style dialog box, set the Blend Mode to Normal and the Opacity to 50%.

4 Crop the image to the white area behind the sign (Figure 7–49).

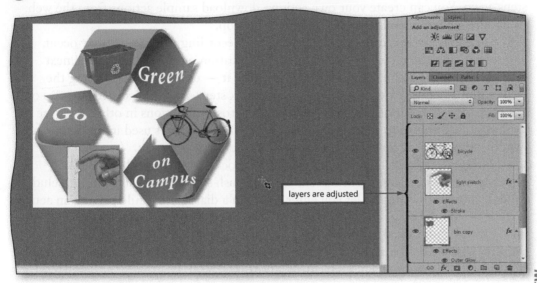

Figure 7–49

BTW

Quick Reference
For a table that lists how to complete the tasks covered in this book using touch gestures, the mouse, shortcut menu, and keyboard, see the Quick Reference Summary at the back of this book, or visit the Quick Reference resource on the Student Companion Site located on www.cengagebrain.com.

To Save the File

After adding many layers and effects, it is a good time to save the file again in the following step.

1 Press CTRL+S. If Photoshop displays a dialog box, tap or click the OK button.

To Flatten and Save

The following steps merge the visible layers and then save the document with a new file name. Photoshop uses the name of the layer that was selected when the merge command was executed.

1 On the Layers panel, select the Recycle Symbol layer.

2 Press SHIFT+CTRL+E to merge the visible layers into a single layer.

3 Tap or click File on the Application bar, and then tap or click Save As to display the Save As dialog box.

4 Type **Campus Recycling Sign Merged** in the File name box and ensure the file type is set to Photoshop (*.PSD;*.PDD).

5 If necessary, browse to your storage location. Tap or click the Save button to save the merged file.

6 If Photoshop displays a Photoshop Format Options dialog box, tap or click the OK button.

Break Point: If you wish to take a break, this is a good place to do so. Press CTRL+Q to quit Photoshop. To resume at a later time, start Photoshop, open the file named Campus Recycling Sign, and continue following the steps from this location forward.

Actions

BTW

Creating Actions
You must be careful when you record actions that involve selecting a named layer. When you play back the action in a different file, Photoshop will look for that layer. If the named layer does not exist in the file, the action will not function correctly.

An **action** is an automation task that stores a series of commands and keystrokes for repeated use later. For example, because of the large number of pixels generated by digital cameras, Photoshop typically imports those photos with very large document dimensions. If you often use a digital camera to generate the images you use in Photoshop, you could save the resize process as an action. Then, each time you edit a photo from your camera, you could use a single command to play the action and perform the steps again. You can create your own actions, download sample actions from the web, or use predefined actions that come with Photoshop.

The process of creating an action involves recording the steps as they occur, and then saving the recorded steps as a file in a location on your system. The next time you need the action, you can load it and play it — effectively performing the steps automatically. Action recording and playback steps are not recorded as states on the History panel. Actions are comparable to macros or functions in other software applications. Photoshop records nearly all commands and tools used in the Photoshop window; it will not record steps performed in other windows.

BTW

Actions with Prerequisites
If you see parentheses around the action name, the action will only work at certain times. For example, if the word, Type, is in parentheses, you must have a text box selected. If the word, Selection, is in parentheses, the action will work only if you have a current selection marquee.

Actions might include **stops** or pauses that occur during playback. Stops typically require user input, such as choosing a brush size. Actions also might include **modal** controls that stop to let you enter values in a dialog box while playing an action. If there are modal controls in an action, you can choose not to display the various dialog boxes and instead automatically accept the values that were used when the action was created. When you toggle modal controls off, the playback runs through the steps seamlessly, without any visible dialog boxes.

Plan Ahead

Record actions for repetitive tasks.
If you perform the same Photoshop tasks repeatedly, record the keystrokes for quick playback using an action. When creating and saving an action, the general workflow is as follows:

1. Practice the action and write down the steps.

2. Create a new action set, or select one you have previously created.

3. Create a new action, giving it a name and keyboard shortcut.

4. Tap or click the Record button.

5. Carefully proceed through the steps of your task.

6. Tap or click the Stop button.

7. Turn on dialog boxes and then edit stop points as necessary.

8. Save the set as an atn file for use in other Photoshop documents.

If you make a mistake while recording the action, the best solution may be to stop the recording and begin again. If you decide to edit an action, you can double-tap or double-click an individual step in the Actions panel and then change its settings. To omit a recorded step during playback, tap or click the Toggle item on/off box in the left column of the Actions panel.

BTW

Organizing Actions
You can organize sets of actions for different types of work, such as online publishing or print publishing, and then transfer sets to other computers. Normally, user-defined action sets are stored with the file in which they are created. You can save your sets and actions to a separate actions file, however, so you can recover them if the file in which they were created in is destroyed.

BTW

Photoshop Actions
Many Photoshop actions use a beginning step of creating a snapshot in the History panel. That way, you can see what the image looked like before the changes were made.

The Actions Panel

The Actions panel helps you manage actions you have created and those predefined actions that come with Photoshop (Figure 7–50). Each time you create a new action, it is added to the panel. An **action set** is an organizational folder that includes multiple actions, and can be opened or expanded by clicking the triangle to the left of the action set.

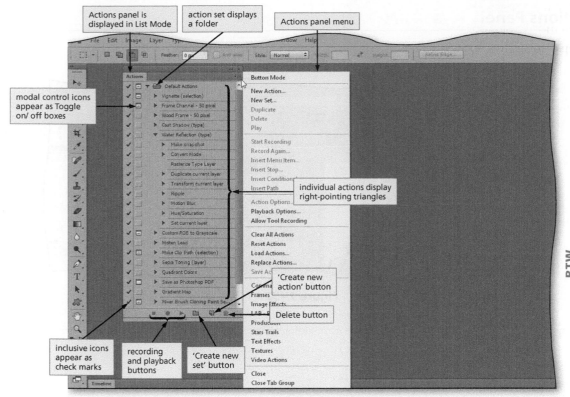

Figure 7–50

BTW

Modal Icons
Each step in an action can have its own modality, which means that the action will stop at every dialog box. You might want the playback to stop at certain points to allow user decisions, while at other steps, you might want to mandate settings. If an action set contains steps with mixed modalities, the modal icon beside the action set is displayed in red. If all steps are modal, the modal icon will be displayed in black.

BTW

Droplets
The Droplet command automation feature converts an action into a standalone program with its own icon. Dragging a file onto the droplet icon will start Photoshop and perform the action on the image. Droplets are cross-platform and transferable. Most graphic intensive publications - from yearbooks to directories - use droplets to standardize size and resolution of photos.

BTW

Editing Actions
Other edits that you can perform on the recorded steps include deselecting some check boxes, dragging a command to the Delete button on the status bar to remove it permanently, and setting playback options on the Actions panel menu.

In Figure 7–50, the Default Actions set is expanded to display the predefined actions. The Water Reflection action is expanded to display the individual commands. On the left, a column of check marks indicates each command's inclusion in the action. Photoshop allows you to exclude specific commands during playback, if you wish. The second column indicates whether the action is modal. To enable modal controls so that you can enter your own values in dialog boxes used in the action, tap or click the Toggle dialog on/off box on the Actions panel. On the panel's status bar are media player-style buttons for stop, record, and play, as well as buttons to create sets and actions. The Actions panel menu displays commands to manage actions, set options, and load new sets of predefined actions. Action sets can be saved independently for use in other images. A saved action displays a file extension of atn. In the Save Action dialog box, Photoshop opens the folder where it stores other atn files by default.

The Actions panel can be displayed in two modes. The list mode, shown in Figure 7–50, allows you to make more choices about selecting, editing, playing, and managing your actions. The button mode, shown in Figure 7–51, is used for quick playbacks. To switch modes, choose the desired mode from the Actions panel menu.

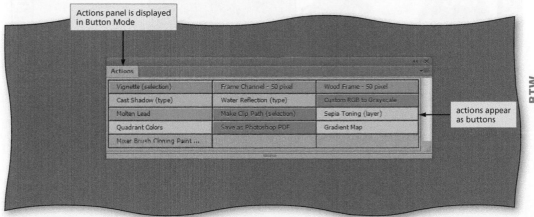

Figure 7–51

To Display the Actions Panel

The following step displays the Actions panel.

- Tap or click Window on the Application bar, and then tap or click Actions to display the Actions panel (Figure 7–52).

Figure 7–52

Other Ways

1. Press ALT+F9

2. Press F9

To Append Action Sets

The Actions panel contains a Default Actions set that provides 13 different actions. In addition to the Default Actions set, nine other sets are available on the Actions panel menu. In the following steps, you will append one of those sets to the list of default actions in the Actions panel.

- Tap or click the Actions panel menu button to display the Actions panel menu (Figure 7–53).

Q&A What does the Load Actions command do?
It opens a dialog box so you can navigate to the location of an action set. Any actions or action sets not saved previously with the image must be loaded into the current file.

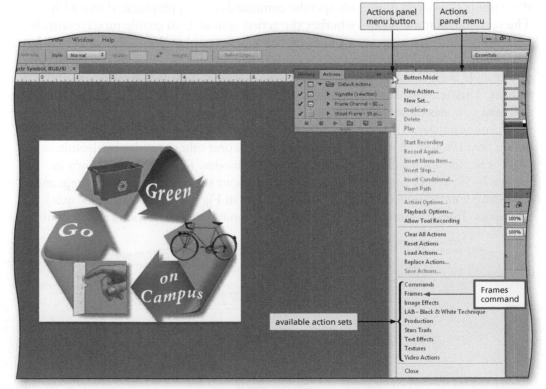

Figure 7–53

2
- Tap or click Frames to select the action set.
- Drag the bottom-right corner of the Actions panel down to make the Actions panel taller and display more items.
- Scroll in the panel to display the Frames set, and then tap or click the name, Brushed Aluminum Frame to select the action (Figure 7–54).

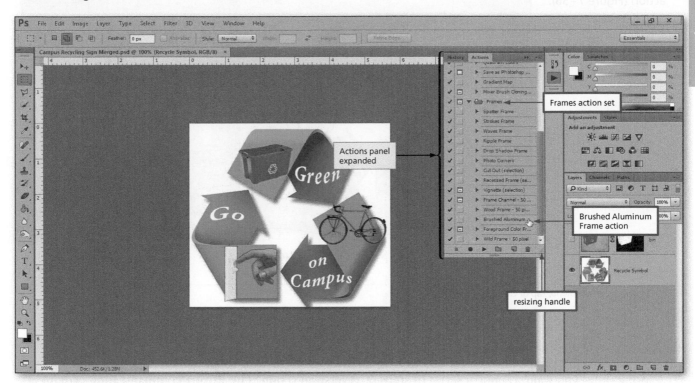

Figure 7–54

To Play an Action

To play an action, you tap or click the Play selection button on the Actions panel status bar. In the steps that follow, the Brushed Aluminum Frame action is played to create a picture frame around the advertisement. Later in this chapter, you will create a custom action.

1
- Tap or click the Play selection button to play the action (Figure 7–55).

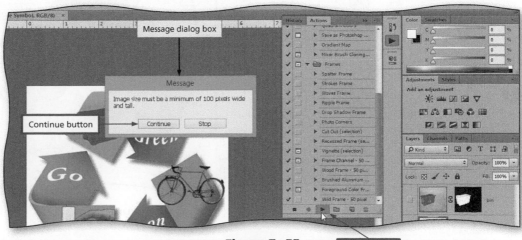

Figure 7–55

2

• In the Message dialog box, tap or click the Continue button to apply the action (Figure 7–56).

Q&A What are the right-pointing triangles on the Actions panel?
If you tap or click a right-pointing triangle, Photoshop displays the steps taken in the action.

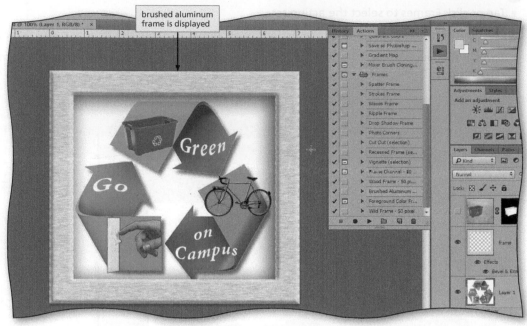

Figure 7–56

Other Ways

1. On Actions panel menu, tap or click Play

To Revert

Sometimes you want to undo a series of steps or reverse an action. The Revert command allows you to go back to the last saved version of the file.

1

• Tap or click File on the Application bar to display the File menu (Figure 7–57).

Q&A Could I have closed the file without saving and then reopened it?
Yes, but the menu or even the F12 function key is faster.

2

• Tap or click Revert to go back to the last saved version of the file.

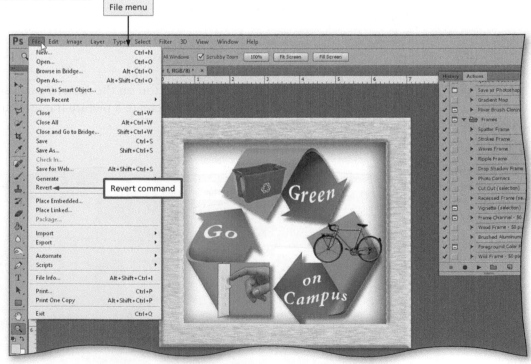

Figure 7–57

Other Ways

1. On History panel, tap or click the original state at the top of the panel

2. Press F12

To Create a New Action Set

The following steps create a new action set named Recycling Sign Action in the Campus Recycling Sign Merged file. Saving your actions in a new action set keeps them separate from the built-in actions included in Photoshop.

 1

- On the Actions panel status bar, tap or click the 'Create new set' button to display the New Set dialog box.

- Type **Recycling Sign Action** in the Name text box to name the action set (Figure 7–58).

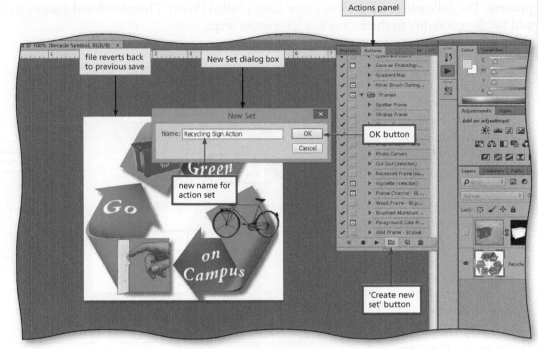

Figure 7–58

2

- Tap or click the OK button to create the action set, and add it to the Actions panel (Figure 7–59).

Figure 7–59

Other Ways

1. On Actions panel menu, tap or click New Set

To Create a New Action

When you tap or click the 'Create new action' button, the New Action dialog box is displayed. The New Action dialog box allows you to name the action, position it within a set, assign a function key, and choose a display color for the action in the panel. After you edit the settings, you use the Record button to begin the process. The following step creates a new action called Poster Thumbnail and assigns an identification color. You add the functionality to the action in a later set of steps.

- On the Actions panel status bar, tap or click the 'Create new action' button to display the New Action dialog box.

- Type **Poster Thumbnail** in the Name text box to name the action.

- Tap or click the Function Key button, and then tap or click F11 in the list to assign a function key to the action.

- Tap or click the Color button and then tap or click Red in the list to assign a color to the new action (Figure 7–60).

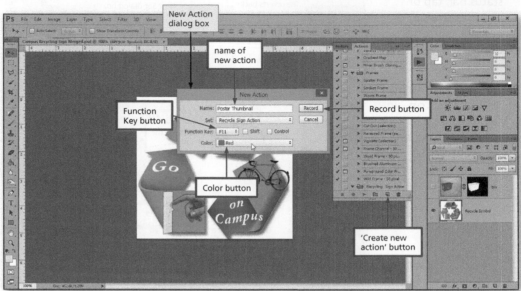

Figure 7–60

Other Ways

1. On Actions panel menu, tap or click New Action

To Record an Action

The next steps record an action that applies the Poster Edges artistic filter and reduces the size of the document to 300 pixels wide. This is an appropriate size to include on a webpage or to use for e-mailing a client a sample of the artwork.

- In the New Action dialog box, tap or click the Record button to close the dialog box and begin recording keystrokes (Figure 7–61).

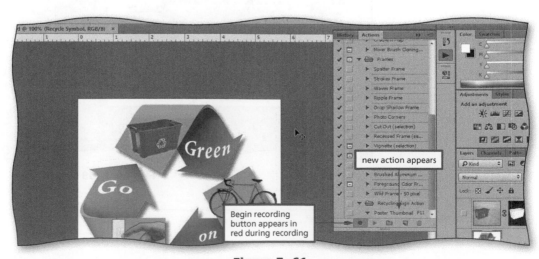

Figure 7–61

2

- Press the D key to reset the default colors in preparation for the filter.

- Tap or click Filter on the Application bar to display the Filter menu (Figure 7–62).

Q&A

What if I make a mistake while recording an action? If you tap or click inadvertently while creating an action, you can press CTRL+Z to cancel the recording and then start over.

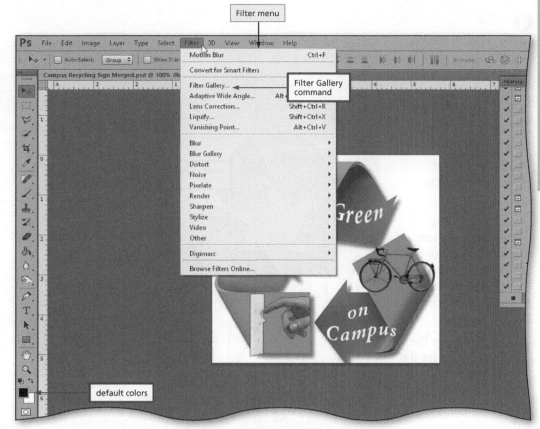

Figure 7–62

3

- Tap or click Filter Gallery to display the Filter Gallery window.

- Tap or click the Artistic category, and then tap or click Poster Edges to record the first step of the action.

- Slide the Edge Thickness slider to 1.

- Slide the Edge Intensity slider to 2.

- Slide the Posterization slider to 2 (Figure 7–63).

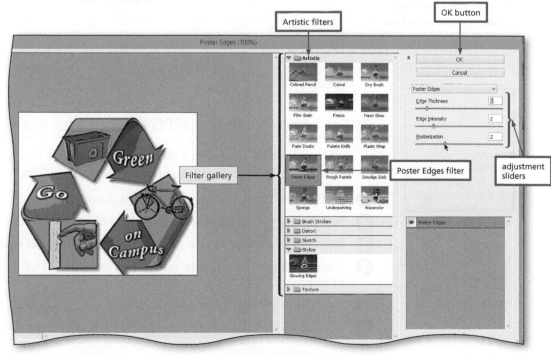

Figure 7–63

4

- Tap or click the OK button to accept the new settings and apply the filter.

- Press ALT+CTRL+I to display the Image Size dialog box.

- Set the unit of measurement to **Pixels**.

- Tap or click the Resample button, and then tap or click 'Bicubic Sharper (reduction)' to assign a reduction algorithm.

- Type **300** in the Width box to set the new width to 300 pixels (Figure 7–64).

5

- Tap or click the OK button to resize the image and close the Image Size dialog box.

- Tap or click the 'Stop playing/recording' button to stop the recording.

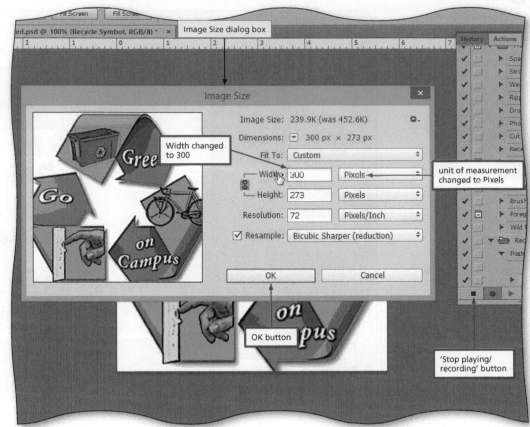

Figure 7–64

To Save the File in the JPEG Format and Revert

The following steps save a copy of the altered file in a format appropriate for sharing with a client by e-mail. You then revert the file back to its original state.

1 Press SHIFT+CTRL+S to display the Save As dialog box.

2 Navigate to your storage location and the Chapter 07 folder.

3 Type **Recycling Sign Sample** in the File name text box.

4 Tap or click the 'Save as type' button and select JPEG (*.JPG;*.JPEG;*.JPE) from the list of options.

5 Tap or click the Save button to save the document as a JPEG file.

6 Tap or click the OK button to accept the default settings in the JPEG Options dialog box.

7 Press the F12 key to revert the document to its last saved state and undo all the changes made by the action.

To Test the Action

To test the action, the following steps open a new file and then play back the action using the function key to confirm that it works.

- Open the file called Test Action from the Chapter 07 folder of the Data Files for Students, or a location specified by your instructor.

- Press the F11 key to play the action and apply the effect.

- Press CTRL+1 (ONE) to zoom to 100% (Figure 7–65).

2

- Close the Test Action file.

- Tap or click the No button to confirm closing the file without saving any changes.

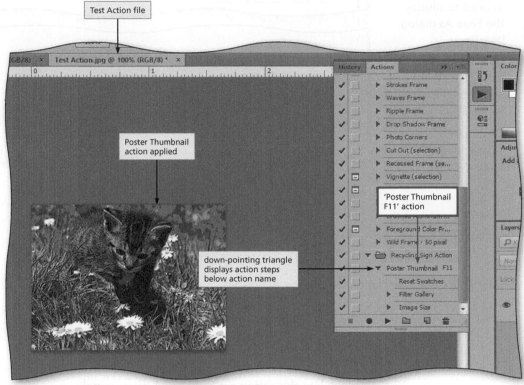

Figure 7–65

To Save an Action Set

The following steps save a new action set using the Actions panel menu.

1

- On the Actions panel, tap or click the Recycling Sign Action set.

- Tap or click the Actions panel menu button to display the menu (Figure 7–66).

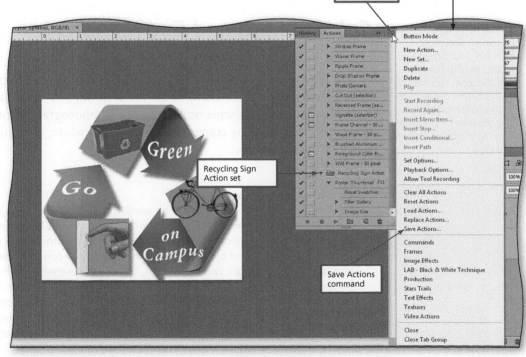

Figure 7–66

2

- Tap or click Save Actions to display the Save As dialog box.

- Navigate to your storage location and the Chapter 07 folder (Figure 7–67).

 Q&A Could I save the action set in the Actions folder with the installed Photoshop actions?
Yes; however, saving on a personal storage device keeps lab installation actions unchanged for other students.

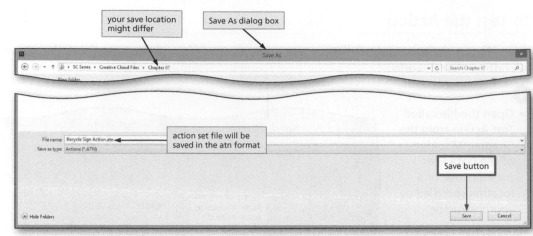

Figure 7–67

3

- Tap or click the Save button to save the Action Set.

To Delete an Action Set

Because you have finished with the action set and have saved it, the following steps delete the action set from the Actions panel.

1 On the Actions panel, tap or click the Recycling Sign Action set.

2 Tap or click the Actions panel menu button, and then tap or click Delete.

3 When Photoshop displays a confirmation message, tap or click the OK button.

4 Tap or click the Collapse Panel button to collapse the Actions panel.

Color Toning and Conversions

Color toning is the process of changing or intensifying the color of a photograph after it has been processed by the camera. In traditional photography, toning was a darkroom technique that changed the black colors in a black-and-white photograph to a chosen color, such as sepia or blue. In digital photography, toning includes a variety of techniques, including converting to black and white, creating duotones or split tones, and adding tints.

Plan Ahead

Create print versions.
Consider where your artwork will be used. If it will be used on a website, mobile application, computer game, or for another purpose in electronic format, the RGB color mode is the best choice because all colors in the image are created by a combination of red, green, and blue pixels. This matches how computer screens generate color images. If your artwork will be printed, then cyan, magenta, yellow, and black inks will be used to create the color print. Images in the RGB color mode often print darker than expected or suffer significant changes in color when printed. Converting the image from RGB to CMYK allows you to see more precisely how the image will print and allows you to make adjustments in the overall color before sending the image to a printer.

Many of the color toning adjustments are located on the Adjustments panel, but some are available only through the menu system. Recall that you previously used the Replace Color command to change the color of the bicycle. Most of the tools work in the same way — they map or plot an existing range of pixel values to a new range of values. The main difference is the amount of control each tool provides. For example, the various color adjustment commands on the Image menu alter the pixels in the current layer.

Another way to adjust color is to use an adjustment layer created using the Layer menu. This approach allows you to experiment with color and tonal adjustments first, before committing them to the image.

You also can use the New Adjustment Layer submenu on the Layers menu to make color adjustments. The difference is that when you access the settings using the menu system, Photoshop opens a dialog box allowing you to name and color the layer as you create it. You fine-tune the settings using the Adjustments panel either way.

Table 7–4 displays color adjustment commands that are not located on the Adjustments panel and therefore must be accessed through the menu system.

BTW

Pantone
Duotones are ideal for two-color print jobs with a spot color such as a PANTONE color used for accent. The PANTONE color matching system is a standardized system in which users and printing professionals can make sure colors match without direct contact with one another.

Table 7–4 Menu-Only Adjustment Controls

Option	Use	Menu Access
Desaturate	Produces a grayscale image but leaves the image in the same color mode	Image | Adjustments
Equalize	Redistributes the brightness values of all pixels so they represent the entire range of brightness levels more evenly	Image | Adjustments
Match Color	Matches the color across selections, layers, or photos as well as adjusts luminance, color range, and color casts in an image	Image | Adjustments
Replace Color	Replaces specified colors in an image with new color values	Image | Adjustments
Shadows/Highlights	Lightens or darkens based on surrounding pixels to correct photos with strong backlighting or other lighting errors	Image | Adjustments
Variations	Adjusts the color balance, contrast, and saturation of an image using thumbnail samples	Image | Adjustments

Black and White

Recall that converting a color image to the Grayscale mode on the Image Mode submenu is one way to discard color information from the pixels in the image. If you change the color mode to Lab Color, a Lightness channel also creates a black-and-white image. The Adjustments panel contains several settings that you can use to create a black-and-white or grayscale image. Additionally, some graphic artists create two adjustments layers, one for black and one for white, to emulate the film and filter process of traditional photography.

First, you will use the Desaturate command to view the image in grayscale; then you will undo and use the Black & White settings on the Adjustments panel.

To Desaturate

The following steps use the Desaturate command on the Adjustments submenu to produce a grayscale image for use in black and white advertising or for use as on letterhead printed on a black-and-white printer.

1

- If necessary, tap or click the Recycling Symbol layer to select it on the Layers panel.

- On the Application bar, tap or click Image and then point to Adjustments to display the Adjustments submenu (Figure 7–68).

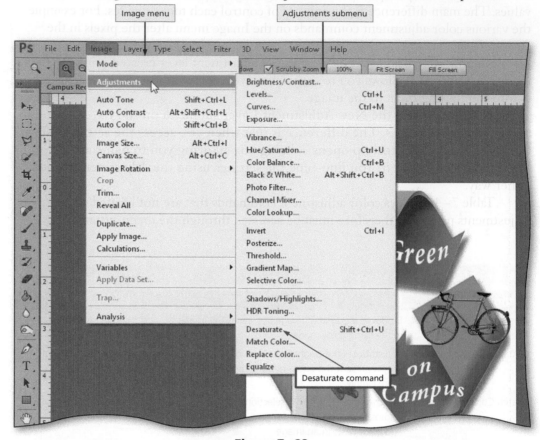

Figure 7–68

2

- Tap or click Desaturate to produce a grayscale image (Figure 7–69).

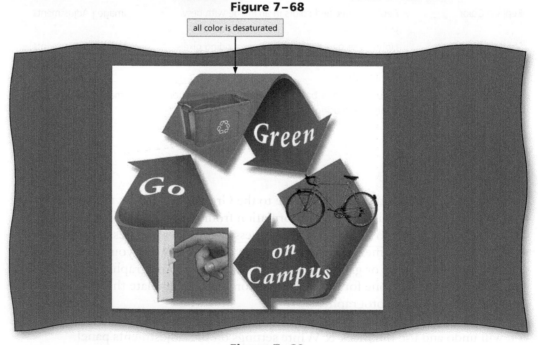

Figure 7–69

Other Ways

1. Press SHIFT+CTRL+U

To Undo the Desaturate Command

While the Desaturate command is appropriate for technical illustrations or when you want to neutralize or de-emphasize a background, it leaves the image in the same color mode, usually rendering a flat, lifeless version compared to other methods. Additionally, it sometimes reduces the contrast between foreground and background objects, making them difficult to see. Therefore, the following step undoes the Desaturate command.

 Press CTRL+Z to undo the previous command.

To Create a Black-and-White Adjustment

The Adjustments panel and its Black & White settings allow you to customize the shades of gray in the document window. By customizing the shades, you can create more diversity among the various shaded elements. For example, the recycle bin did not stand out when the Desaturate command was used. By adjusting a channel, the black-and-white version will appear with more variety. In the following steps, the items in the image are adjusted.

- Tap or click the Black & White icon on the Adjustments panel to display the black and white settings.

- On the Properties panel status bar, tap or click the 'Clip to layer' button so that the changes affect only the Recycling Symbol layer.

- Tap or click the 'Modify a slider' button to enable changes based on tapping, clicking, or dragging in the document itself (Figure 7–70).

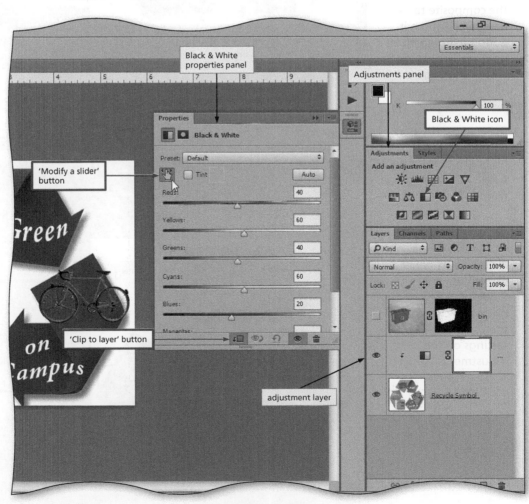

Figure 7–70

2

- In the document window, drag across the recycle bin to adjust the shading of the blues in the image (Figure 7–71).

Q&A Could I have used the sliders on the Adjustments panel to make the changes?
Yes, the sliders work the same way on the panel as they do in the document window.

 Experiment

- Try dragging other areas of the composite to darken or lighten it. Continue dragging until you are satisfied with the changes.

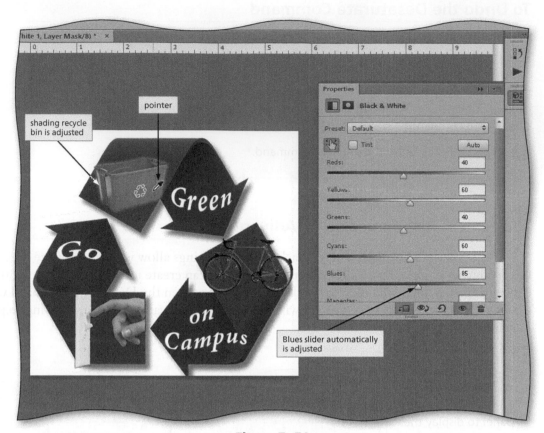

Figure 7–71

3

- Drag across the bars in the bicycle to highlight the bicycle frame in the image (Figure 7–72).

4

- At the top of the Adjustments panel, tap or click the Collapse Panel button to close the Black & White settings on the Adjustments panel.

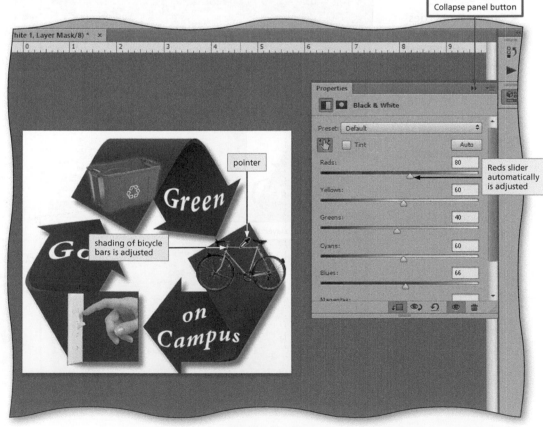

Figure 7–72

To Save the Black-and-White Image

The black-and-white image is complete. The next steps save the file.

1 Press SHIFT+CTRL+S to open the Save As dialog box.

2 Type **Campus Recycling Sign Black and White** to enter the file name.

3 Tap or click the Save button to save the image. If Photoshop displays a dialog box, tap or click the OK button.

Sepia

Sepia is a color toning technique resulting in a reddish-brown tint. Originally created through a pigmenting process for preservation of photos, it has become a popular kind of tinting to emulate older photos or for special effects. As with black-and-white conversions, Photoshop has many ways to create a sepia tone, including tints, channel mixing, selective coloring, filters, and processing raw data from a digital camera.

To Create a Sepia Image using Selective Color

The following steps create a sepia version of the Recycling Sign ad using the Selective Color settings on the Adjustments panel.

1
- With the adjustment layer still selected on the Layers panel, tap or click the Selective Color icon on the Adjustments panel, to display its settings.
- Tap or click the 'Clip to layer' button on the status bar so that only the Recycling Symbol layer is affected.
- Tap or click the Colors button to display its list (Figure 7–73).

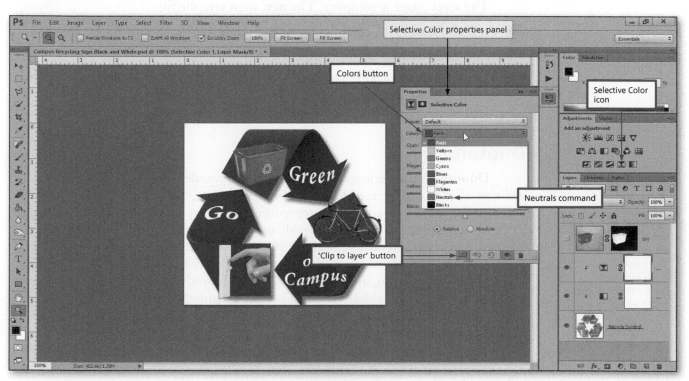

Figure 7–73

2

- Tap or click Neutrals to adjust the neutral colors in the image.

- Drag the Cyan slider to –53, drag the Magenta slider to –31, drag the Yellow slider to –18, and drag the Black slider to approximately 15 until a warm brown color is attained (Figure 7–74).

Q&A | What do the Relative and Absolute option buttons do?
If you select the Relative option button, the percentage of change is multiplied by the current color. If you select the Absolute option button, the percentage of change is added to the current color.

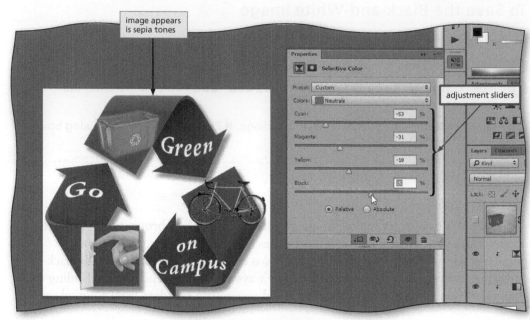

Figure 7–74

3

- At the top of the Properties panel, tap or click the 'Collapse to Panel' button.

To Save the Sepia Image

The sepia image is complete. The next steps save the file.

1 Press SHIFT+CTRL+S to open the Save As dialog box.

2 Type **Recycling Sign Sepia** as the file name.

3 Tap or click the Save button to save the image. If Photoshop displays a dialog box, tap or click the OK button.

Duotone

Duotone is a generic term for a variety of grayscale images printed with the addition of one, two, three, or four inks. In these images, colored inks, rather than different shades of gray, are used to reproduce tinted grays, increasing the tonal range of a grayscale image. Although a grayscale image displays up to 256 shades of gray, a printing press can reproduce only about 50 shades. For this reason, a grayscale image printed with only black ink can look significantly coarser than the same image on the screen. Printing with two, three, or four inks, each reproducing up to 50 levels of gray, produces an image with a slight tint and a wider dynamic range.

Because duotones affect only the gray levels, they contain only one channel; however, you can manipulate a wide range of tints using the Duotone Options dialog box. Creating a duotone version of an image is useful when the image will be printed in a single color, such as in a black and white newspaper, grayscale newsletter, or for a color special effect.

To Convert an Image to Duotone

Because duotone requires a completely grayscale image, you will convert the current image to grayscale and then to duotone in the following steps.

 1

- On the Image menu, point to Mode and then tap or click Grayscale.

- When Photoshop asks to discard adjustment layers, tap or click the OK button.

- When Photoshop asks to discard color information, tap or click the Discard button to accept the change (Figure 7–75).

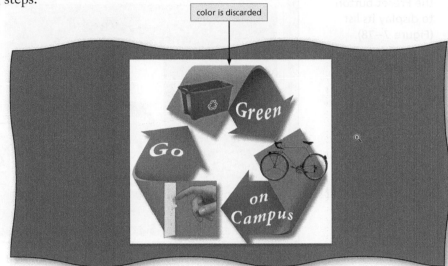

Figure 7–75

2

- On the Image menu, point to Mode and then tap or click Duotone to display the Duotone Options dialog box. Tap or click the Preview check box to preview the image, if necessary.

- Drag the title bar of the dialog box up and to the right to display more of the image.

- Tap or click the Type button to display its list (Figure 7–76).

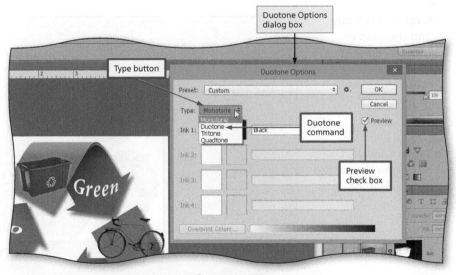

Figure 7–76

3

- Tap or click Duotone to add one color to the original black (Figure 7–77).

Q&A | What do the two boxes in front of the Black label represent?
The first box indicates how the color is spread across the image. The second box is the color itself. Clicking either box allows you to adjust the settings.

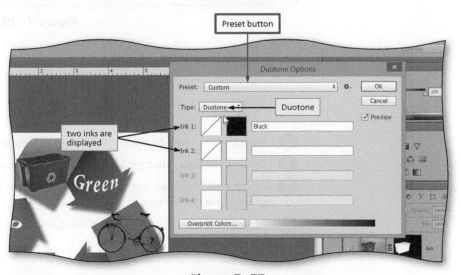

Figure 7–77

4

● To specify the second color, tap or click the Preset button to display its list (Figure 7–78).

Q&A Could I just choose the color using the 'Select an ink' color box?
Yes, but the Preset box list includes standard colors that print shops and service bureaus can match easily.

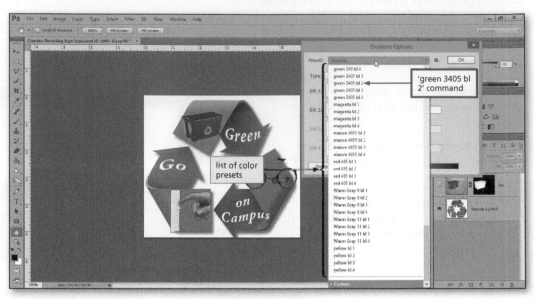

Figure 7–78

5

● Scroll as necessary and then tap or click 'green 3405 bl 2' to select a green duotone (Figure 7–79).

6

● Tap or click the OK button to choose the green duotone.

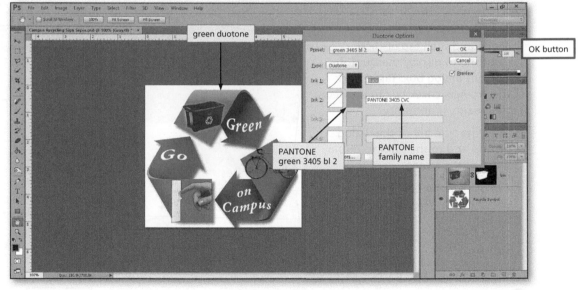

Figure 7–79

To Save the Duotone Image

The duotone image is complete. The next steps save the file.

1 Press SHIFT+CTRL+S to open the Save As dialog box.

2 Type **Campus Recycling Sign Duotone** to enter the file name.

3 Tap or click the Save button to save the image. If Photoshop displays a dialog box, tap or click the OK button.

4 Tap or click the Close button on the Campus Recycling Sign Duotone document window tab.

Preparing for Four-Color Processing

Most digital cameras create an RGB file. While that is fine for online viewing and web graphics, recall that many traditional full-color printing presses can print only four colors: cyan, magenta, yellow, and black (CMYK). Other colors in the spectrum are simulated using various combinations of those colors. When you plan to print a photo professionally, you might have to convert it from one color model to the other. The recycle bin image was taken with a digital camera and uses the RGB color model. The university wants a professional color print of the advertisement. The service bureau that will print the ad uses the Trumatch 4-color matching system, which requires the CMYK color model.

Photoshop allows you to convert directly from RGB to CMYK; however, using the intermediary Lab color mode gives you more flexibility in color changes and contrast.

Using Lab Color

Lab Color is an internationally accepted color mode that defines colors mathematically using a lightness or luminance setting, and two color or chromatic channels — an A-axis color for colors from magenta to green, and a B-axis color for colors from yellow to blue. The Lab Color mode, which tries to emulate the colors viewable by the human eye, incorporates all the colors in the RGB and CMYK color spectrums and often is used as an intermediary when converting from one format to another.

In Figure 7–80, the Lab color space is represented by the color spectrum. The black outline represents RGB's color space. The white outline represents CMYK's color space. RGB and CMYK are subsets, but they also are slanted in the color spectrum. For example, when converting from RGB to CMYK, you lose some of the blue's intensity but gain yellow. Reds and greens are better in RGB; cyans (blues) and magentas are better in CMYK, as you would expect. Contrast, a result of how bright the white is and how dark the black is, is represented poorly in CMYK. The printer cannot make white any brighter than the paper on which it is printed. A solid black does not exist in CMYK on a display monitor. Therefore, when adjusting color and contrast during a conversion, it is appropriate to convert RGB to Lab Color first, make your adjustments, and then convert it to CMYK.

BTW

JPEG Artifacts
Sometimes, when converting from RGB to Lab color, a JPEG image will leave behind some small blotches of irregular color, called **artifacts**, because of the compression method involved. Sharpening the image will remove those kinds of artifacts.

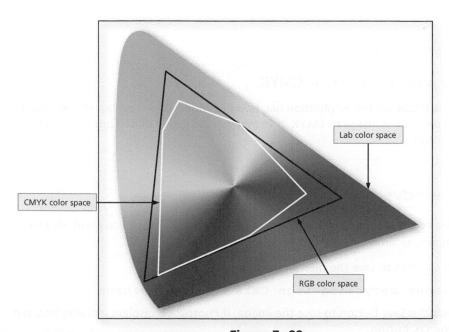

Lab color space

CMYK color space

RGB color space

Figure 7–80

The Lab Color mode calculates each color description, rather than generating it from a combination, as is the case for RGB. Because RGB colors are combinations of colors, they may look different on different devices. For example, a row of televisions or monitors in a store displaying the same program will look different because different television manufacturers combine red, green, and blue in slightly different ways. Working with Lab colors usually provides colors that are more consistent across platforms.

The Lab Color mode is independent of the type of device or media, and may be used for either display or printing. Many photo CD images use Lab colors where the luminance and color values are edited independently.

To Convert to Lab Color

The Lab Color mode will be used in the conversion process for the advertisement. Converting to Lab color rasterizes or changes vector-based text layers to pixel-based images. The conversion process also merges the layers. The following step converts to Lab color.

- Open the Campus Recycling Sign Merged file from the Chapter 07 folder of your storage location.

- Adjust the magnification as necessary.

- Tap or click Image on the Application bar, point to Mode, and then tap or click Lab Color to begin the conversion (Figure 7–81).

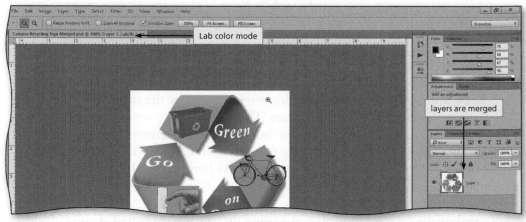

Figure 7–81

- When Photoshop displays a message about merging layers, tap or click the Merge button.

To Convert to CMYK

BTW

Certification
The Adobe Certified Expert (ACE) program provides an opportunity for you to obtain a valuable industry credential – proof that you have the Photoshop CC skills required by employers. For more information, visit the Certification resource on the Student Companion Site located on www .cengagebrain.com.

The following step converts to CMYK.

1 Tap or click Image on the Application bar, point to Mode, and then tap or click CMYK Color to convert the image to CMYK. If Photoshop displays a dialog box, tap or click the OK button.

To Save the Advertisement

After the conversion to Lab and the conversion to CMYK, it is a good idea to save the file again, as shown in the following steps.

1 Press CTRL+SHIFT+S to save the file.

2 Type **Campus Recycling Sign CMYK** to enter the file name.

3 Tap or click the Save button to save the image. If Photoshop displays a dialog box, tap or click the OK button.

Printing Color Separations

Graphic professionals sometimes use print shops, labs, or service bureaus for their advanced printing needs. Service bureaus typically use image setters to create high-quality prints. An **image setter** is a high-resolution output device that can transfer electronic files directly to photosensitive paper, plates, or film. While many service bureaus can resize and edit color at the time of printing, you save both time and money by performing these prepress tasks ahead of time in Photoshop. **Prepress tasks** are the various printing-related services performed before ink actually is put on the printed page.

When preparing your image for prepress, and working with CMYK images or images with spot color, you can print each color channel as a separate page. Photoshop also has a Split Channels command on the Channels panel menu that splits the channels into separate document windows for view and adjusting, if desired. Different service bureaus and labs require different kinds of submissions that are highly printer-dependent. Even when supplying a composite for reference by the service bureau, you might want to print color separations for proofing purposes. Separations help you see if your composite file will separate correctly, and help you catch other problems that might not be apparent by looking at the composite.

BTW

Flash Cards
The Student Companion Site has interactive flash cards of the important concepts in each chapter. Visit For detailed instructions about accessing available resources, visit solutions .cengage.com/ctdownloads or contact your instructor for information about the flash cards.

To Print Color Separations

Printing the project in color separations allows you to determine whether your composite will separate properly and helps you spot problems before going to press. The following steps print the Recycling Sign CMYK document as color separations.

- Ready the printer attached to your computer.

- Tap or click File on the Application bar, and then tap or click Print to display the Photoshop Print Settings dialog box.

- Tap or click the Color Handling box arrow to display its list (Figure 7–82).

Q&A How can I resize the dialog box?
You can drag any edge of the dialog box to resize it. Other system dialog boxes, such as Save As, can be resized by double-clicking the title bar.

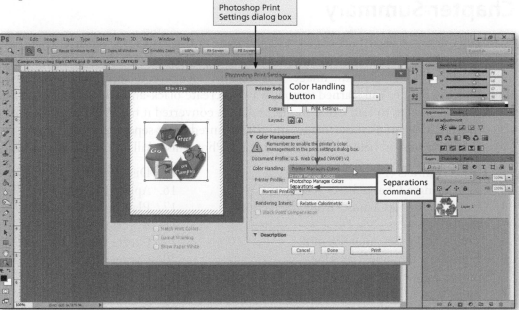

Figure 7–82

2

● Tap or click Separations in the list.

● Tap or click the Print button to display your printer-dependent Print dialog box.

● Tap or click the Print button or the appropriate button for your printer to print the image.

● Retrieve your four printouts from the printer.

Q&A Why do I have four different printouts?
You printed separations. Just as the RGB channels you examined earlier in this chapter showed different grayscale versions of an image depending on how much red, green, or blue was present, the printed color separations show the same thing — but for the cyan, magenta, yellow, and black channels.

To Save and Close the Four-Color Version

The following steps save and close the CMYK four-color version of the Recycling Sign document.

1 Press CTRL+S to save the file with the same name.

2 Tap or click the Close button on the document window title bar to close the image.

To Quit Photoshop

The chapter is complete. The final step is to quit Photoshop.

1 Tap or click the Close button on the right side of the Photoshop title bar to quit Photoshop.

Chapter Summary

In this chapter, you used a master copy of an image as the basis for creating several new versions. First, you used channels to aid in the creation of complex selections, which were later used as masks. You added warped text and used an action to embellish the image. You recorded an action to apply an artistic filter and resize a thumbnail version of the image. You learned various ways to create black-and-white, sepia, and duotone images. Finally, you converted the image to Lab Color mode, and then converted it to CMYK color. Among the prepress activities, you resized and resampled the image, and then printed color separations.

The items listed below include all the new Photoshop skills you have learned in this chapter:

1. View Channels (PS 405)
2. Select using a Channel (PS 406)
3. Create an Alpha Channel from a Selection (PS 408)
4. Edit an Alpha Channel (PS 408)
5. Duplicate a Channel (PS 413)
6. Paint in Brush Overlay Mode (PS 414)
7. Complete the Alpha Channel (PS 416)
8. Replace a Color (PS 418)
9. Create a Transparent Background and Save (PS 421)
10. Create a Layer Mask from an Alpha Channel (PS 423)
11. Use the Refine Mask Tool (PS 425)
12. Load and Move a Selection (PS 428)
13. Add Point Text (PS 430)
14. Warp Text (PS 432)

15. Display the Actions Panel (PS 438)
16. Append Action Sets (PS 438)
17. Play an Action (PS 439)
18. Revert (PS 440)
19. Create a New Action Set (PS 441)
20. Create a New Action (PS 442)
21. Record an Action (PS 442)
22. Test the Action (PS 445)
23. Save an Action Set (PS 445)
24. Delete an Action Set (PS 446)
25. Desaturate (PS 448)
26. Create a Black-and-White Adjustment (PS 449)
27. Create a Sepia Image using Selective Color (PS 451)
28. Convert an Image to Duotone (PS 453)
29. Convert to Lab Color (PS 456)
30. Print Color Separations (PS 457)

Apply Your Knowledge

Reinforce the skills and apply the concepts you learned in this chapter.

Creating an Alpha Channel

Note: To complete this assignment, you will be required to use the Data Files for Students. Visit solutions.cengage.com/ctdownloads for detailed instructions or contact your instructor for information about accessing the required files.

Instructions: Start Photoshop and perform the customization steps found on pages PS 6 through PS 11. Open the Apply 7-1 Dark Sky file from the Chapter 07 folder of the Data Files for Students. You will edit the file to create an alpha channel, hide the dark sky background, and insert a new sky background to create the photo shown in Figure 7–83.

Courtesy of Alec Fehl

Figure 7–83

Perform the following tasks:

1. On the File menu, tap or click Save As. Save the image on your storage device as a PSD file, with the file name Apply 7-1 Sky Complete.
2. On the Layers panel, press and hold or right-click the Background layer and then tap or click Duplicate Layer. Name the new layer, Foreground. Select only the Foreground layer, and hide the Background layer by clicking its visibility icon.
3. Tap or click the Channels panel and then, one at a time, view each channel independent of the others. Decide which channel has the most contrast to facilitate removing the sky background.
4. Press and hold or right-click the Blue channel and then tap or click Duplicate Channel. Name the new channel Old Background.

Continued >

Apply Your Knowledge *continued*

5. If necessary, tap or click the Old Background channel to select it and ensure it is the only visible channel. All other channels should have their visibility icons toggled off.

6. To define the foreground:

 a. Use the Brush Tool set to Overlay mode and black as the foreground color. Drag across the top of the trees and grass where they meet the sky to paint them black.

 b. Drag a second time across the trees and grass below the initial swatch of black to paint more of the trees and grass black.

 c. Change the brush to Normal mode and paint the rest of the bottom portion of the image black.

7. To define the background:

 a. Change the brush back to Overlay mode and change the foreground color to white.

 b. Drag just above the trees to paint the bottom portion of the sky white. You may need to tap or click any trouble spots to turn them white.

 c. Continue painting the sky white where it is close to the trees.

 d. Change the brush to Normal mode and paint the remaining top portion of the image and the rest of the sky white.

 e. Continue to switch between black and white and Normal and Overlay modes until the top portion of the Image (sky) is completely white, and the foreground (trees and grass) is black.

8. Because the black areas will hide pixels when used as a mask while the white areas will allow the pixels to show through, you must reverse the colors within the channel. Black needs to become white, and white needs to become black. Press CTRL+I to invert the colors of the channel.

9. To view all channels and return to the Layers panel:

 a. Tap or click the RGB channel.

 b. Tap or click the Layers panel.

 c. Tap or click the Foreground layer to select it, if necessary.

10. To load the channel as a selection and create a mask:

 a. Tap or click Select on the Application bar.

 b. Tap or click Load Selection.

 c. From the Channel menu, choose Old Background and tap or click OK.

 d. Tap or click the 'Add layer mask' button on the Layers panel status bar.

11. To refine the mask:

 a. Tap or click the mask thumbnail to select it.

 b. Tap or click Select on the Application bar, and then tap or click Refine Mask to display the Refine Mask dialog box.

 c. Tap or click the View button to display the list of views, and then choose On Layers.

 d. Drag the slider as necessary to refine the edges to approximately 5 to increase the size of the selection border where the edge refinement occurs.

 e. Tap or click the Output To button to display its list, and then tap or click New Layer so that Photoshop creates a new layer with the refined mask applied.

 f. Tap or click the OK button to apply the refinement.

12. To insert the new background file:

 a. Open the Apply 7 - 1 Good Sky file from the Chapter 07 folder of the Data Files for Students.

 b. Position the two open documents side by side.

   c. Use the Move Tool to drag the good sky image to the Apply 7-1 Sky Complete document.

   d. Close the Apply 7-1 Good Sky document.

   e. Rename the new layer, Layer 1, to New Sky.

13. To position the new background:

   a. Drag the layers in the Layers panel to restack them, if necessary, so the Foreground layer is the top layer and the New Sky layer is beneath it.

   b. Use the Move Tool to position the New Sky layer as necessary.

14. Save the image.

15. To resize the image for printing on a desktop printer:

   a. On the Image menu, tap or click Image Size.

   b. Tap or click the Resample check box to deselect it.

   c. Type **9** in the Width box.

   d. Tap or click the OK button.

16. Ready your printer. Print color separations in Landscape mode and turn them in to your instructor.

17. Quit Photoshop without saving the resized file.

Extend Your Knowledge

Extend the skills you learned in this chapter and experiment with new skills. You may need to use Help to complete the assignment.

Adding Spot Colors to a Print

Note: To complete this assignment, you will be required to use the Data Files for Students. Visit solutions.cengage.com/ctdownloads for detailed instructions or contact your instructor for information about accessing the required files.

Instructions: Start Photoshop and perform the customization steps found on pages PS 6 through PS 11. Open the file Extend 7–1 Spot Color file from the Chapter 07 folder of the Data Files for Students. The purpose of this exercise is to add two spot colors to a four-color travel flyer. The two inks are PANTONE shades, not contained in the standard CMYK range. The file contains two extra channels with saved text selections that will be loaded and recolored. The final edited photo is displayed in Figure 7–84 on the next page.

Perform the following tasks:

1. Press SHIFT+CTRL+S to save the image on your storage device as a PSD file, with the file name Extend 7–1 Spot Color Complete.

2. To convert the image from RGB mode to CMYK mode:

   a. Point to Mode on the Image menu, and then tap or click CMYK Color.

   b. If Photoshop displays a dialog box warning you about converting to CMYK, tap or click the OK button.

3. Tap or click the Channels panel tab to activate the panel.

4. Tap or click Select on the Application bar, and then tap or click Load Selection to open the Load Selection dialog box.

5. Tap or click the Channel box arrow, tap or click the Stonehenge channel, and then tap or click the OK button to load the first text channel and display the selection marquee in the document window.

Continued >

Extend Your Knowledge *continued*

Courtesy of Alec Fehl

Figure 7–84

6. Tap or click the Channels panel menu button, and then tap or click New Spot Channel to open the New Spot Channel dialog box.

7. Type `100` in the Solidity box, and tap or click the color box to access a color selection dialog box. If the Color Picker (Spot Color) dialog box appears, tap or click the Color Libraries button to display the Color Libraries dialog box.

8. Tap or click the Book box arrow and then tap or click 'PANTONE+ Pastels & Neons Uncoated' in the list. Scroll in the color bar and select an appropriate color.

9. Tap or click the OK button to close the Color Libraries dialog box. Tap or click the OK button again to close the New Spot Channel dialog box.

10. Repeat Steps 4 through 9 for the Legendary Travel channel. Choose a color from the PANTONE+ Metallic Coated colors.

11. Save the image again.

12. Use the Save As command to save a copy of the file as Extend 7-1 Spot Color Complete in the Photoshop DCS 2.0 (*.EPS) in the format, which saves the file in a format that contains the extra spot channels.

13. Submit the assignment in the format specified by your instructor.

Make It Right

Analyze a project and correct all errors and/or improve the design.

Fixing a Grainy Photo Using Channels

Note: To complete this assignment, you will be required to use the Data Files for Students. Visit solutions.cengage.com/ctdownloads for detailed instructions or contact your instructor for information about accessing the required files.

Instructions: Start Photoshop and perform the customization steps found on pages PS 6 through PS 11. Open the Make It Right 7-1 Grainy file from the Data Files for Students and save it as Make It Right 7-1 Grainy Complete in the PSD file format. You have a poor quality photo of an image (Figure 7–85) that you need for a brochure. Because the ISO settings on your camera were set too high, there is a lot of visual noise in the pixels, which makes the image appear grainy. You will use channels to fix the problem.

Perform the following tasks:

Access the Channels panel and tap or click each color channel one at a time. Notice that the Red and Blue channels appear fine but the Green channel is full of noise and pixilation. With the Green channel selected, tap or click the visibility icon next to the RGB master channel. On the Application bar, tap or click Filter, point to Blur, and then tap or click Gaussian Blur to open the Gaussian Blur dialog box. Adjust the Radius, blurring the Green channel to reduce some of the noise in the photo. On the Application bar, tap or click Filter, point to Noise, and then tap or click Reduce Noise. Adjust the settings to reduce the noise and pixilation further. When you are happy with the outcome, save the file with the name, Make It Right 7-1 Grainy Fixed, and submit it to your instructor.

Courtesy of Alec Fehl

Figure 7–85

In the Labs

Design and/or create a project using the guidelines, concepts, and skills presented in this chapter. Labs are listed in order of increasing difficulty.

Lab 1: **Creating a Frost Effect Using Channels**

Note: To complete this assignment, you will be required to use the Data Files for Students. Visit solutions.cengage.com/ctdownloads for detailed instructions or contact your instructor for information about accessing the required files.

Problem: You need a photo of a field with an early frost on the ground for a collage, but it is the middle of the summer and everything is green. You will use your knowledge of channels to make the grass and trees look as though they have frost on them. The finished product is displayed in Figure 7–86.

Instructions: Perform the following tasks:

1. Start Photoshop. Perform the customization steps found on pages PS 6 through PS 12.

2. Open the file Lab 7-1 Green Grass from the Chapter 07 folder of the Data Files for Students.

3. Save the file as Lab 7-1 White Frost. Navigate to your storage device.

4. If necessary, tap or click the Layers panel tab to display the layers. Press and hold or right-click the Background layer and then tap or click Duplicate Layer on the context menu. Name the new layer, frost.

5. At the top of the Layers panel, tap or click the Blending Mode box arrow and then tap or click Lighten.

Figure 7–86

6. Tap or click the Adjustments panel tab to access the Adjustments panel. Tap or click the Channel Mixer icon to display its settings. (*Hint:* The Channel Mixer icon is the next-to-last one in the second row.)

   a. Tap or click the Monochrome check box to select it.

   b. Type **200** in the Red box.

   c. Type **150** in the Green box.

   d. Type **-150** in the Blue box.

   e. Type **0** in the Constant box, if necessary.

   f. Collapse the Channel Mixer panel.

7. On the Layers tab, select the Background layer.

8. To select the sky:

   a. Tap or click the Channels panel tab to access the Channels panel.

   b. Notice that an alpha channel has been created previously and was named, sky.

   c. Tap or click the Layers panel tab.

   d. On the Application bar, tap or click Select and then tap or click Load Selection to display the Load Selection dialog box.

   e. Tap or click the Channel box arrow and then tap or click sky in the list, if necessary.

   f. Tap or click the OK button to close the Load Selection dialog box and to display the selection marquee in the document window.

   g. Press CTRL+J to create a new layer. Name the layer, sky.

   h. On the Layers panel, drag the new Sky layer above the others.

9. Save the file again.

10. To adjust the amount of frost:

    a. On the Layers panel, tap or click the Channel Mixer layer.

    b. At the top of the Layers panel, change the opacity to 70%.

    c. Save your changes.

11. Flatten the image and then save the file in the JPEG format and submit it to your instructor as directed.

Lab 2: **Using Predefined Actions**

Note: To complete this assignment, you will be required to use the Data Files for Students. Visit solutions.cengage.com/ctdownloads for detailed instructions or contact your instructor for information about accessing the required files.

Problem: Your neighbor wants you to use her photo of homegrown berries to create flyer for a farmer's market. You decide to investigate Photoshop's predefined actions to look for a specialized frame that you can apply to the photo. The finished product is displayed in Figure 7–87 on the Next page.

Instructions: Perform the following tasks:

1. Start Photoshop. Perform the customization steps found on pages PS 6 through PS 11.

2. Open the file Lab 7-2 Berries from the Chapter 07 folder of the Data Files for Students.

3. Tap or click the Save As command on the File menu. Type **Lab 7-2 Flyer** as the file name and set the format to the Photoshop PSD format, if necessary. Navigate to your storage device. Tap or click the Save button. If Photoshop displays a dialog box, tap or click the OK button.

4. Press ALT+F9 to display the Actions panel. If the Frames action set is not listed, tap or click the panel menu button, and then tap or click Frames. If necessary, tap or click the right-pointing triangle of the Frames action set to display the actions stored in the set. Scroll down and tap or click the Photo Corners action.

Continued >

In the Labs continued

Courtesy of Alec Fehl

Figure 7–87

5. Tap or click the Play selection button on the Actions panel status bar. When the action is complete, close the Actions panel.

6. On the Layers panel, select the photo corners layer, if necessary.

7. To size and rotate the berries:

   a. Press CTRL+T to freely transform the layer.

   b. SHIFT+drag the lower-left corner of the selection border up and to the right until the pointer is positioned approximately in the center of the document.

   c. Point to the outside of the selection border until the pointer appears as a curved arrow and then drag up to rotate the selection.

   d. Point to the inside of the selection border and drag the berries into position.

   e. Press the ENTER key to apply the transformation.

8. To change the background color:

   a. Tap or click the 'Set foreground color button' at the bottom of the Tools panel to display the Color Picker.

   b. In the R box, type `250`. In the G box, type `131`. In the B box, type `4`. Alternatively, choose a color of your liking.

   c. Tap or click the OK button to set the foreground color.

   d. Tap or click the new background layer in the Layers panel to select it.

   e. Press SHIFT+G repeatedly until the Paint Bucket Tool is selected.

   f. Tap or click in the document window to fill the new background layer with the new color.

9. Tap or click the 'Horizontal Type Tool' button on the Tools panel.

10. To adjust the text settings:

   a. On the options bar, select the Cooper Std font family or a similar font.

   b. Set the font size to 12.

   c. Set the anti-aliasing method to Smooth.

   d. Tap or click the Center text button.

   e. Choose a white font color.

11. Drag a text box that fills the left side of the image. In the text box, type **Farmer's Market every Saturday 7am - noon Community Center parking lot**, pressing the ENTER key as necessary to create the lines shown in Figure 7–96. (*Hint:* If your line spacing is too large, tap or click Paragraph on the Window menu and make sure all line spacing boxes are set to 0 (zero) in the Paragraph panel.) When you are finished, tap or click the 'Commit any current edits' button on the options bar. Use the Move Tool to adjust the placement of the text box or the berries if needed. Save your changes.

12. When you are finished, press CTRL+SHIFT+S to display the Save As dialog box. Save the file with the name, Lab 7-2 Flyer Complete, in the JPG format.

13. E-mail your instructor with the Lab 7-2 Flyer Complete file as an attachment, or see your instructor for another way to submit this assignment.

Lab 3: **Changing Band Membership**

Note: To complete this assignment, you will be required to use the Data Files for Students. Visit solutions.cengage.com/ctdownloads for detailed instructions or contact your instructor for information about accessing the required files.

Problem: A local band has contracted you to alter a concert photo to include their new bass player. They have provided you with a photo of their band in concert and a separate photo of the bass player. You are to edit the bass player photo and place him on the concert stage, creating a picture the band can use for promotional purposes. The edited photo is shown Figure 7–88.

Instructions: Perform the following tasks:
Start Photoshop. Perform the customization steps found on pages PS 6 through PS 11. Open the Lab 7-3 Bassist photo from the Chapter 07 folder of the Data Files for Students. Select the background and create an alpha channel. Hide or delete the background and edit as necessary to display only the bassist. Open the file named Lab 7-3 Concert. Arrange the documents side by side and then use the Move Tool to drag the bassist image into the Lab 7-3 Concert document window. Adjust and scale the layers as necessary.

Courtesy of Alec Fehl

Figure 7–88

Continued >

In the Labs *continued*

Refine the bass player's mask to decontaminate the edge colors. Use the Adjustments panel to adjust the levels and contrast so the bassist matches the concert scene. Delete portions of the bass player or create a mask so he appears behind the stage speakers and other band members. Create a Warped text box with the band name, as shown in Figure 7–88. Sample the blue in the guitar strap for the color of the text and apply a layer style to emphasize the text. Save the file as Lab 7-3 New Bass Player in the PSD format.

Cases and Places

Apply your creative thinking and problem-solving skills to design
and implement a solution.

1: Converting to Black and White

Academic

Your school prints a monthly newsletter in black and white. Open the Case 7-1 School image that is located in the Chapter 07 folder of the Data Files for Students. Use the Adjustments panel and the Black & White adjustment to create a black-and-white version of the image that maintains good contrast and is not washed out. Write down the settings you used, and then revert the image to its original state. Using the Case 7-1 School image, record a new action named Convert to B&W, and apply the settings you wrote down earlier as you record the action. Apply the saved action to the Case 7-1 Football and Case 7-1 Graduation images located in the Chapter 07 folder. Save the three black-and-white images with the description, B&W, appended to the end of the default file name.

2: Reusing an Action Set

Personal

You are volunteering your graphic design skills to help a local church prepare a poster thumbnail of their church building. In this chapter, you created an action set named Recycling Sign Action. You decide to try to reload the action set and apply the Poster Thumbnail action to the image of the church. If you did not create the action in the chapter, see your instructor for ways to complete this assignment. Open the Case 7-2 Church image located in the Chapter 07 folder of the Data Files for Students. Display the Actions panel and access the panel menu. Use the Load Actions command and navigate to your storage device to load the Recycle Sign Action set. Play the Poster Thumbnail action. Save the file as Case 7-2 Church Poster Thumbnail.psd and submit it to your instructor. Delete the action set from the Actions panel.

3: Converting to Duotone

Professional

A wedding planner wants to use a picture of a tulip on her business cards. The tulip is in full color, but her business cards are going to use brown spot color on ivory paper. Open the Case 7-3 Tulip image located in the Chapter 07 folder of the Data Files for Students. Save the image on your storage device with the name Case 7-3 Tulip Edited. Use an alpha channel to remove the background. Flatten the image. Convert the image to grayscale and then convert the image to duotone. When the Duotone dialog box is displayed, double-tap or double-click the Color Picker and choose a sepia color. Type **sepia** in the Name text box. Tap or click the OK button. Convert the image to CMYK color. Save the image again, and then print a copy. See your instructor for ways to submit this assignment.

Ps File Edit Image Layer Type Select Filter 3D View Window Help

Adobe Photoshop CC   Feather: 0 px   ☐ Anti-alias   Style: Normal ◆   Width: ⇄   Height: Refine Edge...

8 | Working with Vector Graphics and 3D Tools

Objectives

You will have mastered the material in this chapter when you can:

- Describe the characteristics of clip art and vector graphics
- Differentiate between vector and raster graphic images
- Create shape layers and paths with the Pen Tool
- Draw line segments and curved paths
- Add and convert anchor points
- Use the Freeform Pen Tool with the magnetic pen option

- Stroke a path
- Move and modify paths using the Path Selection and Direct Selection Tools
- Manage paths on the Paths panel
- Create a 3D extrusion from a 2D image
- Employ 3D tools
- Create a dashed line using the Line Tool
- Use the Note Tool

Ps File Edit Image Layer Type Select Filter 3D View Window Help

Adobe **Photoshop** CC   Feather: 0 px   Anti-alias   Style: Normal ⬦   Width: Height: Refine Edge...

8 | Working with Vector Graphics and 3D Tools

Introduction

With the advent of page layout and word processing software, images have become common in all kinds of documents. Websites without graphics are passé. Business stationery now includes artwork and logos in addition to the standard address fields. Content data, lectures, and oral presentations are considered uninteresting without graphics and multimedia effects, and textbooks are loaded with graphics to help improve students' focus and comprehension. Students routinely insert clip art into papers and presentations.

The term **clip art** refers to individual images or groups of vector graphics that can be transferred across computer applications and platforms. Clip art commonly is an illustrative, vibrant drawing that features solid blocks of color, rather than a photo, but the term is applied loosely to any image that accompanies or decorates text, including black-and-white images. The term, clip art, also is applied to visual elements such as bullets, lines, shapes, and callouts.

Project — Creating a Ticket

A local racetrack wants to improve its image by creating a more exciting ticket for its events. Tickets come in all sizes, and are used for events, performances, raffles, exchanges, or even as proof of receipt. Tickets may be numbered and may identify certain seating, dates, times, and charges. Tickets sometimes have a tear-off or ticket stub that is detached once the ticketholder has been admitted to the event, or when service is rendered. You will begin the process of designing the ticket by creating a piece of clip art from a photo. Using the Pen Tool and paths, portions of the image are recolored to create a cartoon look and feel. You then will use Photoshop's 3D tools to add depth and interest to the clip art and text. You will add other text and clip art to create the ticket displayed Figure 8–1.

Overview

As you read this chapter, you will learn how to create the ticket shown in Figure 8–1 by performing these general tasks:

- Use the Path and Pen Tools to create shapes.
- Create vector graphics using paths.
- Save paths using the Paths panel.
- Merge paths.
- Extrude a 3D object.
- Use 3D tools.
- Create 3D text.
- Annotate a clip art image using the Note Tool.

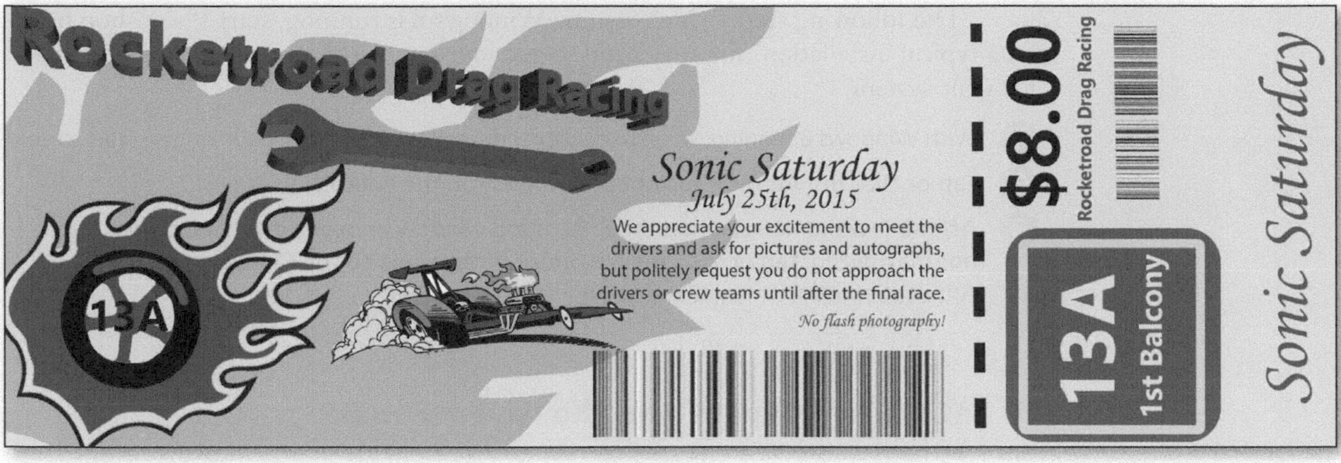

© iStockphoto.com/KeithBishop;courtesy Mike Flaherty

Figure 8–1

Plan Ahead

General Project Guidelines

When editing a photo, the actions you perform and decisions you make will affect the appearance and characteristics of the finished product. As you edit photos, such as the one shown in Figure 8–1, you should follow these general guidelines:

1. **Add detail to enhance clip art.** Good clip art uses strong lines and colors with enough detail to highlight the image's purpose. Keep the purpose, context, and audience in mind as you add detail such as movement, depth, and light to the clip art.
2. **Use vector graphics for clip art.** When creating clip art, use vector graphics. Vector graphics are high-quality graphics used in illustrations, typography, logos, and advertisements. They retain their crisp edges when resized, moved, or recolored. Vector graphics do not pixelate when transferred to other applications.
3. **Create 3D objects to add depth and interest.** When you convert a 2D picture into a 3D object, you add a sense of realism. Keep the angles, depth, and shadows the same across all 3D objects in the same scene.
4. **Annotate graphics within the file.** Consider adding notes within the file itself, rather than using email with an attached photo, to provide documentation and explanations. That way, the information stays with the graphic and can be accessed by others.

When necessary, more specific details concerning the preceding guidelines are presented at appropriate points in the chapter. The chapter also will identify the actions performed and decisions made regarding these guidelines during the creation of the document shown in Figure 8–1.

To Start Photoshop

If you are stepping through this project on a computer and you want your screen to match the figures in this book, then you should change your computer's resolution to 1366 × 768 and reset the panels, tools, and colors. For more information about how to change the resolution on your computer and other advanced Photoshop settings, read the Editing Preferences Appendix.

The following steps, which assume Windows 8 is running, start Photoshop based on a typical installation. You may need to ask your instructor how to start Photoshop for your system.

1 With Windows 8 running, scroll to display the Adobe Photoshop CC tile on the Start screen.

2 Tap or click the Adobe Photoshop CC tile to run the Photoshop app.

3 After a few moments, when the Photoshop window appears, if the window is not maximized, tap or click the Maximize button next to the Close button on the Application bar to maximize the window.

To Set the Workspace and the Layers Panel

The following steps select and reset the Essentials workspace, as well as setting options on the Layers panel.

1 Tap or click the workspace switcher on the options bar to display the list and then tap or click Essentials to select the default workspace panels.

2 Tap or click the workspace switcher on the options bar again, to display the list and then tap or click Reset Essentials to restore the workspace to its default settings and reposition any panels that might have been moved by previous users.

3 Tap or click the Layers panel menu button and then tap or click Panel Options. In the Panel Options dialog box, tap or click the medium thumbnail, and tap or click to select the Layer Bounds options button. Tap or click the OK button.

To Reset the Tools and the Options Bar

Recall that the Tools panel and the options bar retain their settings from previous Photoshop sessions. The following steps select the Rectangular Marquee Tool and reset all tool settings in the options bar.

1 If the tools in the Tools panel appear in two columns, tap or click the double arrow at the top of the Tools panel.

2 If necessary, tap or click the 'Rectangular Marquee Tool' button on the Tools panel to select it.

3 On the options bar, press and hold or right-click the 'Rectangular Marquee Tool' icon to display the context menu, and then tap or click 'Reset All Tools'. When Photoshop displays a confirmation dialog box, tap or click the OK button to restore the tools to their default settings.

To Set the Interface and Default Colors

Recall that Photoshop retains the interface color scheme, as well as the foreground and background colors from session to session. The following steps set the interface to Medium Gray and the foreground and background colors to black over white.

1 Tap or click Edit on the Application bar to display the Edit menu. Tap or click Preferences and then tap or click Interface on the Preferences submenu to display the Preferences dialog box.

2 If necessary, tap or click the third button, Medium Gray, to change the interface color scheme.

3 Tap or click the OK button to close the Preferences dialog box.

4 Tap or click the 'Default Foreground and Background Colors' button on the Tools panel to set the default colors to black and white. If black is not over white on the Tools panel, tap or click the 'Switch Foreground and Background Colors' button.

MAC For a detailed example of this procedure using the Mac operating system, refer to the For Mac Users Appendix.

Clip Art

Clip art images can be created from scratch, produced from a photo, copied and pasted from another source, or imported directly as a file into some applications. The use of clip art can save artists time and money; and in some cases, using clip art in a project allows artwork to be included when it would otherwise not be possible to do so. Clip art galleries that come with some page layout and word processing applications often contain hundreds of images.

Plan
Ahead

> **Add detail to enhance clip art.**
> There are many ways to add detail to vector graphics and clip art, including overlays, layer styles, shadows, blending modes, and reflections. Make sure each of your edits is purposeful and not distracting. It is best to create a new layer for each enhancement.

Clip art comes in a variety of file formats. **Bitmap images** work best in the size and orientation at which they are created, and typically are stored in the GIF, JPG, BMP, TIF, or PNG formats. **Vector images** are resolution-independent and do not pixelate when resized. They commonly are stored as EPS, SVG, WMF, SWF, or PDF files. Choosing the appropriate file format often depends on the purpose of the graphic — print, web, or file transfer — as well as the scalability and resolution.

For print publications, vector images can be resized, rotated, and stretched easily. The disadvantage is that many vector formats are specific to the software in which the image was created. For example, Windows Metafile is a format used with Microsoft products and associated clip art. It is saved with the extension WMF. A graphic created with Adobe Flash has the extension SWF. While you can copy and import those types of vector images between applications, you might not be able to edit them without using the original software.

Clip art is not always free. Application software companies provide a license for registered users to import and distribute the clip art provided with the package without charge. Some web clip art galleries might specify royalty-free images for one-time use, but not for commercial use intended to generate profit. For other uses, you must purchase clip art. It is important to read all licensing agreements carefully. The usage of some artwork requires written permission. Copyright laws apply to all images equally — the right of legal use depends on the intended use and conditions of the copyright owner. All images are copyrighted, regardless of whether they are marked as copyrighted.

Table 8–1 on the next page displays some of the categories, descriptions, and usages of clip art sources.

Table 8–1 Clip Art

Clip Art Category	Warnings	Use
Free — An image that is given or provided free of charge	It is important to check the website owner's motive for giving away clip art. Some free graphics are unlabeled, copyrighted images. Images might contain spyware or viruses.	Appropriate for personal use and sometimes for educational purposes, but because the original source might be obscure, free clip art is not recommended for business use.
Published clip art — images in print or online	Ask for written permission to use the image. Do not use the image unless you can track it to its original source.	Published clip art is appropriate for personal use, educational purposes, and one-time use on a website. With permission, it may be used commercially.
Copyrighted — trademarked images that have legal owners	Do not use unless you have a written agreement with the copyright holder.	Copyrighted clip art has limited legal use. Only fully licensed resellers may use copyrighted clip art. It is not appropriate for any personal or educational use.
Royalty-free — images provided at little or no cost by the owner	Carefully read the rights and usages. Trading post websites require the permission of the artist or photographer. Even legitimate images might contain spyware or viruses.	With written permission from the owner, royalty-free clip art and stock images normally can be used by anyone — even for commercial use such as on websites and business stationery — but without redistribution rights.
Rights-protected — images created and sold for a specific use	You must buy the right to use the image exclusively. You may not use the image for any use other than its intended purpose.	Written businesses contract with artists to design rights-protected logos and artwork. The seller promises not to sell that image to anyone else for that purpose.
Editorial rights — photos used in public interest	Some editorial-use images also are copyrighted. Read the agreement carefully.	Editorial-rights images are used with written permission for news, sports, entertainment, and other public purposes with appropriate citation. These images are usually less restrictive and less expensive than rights-protected images.

In this chapter, you will create your own clip art — clip art that has no legal restrictions because you are designing it yourself. Artists, graphic design professionals, typographers, and casual users all use Photoshop to create specialized graphics such as clip art to avoid potential copyright problems.

To Create a New File

The following steps use a shortcut key to display the New dialog box and then set the attributes for a new image. You will create the ticket in RGB mode to be able to use all of the features and 3D tools in Photoshop.

1 Press CTRL+N to display the New dialog box.

2 Type **Racing Ticket** in the Name box to name the graphic.

3 Tap or click the Width unit button, and then tap or click Inches in the list, if necessary.

4 Set the Width to 6 inches and the Height to 2 inches.

5 Set the Resolution to 300 Pixels/Inch.

6 Set the Color Mode to RGB Color, 8 bit.

7 Set the Background Contents to Transparent (Figure 8–2).

8 Tap or click the OK button to create the document.

9 Press CTRL+0 (ZERO) to maximize the canvas.

10 On the Layers panel, double-tap or double-click the name of the layer, Layer 1.
    Type **Background** and then press the ENTER key to rename the layer.

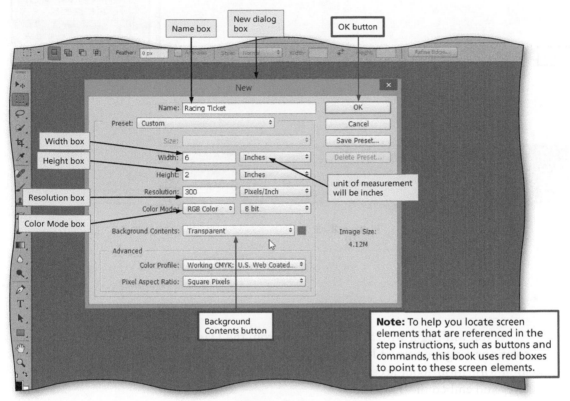

Figure 8–2

To Set Background Color

The following steps fill the background with an almond color based on CMYK colors. Recall that the CMYK color mode is used for most commercial printing. You will convert the image to CMYK later in the chapter, before printing.

1 On the Color panel, tap or click the panel menu button and select CMYK sliders.

2 On the Colors panel, enter 0 in the C box, 2 in the M box, 20 in the Y box, and 5 in the K box to choose an almond color.

3 On the Tools panel, select the 'Paint Bucket Tool'.

4 Tap or click the canvas to fill the background with almond (Figure 8–3 on the next page).

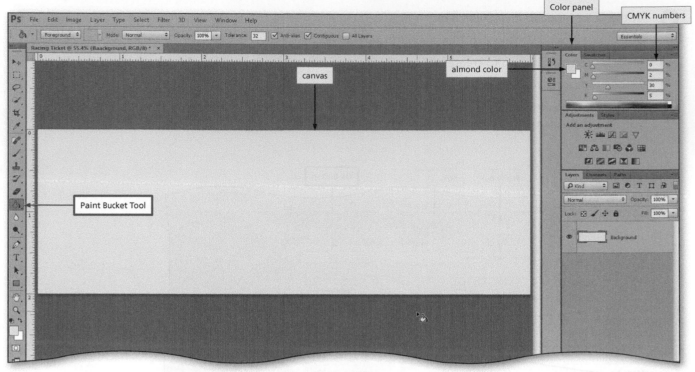

Figure 8–3

To Embed the Tire Graphic

You will begin with a photo of a tire from the Data Files for Students. Visit solutions.cengage.com/ctdownloads for detailed instructions or contact your instructor for information about accessing the required files. The following steps create a new layer and embed the Tire file.

1. Press SHIFT+CTRL+N to display the New Layer dialog box. Name the layer, tire, and choose a yellow identification color.

2. On the File menu, tap or click Place Embedded.

3. Navigate to the Photoshop Data Files for Students and the Chapter 08 folder.

4. Double-tap or double-click the Tire file to embed it on the new layer.

5. On the options bar, type 2 in both the W and H boxes.

6. In the document window, move the tire graphic to the lower-left corner of the canvas, as shown in Figure 8–4.

7. On the options bar, tap or click the 'Commit transform (Enter)' button to complete the transformation.

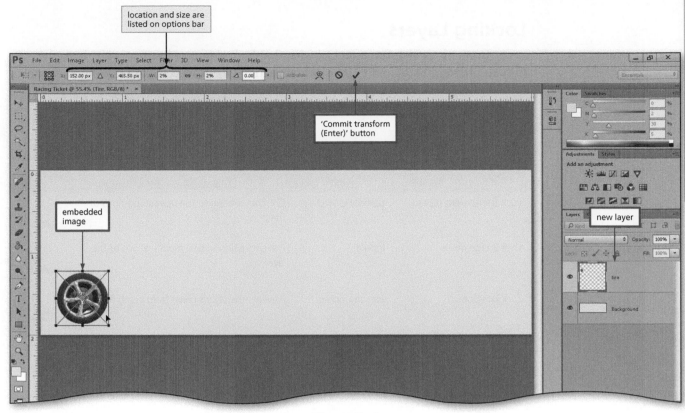

Figure 8–4

To Create a New Group from Layers

The following steps create a new group from the tire layer. Recall that creating a group from a layer or layers, automatically places those layers in the layer group.

1 Tap or click Layer on the Application bar, tap or click New on the Layer menu, and then tap or click 'Group from Layers' to display the New Group from Layers dialog box.

2 Name the new group, Tire Graphic, and choose a yellow identification color.

3 Tap or click the OK button to create the group (Figure 8–5).

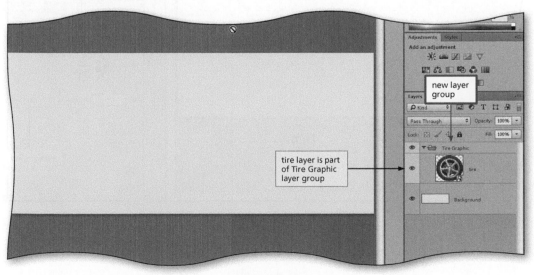

Figure 8–5

Locking Layers

In previous chapters, you locked and unlocked layers. Layers can be locked fully to prevent further editing or locked partially to allow certain functions without disturbing other effects and settings. Table 8–2 displays information about the four locking buttons on the Layers panel.

Table 8–2 Locking Buttons			
Name of Lock	**Type of Lock**	**Description**	**Button**
Lock transparent pixels	partially locked	Confines editing to the opaque portions of the layer	
Lock image pixels	locked	Prevents painting tool modifications of the layer	
Lock position	partially locked	Prevents the layer's pixels from being moved	
Lock all	locked	Locks transparent pixels, image pixels, and position	

To Lock Layers

The following steps use the Lock all button to lock the background fully, and use the Lock position button to partially lock the tire layer. Partially locking the tire layer will protect it from accidental editing or movement.

- On the Layers panel, select the Background layer.

- Tap or click the Lock all button to lock the layer and to display the solid lock icon (Figure 8–6).

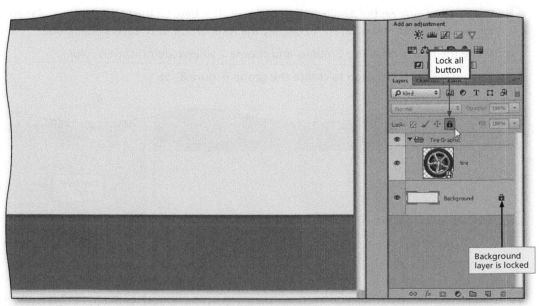

Figure 8–6

Q&A

When should I lock a layer?
You might want to lock a layer fully when you finish working with it. You might want to lock a layer partially if it has the correct transparency and styles, but you still are deciding on the layer's position.

2
- Select the tire layer.
- Tap or click the Lock position button to lock the layer partially and to display a hollow lock icon (Figure 8–7).

Figure 8–7

To Save the File in the PSD Format

The following steps save the file in the PSD format for maximum editing flexibility.

1 Tap or click File on the Application bar to display the File menu and then tap or click Save As to display the Save As dialog box.

2 Navigate to your storage location (or the Creative Cloud Files location) by using the Navigation pane or the Previous Locations box arrow to select that drive as the new save location.

3 Tap or click the New folder button on the Save As dialog box toolbar to create a new folder on the selected storage device.

4 When the new folder appears, type **Chapter 08** to change the name of the folder, and then press the ENTER key. Double-tap or double-click the new folder to open it.

5 If necessary, tap or click the 'Save as type' button to display the list of available file formats, and then tap or click Photoshop (*.PSD;*.PDD) in the list to select the file type.

6 Tap or click the Save button to save the document on the selected drive, in the new folder, and with the new file name.

BTW

Quick Reference
For a table that lists how to complete the tasks covered in this book using touch gestures, Application bar menus, shortcut menu, and keyboard, see the Quick Reference Summary at the back of this book, or visit the Quick Reference resource on the Student Companion Site located on www.cengagebrain.com.

Vector Graphics

Vector and bitmap are the two image file types available in Photoshop. As you have learned, vectors — also called vector graphics — are made up of shapes, lines, and curves that are defined by mathematical objects, or vectors. **Vector graphics** are high-quality graphics used in illustrations, typography, logos, and advertisements. Vector graphics retain their crisp edges when resized, moved, or recolored because they are made up of individual, scalable lines and objects rather than bitmapped pixels. Therefore, vector graphics are not directly editable at the pixel level. You can change a vector graphic, but not in the same way as you change a non-vector graphic. When you edit a vector graphic, you change its attributes such as color, fill, and outline. For example, if you create a circle as a shape layer, the vector graphic is generated using the current color scheme and style displayed on the options bar. You cannot edit a vector graphic with brush or eraser tools, nor can you fill it with color using the Paint Bucket Tool. If you change your mind about the color, for instance, you must select the shape layer and then change the color using the options bar. Changing the attributes of a vector object does not affect the object itself; it merely applies the change as it manipulates the layer along a path. In a previous chapter, you used the Shape layers button on the Shape options bar to create a vector graphic automatically. You might have seen or used vector graphics as clip art in page layout and word processing apps.

Because vector graphics are drawn, rather than compiled from pixels, they are more difficult to edit. If you want to edit the pixels, you must convert a vector graphic to a flat raster image, in a process called **rasterizing**. When you rasterize, you might need to set the pixel dimensions, color mode, anti-aliasing, dithering, and resolution. The disadvantage of rasterizing is that the image becomes resolution dependent, making it difficult to resize without sacrificing a degree of image quality. While raster images are scaled successfully in page layout apps, a permanent change in size is harder to interpolate.

The other graphic file type is a bitmap image, also called a raster image. **Raster images** are made up of pixels of color and are resolution dependent; thus, they are appropriate for photographs and artwork with continuous color, such as paintings. Images from scanners and digital cameras are raster images because they need to use continuous color to form the image.

Plan Ahead

> **Use vector graphics for clip art.**
> Begin with a good photo of the subject to use as a pattern. Study the shapes, angles, lines, and lighting. Because composition is such an important factor in clip art, consider using the photo as your outline to create the vector graphic or vector art. As you use paths to draw the vectors, experiment with different colors for each part of the vector graphic to differentiate it. Create each shape before adding detail.
>
> By creating an original piece of vector art, you can express exactly what you or your client wants to convey through an image.

The Pen Tools

Although you can use any of Photoshop's shape tools to create vector graphics, the most versatile are the Pen Tool and the Freeform Pen Tool. Both tools create shapes by drawing. The Pen Tool uses lines and curves; the Freeform Pen Tool allows you draw in a freehand fashion. Whereas the Shape Tool creates predetermined shapes, the pen tools allow you to tap, click, and drag to create unusual shapes.

The pen tools are different from selection tools in that they create a path or shape rather than a selection. A **path** is an outline that you can use later for things such as shapes, selections, fills, or strokes. A path is different from a regular selection, in that it uses vector graphic qualities while still being adjustable.

As you use the Pen Tool, each tap or click in the document window becomes an **anchor point**, also called a handle or node. An anchor point is displayed as a small square. The current or latest anchor point is always a solid square, indicating that it is selected. Non-selected anchor points are displayed as hollow squares and are used to alter the shape and angle of lines at adjacent segments along the path.

When you are finished with the Pen Tool, you have two choices: create an open path or a closed path. You can CTRL+click to create an open path. The ends of an **open path** do not connect, thus creating a **path line** or curve, rather than a polygon or ellipse. Open paths can be used to create outlines or color strokes, or they can be used to place text such as words that appear contoured along a curve. If you finish a path by joining the ends, it is called a **closed path** and creates a two-dimensional shape on the canvas. When

BTW

Path Lines
Not all paths have to be two-dimensional shapes; a path can be as simple as a line. To create a straight line path, you tap or click the document window using the Pen Tool, creating an anchor point. When you tap or click again, a second anchor point is displayed and a path line connects the two in the document window.

your pointer gets close to the first anchor point, a small circle is displayed next to the tip of the pointer. Tapping or clicking then connects the anchor points and closes the path.

Table 8–3 displays some of the possible tasks when creating path lines.

Table 8–3 Creating Path Lines		
Task	**Steps**	**Result**
Create a straight line path.	Tap or click a beginning point. Tap or click an ending point.	
Add an anchor point.	Tap or click along a path.	
Delete an existing anchor point.	If the Auto Add/Delete option is selected on the options bar, you can tap or click an existing point to delete it.	
Create an arc or curve.	Tap or click to create a first anchor point. Drag a second anchor point in the opposite direction.	
Create an S curve.	Drag a first anchor point down. Drag a second anchor point in the same direction.	
Create a polygon.	Click at least three times to create anchor points, and then tap or click the original anchor point again.	
Create an ellipse.	Create a line. Drag the beginning point. Drag the ending point in the opposite direction. Tap or click the beginning point.	
Simple Drag	Creates an anchor point and two direction lines with end point diamonds.	

When you drag, rather than tap or click, the Pen Tool creates an anchor point and two direction lines with **end point** diamonds (Figure 8–8). This process allows you to create curves and bumps. As you drag, the direction lines move outward; the direction of the drag determines the eventual direction of the curve. For instance, if you drag to the right, the bump of the curve will be to the right. The length of the drag

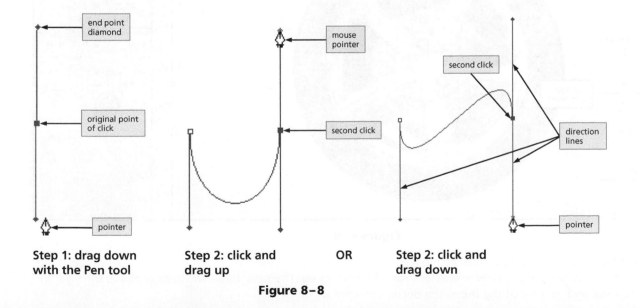

Step 1: drag down with the Pen tool   **Step 2: click and drag up**   **OR**   **Step 2: click and drag down**

Figure 8–8

determines how much influence the anchor point will have over the curve — the longer the drag, the more exaggerated the curve. To create the other end of the curved line, simply tap or click the desired end point diamond and drag again. Dragging the end point in the opposite direction creates an arc; dragging in the same direction creates an S curve. Once the curve is completed, the direction lines no longer appear; the curve is the only thing that is displayed in the document window.

Shape Layers

The Pen Tool's **Shape mode** allows you to create a **shape layer** or **vector shape**. The Shape mode displays an option bar similar to the Shape Tool option bar — the difference is that you do not have to use a predefined shape. You can draw the shape yourself. The new vector shape is filled with the color visible on the options bar. Because they are easily moved, aligned, resized, and distributed, shape layers are ideal for making graphics for clip art and for webpages.

To Use the Pen Tool in Shape Mode

The following steps create a closed path with the Pen Tool to highlight in yellow the areas between the hubcap spokes. Each path will become a shape layer on the Layers panel.

1

- On the Layers panel, select the tire layer if necessary.

- In the document window, zoom in on the tire.

- Tap or click the Swatches panel tab to display the Swatches panel, and then tap or click CMYK Yellow to change the foreground color.

- On the Tools panel, press and hold or right-click the current pen tool button to display the context menu (Figure 8–9).

Figure 8–9

Q&A

If I locked that layer earlier, why am I selecting it?

Remember that layers—and paths—are created from the bottom up. The new shape will appear above the layer in the Layers panel and in front of the tire in the document window.

2

- Tap or click Pen Tool to select it.

- On the options bar, tap or click the 'Pick Tool Mode' button to display the Pen Tool modes (Figure 8–10).

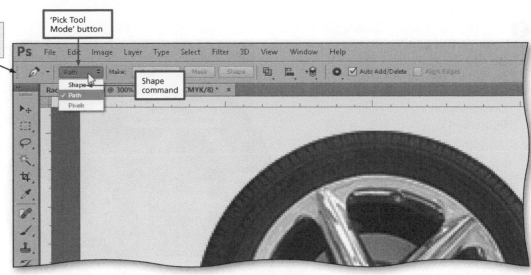

Figure 8–10

3

- Tap or click Shape in the list.

- If necessary, tap or click the Stroke box to display the pop-up panel and then tap or click the No Color button to create a shape layer with no stroke.

- In the document window, tap or click the edge of one of the hubcap spokes, as shown in Figure 8–11 to display the first anchor point.

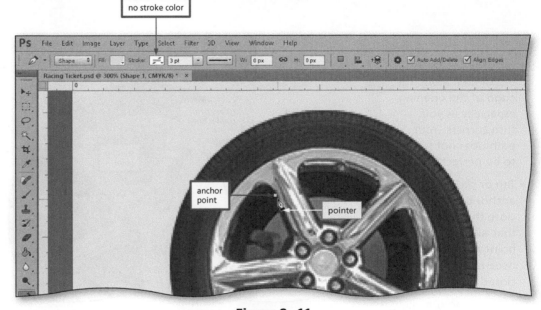

Figure 8–11

4

- Move the pointer along the edge of the spoke. Tap or click again to display the second anchor point and the path line (Figure 8–12).

Q&A How can I tell which anchor point is selected?
The first anchor is displayed hollow and the second one is a solid square, indicating that the second anchor point is selected or current.

Figure 8–12

5

● Tap or click to add a third anchor point along the opening between the hubcap spokes (Figure 8–13).

Q&A Why did a yellow shape appear?
When you create more than two anchor points, Photoshop begins to fill the shape layer with the selected color.

path begins to fill with foreground color

third anchor point

Figure 8–13

6

● Moving clockwise, tap or click along the edge of the opening, especially as you turn corners. Your path does not have to be perfect.

● Tap or click the first anchor point to close the path. Note that all the anchor point are now solid because the path is closed (Figure 8–14).

Q&A What if I do not like the path or parts of it are wrong?
You can back up through your steps on the History panel or delete the path entirely and start again. Later in this chapter, you will learn how to adjust path anchor points by adding, deleting, converting, or moving them.

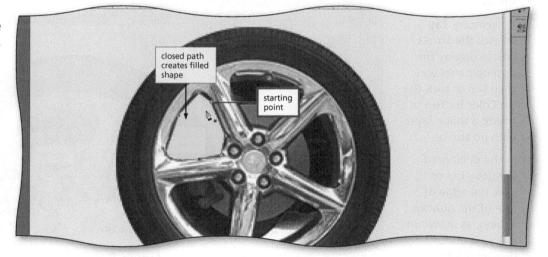

closed path creates filled shape

starting point

Figure 8–14

Other Ways

1. Press P or SHIFT+P, tap or click 'Pick Tool Mode' button on options bar, tap or click Shape, tap or click points in image

BTW | **Deleting Anchors**
Before you close a path, if you make a mistake, you can press the BACKSPACE key to delete the current anchor point.

BTW | **Viewing Anchor Points**
If you want to see a line while you create new anchor points, you can tap or click the Geometry options button on the options bar (Figure 8–15). One of the geometry options for the Pen Tool is a Rubber Band check box. The Rubber Band feature will help you guide your next anchor point by displaying a stretch line between anchor points, even before you click.

To Add Anchor Points to a Shape

For precise adjustments along path segments, you sometimes need to insert additional anchor points. Photoshop creates direction lines automatically with each added anchor point to give you more flexibility in editing. The following steps add anchor points using the 'Add Anchor Point' Tool.

- On the Tools panel, press and hold or right-click the Pen Tool button to display the context menu (Figure 8–15).

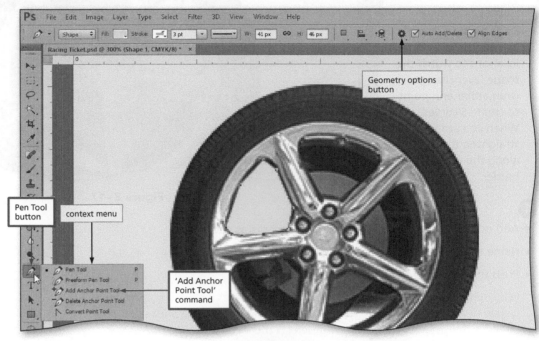

Figure 8–15

- Tap or click 'Add Anchor Point Tool' in the list.

- In the document window, locate an area of yellow that could be improved by adjusting the path.

- Zoom as necessary to tap or click the edge of the yellow to add an anchor point (Figure 8–16).

Q&A Why did the pointer display a plus sign? The pointer displays a plus sign (+) next to the tip of the pen when you add anchor points.

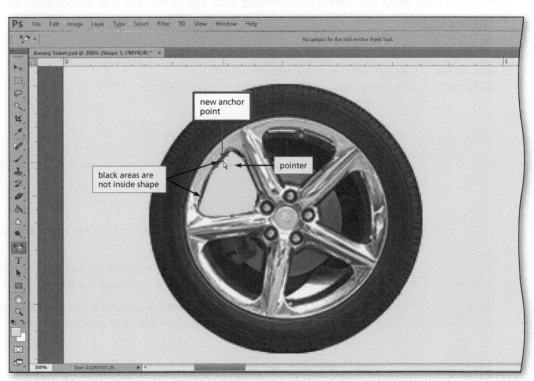

Figure 8–16

* Drag the newly created anchor point until the edge aligns with the hubcap, as shown in Figure 8–17.

 Experiment

* Drag the new anchor point to different locations to watch the shape layer change. Drag either end point to create S curves. When you are finished, straighten the line along the original border.

anchor point moved to edge

Figure 8–17

❹

* Add other anchor points and make adjustments as necessary.
* Name the new layer, yellow insert 1 on the Layers panel.
* Press the ENTER key to commit the shape.

Q&A | Why do I need to press the ENTER key?
Unless you choose a different tool or create a new layer, the path stays active or selected. Pressing the ENTER key commits or deselects the shape.

 **Experiment**

* Add another anchor point. On the Tools panel, press and hold or right-click the Pen Tool button and then select the 'Delete Anchor Point' Tool. Tap or click the new anchor point to delete it. Deselect.

Other Ways

1. Press and hold or right-click path, tap or click 'Add Anchor Point'
2. On Pen Tool options bar, tap or click Auto Add/Delete check box, tap or click path

To Create More Shape Layers

The following steps create four more shape layers to fill the other open spots in the hubcap.

❶ Select the Pen Tool.

❷ Tap or click to create an anchor point in the next open area of the hubcap, at the edge of the spoke.

❸ Continue to tap or click along the edge of the opening. When you get back to the original anchor point, tap or click it to close the path.

❹ Select the Add Anchor Point tool and make adjustments as necessary. Remember to tap or click first, before trying to drag the new anchor point.

⑤ Name the new layer `yellow insert 2` on the Layers panel.

⑥ Press the ENTER key to commit the shape.

⑦ Repeat Steps 1 through 6 to create shapes to cover the other open areas of the hubcap (Figure 8–18).

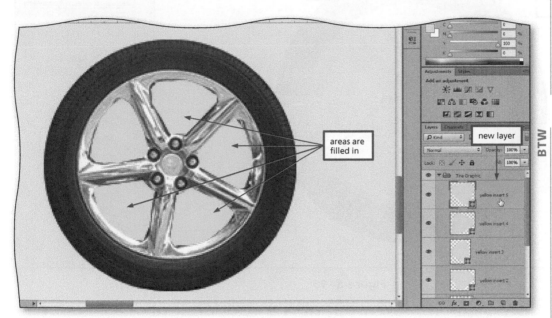

areas are filled in

new layer

Figure 8–18

To Change to the Default Colors

The following step resets the colors.

① Press the D key to choose the default colors.

To Use the Freeform Pen Tool

The next step in creating a clip art version of the tire is to color the tire itself. The following steps use the Freeform Pen Tool to create a black rim on the tire.

①

- On the Layers panel, select the tire layer.
- Press and hold or right-click the current pen tool and then tap or click 'Freeform Pen Tool' on the context menu to select it.
- On the options bar, tap or click to select the Magnetic check box.
- Tap or click the edge of the tire and then begin to drag around the outside of the tire (Figure 8–19 on the next page).

 Will the new shape cover the other shapes?
No. By selecting the tire layer, the new shape will appear in front of the tire, but behind the other shapes.

Figure 8–19

Q&A What does the Magnetic setting do?

Like the Magnetic Lasso Tool, the Magnetic setting on the Freeform Pen Tool options bar creates an attraction for anchor points. The pointer displays a horseshoe magnet shape.

2

- Slowly finish dragging around the outside edge of the tire. When you return to the starting point, tap or click it to close the path and fill the shape with black (Figure 8–20).

Q&A How can I tell when I return to the starting point?

Like the lasso tools, when you get close to the starting point, the pointer will display a small circle.

3

- On the Layers panel, rename the new shape layer tire rim.

- Hide the original tire layer.

Figure 8–20

TO CONVERT TO CORNER POINT

When you convert anchor points to corner points, the direction line extends in a single direction on one side only of the anchor point. If you wanted to convert an anchor point to a corner point, you would perform the following steps.

1. Tap or click the current pen tool button on the Tools panel to display the context menu.

2. Tap or click 'Convert Point Tool' to select it.

3. On the canvas, tap or click a previously created anchor point to convert it to a corner point.

4. Drag the anchor point to create a single-sided direction line.

TO DELETE AN ANCHOR POINT

If you wanted to delete an anchor point to a corner point, you would perform the following steps.

1. Tap or click the current Pen Tool button on the options bar to display the context menu.

2. Tap or click 'Delete Anchor Point Tool' to select it.

3. On the canvas, tap or click a previously created anchor point to delete it.

Path Mode

The Pen Tool's Path mode creates a line or path. In Path mode, you can create anchor points, drag direction lines, and drag end points. The Path mode options bar (Figure 8–21) contains buttons to convert the path into selections, masks, and shapes, as well as buttons for placement, alignment, and stacking order of multiple shapes and paths.

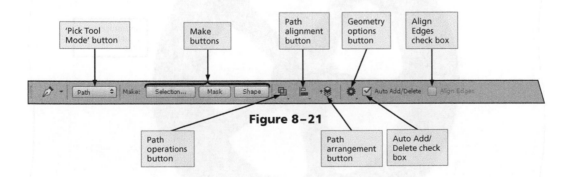

Figure 8–21

To Use the Pen Tool in Path Mode

Earlier you learned that anchor points contain a direction line that extends in opposite directions out from the anchor point. The direction line contains a direction point on either end, as well as the center anchor point itself. Dragging a direction point alters the length and angle of the direction line, which in turn changes the shape of the path. The steps on the next page use the Pen Tool in Path mode, to create a curved path in preparation for adding detail to the clip art.

1

- Press SHIFT+CTRL+N to create a new layer and name it gray stripe.

- Select the Pen Tool.

- On the options bar, tap or click the 'Pick Tool Mode' button and then tap or click Path to use the Path mode.

- Tap or click to create an anchor in the upper-left corner of the tire rim, as shown in Figure 8–22.

Figure 8–22

2

- Position the pointer on the right side of the tire rim, and then drag a direction line down and slightly right to create a curved path. Adjust the position of the pointer as necessary to keep the path on the tire (Figure 8–23).

Q&A Why is there no display on the Layers panel?
There is no display because you are creating a path — not a shape. As you will learn later in the chapter, Paths appear on the Paths panel.

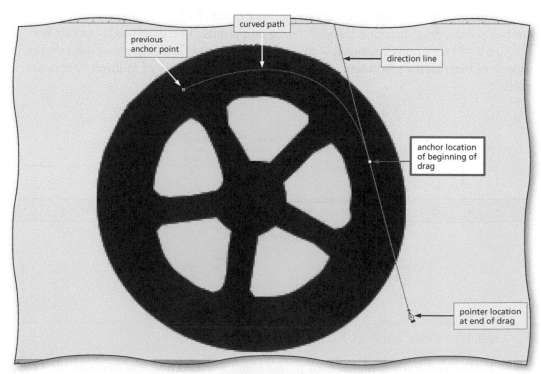

Figure 8–23

To Stroke a Path

Stroking a path is similar to stroking a selection or text — you are adding color to the edges. When you stroke a path, you need to choose your color and brush before applying it to the path. The following steps stroke the path with a gray color and a soft round brush.

1

- On the Swatches panel, tap or click 70% Gray to choose a gray foreground color.

- Select the Brush Tool.

- Press and hold or right-click the canvas to display the Brush Preset picker's pop-up panel.

- Tap or click the Soft Round brush preset or a similar preset with a size of approximately 13 px (Figure 8–24).

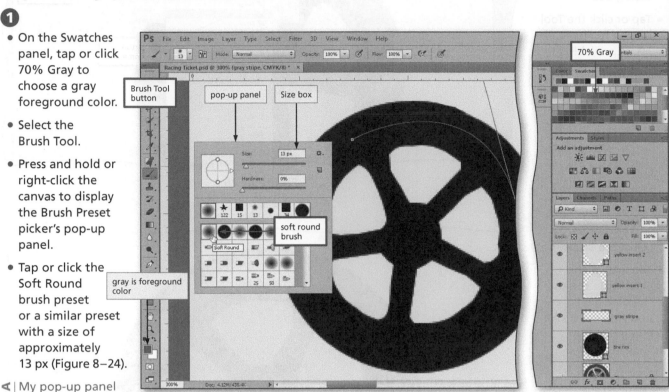

Q&A My pop-up panel displays different brushes. Did I do something wrong?
No. Each user will have a different brushes in the recently used brushes bar.

Figure 8–24

2

- Select the Pen Tool.

- Press and hold or right-click the curved path to display the context menu (Figure 8–25).

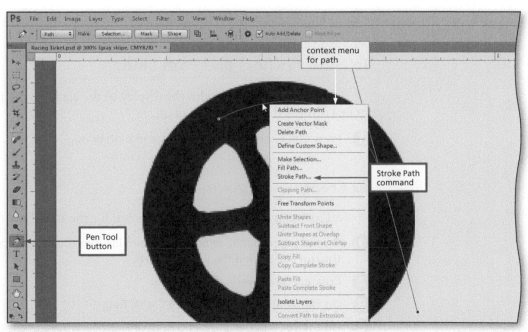

Figure 8–25

3

- Tap or click Stroke Path to display the Stroke Path dialog box.

- Tap or click the Tool button to display the list of available tools (Figure 8–26).

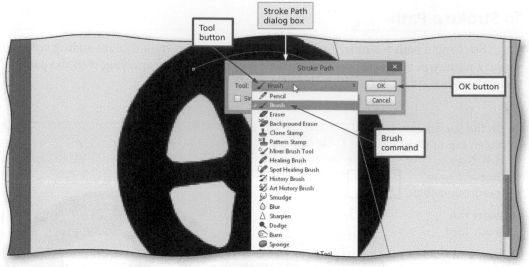

Figure 8–26

4

- Tap or click Brush to select the Brush Tool.

- Tap or click the OK button to close the dialog box, applying the stroke (Figure 8–27).

Q&A Is the stroke a shape layer?
No. The stroke was created by the Brush tool, so it appears on the Layers panel as a painted area, not a shape or smart object.

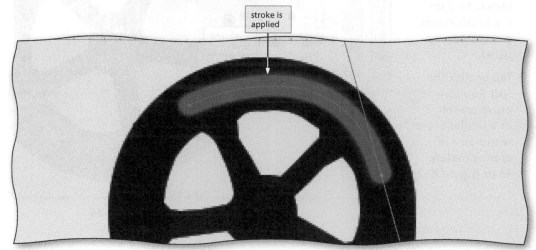

Figure 8–27

Other Ways

1. On Paths panel status bar, tap or click 'Stroke path with brush' button

To Hide Anchors and Path Lines

The following step hides the display of the anchors and path lines. Pressing CTRL+H turns the display on and off.

1 Press CTRL+H to hide the anchors and path lines.

To Create the Spokes

The following steps create red spokes for the tire clip art.

1 On the Layers panel, select the tire rim layer so the new shape will appear in front of the rim but behind the yellow inserts.

2 Create a new layer named spokes.

3 On the Swatches panel, choose CMYK Red.

4 On the Tools panel, press and hold or right-click the current shape tool and then tap or click Ellipse Tool on the context menu to select it.

5 SHIFT+drag a circle around the yellow shapes to create red spokes as shown in Figure 8–28. If you need to reposition as you are drawing, press the space bar, and continue dragging.

Figure 8–28

To Insert the Text

The final steps to complete the tire graphic insert the seat number text.

1 On the Layers panel, select the top layer in the Tire Graphic group, so the text will appear in front of the tire on the canvas.

2 Set the default colors to black over white.

3 Select the Horizontal Type Tool.

4 On the options bar, select the 'Segoe UI Bold' font or a similar font. Set the font size to 14. Set the anti-aliasing to Crisp. Tap or click the 'Left align text' button.

5 In the document window, drag a text box over the center of the tire. Type `13A` to enter the text (Figure 8–29).

6 On the options bar, tap or click the 'Commit any current edits' button to finish the text.

Figure 8–29

To Save the File

The tire clip art is complete. The following step saves the file.

❶ Press SHIFT+S to save the file with the same name in the same location.

Break Point: If you wish to take a break, this is a good place to do so. Press CTRL+Q to quit Photoshop. To resume at a later time, start Photoshop, open the file named Racing Ticket, and continue following the steps from this location forward.

Creating the Flame Shape

The next portion of the ticket that you will create is the flame. First, you will embed a flame image, and then you will use the image to create a shape layer to appear in the background. Repeating the outline of the flame will add consistency and a professional look to the ticket.

To Embed the Flame Image

The following steps embed the Flame image.

❶ Press CTRL+0 (ZERO) to zoom out and display the entire ticket.

❷ On the Layers panel, tap or click the Tire Graphic group arrow to collapse the group. Select the Background layer.

❸ Press SHIFT+CTRL+N to display the New Layer dialog box. Name the layer **flame** and choose a red identification color.

❹ On the File menu, tap or click Place Embedded. Navigate to the Photoshop Data Files for Students and the Chapter 08 folder. Double-tap or double-click the Flame file to embed it on the new layer.

❺ On the options bar, enter **35** in both the W and H boxes. Enter **15** in the Set Rotation box (Figure 8-30).

❻ Move the image to the lower-left corner of the canvas so that the tire is approximately centered within the flame. Tap or click the 'Commit transform (Enter)' button.

Figure 8–30

To Manage Layers

The following steps create a new group from the flame layer and hide the Tire Group layer.

1 With the flame layer selected, tap or Layer on the Application bar, tap or click New on the Layer menu, and then tap or click 'Group from Layers' to display the New Group from Layers dialog box.

2 Name the new group, Flame Graphic, with a red identification color.

3 Tap or click the OK button to create the group.

4 Hide the Tire Graphic group.

5 In the document window, zoom in on the flame (Figure 8–31).

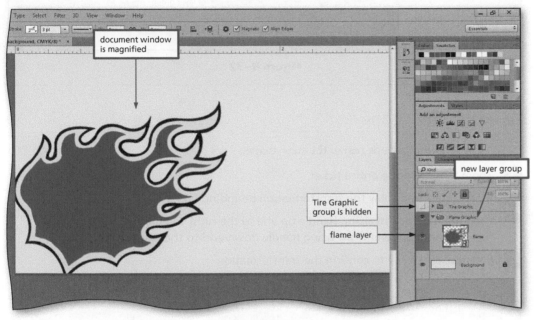

Figure 8–31

To Create Another Shape Layer

The following steps use the flame as a pattern to create a background.

1 On the Swatches panel, tap or click Pastel Yellow Orange to select the color. On the Layers panel, select the Background layer.

2 Press and hold or right-click the current pen tool and then tap or click 'Freeform Pen Tool' on the context menu to select it.

3 On the options bar, tap or click the 'Pick tool mode' button and then tap or click Shape, if necessary. Tap or click to select the Magnetic check box, if necessary.

4 Slowly drag around the outside of the flame image. When you return to the starting point, tap or click it to close the path.

5 Rename the new shape layer, flame background.

6 Press CTRL+RIGHT BRACE [}] to move the layer up into the Flame Graphic group (Figure 8–32 on the next page).

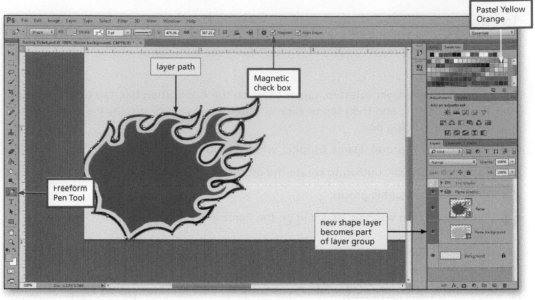

Figure 8–32

To Resize the Shape

The following steps resize the new shape.

1 Zoom to display the entire ticket.

2 Press CTRL+T to display the transformation bounding box.

3 Drag the upper-right sizing handle up and to the right to enlarge the background flame. Drag the lower-right sizing handle down and to the right (Figure 8–33).

4 Press the ENTER key to confirm the transformation.

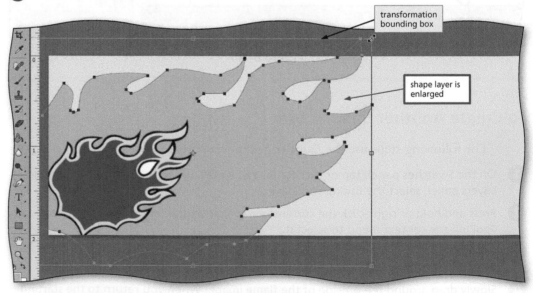

Figure 8–33

The Paths Panel

When you use the Path mode on the Pen Tool option bar, the path does not create a shape layer on the Layers panel; instead, it becomes a path or work path on the Paths panel. The Paths panel (Figure 8–34) lists the name and displays a thumbnail image of each saved path, the current work path, and any current vector mask. Once created,

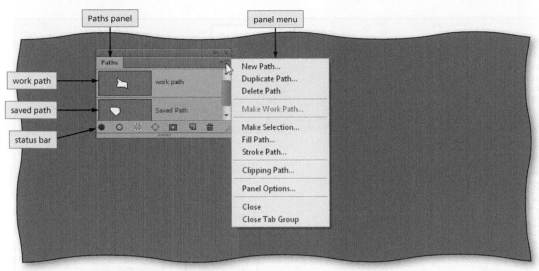

Figure 8–34

you can use a path to make a selection, create a vector mask, or fill and stroke with color to create raster graphics. A **work path** is a temporary path that opens in the Paths panel and defines the outline of the shape until you save or rename it. If you need to create a complex shape, you can begin by creating multiple paths and then combine them into a single shape. Many people use the Paths panel to save selections. For example, you might spend a lot of time carefully selecting a tedious portion of your image. If you are called away to another task and have to quit Photoshop, the selection is lost. Creating a path allows you to save the area so you can reselect it later.

To Embed the Wrench Graphic

A second piece of clip art will display a wrench, created using the Paths panel. First, you will embed a photo of a wrench to use as a pattern from the Data Files for Students. Visit solutions.cengage.com/ctdownloads for detailed instructions or contact your instructor for information about accessing the required files. The following steps create a new layer and embed the Wrench file.

1 Change back to the default colors.

2 On the Layers panel, tap or click the arrow next to the Flame Graphic group layer to collapse it.

3 Tap or click the Tire Graphic group so the embedded graphic will appear above it on the Layers panel. Make the Tire Graphic group visible.

4 Press SHIFT+CTRL+N to display the New Layer dialog box. Name the layer `wrench` and choose an orange identification color.

5 On the File menu, tap or click Place Embedded.

6 Navigate to the Photoshop Data Files for Students and the Chapter 08 folder.

7 Double-tap or double-click the Wrench file to embed it on the new layer.

8 Rename the layer, wrench.

9 Resize the wrench down to 30% and move it to the location shown in Figure 8–35 on the next page.

10 Tap or click the 'Commit transform (Enter)' button to place the file.

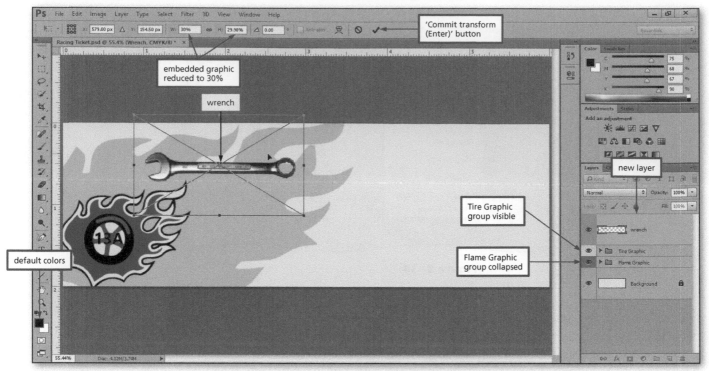

Figure 8–35

To Create a Work Path using the Pen Tool

You will use the Pen Tool to create two paths — one for the wrench and one for the aperture or space inside the handle. You will then combine the two paths into a single shape using the Paths panel. The following steps create a work path around the wrench using the Pen Tool.

1

- If necessary, select the wrench layer and zoom to approximately 170% so the wrench fills the screen.

- Select the Pen Tool.

- On the options bar, tap or click the 'Pick tool mode' button and then tap or click Path to select the mode that creates a path on the Paths panel.

- Tap or click the top of the wrench handle, on the left, to create the first anchor point.

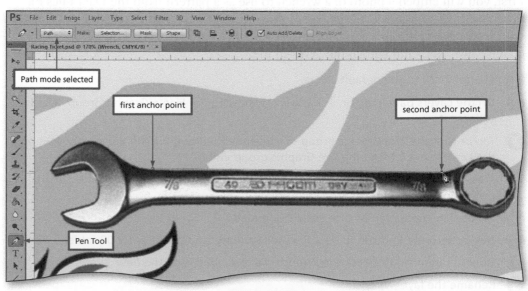

Figure 8–36

- Tap or click the top of the wrench handle, on the right, to create a second anchor point (Figure 8–36).

2

- Tap or click again at a location where the edge of the wrench handle begins to go up, creating a third anchor point.

- Position the pointer on the right side of the wrench, and then drag slowly down to create a curve along the rim (Figure 8–37).

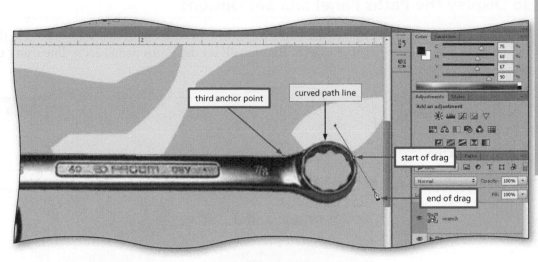

Figure 8–37

3

- ALT+tap or ALT+click the center anchor point of the direction line to convert it to a corner point (Figure 8–38).

Q&A What was the symbol attached to the pointer?

When you ALT+click you are actually changing to the Convert Point tool. The pointer changes to display a V-shape below the pen tip.

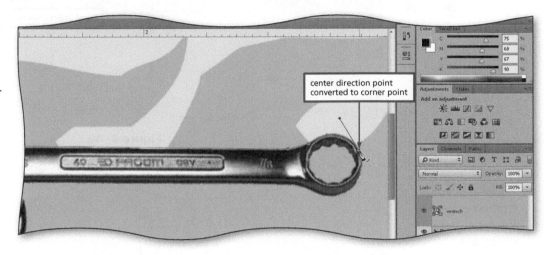

Figure 8–38

4

- Continue around the edge of the wrench. When the path is straight, tap or click. When the path is curved, slowly drag in the opposite direction to create a curved segment.

- When you get back to the beginning anchor point, tap or click it to close the path (Figure 8–39).

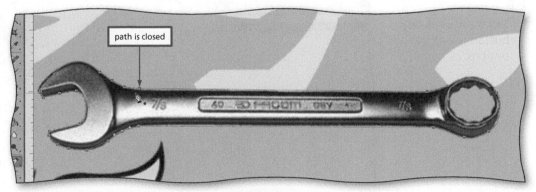

Figure 8–39

To Display the Paths Panel and Set Options

The following step displays the Paths panel and the work path that was created in the previous steps. Like the Layers panel, there are three sizes of thumbnails on the Paths panel, accessible using the panel menu.

- Tap or click the Paths panel tab to display the Paths panel.
- Tap or click the panel menu button to display the menu (Figure 8–40).

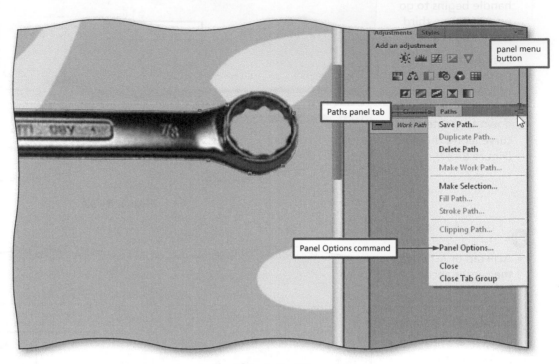

Figure 8–40

- Tap or click Panel Options to display the Panel Options dialog box.
- Tap or click the largest thumbnail (Figure 8–41).

- Tap or click the OK button to accept the options.

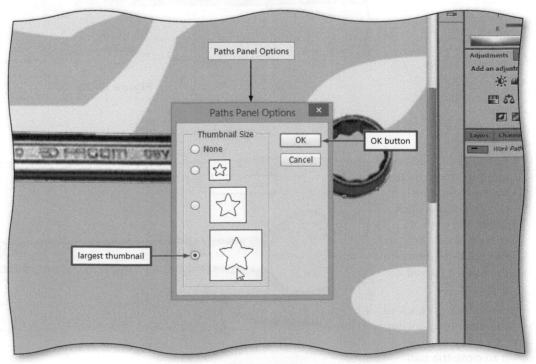

Figure 8–41

To Save a Work Path as a Named Path

Because work paths are temporary, the following steps save and name the path.

- On the Paths panel, double-tap or double-click the Work Path name to display the Save Path dialog box.

- In the Name box type **wrench outline** to assign the path name (Figure 8–42).

Q&A
Why should I rename the path?
Renaming a Work Path saves the path. If you did not rename the Work Path, it would disappear as soon as the path was deselected.

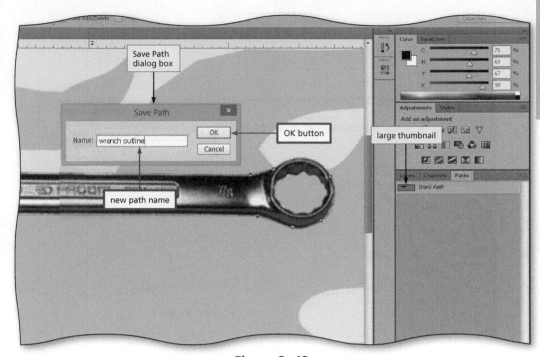

Figure 8–42

- Tap or click the OK button to close the dialog box.

- Tap or click the gray area of the Paths panel below the wrench outline path to deselect it.

Other Ways

1. On Paths panel menu, tap or click Save Path, enter name, deselect

To Create a New Work Path

The following step creates a new work path around the inside of the aperture on the right end of the wrench. You will use the magnetic option of the Freeform Pen Tool to draw around the inside of the handle.

- Select the Freeform Pen Tool.

- If necessary, tap or click the Magnetic check box on the options bar so that it displays a check mark.

- Tap or click inside the aperture along the edge, and then release the mouse button.

- Drag slowly around the inside of the aperture, keeping the point of the pen icon on the inside edge.

- When you return to the starting point, tap or click the first anchor point to close the path (Figure 8–43 on the next page).

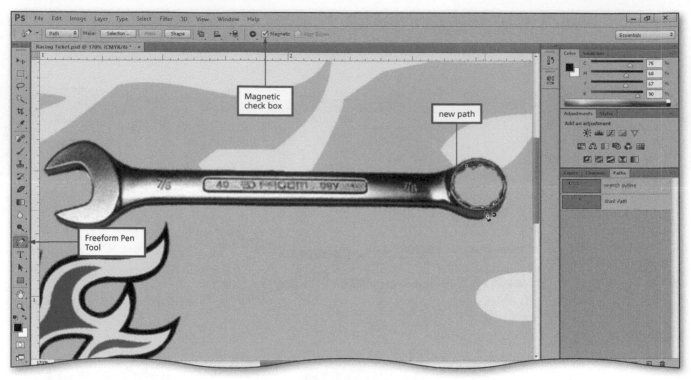

Figure 8–43

To Save the Second Path

The following step saves the work path.

1 On the Paths panel, double-tap or double-click the Work Path name, type `inside handle` to rename the path, and press the ENTER key to rename the path.

TO CREATE A SELECTION FROM A PATH

If you wanted to create a selection from a path, you would perform the following steps.

1. Open a file with a saved path.
2. Display the Paths panel.
3. Tap or click the 'Load path as a selection' button on the Paths panel status bar.

TO CREATE A PATH FROM A SELECTION

If you wanted to create a path from a selection, you would perform the following steps.

1. Use a selection tool to create a selection in the document window.
2. Display the Paths panel.
3. Tap or click the 'Make work path from selection' button on the Paths panel status bar.
4. Rename the work path and save the file.

The Path Selection and Direct Selection Tools

Two tools are particularly useful to edit the shape and placement of paths by moving lines and anchor points. The Path Selection Tool transforms a vector shape or an entire path. It also can be used to merge paths. The Direct Selection Tool moves a path segment — the line between two anchor points — or individual anchor points. The options bar for both tools is similar to the options bar on any of the shape tools. The only difference is the addition of a Select button where you can choose the active layer or all of the layers.

To Merge Paths

In the next steps, the paths are merged using the Path Selection Tool. Merging makes the wrench outline and the space inside the handle into a single shape, so that if you move the wrench, the space inside the handle moves too.

- On the Tools panel, tap or click the 'Path Selection Tool' to select it.

- In the document window, tap or click the outline of the path inside the aperture to select it. Adjust the magnification as necessary to select it (Figure 8–44).

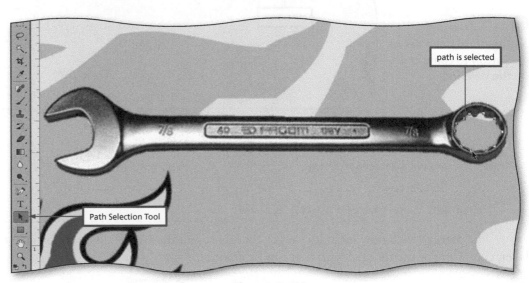

Figure 8–44

- Press CTRL+C to copy the path.

- On the Paths panel, tap or click the wrench outline path to select it.

- Press CTRL+V to paste the copied path onto the wrench outline path (Figure 8–45).

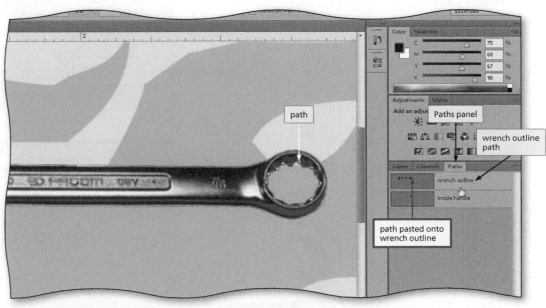

Figure 8–45

To Delete a Path

Because the two paths have been combined into a single path, the inside handle path no longer is needed. The following steps delete the inside handle path.

- Tap or click the 'inside handle path' on the Paths panel to select it.

- Tap or click the 'Delete current path' button on the Paths panel status bar to display a confirmation dialog box (Figure 8–46).

- Tap or click the Yes button to complete the deletion.

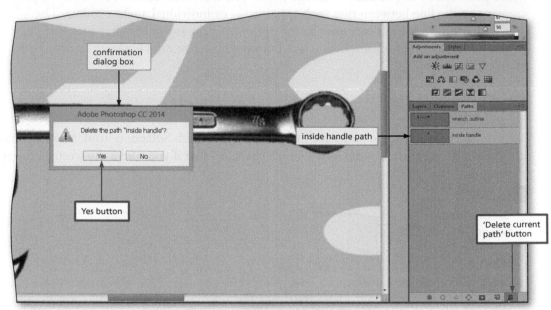

Figure 8–46

Other Ways

1. Select path on Paths panel, press DELETE key

To Create a Shape Layer from a Path

The merged path now includes shapes that represent the wrench. The following steps create a new shape layer, consisting of the merged path that can be colored.

1

- With the wrench outline path selected, tap or click Layer on the application bar, and then tap or click 'New Fill Layer' to display the fill choices (Figure 8–47).

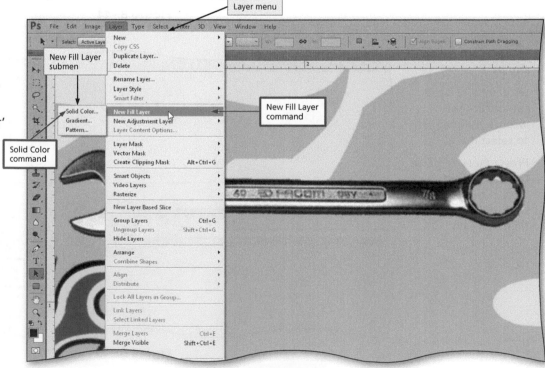

Figure 8–47

2

- Tap or click Solid Color to display the New Layer dialog box.

- In the Name box, type **wrench shape** to name the new shape layer. Choose an orange identification color (Figure 8–48).

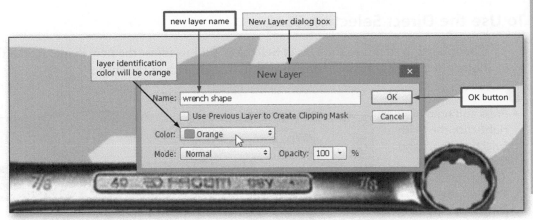

Figure 8–48

3

- Tap or click the OK button to display the Color Picker (Solid Color) dialog box.

- Move the eyedropper pointer into the document window, and tap or click the red color of the flame to select it (Figure 8–49).

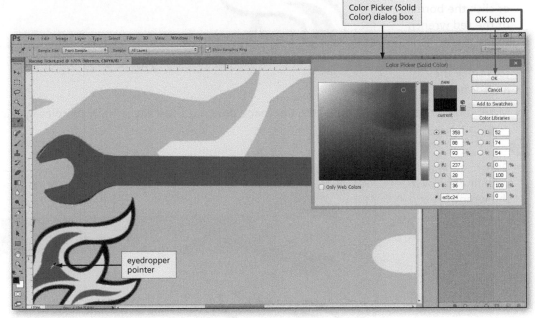

Figure 8–49

4

- Tap or click the OK button to close the Color Picker and set the color of the shape.

- Tap or click the Layers panel tab to display the layers (Figure 8–50).

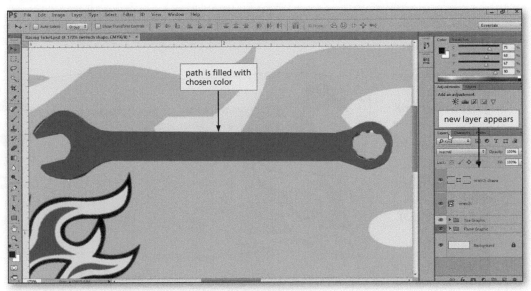

Figure 8–50

To Use the Direct Selection Tool

The following steps use the Direct Selection Tool to adjust the new shape. Recall that the Direct Selection Tool allows you edit any anchor point, direction line, or path in the shape.

 1

- Press and hold or right-click the 'Path Selection Tool', and then tap or click 'Direct Selection Tool' on the context menu to select it.

- If necessary, tap or click the border of the red wrench shape in the document window to display the anchor points.

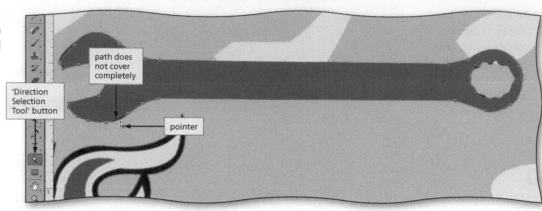

Figure 8–51

- Move the pointer to a location where the shape does not cover the wrench completely (Figure 8–51).

2

- Drag the shape's path line to cover the wrench (Figure 8–52).

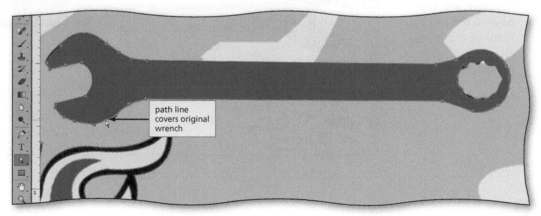

Figure 8–52

 3

- Drag any other path lines where the original wrench still appears.

- Press CTRL+H to hide the anchor paths.

- On the Layers panel, hide the wrench layer (Figure 8–53).

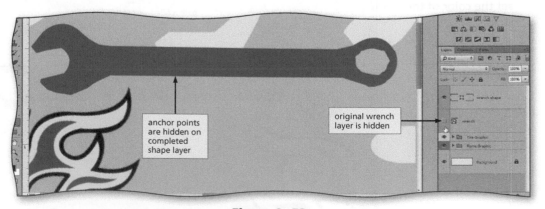

Figure 8–53

To Save the File Again

The following step saves the document.

1 Press CTRL+S to save the document.

Break Point: If you wish to take a break, this is a good place to do so. Press CTRL+Q to quit Photoshop. To resume at a later time, start Photoshop, open the file named Racing Ticket, and continue following the steps from this location forward.

Using 3D Tools

Photoshop CC includes 3D tools that previously were included only in the extended version of Photoshop CS6. The 3D tools allow you to design and print 3D objects. You have the ability to rotate, scale, drag, and move objects, while working with meshes, materials, textures, surfaces, or lights. In this chapter, you will use the 3D tools to create 3D clip art and 3D text. You will learn more about 3D Modeling in a future chapter.

BTW

System Requirements
To use the 3D Tools you must have at least 2 GB (gigabytes) of RAM and at least 512 MB (megabytes) of vRAM (video memory). You also should update the driver on your graphics card.

Plan Ahead

Create 3D objects to add depth and interest.
To add a sense of reality to a scene, consider converting a 2D image into a 3D object. Elements that are near each other in a scene should be formatted in a similar manner using the same angles, depth, and shadows. Do not be afraid to experiment as you edit the lighting, rotation, scaling, and perspective.

One of the easiest ways to work with 3D tools is to create a 3D object from a layer or path in a process called extrusion. **Extrusion** converts or extends a flat object into a 3D object with a cross-sectional profile. Extrusion creates a new layer on the Layers panel with a cube icon, and enables the 3D Mode buttons on the options bar. The 3D Mode buttons allow you to manipulate the object by dragging. Table 8–4 describes the 3D Mode buttons; the best way to learn their capabilities and see the effects is to experiment with them.

Table 8–4 3D Mode Buttons		
Function	**Description**	**Button**
Rotate	Drag up or down to rotate the object on its x-axis. Drag side to side to rotate it around its y-axis.	
Roll	Drag side to side to rotate the model around its z-axis or 3D axis.	
Drag or Pan	Drag up or down to move the object vertically. Drag side to side to move it horizontally.	
Slide or Move	Drag up or down to move the object closer or farther away. Drag side to side to move the object horizontally.	
Scale or Resize	Drag up or down to change the size of the object.	

3D objects and settings also are manipulated using the 3D panel. If you have not selected a 3D object on the Layers panel, the 3D panel displays tools to create one (Figure 8–54a). If you are working with a 3D object already, the panel displays tools to filter and adjust 3D settings (Figure 8–54b). Each setting on the 3D panel displays its own Properties panel with content-specific settings.

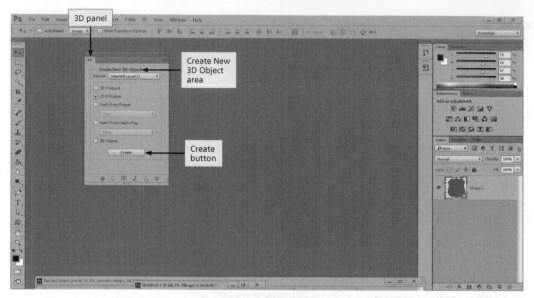

Figure 8–54a

a) **3D panel before creating object**

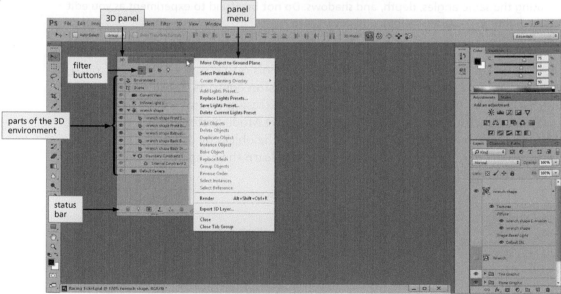

Figure 8–54b

b) **3D panel after creating object**

You can display the 3D panel by extruding an object from the 3D menu, by using the Window menu, or by accessing the 3D workspace. The top section of the panel (Figure 8–54b) has buttons to filter by scene, meshes, materials, and lights. Photoshop uses the term **scene** to indicate the environment or stage associated with the wide range of 3D tools and views. The bottom section of the panel is context sensitive, showing the settings and options for the 3D component selected at the top. Settings appear as layered states in the panel with grouping and visibility options.

In the following sections, you will convert the wrench shape into a 3D object, edit the lighting, and manipulate it. Then you will create 3D text for the title.

To Create a 3D Extrusion

The following steps display the 3D panel and then convert the wrench layer to a 3D object using extrusion.

1

- Zoom to display the entire ticket.

- On the Window menu, tap or click 3D to display the 3D panel.

- On the 3D panel, tap or click the 3D Extrusion option button to select it (Figure 8–55).

Q&A My 3D commands are grayed out. What should I do?

It is possible that your graphics processor is turned off. Save your file and close it. Press CTRL+K to display the Preferences dialog box, and then tap or click Performance. Place a check mark in the 'Use Graphics Processor' check box, and then tap or click the OK button. Restart Photoshop and open your file again. Select the wrench shape layer. The 3D menu commands should be enabled.

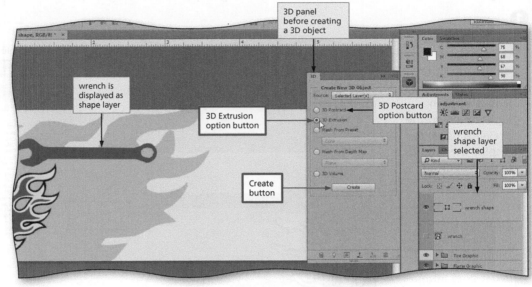

Figure 8–55

2

- Tap or click the Create button to extrude the layer.

- If Photoshop asks if you want to switch to the 3D workspace, tap or click the No button (Figure 8–56).

Q&A Why did the color change?

The default 3D lighting settings use darker shades for the foreground and lighter shades for shadows. You will adjust those in the next steps.

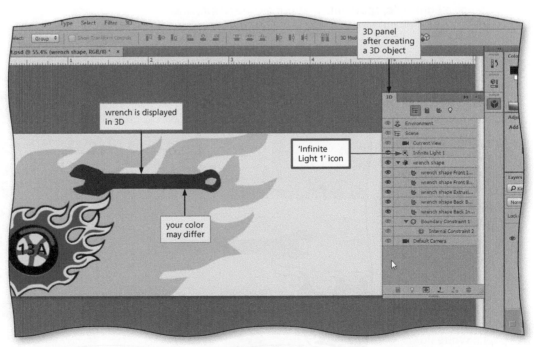

Figure 8–56

Other Ways

1. Tap or click 3D on Application bar, tap or click 'New 3D Extrusion from Selected Layer'

BTW

Postcard Extrusion
The 3D Postcard option (Figure 8–55) adds a sense of dimension to a flat file such as a screenshot, webpage, or pictures of printed documents. It is not a true extrusion. It is similar to the dimension commands in page layout or word processing apps.

To Edit 3D Lights

3D lights illuminate objects from different angles, adding realistic depth and shadows. The lighting settings affect the color of the object. The following steps adjust the lighting.

- On the 3D panel, double-tap or double-click the 'Infinite Light 1' icon (shown in Figure 8–56 on the previous page) to display the Infinite Light Properties panel.

- Tap or click the Preset button to display its list (Figure 8–57).

Q&A What does Infinite Light mean?
Infinite lights shine from one directional plane, like sunlight. Other options include point lights similar to a light bulb, spotlights that use a cone shape, and image-based lights based on an external lighting map.

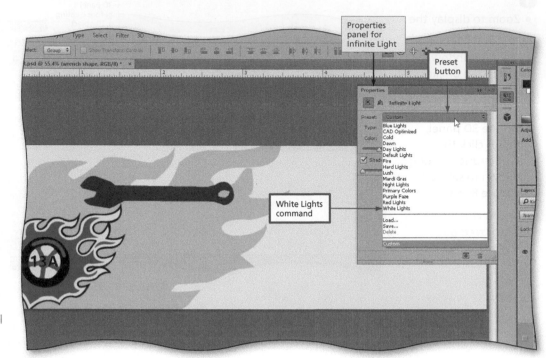

Figure 8–57

- Tap or click White Lights to select the lighting preset.

- Drag the Color slider to the right until the wrench displays a dark red color, approximately 139% (Figure 8–58).

Q&A What does the White Lights setting do?
In the case of the wrench, which will be printed as part of the ticket on white paper, white lights will provide a more realistic preview of the ticket.

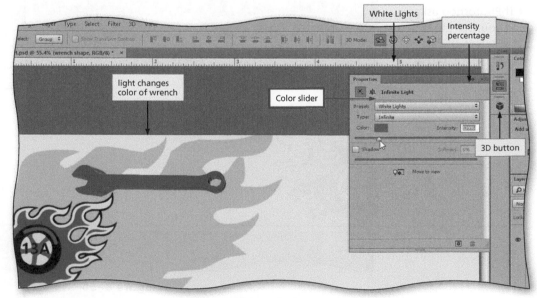

Figure 8–58

- Tap or click the 3D button on the vertical dock to display the panel.

To Use the 3D Mode Buttons

3D Mode buttons manipulate objects by rotating, rolling, dragging, moving or resizing them. It takes practice to use these tools effectively; whether an edit is successful and pleasing can be a matter of personal opinion. The following steps increase the 3D look for the wrench by using the 3D Mode buttons.

- On the Layers panel, select the 3D object, in this case, the wrench shape.

- On the 3D panel, select the wrench shape state.

- If necessary, tap or click the 'Rotate the 3D Object' button on the options bar to select it.

- In the document window, drag to the right to add perspective to the wrench (Figure 8–59).

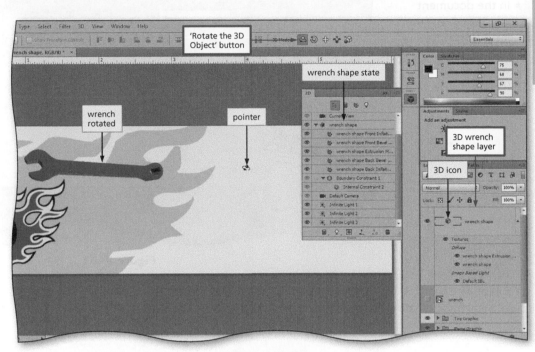

Figure 8–59

- Drag up slightly to add depth to the wrench by increasing the width of the shadow (Figure 8–60).

Experiment

- Tap or click the 'Drag the 3D Object' button. Drag in different directions to become familiar with the tool. After each drag, press CTRL+Z to undo the rotation.

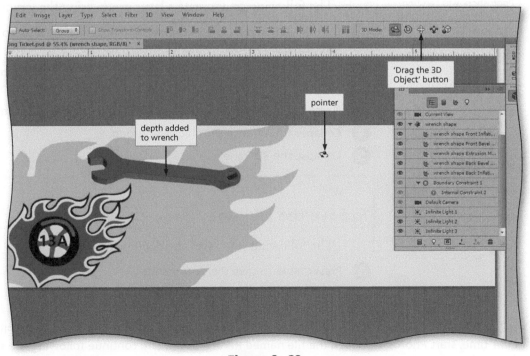

Figure 8–60

3

- On the options bar, tap or click the 'Scale the 3D Object' button to select it.

- In the document window, drag from left to right to reduce the size of the wrench (Figure 8–61).

Q&A

Could I use the Transform tools to scale the wrench? No. The Transform tools do not work on 3D objects due to the difficulty of maintaining all of the 3D aspects.

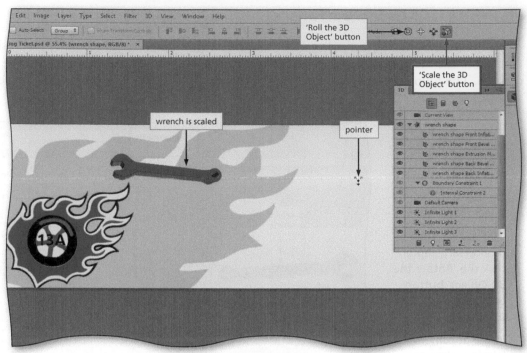

Figure 8–61

 **Experiment**

- Tap or click the 'Roll the 3D Object' button. Drag in different directions to become familiar with the tool. After each drag, press CTRL+Z to undo the roll.

BTW

Photoshop Help
At anytime while using Photoshop, you can find answers to questions and display information about various topics through Photoshop Help. Used properly, this form of assistance can increase your productivity and reduce your frustrations by minimizing the time you spend learning how to use Photoshop. For instruction about Photoshop Help and exercises that will help you gain confidence in using it, read the Using Photoshop Help Appendix.

To Create a New Layer Group

The following steps create a layer group using the wrench layers.

1 On the Layers panel, select the wrench shape layer. CTRL+tap or CTRL+click the wrench layer to select it also.

2 Tap or click Layer on the Application bar, tap or click New, and then tap or click 'Group from Layers' to display the New Group from Layers dialog box.

3 Name the group Wrench Graphic and choose an orange identification color.

4 Collapse the Wrench Graphic layer group.

5 Collapse the 3D Panel.

To Save the File Again

The following step saves the document.

1 Press CTRL+S to save the document.

Break Point: If you wish to take a break, this is a good place to do so. Press CTRL+Q to quit Photoshop. To resume at a later time, start Photoshop, open the file named Racing Ticket, and continue following the steps from this location forward.

To Create 3D Text

Photoshop displays a special 3D button on each of the type tool options bars. If you tap or click the 3D button while on a text layer, Photoshop converts the text into a 3D object, complete with the 3D characteristics and 3D tool buttons on the Move Tool options bar. You then can use the 3D Mode buttons and the 3D panel tools on the text.

- Use the Swatches panel to select the CMYK Red color.

- Press the T key to access the Horizontal Type tool. If necessary, select the 'Segoe UI Bold' font or a similar font. Set the font size to 14. Set the anti-aliasing to Crisp. Tap or click the 'Left align text' button.

- Tap the upper-left corner of the ticket to begin point text.

- Type **Rocketroad Drag Racing** to enter the text (Figure 8–62).

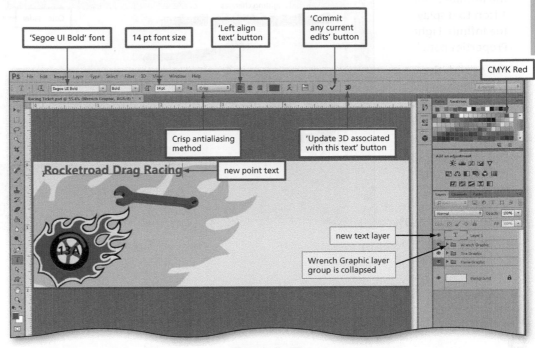

Figure 8–62

- On the options bar, tap or click the 'Commit any current edits' button to finish the text.

- Tap or click the 'Update 3D associated with this text' button to create a 3D version of the text. If Photoshop asks if you would like to switch to the 3D workspace, tap or click the No button (Figure 8–63).

Figure 8–63

- To apply the same lighting setting to the text as you did with the wrench, double-tap or double-click the Infinite Light 1 icon to display the Infinite Light Properties panel.

- Tap or click the Preset button to display its list and then choose White Lights.

- Drag the Color slider to the right until the text displays a dark red color, approximately 139% (Figure 8–64).

Figure 8–64

- Tap or click the 3D button on the vertical dock to display the panel.

- On the 3D panel, select the 'Rocketroad Drag Racing' state.

- On the options bar, tap or click the 'Rotate the 3D Object' button and drag to the right to add perspective. Part of your text might move off the canvas.

- Drag up slightly to add depth to the text (Figure 8–65).

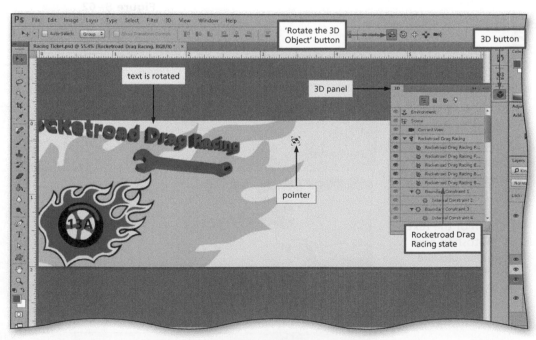

Figure 8–65

5

- On the options bar, tap or click the 'Drag the 3D Object' button and drag the object to the right as shown in Figure 8–66.

Q&A Is it OK if my text overlaps the wrench?
Yes. A slight overlap is fine. You will adjust the wrench later in the chapter.

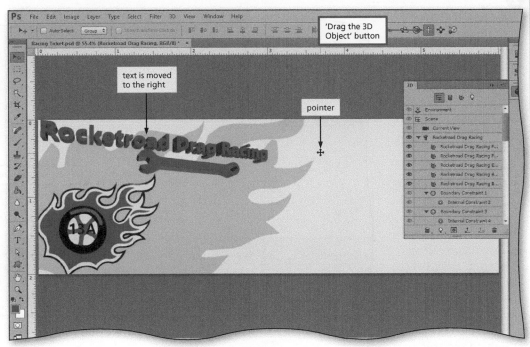

Figure 8–66

To Rasterize

When you rasterize a 3D layer or object, it becomes a non-vector graphic capable of being edited. There are several reasons you might want to rasterize a 3D object. You might want to apply a filter, use it as a pattern, add subtle gradients, change its color, transform, or erase part of the object. It is a good practice to make a copy of the layer before rasterizing, so if you make a mistake you can return to the original. The following steps make a copy of the wrench shape layer and then rasterize it so that you can edit it further.

1

- On the Layers panel, expand the Wrench Graphic layer group.

- Press and hold or right-click the wrench shape layer, and then tap or click Duplicate Layer on the context menu.

- Name the new layer **wrench rasterized**.

- Hide the wrench shape layer (Figure 8–67).

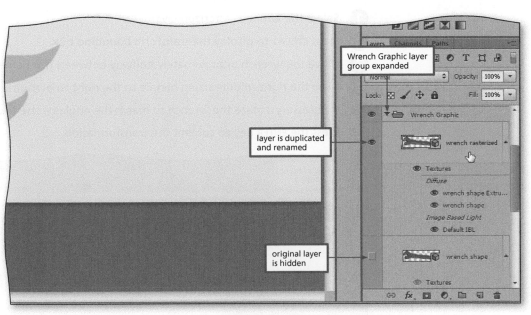

Figure 8–67

- Press and hold
  or right-click the
  wrench rasterized
  layer to display
  its context menu
  (Figure 8–68).

What is the
difference between
render and
rasterize?
The processes are
similar. Rasterizing
converts a vector
image into a pixel-
based raster image.
Render is used
more commonly
for animation,
video generation,
or modeling.
Behind the scenes,
Photoshop uses different algorithms.

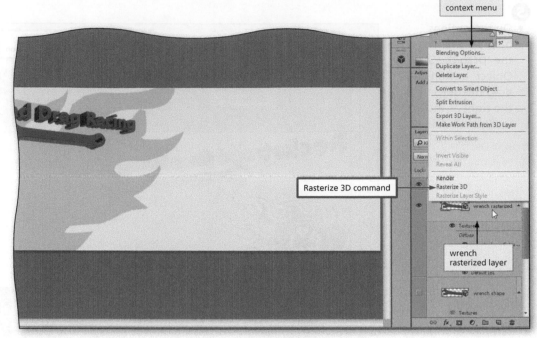

Figure 8–68

- Tap or click Rasterize 3D to rasterize the image.

Other Ways

1. Tap or click Rasterize on Layer menu, tap or click 3D

To Further Edit the Wrench

The following steps make further edits to the wrench.

1. Select the wrench rasterized layer.

2. Press CTRL+T to display the transform bounding box.

3. Move the wrench approximately halfway between the flame and the text.

4. Drag the right-middle sizing handle to the right to elongate the wrench.

5. If necessary, rotate the wrench to match the angle of the text (Figure 8–69).

6. Press the ENTER key to commit the transformation.

Figure 8–69

To Insert Other Text

The following steps insert other text in the ticket. Zoom as necessary.

1 On the Layers panel, select the Rocketroad Drag Racing layer.

2 Select the Horizontal Type Tool.

3 Change the font to Monotype Corsiva Regular. Change the font size to 15.

4 Change the font color to black, and center align.

5 Tap or click in the document window to create point text on the right side of the wrench. Type `Sonic Saturday` to enter the text. Tap or click the 'Commit any current edits' button to finish the text.

6 Create another line of text below the previous one with a font size of 10. Type `July 25th, 2015` and commit the text.

7 Drag a text box below the previous text, approximately 1.75 inches wide and .5 inches tall. Change the font to Myriad Pro Regular. Change the font size to 6 and tap or click the 'Right align text' button. Enter the text, `We appreciate your excitement to meet the drivers and ask for pictures and autographs, but politely request you do not approach the drivers or crew teams until after the final race.`

8 Below the previous text, create a final text box. Change the font back to Monotype Corsiva Regular. If necessary, change the font size to 6. Set the color to CMYK Red. Type `No flash photography!` as shown in Figure 8–70.

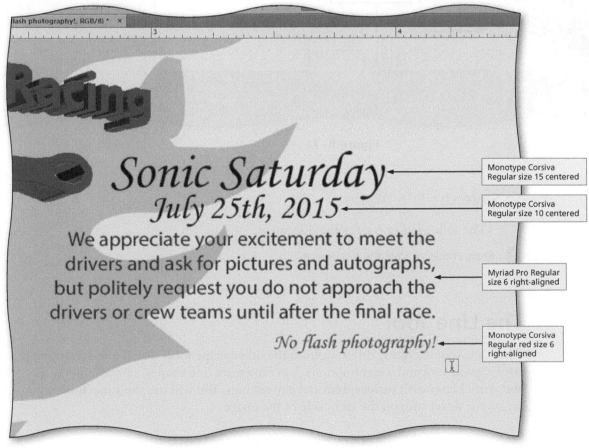

Figure 8–70

To Embed Other Images

The following steps embed two more images.

1 Zoom to display the entire ticket.

2 Use the File menu and the Place Embedded command to insert the Bar Code image. Resize it to fit below the text and use the pink smart guides to right-align it with the text.

3 Embed the Racecar image and place it to the left of the bar code.

4 Select all of the layers not currently in a layer group. Use the 'Group from Layers' command to group them with the name, Body Content. Use a blue identification color (Figure 8–71).

6 Collapse the Body Content group if necessary.

Figure 8–71

To Save the File Again

The following step saves the document.

1 Press CTRL+S to save the document.

The Line Tool

The Line Tool is slightly different from the other shape tools. It has a wider array of stroke, geometry, and weight options. You can create line shapes, arrows, hollow lines, and dotted lines with various dash and gap settings. You will use the Line Tool as you create the ticket stub on the right side of the image.

To Create a Dashed Line

The following steps create a vertical dashed line.

- Zoom to display the entire ticket, if necessary, and reset the colors back to their default settings.

- Press and hold or right-click the current shape tool and then tap or click Line Tool on the context menu.

- On the options bar, set the stroke width to 6 pt. Set the weight to 15 px.

- Tap or click the 'Set shape stroke type' button to display the Stroke Options pop-up panel.

- In the pop-up panel, tap or click the dashed line (Figure 8–72).

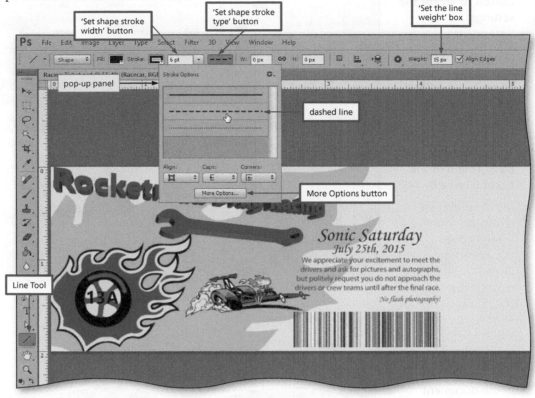

Figure 8–72

- Tap or click the More Options button to display the Stroke dialog box.

- In the Dash box, type **1**. In the Gap box, type **2** (Figure 8–73).

Q&A Could I save this as a custom preset?
Yes. If you click the Save button, your settings will be saved for future use. If you want to delete your saved preset, tap or click the Preset button, and then tap or click 'Delete Current Preset'.

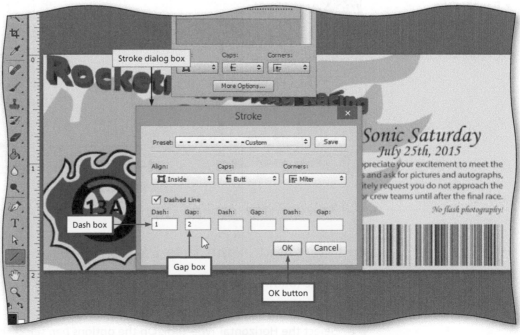

Figure 8–73

③

- Tap or click the OK button to accept the settings.

- Tap or click the 'Set the stroke color' box. In the pop-up panel, tap or click the almond color you chose earlier, so the gap color will match the background of the ticket (Figure 8–74).

My almond color is missing. What should I do?

Tap or click the Color Picker. On the Colors panel, enter 0 in the C box, 2 in the M box, 20 in the Y box, and 5 in the K box to choose an almond color.

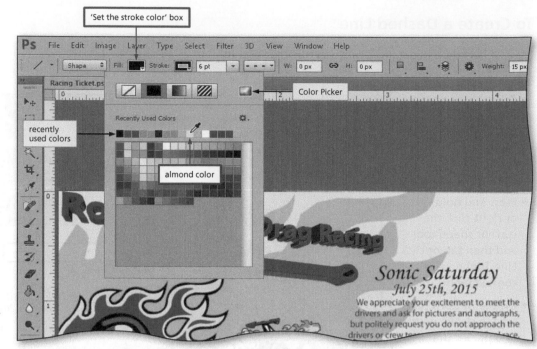

Figure 8–74

④

- In the document window, drag a straight vertical line down the right side of the current objects to create a ticket stub.

- Rename the new shape layer, **dashed line** (Figure 8–75).

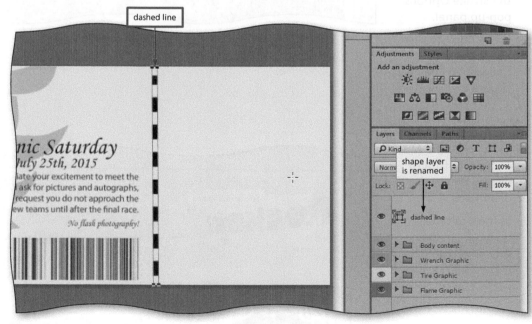

Figure 8–75

To Insert Text in the Ticket Stub

The following steps insert text in the ticket stub. Zoom as necessary.

① Select the default colors.

② Select the Horizontal Type Tool. On the options bar, select the 'Segoe UI Bold' font or a similar font. Set the font size to 24. Set the anti-aliasing to Crisp. Tap or click the 'Left align text' button.

③ Tap or click in the ticket stub to create point text. Type **$8.00** to enter the text. On the options bar, tap or click the 'Commit any current edits' button.

④ Press CTRL+T to display the transform bounding box. Rotate the text 90 degrees counterclockwise. Move the text into place as shown in Figure 8–76.

⑤ Use the Horizontal Type Tool to repeat the process with CMYK Red text, size 6. Enter **Rocketroad Drag Racing**. Rotate the text and place it to the right of the previous text.

⑥ Repeat the process again, this time using the font, Monotype Corsiva Regular. Change the font size to 22. Type the text **Sonic Saturday**. Rotate the text and place it on the end of the ticket stub as shown in Figure 8–76.

Figure 8–76

To Finish the Ticket Stub

The following steps complete the ticket stub, inserting the bar code, adding a red shape to serve as a background for the seat number, a decorative almond outline, and the text itself.

① Use the Swatches panel to select CMYK Red.

② Use the File menu and the Place Embedded command to insert the Bar Code image. Rotate it 90 degrees counterclockwise. Resize it to fit to the area shown in Figure 8–77 on the next page. Name the new layer, small bar code.

③ To create the red background for the seat number, press and hold or right-click the current shape tool, and then tap or click 'Rounded Rectangle Tool' in the list.

④ On the options bar, tap or click the Fill color box and then choose CMYK Red, if necessary. Tap or click the Stroke box and then tap or click No Color on the pop-up panel. SHIFT+drag to create a rounded rectangle on the ticket stub as shown in Figure 8–77. Name the new layer, rounded rectangle.

⑤ Create a new layer named almond outline.

⑥ To create a decorative outline near the edge of the red rectangle, select the Rounded Rectangle Tool if necessary. On the options bar, change the Fill color to No Color and the Stroke color to almond. Change the stroke width to 3 pt. Change the stroke type to a solid line. SHIFT+drag to create a slightly smaller rounded rectangle over the top of the previous one.

⑦ Use the Eyedropper tool to sample the almond color.

⑧ To create the text for the seat, select the almond outline layer on the Layers panel to make sure the text will be visible in front of the other layers.

⑨ Select the Horizontal Type Tool. On the options bar, select the 'Segoe UI Bold' font or a similar font. Set the font size to 24. Set the anti-aliasing to Crisp. Tap or click the 'Left align text' button. Tap or click the document window and then type `13A` and commit the text. Rotate the text and place it as shown in Figure 8–77.

⑩ Create a new layer. On the options bar, change the font size to 10. Tap or click the document window, type `1st Balcony,` and then commit the text. Rotate the text and place it as shown in Figure 8–77.

⑪ Group all ungrouped layers except the Background layer. Name the group, `Ticket Stub Content`. Use a green identification color.

Figure 8–77

To Save the File Again

The following step saves the document.

❶ Press CTRL+S to save the document.

The Note Tool and Notes Panel

In Photoshop, an **annotation** is an explanatory note or comment included within the file for the purpose of storing information about the file. The Note Tool, included with the Eyedropper Tool on the Tools panel, opens the Notes panel, in which you can enter comments. Notes in the Notes panel have scrolling capabilities, standard editing functions, and a Close button in the corner. A yellow note icon appears in the document window when you tap or click the Note Tool button and the Note options bar is displayed. The Note options bar contains choices for author, color, and font size. The name you enter in the Author box becomes the text on the Notes panel title bar. You can edit, delete, or reposition notes anywhere on the image for greater emphasis; they stay with the file until they are deleted. These notes are different from the metadata and keywords stored by Adobe Bridge. Annotations are more like the popular, small, yellow sticky notes that you might attach physically, a comment inserted in many Office programs, or a short phone or text message.

BTW

Adobe Bridge
If you want to learn more about file management, metadata, and keywords, read the Using Adobe Bridge CC Appendix.

Annotate graphics within the file.
Photoshop lets you save notes with any image file. You might want to write a note to another person on your team about the use of the graphic, or you might want to keep some notes for yourself about which filter you used, or which settings you changed on a blend mode. Still other times, you might want to list some special instructions.

Plan Ahead

Once it is created, to read a note, double-tap or double-click it — you do not have to tap or click the Note Tool to read notes. Notes do not print, and they are unique to Photoshop; a note in a Photoshop document is not visible in other graphic-editing software packages.

To Create a Note

The next steps create a note in the Racing Ticket image. The note will remind a coworker to add keywords to the image in Adobe Bridge.

1

• Press and hold or right-click the Eyedropper Tool button to display its context menu (Figure 8–78).

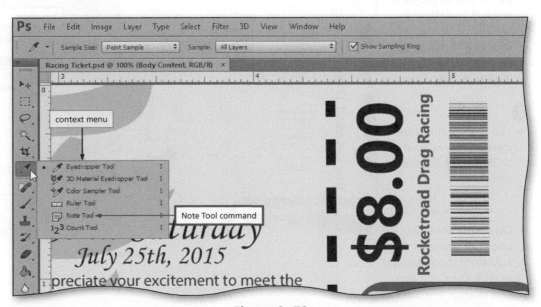

Figure 8–78

- Tap or click Note Tool in the menu.

- Tap or click the outside of the canvas to place the note location and open the Notes panel.

- In the Notes panel window, type **Katie, don't forget to add keywords to this image using Adobe Bridge before you upload it to the server.** to complete the note (Figure 8–79).

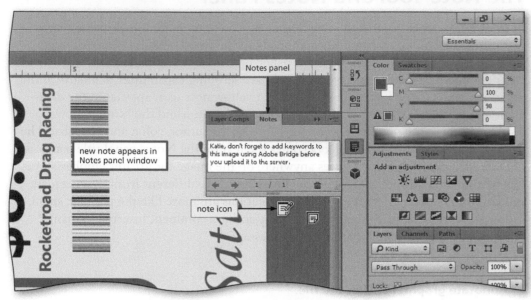

Figure 8–79

- Tap or click the Notes icon on the vertical docking to hide the panel.

To View a Note

The next steps view the note as a different user would.

- Double-tap or double-click the note button on the canvas to open the Notes panel and display the note. If you do not see the note, tap or click the Notes button on the vertical dock (Figure 8–80).

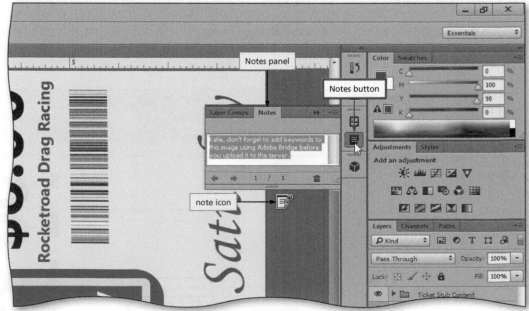

- Tap or click the Notes icon on the vertical docking to hide the panel.

⊘ Experiment

- On the options bar, add your name as the author of the note. Tap or click the Color box and change the color of the note

Figure 8–80

The Ruler and Count Tools

In the same group as the Eyedropper and Note Tools, Photoshop includes the Ruler Tool and the Count Tool. The Ruler Tool works in conjunction with the Info panel to position images or elements precisely by measuring. The Ruler Tool creates a non-printing line; the location and length are displayed on the Info panel. If you have two ruler lines, the Info panel also displays the angle. To Use the Ruler Tool, tap or click at one edge of the object you want to measure and then drag to the other side. All measurements except the angle are calculated in the unit of measure currently set in Photoshop preferences. The Ruler Tool is useful for measuring objects in an image that are not selections or layers.

The Count Tool allows you to count specific items in the document window and number them with non-printing numbers. After selecting the Count Tool, you simply tap or click each thing you want to count. The Count Tool options bar allows you to change the color, size, and visibility of the numbers, as well as creating multiple groups of counts. The Count Tool is used by scientists and doctors to count specific items in slides. You also can use the Count Tool to count people in a picture or any repeated item in the scene.

TO USE THE RULER TOOL

If you wanted to use the Ruler Tool, you would perform the following steps.

1. Press and hold or right-click the Eyedropper Tool to display the context menu. Tap or click Ruler Tool in the list.

2. In the document window, tap or click the left side of an object, such as the wrench. Drag to the other end of the object. SHIFT+drag to draw a straight line or use the options bar.

3. Press the F8 key to display the Info panel and read the measurements of the ruler line.

TO USE THE COUNT TOOL

If you wanted to use the Count Tool, you would perform the following steps.

1. Press and hold or right-click the Eyedropper Tool to display the context menu. Tap or click Count Tool in the list.

2. In the document window, tap or click several objects, such as the points on the flame

3. Use the options bar to adjust settings.

4. Tap or click the Clear button to clear the numbers.

To Save the Finished Racing Ticket

The following step saves the fully layered, PSD version of the image.

1 Press CTRL+S.

BTW

Numbering Tickets
If you want to create numbered documents, such as tickets, yourself, page layout programs such as Microsoft Publisher, Quark, and Adobe InDesign have easy ways to generate individual tickets using a field linked to a database of ticket numbers.

To Prepare the Ticket for Professional Printing

BTW

Printing Tickets
If you are having tickets
professionally printed, the
print shop typically wants
the following:

- File Format: TIFF, JPG,
  or PDF

- Resolution: 300 DPI

- Color Mode: CMYK or
  Grayscale for black and
  white

- Bleed Space: .25" on
  each side ensures that no
  text or pictures near the
  edge will be cut off.

The following steps remove the ticket number, as it will be added at the print shop. The steps also flatten the image, add .25 inches of white space around the edge to accommodate most printers, convert the ticket to CMYK, and save it in the TIFF format.

1 On the Layers panel, delete the layer 13A in the Tire Graphic group. In the Ticket Stub group, delete both the 13A layer and the 1st Balcony layer.

2 Flatten all layers. If Photoshop asks if you want to discard the hidden layers, tap or click the Yes button.

3 Press CTRL+A to select all of the ticket. Press CTRL+T to display the bounding box. SHIFT+drag a corner sizing handle to create approximately .25 inch of white space on all four sides. Confirm the transformation.

4 Using the Mode submenu on the Image menu, convert the image to CMYK.

5 Use the Save As dialog box to save the file on your storage device, with the file name Racing Ticket for Print, in the TIFF format.

To Close All Document Windows and Quit Photoshop

The ticket is complete, so the following steps close the document window and quit Photoshop.

1 Tap or click the Close button in any open document window. If Photoshop asks to save the file, tap or click the No button.

2 Tap or click the Close button on the Photoshop title bar.

Chapter Summary

In this chapter, you converted photos into clip art and created a ticket. You learned about the general characteristics of clip art, and the difference between vector and raster graphics.

As you created both paths and shape layers, you used the Pen and Freeform Pen Tools to draw line segments and anchor points. You added and converted anchor points to create straight lines and curves. The Path Selection and Direct Selection Tools helped position paths and shapes. You created a 3D shape and 3D text to add depth and perspective to the ticket. Finally, you used the Note Tool to annotate your file before converting it to a format ready for printing.

The items listed below include all the new Photoshop skills you have learned in this chapter:

1. Lock Layers (PS 478)
2. Use the Pen Tool in Shape Mode (PS 482)
3. Add Anchor Points to a Shape (PS 485)
4. Use the Freeform Pen Tool (PS 487)
5. Convert to Anchor Point (PS 489)
6. Delete an Anchor Point (PS 489)
7. Use the Pen Tool in Path Mode (PS 489)
8. Stroke a Path (PS 491)
9. Create a Work Path using the Pen Tool (PS 498)
10. Display the Paths Panel and Set Options (PS 500)
11. Save a Work Path as a Named Path (PS 501)
12. Create a New Work Path (PS 501)
13. Create a Selection from a Path (PS 502)
14. Create a Path from a Selection (PS 502)
15. Merge Paths (PS 503)
16. Delete a Path (PS 504)
17. Create a Shape Layer from a Path (PS 504)
18. Use the Direct Selection Tool (PS 506)
19. Create a 3D Extrusion (PS 510)
20. Edit 3D Lights (PS 510)
21. Use the 3D Mode Buttons (PS 511)
22. Create 3D Text (PS 513)
23. Rasterize (PS 515)
24. Create a Dashed Line (PS 519)
25. Create a Note (PS 523)
26. View a Note (PS 524)
27. Use the Ruler Tool (PS 525)
28. Use the Count Tool (PS 525)

Apply Your Knowledge

Reinforce the skills and apply the concepts you learned in this chapter.

Converting a Birdhouse to Clip Art

Note: To complete this assignment, you will be required to use the Data Files for Students. Visit solutions.cengage.com/ctdownloads for detailed instructions or contact your instructor for information about accessing the required files.

Instructions: Start Photoshop and perform the customization steps found on pages PS 6 through PS 11. Open the Apply 8-1 Birdhouse file from the Chapter 08 folder of the Data Files for Students. The purpose of this exercise is to create a clip art image from part of a digital photograph. The photo you open is a picture of a birdhouse, shown in Figure 8–81a. You will convert the image to a clip art image as shown in Figure 8-81b.

Courtesy of David Reneau

| **Figure 8–81a** | **Figure 8–81b** |

Perform the following tasks:

1. On the File menu, tap or click Save As. Save the image on your storage device in the PSD format, with the file name Apply 8-1 Birdhouse Complete. If the Photoshop Format options dialog box is displayed, tap or click the OK button.

2. Select the Pen Tool on the Tools panel. On the options bar, tap or click the Mode button and select Shape for the drawing mode. With black as the foreground color, tap or click the lower-left corner of the pole. Tap or click again toward the upper-left corner of the pole. Tap or click two more times at the corners to create a closed path around the pole. Name the new layer, pole.

3. Create another black curved path for the top of the ornament of the birdhouse. Rename the layer, tip.

Continued >

Apply Your Knowledge *continued*

4. Create a new layer with the name, topper. Change the foreground color to red. Use the Pen Tool to draw around the red topper as shown in Figure 8–81b on the previous page.

5. Create a new layer with the name, walkway. Change the foreground color to orange. Zoom in on the birdhouse itself.

6. If necessary, select the Pen Tool. Create a path around the walkway that hangs down on the left side of the birdhouse.

7. Create a new layer. Use the Eyedropper Tool to sample the green in the bird house. Select the 'Freeform Pen Tool' on the Tools panel. On the options bar, tap or click the Magnetic check box, if necessary. Tap or click the lower-left corner of the lower level green area. Move around the green area, tapping or clicking as needed at the corners. When you finish, tap or click the first anchor point to close the path. Use the 'Add Anchor Point' Tool to add anchor points to any areas missed by the Freeform Pen Tool. When you are finished, name the layer, first floor green.

8. Repeat Step 6 to create a second floor green layer.

9. Repeat Step 6 to create a green roof layer.

10. Create a new layer. Change the foreground color to white. Use the Pen Tool or the Freeform Pen Tool to outline the area between the first floor green shape and the second floor green shape. Do not worry about the holes. Name the layer, first floor white.

11. Repeat Step 9 to create a second floor white layer.

12. Create a new layer named, holes. Hide all of the white and green shape layers.

13. To create the holes:

    a. Press CTRL+J to create a layer via copy. Name the layer, holes.

    b. Select the 'Elliptical Marquee Tool'. On the options bar, tap or click the 'Add to selection' button.

    c. One at a time, SHIFT+drag a circle around each of the four circular holes in the bird house.

    d. One at a time, drag to create an ellipse around the two holes on the right of the bird house.

    e. Press SHIFT+F5 to display the Fill dialog box. Tap or click the Use button and then tap or click Black to fill the shapes with black. Rearrange layers as necessary.

14. Use the Note Tool to insert a note into the file. In the note, insert your name, course number, and school.

15. Save the image again. See your instructor for ways to submit this assignment.

Extend Your Knowledge

Extend the skills you learned in this chapter and experiment with new skills. You may need to use Help to complete the assignment.

Designing a 3D Poster

Note: To complete this assignment, you will be required to use the Data Files for Students. Visit solutions.cengage.com/ctdownloads for detailed instructions or contact your instructor for information about accessing the required files.

Instructions: Start Photoshop and perform the customization steps found on pages PS 6 through PS 11. Open the Extend 8-1 Camera file from the Chapter 08 folder of the Data Files for Students. You have been asked to create some artwork to use at a retro camera exhibit. You decide to investigate Photoshop's 3D lighting and scene presets, using a picture of a 35 mm camera, and provide four different views for the exhibit organizer.

Perform the following tasks:

1. On the File menu, tap or click Save As. Save the image on your storage device in the PSD format, with the file name, Extend 8-1 Camera Edited.

2. Duplicate the camera 1 layer three times. Name the layers camera 2, camera 3, and camera 4. Move camera 1 to the upper-left corner, camera 2 to the upper-right corner, camera 3 to the lower-left corner, and camera 4 to the lower-right corner.

3. Use Photoshop Help to read about the topic, '3D Lights Settings' and note the various ways to change the lighting.

4. Select the camera 1 layer. On the 3D menu, tap or click 'New 3D Extrusion from Selected Layer' to create a 3D object. If Photoshop asks if you wish to change to the 3D workspace, tap or click the Yes button. On the 3D panel, select 'Infinite Light 1'. On the Properties panel, tap or click the Preset button and change the light to Day Lights. Drag the intensity slider to 125%, creating a black-and white-retro feel.

Courtesy of Fred Starks

Figure 8–82

5. Select the camera 2 layer. On the 3D menu, tap or click 'New 3D Extrusion from Selected Layer' to create a 3D object. On the 3D panel, select 'Infinite Light 1'. On the Properties panel, tap or click the Preset button and change the light to Mardi Gras. Drag the intensity slider to 200. Remove the check mark in the Shadow check box. On the 3D panel, select camera 2. On the options bar, tap or click the 'Rotate the 3D Object' button. In the document window, drag the camera to show off some of the Mardi Gras colors.

Continued >

Extend Your Knowledge *continued*

6. Use Photoshop Help to read about the topic, 'Change 3D Render Settings' and note the various presets for scene rendering.

7. Select the camera 3 layer. On the 3D menu, tap or click 'New 3D Extrusion from Selected Layer' to create a 3D object. On the 3D panel, select 'Infinite Light 1'. On the Properties panel, tap or click the Preset button and change the light to White Lights. Drag the intensity slider to 200. On the 3D panel, select Scene. On the Properties panel, tap or click the Presets button to display its list. Tap or click Sketch Scattered to create a kind of line drawing.

8. Select the camera 4 layer. On the 3D menu, tap or click 'New 3D Extrusion from Selected Layer' to create a 3D object. On the 3D panel, select 'Infinite Light 1'. On the Properties panel, tap or click the Preset button and change the light to White Lights. Drag the intensity slider to 200. On the 3D panel, select Scene. On the Properties panel, tap or click the Style button to display its list. Tap or click Cartoon to create a kind of clip art scene. If necessary, tap or click the Lines check box so it displays a check mark. On the 3D panel, select camera 4. On the Properties panel, change the Extrusion depth, or amount of shadow, to .8 inches. On the options bar, select the 'Rotate the 3D Object' button and rotate the camera in the document window.

9. If you have 3D printing capabilities, print a copy of the file.

10. Save the file again and turn it in to your instructor.

Make It Right

Analyze a project and correct all errors and/or improve the design.

Music Store Rock Camp

Note: To complete this assignment, you will be required to use the Data Files for Students. Visit solutions.cengage.com/ctdownloads for detailed instructions or contact your instructor for information about accessing the required files.

Problem: The music store needs help completing a new logo for its summer camp. A previous graphic designer started the project but did not finish it. A photo of a young guitarist (Figure 8–83) needs to be converted to a silhouette.

Perform the following tasks:

1. Start Photoshop and perform the customization steps found on pages PS 6 through PS 11. Open the file Make It Right 8-1 Rock Camp file from the Data Files for Students and save it as Make It Right 8-1 Rock Camp Edited in the PSD file format.

2. Look through the layers on the Layers panel. Select the Guitarist layer, if necessary. Use the Pen Tool in Path mode to trace slowly around the entire outline of the guitarist and the guitar, stopping at her knees. Do not be concerned with tracing her perfectly. You may ignore details such as the curly hair, bracelet, and spaces between the guitar's tuning pegs. If necessary, use the 'Direct Selection Tool' to make adjustments.

Courtesy of Alec Fehl

Figure 8–83

3. Create a new layer and name it, Silhouette. Tap or click the Paths panel tab and notice that the guitarist outline is named Work Path in the panel. Rename the path, Guitarist Path. On the Paths panel status bar, tap or click the 'Load path as a selection' button. Tap or click the Paths panel in the gray area below the paths to deselect the current path. Use the Eyedropper Tool to sample the gold color from the text surrounding the logo. Press ALT+BACKSPACE to fill the selection with gold. Tap or click the Layers panel tab to switch to the Layers panel. Press CTRL+D to deselect the selection. Hide the Guitarist layer , and then select the Silhouette layer. Move the silhouette layer so the knees slightly overlap the gold ring at the bottom and the guitarist appears to be rising inside the logo. In the Layers panel, drag the Silhouette layer down below the Gold Ring layer.

4. Add an inner shadow to the silhouette. Add a drop shadow to the gold ring layer. Save the file and submit it to your instructor when you are happy with the results.

In the Labs

Design and/or create a project using the guidelines, concepts, and skills presented in this chapter. Labs are listed in order of increasing difficulty.

Lab 1: Creating a Sign with Paths

Note: To complete this assignment, you will be required to use the Data Files for Students. Visit solutions.cengage.com/ctdownloads for detailed instructions or contact your instructor for information about accessing the required files.

Problem: Your summer job is working at the public library. Your supervisor has asked you to make a sign for the Bookworm Corner — a section of the children's library with carpeting and bean bag chairs. He would like the same image in a scalable format for use in the desktop publishing products of the library. You have taken a picture of some books and decide to add a clip art of a worm as shown in Figure 8–84. You will save it in both the PSD and GIF formats to preserve the transparency.

Courtesy of Joy Starks

Figure 8–84

Instructions: Perform the following tasks:

1. Start Photoshop. Perform the customization steps found on pages PS 6 through PS 11.

2. Open the file, Lab 8-1Books, from the Chapter 08 folder in the Data Files for Students.

3. Save the file in the PSD format with the name, Lab 8-1 Books Clip Art on your storage device.

4. Zoom the photo to 16.67% magnification, if necessary.

5. To create a transparent background:

   a. Press the w key to access the Magic Wand tool. On the options bar, tap or click the 'Add to selection' button.

   b. Select all of the white areas.

   c. On the Select menu, tap or click Inverse.

   d. On the Layer menu, point to New, and then tap or click 'Layer Via Cut'. Name the new layer, books.

   e. Delete the Background layer.

6. To create a color shape layer of an individual book:

   a. Select the Swatches panel. Choose a bright color in the red family.

   b. Select the Pen Tool. On the options bar, tap or click the 'Pick Tool Mode' button, and then tap or click Shape. If necessary, change the Fill color to red. Change the Stroke color to No Color.

   c. Choose a book in the document window and then tap or click each corner to create a red shape layer.

   d. Add and subtract anchor points as necessary to match the edges. Convert any anchor points that need moving and adjust the path as necessary. Use the Path Selection tool to adjust anchor points along the path.

7. Repeat Step 6, choosing a different color from the Swatches panel for each book.

8. To add a special effect:

   a. Select the Shape 1 layer.

   b. Tap or click the 'Add a layer style' button and then tap or click Bevel & Emboss on the shortcut menu.

   c. When the Layer Style dialog box is displayed, choose the settings displayed in Table 8–5.

Table 8–5 Layer Style Setting for the Books Clip Art	
Name	**Setting**
Style	Inner Bevel
Technique	Smooth
Depth	100%
Direction	Down
Size	24 px
Soften	3 px
Angle	-138°
Altitude	21°
Gloss Contour	Linear
Highlight Mode	Screen
Highlight Mode Opacity	75%
Shadow Mode	Multiply
Color	Black
Shadow Mode Opacity	75%

Continued >

In the Labs *continued*

9. To copy the layer style to the other shape layers:

   a. Press and hold or right-click the Shape 1 layer. When the shortcut menu is displayed, tap or click 'Copy Layer Style'.

   b. SHIFT+tap or SHIFT+click each of the other shape layers.

   c. Press and hold or right-click the selected layers and then tap or click Paste Layer Style on the context menu.

10. Merge all layers.

11. Use a selection tool to select the six books sitting on top. Press SHIFT+CTRL+J to make a layer via cut. Name the new layer top books.

12. To add the worm graphic:

   a. Tap or click the books layer, so the new worm graphic will be inserted between the books and top books layers.

   b. Open the file named, Lab 8-1 Worm, from the Chapter 08 folder in the Data Files for Students. Arrange the windows beside each other.

   c. Select the 'Rectangular Marquee Tool'. Drag a rectangle around the right half of the worm. Press the v key to access the Move Tool. Drag the selection and drop it in the Books Clip Art window. Place it on the right side of the books as shown in Figure 8–84. Press CTRL+T and resize the layer as necessary. Name the layer, right worm.

   d. Tap or click the Worm window again. Select the Rectangular Marquee Tool. Drag a rectangle around the left half of the worm. Press the v key to access the Move tool. Drag the selection and drop it in the Books Clip Art window. Place it on the left side of the books as shown in Figure 8–84. Press CTRL+T and resize the layer as necessary. Name the layer, left worm.

13. Save the file again.

14. Use the Save As command to save the file in the GIF format with the same name. Accept the default settings in the GIF dialog boxes.

15. Print a copy and submit it to your instructor.

Lab 2: Creating a Magazine Cover with 3D

Note: To complete this assignment, you will be required to use the Data Files for Students. Visit solutions.cengage.com/ctdownloads for detailed instructions or contact your instructor for information about accessing the required files.

Problem: You are to create a magazine cover for a new magazine about dragons. You decide to use 3D text and layers (Figure 8–85).

Instructions: Perform the following tasks:

1. Start Photoshop. Perform the customization steps found on pages PS 6 through PS 11.

2. Open a new file, 8.5 × 11 inches, in the RGB format with a resolution of 150. Choose a white background. Use the name, Lab 8-2 Magazine Cover.

© iStockphoto.com/LindaMarieB

Figure 8–85

3. Select the Gradient Tool. Tap or click the Gradient picker on the options bar, and then choose the Chrome gradient. On the options bar, tap or click the Radial Gradient button.

4. In the document window, drag from the middle of the page down and right, to the lower-right corner to create the background.

5. Use the Place Embedded command on the File menu to place the Lab 8-2 Dragon file as shown in Figure 8–58. Resize as necessary. Rename the layer, dragon.

6. Select the Horizontal Type Tool. On the options bar, choose Myriad Pro Bold, size 30, centered. Change the color to navy blue. Drag a text box across the top of the page. Type **Everything You Wanted to Know About** and then tap or click the 'Commit any current edits' button.

7. Create a new layer on the Layers panel. On the options bar, change the font to Old English Text MT Regular. Change the color to black. Change the size to 144 and center align. Type **Dragons** and then tap or click the 'Commit any current edits' button.

Continued >

In the Labs *continued*

8. On the options bar, tap or click the 3D button to convert the text to 3D. If Photoshop asks if you want to change to the 3D workspace, tap or click the Yes button.

9. On the 3D panel, select the 'Infinite Light 1' content. On the Properties panel, change the lighting to White Lights with an intensity of 250.

10. On the 3D panel, select the Dragons content. On the options bar, use the 'Rotate the 3D Object' button to rotate the text slightly upward

11. Use the Window menu to access the Styles panel. On the styles panel, tap or click the Nebula (Texture) style to apply the style to the text.

12. Select the Layers panel and the dragon layer. Tap or click 3D on the Application bar, and then tap or click 'New 3D Extrusion from Selected Layer'. If Photoshop asks if you want to change to the 3D workspace, tap or click the Yes button.

13. In the Mesh Properties panel, change the Extrusion depth to 0.

14. On the 3D panel, select the 'Infinite Light 1' content. On the Infinite Light Properties panel, change the Preset to Default Lights with an intensity of 125. If necessary, select the Shadow text box and drag the Softness slider to 27.

15. Save the file on your storage device in the TIFF format.

16. Rasterize each 3D layer and then print a copy for your instructor.

17. For extra credit, draw a dashed line approximately 2 inches from the bottom of the page. Insert the date below the line. Match either the font of the Dragons layer or the font of the other text layer.

Lab 3: Creating a Promotional Flyer

Note: To complete this assignment, you will be required to use the Data Files for Students. Visit solutions.cengage.com/ctdownloads for detailed instructions or contact your instructor for information about accessing the required files.

Problem: A local bakery is hosting their annual "cupcake day" when they will sell their gourmet cupcakes (normally $3 each) for only 50¢. They have asked you to create a promotional flyer for the event in the style of a postage stamp (Figure 8–86).

Instructions: Perform the following tasks:
Start Photoshop. Perform the customization steps found on pages PS 6 through PS 11. Create a new document with a white background, 3 inches wide and 4 inches tall, and save the file in the Photoshop PSD format as Lab 8-3 Cupcake Flyer on your storage device.

Use the Custom Shape Tool to create a stamp shape that almost fills the page. (*Hint:* on the Custom Shape Tool options bar, tap or click the Custom Shape picker to display the pop-up panel. Tap or click the menu button and then load the Objects library of shapes. Select the Stamp 1 shape.) Name the layer, stamp. Use the 'Add a layer style' button to apply a 3-pixel black stroke. Apply a Gradient Overlay layer style with the colors of your choice to add texture to the background of the stamp shape. Add text similar to that shown in Figure 8–86. Create a layer group named, Type, and drag the type layers into it.

© Courtesy of Alech Fehl

Figure 8–86

Open the Lab 8-3 Cupcake file from the Chapter 08 folder of the Data Files for Students. Drag the cupcake photo into the Lab 8-3 Cupcake Flyer document. Hide the Stamp layer and Type layer group so you can focus on the cupcake. Use the Pen Tool and Freeform Pen Tool to trace the different parts of the cupcake. It may be helpful to zoom in so the cupcake is enlarged. Color the shapes appropriately and add layer styles, such as a Pattern Overlay, to add texture. Create a new layer group named, Cupcake, to store all the cupcake layers. Hide the original cupcake photo layer and resize the Cupcake layer group to enlarge your clip art cupcake. Rearrange the stacking order of the layer groups, if necessary.

Rotate, resize, and reposition any layers and then apply any additional layer styles you think benefit the design. Save the file.

Cases and Places

Apply your creative thinking and problem-solving skills to design and implement a solution.

Note: To complete this assignment, you will be required to use the Data Files for Students. Visit solutions.cengage.com/ctdownloads for detailed instructions or contact your instructor for information about accessing the required files.

1: Map Demographics

Academic

Your political science professor has given you the assignment of creating an electoral map for your state from the last presidential election. Find a free graphic of your state map that shows county outlines. Research county election results using your state government's website. With the Freeform Pen Tool and the Shape layers button, draw around each county, filling it with either red for Republican or blue for Democrat. Save and print the file.

2: Create an Invitation

Personal

You are throwing a birthday party for a friend and need to make invitations. Create a new document in Photoshop with a solid, bright background. Take a digital picture of some gift boxes and another digital picture of a fun location, such as a swimming pool, roller rink, or bowling alley. If you do not have access to a digital camera or cannot find gift boxes or an appropriate location, download gift box or location photos from a free clip art site on the web. Copy the location image into your new document, and then convert it into a vector graphic using the various pen tools. Convert just enough of the photograph so that the location is recognizable. You do not need to convert every detail. Add the gift box photo to your new document and convert the gift box to a vector graphic. Delete the layers containing the original photos. Use the Horizontal Type Tool to insert invitation text, such as the name of your friend and the location and date/time of the party. Add 3D elements to the text. Save the file in the format specified by your instructor.

3: Creating a Game Graphic

Professional

You recently took a job with a company that produces graphical adventure games for computers. Your assignment is to convert an image of a historical ruin into a clip art type of graphic to display on the CD liner. The photo, Case 8-3 Archway, is located in the Chapter 08 folder of the Data Files for Students. Open the photo. Use the Pen Tool in Shape mode to create shape layers for each vertical column in the image. Choose a dark tan color with no stroke for each shape. Select all of the shape layers and group them in a layer group named Columns. Use the Freeform Pen Tool, and anchor point tools to draw around other parts of the archway with darker and lighter shades. Do not recolor the blue sky. Save the file in the PSD format and submit a copy to your instructor.

9 | Web Tools, 3D Modeling, and Animation

Objectives

You will have mastered the material in this chapter when you can:

- Explain why planning is the most important step in web design
- Generate a contact sheet and save it as a webpage
- Differentiate between a webpage and a website
- Create a graphic using Perspective Warp
- Slice an image
- Apply slice settings
- Use meshes, lighting, and materials to create a 3D model

- Manipulate 3D models using alternative displays and widgets
- Create animation frames
- Describe the process of creating an animation
- Tween an animation
- Loop an animation
- Optimize an animation
- Preview an animation

Ps File Edit Image Layer Type Select Filter 3D View Window Help

Adobe **Photoshop CC**   Feather: 0 px   Anti-alias   Style: Normal   Width: Height: Refine Edge...

9 | Web Tools, 3D Modeling, and Animation

Introduction

Photoshop has several tools to help you design webpages, perform advanced editing of 3D objects, and create animations. In previous chapters, you have used the Save for Web command to save photos in the proper format for the web and to generate the HTML to display your photo in a web browser. Although Photoshop does not have a full complement of webpage creation features, you can use it to create a mockup of a webpage as a sample or prototype in advance of creating a fully featured site. In this chapter, you will create a **contact sheet,** which is a set of multiple images that appear on one page. That contact sheet, or gallery, will appear from a link on a home page, which is the first page or starting point of a website. Photoshop optimizes or enhances webpages to make them more interactive by using slices with hyperlinks or hot spots. In addition, you will use 3D modeling tools to design a piece of artwork for the webpage. Finally, you will use the Timeline panel to animate the artwork for display on the web. You will combine all of these elements into an interactive website for a fictitious company named Creative Weddings.

Project — Creating a Wedding Planner's Home Page

This chapter examines some of the web, animation, and 3D modeling tools available in Photoshop as you create a home page for a wedding planner. A **home page** is a webpage designated as the first page and point of entry into a **website**, which is a collection of related webpages owned or operated by the same entity. Also called the main page or index page, a home page typically welcomes the visitor by introducing the purpose of the site, indicating the business name or personal name of the website's owner, and providing links to the lower-level pages of the site.

The Creative Weddings home page uses a sage, cream, and dark red color scheme. A **masthead** is the top portion of a document's design and is usually the first thing people notice when looking at a webpage. Therefore, the masthead is the ideal place to locate the company name, eye-catching imagery, contact information, and anything else you want to be sure your visitors see. A group of links to other webpages in the Creative Weddings site appears below the masthead. One of the links will take visitors to a gallery contact sheet. Finally, when the home page first appears, a 3D wedding ring will move from the bottom of the page to the top using animation. The webpage is illustrated in Figure 9–1a. The gallery contact sheet, opened from a link on the webpage, is illustrated in Figure 9–1b.

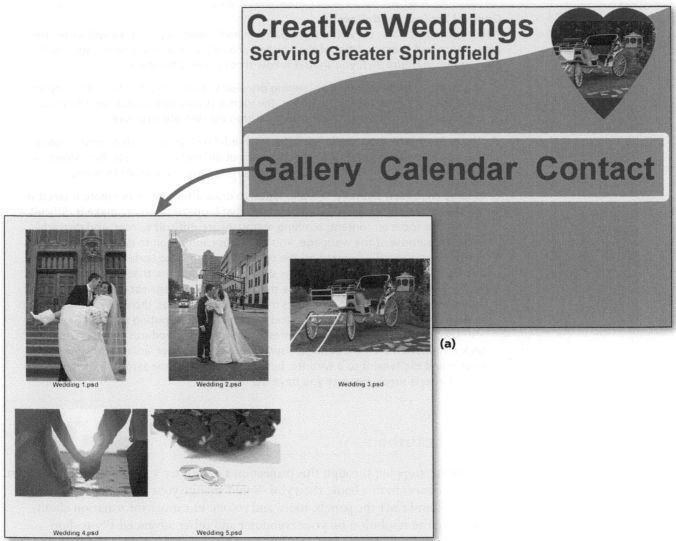

(a)

(b)

Figure 9–1

Overview

As you read this chapter, you will learn how to create the website shown in
Figure 9–1 by performing these general tasks:

- Generate a contact sheet.
- Create slices from text for navigation.
- Set slice options for hyperlinks.
- Create a 3D model using a predefined mesh.
- Manipulate a 3D model.
- Create multiple layers and position them for animation.
- Create frames in the Timeline panel.
- Create new frames using tweening.
- Use the Timeline panel to set animation options.
- Preview the animation.

General Project Guidelines

When editing a photo, the actions you perform and decisions you make will affect the appearance and characteristics of the finished product. As you edit photos, such as the ones shown in Figure 9–1, you should follow these general guidelines:

1. **Use standard web design and planning principles.** As you develop the site, keep in mind the site's purpose, the audience, the elements you plan to include, the visual impact, and the placement of the pages within the website structure.

2. **Create 3D objects from predefined shapes.** Predefined shapes such as cones, cubes, and cylinders can be used to create hundreds of different 3D objects. Beginning with a mathematically correct shape gives you a strong base from which to work.

3. **Employ animation carefully.** Use animation to draw attention to or create interest in a website, but do not overdo it. Animations that loop continuously make it difficult for users to focus on content; scrolling marquees are difficult to read and distract from the purpose of the webpage. You should use animation to draw the viewer's attention to a specific element on the page, alert readers to updated information, or create hot spots. Animation always should have a purpose that is related to the content in the page. Weigh the value the animation adds against its disadvantages: animation reduces performance, uses more system resources, increases load time, and seldom runs optimally on both low-end and high-end computing systems. Research also suggests that animation sometimes is distracting and reduces the user's ability to seek information on the webpage. Used judiciously however, animation adds visual appeal and excitement to a website, but you should resist the temptation to include special effects simply because you have the expertise.

To Start Photoshop

If you are stepping through this project on a computer and you want your screen to match the figures in this book, then you should change your computer's resolution to 1366 × 768 and reset the panels, tools, and colors. For more information about how to change the resolution on your computer and other advanced Photoshop settings, read the Editing Preferences Appendix.

The following steps, which assume Windows 8 is running, start Photoshop based on a typical installation. You may need to ask your instructor how to start Photoshop for your system.

1 With Windows 8 running, scroll to display the Adobe Photoshop CC tile on the Start screen.

2 Tap or click the Adobe Photoshop CC tile to run the Photoshop app.

3 After a few moments, when the Photoshop window appears, if the window is not maximized, tap or click the Maximize button next to the Close button on the Application bar to maximize the window.

To Set the Workspace and the Layers Panel

The following steps select and reset the Essentials workspace, as well as setting options on the Layers panel.

1 Tap or click the workspace switcher on the options bar to display the list, and then tap or click Essentials to select the default workspace panels.

2   Tap or click the workspace switcher on the options bar again to display the list, and then tap or click Reset Essentials to restore the workspace to its default settings and reposition any panels that might have been moved by previous users.

3   Tap or click the Layers panel menu button and then tap or click Panel Options. In the Panel Options dialog box, tap or click the medium thumbnail, and tap or click to select the Layer Bounds options button. Tap or click the OK button.

To Reset the Tools and the Options Bar

Recall that the Tools panel and the options bar retain their settings from previous Photoshop sessions. The following steps select the Rectangular Marquee Tool and reset all tool settings in the options bar.

1   If the tools in the Tools panel appear in two columns, tap or click the double arrow at the top of the Tools panel.

2   If necessary, tap or click the 'Rectangular Marquee Tool' button on the Tools panel to select it.

3   On the options bar, press and hold or right-click the 'Rectangular Marquee Tool' icon to display the context menu, and then tap or click 'Reset All Tools'. When Photoshop displays a confirmation dialog box, tap or click the OK button to restore the tools to their default settings.

To Set the Interface and Default Colors

Recall that Photoshop retains the interface color scheme, as well as the foreground and background colors from session to session. The following steps set the interface to Medium Gray and the foreground and background colors to black over white.

1   Tap or click Edit on the Application bar to display the Edit menu. Tap or click Preferences, and then tap or click Interface on the Preferences submenu to display the Preferences dialog box.

2   If necessary, tap or click the third button, Medium Gray, to change the interface color scheme.

3   Tap or click the OK button to close the Preferences dialog box.

4   Tap or click the 'Default Foreground and Background Colors' button on the Tools panel to set the default colors to black and white. If black is not over white on the Tools panel, tap or click the 'Switch Foreground and Background Colors' button.

MAC For a detailed example of this procedure using the Mac operating system, refer to the For Mac Users Appendix.

Contact Sheets

Contact sheets combine multiple small images into a single document or page for the purpose of previewing or comparing the images. In film photography, contact sheets often were used to scan quickly for the highest quality images from a roll of film. In digital photography, thumbnail images are printed for quick reference or to display on the web. Also known as an index sheet or proof sheet, contact sheets are useful to show clients how a finished photo might look.

BTW | **Web Galleries**
Previous versions of Photoshop and Adobe Bridge included the ability to create web galleries, an interactive web contact sheet that displayed one photo at a time. Photoshop CC and Bridge CC no longer include web galleries. Adobe offers web galleries as an optional download or add-in app. Or, you can create web galleries using the Adobe Lightroom CC application.

In Photoshop, the Contact Sheet command is one of several advanced automation commands including **droplets**, which are executable scripts that can process multiple photos, and **PDF presentations**, which save multiple photos as a PDF file or automate them into a slide show.

To Create a Contact Sheet

The owner of Creative Weddings would like to showcase her services on her website by displaying photos related to her business. The following steps create a contact sheet with five photos from the Data Files for Students. In business situations, you can include many more photos and create multiple sheets. Because the contact sheet will be displayed on the web, you will create a sheet with the dimensions of 800 × 600 pixels. For fast loading, you will set the resolution to 72 dpi (dots per inch).

1

- Tap or click File on the Application bar, and then tap or click Automate to display the Automate submenu (Figure 9–2).

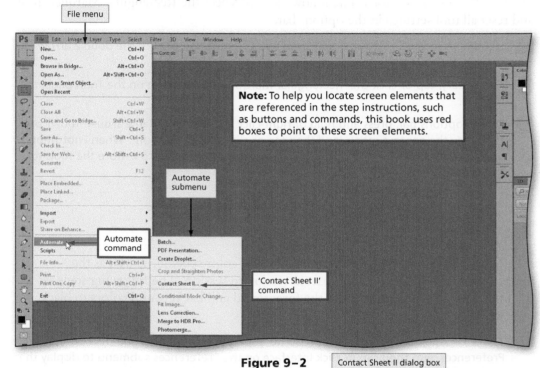

Note: To help you locate screen elements that are referenced in the step instructions, such as buttons and commands, this book uses red boxes to point to these screen elements.

Figure 9–2

2

- Tap or click 'Contact Sheet II' to display the Contact Sheet II dialog box.

- In the Source Images area, tap or click the Use button to display its list (Figure 9–3).

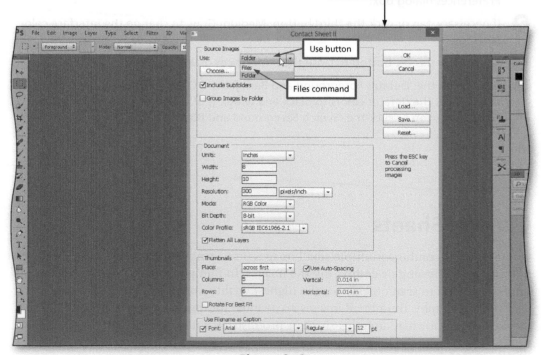

Figure 9–3

3

- Tap or click Files in the list because you want to create a contact sheet from files.

- Tap or click the Browse button to display the Open dialog box.

- Navigate to the Data Files for Students and the Chapter 09 folder.

- Tap or click the Wedding 1 file to select it.

- SHIFT+tap or SHIFT+click the Wedding 5 file to add it, and all the Wedding files in between, to the selection (Figure 9–4).

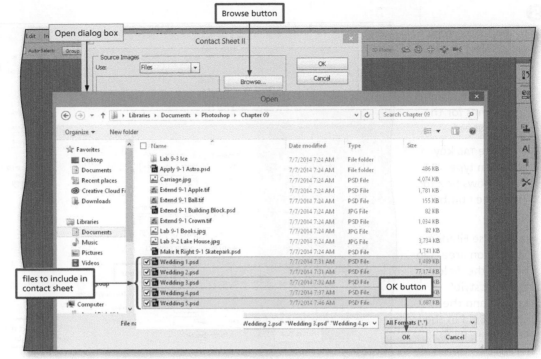

Figure 9–4

Q&A Could I choose a folder of images?

Yes. You can tap or click the Use button and then choose Folder, if all of your images are in a unique folder on your system.

4

- Tap or click the OK button or Open button to add the photos to the contact sheet list.

- In the Document area, tap or click the Units button and then tap or click pixels in the list.

- Press the TAB key and then type 800 in the Width box.

- Press the TAB key and then type 600 in the Height box.

- Press the TAB key and then type 72 in the Resolution box (Figure 9–5).

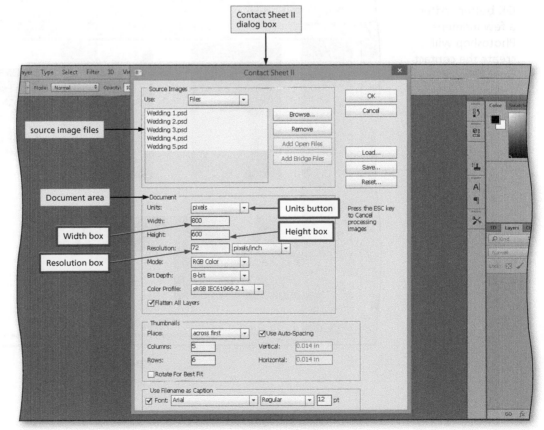

Figure 9–5

5

- In the Thumbnails area, select the text in the Columns box and then type   3 to enter the number of columns for the contact sheet.

- Press the TAB key and then type   2 in the Rows box to enter the number of rows.

- In the Use Filename as Caption area, tap or click the 'Select the font style' button and then choose Bold in the list (Figure 9–6).

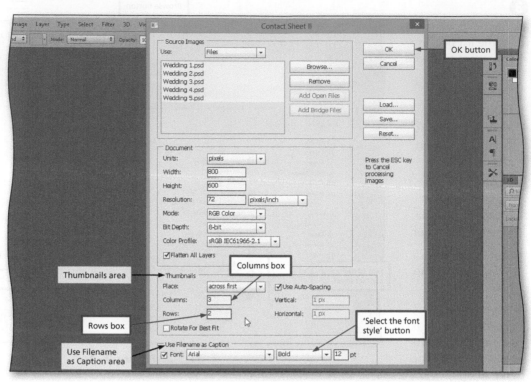

Figure 9–6

6

- Tap or click the OK button. After a few moments, Photoshop will create the contact sheet (Figure 9–7).

contact sheet displays two rows and three columns of pictures

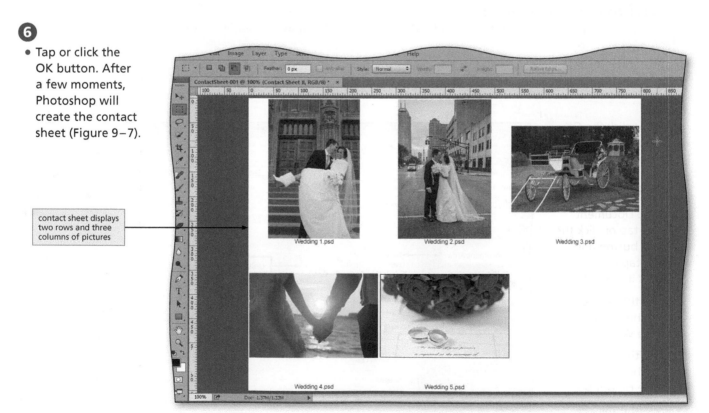

Figure 9–7

To Change the Background Color

The Creative Weddings company uses a sage, cream, and dark red color scheme. The following steps change the background color.

1 On the Tools panel, double-tap or double-click the 'Set foreground color' button to display the Color Picker (Foreground Color) dialog box.

2 In the hexadecimal # box, enter `f9f2ca` to create a cream color.

3 Tap or click the OK button to close the dialog box.

4 On the Tools panel, select the 'Paint Bucket Tool'.

5 Tap or click the white background in the document window to change it to a cream background (Figure 9–8).

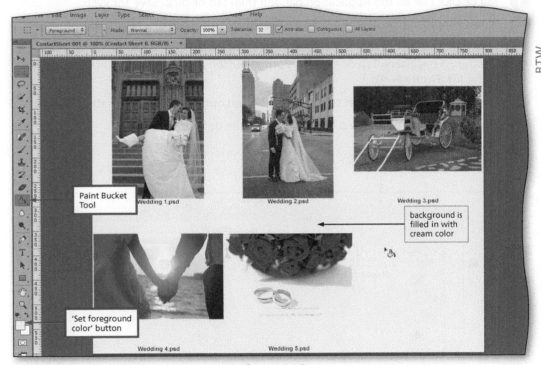

Paint Bucket Tool

Wedding 1.psd

Wedding 2.psd

Wedding 3.psd

background is filled in with cream color

'Set foreground color' button

Wedding 4.psd

Wedding 5.psd

Figure 9–8

BTW

The Photoshop Window
The chapters in this book begin with the Photoshop window appearing as it did at the initial installation of the software. Your Photoshop window might look different depending on your screen resolution and other Photoshop settings.

To Save the Contact Sheet in the PSD Format

The following steps save the file in the PSD Format, and create a new Chapter 09 folder on your storage device.

1 Tap or click File on the Application bar and then tap or click Save As to display the Save As dialog box.

2 In the File name text box, type `Contact Sheet` to rename the file. Do not press the ENTER key after typing the file name.

3 Navigate to your storage location (or the Creative Cloud Files location).

4 Tap or click the New folder button on the Save As dialog box toolbar to create a new folder on the selected storage device.

5 When the new folder appears, type `Chapter 09` to change the name of the folder, and then press the ENTER key. Double-tap or double-click the new folder to open it.

⑥ If necessary, tap or click the 'Save as type' button to display the list of available file formats, and then tap or click Photoshop (*.PSD;*.PDD) in the list to select the file type.

⑦ Tap or click the Save button to save the document on the selected drive, in the new folder, and with the new file name. If Photoshop displays a dialog box, tap or click the OK button.

To Save the Contact Sheet as a Web Graphic

The following steps save the contact sheet as a web graphic. Recall that a graphic destined for the web commonly is saved as a GIF file, which will display quickly in a browser. Saving it as a single image file, rather than as an HTML file with a supporting folder, will save space.

① Tap or click File on the Application bar and then tap or click 'Save for Web'.

② When Photoshop displays the Save for Web dialog box, tap or click the Save button.

③ When Photoshop displays the Save Optimized As dialog box, navigate to your storage location, if necessary. Tap or click the Format button and then tap or click Images only in the list (Figure 9–9).

④ Tap or click the Save button to save the file as an optimized image for the website.

⑤ Close the file and press the D key to return to the default colors.

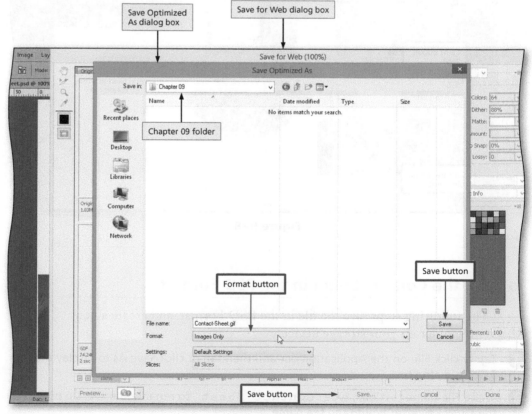

Figure 9–9

Designing a Webpage

Planning is the most important step when designing webpages and websites. A **webpage** is a single page of graphics and information that you view using web browser software. A **website** is a collection of webpages that are linked logically, and located together on a hosting computer. Webpages within websites typically share a common design and are navigated, or browsed, using some kind of graphic elements — buttons or images — that move the browser from page to page. To be an effective web designer, you need to understand and apply principles of web design and programming protocols, and become proficient with many planning and design tools, including web programming languages and scripting tools. As a graphic designer, however, you might need to use Photoshop to prepare graphics for the webpage or to plan the site with galleries, graphics, color, links, and animation. Without the visual impact of color, shapes, and contrast, webpages are neither interesting nor motivating.

Use standard web design and planning principles.

When planning webpages, you should consider several important issues:

- **Purpose** — Decide on the site's intended use; for example, advertising, direct sales, business-to-business tasks, prospect generation, employee communications, customer support, information, or education.

- **Audience** — Take into account the target population and the characteristics, preferences, web experience, and computer systems of the audience, and adapt the site design accordingly.

- **Viewer expectations** — Examine the webpage to see if links and other elements are located in common places, test the ease of navigation and form fields, check for usability issues, and so on. Navigation elements, such as buttons and tabs, typically are placed on the top or left side of a webpage.

- **Visual characteristics of planned elements or content** — Make sure that text, images, color, and animation are used judiciously and with purpose.

- **Viewer's visual impact** — Research shows that web users form first impressions of webpages in as little as 50 milliseconds, making nearly instantaneous judgments of a website's visual appeal, including the loading speed, perceived credibility, usability, and attraction.

- **Page's placement within the website structure** — Careful planning of the home page, secondary page(s), links, and accompanying folders involves the design and application of naming conventions, file hierarchy, and structure.

Plan Ahead

You begin creating the Creative Weddings website by designing a home page, which serves as a starting place from which to access several other pages. Colors on a home page should be web-safe and should match theme or company colors. A graphic, clipped within a shape, will add interest. You also will insert a title heading and subheading.

BTW

Student Companion Site
Visit the Student Companion Site located on www.cengagebrain.com. For detailed instructions about accessing available resources, visit www.cengage.com/ct/studentdownload or contact your instructor for information about accessing the required files.

Setting Webpage Dimensions and Colors

Webpages come in a variety of sizes; however, most pages usually fall within certain height and width limits. It is important to choose a size for your webpage that will accommodate the majority of users' monitors and screen size settings. Oversized webpages designed on larger screens with resolutions of 1024×768 or higher become unreadable when viewing the page using narrower browser widths. The graphics might be too wide to fit the browser window, and unwrapped text might create long, unreadable lines. Web designers constantly analyze and compare existing websites for usage guidelines related to screen colors, screen size, scrolling, graphics, and readability of text.

Another consideration is the possibility that the site visitor will want to print the webpage. Setting the dimensions of the webpage to 800 × 600 pixels will accommodate most users visually, but for webpages destined for print on 8.5 × 11-inch paper, you should try to keep text and graphics within 760 pixels wide and 410 pixels high to account for margins when printed.

A final consideration is the color scheme. You should work in RGB colors that display better on screens than CMYK. Make sure you choose web-safe colors.

To Set Attributes for a New Document

The following steps set the attributes for a new web document that will be used as the Creative Weddings home page. Recall that a common resolution for web products is 72 pixels per inch (PPI). By using 800 × 600 pixels, most visitors to the webpage will not have to scroll to see the information. Later, as part of a complete website solution, HTML code could be added to create more flexibility and to adjust screen size further.

1 Press CTRL+N to display the New dialog box and type **Creative Weddings Home Page** in the Name text box.

2 Tap or click the Width unit button and then tap or click Pixels in the list, if necessary.

3 Double-tap or double-click the Width box and then type **800**.

4 Double-tap or double-click the Height box and then type **600**.

5 Double-tap or double-click the Resolution box and then type **72**. Tap or click the Resolution unit button and then tap or click Pixels/Inch in the list, if necessary.

6 Change the Color Mode to RGB Color, 8 bit.

7 If necessary, tap or click the Background Contents button and then tap or click White in the list to finish setting the attributes for the new file (Figure 9–10).

8 Tap or click the OK button to create the new document.

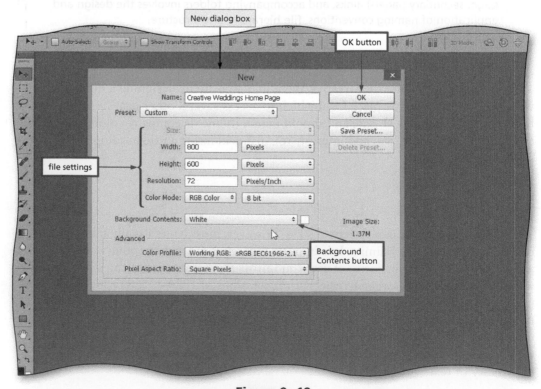

Figure 9–10

To Set the Rulers to Pixels

Using pixels as the unit of measurement in the rulers allows you to keep in mind the page layout, both for browsers and printing of graphics and text. The following steps display the rulers and change the units to pixels.

- If the rulers are not displayed in the document window, press CTRL+R.
- Press and hold or right-click either of the rulers to display the context menu (Figure 9–11).

- Tap or click Pixels in the list to change the ruler units to pixels.

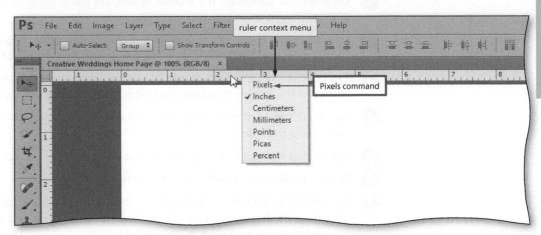

Figure 9–11

To Choose RGB Sliders

Because webpages will be displayed on the screen, it is appropriate to use the RGB colors. The following steps choose RGB sliders and the RGB spectrum.

1 Tap or click the Color panel menu button, and then tap or click RGB Sliders on the context menu.

2 Tap or click the Color panel menu button, and then tap or click RGB Spectrum on the context menu.

To Color the Background

The following steps set the background color to a web-safe sage color. You can use the sliders or enter numbers in the Color boxes.

1 On the Color panel, set the R color to 135. Set the G color to 145. Set the B color to 118.

2 On the Tools panel, select the 'Paint Bucket Tool'.

3 Tap or click the canvas to change the color of the background (Figure 9–12).

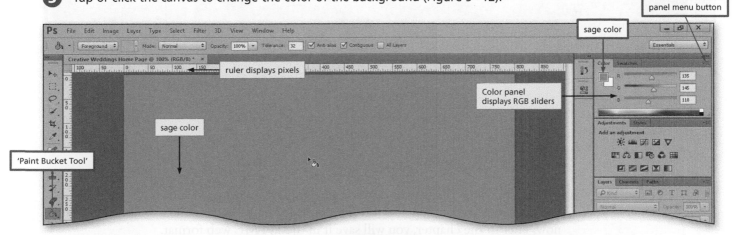

Figure 9–12

To Add a Contrast Color

The following steps use the Pen Tool to create a shape in the upper-left corner of the website, using a contrasting cream color.

1 On the Color panel, set the R color to 249. Set the G color to 242. Set the B color to 202, creating a cream color.

2 Select the Pen Tool. On the options bar, set the Mode to Shape. If necessary, tap or click the Fill box and then choose the cream color in the list of recently used colors.

3 Tap or click the upper-left corner of the canvas and then tap or click the upper-right corner of the canvas to create the first path line along the top border of the canvas.

4 Tap or click the left margin at approximately 225 pixels as shown on the vertical ruler to create a triangle.

5 Tap or click the upper-left corner anchor point to close the path.

6 On the Tools panel, select the 'Add Anchor Point Tool'.

7 Tap or click to add an anchor point on the diagonal side, at approximately 175 as shown on the horizontal ruler. Drag the anchor point up and slightly right to create an inward curve, as shown in Figure 9–13.

8 Tap or click to add another anchor point, at approximately 475 as shown on the horizontal ruler. Drag the anchor point down and slightly left to create an outward curve, as shown in Figure 9–13.

9 Rename the layer, cream accent corner.

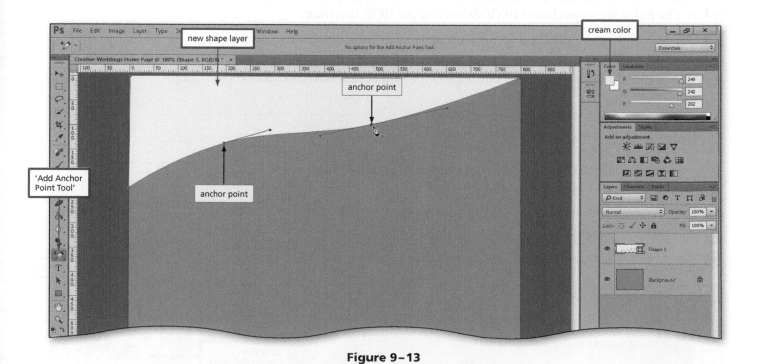

Figure 9–13

To Save the New Document

With the settings and background complete, it is a good time to save the document on your storage device. The following steps save it in the PSD format for now; later in the chapter, you will save it in the HTML web format.

1 Tap or click File on the Application bar to display the File menu and then tap or click Save As to display the Save As dialog box.

2 If necessary, type `Creative Weddings Home Page` in the File name text box. Do not press the ENTER key after typing the file name.

3 Navigate to your storage location (or the Creative Cloud Files location).

4 Double-tap or double-click the Chapter 09 folder to open it.

5 If necessary, tap or click the 'Save as type' button to display the list of available file formats, and then tap or click Photoshop (*.PSD;*.PDD) in the list to select the file type.

6 Tap or click the Save button to save the document on the selected drive, in the new folder, and with the new file name. If Photoshop displays a dialog box, tap or click the OK button.

Perspective Warp and Puppet Warp

Perspective Warp allows you to warp an image based on vertical and horizontal planes. With Perspective Warp, you create a grid over the image and drag points on the grid to define the perspective of the original image, indicating planes. If necessary, you can create multiple grids for strong corners in the image. You then manipulate or warp the image so you can view it from a range of different angles, as if you were walking around it. It is ideal for focusing one part of an image such as a specific side of a building, or to change the perspective on a layer so that it matches other layers in the image.

Another warp feature in Photoshop is the Puppet Warp. **Puppet Warp** provides a visual mesh or grid that lets you distort specific image areas by creating points in the mesh. Dragging a point distorts or moves the specific portion of the image, while leaving other areas intact. Options bar settings include Mode to determine the elasticity of the mesh, Density to determine the spacing, and Expansion to change the outer edge of the mesh. You might use Puppet Warp to apply subtle retouching and reshaping of a specific portion of the image, or for larger transformations such as moving an arm or a leg. It is common to use Puppet Warp on smart object layers or vector masks. You will apply warp adjustments to one of the wedding photos.

To Use Perspective Warp

The steps on the next page place an image of a wedding carriage on the canvas. Visit solutions.cengage.com /ctdownloads for detailed instructions or contact your instructor for information about accessing the required files. You then will use Perspective Warp to focus on the passenger seat. As with the 3D tools from the previous chapter, the Perspective Warp command needs to use the graphics accelerator feature on your system.

1

• On the File menu, tap or click Place Embedded. Navigate to the Photoshop Data Files for Students and the Chapter 09 folder.

• Double-tap or double-click the Carriage file to place the image.

• Press the ENTER key to finish embedding the image (Figure 9–14).

Figure 9–14

2

• Tap or click Edit on the Application bar to display the Edit menu (Figure 9–15).

Q&A My Perspective Warp command is grayed out. What should I do?
Your graphics processor might not be turned on. If necessary, close your file without quitting Photoshop. Press CTRL+K to display the Preferences dialog box, and then tap or click Performance. Place a check mark in the 'Use Graphics Processor' check box, and then tap or click the OK button.

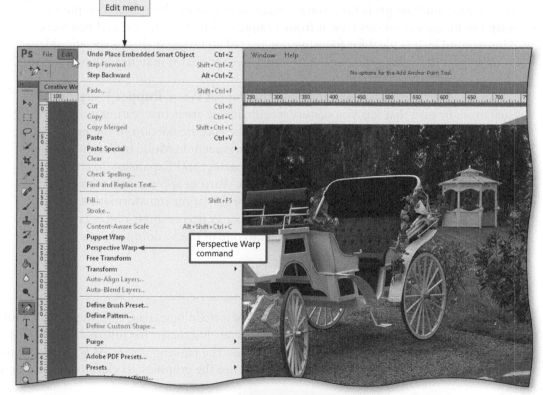

Figure 9–15

Restart Photoshop and open your file again. Select the carriage layer. The Perspective Warp command now should be enabled.

- Tap or click
  Perspective Warp
  to display the
  Perspective Warp
  options bar and
  pointer.

- If necessary,
  tap or click the
  Layout button on
  the options bar
  (Figure 9–16).

Q&A What do the other
buttons do?
The three buttons to
the right of the Warp
button straighten
and level the vertical
and horizontal
layout lines.

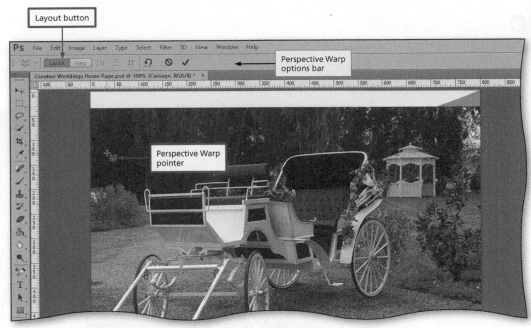

Figure 9–16

- In the document
  window, drag
  to create a grid
  that includes the
  passenger seat and
  the right side of the
  image, as shown in
  Figure 9–17.

Experiment

- Drag internal grid
  lines to practice
  moving the grid.
  Press CTRL+Z to undo
  the move. Drag a
  corner to watch the
  grid change. Press
  CTRL+Z to undo the
  move. Drag a second
  grid near the first
  and watch Photoshop
  join the grids. Press
  CTRL+Z to remove the
  second grid.

Figure 9–17

5

- Drag the lower-right corner up, to match the plane or angle in the lower part of the scene (Figure 9–18).

Q&A What do I do if an image has a strong corner and each side has different planes? In the case of strong corners, you should create two grids that meet along the corner; that way, you can adjust different angles for each side of the photo.

point adjusted so line matches angle of driveway

Figure 9–18

6

- Drag the upper-right corner down to match the straight line of the gazebo (Figure 9–19).

Q&A Does the image have multiple planes? Yes. It is common for images to have different planes and angles in the foreground and background. The Perspective Warp works best when you identify all of the angles.

point adjusted

gridline matches angle of gazebo

Figure 9–19

7

- On the options bar, tap or click the Warp button to display a warp bounding box in the document window.

- In the document window, SHIFT+tap or SHIFT+click the left vertical line to select it (Figure 9–20).

Q&A Why did I select the line?
Selecting the line will ensure that the warp affects all of the image vertically. In the warp mode, if you drag only a corner, the warp transforms using a corner perspective.

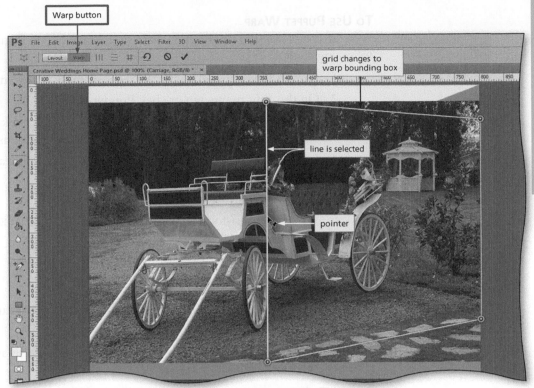

Warp button

grid changes to warp bounding box

line is selected

pointer

Figure 9–20

8

- Drag the lower-left handle further to the left to focus on the passenger seat (Figure 9–21).

 Experiment

- Drag other handles and watch the image change. After each transformation, press CTRL+Z. SHIFT+tap or SHIFT+click the vertical line to deselect it. Drag a handle and watch the image change. Press CTRL+Z to undo.

9

- Press the ENTER key to commit the warp.

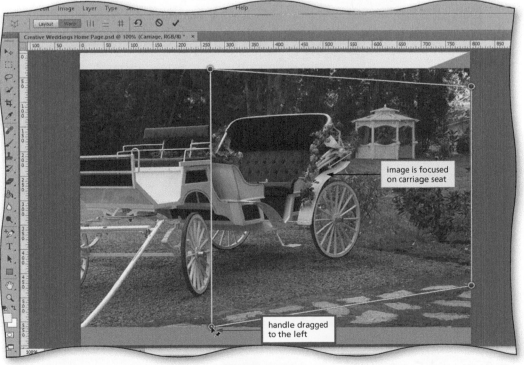

image is focused on carriage seat

handle dragged to the left

Figure 9–21

TO USE PUPPET WARP

If you wanted to use Puppet Warp on an image, you would perform the following steps.

1. On the Layers panel, select the layer or mask you want to transform.

2. On the Edit menu, tap or click Puppet Warp.

3. On the options bar, tap or click the Show Mesh check mark, if necessary to display the mesh. Adjust the mode, density, and expansion.

4. In the image window, click to add pins to areas you want to transform and areas you want to anchor in place.

5. Drag the pins to warp the mesh.

6. When the transformation is complete, press the ENTER key.

To Resize and Move the Carriage

The following steps resize and move the carriage to the upper-right corner of the webpage.

1 Press CTRL+T to display the bounding box. If Photoshop displays an information dialog box, tap or click the OK button.

2 SHIFT+drag a corner handle and resize the carriage image to approximately .10% as shown on the options bar.

3 Drag the image to the upper-right corner of the canvas as shown in Figure 9–22.

4 Press the ENTER key to commit the transformation.

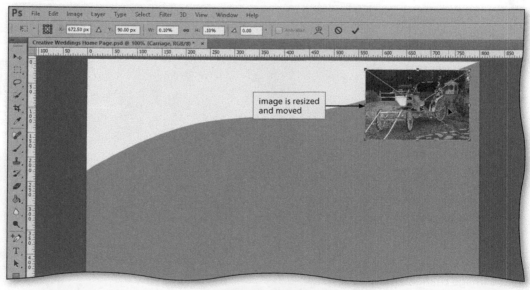

Figure 9–22

To Append Custom Shapes

The following steps append new shapes to the Custom Shapes tool in preparation for creating a heart-shaped clipping mask.

- On the Tools panel, press and hold or right-click the current shape tool button and then tap or click 'Custom Shape Tool' to choose the tool.

- On the options bar, tap or click the Custom Shape picker to display the pop-up panel.

- Tap or click the panel menu button to display the list of shape libraries (Figure 9–23).

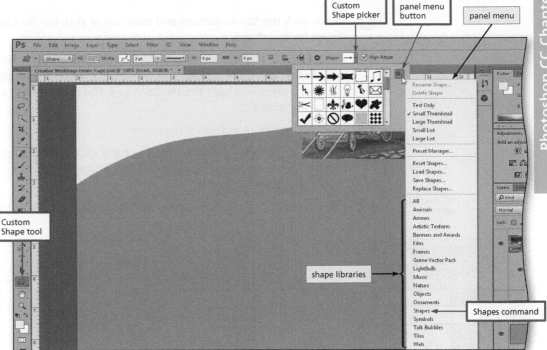

Figure 9–23

- Tap or click Shapes. When Photoshop asks if you want to append the library, tap or click the Append button.

- In the pop-up panel, scroll as necessary and then tap or click the Heart shape (not the Heart Card shape) (Figure 9–24).

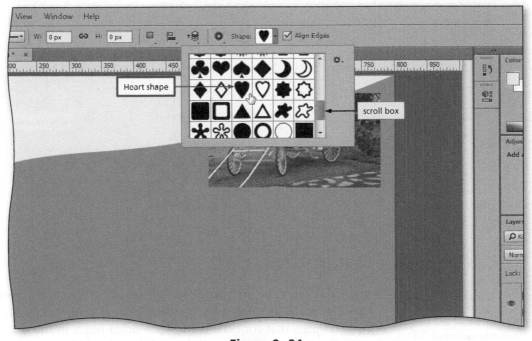

Figure 9–24

To Create a Clipping Shape

The following steps create a heart shape and use it to outline the carriage.

1 On the Layers panel, select the cream accent corner layer so the new layer will appear above it.

2 Press SHIFT+CTRL+N to create a new layer. Name the layer, heart.

3 On the Custom Shape options bar, tap or click the Fill button to display the pop-up panel and then tap or click Dark Red to select the fill color.

4 Tap or click the Stroke button and then tap or click the No Color button to specify to stroke for the shape.

5 In the document window, slowly drag a heart over the passenger seat of the carriage. Include the gazebo, if possible. As you drag, if you need to adjust the placement of the heart, press and hold the SPACEBAR key. The heart should extend slightly above and below the graphic.

6 Release the mouse button, if necessary.

7 On the Layers panel, press and hold or right-click the Carriage layer to display the context menu, and then tap or click 'Create Clipping Mask' to clip the picture to the shape of the layer below it.

8 Use the Move Tool, if necessary to adjust the heart or the carriage layer (Figure 9–25).

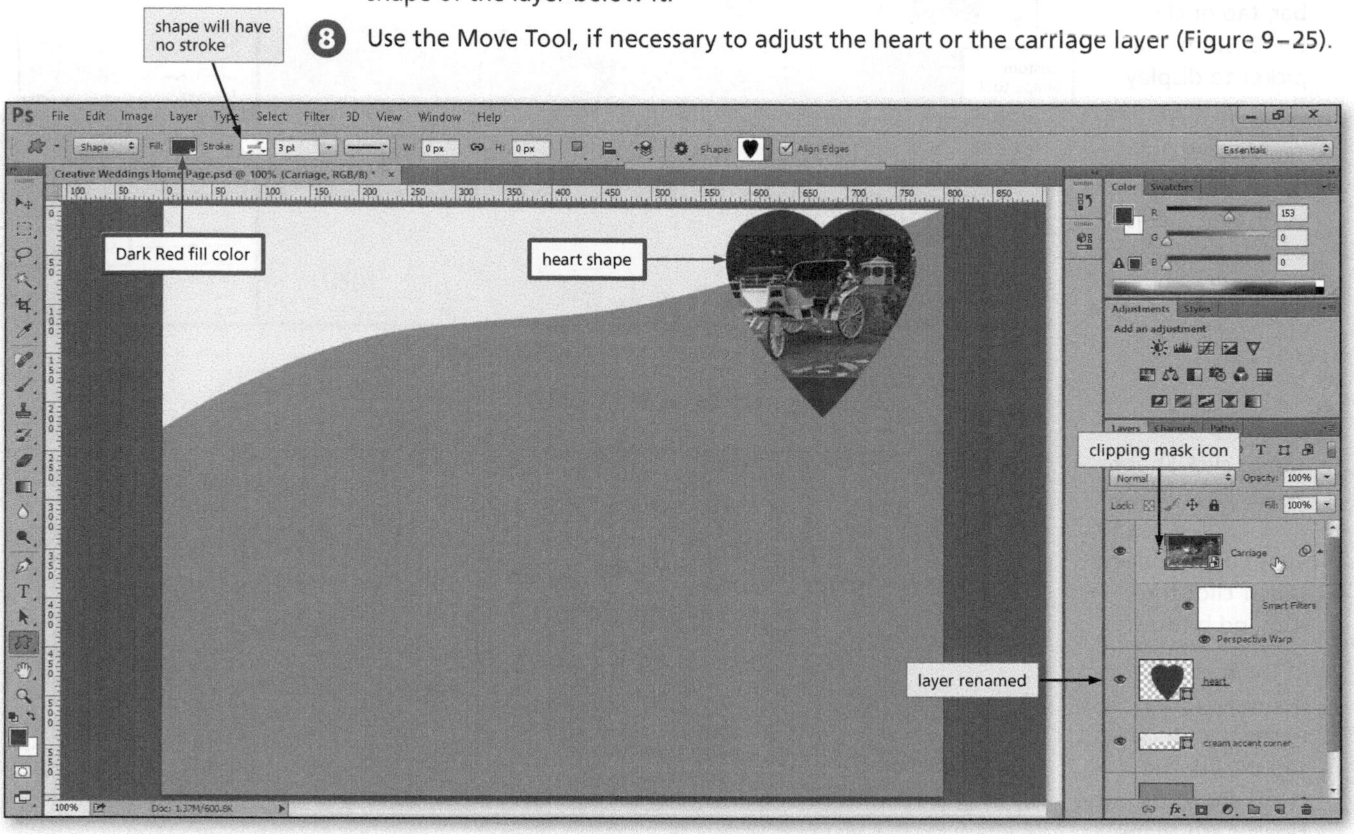

shape will have no stroke

Dark Red fill color

heart shape

clipping mask icon

layer renamed

Figure 9–25

Navigation Bars

BTW

Web Fonts
The Arial and Helvetica fonts look very similar to each other, and to the average casual reader, may even be indistinguishable. Between the systems that have the Arial font and those with the Helvetica font, the combination covers most of the commercially sold operating systems. Using HTML code, you can specify the combination "Helvetica, Arial, sans-serif" so that if the Helvetica typeface is available, it will be used in preference to Arial.

After looking at the masthead to identify the website, most users look for a text heading and a **navigation bar** to identify a site's content. A navigation bar is an area on a webpage that contains the links to other pages in the site. Navigation elements typically are buttons or text links, and they should be consistent in their appearance, with text characteristics that differentiate the navigational elements from other elements on the page. Using placement, font size, and font style appropriately and consistently for various text elements helps users identify the webpage heading, navigation bar links, and regular page content. Many websites use a sans serif font because it is easy to read on a computer monitor. In the Creative Weddings website, you will use an Arial font that should appear correctly in most browsers. Color is a secondary consideration for text because not all users will be able to distinguish colors. Choosing colors with high contrast is the best choice for accessibility and readability. For more information about colors and contrast, read the Graphic Design Overview Appendix.

In the Creative Weddings website, you will use a dark red color for the text, which will provide contrast against the cream and sage backgrounds.

To Create Heading Text

The following steps create text using the secondary color, Dark Red.

1 On the Layers panel, select the Carriage layer.

2 Select the 'Horizontal Type Tool'. On the options bar, select the Arial Bold font, a Bold font style, a size of 60 pt, a Crisp anti-aliasing method, and left aligned.

3 If the font color is not Dark Red, tap or click the Color box, tap or click the heart in the document window, and then tap or click the OK button to close the Color Picker (Text Color) dialog box.

4 Tap or click the upper-left corner of the canvas to create point text. Type `Creative Weddings` to create the heading. Confirm the text on the options bar.

5 Tap or click below the previous text. Change the font size to 36 pt. Type `Serving Greater Springfield` to create the subheading. Confirm the text on the options bar (Figure 9–26).

new text is Arial Bold 60

new text is Arial Bold 36

Figure 9–26

To Create the Navigation Bar

The following step creates the text that will later become the navigation bar. The navigation bar will include the elements that allow a user to navigate around the site.

1

- Using the same settings on the Horizontal Type Tool options bar, tap or click in the document window at 300 pixels on the vertical ruler and about 25 on the horizontal ruler (be sure that the vertical position is at or hi-gher than 300 pixels). Change the font size back to 60.

new text

Figure 9–27

- Type `Gallery` and then press the SPACEBAR two times.

- Type `Calendar` and then press the SPACEBAR two times.

- Type `Contact` to complete the navigation bar text. Confirm the text on the options bar (Figure 9–27).

To Organize Layers

The following steps create two layer groups: one for the heading objects and one for the navigation bar. The Heading Objects group will contain the picture and text layers at the top. The Navigation Bar group will contain the text in the middle, a border you will create later, and future hyperlinked slices.

1 Select the cream accent corner layer, the heart layer, the Carriage layer, the Creative Weddings layer, and the Serving Greater Springfield layer.

2 Press and hold or right-click the selected layers, and then tap or click 'Group from Layers'. Name the group, **Heading Objects**, and use a green identification color.

3 Select the Gallery Calendar Contact layer.

4 On the Layer menu, tap or click New, and then tap or click 'Group from Layers'. In the Name text box, type **Navigation Bar** and use a red identification color.

5 Minimize the Heading Objects group on the Layers panel, if necessary, and select the Gallery layer (Figure 9–28).

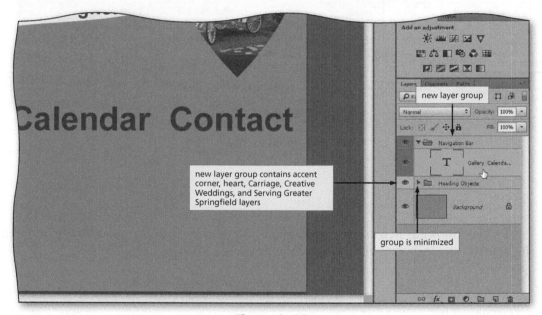

Figure 9–28

To Save the File Again

Because you have completed entering the text for the site, the following step saves the file.

1 Press CTRL+S. If Photoshop displays a dialog box, tap or click the OK button.

Break Point: If you wish to take a break, this is a good place to do so. Press CTRL+Q to quit Photoshop. To resume at a later time, start Photoshop, open the file named Creative Weddings Home Page, and continue following the steps from this location forward.

Creating Slices

The navigation functionality — the visitor's ability to move from one webpage to another — will be assigned to the navigation bar you just created. You will convert each of the navigation text elements to a slice. A **slice** is a defined rectangular area in a document that performs a specific function, such as opening a different webpage, when the page is viewed in a web browser. Another common application of slices is the creation of image maps. An **image map** is a graphic containing one or more invisible regions, called **hot spots**, that are hyperlinked. For example, you could slice a map of the United States into an image map by assigning hot spots to each state. Tapping or clicking an individual state then would cause the browser to perform a designated task such as displaying a different webpage or moving to another location on the current page. Slices give you better control over the function and file size of your image because you can optimize slices to load individually. When you save a sliced image for the web, each slice is saved as an independent file with its own settings and color table; the slice preserves hyperlinks and special effects; however, when viewed in a browser, the slices will appear as a single webpage.

You create a slice by dividing a single object into smaller segments using the Slice Tool or by creating layer-based slices, which are slices that are created automatically from the contents of a layer. The Slice Tool is located with the Crop Tool on the Tools panel. Once you create a slice, you can select, move, resize, or align it. You can assign each slice an individual hyperlink.

Photoshop displays a number and a badge on the slice when you create it. A **slice badge** is an icon that appears next to the slice number, indicating certain information about the slice. A slice badge indicates whether the slice is image based, layer based, or has no content. Photoshop displays a blue slice number and blue slice badge on user-defined slices; automatically created slices display gray slice numbers and gray slice badges. Numbering of slices is from left to right and top to bottom, beginning in the upper-left corner of the image. If you change the arrangement or total number of slices, Photoshop updates the slice numbers to reflect the new order.

The Slice Tool options bar allows you to designate an exact size for the slice or use guides to create a slice.

To Create Slices

The following steps create slices in the Creative Weddings home page. You will slice the Gallery layer into three sections, each of which will serve as a link to other parts of the Creative Weddings website.

1

- On the Layers panel, select the text layer in the Navigation Bar group. On the Tools panel, press and hold or right-click the Crop Tool button to display the context menu (Figure 9–29).

Figure 9–29

2

- Tap or click Slice Tool to select it.

- In the document window, position the pointer at the left margin, just above the word, Gallery. Drag a rectangle around the word, Gallery (Figure 9–30).

Q&A What are all those symbols and lines? After you create your custom slice, Photoshop slices the remaining areas of the page into numbered pieces above, below, and to either side of the Gallery slice. In the slice badge, a mountain icon indicates that the slice has image content.

Figure 9–30

3

- In the document window, drag a rectangle around the word, Calendar, to create a slice. As you drag, allow Photoshop to snap the slice into position so it is the same height as the Gallery slice (Figure 9–31).

Q&A Why are the slices numbered 1, 2, and 3? Photoshop starts slicing the page at the top-left corner. Because your slice began approximately halfway down, slice 1 is the upper portion of the canvas.

Figure 9–31

4
- Create a slice for the word, Contact (Figure 9–32).

Figure 9–32

Other Ways

1. On Layer menu, tap or click 'New Layer Based Slice'

The Slice Select Tool

Once you create a slice, you can select, move, resize, align, distribute, and assign attributes using the Slice Select Tool. With the Slice Select Tool activated, you select a slice by clicking it. To move a slice, tap or click within the slice and drag. To resize a slice, drag its border or drag a handle. The Slice Select Tool options bar displays many buttons to reorder, align, and distribute (Figure 9–33). Other Slice Select Tool options — including the ability to delete, divide, and reorder — are available by pressing and holding or right-clicking the slice.

The Slice Options dialog box (Figure 9–33) appears when you double-tap or double-click a slice; you can use it to set values associated with a slice.

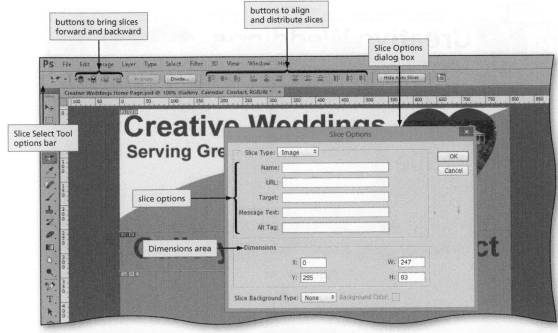

Figure 9–33

Each slice becomes a small image when converted to HTML. Photoshop generates the code behind the scenes to make each slice into an image and a hyperlink. When you save the overall file in the HTML format, Photoshop stores each slice as a gif file in an images folder. The HTML code also is responsible for putting the pieces back together in a browser. The Name box of the Slice Options dialog box automatically generates the name of that image, although you can change it. The URL box holds the webpage address of the hyperlink. The Target box allows you to specify how the link will open — in a new browser window (or browser tab) or as a replacement of the current page. For example, a target setting of _blank will cause the hyperlink to open the webpage in a new browser window or tab. Table 9–1 displays the various values you can use in the Target box.

Table 9–1 Target Box Values	
Value	**Description**
_blank	Opens the linked document in a new window or tab
_self	Opens the linked document in the same frame as it was clicked (default setting)
_parent	Opens the linked document in the parent frame
_top	Opens the linked document in the full body of the window

The Message Text box allows you to specify text that will be displayed in the browser's status bar when a user points to the hyperlink. You can use the Alt Tag box to create alternative text used by screen readers. The alternative text also becomes a tool tip in most browsers; it appears as placeholder text if a user chooses not to download graphics. At the bottom of the Slice Options dialog box are dimension settings and the background type setting.

To Enter Slice Settings

The following steps select a slice with the Slice Select Tool and then enter hyperlink settings for the Gallery slice.

- Press and hold or right-click the Slice Tool button to display the context menu.

- Tap or click 'Slice Select Tool' to choose the tool.

- Double-tap or double-click the Gallery slice badge to display the Slice Options dialog box (Figure 9–34).

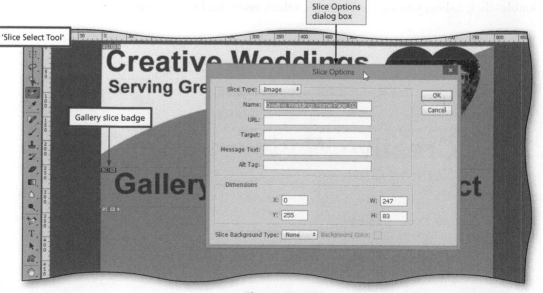

Figure 9–34

2

- Type **Gallery** to replace the text in the Name box.

- Press the TAB key to move to the URL box and then type **Contact-Sheet .gif** as the entry. Recall that this is the name of the gallery contact page created earlier in the chapter.

- Tab to the Target box and then type **_blank** as the entry.

- Tab to the Message Text box and then type **Go to the gallery contact sheet page**. as the entry.

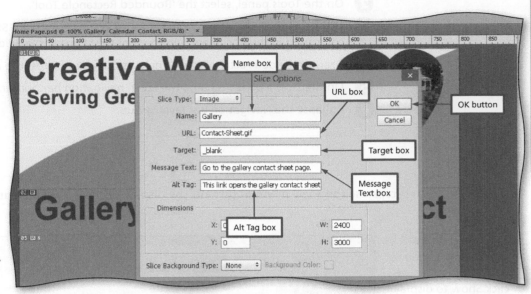

- Tab to the Alt Tag box and then type **This link opens the gallery contact sheet**. as the entry (Figure 9–35).

Figure 9–35

3

- Tap or click the OK button to apply the settings and close the dialog box.

Other Ways

1. Press and hold or right-click slice, tap or click Edit Slice Options, enter settings, tap or click OK button

2. On options bar, tap or click 'Set options for the current slice' button, enter settings, tap or click OK button

To Enter More Slice Settings

The following steps set the options for the remaining slices. The Calendar and Contact slices will point to webpages created by the owner of the company at a future time.

1 Double-tap or double-click the Calendar slice badge to display the Slice Options dialog box, select any existing type in the Name text box, and then type **Calendar**.

2 Tap or click the URL box, select any existing text, and then type **calendar.html** as the entry. Enter **_blank** in the Target box. Enter **Go to the calendar page**. in the Message Text box. Enter **This link opens the calendar**. in the Alt Tag box.

3 Tap or click the OK button to apply the settings and close the dialog box.

4 Double-tap or double-click the Contact slice badge to display the Slice Options dialog box, and then type **Contact** in the Name text box. Enter **contact.html** in the URL box. Enter **_blank** in the Target box. Enter **Go to the contact page**. in the Message Text box. Enter **This link opens the contact page**. in the Alt Tag box.

5 Tap or click the OK button to apply the settings and close the dialog box.

BTW

URL BOX
If your linked files are in a different folder, the Slice URL box must display a / (slash) in between the name of the folder and the file name.

To Finish the Navigation Bar

The following steps add a border around the navigation bar, using a rounded rectangle shape.

1 On the Layers panel, select the Gallery layer, if necessary.

2 On the Tools panel, select the 'Rounded Rectangle Tool'.

3 On the options bar, change the Fill to No Color. Change the Stroke color to the cream color used in the document window. Set the shape stroke width to 10 pt.

4 Drag a rounded rectangle that encloses the words across the middle of the page.

5 On the Layers panel, rename the layer, navigation bar border.

6 Collapse the Navigation Bar layer group.

To Hide Slices

The following steps use the View menu to turn off the display of slices in the document window.

1

- Tap or click View on the Application bar, and then tap or click Show to display the Show submenu (Figure 9–36).

Figure 9–36

2

- Tap or click Slices to turn off the slice display (Figure 9–37).

Figure 9–37

To Save the File

The following step saves the file again.

 Press CTRL+S to save the file again.

Break Point: If you wish to take a break, this is a good place to do so. Press CTRL+Q to quit Photoshop. To resume at a later time, start Photoshop, open the file named Creative Weddings Home Page, and continue following the steps from this location forward.

3D Modeling

3D modeling is the process of developing a three-dimensional image based on two-dimensional surfaces. 3D modeling is a staple of the movie and gaming industries, but also is used in advertising, web design, manufacturing, and interior design, among others.

Create 3D objects from predefined shapes.
Predefined shapes such as cones, cubes, and cylinders can be used to create hundreds of different 3D objects. Beginning with a mathematically correct shape gives you a strong base from which to work.

Plan Ahead

Photoshop CC has many tools and panels to help you perform 3D modeling; in fact, entire books have been written about the 3D modeling process in Photoshop. Even so, Photoshop is not a dedicated modeling app. Professional 3D modeling software programs such as Maya, Lightwave, and 3DS offer many advanced features and scene description languages. Because of their complexity, these apps require a steep learning curve.

As you learned, a 3D image can be extruded from 2D image. However, you also can create a 3D image from scratch or by editing a previously created 3D model. In general, 3D modelers or artists manipulate and designate heights, widths, and depths, but they also have to edit surfaces, lighting, and camera view or eye – the entire scene. You can include more than one model in the scene.

Meshes, Lighting, and Materials

Recall that in Chapter 8, you manipulated an object using 3D rotating and move tools. In this chapter, you will use a mesh. A **mesh** is the underlying structure of a 3D model, often represented by a wireframe or skeleton. A 3D model always has at least one mesh, and may combine multiple meshes. In Photoshop, you can you can change the orientation of a mesh and transform it by scaling along different axes. In addition, you can create your own 3D meshes, using pre-supplied shapes.

In a previous chapter, you edited the lighting of a 3D object. **Lighting types** include Infinite, Spot, Point lights, as well as Image-based lights that wrap around a scene. 3D lights illuminate from different angles to add realistic depth and shadows. With 3D settings turned on, you also see a lighting widget to help you focus the direction from which the light is coming. By default, Photoshop creates one infinite light when you create a 3D scene. You can edit lighting color and intensity and add new lights.

After manipulating the mesh and the lighting, you can change the **material** or surface texture. Photoshop has a material picker; however, you can use a separate 2D file to provide a unique material. For most materials, you can adjust settings such as gloss, shine, opacity, or reflection.

To Create a 3D Mesh using a Predefined Shape

The following steps use a predefined shape from Photoshop's list of meshes. While you design a 3D object, it is easier to hide the other layers and use the full screen to manipulate and edit.

1

- Hide both the Navigation Bar and Heading Objects groups.

- Press SHIFT+CTRL+N to create a new layer. Name it, ring, and use a yellow identification color. Hide all of the layers except the ring layer.

- Tap or click 3D on the Application bar, tap or click 'New Mesh from Layer', and then tap or click Mesh Preset to display the list (Figure 9–38).

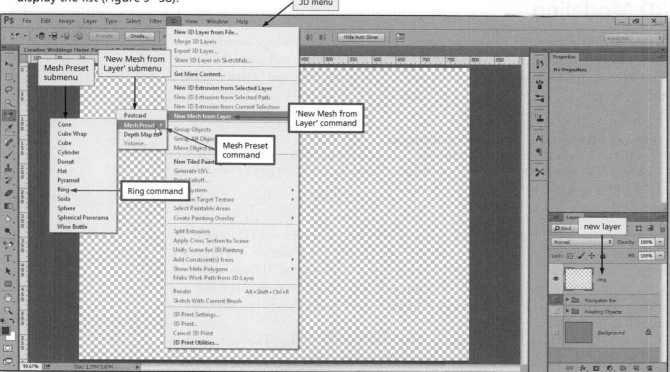

Figure 9–38

2

- Tap or click Ring. When Photoshop asks if you want to display the 3D workspace, tap or click the Yes button (Figure 9–39).

What is displayed in the lower-left corner of the workspace? That symbol is the 3D axis preview. You will learn about the 3D axis in the next series of steps.

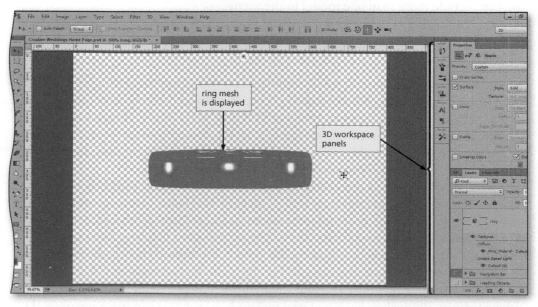

Figure 9–39

Other Ways

1. On 3D panel, tap or click 'Mesh from Preset' option button, tap or click 'Create New 3D Object' button, select shape

3D Display Settings

Several different views can be turned on and off when using the 3D tools. Each of the display settings changes how the the 3D object appears in the document window and turns on and off certain **widgets** or small tools to assist you with 3D editing. Table 9–2 lists the display settings and their purpose.

The '3D Secondary View' command displays its own Secondary View window so you can see the 3D object from a different angle. It also is the called picture-in-picture window, the camera view, or the alternate view window. The 3D axis widget allows you edit any of the three axes in a 3D object. As you point to each part of the axis, a tool tip appears along with a ring to help see the direction and rotating. Each axis has special parts for moving, rotating or compressing. The center of the axis can be used to scale uniformly.

Table 9–2 3D Show Display Settings		
Setting	**Description**	**Purpose**
3D Secondary View	This view displays a floating picture-in-picture window displaying the 3D object from another view.	While you position models and adjust lighting, you can see the affect from two different perspectives, such as from the front and the top.
3D Ground Plane	This view displays a ground mesh, and displays the image as if it is sitting atop something.	The ground plane allows you to preview shadows based on the lighting. It also allows you to change the axis for easier editing.
3D Lights	This view displays Infinite, Spot, and Point light icons in the document window and a lighting widget.	The lighting widget allows you to rotate the lighting around the outside of the model, as if the sun is shining from a different direction,
3D Selection	This view displays a 3D wire box around the object and the 3D axis widget.	The 3D axis widget allows you to rotate the model on any of its three axes.

To Show 3D Views

The following steps view the 3D object in each of the 3D settings.

1

- On the Layers panel, select the 3D layer, in this case the ring, if necessary.

- Tap or click View on the Application bar and then tap or click Show to display the 3D settings. If any of the 3D commands already display a check mark, tap or click the command to remove the check mark. Repeat as necessary to ensure that no commands currently are selected (Figure 9–40).

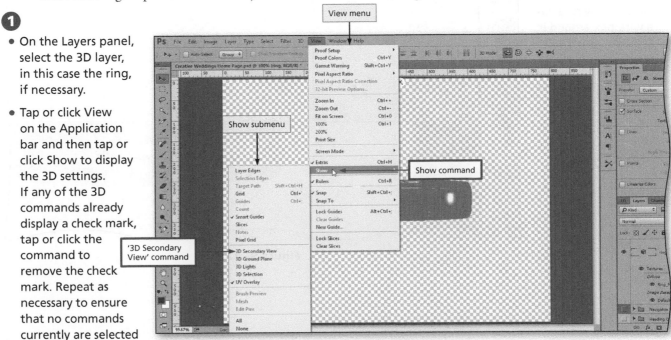

Figure 9–40

2

- Tap or click '3D Secondary View' to display the Secondary View window.

- On the Secondary View window title bar, tap or click the 'Select View/Camera' button to display the list of views (Figure 9–41).

Experiment

- On at a time, tap or click each of the views on the menu to see how the Secondary View window changes. When you are done, tap or click the 'Select View/Camera' button again.

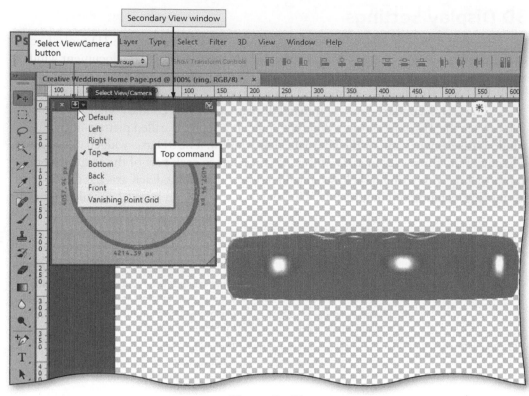

Figure 9–41

3

- Tap or click Top to display the top of the ring in the Secondary View window (Figure 9–42).

Q&A

In the document window, my ring has a wire box around it. Did I do something wrong?

No. Sometimes if you click a 3D object in any of the views, its wire box will be displayed.

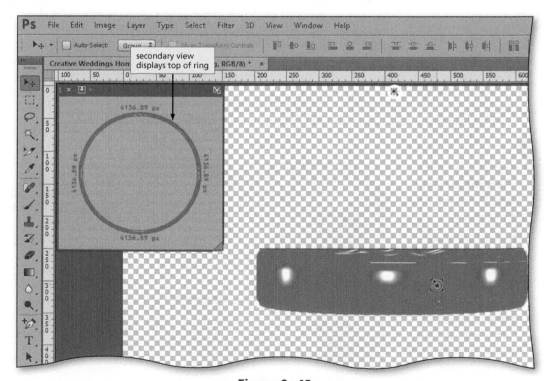

Figure 9–42

- Tap or click View on the Application bar, tap or click Show, and then tap or click 3D Selection to display the 3D Axis widget. If your axis is not displayed, tap or click the ring in the document window.

- Drag down in the document window to see the three axes clearly (Figure 9–43).

 Experiment

- Point to each part of each axis in the widget to see the tool tip and various rings. Practice using the widget to rotate move and scale. After each movement, press CTRL+Z to undo.

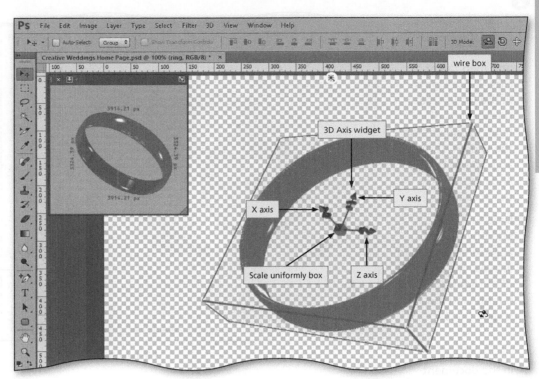

Figure 9–43

To Edit the Lighting

The following steps edit the lighting for the ring. By default, Photoshop creates one light source for you. Different lighting settings create additional lights that appear as small knobs on the lighting widget. Recall that the White Lights setting most resemble daytime lighting and commonly is used for printed and web-based images. White Lights have three lighting sources, one for each axis.

1

- Display the 3D panel.

- On the 3D panel, tap or click the Infinite Light setting to display the Properties panel for Infinite Light, and also to display the lighting widget (Figure 9–44).

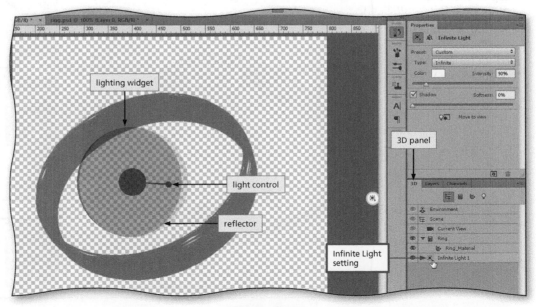 **Experiment**

- On the Properties panel, if necessary, tap or click the Shadow check box to display the shadow on the ring. Drag the Softness slider and view the results. Tap or click the Shadow check box again, to turn off shadows.

Figure 9–44

2

- On the Properties panel, tap or click the Preset button and then tap or click White Lights in the list to create three points of light, or sources, on the widget, three adjustment knobs, and light sources on the 3D panel.

- Drag the Intensity slider to approximately 250 to increase the intensity of the light, thus brightening the ring (Figure 9–45).

Experiment

- In the document

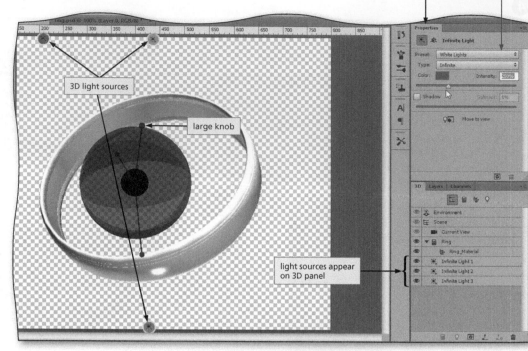

Figure 9–45

window, drag the large knob to make global changes to the lighting. Press CTRL+Z to undo the change. Drag one of the small knobs to create a more precise lighting shift. Notice how the reflector ellipse changes. Press CTRL+Z to undo the change.

To Edit the Materials

The following steps choose a material for the ring using the Material picker. You will choose a gold gradient to simulate a gold wedding ring.

1

- On the 3D panel, tap or click the Ring_Material setting to display the Properties panel for Materials (Figure 9–46).

What happened to the lighting widget? Because the lighting setting is not selected on the 3D panel, Photoshop does not display the widget. You can click individual lighting settings on the panel to redisplay the widget.

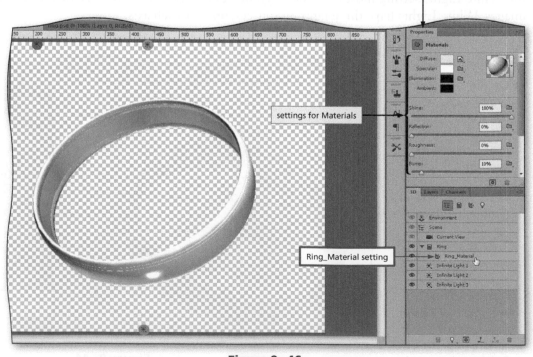

Figure 9–46

2

- On the Properties panel, tap or click the Material picker to display its list. Scroll down to display the gold previews (Figure 9–47).

 Experiment

- Scroll through the rest of the previews. Point to a preview to displays its name in a tool tip.

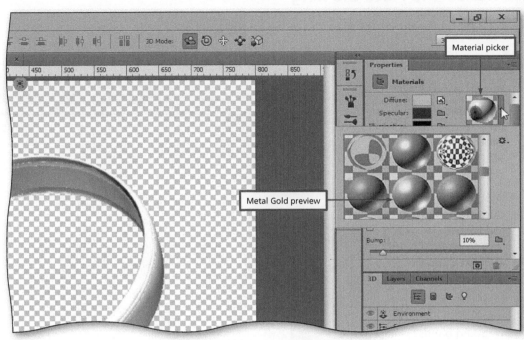

Figure 9–47

3

- Tap or click the Metal Gold preview.

- Tap or click the Material picker again to close the list.

- Drag the Shine slider to 50% to increase the sparkle (Figure 9–48).

 Experiment

- Scroll through the rest of the settings on the Properties panel. Drag the sliders to preview the result. Press CTRL+Z to undo.

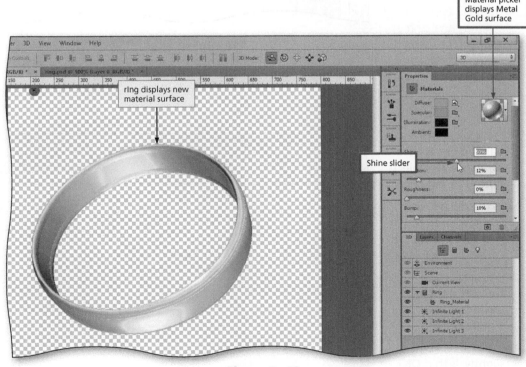

Figure 9–48

To Resize and Place the Ring

The following steps resize and move the ring to better fit in the scene.

1

- On the 3D panel, select the Ring layer.

- On the Move Tool options bar, tap or click the 'Scale the 3D Object' button to select it.

- Drag down in the document window to reduce the size of the ring to approximately 100 pixels square (Figure 9–49).

Q&A Could I duplicate the ring to make two wedding bands?
Yes, if you wanted to do so, you would press and hold or right-click Ring on the 3D panel and then tap or click Duplicate Objects on the context menu.

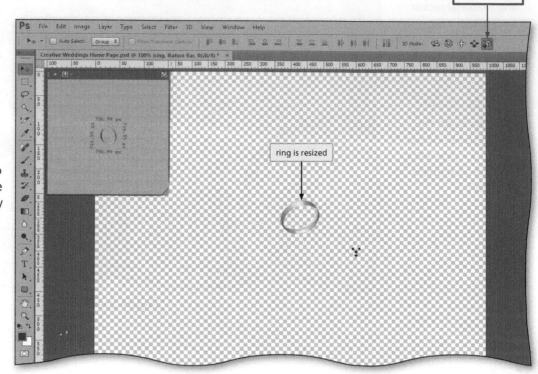

Figure 9–49

2

- On the options bar, tap or click the 'Drag the 3D Object' button to select it.

- In the document window, drag the ring to the lower-left corner of the canvas.

- Press CTRL+H to turn off the 3D settings display (Figure 9–50).

Q&A My ring turned slightly. Is that OK?
Yes, your ring does not have to match the figure exactly.

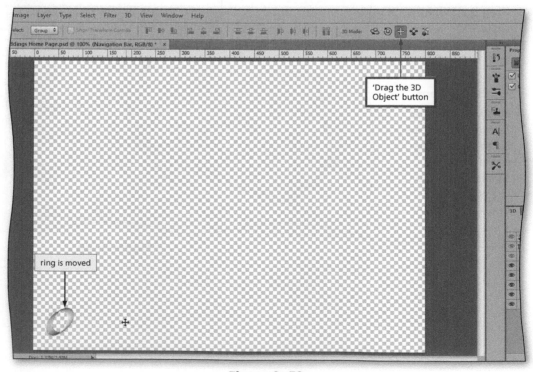

Figure 9–50

To Save the File

The following step saves the file again.

 Press CTRL+S to save the file again.

BTW

3D Instances
On the context menu of a 3D object, you can create an object instance. An instance is an exact copy that inherits any edits you make to the original.

Break Point: If you wish to take a break, this is a good place to do so. Press CTRL+Q to quit Photoshop. To resume at a later time, start Photoshop, open the file named Creative Weddings Home Page, and continue following the steps from this location forward.

Animation

The next step in developing the Creative Weddings website is to create an animation that moves an image across the home page. An **animation** is a sequence of frames or images, displayed over time to convey movement. A **frame** is a single view of the image within the sequence, which can be edited and optimized. Each frame in an animation varies slightly from the preceding frame; the variation is the result of changing effects, filters, or repositioning objects. This variation creates the illusion of movement when the frames are viewed or played in quick succession. Professional animators create hundreds or thousands of frames, each with a tiny change from frame to frame, to emulate smooth movement. In small animations that are used on the web, such as **animated GIFs**, the number of frames varies, but commonly includes from 5 to 50 frames and can run several seconds or longer, depending on how the timing for the animation is set.

Employ animation carefully.
The judicious use of animation in a website can add impact and increase comprehension, but a little goes a long way. Animations that illustrate a dynamic process, enliven a logo, or pace the delivery of information are best. Keep in mind the following rules when creating animations:

- Animations should enhance content. All websites present information, so animated effects should support the content by delivering information, identifying key elements or purpose, or clarifying a complex process.

- Simple animations are more effective than complex ones. Animated effects should enhance, not distract from, content. Choose subtle effects, such as dissolves and fades.

- Keep your animations consistent; do not try to do too many different kinds of animations on a website.

Plan Ahead

Designers create animations using a wide variety of application software. Although Photoshop is a high-end graphic-editing tool, it is not intended for the creation of advanced animations with film or movie quality. You can create basic animations in Photoshop, however.

To learn all of the animation and optimization features in Photoshop takes time and practice. In this chapter, you will create a simple animation with approximately 30 frames. Building this animation presents you with an introduction to the basic techniques and tools used in animation and optimization. Further study will be required to master these tools and techniques.

Creating the Animation for the Creative Weddings Webpage

The animation in the Creative Weddings webpage rotates the ring, starting in the lower-left corner, and finishes near the bottom of the heart shape. First, you will make three more copies of the ring layer on the Layers panel. For each copy, you will manipulate the position and angle of the ring 3D object. Relocation of the layer gives the illusion of motion when viewed in quick succession. Finally, you will place each layer as a frame in the animation and have Photoshop create additional frames for smooth transitions.

To Duplicate 3D Layers

Because animation depends on hiding and showing layers, the following steps duplicate the ring object three times, and make all layers visible.

1 Tap or click the Layers panel title bar to display the Layers panel.

2 Make all layers visible.

3 Double-tap or double-click the ring layer and rename it ring 1.

4 Press and hold or right-click the ring 1 layer and duplicate it. Name the duplicate layer, ring 2.

5 Duplicate the ring 1 layer two more times to create ring 3 and ring 4.

6 On each ring layer, tap or click the 'Reveals layer effects in the panel' button so the effects are collapsed.

7 Drag the top of the Layers panel upward to resize it so you can see all of the new layers. Your layers may be in a different order.

8 Select the ring 2 layer (Figure 9–51).

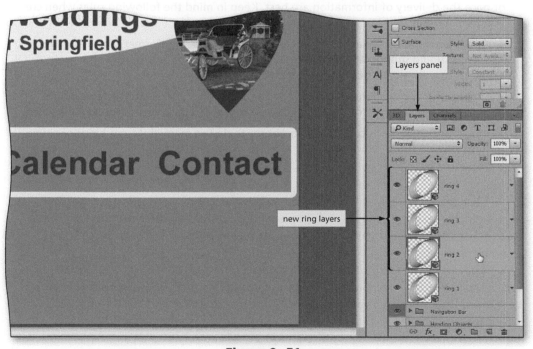

Figure 9–51

To Change the Position of the Ring on Each Layer

Recall that when you created ring 1, you had the ring 3D object placed in the lower-left corner of the canvas. You then created three more copies of the ring. Each copy needs to have the ring placed at a different position and slightly rotated, ending with Ring 4 sitting fairly flat at the top of the page. The following steps change the position of the ring on each of the three duplicated layers.

1

- With ring 2 selected on the Layers panel, tap or click the tab on the 3D panel to display it.
- Tap or click Ring on the 3D panel.
- On the Move Tool options bar, tap or click the 'Drag the 3D Object' button, and then drag the ring upward and to the right.
- Tap or click the 'Rotate the 3D Object' button, and then drag upward in the document window to rotate the ring as shown in Figure 9–52. Your position and rotation do not have to match perfectly.

Figure 9–52

2

- Select the Layers panel and select the ring 3 layer.
- Switch to the 3D panel, and tap or click Ring.
- Use the 3D tools on the options bar to rotate and position the ring as shown in Figure 9–53.

Q&A I am having trouble rotating the ring. What should I do?
Using the 3D tools takes some practice. Make sure you have the Ring selected on the 3D panel. You may want to turn on the 3D axis widget. To do so, tap or click View, tap or click Show, and then tap or click 3D Selection. Your rotation does not have to match the figure perfectly.

Figure 9–53

- Select the Layers panel and select the ring 4 layer.
- Switch to the 3D panel, and tap or click Ring.
- Use the 3D tools on the options bar to rotate and position the ring as shown in Figure 9–54.

ring 4 is rotated and moved

Figure 9–54

The Timeline Panel

You will use the Timeline panel in conjunction with the Layers panel to create animation frames (Figure 9–55). The Timeline usually opens at the bottom of the Photoshop window, with one frame visible to start. As with other panels, you can drag the title bar of the Timeline panel to move it, if necessary. To create an animation, you insert a new frame from the panel menu, and then edit the layers on the Layers panel. Frames are added sequentially from left to right in the panel as you create them.

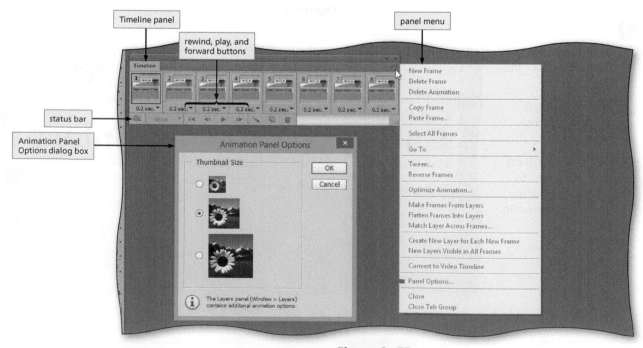

Figure 9–55

The Timeline panel menu displays commands to create, manipulate, and optimize the frames. Below each frame is a button used to set the timing or delay between the current frame and the next frame.

The buttons for manipulating the frames appear at the bottom of the Timeline panel; they allow you to edit how the animation loops; play, rewind, and fast-forward the animation; and tween, duplicate, and delete frames. Additionally, the Timeline panel can operate in a video mode that creates true video files rather than graphic file animations.

To Display the Timeline Panel

The following step uses the menu system to open the Timeline panel.

1

- Tap or click Window on the Application bar and then tap or click Timeline to display the Timeline panel. If the 'Create Frame Animation' button is displayed, tap or click the button.

- Press CTRL+0 (ZERO) to display the entire canvas (Figure 9–56).

Q&A | My button says 'Create Video Timeline'. Did I do something wrong?
No. A previous user may have been creating an animation.
Photoshop remembers the settings. Tap or click the arrow next to the button, tap or click 'Create Frame Animation' in the list, and then tap or click the button.

Figure 9–56

To Create New Frames

To simulate the ring moving and rotating, you will create an animation frame for each ring, hiding the other three ring layers. The steps on the next page build the animation using the Timeline panel. As you create each frame, you will hide the previous ring and display the next one.

- Display the Layers panel.
- Hide rings 2, 3, and 4 (Figure 9–57).

Q&A My timeline frame is very small. Can I make it bigger?
Yes. Tap or click the Timeline panel menu button, tap or click Panel Options, and select a bigger size.

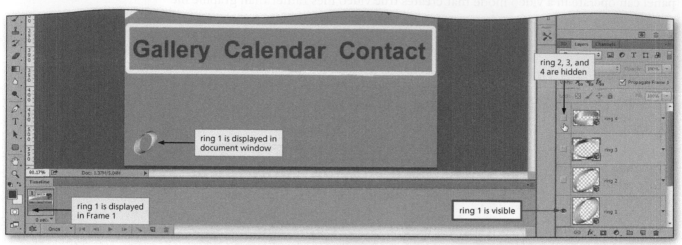

Figure 9–57

- On the Timeline panel status bar, tap or click the 'Duplicates selected frames' button to create a second frame.
- On the Layers panel, hide ring 1 and display ring 2 (Figure 9–58).

Q&A Does it make any difference which layer is selected?
No, in this case, the animation is controlled by visibility and eventually opacity. The selected layer is not important.

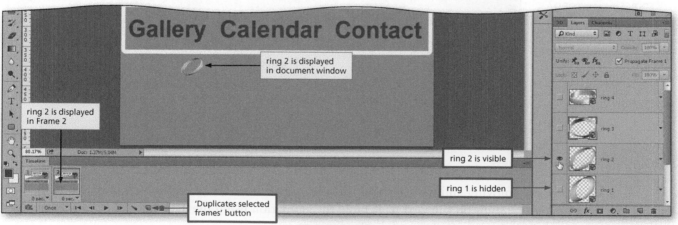

Figure 9–58

- On the Timeline panel status bar, tap or click the 'Duplicates selected frames' button to create a third frame.
- On the Layers panel, hide ring 2 and display ring 3 (Figure 9–59).

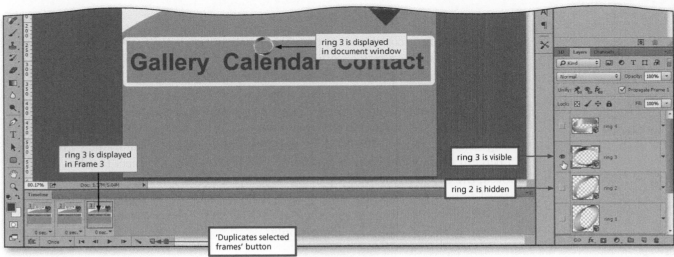

Figure 9–59

4

- On the Timeline panel status bar, tap or click the 'Duplicates selected frames' button to create a fourth frame.

- On the Layers panel, hide ring 3 and display ring 4 (Figure 9–60).

Experiment

- On the Timeline, tap or click the first frame. On the Timeline status bar, tap or click the Play animation button to preview the animation.

Figure 9–60

Other Ways

1. On Animation panel menu, tap or click Copy Frame, tap or click Paste Frame

Disposing of Frames

The Dispose command, available on each frame's context menu, discards the current frame before displaying the next frame. When displayed on the web, the disposal prevents flickering and provides a more consistent flow of animation.

Tweening

Tweening, a corruption of the phrase in-between, is a way to allow Photoshop to create new frames automatically between two existing frames. When you tween between two frames, Photoshop parses the data equally in the frames, creating graduated changes. Photoshop reduces the opacity of the layer evenly across the new frames and increments the layer position equally, and any special effects are interpolated across the new frames. For example, if two frames contain an opacity change from 50 percent to 100 percent, Photoshop creates a tween frame with 75 percent opacity. Similarly, if two frames display a rasterized object that has been moved, the tween frame will display the object placed halfway between the two. A third setting named Effects will tween any layer effects between frames.

In this project, because the rings are 3D layers that have not been rasterized, tweening will display opacity changes only.

To Tween

The following steps create five new frames between each of the current frames, tweening the opacity in an animated effect.

- Tap or click Frame 1.

- On the Timeline status bar, tap or click the 'Tweens animation frames' button to display the Tween dialog box.

- In the 'Frames to Add' box enter **5** to add five frames between Frames 1 and 2 (Figure 9–61).

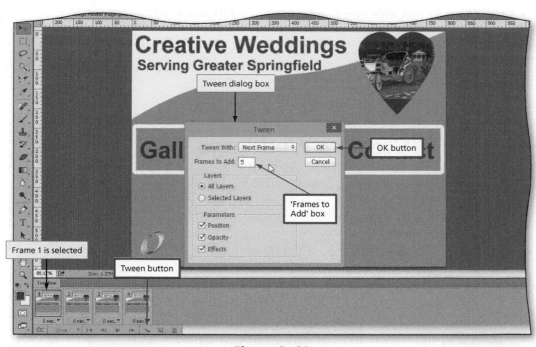

Figure 9–61

- Tap or click the OK button to add five tweened frames between the original first and second frame (Figure 9–62).

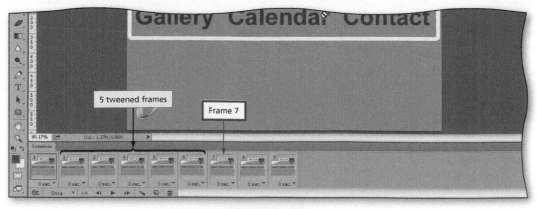

Figure 9–62

3

- Tap or click Frame 7 (which was the original Frame 2).

- Tap or click the 'Tweens animation frames' button to display the Tween dialog box, and then tap or click the OK button to add five more tweened frames.

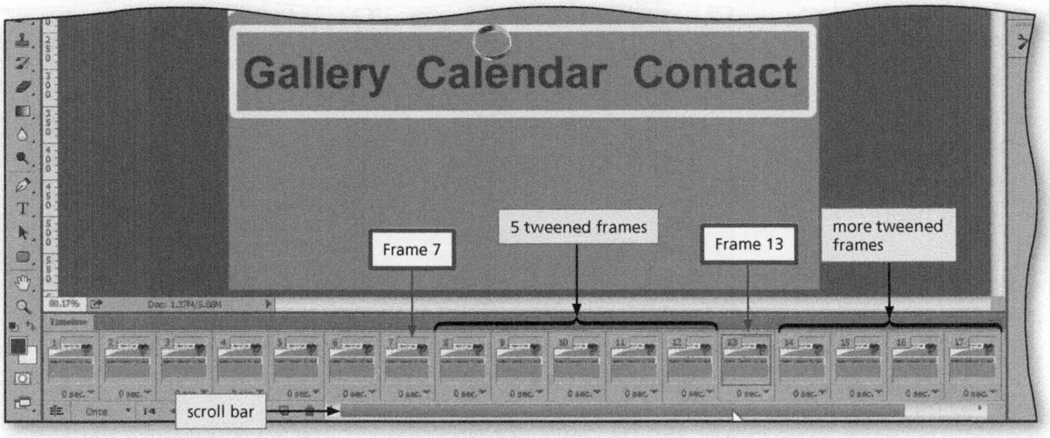

- Tap or click Frame 13.

- Tap or click the 'Tweens animation frames' button to display the Tween dialog box, and then tap or click the OK button to add five more tweened frames (Figure 9–63).

Figure 9–63

Q&A | How many frames should I have in total?
You will have a total of 19 — the four original frames, and three sets of five tweened frames. You can use the scroll bar to see all of the frames.

Other Ways

1. Select frame, on panel menu tap or click Tween

To Set the Timing

The amount of time that Photoshop takes to move from one frame to another during playback is called the **delay time**. In the following steps, you will set the time to .2 seconds so very little time elapses between frames.

1

- Tap or click the Timeline panel menu button to display the context menu (Figure 9–64).

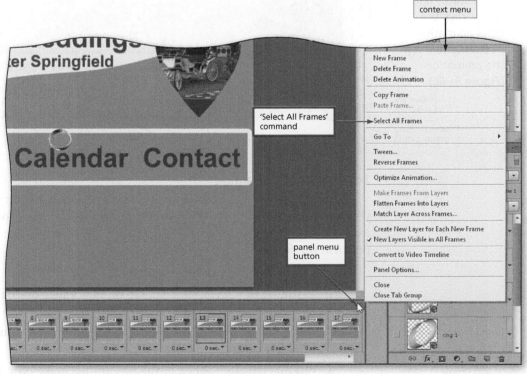

Figure 9–64

2

- Tap or click 'Select All Frames' to select all of the frames.

- Tap or click the bottom of any frame to display its context menu (Figure 9–65).

 3

- Tap or click 0.2 seconds to set the timing between frames to two-tenths of a second.

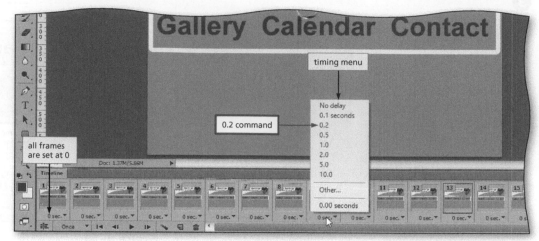

Figure 9–65

Other Ways

1. Press and hold or right-click frame, choose timing

To Preview the Animation

The following steps preview the animation by clicking the Plays animation button on the Timeline status bar.

1

- On the Timeline panel, tap or click Frame 1 to select it.

- On the Timeline panel status bar, tap or click the Plays animation button to preview the animation (Figure 9–66).

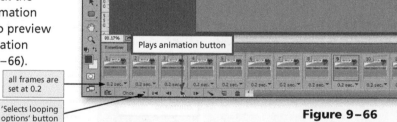

Figure 9–66

TO OFFSET FOR ANIMATION

If you want to create an animation that moves an object without any rotation, you can use a special filter in Photoshop to specify the exact movement in pixels. For example, if you wanted to create a ball that bounces across the screen, you would perform the following steps.

1. Duplicate the layer that contains the ball.
2. With the new layer selected, tap or click Filter on the Application bar, point to Other, and then tap or click Offset.
3. In the Offset dialog box, specify exactly how many pixels to move the object, both horizontally and vertically.
4. On the Timeline panel, in the first frame, make only the original layer visible.
5. Duplicate Frame 1 and make only the filtered frame visible.
6. Repeat Steps 1 through 5 for each new position of the bouncing ball.

Timing Frames
You can set the delay time as soon as you create the first frame. The delay time that you specify in Frame 1 automatically applies to subsequent frames as they are created or tweened.

Animation Settings

You can choose to have an animation display just once, a specified number of times, or repeat continuously, which is called **looping**. The animation you created displayed once. The animation display choices are available through the 'Selects looping options' button, shown in Figure 9–66.

Additionally, you can optimize the animation for both performance and storage with two settings on the Timeline panel menu. Without optimizing, Photoshop includes the entire layer within each frame. Optimizing reduces file size by cropping each frame to include only the area that has changed from the preceding frame. Photoshop uses a bounding box that you access through the Timeline panel menu to automatically crop the frame. Optimizing can lessen the time needed to download the animation when viewed on a webpage. The Redundant Pixel Removal setting identifies the pixels in a frame that are unchanged from the preceding frame and makes them transparent. This can reduce the file size because unneeded pixels are removed. Later, when you save the file as a GIF or HTML file, you must select the Transparency option on the Optimize panel for the setting to work properly.

To Optimize the Animation

The following steps set the optimization for the animation.

1

- Tap or click the Timeline panel menu button to display the menu (Figure 9–67).

Q&A | What does the 'Match Layer Across Frames' command do?
If you added an animation to an existing image, the Match command would make the contents of the selected layer visible throughout every frame of the animation.

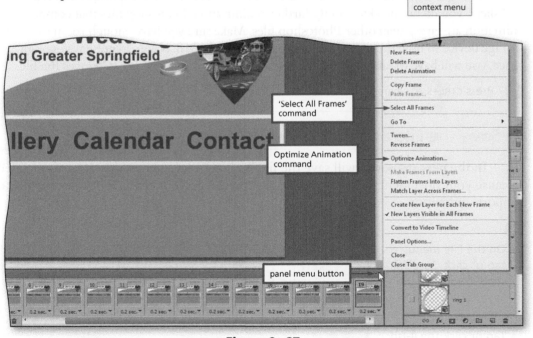

Figure 9–67

- Tap or click 'Select All Frames' to include all of the frames in the animation.

- Tap or click the Timeline panel menu button, and then click Optimize Animation to display the Optimize Animation dialog box.

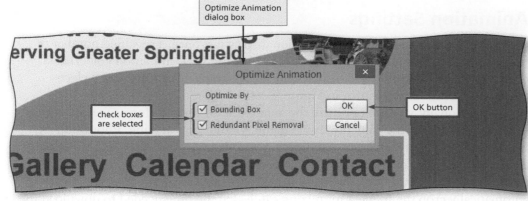

Figure 9–68

- If necessary, place a check mark in both the Bounding Box and 'Redundant Pixel Removal' check boxes to select them (Figure 9-68).

- Tap or click the OK button to close the dialog box.

To Save the File with the Animation

Saving the file preserves the animation. Because you have used appropriate sizes and slices, you do not need to specify further optimization. Photoshop files that contain animation are larger than other Photoshop files. Make sure you have enough room on your storage device to hold the file, which is approximately 24 MB. If you do not have enough space, you will have to save your file in another location. The following step saves the file.

 Press CTRL+S to save the file.

To Save the File as a Webpage

In the next steps, you will save the file in the HTML format that can be uploaded to a web server. Because your document includes animation, you must save in the GIF format because only the GIF format supports animation.

- On the File menu, tap or click 'Save for Web' to display the Save for Web dialog box.

- Tap or click the 4-Up tab, if necessary, to view the original image and three optimized previews.

- Tap or click the upper-right preview to select it.

- Tap or click the Preset box arrow to display the choices (Figure 9–69).

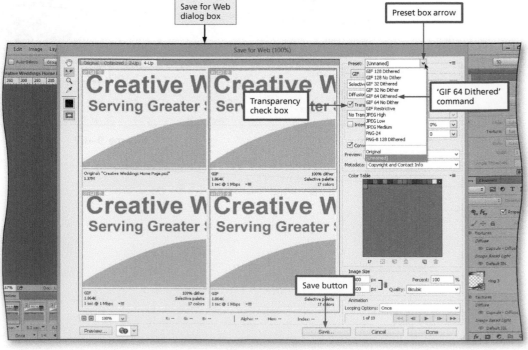

Figure 9–69

- Tap or click 'GIF 64 Dithered' in the Preset menu because that setting offers an acceptable balance between image quality and file size.

- Confirm that a check mark appears in the Transparency check box.

- Tap or click the Save button to display the Save Optimized As dialog box.

- Navigate to the location of your storage device.

- Tap or click the Format button, and then tap or click 'HTML and Images' in the list.

- If necessary, tap or click the Slices button and select All Slices so that all slices are saved (Figure 9–70).

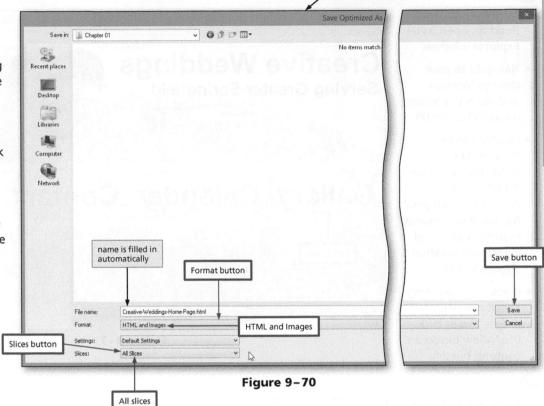

Figure 9–70

- Tap or click the Save button to save the file and a folder of images on the storage device.

To Close the File and Quit Photoshop

The webpage is complete. The final step is to close the file and quit Photoshop.

1 Tap or click the Close button on the Photoshop title bar. If Photoshop displays a message about saving the file, tap or click the No button.

To View the Webpage Interactively

To make a final check of the interactivity of the webpage, the steps on the next page open the Creative Weddings HTML file with a browser for viewing the animation. After you tap or click the Gallery link, the web gallery will open.

1

- On the Windows 8 desktop, open a File Explorer window.

- Navigate to your storage location and open the folder named Chapter 09.

- Double-tap or double-click the HTML file, Creative Weddings Home Page, to launch your default web browser, load the page, and view the animation (Figure 9–71).

- If you see a warning about running scripts, tap or click the 'Allow blocked content' button.

Figure 9–71

2

- When the animation is finished, tap or click the Gallery link to open the contact sheet in a new window (Figure 9–72).

3

- Close all of the open windows.

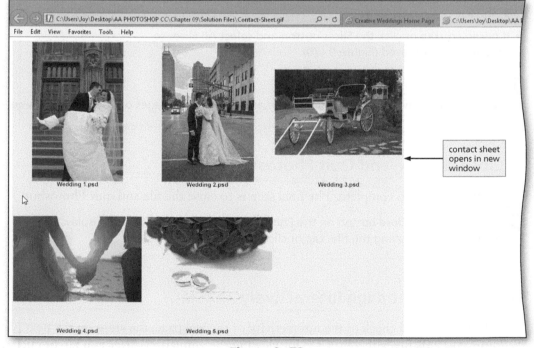

Figure 9–72

3D Printing

Photoshop CC contains many tools to make 3D printing easy. **3D printing** is the printer's ability to handle Photoshop instructions that will convert a 3D digital model to a 2D representation, typically by laying down many successive thin layers of ink. You have the option of printing to your own 3D printer or using a service that prints 3D models. What used to be a tedious and expensive process has become more user-friendly with the ability to build, refine, preview, and prepare 3D files — all within Photoshop. The preview settings are similar to regular print preview tools. You can perform mesh repair, adjust structure, and edit other settings to match your printer's capabilities. Photoshop CC supports the most popular desktop 3D printers, such as the MakerBot Replicator, and also supports a full range of high-quality materials available through third-party vendors such as Shapeways.com.

To Perform 3D Printing

If you wanted to print your 3D object on a printer capable of 3D printing, you would perform the following steps.

1. Select your 3D model or object.
2. Tap or click 3D on the Application bar, and then tap or click 3D Print Settings.
3. In the 3D Print Settings panel, choose whether you want to print to a printer connected to your computer or use an online 3D printing service.
4. Select a unit for the printer volume—inch, centimeter, millimeter, or pixel. The unit is reflected in the Printer Volume dimensions as well as the print plate measurements.
5. Select a Detail Level — Low, Medium, or High—for the 3D print.
6. Choose 'Scale To Print Volume' if you want Photoshop to auto-scale your 3D model, such that it fills up the available print volume of the selected printer.
7. Tap or click the Print icon to display the Photoshop 3D Print Settings dialog box. Adjust any settings.
8. Tap or click the Print button or the Export button.

BTW

Flash Cards
The Student Companion Site has interactive flash cards of the important concepts in each chapter. For detailed instructions about accessing available resources, visit solutions. cengage.com/ctdownloads or contact your instructor for information about the flash cards.

Chapter Summary

In this chapter, you created a website for the Creative Weddings wedding planner company. First, you organized images in a folder and created a contact sheet. After creating a webpage background, you added placeholder text and a navigation bar. You entered text to serve as hyperlinks when the webpage is viewed in a browser. You sliced the image into multiple sections, one for each hyperlink. You used the Slice Options dialog box panel to enter specific settings for the hyperlink, such as the destination URL and Status bar message.

You created a 3D graphic of a ring and adjusted the object's lighting and appearance. Finally, you created a series of frames that animated a graphic of a ring rotating across the screen. You created each part of the animation as a separate layer and then displayed each layer in its own animation frame. You learned about the Timeline panel and animation techniques such as looping, tweening, and optimizing. The completed animation was added to the home page of the website. You prepared the webpage for publishing to the web. With the website complete, you tested the animation and the hyperlink in a web browser.

The items listed below include all the new Photoshop skills you have learned in this chapter:

1. Create a Contact Sheet (PS 544)
2. Set the Rulers to Pixels (PS 551)
3. Use Perspective Warp (PS 553)
4. Use Puppet Warp (PS 558)
5. Append Custom Shapes (PS 558)
6. Create the Navigation Bar (PS 561)
7. Create Slices (PS 563)
8. Enter Slice Settings (PS 566)
9. Hide Slices (PS 568)
10. Create a 3D Mesh Using a Predefined Shape (PS 570)
11. Show 3D Views (PS 571)
12. Edit the Lighting (PS 573)
13. Edit the Materials (PS 574)
14. Resize and Place the Ring (PS 576)
15. Change the Position of the Ring on Each Layer (PS 579)
16. Display the Timeline Panel (PS 581)
17. Create New Frames (PS 581)
18. Tween (PS 584)
19. Set the Timing (PS 585)
20. Preview the Animation (PS 586)
21. Offset for Animation (PS 586)
22. Optimize the Animation (PS 587)
23. Save the File as a Webpage (PS 588)
24. View the Webpage Interactively(PS 589)
25. Perform 3D Printing (PS 591)

Apply Your Knowledge

Reinforce the skills and apply the concepts you learned in this chapter.

Creating a Web Banner

Note: To complete this assignment, you will be required to use the Data Files for Students. Visit solutions.cengage.com/ctdownloads for detailed instructions or contact your instructor for information about accessing the required files.

Instructions: Start Photoshop and perform the customization steps found on pages PS 6 through PS 11. Open the Apply 9-1 Astro file from the Chapter 09 folder of the Data Files for Students. The purpose of this exercise is to create a web banner for an organization that offers astronomy programs for kids. The Apply 9-1 Astro file contains a banner with the name of the program, an image, and a short description. You are to create a folder to hold all of the associated files, add text slices, and animate the image in preparation for hyperlink entries. The animation will resize the planet image to add motion to the page. The final product is shown in Figure 9–73.

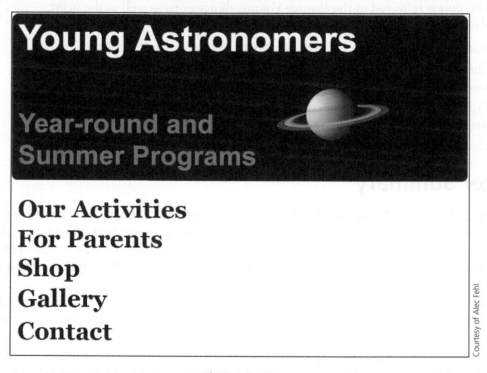

Courtesy of Alec Fehl

Figure 9–73

Perform the following tasks:

1. On the File menu, tap or click Save As. When the Save As dialog box is displayed, navigate to your storage device. Double-tap or double-click the Chapter 09 folder, and then tap or click the 'Create New Folder' button on the toolbar. When the new folder is displayed, type **Apply 9-1 Astronomy Website** as the name, and then press the ENTER key to rename the folder. If necessary, double-tap or double-click the Apply 9-1 Astronomy Website folder to open it. In the File name text box, type **Apply 9-1 Astronomy Edited** to name the file. If necessary, tap or click the 'Save as type' button, and then tap or click Photoshop (*.PSD;*.PDD) in the list. Tap or click the Save button. If Photoshop displays an options dialog box, tap or click the OK button.

2. To create the text hyperlinks:

   a. On the Layers panel, tap or click the Background layer to select it.

   b. On the Tools panel, tap or click the 'Horizontal Type Tool' button. On the options bar, set the font to Georgia or Georgia Bold, set the font style to Bold, set the size to 10, set the anti-aliasing to Sharp, set the alignment to Left, and set the color to black.

   c. Tap or click on the left side of the document window, just below the black masthead shape. Type **Our Activities** and then tap or click the 'Commit any current edits' button on the options bar.

   d. Press the v key to access the Move Tool. Drag the Our Activities text into position so that it resembles Figure 9–73. ALT+drag four copies of the text and position them along the left edge, below each other. One at a time, double-tap or double-click the layer thumbnail of each new layer and type the words shown in Figure 9–73.

   e. Select the five type layers you added on the Layers panel. On the Tools panel, select the Move Tool. On the options bar, tap or click the 'Distribute vertical centers' button and the 'Align left edges' button.

3. To slice the text:

   a. On the Layers panel, select the Our Activities text layer.

   b. On the Tools panel, tap or click the Slice Tool button.

   c. Draw a slice around the Our Activities text element.

   d. Repeat the process for the remaining four type layers.

4. To create new layers for the animation:

   a. On the Layers panel, press and hold or right-click the Saturn layer, tap or click Duplicate Layer, and then tap or click the OK button to duplicate the layer. Repeat the process until you have the Saturn layer and four copies. Rename the five Saturn layers from top to bottom Saturn 22, Saturn 44, Saturn 66, Saturn 88, and Saturn 100 respectively.

   b. Tap or click the Saturn 22 layer and press CTRL+T to display the Transform options bar. On the options bar, tap or click the 'Maintain aspect ratio' button, if necessary, to select it. In the Set horizontal scale box, type **22** to resize the layer to 22 percent of its original size. Press the ENTER key to accept your entry, then press ENTER again to commit the change.

   c. Repeat Step 4b for the Saturn 44, Saturn 66, and Saturn 88 layers, resizing them to 44, 66, and 88 percent, respectively.

   d. On the Layers panel, turn off the visibility of all the Saturn layers except Saturn 22.

5. To create animation frames:

   a. On the Window menu, tap or click Timeline. Tap or click the 'Duplicates selected frames' button.

   b. On the Layers panel, turn off the visibility of the Saturn 22 layer and turn on the visibility of the Saturn 44 layer.

   c. Create a third frame. On the Layers panel, turn off the visibility of the Saturn 44 layer and turn on the visibility of the Saturn 66 layer.

   d. Create a fourth frame. On the Layers panel, turn off the visibility of the Saturn 66 layer and turn on the visibility of the Saturn 88 layer.

   e. Create a fifth frame. On the Layers panel, turn off the visibility of the Saturn 88 layer and turn on the visibility of the Saturn 100 layer.

6. To create tweens:

   a. On the Timeline panel, tap or click Frame 5 to select it, if necessary.

   b. Tap or click the 'Tweens animation frames' button.

   c. Ensure the Tween With box is set to Previous Frame and set the Frames to Add box to 3.

   d. Ensure the All Layers option is selected and all three Parameters check boxes are checked. Tap or click the OK button.

   e. Tap or click Frame 4 and repeat Steps 6b through 6d to create tweened frames between Frames 3 and 4.

   f. Tap or click Frame 3 and repeat Steps 6b through 6d to create tweened frames between Frames 2 and 3.

Continued >

Apply Your Knowledge *continued*

    g. Tap or click Frame 2 and repeat Steps 6b through 6d to create tweened frames between Frames 1 and 2.

    h. If desired, change the time delay by selecting all of the frames and then tapping or clicking the 'Selects frame time delay' button. When you are done, select Frame 1.

    i. If necessary, set the Selects looping options menu to Once. Save the file.

7. Choose 'Save for Web' on the File menu. When the Save for Web dialog box appears, tap or click the 4-Up tab, if necessary, set the Preset menu to GIF 64 Dithered, and then tap or click the Preview button. Wait for the browser window to open; if necessary, tap or click the 'Allow Blocked Content' button. Watch the animation. Close the browser window.

8. Tap or click the Save button in the Save for Web dialog box. If necessary, navigate to the Apply 9-1 Astronomy Website folder. If necessary, type **Astro-Edited** in the File name box. If necessary, tap or click the Format box, and then select HTML and Images in the list. Tap or click the Save button.

9. Close the Apply 9-1 Astro Edited.psd document window. If Photoshop asks if you want to save the file again, tap or click the No button. Quit Photoshop.

10. Submit the Apply 9-1 Astronomy Website folder in the format specified by your instructor.

Extend Your Knowledge

Extend the skills you learned in this chapter and experiment with new skills. You may need to use Help to complete the assignment.

Using 3D with a Vanishing Point Filter

Note: To complete this assignment, you will be required to use the Data Files for Students. Visit solutions.cengage.com/ctdownloads for detailed instructions or contact your instructor for information about accessing the required files.

Instructions: Start Photoshop and perform the customization steps found on pages PS 6 through PS 11. You have been asked to design an ABC block for a children's store advertisement. You will need to create a 3D cube, edit the surface of the cube, and then add pictures in perspective. The completed block is shown in Figure 9–74.

Courtesy of Joy Starks

Figure 9–74

Perform the following tasks:

1. Press CTRL+N to display the New dialog box. Type `Extend 9-1 Building Block` in the Name text box to replace the default name.

2. Set the width to 5 inches. Set the height to 5 inches. Set the resolution to 150.

3. Set the color mode to RGB and 8 bit. Set the background contents to White.

4. Tap or click the OK button to close the dialog box. Press CTRL+O (ZERO) to fit the image on the screen.

5. Press SHIFT+CTRL+S to save the image on your storage device as a PSD file, with the file name Extend 9-1 Building Block Edited.

6. Use Photoshop Help to read about the difference between the Cube and the Cube Wrap meshes.

7. Switch to the 3D workspace. On the 3D panel, tap or click the 'Mesh from Preset' option button. Tap or click the 'Create New 3D Object' button and then choose Cube Wrap from the list. Tap or click the Create button to create the cube.

8. On the 3D panel, select the Cube_Material setting. On the Properties panel, tap or click the Material picker and then choose 'Plastic Glossy (Blue)' from the list.

9. On the 3D panel, select the Infinite Light 1 setting. On the Properties panel, choose the White Lights preset with an intensity of 250%.

10. On the 3D panel, select the Cube Wrap setting. On the Tools panel, select the Move Tool, if necessary. On the options bar, tap or click the 'Rotate the 3D Object' button. In the document window, rotate the scene so you can see three sides of the cube.

11. Use Photoshop Help to read about the Vanishing Point filter.

12. Display the Layers panel. Create a new layer named, apple.

13. Open the Extend 9-1 Apple file from the Chapter 09 folder of the Data Files for Students. Press CTRL+A to select all. Press CTRL+C to copy the image to the Clipboard. Close the file.

14. With the Extend 9-1 Building Block Edited file displayed, tap or click Vanishing Point on the Filter menu. In the Vanishing Point dialog box, press the C key to access the Create Plane Tool. On the cube, tap or click the one of the top corners. Moving around the top of the cube, tap or click each of the other three corners to create a plane.

15. Press CTRL+V to paste the apple image from the Clipboard. Press the T key to access the Transform Tool. Drag the image into the plane and resize as necessary. Tap or click the OK button to close the Vanishing Point dialog box.

16. Repeat Steps 12 through 15 using the Extend 9-1 Ball file. Place the ball image on the front-left plane of the cube.

17. Repeat Steps 12 through 15 using the Extend 9-1 Crown file. Place the crown image on the front-right plane of the cube.

18. Save the file. See your instructor for ways to submit this assignment.

Make It Right

Analyze a project and correct all errors and/or improve the design.

Improving a Skateboard Park Banner Advertisement

Note: To complete this assignment, you will be required to use the Data Files for Students. Visit solutions.cengage.com/ctdownloads for detailed instructions or contact your instructor for information about accessing the required files.

Continued >

Make It Right *continued*

Problem: The Westville Skatepark has a web banner that needs to grab the attention of visitors to their website. They have started work on an animated GIF banner using Photoshop's frame animation but it has several problems that you will need to fix: the background disappears and reappears, the animation is too fast, the phone number flashes, and the path of the skateboarder is incorrect.

Perform the following tasks:

1. Start Photoshop and perform the customization steps found on pages PS 6 through PS 11. Open the Make It Right 9-1 Skatepark file from the Chapter 09 folder of the Data Files for Students. Press SHIFT+CTRL+S to save the image on your storage device as a PSD file, with the file name Make It Right 9-1 Skatepark Edited.

2. Open the Timeline panel. Play the animation and notice how the background disappears and reappears, and the park name and phone number flash on and off. Notice also that the skateboarder's motion is haphazard. Finally, the animation is too fast (Figure 9–75).

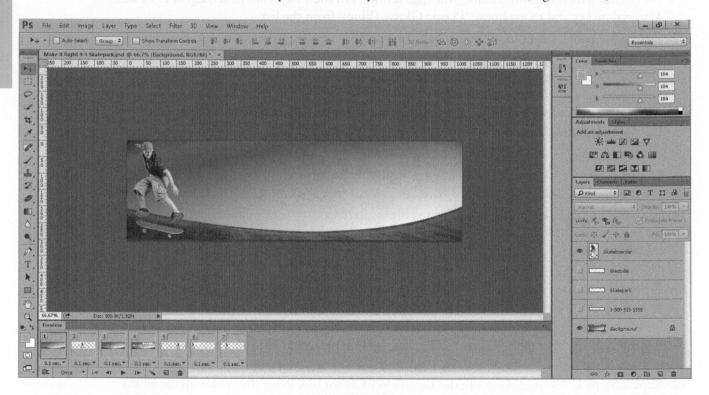

Figure 9–75

3. Select Frame 1 on the Timeline panel. Select the Background layer on the Layers panel. Tap or click the Timeline panel menu button, and then tap or click 'Match Layer Across Frames'. When the dialog box appears, tap or click the OK button.

4. Tap or click the 'Indicates layer visibility' button to show all three layers of text (Westville, Skatepark, and 1-800-555-5555). Tap or click the 1-800-555-5555 layer, and then SHIFT+tap or SHIFT+click the Westville layer to select all three layers. Tap or click the Timeline panel menu button, and then tap or click 'Match Layer Across Frames'. When the Match Layer dialog box appears, tap or click the OK button.

5. On the Layers panel, select the Skateboarder layer. Use the Move Tool to drag the Skateboarder layer to the far left side of the workspace, just off of the document window. Tap or click Frame

2 and then use the Move Tool to position the skateboarder to the right of its location in the previous frame. Continue selecting the frames and moving the Skateboarder layer so the skateboarder's path moves from left to right. Frame 7 should display the skateboarder on the right side of the banner.

6. With Frame 7 selected, add four tween frames between Frames 7 and 6. Select Frame 6 and add two tween frames between Frames 6 and 5. Select all the frames and change their timings from 0.1 sec. to 0.2 sec.

7. Play the animation again and check for accuracy. Fix any other problems and adjust the timing as necessary. Save your changes. Use the 'Save for Web' command to save the file in the GIF format with the name, Make-It-Right-9-1-Skatepark-Animated. Be sure to set the Format box to Images Only so only the GIF, and not the HTML file, is created. See your instructor for ways to submit this assignment.

In the Labs

Design and/or create a project using the guidelines, concepts, and skills presented in this chapter. Labs are listed in order of increasing difficulty.

Lab 1: **Creating an Image Map**

Note: To complete this assignment, you will be required to use the Data Files for Students. Visit solutions.cengage.com/ctdownloads for detailed instructions or contact your instructor for information about accessing the required files.

Problem: As an assignment for your economics class, you decide to make an image map, shown in Figure 9–76. The image map links images of language books to websites that offer English-language tourism guides for the appropriate country. When users view the image map, tapping or clicking any book in the graphic will link them to a website featuring information about that country. Table 9-3 shows the URL of each website you will use for each country.

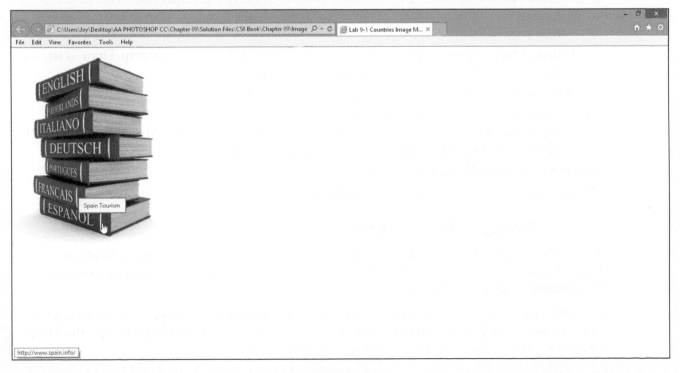

Figure 9–76

Continued >

In the Labs *continued*

Table 9–3 URL Settings	
Language	**URL**
English	http://www.usatourist.com
Nederlands	http://www.holland.com
Italiano	http://www.italia.it
Deutsch	http://www.germany.travel
Portugues	http://www.golisbon.com
Francais	http://www.franceguide.com
Espanol	http://www.spain.info

Instructions: Perform the following tasks:

1. Use File Explorer to open the Computer window, navigate to your storage device, and create a new folder named, Lab 9-1 Tourism Image Map.

2. Start Photoshop. Perform the customization steps found on pages PS 6 through PS 11.

3. Open the file Lab 9-1 Books from the Chapter 09 folder of the Data Files for Students.

4. Tap or click the Save As command on the File menu. Navigate to your storage device and the Lab 9-1 Tourism Image Map folder. Save the file with the file name, Lab 9-1 Tourism Image Map, in the PSD format. If Photoshop displays an options dialog box, tap or click the OK button.

5. To create a slice for each book:

   a. On the Tools panel, select the Slice Tool.

   b. Drag a rectangle around the outline of the English book. Drag around as much of the English book as you can, while selecting as little of the Nederlands book as possible.

   c. Press SHIFT+C to activate the 'Select Slice Tool'. On the options bar, tap or click the 'Set options for the current slice' button to display the Slice Options dialog box. Type English in the Name box. Enter the URL from Table 9–3. Leave the Target box blank. In the Message Text box, type USA as the entry. In the Alt Tag box, type USA Tourism. Tap or click the OK button.

   d. Repeat Steps 5a through 5c for the other books included in the image map. Draw as large a slice as possible, while overlapping other books as little as possible.

6. When all the books are complete, save the PSD file again.

7. Tap or click the Save for Web command on the Photoshop File menu. Choose the best optimization and save the file with the name, Lab-9-1-Tourism-Image-Map, using the HTML and Images format, in the Lab 9-1 Tourism Image Map folder.

8. Quit Photoshop. Preview the website using a browser.

9. See your instructor for ways to submit this assignment.

Lab 2: **Perspective Warp**

Note: To complete this assignment, you will be required to use the Data Files for Students. Visit solutions.cengage.com/ctdownloads for detailed instructions or contact your instructor for information about accessing the required files.

Problem: You have been asked to edit a photo of a lake house to focus more on the waterfront side of the house rather than the current corner view. You decide to use Photoshop's Perspective Warp to edit the photo to look like the version shown in Figure 9–77.

Figure 9–77

Instructions: Perform the following tasks:

1. Start Photoshop. Perform the customization steps found on pages PS 6 through PS 11.

2. Open the file Lab 9-2 Lake House from the Chapter 09 folder of the Data Files for Students.

3. Save the file on your storage device in the Chapter 09 folder with the name, Lab 9-2 Lake House Edited, in the PSD format.

4. On the Edit menu, choose Perspective Warp. Draw a perspective plane that includes only the right side, or front of the house and the rocks and the reflection in the water. Include only trees as necessary.

5. Drag another perspective plane close to the first one, which includes all of the left side of the image. Photoshop will join the grids of the two planes.

6. On the right side, drag the upper-right handle to match the angle of the roof. Drag the lower-right handle to match the ground.

7. On the left side, drag the upper-left handle to match the straight line of the balcony. Drag the lower-left handle to match the ground. (*Hint*: you may not have to make much adjustment on the left side.)

8. On the options bar, tap or click the Warp button. SHIFT+tap or SHIFT+click the center vertical line to select it.

9. Drag the lower-center handle to the left to display more of the right side of the house (waterfront side). Commit the warp.

10. Save the file again, and submit the assignment as specified by your instructor.

Continued >

In the Labs *continued*

Lab 3: Creating a Website Animation

Note: To complete this assignment, you will be required to use the Data Files for Students. Visit solutions.cengage. com/ctdownloads for detailed instructions or contact your instructor for information about accessing the required files.

Problem: As an intern for a web design company, you have been assigned to create an animated GIF for an air conditioning service shop (Figure 9–78). The client has provided several photos of an ice cube melting, which are included with the Data Files for Students.

Instructions: Perform the following tasks:
Copy the folder Lab 9-3 Ice from the Data Files for Students to your storage location. Open the Lab 9-3 Ice Banner file from your storage device. Notice that the dimensions of this file are 120 pixels wide × 240 pixels tall — standard dimensions for a vertical web banner ad. Open each of the Ice photos in the Lab 9-3 Ice folder, and use the Move Tool to copy each photo into the Lab 9-3 Ice Banner document. Move the Blend layer to the top of the layer stack, and arrange the ice photos in order from solid to melted. Create a new text layer at the top of the document with the phrase, Air Conditioner Problems Burning You Up? Select an appropriate font and color so the phrase is readable against the black background. Create another new text layer at the bottom of the document with the company name and phone number, AirPros 1-800-555-5555. Select an appropriate font and color so the name and phone number are readable against the white background. Create a 10-frame animation that animates the ice melting. The text should be visible throughout all frames. Set the animation speed to 1 second for the first frame and 0.2 seconds for all remaining frames. Set the looping to repeat once. Save the file to the Lab 9-3 Ice folder with the name, Lab 9-3 Ice Banner Animated. Save the file for the web, in the HTML and Images format, to the Lab 9-3 Ice folder with the name, Ice-Animated. View it in a browser to watch the ice cube melt.

Courtesy of Alec Fehl

Figure 9–78

Cases and Places

Apply your creative thinking and problem-solving skills to design and implement a solution.

Note: To complete this assignment, you will be required to use the Data Files for Students. Visit solutions.cengage.com/ctdownloads for detailed instructions or contact your instructor for information about accessing the required files.

1: Create a Photoshop Resources Webpage

Academic

Your web design instructor has given you an assignment to create a webpage that includes links to some useful websites. Create a folder in your storage location named Case 9-1 Photoshop Resources. Use a light muted color and draw a large shape for the background. Use the Vertical

Type Tool to create a text element down the left edge of the page. Use a contrasting color for the text. Type your name in the bounding box. Using the same text color, create a horizontal type element heading that says, Photoshop Resources. Below the heading and to the right of your name, create four more horizontal type elements, using placeholder text such as 'replace this', in a complementary font, but use a smaller font size. Using your favorite search tool, find several websites that offer Photoshop tutorials or other Photoshop resources (such as custom brush or shape downloads). Type the name (not the URL) of one such website into the first of the five text elements. Type the names of four additional websites into the remaining text elements. Slice each text element. Use the Slice Options dialog box to insert a URL, a _blank target specification, an Alt tag, and a status bar message for each slice. Save the file to your Photoshop Resources folder in the PSD format with the name, Case 9-1 My Photoshop Resources. Preview the webpage and make any necessary changes. Save the page as HTML and images to the Case 9-1 Photoshop Resources folder with the name, My_Photoshop_Resources. Exchange your Photoshop Resources folder with another student and explore their Photoshop resources webpages.

2: Design a Personalized Web Banner

Personal

You have decided to put your name up in lights! Create a web banner with a bold background color. Create a type bounding box using a large font in a contrasting color. Type your name. Add a layer effect to enhance the text. On the Layers panel, make sure the opacity is set to 100%. Duplicate the layer and set the opacity of the copy to 10%. Turn the visibility off on both text layers. Open the Timeline panel. In the first frame, turn on the visibility of the 10% layer. Create a second frame in which you turn off the 10% layer and turn on the 100% layer. Set the time delay on each frame to .5 seconds. Set the animation to play only once. Tween the two frames with 10 frames in between, applying only opacity changes. Create a folder in your storage location named Case 9-2 Personalized Banner. Save the file in the PSD format to the folder with the name Case 9-2 My Banner. Save the file optimized for the web in HTML and Images format in the Personalized Banner folder with the name My-Banner. View your name up in lights using a browser window.

3: Customize 3D Navigation Buttons

Professional

You need to make buttons for an upcoming slide show presentation and want something more than the traditional clip art buttons that come with your presentation software. Create a new file in Photoshop with a transparent background. Press the U key to access the Rectangle Tool. Draw a rectangle approximately 300 pixels square. Use the Live Shape Properties panel to round the four corners to approximately 50 pixels. Open the Styles panel and choose a style for the rectangle. Create a text layer using a contrasting color and type OK in large letters on the face of the button. Merge the rectangle and the text layer. Use the 3D menu to extrude the layer to a 3D object. On the 3D panel, change the lighting to White Lights. One at a time select each of the material faces of the 3D object. Use the Materials panel to change the surface of each of the faces and the bevel. Save the file to your storage location with the name, Case 9-3 Button.

Ps   File   Edit   Image   Layer   Type   Select   Filter   3D   View   Window   Help

Adobe **Photoshop CC**   Feather: [0 px]   [Anti-alias]   Styles: [Normal]   [Width:] [ ] [ ] [Height:] [ ]   [Refine Edge...]

Appendix A
Project Planning Guidelines

Using Project Planning Guidelines

The process of effectively communicating specific information to others is a learned, rational skill. Computers and software, especially Adobe Photoshop CC, can help you develop ideas and present detailed information to a particular audience.

Using Adobe Photoshop CC, you can edit photos and create original graphics. Computer hardware and image-editing software, such as Adobe Photoshop CC, reduce much of the laborious work of manually drafting and revising projects. Some design professionals use sketch pads or storyboards, others compose directly on the computer, and others have developed unique strategies that work for their own particular thinking and artistic styles.

No matter which method you use to plan a project, follow specific guidelines to arrive at a final product that presents an image or images clearly and effectively (Figure A–1). Use some aspects of these guidelines every time you undertake a project and others as needed in specific instances. For example, in determining content for a project, you may decide an original graphic would communicate the idea more effectively than an existing photo. If so, you would create this graphical element from scratch.

Determine the Project's Purpose

Begin by clearly defining why you are undertaking this assignment. For example, you may want to correct camera errors and adjust image flaws. Or you might want to create a graphic for a specific publishing or marketing purpose. Once you clearly understand the purpose of your task, begin to draft ideas of how best to communicate this information.

Analyze Your Audience

Learn about the people who will use, analyze, or view your work. Where are they employed? What are their educational backgrounds? What are their expectations? What questions do they have? How will they interact with your product? What kind of computer system and Internet connection will they have? Design experts suggest drawing a mental picture of these people or finding photographs of people who fit this profile so that you can develop a project with the audience in mind.

PROJECT PLANNING GUIDELINES

1. DETERMINE THE PROJECT'S PURPOSE
Why are you undertaking the project?

2. ANALYZE YOUR AUDIENCE
Who are the people who will use your work?

3. GATHER POSSIBLE CONTENT
What graphics exist, and in what forms?

4. DETERMINE WHAT CONTENT TO PRESENT TO YOUR AUDIENCE
What image will communicate the project's purpose to your audience in the most effective manner?

Figure A–1

© Cengage Learning

By knowing your audience members, you can tailor a project to meet their interests and needs. You will not present them with information they already possess, and you will not omit the information they need to know.

Example: Your assignment is to raise the profile of your college's nursing program in the community. Your project should address questions such as the following: How much does the audience know about your college and the nursing curriculum? What are the admission requirements? How many of the applicants admitted complete the program? What percent of participants pass the state nursing boards?

Gather Possible Content

Rarely are you in a position to develop all the material for a project. Typically, you would begin by gathering existing images and photos, or designing new graphics based on information that might reside in spreadsheets or databases. Design work for clients often must align with and adhere to existing marketing campaigns or publicity materials. Websites, pamphlets, magazine and newspaper articles, and books could provide insights of how others have approached your topic. Personal interviews often provide perspectives not available by any other means. Consider video and audio clips as potential sources for material that might complement or support the factual data you uncover. Make sure you have all legal rights to any photographs you plan to use.

Determine What Content to Present to Your Audience

Experienced designers recommend identifying three or four major ideas you want an audience member to remember after viewing your project. It also is helpful to envision your project's endpoint, the key fact or universal theme that you want to emphasize. All project elements should lead to this end point.

As you make content decisions, you also need to think about other factors. Presentation of the project content is an important consideration. For example, will the content of your brochure look good when printed on thick, colored paper or transparencies? Will the format in which you save the content affect how your photo will be viewed in a classroom with excellent lighting and a bright projector? How will the content look when viewed on a tablet or mobile device? Determine relevant time factors, such as the length of time to develop the project, how long editors will spend reviewing your project, or the amount of time allocated for presenting your designs to the customer. Your project will need to accommodate all of these constraints.

Decide whether a graphic, photograph, or artistic element can express or emphasize a particular concept. The right hemisphere of the brain processes images by attaching an emotion to them, so in the long run, audience members are more likely to recall themes from graphics rather than those from the text.

Finally, review your project to make sure the theme still is identifiable easily, and has been emphasized successfully. Is the focal point clear and presented without distraction? Does the project satisfy the requirements?

Summary

When creating a project, it is beneficial to follow some basic guidelines from the outset. By taking some time at the beginning of the process to determine the project's purpose, analyze the audience, gather possible content, and determine what content to present to the audience, you can produce a project that is informative, relevant, and effective.

Ps File Edit Image Layer Type Select Filter 3D View Window Help

Adobe Photoshop CC Feather: 0 px Anti-alias Style: Normal Width: Height: Refine Edge...

Appendix B
Graphic Design Overview

Understanding Design Principles

Understanding a few basic design principles can catapult you to the next level of digital artistry. Beyond knowing how to use software, a graphic designer must know how to create effective and readable layouts no matter what the product type. In this Appendix, you will learn the design principles, color theory, typography, and other technical knowledge required to create usable and successful graphic designs.

A major goal in graphic design work, whether for print or webpage layout, is to guide the viewer's eyes toward some key point. Another major goal of design work is to convey a certain emotion — a project can have the effect of making the viewer feel relaxed, energetic, hungry, hopeful, or even anxious. By implementing a few basic principles of design, you can control your viewers' physical focus so they look where you want them to look as you steer them toward a desired emotion. Design principles typically include the following:

- Balance
- Contrast
- Dominance
- Proximity
- Repetition
- Closure
- Continuance
- Negative space
- Unity

Balance

Visual elements can be **balanced** within a design, with visual elements distributed in a horizontal or vertical arrangement. Unbalanced designs can cause viewers to feel anxious or uncomfortable, or even as if they are falling sideways out of their seats. Balance may be achieved symmetrically or asymmetrically. Symmetrical balance mirrors a visual element to achieve equilibrium (Figure B–1). Asymmetrical balance can be achieved by balancing a small, dark element with a large, light element (Figure B–2) or balancing one large element with several smaller elements (Figure B–3).

with symmetrical balance, the left and right halves are mirror reflections, and the two trees, which are identical in size and shape, balance the composition

Adobe product screenshot(s) reprinted with permission from Adobe Systems Incorporated, unless otherwise noted; courtesy of Alec Fehl

Figure B–1

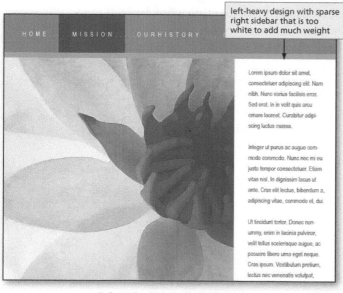

left-heavy design with sparse right sidebar that is too white to add much weight

(a) Unbalanced design

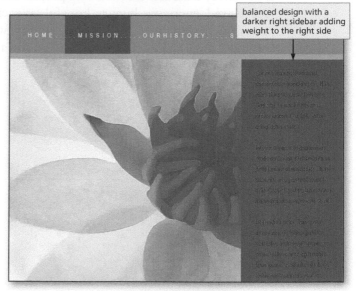

balanced design with a darker right sidebar adding weight to the right side

(b) Balanced design

Figure B–2

large photo at right is asymmetrically balanced by the multiple small thumbnails on left

Figure B–3

Contrast

Contrast describes the visual differences between elements; it adds variety to a design and helps to draw the viewer's focus. Differences in color, scale, quantity, or other characteristics of visual elements help to achieve contrast. The element that is different from the others draws the viewer's attention. In Figure B–4, the words in white contrast against the other words on the page, and the viewer's eye is drawn to the contrasting sentence.

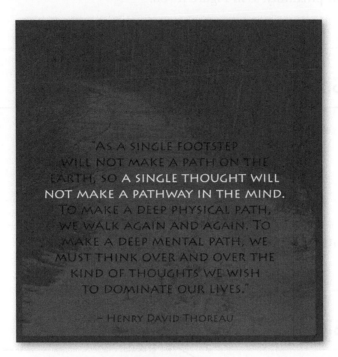

Figure B–4

Dominance

Dominance is a critical principle in controlling viewer focus. The dominant element in a design is the one to which a viewer's eyes and attention usually move first. An element's position within a design or its contrast to other elements can establish dominance. If you want your viewer to focus on a certain area of your design or on a specific design element, make it dominant, like the yellow V.I.P. banner in the discount card shown in Figure B–5, which grabs your attention with its contrasting color, even though it is not the largest element in the design.

BTW | **Dominant Object Placement**
Placing an object at a certain location within a grid, such as the intersection of thirds, or slightly above and to the right of center, helps to establish dominance.

Figure B–5

Proximity

Proximity describes the relative space between elements. Related elements should be close to each other. Headings should be close to their related paragraph text, and product names should be close to their photos and prices. As shown in Figure B–6, when related items are not within close proximity of each other (Figure B–6a), the viewer might not know the items are related. When elements are too close, the design looks cluttered and text can become difficult to read. Strive for balance in your proximity, as in Figure B–6b.

(a) Items without proximity are not clearly related

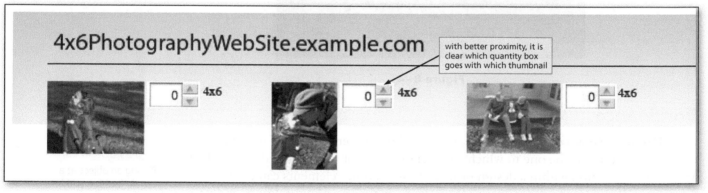

(b) Items with close proximity are clearly related

Figure B–6

Repetition

Repeating a visual element helps to tie a design together. **Repetition** of color, shape, texture, and other characteristics can help to unify your design (Figure B–7), create patterns, or impart a sense of movement. Most websites repeat a design theme across all the pages so users know they are on the same site as they navigate from page to page. Repeated colors and layouts help to unify the overall website design.

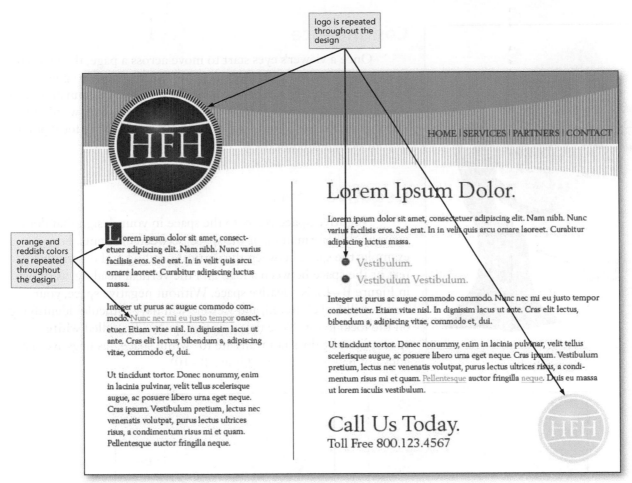

Figure B–7

Closure

Not everything in a design must be composed of solid lines. Composing objects from small parts and spaces allows a design to breathe and creates visual interest. Under the concept of **closure**, the human brain will fill in the blanks to close or complete the object (Figure B–8).

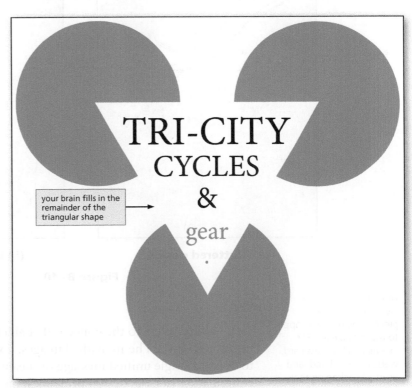

Figure B–8

large dominant dancer captures your attention and her arms direct your eyes straight to the message

Figure B–9

Continuance

Once a viewer's eyes start to move across a page, they tend to keep moving — and you can exploit this **continuance** to guide the viewer's eyes exactly where you want them to go. A dominant object can capture the viewer's initial focus, and diagonal lines within that dominant object can guide the viewer's eyes toward the focal point of your design (Figure B–9).

Negative Space

Negative space refers to the space in your design that does not contain information, or the space between elements. For example, the space between the vertical heading and descriptive text or the space between a logo and the vertical heading, as shown in Figure B–10, is negative space. Without negative space, your design will feel cluttered, and viewers will have difficulty identifying on the focal point. Note that negative space, also called **white space,** literally does not translate to "white space," as negative space does not have to be white (Figure B–10).

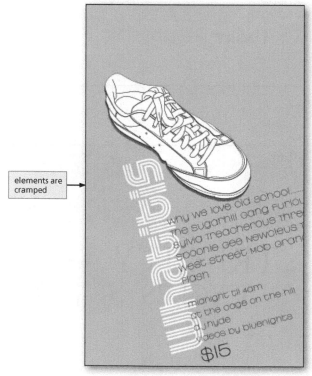

elements are cramped

moving the shoe adds white space and relieves visual tension

(a) Cluttered design   **(b) Uncluttered design**

Figure B–10

Unity

Unity refers to the concept that all elements within a design work well together to form a whole. The individual images, textures, text, and negative space join together to create a single unified message or meaning. Unity can be created by applying a combination of basic design principles. Balanced elements alone do not produce a visually appealing design. The same is true for elements with appropriate proximity and negative space, good contrast, or clear dominance. No single design principle is responsible for a pleasing design. Instead, the combination of these principles creates a single unified design. Without unity, a design degrades into chaos and loses meaning. Of course, that is not a bad thing if chaos is the intentional message.

Layout Grids

A graphic designer needs to know where to place elements within a document or webpage. The use of grids makes it easy to align objects to each other and can help with balance and proximity. You can apply any of the many standard grids to webpage layouts or print layouts for standard paper sizes. One very popular grid system uses thirds, a method that is derived from the golden ratio.

Rule of Thirds and Golden Ratio   The rule of thirds specifies that splitting a segment into thirds produces an aesthetically pleasing ratio. The rule of thirds is derived from a more complex mathematical concept called the golden ratio, which specifies segment ratios of long segment divided by short segment equal to about 1.618, which is close enough to the rule of thirds that designers typically apply the rule of thirds rather than break out their calculators (Figure B–11).

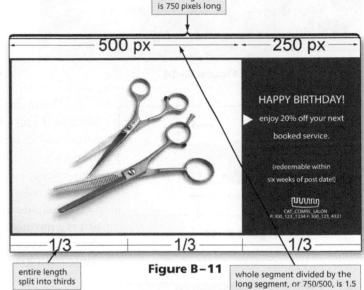

Figure B–11

Color Theory

Color can have a profound effect on the overall message a design conveys. Certain colors evoke specific emotions, and the way colors are combined can make the difference between readable copy and copy that is unable to be read.

Color Properties

Before you begin to work with color, it is important to understand the properties of color, which include hue, saturation, shade, tint, and value.

Hue refers to the tone, or actual color, such as red, yellow, or blue. Many color theorists interpret hue to mean pure color. A pure color, or hue, can be modified to create color variations. A basic color wheel, shown in Figure B–12, displays hue.

Saturation refers to the intensity of a color. As hues become less saturated, they create muted tones and pastels as they approach gray. As hues become more saturated, they appear very bright (Figure B–13).

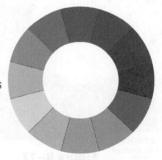

Figure B–12

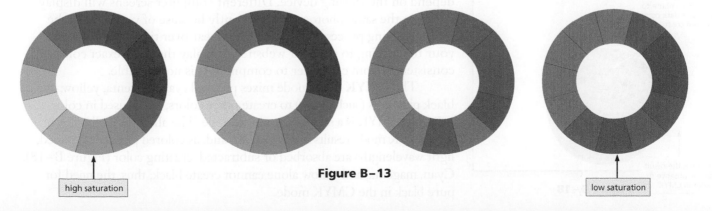

Figure B–13

desaturated hues can have calming effect

Figure B-14

oversaturated hues can be hard on the eyes

Figure B-15

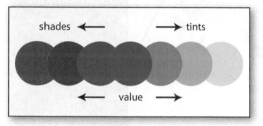

shades ← → tints

← value →

Figure B-16

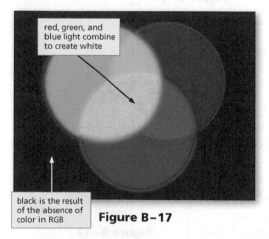

red, green, and blue light combine to create white

black is the result of the absence of color in RGB

Figure B-17

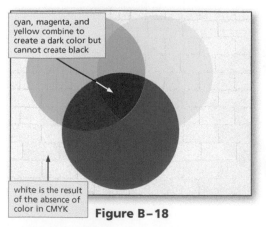

cyan, magenta, and yellow combine to create a dark color but cannot create black

white is the result of the absence of color in CMYK

Figure B-18

Desaturated colors can produce mellow tones and evoke calm feelings (Figure B-14). Oversaturated colors can produce neon-like colors and cause excitement (Figure B-15). Sometimes it is appropriate to use very bright colors, such as in a picture book for children or a high-energy advertisement for a sports drink. Other times, bright, saturated colors produce the wrong feeling for your work.

A **shade** is a mixture of a hue and black, producing a darker color. A **tint** is a mixture of a hue and white, producing a lighter color. A color's **value** describes its overall lightness or darkness. A tint has a higher value, while a shade has a lower value (Figure B-16). Mixing a hue with its shades, tints, and variations of saturation can lead to very harmonious color combinations.

Color Modes

A color mode describes the way in which colors combine to create other colors. The most commonly used color modes are RGB, CMYK, and LAB. Each mode has its strengths and weaknesses, and each is appropriate for a specific type of work.

The **RGB** color mode mixes red, green, and blue light to create other colors. Computer monitors and TV screens use the RGB color mode. All images used on a website must use the RGB color mode because few web browsers can display CMYK images. RGB is an additive color mode, meaning colored light combines (light waves are added) to create other colors. The absence of all color in the RGB mode results in black. As colored light is added, white is created, as shown in Figure B-17. RGB is also device dependent, because the colors you see depend on the viewing device. Different computer screens will display colors in the same photograph differently because of variances in the manufacturing process and component wear over time. Do not waste your time trying to get your website to display the same exact colors consistently from computer to computer. It is not possible.

The **CMYK** color mode mixes physical cyan, magenta, yellow, and black pigments (such as ink) to create other colors, and is used in color printing. CMYK is a subtractive color mode. The absence of all color in the CMYK mode results in white light, and, as colored pigment is added, light wavelengths are absorbed or subtracted, creating color (Figure B-18). Cyan, magenta, and yellow alone cannot create black; thus, the need for pure black in the CMYK mode.

Unlike RGB and CMYK, which combine individual well-defined colors, the **Lab** color mode combines levels of lightness with two color channels, a and b. One color channel ranges from green to magenta, while the other includes blue through yellow. By combining color ranges with lightness values, Lab is able to approximate closely the true human perception of color and thus is able to produce more colors than either RGB or CMYK. This makes it an ideal color mode for photographers wanting to have access to every possible color in a photograph. Lab typically is used during photographic retouching and color correction. The image then is converted to RGB or CMYK for use with electronic media or print.

Psychological Considerations of Color

Colors can evoke both positive and negative emotions in people, and the influence of a color can differ among individuals and cultures. While the effect of color on people is not an exact science, there are some generalities.

White often is associated with cleanliness, purity, and hope. Doctors and brides in most Western cultures wear white. However, white is associated with death and mourning attire in some Eastern cultures. White is the most popular background color and offers great contrast for highly readable dark text.

Black often is used to represent evil, death, or mourning, but also mystery, intelligence, elegance, and power. Black text on a white background is the easiest to read.

Red is used in Western cultures to signify love, passion, and comfort — but also is used to represent sin, anger, hell, and danger. Use dark reds to imply indulgence or fine living and brownish reds for designs dealing with Thanksgiving, harvest, or the autumn season in general.

Green symbolizes many positives such as growth, tranquility, luck, money, ecology, environmentalism, and health, but it also symbolizes jealousy. Green can have a calming effect.

Blue often is cited as the favorite color by men. Like green, it evokes feelings of calmness and serenity. Blue implies authority, stability, loyalty, and confidence. However, it is one of the least appetizing colors, as there are few naturally blue foods. It also is associated with sadness and bad luck, as evidenced in blues music or phrases like "I've got the blues."

Yellow generally makes people happy. It is a highly visible and active color. However, too much yellow can lead to frustration and eye fatigue. Babies cry more in yellow rooms. Avoid using yellow as a page background and use it instead in smaller areas to draw attention.

Print Considerations for Color

The printing process cannot reproduce every color. Gamut refers to the range of printable colors, and colors that cannot be printed are said to be out of gamut. If an out-of-gamut color exists in your document, the printer you are using simply will get as close to it as it can — but it will not be exact. Depending on the printer you have installed, the actual color produced can vary. Photoshop identifies out-of-gamut colors in the Color Picker with a small icon. If your document contains out-of-gamut colors, you have two options: change or replace the out-of-gamut color with one that is in gamut, or accept that the final print may not be exactly what you expected.

Web Considerations for Color

When working with color for the web, the most important thing to remember is that colors will appear differently on different computers. Websites look similar, but not exactly the same, from computer to computer. Years ago, web designers used

BTW | **LAB**
LAB is sometimes written as L*a*b for lightness, color channel a, and color channel b.

BTW | **Shades of White**
The human eye can distinguish more than 200 shades of white.

BTW | **Nature's Colors**
Green is considered the first color of nature and represents fertility, rebirth and freedom. It is the easiest color on the eyes. Blue is a contemplative color in nature, representing water, sky, ice, and temperature.

only the **web-safe colors**, which were a set of 216 colors that supposedly appear the same on all monitors. This was the result of the limitations of video subsystems at the time, as computer monitors could display only 256 specific colors. Microsoft Windows supported 256 specific colors, and Apple Macintosh supported a different 256 colors. Of the two sets, 216 were the same across both platforms; these 216 became the **web-safe palette**. However, designers soon realized that only 22 of those 216 were truly the same between Windows and Macintosh; this subset was called the **really web-safe colors**.

Photoshop displays a warning in the Color Picker for non-web-safe colors. Modern computers (as well as mobile phone browsers) can display millions of distinct colors, so limiting yourself to 216 web-safe colors is no longer a necessity. In fact, it is extremely limiting, because the 216 web-safe colors are generally very bright or very dark with few choices for pastels or saturation and value variances. Most designers do not use web-safe colors for their designs.

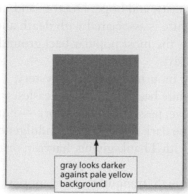

gray looks lighter against brown background

gray looks darker against pale yellow background

Figure B–19

Relativity

A color's relative lightness/darkness value can appear different depending on what other color neighbors it. The gray block in Figure B–19 looks lighter against the brown background and darker against the light yellow background. Keep this in mind as you choose background/foreground relationships. A certain hue (or tint or shade) might look great when it is by itself, but you might not like how it looks in close proximity to another certain color.

Color Schemes and Matching

Choosing colors that work well together and enforce the design's message can be challenging but worth the effort. Successful color matching requires an understanding of **color schemes**, which simply describes an organized method of matching colors based on their positions on a color wheel. The color scheme can make or break a design.

Figure B–12 on page APP 9 displayed a color wheel. While there are various color wheel models, the most popular uses the primary colors red, blue, and yellow (Figure B–20a). Primary colors combine to create the secondary colors green, orange, and purple (Figure B–20b). A primary and a secondary color combine to create a tertiary (third level) color (Figure B–20c). More complex color wheels can include gradients to show varying saturation, tints, and shades (Figure B–21).

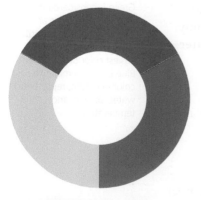
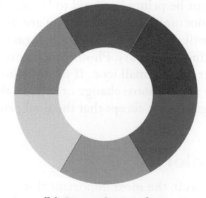
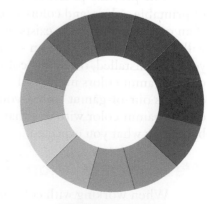

(a) Primary colors   **(b) Secondary colors**   **(c) Tertiary colors**

Figure B–20

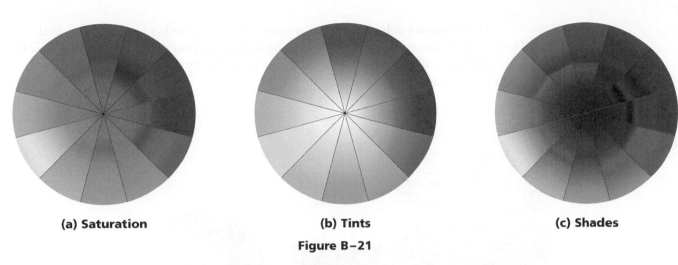

(a) Saturation   (b) Tints   (c) Shades

Figure B–21

Color Schemes   A **monochromatic color scheme** is one that uses a single hue with a variety of shades and tints (Figure B–22). This is an easy color scheme to create. While a monochromatic color scheme can appear soothing, the lack of hue variance can leave it looking a bit boring.

Figure B–22

A **complementary color scheme** uses colors directly across from each other on the color wheel. Their high contrast can look vibrant but also can be hard on the eyes. Avoid using complementary pairs in a foreground/background relationship, as shown in Figure B–23. Adjusting the saturation or substituting tints and shades makes this color scheme more workable.

bright complementary colors do not work well in a foreground/background relationship

adjusting the arrangement of the colors or using a variety of values or saturation can help

Figure B–23

An **analogous color scheme** uses colors next to each other on the color wheel. This color scheme is generally very appealing and evokes positive feelings (Figure B–24). Be careful not to choose colors that are too far apart. A very wide range of analogous colors can appear mismatched.

Figure B–24

The **split-complementary scheme** uses a base color and, instead of its direct complement, the two colors on either side of its complement (Figure B–25). This scheme offers a lot of hue variance, and therefore excitement. However, if all the hues are overly saturated, split-complementary colors can be very harsh. Try keeping one hue saturated and use tints, shades, or desaturated colors for the rest of the scheme.

Figure B–25

Other color schemes such as triadic, tetradic, neutral, and an infinite number of custom schemes also exist. Using a color-matching resource such as software or a website is a good way to help you get started choosing colors and allows you to experiment to see what you and your client like.

Typography

Typography is the art of working with text. Perhaps the two most important factors for graphic designers to address when working with text are visual appeal and readability. A dull text heading will not entice viewers to read the rest of the advertisement, but a text heading that looks beautiful can be useless if it is not readable (Figure B–26).

Readability

Readability is the measurement of how comfortable or easy it is for readers to read the text. Many factors contribute to overall readability. Commonly accepted readability factors include the following:

- Large text passages written in lower-case are easier to read than long text passages in uppercase.
- Regular text is easier to read than italicized text.
- Black text on a white background is easier to read than white text on a black background.
- Legibility affects readability.
- Line length, letterforms, and appearance all influence readability.

Before learning the details of readability, you must understand some type basics. A **font** is a set of characters of a specific family, size, and style. For example, the description Times New Roman, 11 points, italic is a font. What most people consider a font is actually a **typeface** (Times New Roman, in this example). A font represents only a single specific size and style within a family, while a typeface is a set or family of one or more fonts.

Legibility refers to the ease with which a reader can determine what a letter actually is. If readers cannot figure out the letter, they cannot read the text, resulting in low readability and failed message delivery. The difference between legibility and readability is subtle. Figure B–27 shows an exit sign — something that needs to be legible.

Line length refers to the physical length of a line of text. When lines are too long, the reader's eyes can get lost trying to go all the way back to the left side of the page to find the next line. There is no conclusive magic number for how long a line of text should be. Optimal line lengths differ for adults and children, and for people with dyslexia and without. The best choices for line length differ based on the media of the message; printed newspapers, books, text on a website, and the subject lines in an e-mail message all require different line lengths. Some studies recommend line lengths based on physical lengths in inches, while other studies recommend a maximum number of characters per line. However, many designers follow the guideline that line lengths should not exceed 70 characters (about two-and-a-half alphabets' worth of characters).

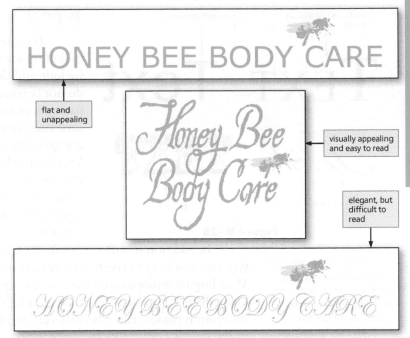

flat and unappealing

visually appealing and easy to read

elegant, but difficult to read

Figure B–26

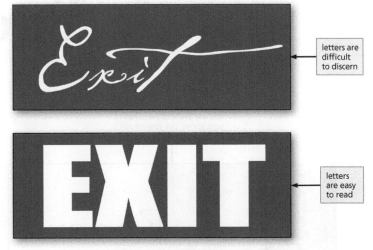

letters are difficult to discern

letters are easy to read

Figure B–27

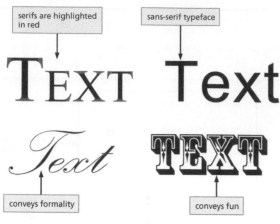

serifs are highlighted in red

sans-serif typeface

conveys formality

conveys fun

Figure B–28

Typeface Categories
In addition to serif, sans serif, and script, fonts can be oldstyle with angled lines and wedge-tipped brushes, modern with vertical stress and no slant, or decorative with whimsical extras around each letter, uneven baselines, and irregular letter heights.

Typeface Categories

Typefaces are organized into several categories, including serif, sans-serif, script, and display. Serif typefaces include additional appendages, while sans-serif typefaces do not (Figure B–28). It is generally accepted that large passages of serif text in print are easy to read, while sans-serif text is easier to read on a webpage. Because headlines are typically small, either serif or sans-serif is appropriate. Varying the headline typeface style from the body copy typeface style is an effective method of adding some visual excitement to an otherwise dull page of text. Script typefaces look like handwriting, and display typefaces are decorative.

In addition to differences in readability, the choice of a serif, sans-serif, or other typeface can help to create an emotion much like the selection of a color scheme. Wedding invitations often use a script typeface to signify elegance, while headlines using display typefaces can grab a reader's attention. The same phrase written in different typefaces can have different implications (Figure B–29). Similarly, differences in the size, weight (boldness), or spacing of a typeface also can influence emotion or meaning (Figure B–30).

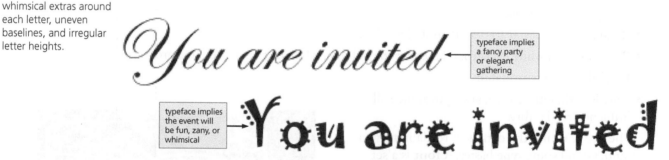

typeface implies a fancy party or elegant gathering

typeface implies the event will be fun, zany, or whimsical

Figure B–29

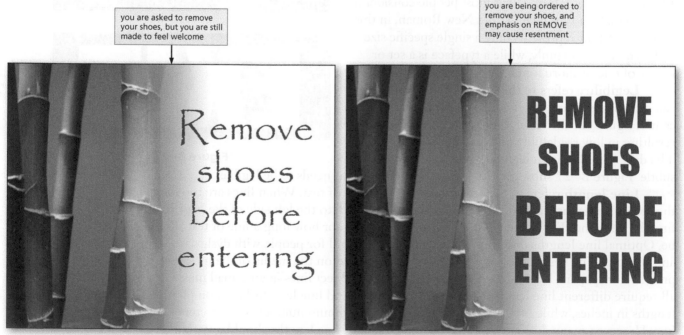

you are asked to remove your shoes, but you are still made to feel welcome

you are being ordered to remove your shoes, and emphasis on REMOVE may cause resentment

Figure B–30

Designing for Web versus Print

Graphic designers must be aware of subtle differences in how print and web projects are created and perceived when designing for these media. While many design principles are common to both, it takes a different mindset to create a design for either medium successfully. Print designs are static, as the layout never varies from print to print (though differences in color may appear because of inconsistencies with the printer or printing press). The appearance of web designs can vary, depending on the device used to view them. Some print designers struggle with the device dependency and fluidity of webpage designs. Some web designers unnecessarily concern themselves about accommodating fluid or shifting content when designing a print advertisement.

Device Dependency and Fluidity

The main differences between print and web design are related to device dependency and fluidity. Webpages are **device dependent**, meaning that the appearance of the page varies depending on the device (computer, cell phone, or PDA) on which they are viewed (Figure B–31). Discrepancies in monitor color calibration, screen resolution, and browser window size can affect how a webpage appears to the viewer. Colors can change, objects can shift, and text can wrap to a new line on different words from one device to another. In comparison, a newspaper or magazine looks the same no matter where it is purchased or where it is read. Designers can work with web programmers to design pages for different devices.

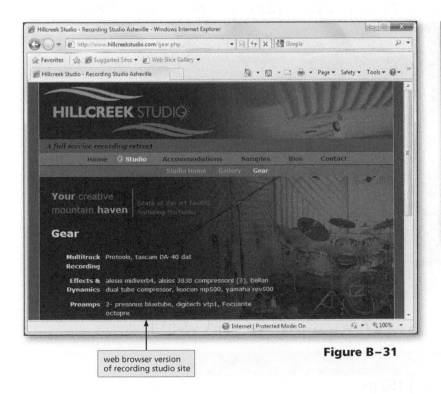

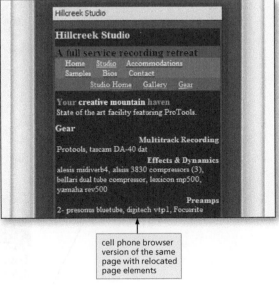

cell phone browser version of the same page with relocated page elements

web browser version of recording studio site

Figure B–31

Pixels, Dimensions, and Resolution

A pixel is the smallest element of a digital image. Magnifying an image reveals the individual pixels (Figure B–32). A pixel, unlike an inch or centimeter, is not an absolute measurement. The physical size of a pixel can change depending on device resolution.

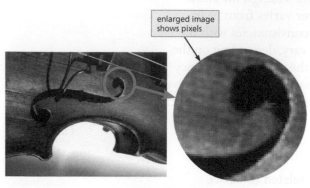

enlarged image shows pixels

Figure B–32

As you learned in Chapter 1, resolution refers to the number of pixels displayed on a computer screen. More pixels produce greater detail. When referring to an image file, the phrase, document dimensions, is used to describe the number of pixels in the file. For example, a document might have the dimensions of 450 × 337, meaning it contains 450 pixels across and 337 pixels vertically, for a total of 151,650 pixels. File size is directly related to document dimension. The more pixels there are in a document, the larger the file size.

When used to describe an image file, the word, resolution, also is used to describe the printed output. The print resolution is given in pixels per inch (PPI) — for example, 72 PPI or 300 PPI. PPI is a linear measurement: 72 PPI means that, when printed, the output will contain 72 pixels across every linear inch. If the document dimensions were 450 × 337, those 450 horizontal pixels would print in groups of 72 PPI, resulting in a printout just over 6 inches wide (Figure B–33).

450 px wide at 72 ppi

inches 1/8   1   2   3   4   5   6

| 72 px | 72 px | 72 px | 72 px | 72 px | 72 px | 18 px |

Note: The rulers are not to scale

image printed at 72 ppi is larger than if it were printed at 300 ppi

450 px wide at 300 ppi

inches 1/8   1   2   3   4   5   6

| 300 px | 150 px |

300 ppi version will be better quality, though smaller, because the pixels are smaller and able to produce more detail

Figure B–33

If the resolution, but not the dimensions, were increased to 300 PPI, then those same 450 pixels would print in groups of 300 per inch, producing a final output about 1.5 inches wide.

Key points to remember when working with resolution are:

- A pixel is not a static measurement. Pixels change in size. They get smaller or larger to fill an inch as defined in the PPI setting.

- Changing the resolution of an image file has no effect on the file size. It affects the physical size of the printed output.

- Changing the document dimensions does affect the file size.

When printing documents, printers create each individual pixel with a group of microscopic dots of ink (or toner or other pigment). The number of dots a printer can generate is measured in dots per inch (DPI). People sometimes incorrectly use the term DPI when they really mean PPI. A printer with a resolution of 2400 DPI means it can squeeze 2400 dots of ink (not pixels) into a single inch. The more dots used to create a pixel, the truer color each pixel can have — resulting in a higher-quality print.

A common misconception related to creating image files is that all graphics for use on the web should be created at a resolution of 72 PPI. However, because PPI affects the output of printing only, the PPI setting has no effect on the screen display of an image.

It is common practice to save web images at 72 PPI, not because it optimizes images for the web, but because the 72 PPI myth so widely is believed.

Working as a Graphic Designer

The business world offers many opportunities for people with creativity and an eye for design. From automotive design to fashion to advertising, the need for talented graphic artists is vast. Many industry experts believe there are generally three levels of professionals working in the graphics field: graphic artists, graphic designers, and people who own graphics editing/design software.

Graphic artists typically receive extensive schooling as art majors and know a lot about design principles and art history. However, schooling does not necessarily mean formal education in a school environment. A graphic artist can be self-educated. The key to the "artist" designation revolves around a personal need to express oneself creatively beyond that of producing commercial work for hire. While graphic artists work with software, they typically also produce art with more traditional media such as paints, pencils, fiber, metals, or other physical materials. Graphic artists may hold the same job as a graphic designer, but very often graphic artists will create and sell their own original artwork. This personal drive to create and the resulting independent production of original artwork is what distinguishes graphic artists from graphic designers.

The line separating graphic artists from graphic designers is a fine one. A **graphic designer** often is knowledgeable about design principles and may possess a wealth of information about art history, but not all graphic designers are graphic artists. They usually create design products for others, such as brochures, advertisements, or websites, using software, but do not create their own original works.

The third category of graphic designers includes people who own and use graphics design software for various purposes. This category, **software owners**, is not a true graphic design designation. Simply owning a copy of Photoshop or knowing how to use a certain software program does not make you a graphic artist/designer. Whereas artists and designers understand principles of design and effective use of color, and possess a certain degree of artistic ability or raw talent, design amateurs rely on the power of the software to help them create projects. Of course, it is possible for an amateur to become a professional designer or artist — but doing so requires education and training, not just purchasing a software suite.

BTW

Certification
The Adobe Certified Expert (ACE) program provides an opportunity for you to obtain a valuable industry credential — proof that you have the Photoshop CC skills required by employers. For more information, visit the Certification resource on the Student Companion Site located on www .cengagebrain.com.

BTW

Educational Requirements
Graphic designers usually need a bachelor's degree in graphic design, computer graphics, or a related field. Employers want to see job candidates who can demonstrate their creativity and originality through a professional design portfolio.

BTW

Jobs in Graphic Design
The U. S. Bureau of Labor statistics predicts a 7% increase in the need for graphic designers by the year 2020.

Jobs in Graphic Design

An understanding of design principles and software skills opens the door to many opportunities in the professional graphics industry. Jobs for graphic designers range from freelance work and self-employment to full-time careers with advertising agencies, web design firms, print houses, software companies, or the marketing team within an organization such as a school or commercial or nonprofit business. Perhaps the most important questions to ask yourself when considering a job in this field are:

- Do I want to work for myself or for someone else?
- Am I truly an artist? Am I creative? Or do I simply follow direction well, understand basic design principles, and know how to use graphics software?
- What is my preferred medium — physical (print) or electronic (web, software interface)?

Once you have secured a position in the graphics field, you will be assigned projects that will call on your design skills and other abilities.

Design Projects

A successful project always begins with solid planning. Proper planning helps you to stay focused and reduces the potential for wasted time and money — both yours and your client's. A project plan must specify the following aspects of the project:

- Scope of design work
- Roles and responsibilities of designer and client
- Expectations and specifications for final product, including time frame

When you and your client agree on the scope of the work and are clear on what the final product should look like, you as the designer know exactly what it is you need to produce. It is better to take the time to plan a project before sitting down with Photoshop, so you have a good idea of what to do once you start the software.

Client and Designer Roles

Both the client and the designer have specific jobs. Defining and agreeing on these roles is crucial for the success of the collaboration.

Simply put, the client must clearly communicate his or her expectations. Clients often need help articulating their wants and needs, and the designer must be able to help draw this information from the client. Additionally, the client must be available to provide feedback when the designer offers a draft for feedback or proofing. A client's responsibilities include the following:

- Clearly communicate the needs of the project
- Provide timely and constructive feedback
- Trust the designer's expertise
- Pay the bills on time

Aside from the obvious (creating the product), the designer also is responsible for making sure the client knows their own responsibilities and avoids poor design choices. Sometimes, a client will request something that is just bad — like certain colors that do not work well together or make text unreadable. The designer is responsible for respectfully steering the client away from the bad options and toward a better alternative.

In a highly competitive job market, you must determine what sets you apart from your competition. A potential client might choose one designer over another not because one is a better or more creative artist, but simply because they like the other designer more.

Customer service is part of your job, as well. Treat your client and your client's time and money with respect, be personable, and appreciate your client, and you will have more to offer than your competitors will. In addition to meeting the responsibilities previously defined, you should do the following:

- Be on time to meetings
- Meet or beat your deadlines so you do not submit work late
- Be able to explain your design choices
- Ensure adherence to copyright law

Defining the Project

As a designer, you must understand you are acting in the role of a hired hand — not an artist with complete creative control. You are being hired to create what your client wants, not what you necessarily prefer. While you need to educate your client as to best practices in design, ultimately the client is paying the bill, so he or she has the final word when it comes to making decisions.

BTW

PPI on the Web
You cannot make an image appear larger on screen by resizing its pixels. Every pixel on the same screen will always be the same size.

Specifying Project Details

You and your client should discuss and agree on the project details before any design work begins. One detail to consider is what the client needs for files. For example, does the client require a 300 PPI TIF file or a layered Photoshop file? How will the files be delivered? Will they be sent by e-mail, burned to a CD and mailed, or downloaded from a website or FTP server? Additionally, you should agree on a timeline of deliverables. A first draft of the design should be sent to the client for approval by a certain date, and pending timely client feedback, the final version should be delivered by the project deadline. The client may have a desired time frame, and the designer must be able to deliver the work within that time frame. Sometimes a compromise must be reached.

Collecting Materials

Existing materials help to speed up the design process. If you are hired to create a website or brochure, ask your client for copies of their existing promotional materials, such as a business card, letterhead, or logo. Ask your client what they like and dislike about these materials and if the product you are creating should be stylistically similar. This approach can prevent you from going down the wrong path, inadvertently creating something the client does not like or need. Additionally, you will need to collect any photographs your client has earmarked for the project.

Next, you must gather other assets for the project — specifically, high-quality artwork and photographs.

Original Artwork   If you have the raw artistic ability or own high-quality camera equipment, you can create your own original artwork or take your own photographs if you are a professional-level photographer. You can outsource some of this work to professional artists or photographers — just make sure to get your client's approval for the cost. Your other option is to use stock art.

Stock Art   **Stock art** includes existing artwork and photographs that can be licensed for use. The cost of a single picture can range from zero to several thousand dollars, depending on the source and license restrictions. Realistically, you should expect to pay between $5 and $40 for each print-quality digital file if you cannot find free sources.

BTW

Photos on CD or DVD
If possible, get photos and images on a CD or DVD. Many times a collection of photographs and other materials are too large to send by e-mail, and even if they are successfully sent, e-mails accidentally get deleted. Having all the materials on CD or DVD also guarantees you always have a backup of the original files as you modify copies with Photoshop or other software.

Public Domain vs. Commercial Stock Art

Public domain stock art sites can be difficult to use because they do not have the funding for the more intuitive style of interface found on the commercial sites. You often can find exactly what you want in the public domain. However, sometimes it is worth the $5 to more easily find exactly what you want on a commercial website.

Stock art is commercially available from many companies, most with a web presence — meaning you can download images or purchase whole collections of stock art on CD or DVD from a website. Thousands of companies sell commercial stock art online. Some of the most popular resources are fotosearch.com, corbis.com, and gettyimages.com.

When searching for stock art, be sure to seek out **royalty-free images**. Images that are royalty free can be reused without paying additional fees. For example, you could spend $100 to purchase an image that is not royalty free and use it on a website. If you want to use the same image in a brochure or another client's website, you might have to pay another fee to reuse the image. Royalty free means that once the initial payment is made, there are no re-usage fees.

If you do not want to pay anything for your images, look into finding **public domain** artwork or photographs. Images in the public domain are completely free to use. The only trick is finding quality artwork in the public domain. Whereas commercial stock art websites typically have millions of high-quality images from which to choose, public domain stock art websites often have far fewer choices. Public domain stock art sites include Flickr, Morgue File, and Uncle Sam's Photos.

Other Licenses   There are usage licenses allowing free unrestricted use of images, audio, video, text, and other content similar to that of the public domain. These licenses include Copyleft, Creative Commons, education use, fair use, GNU general public license, and open source. The definitions of these alternative licenses read like a law book, but it is helpful to recognize the names. Laws related to these licenses allow for limited use of copyright-protected material without requiring the permission of the copyright owner. If you find images or other content offered as one of these alternatives, there is a good chance it will be completely free to use.

Whatever the source for your images, be sure to read the license and usage rights and restrictions carefully. No matter your source for artwork, you need to document its origin. The documentation serves two important purposes. First, it provides a record of the image's origin in case you need to get additional similar artwork. Second, it provides peace of mind should you or your client ever face legal action for copyright infringement. The documentation does not have to be fancy; it can simply be a list of where an image is used in a project and where that image was acquired.

CopyLeft

CopyLeft, a play on the word copyright, has come to mean any work or program that along with its modified and extended versions, is free to use in the public domain.

Summary

Successful design uses the principles of balance, contrast, dominance, proximity, repetition, closure, continuance, negative space, and unity. The properties of color include hue, saturation, shade, tint, and value. Color modes include RGB for web images, CMYK for images you intend to print, and Lab for access to the largest color space possible when working with digital photographs. Adherence to web-safe colors is unnecessary. Colors can have emotional implications and should be used in harmony with neighboring colors. Color schemes include monochrome, complementary, analogous, and split-complementary.

Typeface selections can affect text readability, as can line lengths. Typefaces are organized into several categories, including serif, sans-serif, script, and display. The same website can look different from one monitor or computer to another.

Pixels per inch (PPI) determines the number of pixels printed per inch and affects the printed size of an image only, not how it appears onscreen or its file size. Higher PPI settings produce better quality printouts but have no effect on how an image appears onscreen. Dots per inch (DPI) refers to printer capabilities, and defines how many dots of ink a printer can print in a linear inch. Pixel dimensions, not image resolution, affect how large an image appears on-screen and the size of a file.

Working in graphic design can incorporate a range of creative roles; working with clients in a design role requires specifying project expectations and the responsibilities of both designer and client.

Flash Cards

The Student Companion Site has interactive flash cards of the important concepts in each chapter. Visit For detailed instructions about accessing available resources, visit solutions.cengage.com/ctdownloads or contact your instructor for information about the flash cards.

Ps File Edit Image Layer Type Select Filter 3D View Window Help

Adobe **Photoshop CC**   Feather: 0 px   ☐ Anti-alias   Style: Normal ⬧ Width: ⟷ Height: Refine Edge...

Appendix C
Using Photoshop Help

Photoshop Help

This appendix shows you how to use Photoshop Help. At anytime, whether you are accessing Photoshop currently or not, there are ways to interact with Photoshop Help and display information on any Photoshop topic. The help system is a complete reference manual at your fingertips.

Photoshop Help documentation for Photoshop CC is available in several formats, as shown in Figure C–1 on the following page. The first format is a web-based help system that was introduced in Chapter 1. If you press the F1 key or choose Photoshop Online Help on the Help menu, Adobe Community Help appears in your default browser. You then can use the webpage to search for help topics. The Adobe Community Help page also contains many other kinds of assistance, including tutorials and videos. Your computer must be connected to the web to use this form of Photoshop Help.

A second form of Photoshop Help is available as a PDF file. Again, pressing the F1 key or choosing Photoshop Online Help on the Help menu opens the Adobe Community Help page on the web. Then, you can tap or click the Help PDF link to open a searchable help documentation file, called Using Adobe Photoshop CC, in book format. You can save this help file on your storage device, or continue to use it on the web. If you prefer to view documentation in print form, you can print the Photoshop Help PDF file.

Photoshop Help displays two main panes. The left pane displays a search system. The right pane displays help information on the selected topic. Using Adobe Photoshop CC displays a chapter navigation system on the left, and pages from Photoshop Help documentation on the right.

Using Help

The quickest way to navigate the Photoshop help system is by tapping or clicking topic links on the Help pages. You also can search for specific words and phrases by using the **Search box** in the upper-left corner of the Adobe Community Help webpage. Here you can type words, such as layer mask, hue, or file formats, or you can type phrases, such as preview a web graphic, or drawing with the Pen Tool. Adobe Community Help responds by displaying search results with a list of topics you can tap or click.

Here are some tips regarding the words or phrases you enter to initiate a search:

1. Check the spelling of the word or phrase.

2. Keep your search specific, with fewer than seven words, to return the most accurate results.

3. If you search using a specific phrase, such as, shape tool, put quotation marks around the phrase — the search returns only those topics containing all words in the phrase.

4. If a search term does not yield the desired results, try using a synonym, such as web instead of Internet.

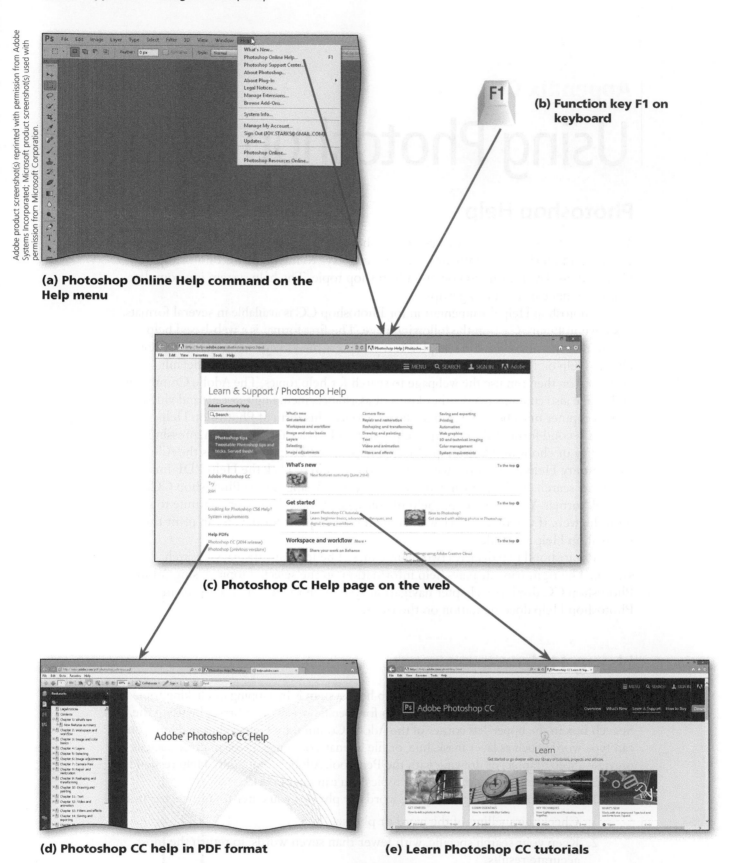

(a) Photoshop Online Help command on the Help menu

(b) Function key F1 on keyboard

(c) Photoshop CC Help page on the web

(d) Photoshop CC help in PDF format

(e) Learn Photoshop CC tutorials

Figure C–1

To Access Photoshop Online Help

The following step shows how to open Photoshop Online Help.

- With Photoshop running on your system, press the F1 key to display the Photoshop Help window.

- When the Photoshop Help window is displayed, double-tap or double-click the title bar to maximize the window, if necessary (Figure C–2).

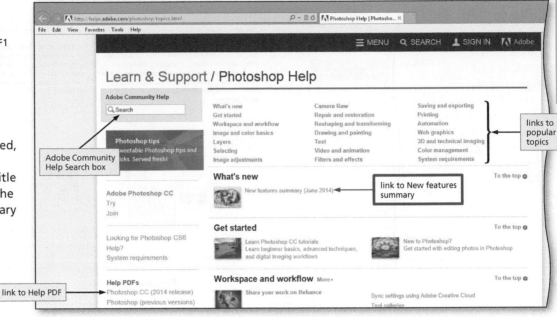

Figure C–2

Other Ways

1. On Help menu, tap or click Photoshop Online Help
2. Open browser, go to helpx.adobe.com/photoshop/topics.html

To Use Help Links

The following steps use a link to look up information about new features in Photoshop CC.

- Tap or click the topic, New features summary, to display its contents (Figure C–3).

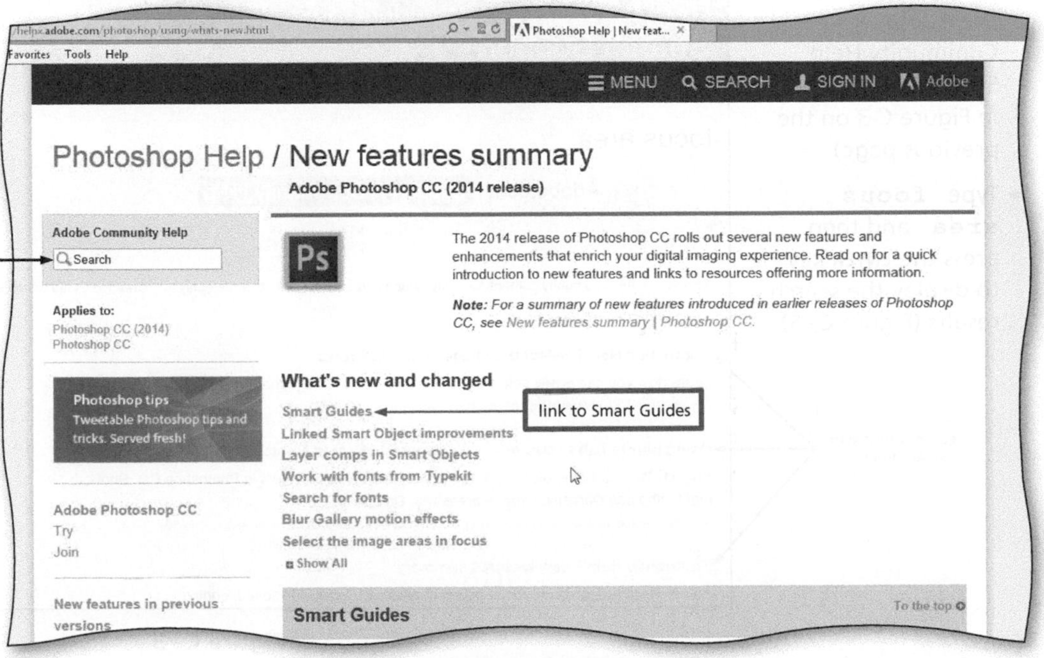

Figure C–3

- Tap or click the link, Smart Guides, to display information about the new tools (Figure C–4).

Q&A

Why does my screen look different?
Adobe routinely updates the online Help files and topics to include the most recent information, videos, and tutorials. Your topics will differ.

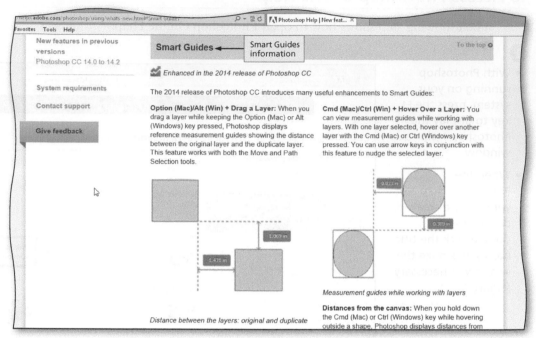

Figure C–4

To Use the Adobe Community Help Search Box

The following steps use the Search box to obtain useful information by entering the keywords, focus area. If none of the topics presents the information you want, you can refine the search by entering another word or phrase in the Search box.

- Scroll to the top of the page, and then tap or click the Adobe Community Help Search box. (shown in Figure C-3 on the previous page)

- Type **focus area** and then press the ENTER key to display the search results (Figure C–5).

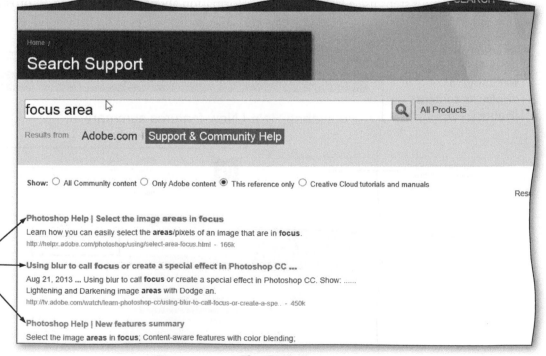

Figure C–5

2

- When the list of Help topics is displayed, tap or click 'Photoshop Help / Select the image areas in focus', or a similar topic in your list.

- Scroll as necessary to display the 'Select the image area in focus' topic (Figure C–6).

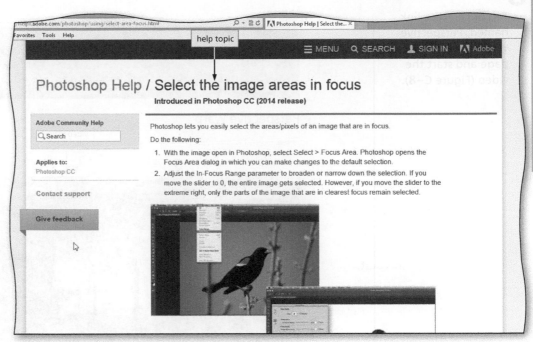

Figure C–6

To View a Video on Adobe TV

Using Photoshop Help while connected to the web, you can view online videos and tutorials. In the following steps, you view a video on Adobe TV.

1

- Scroll as necessary to display the Search box at the top of the page.

- In the Search box, type **adobe tv perspective warp**, and then press the ENTER key to perform the search (Figure C–7).

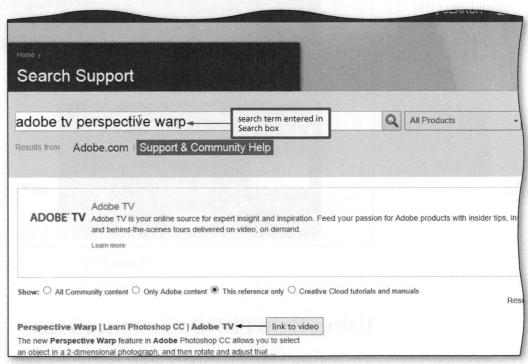

Figure C–7

● Tap or click the link named, Perspective Warp, to open the page and start the video (Figure C–8).

Figure C–8

● When the video is finished playing, tap or click the Close button on the title bar of the browser window to quit Help (Figure C–9).

Figure C–9

Using Help PDF Documentation

The PDF file, Adobe Photoshop Help and Tutorials, is a complete set of documentation for using Photoshop CC. The PDF file is organized into chapter topics with a table of contents like a regular book. You can access Adobe Photoshop Help and Tutorials by tapping or clicking the link on the Photoshop Online Help page.

To Open Adobe Photoshop Help and Tutorials

The following step opens the PDF file, Adobe Photoshop Help and Tutorials, from the Photoshop Online Help page. You can use Adobe Acrobat or Adobe Reader to view the documentation.

1

- Start Photoshop if necessary.

- Press the F1 key to access Photoshop online Help.

- In the Help PDFs area, tap or click Photoshop CC to open the Adobe Photoshop CC Help documentation. (Figure C–10).

Q&A The file would not open because I do not have Acrobat Reader on my system. What should I do? Either download Acrobat Reader or see your instructor for ways to access the file.

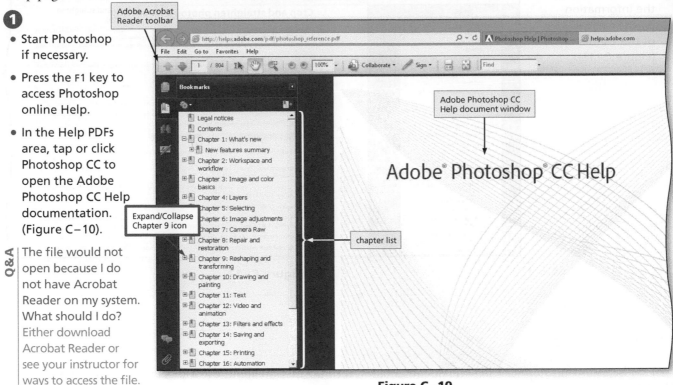

Figure C–10

Other Ways

1. Open browser, go to helpx.adobe.com/pdf/photoshop_reference/pdf

To Navigate the Documentation by Chapter Topic

The following steps use the left pane of the documentation window to find information related to cropping.

1

- With the Adobe Photoshop Help CC documentation file still displayed, tap or click the plus sign next to, Chapter 9: Reshaping and transforming, and then tap or click 'Adjusting crop, rotation, and canvas', to display the topic (Figure C–11).

Q&A What does the light bulb symbol mean? A light bulb icon indicates a Photoshop tip.

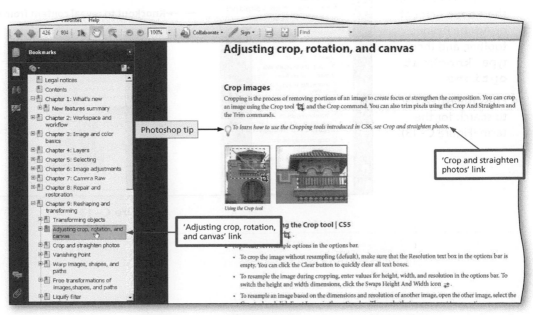

Figure C–11

2

- Tap or click the link, 'Crop and straighten photos', to display the information on the right side of the window (Figure C–12).

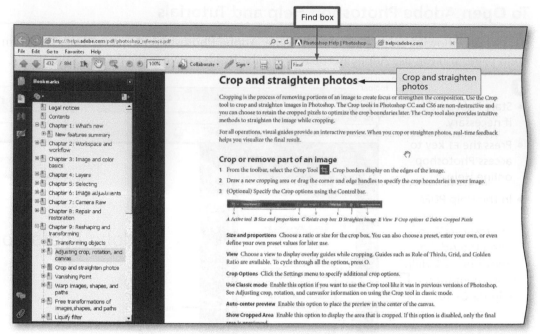

Figure C–12

To Use the Find Box

The following step searches the documentation for information about the topic, knockout, using the Find box.

1

- With the Adobe Photoshop Help and Tutorials documentation window still displayed, tap or click the Find box in the Adobe Acrobat or Adobe Reader toolbar, and then type **knockout options**.

- Press the ENTER key to search for the term (Figure C–13).

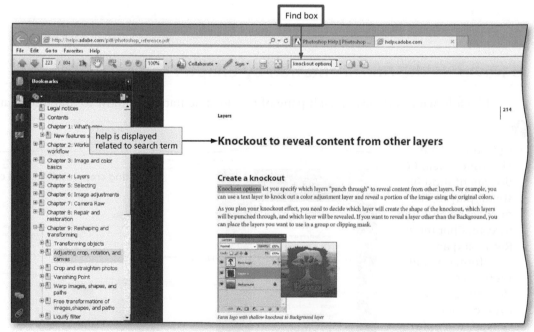

Figure C–13

In the Labs
1: Using Adobe Help on the Web

Instructions: Perform the following tasks using Adobe Community Help.

1. Start Photoshop and then press the F1 key to access Photoshop Help. In the Adobe Community Help Search box, type **art history brush tool** obtain help on using the tool, and then press the ENTER key.

2. When the topics are displayed, tap or click the topic, 'Photoshop Help / Painting stylized strokes with the Art History Brush'.

3. Scroll as necessary to access two additional links and print the information. Hand in the printouts to your instructor. Use the browser's Back and Forward buttons to return to the original page.

4. Use the Search box to search for information on linking layers. Tap or click the 'Photoshop Help / Selecting, grouping, and linking layers' topic in the search results. Read and print the information. One at a time, tap or click the links on the page and print the information for any new page that is displayed.

5. Use the Search box to search for information on tutorials. Navigate to a tutorial of your choice and follow the directions. Write three paragraphs describing your experience, including how easy or difficult it was to follow the tutorial, and what you learned. Turn in the paragraphs to your instructor.

6. Close Photoshop Help.

2: Using Adobe Photoshop CC Documentation

Instructions: Use the Adobe Photoshop CC documentation to understand the topics better, and to answer the questions listed below. Answer the questions on your own paper, or hand in the printed Help information to your instructor.

1. Access the Photoshop Help page on the web. In the Help PDFs area, tap or click Photoshop CC to open the documentation.

2. Use the Find box, and enter **use snapping** as the term. Tap or click the search result entitled, Use snapping, and then print the page. Hand in the printouts to your instructor.

3. Navigate to Chapter 10: Drawing and painting. Tap or click the plus sign to expand the topic. Tap or click the plus sign next to Drawing shapes. Choose three topics that interest you in the expanded area. One at a time, tap or click each link and print the page. Hand in the printouts to your instructor.

Ps File Edit Image Layer Type Select Filter 3D View Window Help

Adobe **Photoshop CC** Feather: 0 px   Anti-alias   Style: Normal   Width: Height: Refine Edge...

Appendix D
Using Adobe Bridge CC

Adobe Bridge

This appendix shows you how to use Adobe Bridge CC. Bridge is a file exploration tool similar to Windows Explorer, but with added functionality related to images. Bridge replaces previous file browsing techniques, and now is the control center for the Adobe Creative Cloud Suite. Bridge is used to organize, browse, and locate the assets you need to create content for print, the web, and mobile devices with drag-and-drop functionality.

You can access Bridge from Photoshop or from the Windows 8 start screen. Bridge can run independently from Photoshop as a stand-alone program.

To Start Bridge Using Windows 8

The following steps start Bridge using Windows 8.

1

- With Windows 8 running, scroll to display the Adobe Bridge CC tile on the Start screen (Figure D–1).

Q&A What is the best way to scroll?
You can scroll by swiping the screen, by tapping or clicking the scroll bar at the bottom of the Start screen, or by using the ARROW KEYS on your keyboard.

Do I have to use the 64 bit version?
No, your computer might run an operating system that uses the 32 Bit version of Photoshop CC. Your steps and screens will work exactly the same way.

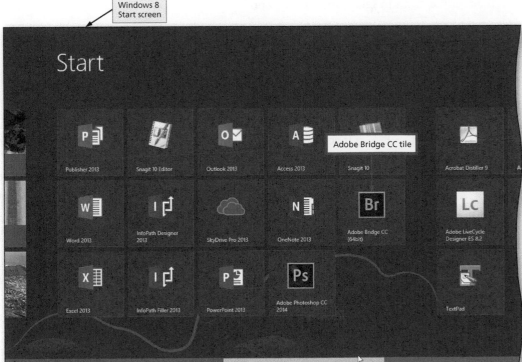

Windows 8 Start screen

Adobe Bridge CC tile

Figure D–1

2

- Tap or click the Adobe Bridge CC tile to run the Bridge CC app.

- After a few moments, when the Bridge window is displayed, if the window is not maximlzed, tap or click the Maximize button next to the Close button on the Application bar to maximize the window.

- Tap or click Computer on the Favorites panel, if necessary (Figure D–2).

Q&A   Can I use a stylus to tap the correct tile?
Yes. You can tap the tile with your finger, click the tile with your mouse, or tap the screen with a stylus to select and run the app.

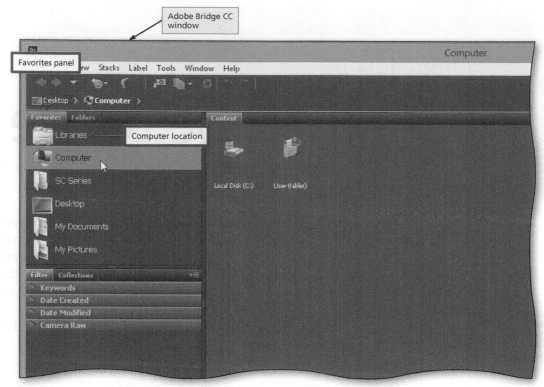

Figure D–2

Other Ways

1. Tap or click Search charm on Charms bar, type `Bridge CC` in search box, tap or click app name in results list	2. In Photoshop, tap or click File on menu bar, tap or click Browse in Bridge	3. Press ATL+CTRL+O

To Start Bridge CC Using Windows 7

If you are using Windows 7, perform these steps to start Photoshop CC instead of the previous steps that use Windows 8.

1. Tap or click the Start button on the Windows 7 taskbar to display the Start menu.

2. Type `Bridge CC` as the search text in the 'Search programs and files' text box, and watch the search results appear on the Start menu.

3. Tap or click Adobe Bridge CC in the search results on the Start menu to start Photoshop CC.

After a few moments, when the Photoshop window is displayed, if the window is not maximized, tap or click the Maximize button next to the Close button on the Application bar to maximize the window.

To Reset the Workspace

To make your installation of Bridge match the figures in this book, you will reset the workspace to its default settings in the following step.

1

- Tap or click Window on the menu bar, and then point to Workspace to display the Workspace submenu (Figure D–3).

2

- Tap or click Reset Workspace on the Workspace submenu.

Q&A | What is the Light Table workspace? The Light Table workspace displays only the Content panel.

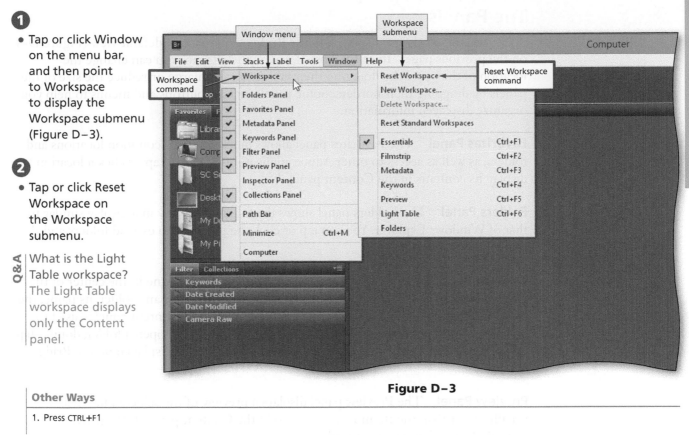

Figure D–3

Other Ways

1. Press CTRL+F1

The Bridge Window

The parts of the Bridge window are displayed in Figure D–4. The window is divided into panels and toolbars.

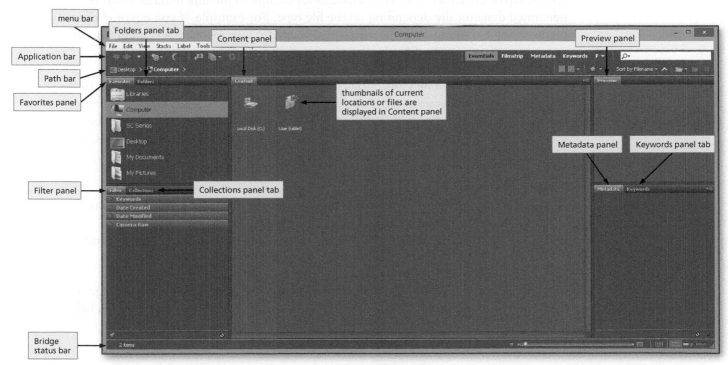

Figure D–4

The Panels

Several panels are displayed in the Bridge workspace in default view (Figure D-4 on the previous page). To select a panel, tap or click its tab. You can change the location of the panels by dragging their tabs. You can enlarge or reduce the size of the panels by dragging their borders. Some panels include buttons and menus to help you organize displayed information.

Favorites Panel The Favorites panel allows quick access to common locations and folders, as well as access to other Adobe applications. You can tap or click a location to display its contents in the Content panel.

Folders Panel The Folders panel shows the folder hierarchy in a display similar to that of Windows Explorer. You can tap or click the plus sign to expand folders and the minus sign to collapse them.

Content Panel The Content panel is displayed in a large pane in the center of the Bridge window. The content panel includes a view of each file and folder, its name, the creation date, and other information about each item. The Content panel is used to select files and open folders. To select a file, tap or click it. To open a folder, double-tap or double-click it. You can change how the Content panel is displayed on the Bridge status bar.

Preview Panel The Preview panel displays a preview of the selected file that is usually larger than the thumbnail displayed in the Content panel. If the panel is resized, the preview also is resized.

Filter Panel The Filter panel is displayed in the lower-left region of the Bridge window. The Filter panel includes many categories of criteria used to filter or control which files are displayed in the Content panel. By default, three categories are displayed when you first start Bridge: Keywords, Date Created, and Date Modified. As you tap or click files, the criteria categories change to include metadata that is generated dynamically depending on the file type. For example, if you tap or click an image in the Content panel, the Filter panel includes criteria such as camera data. If you tap or click an audio file, the criteria include artist, album genre, and so on.

Collections Panel The Collections panel is displayed in the lower-left region of the Bridge window. Collections are a way to group photos in one place for easy viewing, even if the images are located in different folders or on different hard drives. The Collections panel allows you to create and display previously created collections, by identifying files or by saving previous searches.

Metadata Panel The Metadata panel contains metadata information for the selected file. Recall that metadata is information about the file including properties, camera data, creation and modification data, and other pieces of information. If multiple files are selected, shared data is listed such as keywords, date created, and exposure settings.

Keywords Panel The Keywords panel allows you to assign keywords to image files using categories designed by Bridge, or you can create new ones. The keywords help you organize and search your images.

Toolbars

Bridge displays several toolbars to help you work more efficiently (Figure D–5).

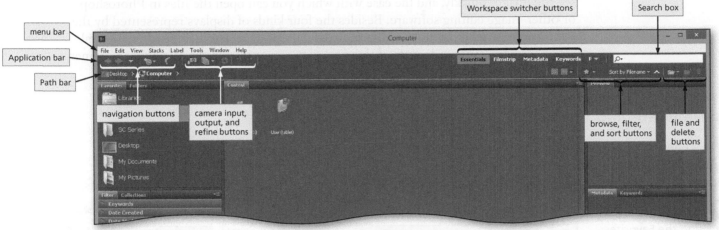

Figure D–5

Menu Bar   The menu bar is displayed at the top of the Bridge window and contains commands specific to Bridge.

Application Bar   Below the menu bar is the Application bar, which includes the navigation buttons, file retrieval and output buttons, buttons for switching workspaces, and other buttons to search for files.

Path Bar   The Path bar displays the path for the current file. To the right of the Path bar are shortcut buttons to help you work with your files. Browse, filter, and sort buttons change the display in the Content panel. The 'Create a new folder' button inserts a new folder in the current location. The rotate buttons are active when an image file is selected in the Content panel. The Delete item button deletes the selected item.

Status Bar   At the bottom of the Bridge window, the status bar displays information and contains buttons (Figure D–6). On the left side of the status bar is information regarding the number of items in the current location and how many files are selected, if any. On the right side of the status bar, the Thumbnail slider sets the size of the thumbnails. To the right of the slider are four buttons used to change the display of the Content panel, including the 'Click to lock thumbnail grid' button, the 'View content as thumbnails' button, the 'View content as details' button, and the 'View content as list' button.

BTW

The Filmstrip Workspace
The Filmstrip workspace displays thumbnails in a scrolling horizontal Content panel. The currently selected items appears in the Preview panel.

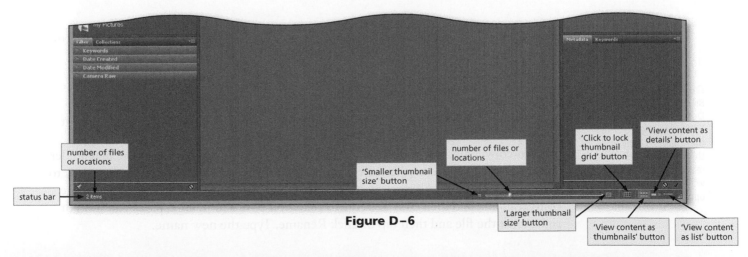

Figure D–6

Bridge Navigation and File Viewing

The advantages of using Bridge to navigate through the files and folders on your computer system include an interface that looks the same in all folders, the ability to see the images quickly, and the ease with which you can open the files in Photoshop or other image editing software. Besides the four kinds of displays represented by the Workspace switcher buttons on the right side of the status bar, Bridge offers several other configurations or layouts of the workspace accessible on the Workspace submenu on the Window menu (Figure D–3 on page APP 35).

To Navigate and View Files Using Bridge

The following step navigates to the Data Files for Students to view files. Visit www.cengage.com/ct /studentdownload for detailed instructions or contact your instructor for information about accessing the required files. You then will use the Workspace switcher buttons to view the Content panel in different styles.

- Using the Favorites panel and the Content panel, navigate to the drive associated with the Data Files for Students.

- When the folders and files are displayed, double-tap or double-click the Photoshop folder, and then double-tap or double-click the Chapter 01 folder to display the files (Figure D–7).

 **Experiment**

- One at a time, tap or click each of the workspace buttons on the options bar and note how the Content panel changes.

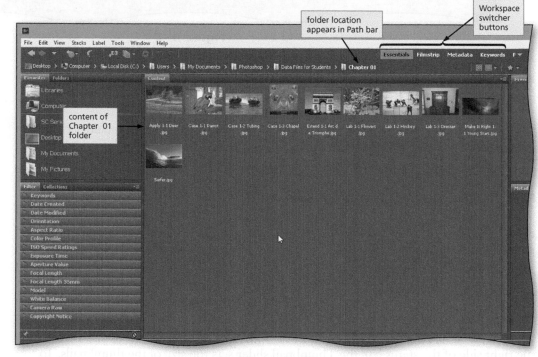

Figure D–7

Other Ways

1. To view Filmstrip workspace, press CTRL+F2
2. To view Metadata workspace, press CTRL+F3
3. To view Output workspace, press CTRL+F4
4. To view Keywords workspace, press CTRL+F5
5. To view Preview workspace, press CTRL+F6

BTW

Duplicating Files
Bridge also offers a Duplicate command on the Edit menu (Figure D–8) that makes a copy in the same folder. Bridge renames the second file with the word, Copy, appended to the file name.

Managing Files

If you want to move a file to a folder that currently is displayed in the Content panel, you can drag and drop the file. The right-drag option is not available. If you want to copy a file, you can choose Copy on the Edit menu, navigate to the new folder and then choose Paste on the Edit menu. At anytime, you can press the DELETE key to delete a file or folder. Alternately, you can press and hold or right-click to display the context menu, and then click Delete. To rename a photo in Bridge, press and hold or right-click the file and then tap or click Rename. Type the new name.

To Copy a File

The following steps copy a file from the Data Files for Students to a USB flash drive using Bridge.

1

- With the Chapter 1 folder contents still displayed in the Content panel, tap or click the Case 1-1 Parrot thumbnail to select it.

- Tap or click Edit on the menu bar to display the Edit menu (Figure D–8).

 Experiment

- Choose a picture and then use one of the rotate commands on the Edit menu to rotate the image. Press CTRL+Z to cancel the rotation. When you are done, tap or click Edit on the menu bar.

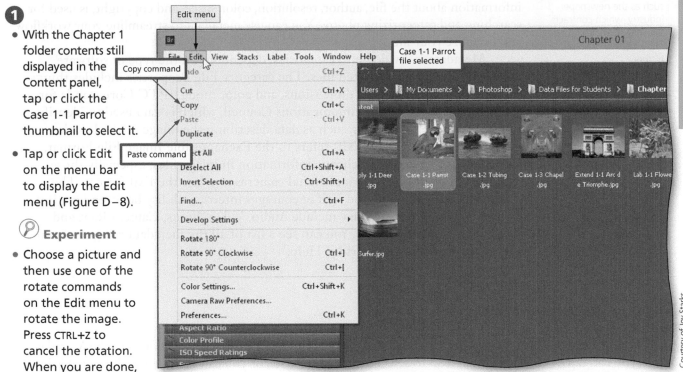

Figure D–8

2

- Tap or click Copy on the Edit menu.

- In the Favorites panel, tap or click Computer.

- When the Computer locations are displayed in the Content panel, navigate to your storage device.

- Tap or click Edit on the menu bar, and then tap or click Paste to display the copy in its new location (Figure D–9).

Q&A I have different folders and files. Did I do something wrong?
No. Your folder structure and files will probably differ.

Figure D–9

Other Ways

1. To copy, press CTRL+C

2. To paste, press CTRL+V

Metadata

A popular use for Bridge allows you to assign metadata to files. Metadata, such as information about the file, author, resolution, color space, and copyright, is used for searching and categorizing photos. You can use metadata to streamline your workflow and organize your files.

Metadata is divided into categories, depending on the type of software you are using and the selected files. The category File Properties includes things like file type, creation date, dimensions, and color mode. IPTC Core stands for International Press Telecommunications Council, which is data used to identify transmitted text and images, such as data describing the image or the location of a photo. Camera Data (Exif) refers to the Exchangeable Image File Format, a standard for storing interchange information in image files, especially those using JPEG compression. Most digital cameras now use the Exif format. The standardization of IPTC and Exif encourages interoperability between imaging devices. Other categories may include Audio, Video, Fonts, Camera Raw, and Version Cue, among others. You can see a list of all the metadata categories and their definitions by using Bridge Help.

To Assign and View Metadata

The Metadata Focus workspace makes it easier to assign or enter metadata for photos. In the Metadata panel, you can tap or click the pencil icon to select fields of metadata, or you can move through the fields by pressing the TAB key. The following steps enter description and location information for the selected file.

 1

- Tap or click the Case 1-1 Parrot thumbnail to select it.

- In the Metadata panel, scroll down to the IPTC Core area.

- Tap or click the arrow next to the heading, IPTC Core to expand the area if necessary (Figure D–10).

Q&A
What are the indications right below the Metadata panel tab in the gray box?
It is called the metadata placard; it displays common camera icons/functions, such as aperture or shutter speed, and their settings.

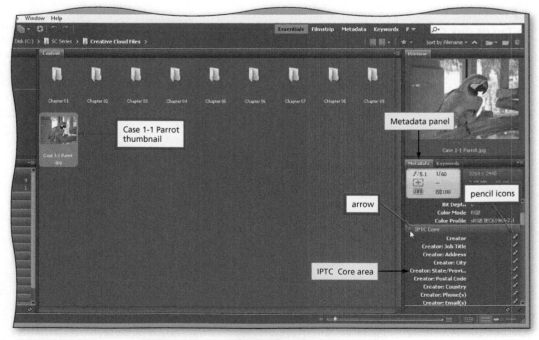

Figure D–10

- Scroll down to the Description field and then tap or click the pencil icon to the right of the Description field. Type **Bubba the parrot** as the description.

- Scroll as needed and then tap or click the pencil icon to the right of the Sublocation field. Type **beach store** as the location.

- Press the TAB key, Type **Palm Island** as the city.

- Press the TAB key. Type **South Carolina** as the state (Figure D–11).

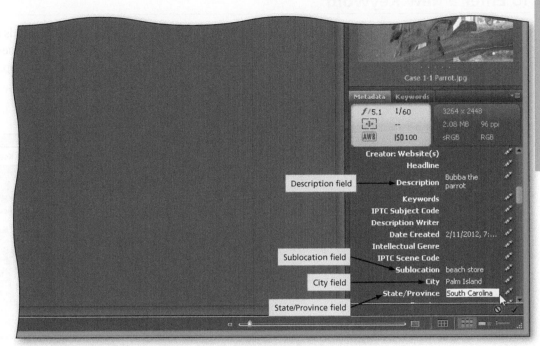

Figure D–11

- Tap or click the Apply button at the bottom of the Metadata panel to assign the metadata to the photo.

- Tap or click File on the menu bar and then tap or click File Info to display the Case 1-1 Parrot.jpg dialog box, and verify the information in the Description field (Figure D–12).

- Tap or click the OK button to close the dialog box.

   Experiment

- Tap or click each of the thumbnail buttons on the Bridge status bar to see how they change the display.

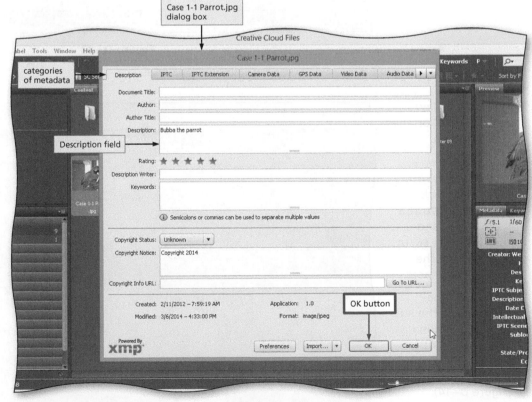

Figure D–12

Other Ways

1. Press CTRL+I, enter data, tap or click OK button

To Enter a New Keyword

The Keywords panel lets you create and apply Bridge **keywords** to files. Keywords can be organized into categories called **sets.** Using keywords and sets, you identify and search for files based on their content. To assign keywords, you tap or click the box to the left of the keyword in the Keywords panel, as shown in the following steps.

- With the Case 1-1 Parrot image still selected, tap or click the Keywords panel tab to display the Keywords panel.

- Press and hold or right-click the word, Places, to display the context menu (Figure D–13).

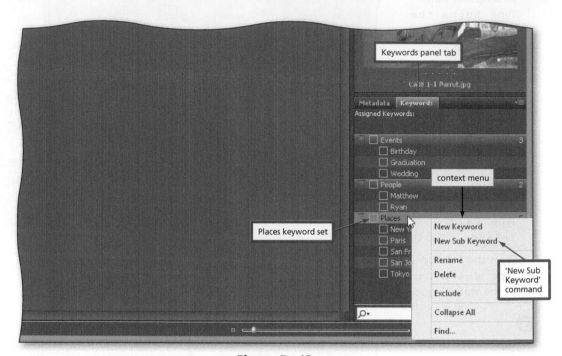

Figure D–13

- Tap or click 'New Sub Keyword' on the context menu.

- When the new field is displayed in the Keywords panel, type `South Carolina` and then press the ENTER key to create the new item in Places.

- Tap or click the check box to the left of South Carolina to assign a South Carolina keyword to the picture (Figure D–14).

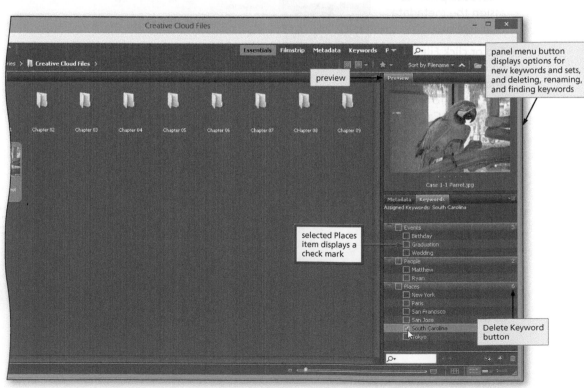

Figure D–14

To Rate a Photo

A rating system from zero stars to five stars is available in Bridge to rate your images and photos. A rating system helps you organize and flag your favorite or best files. Many photographers transfer their digital photos from a camera into Bridge and then look back through them, rating and grouping the photos. You can rate a photo using the Label menu or using shortcut keys. Once the photo is rated, stars are displayed below or above the file name, depending on the workspace view. To change a rating, tap or click Label on the menu bar and then increase or decrease the rating. To remove all stars, tap or click Label on the menu bar and then tap or click No Rating. In some views, you can change a rating by tapping or clicking stars or dots that appear below the thumbnail. You can remove the rating by tapping or clicking left of the stars.

The following step adds a rating to a photo file in Bridge.

1

- With the Case 1-1 Parrot image still selected in the Content panel, press CTRL+3 to assign a three-star rating (Figure D–15).

Q&A How do you remove the stars if you change your mind? Tap or click to the left of the stars in the Content panel, or press CTRL+0 (ZERO) to remove the stars.

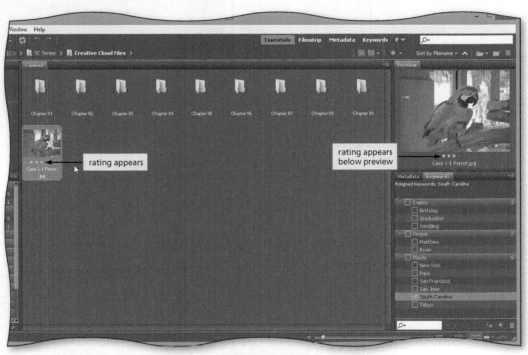

Figure D–15

Other Ways

1. On Label menu, select desired rating

To Label a Photo with Color Coding

Another way to group photos in Bridge is to use a color coding system. Bridge provides five colors that users can use to label or group their photos. Each color has a category keyword that can be used to group photos. Keywords such as Approved, Second, or Review are used in photojournalism to indicate the status of the photo for future usage. Some companies use the colors for sorting and selecting only. The steps on the next page add a green color indicating approval to the Case 1-1 Parrot image using the menu system. Shortcut keys also are available for labeling photos with color coding. You can edit the words associated with the various colors. To do so, press CTRL+K to enter Preferences and then tap or click Labels in the left navigation pane.

BTW

Saving Ratings
Color coding and ratings are portable to other computers only when photos have embedded extensible markup platform (XMP) storage space. Otherwise, the colors and ratings are stored in your system's cached memory.

1

- With the Case 1-1 Parrot image still selected in the Content panel, tap or click Label on the menu bar to display the Label menu (Figure D–16).

Q&A Can I change the colors associated with each label status?

No. Beginning with the Select command on the Label menu and going down, the colors are red, yellow, green, blue, and purple, respectively.

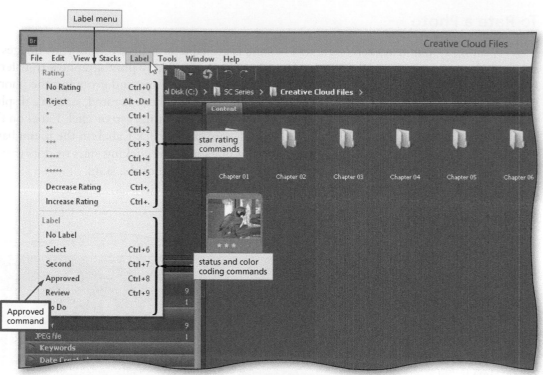

Figure D–16

2

- Tap or click Approved to choose a label status.

- If Bridge displays a dialog box, tap or click its OK button to apply the color (Figure D–17).

Q&A Where will I see the word, Approved, that I chose from the Label menu?

In the Essentials workspace, you only see the green color around the rating. If you tap or click the Metadata workspace switcher button, the status itself is displayed.

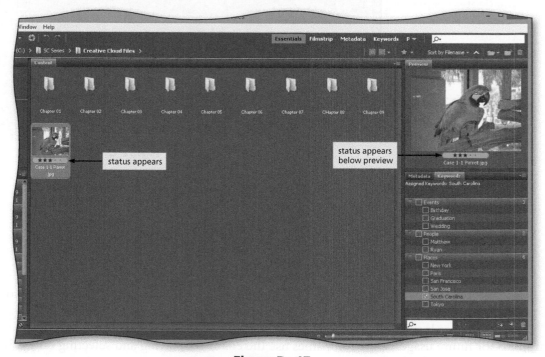

Figure D–17

Other Ways

1. For green color coding, press CTRL+8

Searching Bridge

Searching is a powerful tool in Bridge, especially as the number of stored image files increases on your computer system. It is a good idea to enter keywords, or metadata, for every image file you store, to make searching more efficient. Without Bridge and the search tool, you would have to view all files as filmstrips in Windows, and then look at them one screen at a time until you found what you wanted.

Using the Find Command

In Bridge, you can enter the kind of data or field that you want to search, parameters for that field, and the text you are looking for using the Find command. For example, you could search for all files with a rating of three stars or better, for files less than 1 megabyte in size, files with South Carolina as their location, or files that begin with the letter, m.

To Use the Find Command

The Find dialog box displays many boxes and buttons to help you search effectively. In the following steps, you will look for all files with metadata that includes the word, beach.

- Tap or click Edit on the menu bar, and then tap or click Find to display the Find dialog box (Figure D–18).

Q&A How do I search in other locations? Tap or click the Look in box arrow and choose a location, or tap or click the Browse command in the list to navigate to the desired location.

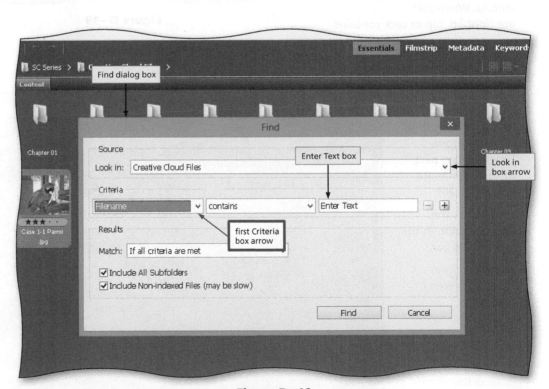

Figure D–18

2

- If necessary, tap or click the first Criteria box arrow, scroll down as necessary, and then tap or click All Metadata to search all of the metadata fields.

- Press the TAB key twice, and then type **beach** in the Enter Text box to enter the criteria (Figure D–19).

 Experiment

- Tap or click the second Criteria box arrow to view the choices for delimiting the criteria. When you are finished, tap or click contains.

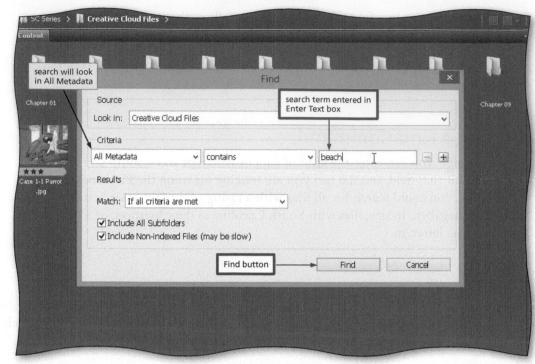

Figure D–19

3

- Tap or click the Find button to display all files that have the word, beach, in any part of their metadata (Figure D–20).

- Tap or click the Cancel button in the Search title bar.

Q&A

Can I search for types of images? Yes, tap or click the first Criteria box arrow, and then tap or click Document Type. The third Criteria box then lists types of images from which you can choose.

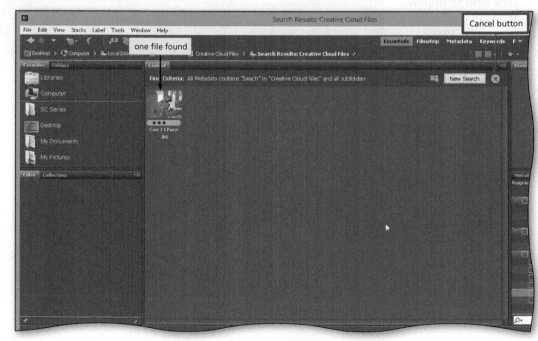

Figure D–20

Other Ways

1. Press CTRL+F, enter search criteria, tap or click Find button

Advanced Searching

The plus sign to the right of the search boxes in the Find dialog box allows you to search multiple fields. You can add additional criteria by tapping or clicking the plus sign. For example, if you wanted to find pictures from your beach vacation that were rated with three stars, you could search for the keyword, beach, in the first line of criteria boxes, and then enter a rating in the second line of criteria boxes to narrow your search even further (Figure D–21). When tapped or clicked, the Match box arrow allows you to match any or all criteria.

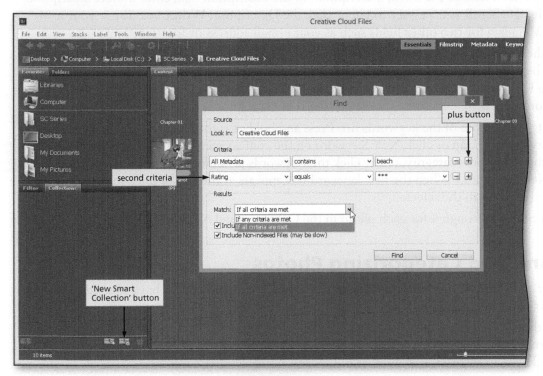

Figure D–21

Bridge offers you a way to save common searches as a **collection** for use later. For example, if you were working for a grocery wholesaler who stores many files for artwork in advertising, searching for pictures related to dairy products would be a common search. Looking through folders of images for pictures of milk or cheese would be very time consuming. To create a stored search collection, tap or click the 'New Smart Collection' button and enter your criteria. Bridge then allows you to name the search. To display stored collections, tap or click Collections in the Favorites panel. Then to perform the search again, double-tap or double-click the collection. With metadata and collection searches, Bridge saves a lot of time.

To Quit Bridge

The final step quits Bridge.

1 Tap or click the Close button on the Bridge title bar.

In the Labs
1: Assigning Metadata

Instructions: You would like to assign metadata to some of the photos you worked on in previous chapters in this book.

1. Start Bridge on your system. When the Bridge window is displayed, tap or click Computer on the Favorites panel. In the Content panel, navigate to your storage location and open a folder that contains a photo or image file.

2. Tap or click to select a file in the folder. In the Metadata panel, scroll down and tap or click the pencil icon next to the word, Description. In the description box, enter a short description of the image. Scroll as necessary to tap or click the Description Writer box. Enter your name. Enter Metadata for two other fields such as your e-mail address or location.

3. With the first photo still selected, tap or click the Keywords panel tab. When the Adobe Bridge dialog box appears, tap or click Apply to apply the changes you just made in the Metadata panel. On the Keywords panel, tap or click to place a check mark next to any keywords that apply to the photo.

4. Scroll to the bottom of the keywords list. Press and hold or right-click the Other Keywords category and then tap or click New Keyword on the context menu. (*Hint*: if you do not have the Other Keywords category, tap or click the Keywords panel menu button, and then tap or click New Keyword.) When the new keyword box appears at the top of the panel, type a new keyword relating to the selected.

5. Repeat Steps 2 through 4 for each photo in the Content panel of the Bridge window.

2: Rating and Categorizing Photos

Instructions: You would like to rate and categorize some of the photos you have created.

1. Start Bridge. Navigate to the location of a Photoshop file you created in a previous chapter.

2. Select the file. Assign a rating to the file on a scale from 1 to 5. On the Label menu, tap or click the number of stars that corresponds to your rating. Repeat the process for other photos as directed by your instructor.

3. Tap or click the file again to select it. Tap or click Label on the menu bar. Choose a label setting, such as Approved. Repeat the process for the previous file you rated, choosing a different label setting.

4. Choose your favorite photo in the folder and then press and hold or right-click the file in the Content panel. Tap or click Add to Favorites on the context menu.

PS File Edit Image Layer Type Select Filter 3D View Window Help

Adobe **Photoshop CC**   Feather: | 0 px | Anti-alias   Style | Normal | Width   Height   Refine Edge...

Appendix E
Editing Preferences

Editing Preferences

This appendix explains how to change the screen resolution in Windows 8 to the resolution used in this book. It also describes how to customize the Photoshop window by setting preferences, menu commands, and resetting user changes. Finally it discusses the experimental features of Photoshop CC, including touch gestures and UI Scaling.

Changing Screen Resolution

Screen resolution indicates the number of pixels (dots) that the computer uses to display the graphics, text, and background you see on the screen. The screen resolution usually is stated as the product of two numbers, such as 1366 × 768. That resolution results in a display of 1,366 distinct pixels on each of 768 lines, or about 1, 049,088 pixels on the screen or monitor. The figures in this book were created using a screen resolution of 1366 × 768.

To Change Screen Resolution

The following steps change your screen's resolution to 1366 × 768 pixels. Your computer already might be set to 1366 × 768 or some other resolution.

1

- Start Windows 8 for your system.

- Tap or click the Desktop app to display the desktop.

- Press and hold or right-click the desktop to display the shortcut menu (Figure E–1).

Q&A How do I change the screen resolution for Windows 7?
The steps are the same. Press and hold or right-click the Windows 7 desktop to display the shortcut menu and continue with the steps.

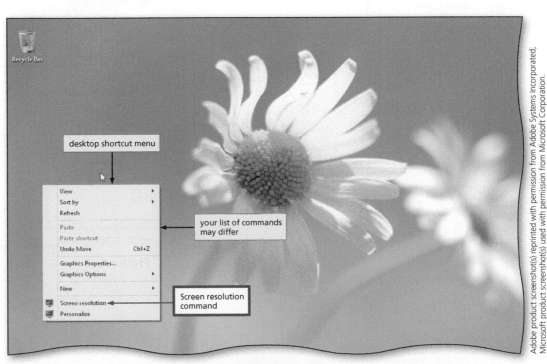

desktop shortcut menu

your list of commands may differ

Screen resolution command

Figure E–1

2

- Tap or click Screen resolution on the shortcut menu to open the Screen Resolution window. Maximize the window if necessary (Figure E–2).

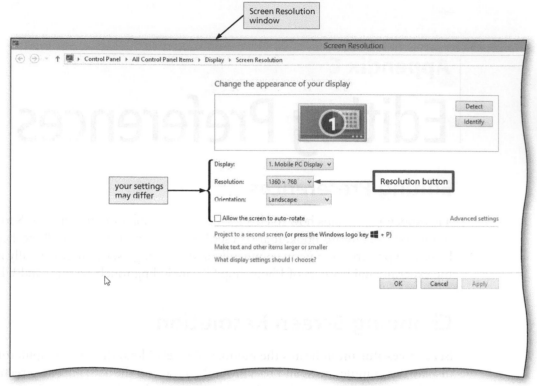

Figure E–2

3

- Tap or click the Resolution button to display the list of available resolutions (Figure E–3).

Q&A | My list is different. Is that a problem?
No. It is likely that your list will be different because each computer system or tablet might have different resolution choices.

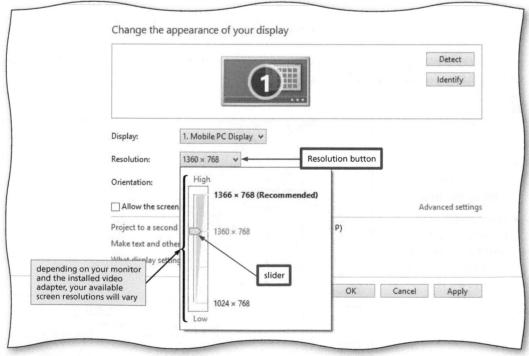

Figure E–3

- Drag the slider in the Resolution list so that the screen resolution changes to 1366 × 768, if necessary, and then tap or click outside of the list to close the list (Figure E–4).

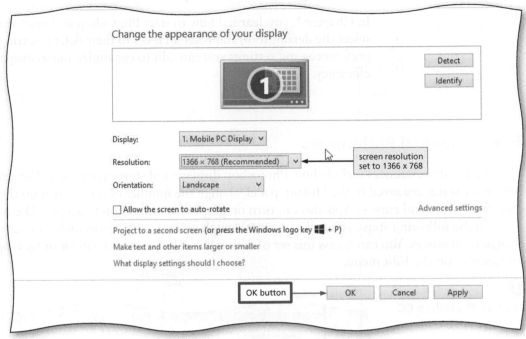

Change the appearance of your display

Detect
Identify

Display: 1. Mobile PC Display ⌄

Resolution: 1366 × 768 (Recommended) ⌄ ← screen resolution set to 1366 x 768

Orientation: Landscape ⌄

☐ Allow the screen to auto-rotate   Advanced settings

Project to a second screen (or press the Windows logo key ⊞ + P)

Make text and other items larger or smaller

What display settings should I choose?

OK button →   OK   Cancel   Apply

Figure E–4

- Tap or click the OK button to change the screen resolution (Figure E–5).

- If Windows displays the Display Settings dialog box, tap or click the Keep changes button to accept the changes.

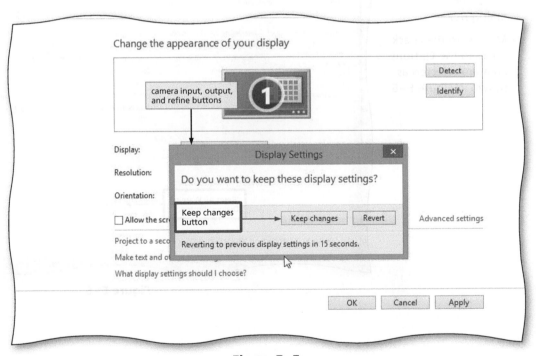

Change the appearance of your display

Detect
Identify

camera input, output, and refine buttons

Display:

Resolution:

Orientation:

Display Settings   ✕

Do you want to keep these display settings?

Keep changes button → Keep changes   Revert   Advanced settings

☐ Allow the scr

Project to a seco

Make text and o

What display settings should I choose?

Reverting to previous display settings in 15 seconds.

OK   Cancel   Apply

Figure E–5

Screen Resolutions

BTW

When you increase the screen resolution, Windows displays more information on the screen, but the information decreases in size. The reverse also is true; as you decrease the screen resolution, Windows displays less information on the screen, but the information increases in size.

Editing Photoshop Preferences

In Chapter 1, you learned how to start Photoshop and reset the default workspace, select the default tool, and reset all tools to their default settings. Photoshop has other preferences and settings you can edit to customize the workspace and maximize your efficiency.

To Edit General Preferences

General preferences include how Photoshop displays and stores your work. For example, you can change how many states are saved in the History panel, change the number of files shown on the Open Recent menu, or reset the display and cursors. You also can turn on graphics acceleration to access 3D commands.

In the following steps, you will navigate through several Preferences dialog boxes to reset values and change preferences. You can access this set of dialog boxes by pressing CTRL+K or by tapping or clicking Preferences on the Edit menu.

- Start Photoshop CC for your system.

- Press CTRL+K to display the Preferences dialog box.

- Make sure the check boxes in the Options area are selected as shown in Figure E–6.

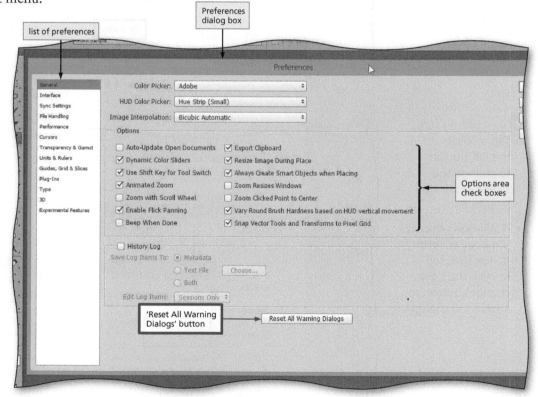

Figure E–6

2

- Tap or click the 'Reset All Warning Dialogs' button, so your dialog boxes will match the ones in this book. When Photoshop displays a Preferences dialog box, tap or click the OK button.

- Tap or click File Handling in the list of preferences on the left side of the Preferences dialog box.

- Tap or click the File Extension button and then tap or click 'Use Lower Case', if necessary, so Photoshop will use lowercase letters when saving.

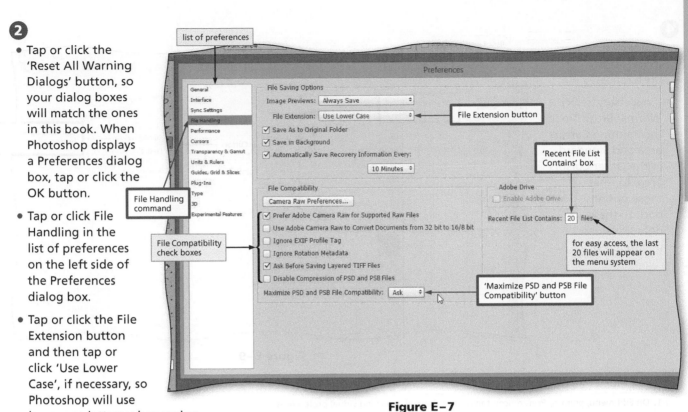

Figure E–7

- Tap or click the 'Maximize PSD and PSB File Compatibility' button and then tap or click Ask, if necessary, so that Photoshop asks about saving files in PSD format.

- Type 20 in the 'Recent File List Contains' box, if necessary, to specify that Photoshop will display the last 20 files (Figure E–7).

3

- Tap or click Performance in the list of preferences.

- If necessary, tap or click the 'Use Graphics Processor' check box so it displays a check mark.

- If necessary, type 50 in the History States box, so Photoshop will allow you to back up through the last 50 steps of any editing session (Figure E–8).

Q&A

My 'Use Graphics Processor' check box is grayed out. What should I do?
See your instructor about updating your graphics card driver, so you can perform 3D and warping commands in Photoshop.

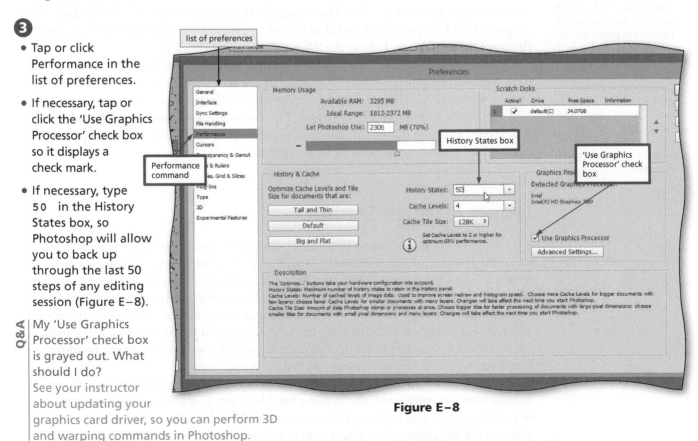

Figure E–8

4

- Tap or click Cursors in the list of preferences.

- If necessary, select 'Normal Brush Tip' in the Painting Cursors area and Standard in the Other Cursors area, to reset those options back to their default values (Figure E–9).

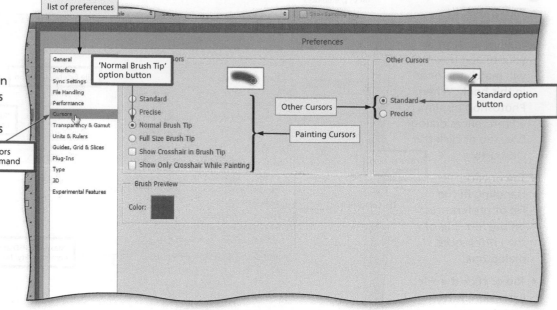

Figure E–9

Other Ways

1. On Edit menu, point to Preferences, tap or click General, select individual preferences

Changing Preferences

If there is one particular setting you wish to change, you can open that specific Preferences dialog box from the menu. For example, if you want to change the color of a ruler guide, you can point to Preferences on the Edit menu and then tap or click Guides, Grid & Slices on the Preferences submenu to go directly to those settings and make your edits.

Changing Other Preferences

The Preferences dialog boxes contain a variety of settings that can be changed to suit individual needs and styles. The 'Reset All Warning Dialogs' button in Figure E–6 on page APP 52 especially is useful to display the dialog boxes if someone has turned them off by tapping or clicking the 'Don't show again' check box.

In Figure E–9, the Normal Brush Tip option causes the mouse pointer outline to correspond to approximately 50 percent of the area that the tool will affect. This option shows the pixels that would be most visibly affected. It is easier to work with Normal Brush Tip than Full Size Brush Tip, especially when using larger brushes. A Standard painting cursor displays mouse pointers as tool icons; a Precise painting cursor displays the mouse pointer as a crosshair.

Using A Touch Screen

The buttons, boxes, and menu options are designed to maximize your workflow, and make the best use of the workspace. At an initial installation, screen elements are set to make use of the mouse or a stylus. That setting is not always the best for those users who work with a touch screen. In addition to using a stylus to **tap** the screen, a touch screen uses gestures made by touching or dragging your fingers on the screen. Therefore, Photoshop CC offers a preference command to turn on touch gestures. These touch gestures work from any touch-capable device such as tables, opaque finger pads, handheld devices, and touch pads.

The typical tap, double-tap, drag, and press and hold gestures work well on menus, buttons, panels, and the options bar. However, you are limited in the number of touch gestures that work on the canvas itself. Table E–1 lists the available touch gestures for the canvas. Two finger canvas gestures do not work in dialog boxes.

Table E–1 Canvas Gestures

Name	Gesture	Result
Pan	Press and hold two fingers down, then drag in any direction, keeping the fingers approximately the same distance apart.	Moves document window in direction of drag
Zoom-Pan	Press and hold two fingers down, then pinch or spread.	Resizes document window
Rotate-Pan	Press and hold two fingers down. Drag one finger.	Rotates document window
Free-form	Press and hold two fingers down for a short time, then pan, zoom, or rotate.	Document window will pan, zoom, or rotate
Single finger double-tap	Use one finger and double-tap the canvas.	On a blank workspace, the Open dialog box will appear
Two fingers double-tap	Double-tap two fingers simultaneously.	Toggles between 'Fit on screen' command and previous canvas size

© Cengage Learning

If you have a very high resolution or large monitor, you can use a preference command to scale the user interface (UI) to 200%. That way, all the buttons and menus are twice as big, allowing you to touch single buttons easily. This procedure is not recommended for tablets or hand-held devices. You must restart Photoshop for any UI change to take effect.

To Turn On Touch Gestures

The following steps turn on the touch gestures feature in Photoshop CC.

1

- If necessary, press CTRL+K to display the Preferences Dialog box.

- Tap or click Experimental Features in the list of preferences to display the settings.

- Tap or click the 'Use Touch Gestures' check box so it displays a check mark (Figure E–10).

🔍 **Experiment**

- Point to each of the options and read the description in the Description area.

 Q&A Should I turn on Scale UI 200% if I am using a touch screen?

Do not turn on UI Scaling unless you have a large monitor. On a tablet or handheld device, the display becomes very large and difficult to use.

Figure E–10

2

- When you are finished, tap or click the OK button to close the Preferences dialog box.

Menu Command Preferences

Photoshop allows users to customize both the application menus and the panel menus in several ways. You can hide commands that you seldom use. You can set colors on the menu structure to highlight or organize your favorite commands. Or, you can let Photoshop organize your menus with color based on functionality. If another user has made changes to the menu structure, you can reset the menus back to their default states.

To Hide and Show Menu Commands

If there are menu commands that you seldom use, you can hide them to access other commands more quickly. A hidden command is a menu command that does not appear currently on a menu. If menu commands have been hidden, a 'Show All Menu Items' command will be displayed at the bottom of the menu list. When you tap or click the 'Show All Menu Items' command or press and hold the CTRL key as you tap or click the menu name, Photoshop displays all menu commands, including hidden ones.

The following steps hide a menu command and then redisplay it.

❶

- Tap or click Edit on the Application bar, and then tap or click Menus to display the Keyboard Shortcuts and Menus dialog box (Figure E–11).

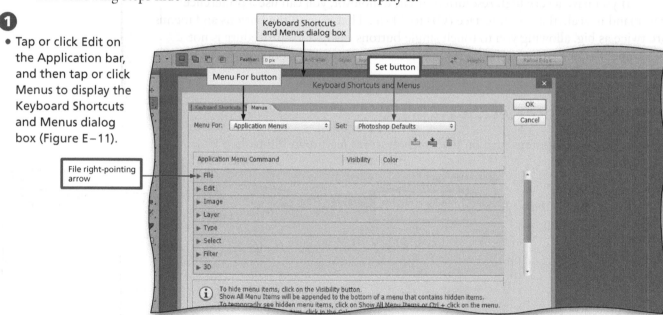

Figure E–11

❷

- If necessary, tap or click the Set button and then tap or click Photoshop Defaults.

- Tap or click the right-pointing arrow next to the word File to display the File commands (Figure E–12).

🔎 **Experiment**

- Tap or click the Menu for button and notice that you can change show and hide panel menu commands as well as Application bar menus.

Figure E–12

• In the Visibility column, tap or click the Visibility button next to the Open Recent command so it no longer displays the eye icon (Figure E–13).

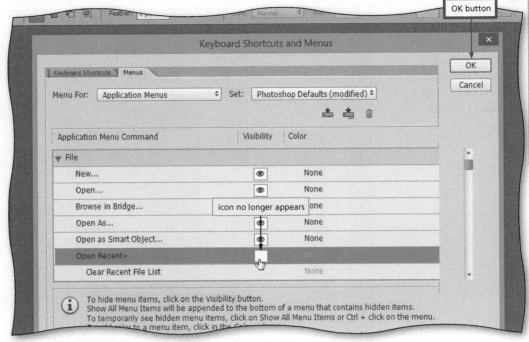

Figure E–13

• Tap or click the OK button to apply the settings.

• Tap or click File on the Application bar to display the File menu (Figure E–14).

Q&A What changed?
The Open Recent command no longer appears on the menu as it first opens.

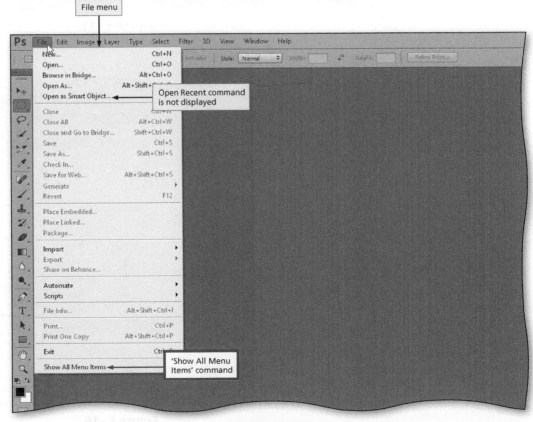

Figure E–14

5

- On the File menu, tap or click 'Show All Menu Items' to redisplay the command that you hid in Step 3 (Figure E–15).

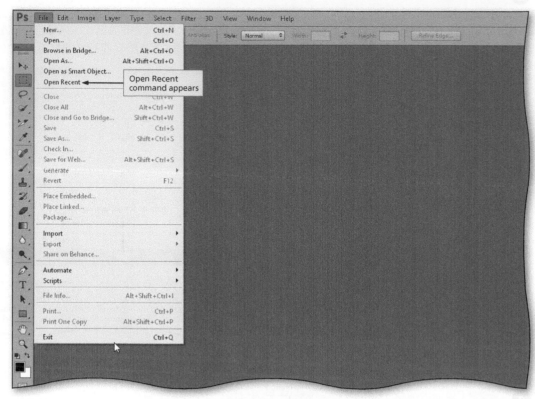

Figure E–15

6

- Tap or click Edit on the Application bar and then tap or click Menus to display the Keyboard Shortcuts and Menus dialog box again.

- If the arrow next to the word, File, is pointing to the right, tap or click it to display the File list.

- Tap or click the Visibility button next to the Open Recent command so it again is displayed (Figure E–16).

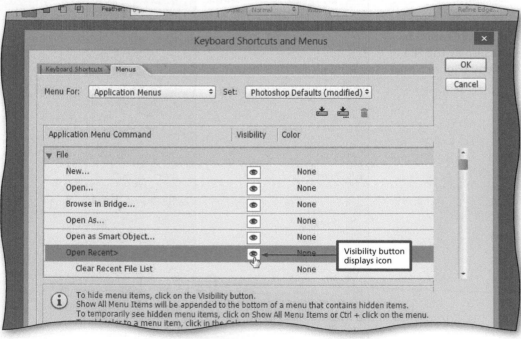

Figure E–16

Other Ways

1. On Window menu, point to Workspace, tap or click 'Keyboard Shortcuts & Menus'

2. Press ALT+SHIFT+CTRL+M

To Add Color to Menu Commands

You can add color to menu commands to help you find them easily or to organize them into groups based on personal preferences. The following steps change the color of the Open and Open As commands.

1

- With the Keyboard Shortcuts and Menus dialog box still displayed, tap or click the word, None, in the row associated with the Open command to display a list of colors (Figure E–17).

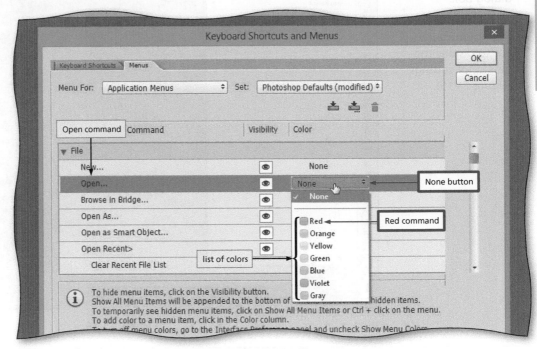

Figure E–17

2

- Tap or click Red in the list to select a red color for the Open command.

- Tap or click the word, None, in the row associated with the Open As command, and then tap or click Red in the list to select a red color for the Open As command (Figure E–18).

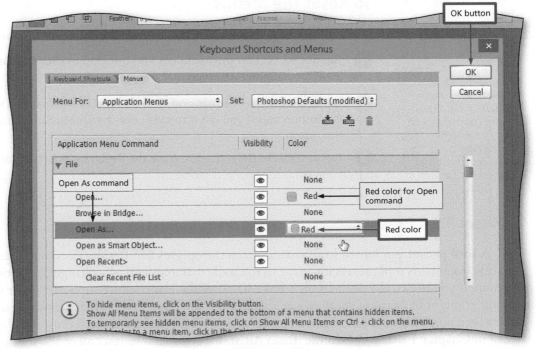

Figure E–18

3

- Tap or click the OK button to close the Keyboard Shortcuts and Menus dialog box.

- Tap or click File on the Application bar to display the new color settings (Figure E–19).

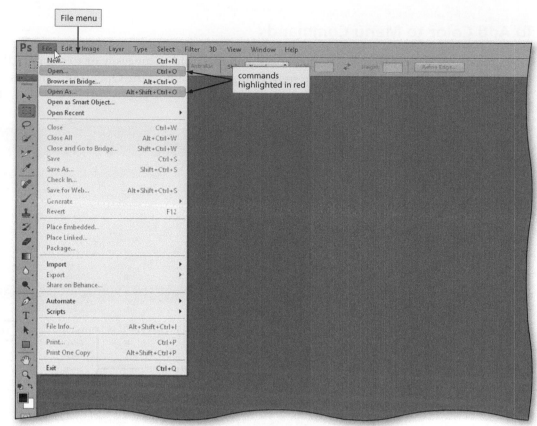

File menu

commands highlighted in red

Figure E–19

BTW

Stored Menu Sets
The Set button (Figure E–17 on the previous page) lists three sets of stored commands: Photoshop Defaults, New in CC, and Photoshop Defaults (modified). Photoshop will display related commands with color. For example, if you choose New in CC, the menu commands that are new will appear in blue.

To Reset the Menus

The following steps reset the menus, removing red from the Open commands.

1 Tap or click Edit on the menu bar and then tap or click Menus to display the Keyboard Shortcuts and Menus dialog box.

2 Tap or click the Set button and then tap or click Photoshop Defaults in the list. When Photoshop asks if you want to save your changes before switching sets, tap or click the No button.

3 Tap or click the OK button to close the Keyboard Shortcuts and Menus dialog box.

To Reset Tool Presets

A **tool preset** is a way to store settings from the options bar. Besides the default settings for each tool, Photoshop contains tool presets for many of the tools that automatically change the options bar. In a lab situation, if you notice that some tools are not working the way they are supposed to, or some presets are missing, it might be because another user changed the settings. A tool preset is not the same as an appended library on a pop-up panel; rather it is the numbers, percentages, and other settings displayed on the options bar. Recall in Chapter 1 that you used the 'Reset All Tools' command to reset all of the tool presets. The following steps reset tools individually.

- On the options bar, tap or click the current tool's Preset picker and then tap or click the menu button to display the Tool Preset menu (Figure E–20).

- Tap or click 'Reset Tool Presets' to reset the tool's preset list.

- If Photoshop displays a dialog box, tap or click the OK button to reload all the default tool presets.

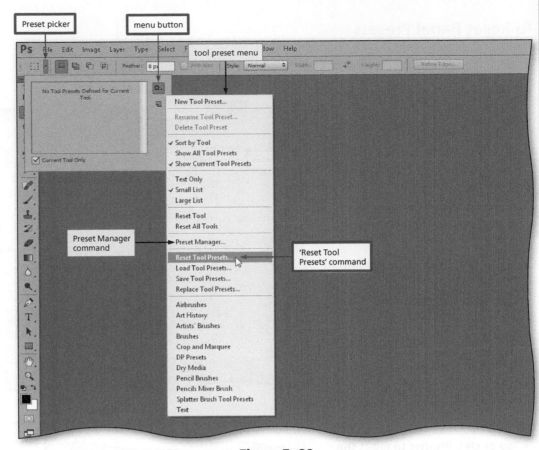

Figure E–20

Other Ways

1. From any panel menu, tap or click 'Reset Tool Presets', tap or click OK button

Resetting Panel Components

Many panels, including the Brushes, Swatches, and Styles panels, display preset samples and libraries with preset shapes, colors, and sizes. A few options bars, including the Gradient and Shape options bars, as well as the Contours box in the Layer Style dialog box, also display similar components — all of which might need to be reset at some time. You can reset these presets using the Preset Manager or individual panel menus.

To Reset Panel Presets

The following steps reset all panels that use presets.

- On the options bar, tap or click the current tool's Preset picker and then tap or click the menu button to display the Tool Preset menu. (See Figure E–20 on the previous page.)

- Tap or click Preset Manager to display the Preset Manager dialog box.

- Tap or click the Preset Type button to display the list of panels that contain presets (Figure E–21).

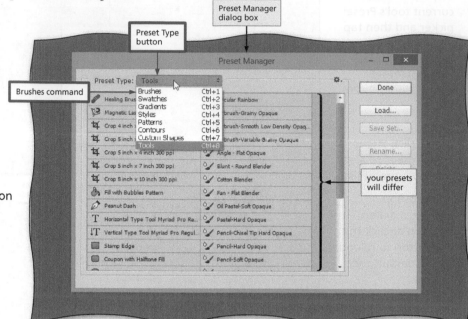

Figure E–21

- Tap or click Brushes to select the Brush presets.

- Tap or click the Preset Manager menu button to display the list of commands and preset libraries (Figure E–22).

- Tap or click Reset Brushes to reset the Brush presets. When Photoshop displays a confirmation dialog box, tap or click the OK button.

- Repeat Steps 1 and 2 for each of the other panels that appear on the Preset Type button list.

- When you are finished resetting all panels, tap or click the Done button to close the dialog box.

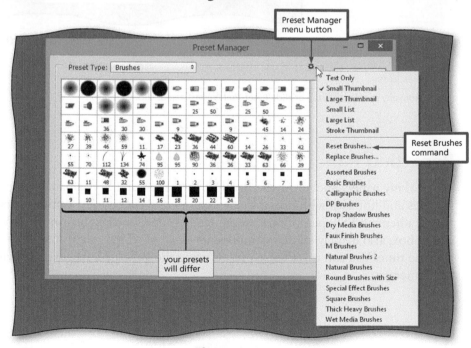

Figure E–22

Other Ways

1. On each panel menu, tap or click Reset command, tap or click OK button
2. On Edit menu, point to Presets, tap or click Preset Manager, edit settings

To Quit Photoshop

The following step quits Photoshop.

- If you are finished setting preferences, press CTRL+Q to quit Photoshop.

In the Labs
1: Changing the Color and Style of Guides and Grids

Instructions: You would like to use some different colors and styles for grids and guides because the current colors are very similar to the colors in your image, making them hard to see. You decide to change the color and style preferences on your system as described in the following steps.

1. Start Photoshop CC.
2. On the Edit menu, point to Preferences, and then tap or click 'Guides, Grid & Slices'.
3. When the Preferences dialog box is displayed, change the Color and Style settings as shown in Figure E–23.

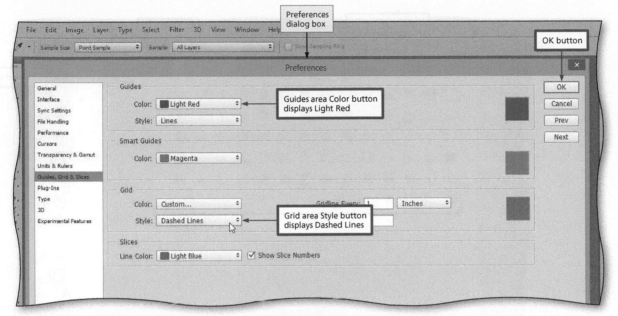

Figure E–23

4. Tap or click the OK button.
5. Open any image file you have saved on your system and drag a guide from the horizontal ruler. Note the Light Red colored line.
6. On the View menu, point to Show, and then tap or click Grid. Note the grid with dashed gray lines.
7. To clear the guides, on the View menu, tap or click Clear Guides.
8. To hide the grid, on the View menu, point to Show and then tap or click Grid.
9. To reset the colors and styles, either change the guide color back to Cyan and the grid style back to Lines, or quit Photoshop and then restart Photoshop while pressing ALT+CTRL+SHIFT. If Photoshop asks if you wish to delete the previous settings, tap or click the Yes button.
10. Quit Photoshop.

2: Resetting Styles

Instructions: Someone has loaded many styles into the style box, making it difficult to find the common styles you prefer. You decide to reset the styles using the following steps.

1. Start Photoshop CC.
2. On the Edit menu, point to Presets, and then tap or click Preset Manager to display the Preset Manager dialog box.
3. Tap or click the Preset Type button to display the Preset list, and then tap or click Styles in the list (Figure E–24).

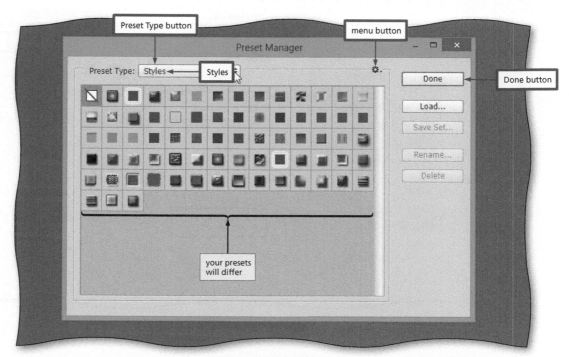

Figure E–24

4. Tap or click the Preset Manager menu button to display a list of commands about the Styles Presets. Tap or tap or click Reset Styles in the list.
5. When Photoshop asks if you want to replace the styles with the default set, tap or click the OK button.
6. Tap or click the Done button to close the Preset Manager dialog box.
7. Quit Photoshop.

3: Searching the Web

Instructions: You want to learn more about optimizing Photoshop settings and your computer system's memory by setting preferences for file size, history states, and cached views. Perform a web search by using the Google search engine at google.com (or any major search engine) to display and print three webpages that pertain to optimizing Photoshop CC. On each printout, highlight something new that you learned by reading the webpage.

Ps File Edit Image Layer Type Select Filter 3D View Window Help

Adobe Photoshop CC Feather: 0 px Anti-alias Style: Normal Width: Height: Refine Edge...

Appendix F

For Mac Users

For the Mac User of this Book

For most tasks, little difference exists between using Photoshop CC with the Windows 8 operating system and using it with the Mac OS X Mavericks 10.9 operating system. With some tasks, however, you will see some differences, or you might need to complete the tasks using different steps. This appendix demonstrates how to start an application, open a file, create a folder and save a file, close a file, display the application menu, and quit an application, using Photoshop CC and the Mac operating system.

Keyboard Differences

One difference between a Mac and a PC is in the use of modifier keys. **Modifier keys** are special keys used to modify the normal action of a key when the two are pressed in combination. Examples of modifier keys include the SHIFT, CTRL, and ALT keys on a PC (Figure F-1a) and the SHIFT, CMD, and OPT keys on a Mac (Figure F-1b). The CMD key sometimes is referred to as the APPLE key.

PC modifier keys

(a) PC keyboard

Mac modifier keys

© Cengage Learning

(b) Mac keyboard

Figure F-1

Table F–1 explains the keystroke equivalencies. For instance, if PC instructions tell you to press CTRL+T to perform a task, Mac users would press CMD+T. In addition, many Mac menus display shortcut notations, using symbols to represent the modifier key.

Table F–1 PC vs. Mac Keystroke Equivalencies		
PC	**Mac**	**Mac Symbol**
CTRL key	CMD key	⌘
ALT key	OPT key	⌥
SHIFT key	SHIFT key	⇧

To Start an Application

The following steps, which assume Mac OS X Mavericks 10.9 is running, start an application based on a typical installation. Other Mac operating systems work in a similar manner. You might need to ask your instructor how to start Photoshop for your computer.

1

- Tap or click the Spotlight button on the Mac desktop to display the Spotlight box.

- Type **Photoshop CC** as the search text in the Spotlight box and watch the search results appear (Figure F–2).

Q&A I have a different operating system. What do I do?
Other Mac operating systems work in a similar manner. See your instructor if you cannot locate the Spotlight box.

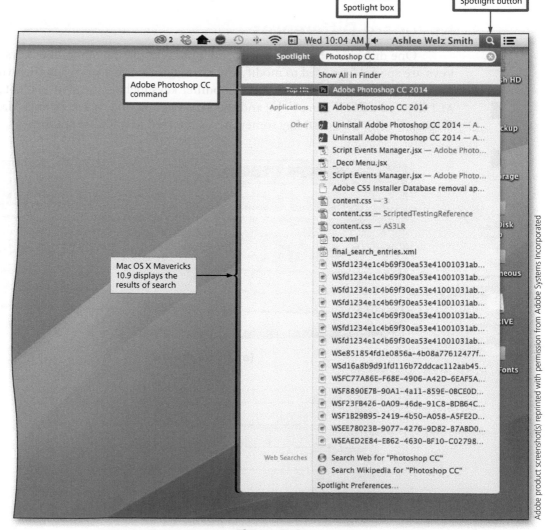

Spotlight box

Spotlight button

Adobe Photoshop CC command

Mac OS X Mavericks 10.9 displays the results of search

Adobe product screenshot(s) reprinted with permission from Adobe Systems Incorporated

Figure F–2

2

- Tap or click Adobe Photoshop CC in the list to start the application.

- If the window is not maximized, tap or click the green Zoom button below the title bar to maximize the window (Figure F–3).

Q&A Does the PC version of Photoshop have a title bar?

No. On the PC platform, Photoshop has an Application bar that combines the menu and clip controls. The clip control functions — minimize, maximize, and close — are inherited from the operating system, and are placed where the system user would expect to find them.

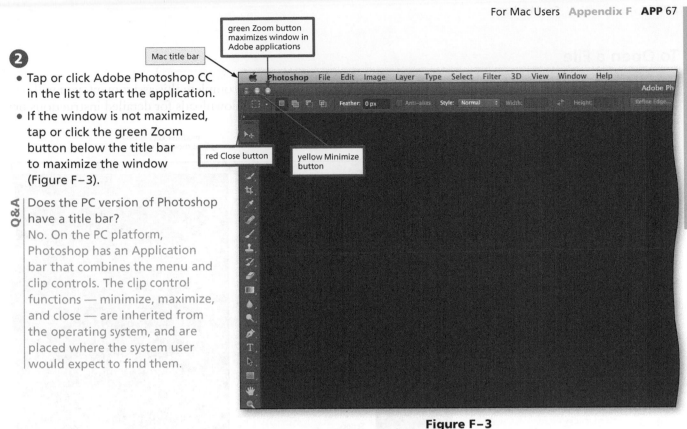

Figure F–3

Customize the Workspace on a Mac

In general, customizing the Photoshop workspace on a Mac is the same as customizing it on a PC. Chapter 1 covers selecting the Essentials workspace, selecting the default tool, and resetting the option bar. When using the Mac OS X operating system, the Preferences submenu is located on the Photoshop menu, rather than the Edit menu. Figure F–4 displays the Preferences submenu, which you use to reset the interface color.

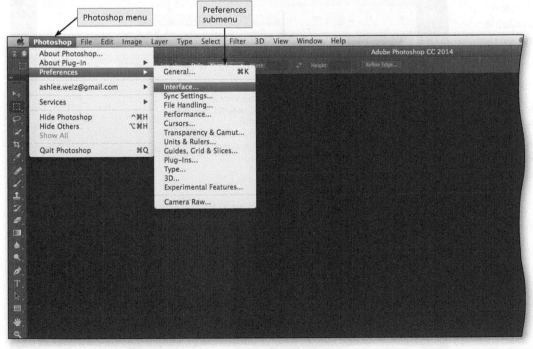

Figure F–4

To Open a File

The following steps open a file from the Data Files for Students. To complete this assignment, you will be required to use the Data Files for Students. Visit solutions.cengage.com/ctdownloads for detailed instructions or contact your instructor for information about accessing the required files.

1

- Start your application, if necessary, and reset the preferences.

- Tap or click File on the title bar to display the File menu (Figure F–5).

Q&A What does it mean when Adobe includes multiple symbols in the shortcut key notation?
Multiple symbols mean that you must hold down several keys. For example, a notation of ⌥ ⌘ o on the menu would mean to press and hold the OPTION and COMMAND keys while you press the o key. Written instructions might say press OPT+CMD+O.

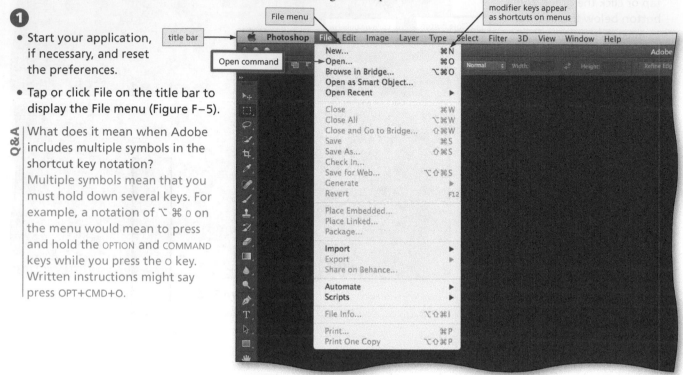

Figure F–5

2

- Tap or click Open on the File menu to display the Open dialog box.

- Tap or click the Where button to display a list of the available storage locations on your system (Figure F–6).

Experiment

- Tap or click a location on the Favorites panel on the left side of the Open dialog box and watch the Where button change. Tap or click the Where button.

Figure F–6

3

- Tap or click the drive associated with the location of the Data Files for Students.

- Navigate to the Photoshop folder, and then the Data Files for Students folder (Figure F–7).

Q&A What is the default location shown in the Open dialog box? By default, the Open dialog box shows the first 10 items in the folder or volume last used during an open or save process. You can use the Icon view, List view, Column view, or Cover Flow view buttons to change the way the contents are presented. Cover Flow view allows you to see the contents of a file as a thumbnail.

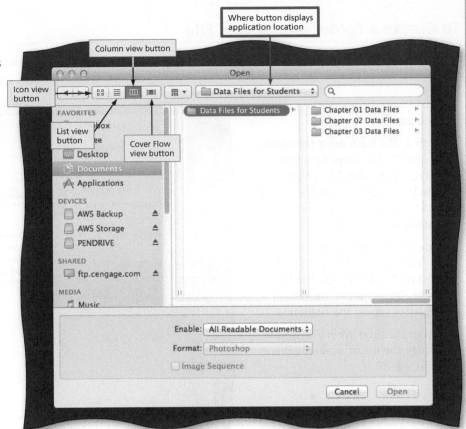

Figure F–7

4

- Double-tap or double-click the Chapter 01 Data Files folder to open it.

- Tap or click the file, Surfer.jpg, to select it (Figure F–8).

5

- Tap or click the Open button to open the selected file and display the open file in the Photoshop workspace.

Figure F–8

To Create a Folder and Save a File

After editing a file, you should save it. The following steps create a folder on a USB flash drive and save a file.

1

- Start Photoshop and open a file, if necessary.

- With a USB flash drive connected to one of the computer's USB ports, tap or click File on the title bar to display the File menu and then tap or click Save As to display the Save As dialog box.

- Type the name of your file, such as **Surfer Edited**, in the Save As box to change the file name. Do not press the RETURN key after typing the file name.

- Tap or click the Where button to display the list of available drives (Figure F–9).

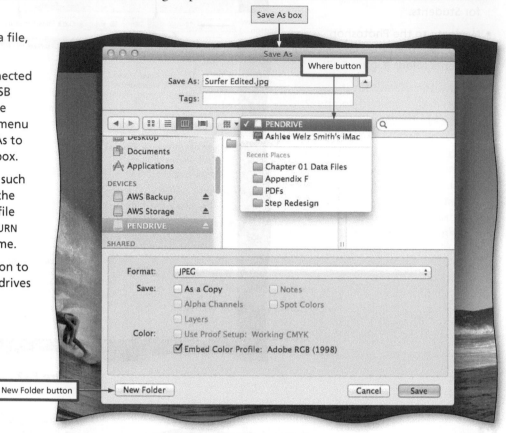

Figure F–9

2

- Tap or click the name of your USB flash drive, in the list of devices to select that drive as the new save location.

- Tap or click the New Folder button to create a new folder on the selected storage device.

- When the new folder appears, type a new folder name such as **Appendix F**, to change the name of the folder, and then press the RETURN key (Figure F–10).

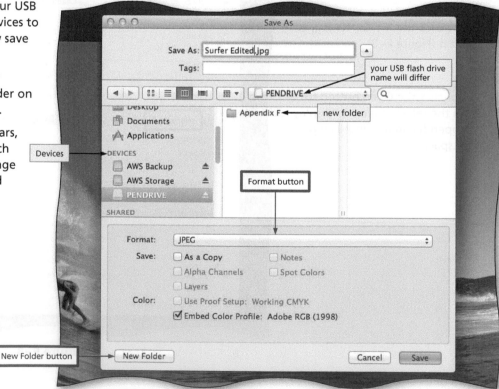

Figure F–10

- If necessary, tap or click the new folder to open it.

- If necessary, tap or click the Format button to display the list of available file formats. Choose the format appropriate for your application and purpose, in this case, the JPEG format (Figure F–11).

4

- Tap or click the Save button to save the document on the selected drive with the new file name.

Figure F–11

To Close a File

The following steps close an open file.

1

- Start Photoshop and open a file, if necessary.

- Tap or click File on the title bar to display the File menu (Figure F–12).

Q&A | Is the File menu different on a Mac?
The File menu is essentially the same. The commands might be grouped in a slightly different manner. The File menu does not contain the Exit command as it does on a PC. You will learn in the next steps that the Quit command is on the Photoshop menu.

2

- Tap or click the Close command on the File menu to close the current open file without quitting the application.

Figure F–12

To Display the Application Menu and Quit the Application

Using the Mac operating system, Photoshop CC includes a Photoshop menu to the left of the typical menu used in Windows. This application menu includes commands that you find in different locations on a PC, the most notable of which are the preferences, services, and the Quit command for each application. The following steps open the Photoshop menu to quit the application.

1

- Start Photoshop, if necessary.

- On the title bar, tap or click Photoshop to open the Photoshop menu (Figure F–13).

Q&A What does the Services command do?
Mac OS X includes a Services submenu in many applications for tasks such as looking up a word in the dictionary, rotating an image, sending an e-mail, or compressing a video. Any service installed on your Mac that manipulates files related to your application will be displayed on the Services submenu.

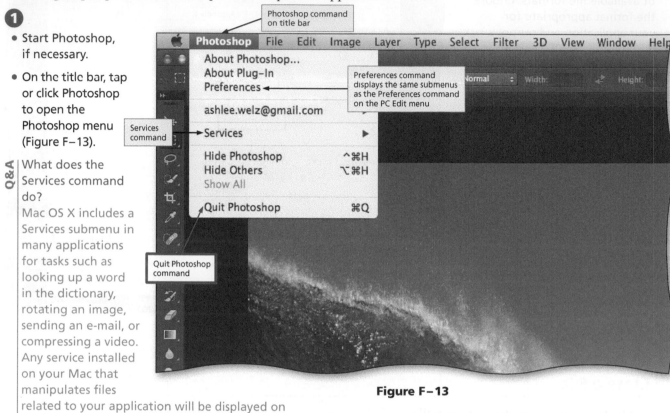

Figure F–13

2

- Tap or click Quit Photoshop to quit the application.

Q&A Can I tab or click the red Close button to quit the application?
The red button closes the application window, but the application will continue to run until you quit the application.

Index

Quick Reference Summary

Adobe Photoshop CC Quick Reference Summary

Task	Page Number	Workspace	Menu	Context Menu	Keyboard Shortcuts
3D Extrusion	PS 509	3D Extrusion option button on 3D panel	3D | select 3D extrusion		
3D Layer, Create	PS 509	3D Extrusion option button on 3D panel	3D | 'New 3D Layer from File'		
3D Lighting, Edit	PS 510	Infinite Light Properties panel			
3D Materials, Edit	PS 574	Materials Properties panel			
3D Mesh, Create	PS 570	'Mesh from Preset' option button on 3D panel	3D | 'New Mesh from Layer' | Mesh Preset | select mesh		
3D Object, Drag	PS 576	'Drag the 3D Object' button on Move Tool options bar			
3D Object, Rotate	PS 579	'Rotate the 3D Object' button on Move Tool options bar			
3D Object, Scale	PS 576	'Scale the 3D Object' button on Move Tool options bar			
3D Printing	PS 591		3D | '3D Print Settings'		
3D Text, Create	PS 513	3D button on 'Horizontal Type Tool' options bar			
3D Views, Show	PS 571		View | Show | select 3D view		
Action Set, Append	PS 438	Select action set on Actions panel menu			
Action Set, Create	PS 441	'Create new set' button on Actions panel status bar			
Action Set, Save	PS 445	Save Actions button on Actions panel menu			
Action, Create	PS 442	'Create new action' button on Actions panel status bar			
Action, Play	PS 445	Play selection button on Actions panel status bar			
Action, Record	PS 442	Record button in New Action dialog box			
Actions Panel, Display	PS 438		Window | Actions		
Add to Selection	PS 81	'Add to selection' button on options bar			SHIFT+drag
Adjustment Layer	PS 187	'Clip to Layer' button on Adjustments panel	Image | Adjustment Layer		CTRL+L
Align and Distribute Layers	PS 372	Align and Distribute buttons on Move Tool options bar			

Adobe Photoshop CC Quick Reference Summary *(continued)*

Task	Page Number	Workspace	Menu	Context Menu	Keyboard Shortcuts
Alpha Channel, Create from Selection	PS 408	'Save selection as channel' button on Channels panel status bar or 'Create New Channel' on Channels panel menu			
Anchor Point Tool	PS 485	'Add Anchor Point Tool' button on Tools panel			
Animation, Optimize	PS 587	Optimize Animation on Timeline panel menu			
Animation, Preview	PS 586	Plays animation button on Timeline status bar			
(Animation) Timing, Set	PS 585	'Selects frame delay time' button on Frame			
Append a Brush Library	PS 243	Preset picker button on Brush options bar, menu button on pop-up panel	Brushes Presets panel menu | select library		
Arrange Windows	PS 152		Window | Arrange | select arrangement		
Background Eraser Tool	PS 178	'Background Eraser Tool' button on Tools panel			SHIFT+E
Baseline Shift	PS 252	'Set the baseline shift' box on Character panel			
Blending Mode, Apply	PS 315	Blending Mode button on Layers panel, select blending mode			
Blur Filter	PS 336, PS 356		Filter | Blur, select filter		
Border, Create	PS 39 – PS 42		Select | Select All; Edit | Stroke		
Border, Modify	PS 43		Select | Modify | Border		
Brightness/Contrast, Adjust	PS 189	Brightness/Contrast icon on Adjustments panel or 'Create new fill or adjustment layer' button on Layers panel status bar, Brightness/Contrast	Layer | 'New Adjustment Layer' | Brightness/Contrast		
Brush Panel, Display	PS 246	'Toggle the Brush panel' button on Brush Presets panel	Window | Brush		F5
Brush Presets, Append Library	PS 243	Brush Presets panel menu button, select library, Append button or Brush Preset picker menu button, select brush preset			
Brush Tool, Select	PS 240	Brush Tool button on Tools panel			B or SHIFT+B
Burn Tool	PS 286	Burn Tool button on Tools panel		Dodge Tool button | Burn Tool	O or SHIFT+O
Camera Shake, Reduce	PS 345		Filter | Sharpen | Shake Reduction		
Channel, Duplicate	PS 413	Duplicate Channel on Channel panel menu		Duplicate Channel	

Adobe Photoshop CC Quick Reference Summary (continued)

Task	Page Number	Workspace	Menu	Context Menu	Keyboard Shortcuts
Character Panel, Show	PS 251	'Toggle the Character and Paragraph panels' button on Horizontal Type Tool option bar	Window | Character		
Clone Source Panel, show	PS 304		Window | Clone Source		
Clone Stamp Tool	PS 304	'Clone Stamp Tool' button on Tools panel			S
Close	PS 46	Close button on document window tab	File | Close		CTRL+W
Color Separations, Print	PS 457	Color Handling button in Print dialog box	File | Print		
Color Sliders, Change on Color Panel	PS 332	CMYK sliders on Color panel menu			
Color, Choose on Swatches Panel	PS 238	select color on Swatches panel			
Colors, Reset Default	PS 8	'Default Foreground and Background Colors' button on Tools panel			D
Colors, Switch Between Background and Foreground	PS 44	'Switch Foreground and Background Colors' button on Tools panel			X
Commit Change (transformation)	PS 165	'Commit transform (Enter) button' on options bar			ENTER
Commit Edits (text)	PS 53	'Commit any current edits' button on Type Tool options bar			
Consolidate Windows	PS 154		Window | Arrange | 'Consolidate All to Tabs'	Document tab | 'Consolidate All to Here'	
Contact Sheet, Create	PS 544		File | Automate | Contact Sheet II		
Content-Aware Move Tool	PS 299	'Content-Aware Move Tool ' button on Tools panel		'Spot Healing Brush Tool' button | 'Content-Aware Move Tool'	J or SHIFT+J
Content-Aware Tool	PS 300		Edit | Fill		DELETE
Convert to Duotone	PS 453		Image | Mode | Duotone		
Convert to Lab Color	PS 456		Image | Mode | Lab Color		
Copy File in Bridge	APP 39		(Bridge) Edit | Copy; Edit | Paste	Copy; Paste	CTRL+C; CTRL+V
Count Tool	PS 525	Count Tool button on Tools panel		Eyedropper Tool button | Count Tool	I or SHIFT+I
Crop Image	PS 36	Crop Tool button on Tools panel	Image | Crop		C or SHIFT+C
Curves	PS 282	Curves button on Adjustments panel	Layer | 'New Adjustment Layer' | Curves		
Custom Shape Tool	PS 237	'Custom Shape Tool' button on Tools panel		Rectangle Tool button | 'Custom Shape Tool'	U or SHIFT+U
Custom Shapes, Append	PS 558	Append button on Shapes panel			
Dashed Line, Create	PS 519	'Set Shape Stroke Type' button on Stroke Options panel			

Adobe Photoshop CC Quick Reference Summary *(continued)*

Task	Page Number	Workspace	Menu	Context Menu	Keyboard Shortcuts
Default Foreground and Background Colors	PS 8	'Default Foreground and Background Colors' button on Tools panel			D
Desaturate	PS 448		Image | Adjustments | Desaturate		
Deselect Selection	PS 45		Select | Deselect		CTRL+D
Direct Selection Tool	PS 506	'Direct Selection Tool' button		'Path Selection Tool' button | 'Direct Selection Tool'	∧ or SHIFT+∧
Distort Selection	PS 162		Edit | Transform | Distort	Distort	
Dodge Tool	PS 287	Dodge Tool button on Tools panel			O or SHIFT+O
Download Speed, Choose	PS 58	'Select download speed' button in Save for Web dialog box	File | 'Save for Web'		ALT+SHIFT+ CTRL+S
Draw using Brush Tool	PS 241	Select brush, drag in document window			
Duplicate Channel	PS 413	Channels panel menu | Duplicate Channel		Duplicate Channel	
Duplicate Selection	PS 86		Edit | Copy; Edit Paste		ALT+drag
Elliptical Marquee Tool	PS 80	'Elliptical Marquee Tool' button on Tools panel		'Rectangular Marquee Tool' button | 'Elliptical Marquee Tool'	M or SHIFT+M
Eraser Tools	PS 173	Eraser Tool button on Tools panel			E or SHIFT+E
Essentials Workspace, Select	PS 6	Essentials button on options bar	Window | Workspace | Essentials		
Eyedropper Tool	PS 231	Eyedropper Tool on Tools panel			I or SHIFT+I
Filter Gallery	PS 348		Filter | Filter Gallery		
Find File in Bridge	APP 45		Edit | Find		CTRL+F
Fit on Screen	PS 115	Fit screen button on Zoom Tool options bar	View | 'Fit on Screen'		CTRL+0 (ZERO)
Flatten Image	PS 197	Flatten Image on Layers panel menu	Layer | Flatten Image	Flatten Image	
Flip Selection Horizontally	PS 87		Edit | Transform | Flip Horizontal	Flip Horizontal	
Flip Selection Vertically	PS 87		Edit | Transform | Flip Vertical	Flip Vertical	
Font Options, Set	PS 52	'Set the font family' button on Horizontal Type Tool options bar			
Frames, Create for Animation	PS 581	New Frame on Timeline panel menu			
Free Transform Selection	PS 165	'Show Transform Control' check box on Move Tool options bar	Edit | Free Transform	Free Transform	CTRL+T
Freeform Pen Tool	PS 487	'Freeform Pen Tool' button on Tools panel		Pen Tool button | 'Freeform Pen Tool'	P or SHIFT+P
Generate Image Assets	PS 381		File | Generate | Image Assets		
Gradient, Create	PS 220	Gradient button on Tools panel			G or SHIFT+G

Adobe Photoshop CC Quick Reference Summary *(continued)*

Task	Page Number	Workspace	Menu	Context Menu	Keyboard Shortcuts
Gradient, Draw	PS 225	With Gradient Tool selected, drag in document window			
Gradient, Edit	PS 223	Gradient box on Gradient Tool options bar			
Grid, Hide or Show	PS 90		View | Show | Grid		CTRL+ APOSTROPHE (')
Grow Selection	PS 105		Select | Grow		
Guides, Create	PS 91	Drag from ruler	View | New Guide		
Guides, Hide or Show	PS 91		View | Show | Guides		CTRL+SEMICOLON (;)
Hand Tool	PS 31	Hand Tool button on Tools panel			H
Healing Brush Tool	PS 295	'Healing Brush Tool' button on Tools panel		'Spot Healing Brush' tool button | 'Healing Brush Tool'	J or SHIFT+J
Help	PS 62, Appendix C		Help | Photoshop Help		F1
History Panel, Display	PS 100	History button on vertical dock	Window | History		
History, Step Backward	PS 101	Previous state on History panel or History panel menu | Step Backward			CTRL+ALT+Z
History, Step Forward	PS 101	Next state on History panel or History panel menu | Step Forward			CTRL+SHIFT+Z
Horizontal Type Tool	PS 53	'Horizontal Type Tool' button on Tools panel			T or SHIFT+T
Hue/Saturation, Adjust	PS 307	Hue/Saturation icon on Adjustments panel or 'Create new fill or adjustment layer' button on Layers panel' | Hue/Saturation	Layer | 'New Adjustment Layer' | Hue/Saturation		CTRL+U
Intersect with Selection	PS 81	'Intersect with selection' button on options bar			SHIFT+ALT+drag
Keyboard Shortcut, Execute	PS 122				DESIGNATED SHORCUT
Keyboard Shortcuts, Create	PS 120		Edit | Keyboard Shortcuts		ALT+SHIFT+CTRL+K
Keyboard Shortcuts, Reset Default	PS 123	Set button in Keyboard Shortcuts and Menus dialog box	Edit | Keyboard Shortcuts		
Lasso Tool	PS 93	Lasso Tool button on Tools panel			L or SHIFT+L
Layer From Background, Create	PS 280	Double-tap or double-click Background layer	Layer | New | 'Layer from Background'	'Layer From Background'	
Layer Group, Create	PS 160	'New Group from Layers' on Layers panel menu	Layer | New | 'Group from Layers'	'Group from Layers'	
Layer Mask, Create	PS 182	'Add layer mask button' on Layers panel status bar			
Layer Mask, Create from Alpha Channel	PS 423		Select | Load Selection		

Adobe Photoshop CC Quick Reference Summary *(continued)*

Task	Page Number	Workspace	Menu	Context Menu	Keyboard Shortcuts
Layer Style, Add	PS 192	'Add a layer style' button on Layers panel status bar	Layer | Layer Style, select style		
Layer Style, Copy	PS 193		Layer | Layer Style | 'Copy Layer Style'	'Copy Layer Style'	
Layer via Cut, Create	PS 146		Layer | New | 'Layer Via Cut'	'Layer Via Cut'	SHIFT+CTRL+J
Layer, Assign a Color	PS 149			select color	
Layer, Create	PS 153	New Layer on Layers panel menu	Layer | New | Layer		SHIFT+CTRL+N
Layer, Display Current	PS 177	ALT+tap or ALT+ click 'Indicates layer visibility' icon on Layers panel			
Layer, Duplicate	PS 158		Layer | Duplicate Layer	Duplicate Layer	
Layer, Hide	PS 150	'Indicates layer visibility' icon on Layers panel	Layer | Hide Layers	'Hide this layer'	
Layer, Move	PS 153	Move Tool button on Tools panel; drag layer in document window			
Layer, Rename	PS 148	Double-click layer name | enter new name or Layer Properties on Layers panel menu		Layer Properties | enter new name	
Layer, Show	PS 149	'Indicates layer visibility' icon on Layers panel	Layer | Show Layers		
Layer, Show Only Current	PS 177	ALT+tap or ALT+click 'Indicates layer visibility' icon on Layers panel			
Layers Panel Options, Change	PS 142	Panel Options on Layers panel menu			
Layers, Lock	PS 480	Lock All button on Layers panel			
Lens Correction Dialog Box	PS 310		Filter |Lens Correction		SHIFT+CTRL+R
Levels, Adjust	PS 187	Levels icon on Adjustments panel or 'Create new fill or adjustment layer button' on Layers panel status bar	Image | Adjustments | Levels		CTRL+L
Lock Transparent Pixels	PS 478	'Lock transparent pixels' button on Layers panel			
Magic Eraser Tool	PS 175	'Magic Eraser Tool' button on Tools panel		Eraser Tool button | 'Magic Eraser Tool'	E or SHIFT+E
Magic Wand Tool	PS 108	'Magic Wand Tool' button on Tools panel		'Quick Selection Tool' | 'Magic Wand Tool'	W or SHIFT+W
Magnetic Lasso Tool	PS 95	'Magnetic Lasso Tool' button on Tools panel		Lasso Tool | 'Magnetic Lasso Tool'	L or SHIFT+L
Magnification, Change	PS 32	Enter number in Magnification box on status bar			
Masking Error, Correct	PS 183		Layer | Layer Mask | Reveal All	Disable Mask	
Menus, Hide or Show	APP 56		Edit | Menus		ALT+SHIFT+ CTRL+M
Metadata, Add	APP 40	(Bridge) Description field on Metadata panel, enter description			

Adobe Photoshop CC Quick Reference Summary *(continued)*

Task	Page Number	Workspace	Menu	Context Menu	Keyboard Shortcuts
Move Tool	PS 84	Move Tool button on Tools panel			V
Navigate Files using Bridge	APP 45	(Bridge) Double-tap or double-click file location, click workspace buttons			
New Adjustment Layer, Create	PS 189	'Create new fill or adjustment layer' button on Layers panel status bar	Layer	'New Adjustment Layer', select adjustment		
New Photoshop File, Start	PS 215		File	New		CTRL+N
Note Tool	PS 523	Note Tool button on Tools panel		Eyedropper Tool button	Note Tool	
Note, View	PS 524	Double-click note in document window			
Offset for Animation	PS 586		Filter	Other	Offset		
Opacity, Change	PS 184	Drag Opacity scrubby slider on Layers panel			
Open	PS 12	Double-tap or double-click workspace	File	Open	Document tab	Open Document	CTRL+O
Open Recent	PS 47		File	Open Recent		
Optimize Animation	PS 587	'Select All Frames' on Timeline panel menu, Optimize Animation on Timeline panel menu			
Paint Bucket Tool	PS 368	'Paint Bucket Tool' button on Tools panel		Gradient Tool button	'Paint Bucket Tool'	G or SHIFT+G
Painting Workspace, Select	PS 214	Workspace switcher on options bar	Painting	Window	Workspace	Painting		
Panel, Collapse	PS 18	Double arrow on panel		Panel tab	'Collapse to Icons'	
Panel, Open	PS 28	Panel button on vertical dock	Window	panel name		
Paste	PS168		Edit	Paste	Paste	CTRL+V
Paste Into	PS 195		Edit	Paste Special	Paste Into		ALT+SHIFT+CTRL+V
Patch	PS 290	Patch Tool button on Tools panel		'Spot Healing Brush Tool' button	Patch Tool	J or SHIFT+J
Path, Create using Pen Tool	PS 498	'Pick tool mode' button on Pen Tool options bar			
Path, Delete	PS 504	'Delete current path' button on on Paths panel status bar			
Path, Save	PS 501	'Make Work Path from Selection' button on Paths panel status bar			
Paths Panel, Display	PS 500	Paths panel tab			
Paths, Merge	PS 503			Direct Selection Tool	'Path Selection Tool', copy and paste	
Pattern, Define	PS 366		Edit	Define Pattern		

Adobe Photoshop CC Quick Reference Summary *(continued)*

Task	Page Number	Workspace	Menu	Context Menu	Keyboard Shortcuts
Pen Tool	PS 482	Pen Tool button on Tools panel			P
Perspective Warp	PS 553		Edit | Perspective Warp		
Perspective, Change	PS 165		Edit | Transform | Perspective	Selection | Perspective	
Polygonal Lasso Tool	PS 97	Polygonal Lasso Tool button on Tools panel		Lasso Tool button | Polygonal Lasso Tool	L or SHIFT+L
Preferences, Edit	APP 52		Edit | Preferences | General		CTRL+K
Preview, Web	PS 60	Preview button in Save for Web & Devices dialog box	File | 'Save for Web & Devices'		ALT+CTRL+SHIFT+S
Print	PS 56		File | Print		CTRL+P
Puppet Warp	PS 558		Edit | Puppet Warp		
Quick Selection Tool	PS 110	'Quick Selection Tool' button on Tools panel			W or SHIFT+W
Quit Photoshop	PS 64	Close button on Application bar	File | Exit		CTRL+Q
Rasterize	PS 515		Layer | Rasterize | Layer	Rasterize 3D	
Rate File in Bridge	APP 43		(Bridge) Label | select rating		CTRL+1 through CTRL+5
Rectangular Marquee Tool	PS 83	'Rectangular Marquee Tool' button on Tools panel			M or SHIFT+M
Red Eye Tool	PS 297	'Red Eye Tool' button on Tools panel		'Spot Healing Brush Tool' button | 'Red Eye Tool'	J or SHIFT+J
Refine Edge	PS 103	Refine Edge button on options bar	Select | Refine Edge	Refine Edge	ALT+CTRL+R
Refine Mask Tool	PS 425		Select | Refine Mask		
Reselect	PS 112		Select | Reselect		SHIFT+CTRL+D
Reset All Tools	PS 8			Tool Preset picker | Reset All Tools	
Resize File with Resampling	PS 49		Image | Image Size		
Resize Image	PS 49		Image | Image Size		ALT+CTRL+I
Rotate Selection	PS 113	Set rotation box on transform options bar	Edit | Transform | Rotate	Rotate	
Rotate Selection 180°	PS 113	Set rotation box on transform options bar	Edit | Transform | Rotate 180°	Rotate 180°	
Rotate Selection 90° CCW	PS 113	Set rotation box on transform options bar	Edit | Transform | 'Rotate 90° CCW'	Rotate 90° CCW	
Rotate Selection 90° CW	PS 113	Set rotation box on transform options bar	Edit | Transform | 'Rotate 90° CW'	Rotate 90° CW	
Rule of Thirds Overlay, Position	PS 36	Drag overlay			
Ruler Tool	PS 525	Ruler Tool button on Tools panel		Eyedropper Tool button | Ruler Tool	I or SHIFT+I
Rulers, Show or Hide	PS 33		View | Rulers		CTRL+R
Save	PS 21		File | Save		CTRL+S

Adobe Photoshop CC Quick Reference Summary *(continued)*

Task	Page Number	Workspace	Menu	Context Menu	Keyboard Shortcuts
Save for Web	PS 60		File | 'Save for Web & Devices'		ALT+SHIFT+CTRL+S
Save in PDF Format	PS 117	'Save as type' button in Save As dialog box, Photoshop PDF (*.PDF;*.PDP)	File | Save As		
Save with New Name	PS 55		File | Save As, enter new name		SHIFT+CTRL+S
Scale Selection	PS 112	Scale (W and H) boxes on transform options bar	Edit | Transform | Scale	Scale	SHIFT+drag corner sizing handle
Scale Text	PS 352	Horizontally scale box on Character panel			
Screen Mode, Change	PS 32	Screen Mode button on Tools panel	View | Screen Mode | select mode		F
Select All	PS 39		Select | All		CTRL+A
Select using a Channel	PS 406	'Load channel as selection' button on Channels panel status bar			
Sepia Image, Create	PS 451	Selective Color icon on Adjustments panel			
Shape Layer, Create with Pen Tool	PS 482	Pen Tool button on Tools panel, create shape			P or SHIFT+P
Shape, Create	PS 234	Shape Tool on Tools panel		Shape Tool button, select shape	U or SHIFT+U
Shape, Fill with a Pattern	PS 368	'Paint Bucket Tool' button on Tools panel; 'Set source for fill area' button on Paint Bucket Tool options bar			
Sharpen Tool	PS 318	Sharpen Tool button on Tools panel		Blur Tool button | Sharpen Tool	
Single Column Marquee Tool	PS 80	'Single Column Marquee Tool' button on Tools panel		'Rectangular Marquee Tool' button | 'Single Column Marquee Tool'	
Single Row Marquee Tool	PS 80	'Single Row Marquee Tool' button on Tools panel		'Rectangular Marquee Tool' button | 'Single Row Marquee Tool'	
Skew Selection	PS 167	Skew (H and V) boxes on transform options bar	Edit | Transform | Skew	Skew	
Slice Select Tool	PS 566	'Slice Select Tool' button on Tools panel		Crop tool button | 'Slice Select Tool'	C or SHIFT + C
Slices, Create	PS 563	Slice Tool button on Tools panel	Layer | 'New Layer Based Slice'	Slice Tool	C or SHIFT + C
Slices, Hide	PS 568		View | Show | Slices		CTRL+H
Smart Filter, Create	PS 348		Filter | 'Convert to Smart Filter'		
Smart Object, Create using Place Command	PS 227		File | Place	'Convert to Smart Object'	
Smart Object, Layer	PS 379	'Convert to Smart Object' on Layers panel menu	Layer | Smart Objects | 'Convert to Smart Object'	'Convert to Smart Object'	
Smooth, Modify	PS 43		Select | Modify | Smooth		
Smudge	PS 317	Smudge Tool on Tools panel		Blur Tool button | Smudge Tool	

Adobe Photoshop CC Quick Reference Summary

Task	Page Number	Workspace	Menu	Context Menu	Keyboard Shortcuts
Snap Selection	PS 90	Drag selection near object or guide			
Snapping, Turn On	PS 97		View | Snap		SHIFT+CTRL+ SEMICOLON (;)
Sponge Tool	PS 286	Sponge Tool button on Tools panel		Dodge Tool button | Sponge Tool	O or SHIFT+O
Spot Healing Brush Tool	PS 294	'Spot Healing Brush Tool' on Tools panel			J or SHIFT+J
Straighten a Photo using Lens Correction	PS 310	Straighten Tool button in Lens Correction dialog box			
Straighten Photo using Crop Tool	PS 36	Straighten button on Crop Tool options bar			
Stroke Layer, Create	PS 192	'Add a layer style' button on Layers panel status bar, Stroke	Layer | Layer Style | Stroke		
Subtract From Selection	PS 81	'Subtract from selection' button on options bar			ALT+drag
Switch Between Background and Foreground Colors	PS 44	'Switch Foreground and Background Colors' button on Tools panel			X
Text, Insert	PS 53	'Horizontal Type Tool' button on Tools panel			T OR SHIFT+T
Timeline Panel, Display	PS 581		Window | Timeline		
Timing, Set	PS 585	'Selects frame delay time' button on Frame			
Tracking	PS 250	'Set the tracking' box on Character panel			
Transform Controls, Display	PS 84	'Show Transform Controls' check box on Move Tool options bar	Edit | Free Transform		CTRL+T
Transform Selection Perspective	PS 165		Edit | Transform | Perspective	Perspective	
Tween	PS 584	'Tweens animation frames' button on Timeline panel status bar or Tween on Timeline panel menu			
Undo	PS 101	Previous state on History panel	Edit | Undo		CTRL+Z
View Channels	PS 405	Channels panel tab			
Warp Selection	PS 162	Warp button on transform options bar	Edit | Transform | Warp	Warp	
Warp Text	PS 434	'Create warped text' button on Horizontal Type Tool options bar			
Web Page, View Interactively	PS 589	Double-tap or double-click HTML file			
Windows, Consolidate	PS 154		Window | Arrange | 'Consolidate All to Tabs'	Document tab | 'Consolidate All to Here'	
Zoom In	PS 26	Zoom In button on Navigator panel	View | Zoom In	Zoom In	CTRL+PLUS SIGN (+)
Zoom Out	PS 26	Zoom Out button on Navigator panel	View | Zoom Out	Zoom Out	CTRL+MINUS SIGN (−)
Zoom Tool	PS 26	Zoom Tool button on Tools panel			Z
Zoomify	PS 57		File | Export | Zoomify